BACKPROPAGATION

Theory, Architectures, and Applications

DEVELOPMENTS IN CONNECTIONIST THEORY
David E. Rumelhart, Editor

BACKPROPAGATION

Theory, Architectures, and Applications

Edited by
Yves Chauvin
*Stanford University
and Net-ID, Inc.*
David E. Rumelhart
*Department of Psychology
Stanford University*

Psychology Press
Taylor & Francis Group

New York London

First Published by
Lawrence Erlbaum Associates, Inc., Publishers
365 Broadway
Hillsdale, New Jersey 07642

Transferred to Digital Printing 2009 by Psychology Press
270 Madison Ave, New York NY 10016
27 Church Road, Hove, East Sussex, BN3 2FA

Library of Congress Cataloging-in-Publication Data

Backpropagation : theory, architectures, and applications / edited by Yves Chauvin and David E.
Rumelhart.
    p. cm.
   Includes bibliographical references and index.
   ISBN 0-8058-1258-X (alk. paper). — ISBN 0-8058-1259-8 (pbk. : alk. paper)
   1. Backpropagation (Artificial intelligence)   I. Chauvin, Yves, Ph. D.   II. Rumelhart,
David E.
Q327.78.B33   1994
006.3—dc20
                                           94-24248
                                              CIP

Publisher's Note
The publisher has gone to great lengths to ensure the quality of this reprint
but points out that some imperfections in the original may be apparent.

Contents

v

Preface

Almost ten years have passed since the publication of the now classic volumes *Parallel Distributed Processing: Explorations in the Microstructure of Cognition*. These volumes marked a renewal in the study of brain-inspired computations as models of human cognition. Since the publication of these two volumes, thousands of scientists and engineers have joined the study of Artificial Neural Networks (or Parallel Distributed Processing) to attempt to respond to three fundamental questions: (1) how does the brain work? (2) how does the mind work? (3) how could we design machines with equivalent or greater capabilities than biological (including human) brains?

Progress in the last 10 years has given us a better grasp of the complexity of these three problems. Although connectionist neural networks have shed a feeble light on the first question, it has become clear that biological neurons and computations are more complex than their metaphorical connectionist equivalent by several orders of magnitude. Connectionist models of various brain areas, such as the hippocampus, the cerebellum, the olfactory bulb, or the visual and auditory cortices have certainly helped our understanding of their functions and internal mechanisms. But by and large, the biological metaphor has remained a metaphor. And neurons and synapses still remain much more mysterious than hidden units and weights.

Artificial neural networks have inspired not only biologists but also psychologists, perhaps more directly interested in the second question. Although the need for brain-inspired computations as models of the workings of the mind is still controversial, PDP models have been successfully used to model a number of behavioral observations in cognitive, and more rarely, clinical or social psychology. Most of the results are based on models of perception, language, memory, learning, categorization, and control. These results, however, cannot pretend to represent the beginning of a general understanding of the human psyche. First, only a small fraction of the large quantity of data amassed by experimental psychologists has been examined by neural network researchers. Second, some higher levels of human cognition, such as problem solving, judgment, reasoning, or decision making rarely have been addressed by the connectionist community. Third, most models of experimental data remain qualitative and limited in scope: No general connectionist theory has been proposed to link the various aspects of cognitive processes into a general computational framework. Overall, the possibility of an artificial machine that could learn how to function in the world with a reasonable amount of intelligence, communication, or "common sense" remains far away from our current state of knowledge.

It is perhaps on the third problem, the design of artificial learning systems, expert in specific tasks, that connectionist approaches have made their best contribution. Such models have had an impact in many different disciplines, most of them represented in this volume. This trend is in part the result of advances in computer, communication, and data acquisition technologies. As databases of information are becoming ubiquitous in many fields, corresponding accurate models of the data-generating process are often unavailable. It is in these areas that machine learning approaches are making their greatest impact. And it is here that connectionist approaches are beneficially interbreeding with several other related disciplines such as statistical mechanics, statistical pattern recognition, signal processing, statistical inference, and information and decision theory.

It may be seen as somewhat of a disappointment to the great excitement of the late 1980s that the idea of "intelligent general learning systems" has to yield to local, specialized, often handcrafted neural networks with limited generalization capabilities. But it is also interesting to realize that prior domain knowledge needs to be introduced to constrain network architectures and statistical performance measures if these networks are to learn and generalize. With hindsight, this realization certainly appears to be a sign of maturity in the field.

The most influential piece of work in the PDP volumes was certainly Chapter 8, "Learning Interal Representations by Error Propagation." Since the original publication of the PDP volumes, the back propagation algorithm has been implemented in many different forms by many different researchers in different fields. The algorithm shows that complex mappings between input and target patterns could be learned in an elegant and practical way by non-linear connectionist networks. It also overcomes many limitations associated with neural network learning algorithms of the previous generation, such as the perceptron algorithm. At the same time, the back-propagation algorithm includes the basic ingredients of the general connectionist recipe: local computations, global optimization, and parallel operation. But most interestingly, the algorithm showed that input-output mappings could be created during learning by the discovery of internal representations of the training data. These representations were sometimes clever, nontrivial, and not originally intended or even imagined by the human designer of the back-propagation network architectures. In the 1960s and 1970s, the cognitive psychology revolution was partially triggered by the realization that such internal representations were necessary to explain intelligent behavior beyond the scope of stimulus-response theory. The internal representations learned by the back-propagation algorithm had an "intelligent flavor" that was difficult for artificial intelligence researchers to ignore. Altogether, these features contributed to the success of back propagation as a versatile tool for computer modellers, engineers, and cognitive scientists in general.

This present volume can be seen as a progress report on the third problem achieved through a deeper exploration of the back-propagation algorithm. The volume contains a variety of new articles that represent a global perspective on the algorithm and show new practical applications. We have also included a small number of articles that appeared over the last few years and had an impact on our understanding of the back-propagation mechanism. The chapters distinguish the theory of back propagation from architectures and applications. The theoretical chapters relate back-propagation principles to statistics, pattern recognition, and dynamical system theory. They show that back-propagation networks can be viewed as non-parametrized, non-linear, structured, statistical models. The architectures and applications chapters then show successful implementations of the algorithm for speech processing, fingerprint recognition, process control, etc.

We intend this volume to be useful not only to students in the field of artificial neural networks, but also to professionals who are looking for concrete applications of learning machine systems in general and of the back-propagation algorithm in particular. From the theory section, readers should be able to relate neural networks to their own background in physics, statistics, information or control theory. From the examples, they should be able to generalize the design principles and construct their own architectures optimally adapted to their problems, from medical diagnosis to financial prediction to protein analysis.

Considering our current stage of knowledge, there is still a lot of terrain to be explored in the back-propagation landscape. The future of back propagation and of related machine learning techniques resides in their effectiveness as practical solutions to real world problems. The recent creation of start-up companies with core technologies based on these mechanisms shows that the engineering world is paying attention to the computational advantages of these algorithms. Success in the competition for cost effective solutions to real-world problems will probably determine if back-propagation learning techniques are mature enough to survive. We believe it will be the case.

Yves Chauvin and David E. Rumelhart

Acknowledgments

It would probably take another volume just to thank all the people who contributed to the existence of this volume. The first editor would like to mention two of them: Marie-Thérèse and René Chauvin.

Editors' note: Recent usage of the term "backpropagation" in neural networks research appears to favor treating it as one word. While the editors acknowledge this trend with the title of this book, we also respect the fact that different researchers in different disciplines have tended to handle the term differently. Therefore, for the purposes of this volume we have respectfully allowed the contributing authors free license to their own preferred usage.

BACKPROPAGATION

Theory, Architectures, and Applications

1 Backpropagation: The Basic Theory

David E. Rumelhart
Richard Durbin
Richard Golden
Yves Chauvin
Department of Psychology, Stanford University

INTRODUCTION

Since the publication of the PDP volumes in 1986,[1] learning by backpropagation has become the most popular method of training neural networks. The reason for the popularity is the underlying simplicity and relative power of the algorithm. Its power derives from the fact that, unlike its precursors, the perceptron learning rule and the Widrow-Hoff learning rule, it can be employed for training nonlinear networks of arbitrary connectivity. Since such networks are often required for real-world applications, such a learning procedure is critical. Nearly as important as its power in explaining its popularity is its simplicity. The basic idea is old and simple; namely define an error function and use hill climbing (or gradient descent if you prefer going downhill) to find a set of weights which optimize performance on a particular task. The algorithm is so simple that it can be implemented in a few lines of code, and there have been no doubt many thousands of implementations of the algorithm by now.

The name *back propagation* actually comes from the term employed by Rosenblatt (1962) for his attempt to generalize the perceptron learning algorithm to the multilayer case. There were many attempts to generalize the perceptron learning procedure to multiple layers during the 1960s and 1970s, but none of them were especially successful. There appear to have been at least three independent inventions of the modern version of the back-propagation algorithm: Paul Werbos developed the basic idea in 1974 in a Ph.D. dissertation entitled

---

[1]*Parallel distributed processing: Explorations in the microstructure of cognition.* Two volumes by Rumelhart, McClelland, and the PDP Research Group.

1

"Beyond Regression," and David Parker and David Rumelhart apparently developed the idea at about the same time in the spring of 1982. It was, however, not until the publication of the paper by Rumelhart, Hinton, and Williams in 1986 explaining the idea and showing a number of applications that it reached the field of neural networks and connectionist artificial intelligence and was taken up by a large number of researchers.

Although the basic character of the back-propagation algorithm was laid out in the Rumelhart, Hinton, and Williams paper, we have learned a good deal more about how to use the algorithm and about its general properties. In this chapter we develop the basic theory and show how it applies in the development of new network architectures.

We will begin our analysis with the simplest cases, namely that of the feedforward network. The pattern of connectivity may be arbitrary (i.e., there need not be a notion of a layered network), but for our present analysis we will eliminate cycles. An example of such a network is illustrated in Figure 1.[2]

For simplicity, we will also begin with a consideration of a training set which consists of a set of ordered pairs $[\langle \vec{x}, \vec{d} \rangle_i]$ where we understand each pair to represent an observation in which outcome $\vec{d}$ occurred in the context of event $\vec{x}$. The goal of the network is to learn the relationship between $\vec{x}$ and $\vec{d}$. It is useful to imagine that there is some unknown function relating $\vec{x}$ to $\vec{d}$, and we are trying to find a good approximation to this function. There are, of course, many standard methods of function approximation. Perhaps the simplest is linear regression. In that case, we seek the best linear approximation to the underlying function. Since multilayer networks are typically nonlinear it is often useful to understand feedforward networks as performing a kind of *nonlinear* regression. Many of the issues that come up in ordinary linear regression also are relevant to the kind of nonlinear regression performed by our networks.

One important example comes up in the case of "overfitting." We may have too many predictor variables (or degrees of freedom) and too little training data. In this case, it is possible to do a great job of "learning" the data but a poor job of generalizing to new data. The ultimate measure of success is not how closely we approximate the training data, but how well we account for as yet unseen cases. It is possible for a sufficiently large network to merely "memorize" the training data. We say that the network has truly "learned" the function when it performs well on unseen cases. Figure 2 illustrates a typical case in which accounting exactly for noisy observed data can lead to worse performance on the new data. Combating this "overfitting" problem is a major problem for complex networks with many weights.

Given the interpretation of feedforward networks as a kind of nonlinear regression, it may be useful to ask what features the networks have which might

---

[2]As we indicate later, the same analysis can be applied to networks with cycles (recurrent networks), but it is easiest to understand in the simpler case.

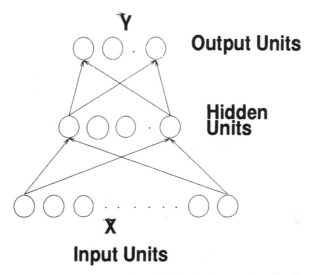

Figure 1.   A simple three-layer network. The key to the effectiveness of the multilayer network is that the hidden units learn to represent the input variables in a task-dependent way.

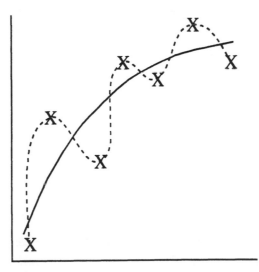

Figure 2.   Even though the oscillating line passes directly through all of the data points, the smooth line would probably be the better predictor if the data were noisy.

give them an advantage over other methods. For these purposes it is useful to compare the simple feedforward network with one hidden layer to the method of polynomial regression. In the case of polynomial regression we imagine that we transform the input variables $\vec{x}$ into a large number of variables by adding a number of the cross terms $x_1x_2, x_1x_3, \ldots, x_1x_2x_3, x_1x_2x_4, \ldots$. We can also add terms with higher powers $x_1^2, x_1^3, \ldots$ as well as cross terms with higher powers. In doing this we can, of course approximate any output surface we please. Given that we can produce any output surface with a simple polynomial regression model, why should we want to use a multilayer network? The structures of these two networks are shown in Figure 3.

We might suppose that the feedforward network would have an advantage in that it might be able to represent a larger function space with fewer parameters. This does not appear to be true. Roughly, it seems to be that the "capacity" of both networks is proportional to the number of parameters in the network (cf. Cover, 1965; Mitchison & Durbin, 1989). The real difference is in the different kinds of constraints the two representations impose. Notice that for the polynomial network the number of possible terms grows rapidly with the size of the input vector. It is not, in general, possible, even to use all of the first-order cross terms since there are $n(n + 1)/2$ of them. Thus, we need to be able to select that subset of input variables that are most relevant, which often means selecting the lower-order cross terms and thereby representing only the pairwise or, perhaps, three-way interactions.

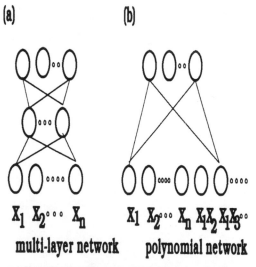

Figure 3. Two networks designed for nonlinear regression problems. The multilayer network has a set of hidden units designed to discover a "low-order" representation of the input variables. In the polynomial network the number of terms expands exponentially.

In layered networks the constraints are very different. Rather than limiting the *order of the interactions*, we limit only the *number of interactions* and let the network select the appropriate combinations of units. In many real-world situations the representation of the signal in physical terms (for example, in terms of the pixels of an image or the acoustic representation of a speech signal) may require looking at the relationships among many input variables at a time, but there may exist a description in terms of a relatively few variables if only we knew what they were. The idea is that the multilayer network is trying to find a low-order representation (a few hidden units), but that representation itself is, in general, a nonlinear function of the physical input variables which allows for the interactions of many terms.

Before we turn to the substantive issues of this chapter, it is useful to ask for what kinds of applications neural networks would be best suited. Figure 4 provides a framework for understanding these issues. The figure has two dimensions, "Theory Richness" and "Data Richness." The basic idea is that different kinds of systems are appropriate for different kinds of problems. If we have a good theory it is often possible to develop a specific "physical model" to describe the phenomena. Such a "first-principles" model is especially valuable when we

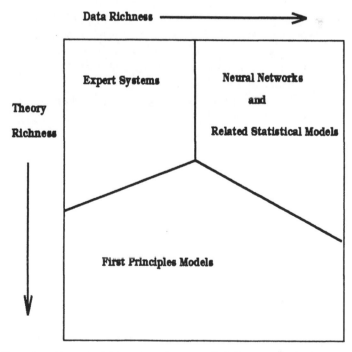

Figure 4.   Neural networks and back propagation can be of the most value for a problem relatively poor in theory and relatively rich in data.

have little data. Sometimes we are "theory poor" and also "data poor." In such a case, a good model may be best determined through asking "experts" in a field and, on the basis of their understanding, devise an "expert system." The cases where networks are particularly useful are domains where we have lots of data (so we can train a complex network) but not much theory, so we cannot build a first-principles model. Note that when a situation gets sufficiently complex and we have enough data, it may be that so many approximations to the first principles models are required that in spite of a good deal of theoretical understanding better models can be constructed through learning than by application of our theoretical models.

SOME PRELIMINARY CONSIDERATIONS

There are three major issues we must address when considering networks such as these. These are:

1. *The representation problem.* What is the representational capacity of a networks of this sort? How must the size of the network grow as the complexity of the function we are attempting to approximate grows?
2. *The learning problem.* Given that a function can be approximated reasonably closely by the network, can the function be learned by the network? How does the training time scale with the size of the network and the complexity of the problem?
3. *The generalization problem.* Given a network which has learned the training set, how certain can we be of its performance on new cases? How must the size of the data set grow as the complexity of the to be approximated function grows? What strategies can be employed for improving generalization?

Representation

The original critique by Minsky and Pappert was primarily concerned with the representational capacity of the perceptron. They showed (among other things) that certain functions were simply not representable with single-layer perceptrons. It has been shown that multilayered networks do not have these limitations. In particular, we now know that with enough hidden units essentially any function can be approximated as closely as possible (cf. Hornik et al., 1989). There still is a question about the way the size of the network must scale with the complexity of the function to be approximated. There are results which indicate that smooth, continuous functions require, in general, simpler networks than functions with discontinuities.

Learning

Although there are results that indicate that the general learning problem is extremely difficult—certain representable functions may not be learnable at all—empirical results indicate that the "learning" problem is much easier than expected. Most real-world problems seem to be learnable in a reasonable time. Moreover, learning normally seems to scale linearly; that is, as the size of real problems increase, the training time seems to go up linearly (i.e., it scales with the number of patterns in the training set). Note that these results were something of a surprise. Much of the early work with the back-propagation algorithm was done with artificial problems, and there was some concern about the time that some problems, such as the parity problem, required. It now appears that these results were unduly pessimistic. It is rare that more than 100 times through the training set is required.

Generalization

Whereas the learning problem has turned out to be simpler than expected, the generalization problem has turned out to be more difficult than expected. It appears to be possible to easily build networks capable of learning fairly large data sets. Learning a data set turns out to be little guarantee of being able to generalize to new cases. Much of the most important work during recent years has been focused on the development of methods to attempt to optimize generalization rather than just the learning of the training set.

A PROBABILISTIC MODEL FOR
BACK-PROPAGATION NETWORKS

The goal of the analysis which follows is to develop a theoretical framework which will allow for the development of appropriate networks for appropriate problems while optimizing generalization. The back-propagation algorithm involves specifying a cost function and then modifying the weights iteratively according to the gradient of the cost function. In this section we develop a rationale for an appropriate cost function. We propose that the goal is to find that network which is the most likely explanation of the observed data sequence. We can express this as trying to maximize the term

$$P(\mathcal{N}|\mathcal{D}) = \frac{P(\mathcal{D}|\mathcal{N})P(\mathcal{N})}{P(\mathcal{D})},$$

where $\mathcal{N}$ represents the network (with all of the weights and biases specified), $\mathcal{D}$ represents the observed data, and $P(\mathcal{D}|\mathcal{N})$ is the probability that the network $\mathcal{N}$ would have produced the observed data $\mathcal{D}$. Now since sums are easier to work with than products, we will maximize the log of this probability. Since the log is a monotonic transformation, maximizing the log is equivalent to maximizing the probability itself. In this case we have

$$\ln P(\mathcal{N}|\mathcal{D}) = \ln P(\mathcal{D}|\mathcal{N}) + \ln P(\mathcal{N}) - \ln P(\mathcal{D}).$$

Finally, since the probability of the data is not dependent on the network, it is sufficient to maximize $\ln P(\mathcal{D}|\mathcal{N}) + \ln P(\mathcal{N})$.

Now, it is useful to understand the meaning of these two terms. The first term represents the probability of the data given the network; that is, it is a measure of how well the network accounts for the data. The second term is a representation of the probability of the network itself; that is, it is a prior probability or a prior constraint on the network. Although it is often difficult to specify the prior, doing so is an important way of inserting knowledge into the learning procedure. More will be said about this later. For the time being, however, we focus on the first term, the performance.

It is useful to begin by noticing that the data can be broken down into a set of observations, each, we will assume, chosen independently of the others. Thus, we can write the probability of the data given the network as

$$\ln P(\mathcal{D}|\mathcal{N}) = \ln P([\langle \vec{x}, \vec{d_i} \rangle]|\mathcal{N})$$

$$= \ln \prod_i P(\langle \vec{x}, \vec{d_i} \rangle|\mathcal{N}) = \sum_i \ln P(\langle \vec{x}, \vec{d_i} \rangle|\mathcal{N}).$$

Note that again this assumption allows us to express the probability of the data given the network as the sum of terms, each term representing the probability of a single observation given the network. We can take still another step. We can break the data into two parts: the outcome $\vec{d_i}$ and the observed event $\vec{x_i}$. We can write

$$\ln P(\mathcal{D}|\mathcal{N}) = \sum_i \ln P(\vec{d_i}|\vec{x_i} \wedge \mathcal{N}) + \sum_i \ln P(\vec{x_i}).$$

Now, since we suppose that the event $\vec{x_i}$ does not depend on the network, the last term of the equation will not affect the determination of the optimal network. Therefore, we need only maximize the term $\Sigma_i \ln (P(\vec{d_i}|\vec{x_i} \wedge \mathcal{N})$.

So far we have been very general; the only real assumption made is the independence of the observed data points. In order to get further, however, we need to make some specific assumptions, particularly about the relationship between the output of the network $\vec{y_i}$ and the observed outcome $\vec{d_i}$, a probabilistic assumption. First, we assume that the relationship between $\vec{x_i}$ and $\vec{d_i}$ is not deterministic, but that, for any given $\vec{x_i}$, there is a distribution of possible values of $\vec{d_i}$. The network, however, *is deterministic,* so rather than trying to predict the actual outcome we are only trying to predict the expected value of $\vec{d_i}$ given $\vec{x_i}$. Thus, the network output $\vec{y_i}$ is to be interpreted as the mean of the actual observed value. This is, of course, the standard assumption.

The Gaussian Case

To proceed further, we must specify the form of the distribution of which the network output is the mean. To decide which distribution is most appropriate, it is necessary to consider the nature of the outcomes, $\vec{d}$. In ordinary linear regression, there is an underlying assumption that the noise is normally distributed about the predicted values. In situations in which this is so, a Gaussian probability distribution is appropriate, even for nonlinear regression problems in which nonlinear networks are required. We begin our analysis in this simple case.

Under the assumption of normally distributed noise in the observations we can write

$$P(\vec{d}_i|\vec{x}_i \wedge \mathcal{N}) = K \exp\left(\sum_j \frac{(y_{ij} - d_{ij})^2}{2\sigma^2}\right),$$

where K is the normalization term for the Gaussian distribution. Now we take the log of the probability:

$$\ln P (\vec{d}_i|\vec{x}_i \wedge \mathcal{N}) = -\ln K - \frac{\Sigma_j(y_{ij} - d_{ij})^2}{2\sigma^2}.$$

Under the assumption that σ is fixed, we want to maximize the following term, where $\mathcal{C}$ is the function to be maximized.

$$\mathcal{C} = -\sum_i \sum_j \frac{(y_{ij} - d_{ij})^2}{2\sigma^2}.$$

Now we must consider the appropriate transfer functions for the output units. For the moment, we will consider the case of what we have termed *quasi-linear* output units in which the output is a function of the *net input* of the unit, where[3] the net input is simply a weighted sum of the inputs to the unit. That is, the net input for unit j, η_j, is given by $\eta_j = \Sigma_k w_{jk}h_k + \beta_j$. Thus, we have $y_j = \mathcal{F}(\eta_j)$.[4]

Recall that the back-propagation learning rule is determined by the derivative of the cost function with respect to the parameters of the network. In this case we can write

$$\frac{\partial \mathcal{C}}{\partial \eta_j} = \frac{(d_{ij} - y_{ij})}{\sigma^2} \frac{\partial \mathcal{F}(\eta_j)}{\partial \eta_j}.$$

This has the form of the difference between the predicted and observed values divided by the variance of the error term times the derivative of the output

---

[3]Note, this is not necessary. The output units could have a variety of forms, but the quasi-linear class is simple and useful.

[4]Note that η_j itself is a function of the input vector $\vec{x}_i$ and the weights and biases of the entire network.

function with respect to its net input. As we shall see, this is a very general form which occurs often.

Now what form should the output function take? It has been conventional to take it to be a sigmoidal function of its net input, but under the Gaussian assumption of error, in which the mean can, in principle, take on *any* real value, it makes more sense to let $\vec{y}$ be linear in its net input. Thus, for an assumption of Gaussian error and linear output functions we get the following very simple form of the learning rule:

$$\frac{\partial \mathscr{C}}{\partial \eta_j} \propto (d_{ij} - y_{ij}).$$

The change in η should be proportional to the difference between the observed output and its predicted value. This model is frequently appropriate for prediction problems in which the error can reasonably be normally distributed. As we shall see, classification problems in which the observations are binary are a different situation and generate a different model.

The Binomial Case

Often we use networks for classification problems—that is, for problems in which the goal is to provide a binary classification of each input vector for each of several classes. This class of problems requires a different model. In this case the outcome vectors normally consist of a sequence of 0's and 1's. The "error" cannot be normally distributed, but would be expected to be binomially distributed. In this case, we imagine that each element of $\vec{y}$ represents the *probability* that the corresponding element of the outcome vector $\vec{d}$ takes on the value 0 or 1. In this case we can write the probability of the data given the network as

$$P(\vec{d}|\vec{x} \wedge \mathcal{N}) = \prod_j y_j{}^{d_j}(1 - y_j)^{1-d_j}.$$

The log of probability is $\Sigma_j \, d_j \ln y_j + (1 - d_j) \ln (1 - y_j)$ and, finally,

$$\mathscr{C} = \sum_i \sum_j d_j \ln y_j + (1 - d_j) \ln(1 - y_j).$$

In the neural network world, this has been called the cross-entropy error term. As we shall see, this is just one of many such error terms. Now, the derivative of this function is

$$\frac{\partial \mathscr{C}}{\partial \eta_j} = \frac{d_j - y_j}{y_j(1 - y_j)} \frac{\partial \mathscr{F}(\eta_j)}{\partial \eta_j}.$$

Again, the derivative has the same form as before—the difference between the predicted and observed values divided by the variance (in this case the variance of the binomial) times the derivative of the transfer function with respect to its net input.

We must now determine the meaning of the form of the output function. In this case, we want it to range between 0 and 1, so a sigmoidal function is natural. Interestingly, we see that if we choose the logistic $\mathcal{F}(\eta_j) = 1/(1 + e^{-\eta_j})$, we find an interesting result. The derivative of the logistic is $\mathcal{F}(\eta_j)(1 - \mathcal{F}(\eta_j))$ or $y_j(1 - y_j)$. It happens that this is the variance of the binomial, so it cancels the denominator in the previous equation, leaving the same simple form as we had for the Gaussian case:

$$\frac{\partial \mathcal{C}}{\partial \eta_j} \propto (d_j - y_j).$$

In the work on generalized linear models (cf. McCullagh & Nelder, 1989) such functions are called *linking functions,* and they point out that different linking functions are appropriate for different sorts of problems. It turns out to be useful to see feedforward networks as a generalization into the nonlinear realm of the work on generalized linear models. Much of the analysis given in the McCullagh and Nelder applies directly to such networks.

The Multinomial Case

In many applications we employ not multiple classification or binary classification, but "1-of-n" classification. Here we must employ still another transfer function. In this case, choose the normalized exponential output function[5]

$$\mathcal{F}_j(\vec{\eta}) = \frac{e^{\eta_j}}{\Sigma_k e^{\eta_k}}.$$

In this case, the $\vec{d}$ vector consists of exactly one 1 and the remaining digits are zeros. We can then interpret the output unit j, for example, as representing the probability that the input vector was a member of class j. In this case we can write the cost function as

$$\mathcal{C} = \sum_i \sum_j d_{ij} \ln \frac{e^{\eta_j}}{\Sigma_k e^{\eta_k}}.$$

and, again, after computing the derivative we get

$$\frac{\partial \mathcal{C}}{\partial \eta_j} \propto (d_{ij} - y_{ij}).$$

---

[5]This is sometimes called the "soft-max" or "Potts" unit. As we shall see, however, it is a simple generalization of the ordinary sigmoid and has a simple interpretation as representing the posterior probability of event j out of a set n of possible events.

The General Case

The fact that these cases all end up with essentially the same learning rule in spite of different models is not accidental. It requires exactly the right choice of output functions for each class of problem. It turns out that this result will occur whenever we choose a probability function from the *exponential family* of probability distributions. This family, which includes, in addition to the normal and the binomial, the gamma distribution, the exponential distribution, the Poisson distribution, the negative binomial distribution, and most other familiar probability distributions. The general form of the exponential family of probability distributions is

$$P(\vec{d}|\vec{x} \wedge \mathcal{N}) = \exp\left[\sum_i \frac{(d_i\theta - B(\theta)) + C(\vec{d}\phi)}{a(\phi)} \right],$$

where θ is the "sufficient statistic" of the distribution and is related to the mean of the distribution, ϕ is a measure of the overall variance of the distribution, and the $B(\ )$, $C(\ )$ and $a(\ )$ are different for each member of the family. It is beyond the scope of this chapter to develop the general results of this model.[6] Suffice it to say that for all members of the exponential family we get

$$\frac{\partial \mathcal{C}}{\partial \eta_j} \propto \frac{d_j - y_j}{\text{var}(y_j)}.$$

We then choose as an output function one whose derivative with respect to η is equal to the variance. For members of the exponential family of probability distributions we can always do this.

The major point of this analysis is that by using one simple cost function, a log-likelihood function, and by looking carefully at the problem at hand, we see that, unlike the original work, in which the squared error criterion was normally employed in nearly all cases, different cost functions are appropriate for different cases—prediction, cross-classification, and 1-of-n classification all require different forms of output units. The major advantage of this is not so much that the squared error criterion is wrong, but that by making specific probability assumptions we can get a better understanding of the *meaning* of the output units. In particular, we can interpret them as the means of underlying probability distributions. As we shall show, this understanding allows for the development of rather sophisticated architecture in a number of cases.

SOME EXAMPLES

Before discussing priors and analyzing hidden units, we sketch how to use this method of analysis to design appropriate learning rules for complex networks.

---

[6]See McCullagh and Nelder (1989, pp. 28–30) for a more complete description.

A Simple Clustering Network

Consider the following problem. Suppose that we wish to build a network which received a sequence of data and attempted to cluster the data points into some predefined number of clusters. The basic structure of the network, illustrated in Figure 5, consists of a set of input units, one for each element of the data vector $\vec{x}$, a set of hidden "cluster" units, and a single linear output unit. In this case, we suppose that the hidden units are "Gaussian"; that is, their output values are given by $K \exp [\Sigma_j (x_j - w_{jk})^2 / 2\sigma^2]$. In this case, the weights $\vec{w}_k$ can be viewed as the center of the kth cluster. The parameter σ, constant in this case, determines the spread of the cluster. We want the output unit to represent the probability of the data given the network, $P(\vec{x}_i|\mathcal{N})$.

Now if we assume that the clusters are mutually exclusive and exhaustive we can write

$$P(\vec{x}_i|\mathcal{N}) = \sum_k P(\vec{x}_i|\vec{x}_i \in c_k)P(c_k),$$

where c_k indexes the kth cluster. For simplicity we can assume that the clusters are to be equally probable, so $P(c_k) = 1/N$, where N is the number of clusters. Now, the probability of the data given the cluster is simply the output of the kth hidden unit, h_k. Therefore, the value of the output unit is $1/N \sum_k h_k$ and the log-likelihood of the data given the input is

$$\mathcal{C} = \ln \left(\sum_k h_k \frac{1}{N} \right).$$

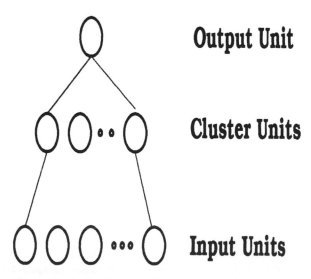

Output Unit

Cluster Units

Input Units

Figure 5.   A simple network for clustering input vectors.

The derivative of $\mathscr{C}$ with respect to the weights is

$$\frac{\partial \mathscr{C}}{\partial w_{jk}} = \left(\frac{(K/N)\exp[\Sigma_j(x_j - w_{jk})^2/2\sigma^2]}{\Sigma_k(K/N)\exp - \Sigma_j[(x_j - w_{jk})^2/2\sigma^2]} \right) \frac{x_j - w_{jk}}{\sigma^2}.$$

The term in parentheses represents the posterior probability that the correct cluster is c_k given the input in a member of one of the clusters. We can call this posterior probability p_k. We can now see that the learning rule is again very simple:

$$\frac{\partial \mathscr{C}}{\partial w_{jk}} \propto p_k(x_j - w_{jk}).$$

This is a slight modification of the general form already discussed. It is the difference between the observed value x_j and the estimated mean value w_{jk} weighted by the probability that cluster k was the correct cluster p_k.

This simple case represents a classic mixture of Gaussian model. We assumed fixed probabilities per cluster and a fixed variance. It is not difficult to estimate the probabilities of each cluster and the variance associated with the clusters. It is also possible to add priors of various kinds. As we will explain, it is possible to order the clusters and add constraints that nearby clusters ought to have similar means. In this case, this feedforward network can be used to implement the elastic network of Durbin and Willshaw (1987) and can, for example, be used to find a solution to the traveling salesman problem.

Society of Experts

Consider the network proposed by Jacobs, Jordan, Nowlan, and Hinton (1991) and illustrated in Figure 6. The idea of this network is that instead of having a single network to solve every problem, we have a set of networks which learn to subdivide a task and thereby solve it more efficiently and elegantly. The architecture allows for all networks to look at the input units and make their best guess, but a normalized exponential "gateing" is used to weight the outputs of the individual network providing an overall best guess. The gateing network also looks at the input vector.

We must train both the gateing network and the individual "expert" networks. As before, we wish to maximize the log-likelihood of the data given the network. The final output of the network is

$$y_{ij\cdot} = \sum_k r_k y_{ijk},$$

where r_k is the probability estimated by the normalized exponential "relevance" network that subnetwork k is the correct network for the current input. At first, it may not be obvious how to train this network. Perhaps we should look at the difference between the output of the network and the observed outcome and use

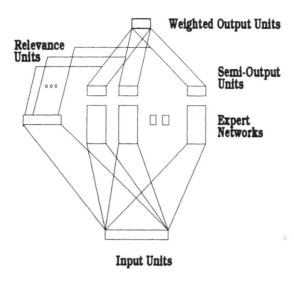

Figure 6. A simple network for clustering input vectors.

that as the error signal to be propagated back through the network. It turns out that the probabilistic analysis we have been discussing offers a different, more principled solution. We should, of course, maximize the log-likelihood—the probability of the data given the network. On the assumption that each input vector should be processed by one network and that the relevance network provides the probability that it should be network *k,* we can write

$$\mathscr{C} = \ln P(\vec{d}_i|\vec{x}_i \wedge \mathscr{N}) = \ln \sum_k P(\vec{d}_i|\vec{x}_i \wedge \mathscr{S}_k)r_k,$$

where $\mathscr{S}_k$ represents the *k*th subnet.

We must now make some specific assumptions about the form of $P(\vec{d}_i|\vec{x}_i \wedge \mathscr{S}_k)$. For concreteness, we assume a Gaussian distribution, but we could have chosen any of the other probability distributions we have discussed. In this case

$$\mathscr{C} = \ln \sum_k Kr_k \exp\left[\sum_j \frac{(d_j - y_{jk})^2}{2\sigma^2} \right].$$

We now must compute the derivative of the log-likelihood function with respect to η_{jk} for each subnetwork and with respect to η_k for the relevance network. In the first case we get

$$\frac{\partial \mathscr{C}}{\partial \eta_{jk}} = \left(\frac{r_k \exp[\Sigma_j(d_j - y_{jk})^2/2\sigma^2]}{\Sigma_i r_i K \exp[\Sigma_j(d_j - y_{jk})^2/2\sigma^2]} \right) \frac{d_j - y_{jk}}{\sigma^2} = p_k \frac{d_j - y_{jk}}{\sigma^2}.$$

Note that this is precisely the same form as for the clustering network. The only real difference is that the probabilities of each class given the input were independent of the input. In this case, the probabilities are input dependent. It is slightly more difficult to calculate, but it turns out that the derivative for the relevance units also has the simple form

$$\frac{\partial \mathscr{C}}{\partial \eta_k} = p_k - r_k,$$

the difference between the position and the prior probability that subnetwork k is the correct network.

This example, although somewhat complex, is useful for seeing how we can use our general theory to determine a learning rule in a case where it might not be immediately obvious and in which the general idea of just taking the difference between the output of the network and the target and using that as an error signal is probably the wrong thing to do. We now turn to one final example.

Integrated Segmentation and Recognition Network

A major problem with standard back-propagation algorithms is that they seem to require carefully segmented and localized input patterns for training. This is a problem for two reasons: first, it is often a labor-intensive task to provide this information and, second, the decision as to how to segment often depends on prior recognition. It is possible, however, to design a network and corresponding back-propagation learning algorithm in which we simultaneously learn to identify and segment a pattern.[7]

There are two important aspects to many pattern recognition problems which we have built directly into our network and learning algorithm. The first is that the exact location of the pattern, in space or time, is irrelevant to the classification of the pattern. It should be recognized as a member of the same class whereever or whenever it occurs. This suggests that we build translation independence directly into our network. The second aspect we wish to build into the network is that feedback about *whether* or not a pattern is present is all that should be required for training. Information about the exact location and relationship to other patterns ought not be required. The target information thus does not include information about *where* the patterns occur, but only about *whether* a pattern occurs.

We have incorporated two basic tricks into our network design to deal with these two aspects of the problem. The first is to build the assumption of translation independence into the network by using local linked receptive fields, and the

---

[7]The algorithm and network design presented here were first proposed by Rumelhart in a presentation entitled "Learning and generalization in multilayer networks" given at the NATO Advanced Research Workshop on Neurocomputing, Algorithms, Architecture and Applications held in Les Arcs, France, in February 1989. The algorithm can be considered a generalization and refinement of the TDNN network developed by (Waibel et al., 1989). A version of the algorithm was first published in Keeler, Rumelhart, and Loew (1991).

second is to build a fixed "forward model" (cf. Jordan & Rumelhart, 1992) which translates a location-specific recognition process into a location-independent output value and then is used to back-propagate the nonspecific error signal back through this fixed network to train the underlying location-specific network. The following sections show how these features can be realized and provide a rationale for the exact structure and assumptions of the network. The basic organization of the network is illustrated in Figure 7.

We designate the stimulus pattern by the vector $\vec{x}$. We assume that any character may occur in any position. The input features then project to a set of hidden units which are assumed to abstract hidden features from the input field. These feature abstraction units are organized into rows, one for each feature type. Each unit within a row is constrained to have the same pattern of weights as every other unit in the row. The units are thus simply translated versions of one another. This is enforced by "linking" the weights of all units in a given row, and

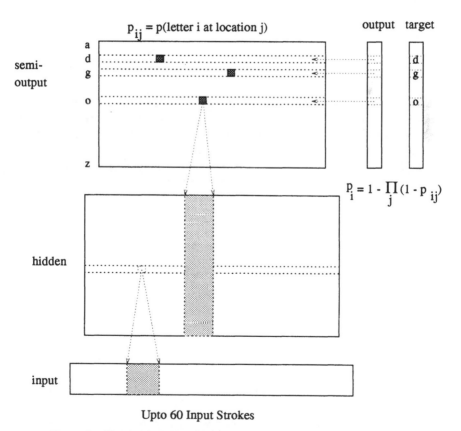

Figure 7. The basic recognition network. See text for detailed network description.

whenever one weight is changed all linked weights are changed. This is the same trick used by Rumelhart et al. (1986) to solve the so-called T/C problem and by LeCun et al. (1990) in their work on zip code recognition. We let the activation value of a hidden unit of type i at location j be a sigmoidal function of its net input and designate it h_{ij}. We interpret the activation of hidden unit h_{ij} as the probability that hidden feature f_i is present in the input at position j. The hidden units themselves have the conventional *logistic* sigmoidal transfer functions.

The hidden units then project onto a set of position-specific letter detection units. There is a row of position-specific units for each character type. Each unit in a row receives inputs from the feature units located in the immediate vicinity of the recognition unit. As with the hidden units, the units in a given row are translated versions of one another. We designate the unit for detecting character i at location j as p_{ij}. We let

$$p_{ij} = \frac{1}{1 + e^{-\eta_{ij}}},$$

where

$$\eta_{ij} = \sum_k w_{ik} h_{kj} + \beta_i$$

and w_{ik} is the weight from hidden unit h_{kj} to the detector p_{ij}. Note that since the weights from the hidden unit to the detection units are linked, this same weight will connect each feature unit in the row with a corresponding detection unit in the row above. Since we have built translational independence into the structure of the network, anything we learn about features or characters at any given location is, through the linking of weights, automatically transferred to every location.

If we were willing, or able, to carefully segment the input and tell the network exactly where each character was, we could use a standard training technique to train the network to recognize any character at any location. However, we are interested in a training algorithm in which we do not have to provide the network with specific training information. We are interested in simply telling the network which characters were present in the input, not where each character is. To implement this idea, we have built an additional network which takes the output of the p_{ij} units and computes, through a fixed output network, the probability that at least one character of a given type is present anywhere in the input field. We do this by computing the probability that at least one unit of a particular type is on. This can simply be written as

$$y_i = 1 - \prod_j (1 - p_{ij}).$$

Thus, y_i is interpreted as representing directly the probability that character i occurred at least once in the input field.

Note that *exactly the same target* would be given for the word "dog" and the word "god." Nevertheless, the network learns to properly localize the units in the p_{ij} layer. The reason is, simply, that the individual characters occur in many combinations and the only way that the network can learn to discriminate correctly is to actually detect the particular letter. The localization that occurs in the p_{ij} layer depends on each character unit seeing only a small part of the input field and on each unit of type i constrained to respond in the same way.

Important in the design of the network was an assumption as to the *meaning* of the individual units in the network. We will show why we make these interpretations and how the learning rule we derive depends on these interpretations.

To begin, we want to interpret each output unit as the probability that at least one of that character is in the input field. Assuming that the letters occurring in a given word are approximately independent of the other letters in the word, we can also assume that the probability of the target vector given the input is

$$p(\vec{d}|\vec{x}) = \prod_j y_j^{d_j}(1 - y_j)^{(1-d_j)}.$$

This is obviously an example of the binomial multiclassification model. Therefore, we get the following form of our log-likelihood function:

$$\mathscr{C} = \sum_j d_j \ln y_j + (1 - d_j)\ln(1 - y_j),$$

where d_j equals 1 if character j is presented, and zero otherwise.

On having set up our network and determined a reasonable performance criterion, we straightforwardly compute the derivative of the error function with respect to η_{ij}, the net input into the detection unit p_{ij}. We get

$$\frac{\partial \mathscr{C}}{\partial \eta_{ij}} = (d_j - y_i) \frac{p_{ij}}{y_i}.$$

This is a kind of *competitive* rule in which the learning is proportional to the relative strength of the activation of the unit at a location in the ith row to the strength of activation in the entire row. This ratio is the conditional probability that the target was at position j under the assumption that the target was, in fact, presented. This convenient interpretation is not accidental. By assigning the output units their probablistic interpretations and by selecting the appropriate, though unusual, output unit $y_i = 1 - \Pi(1 - p_{ij})$, we were able to ensure a plausible interpretation and behavior of our character detection units.

Concluding Remarks

In this section we have shown three cases in which our ability to provide useful analyses of our networks has given us important insights into network design. It is the general theory that allows us to see what assumptions to make, how to put our networks together, and how to interpret the outputs of the networks. We have, however, attended only to one portion of the problem, namely the measure of performance. Equally important is the other term of our cost function, namely the priors over the networks. We now turn to this issue.

PRIORS

Recall that the general form of the posterior likelihood function is

$$\mathscr{C} = \sum_i \sum_j \ln P(d_{ij}|\vec{x}_i \wedge \mathscr{N}) + \ln P(\mathscr{N}).$$

In the previous section we focused on the performance term. Now we focus on the priors term. As indicated, the major point of this term is to get information and constraints into the learning procedure. The basic procedure is to modify the parameters of the network based on the derivatives of both terms of the entire cost function, not just the performance term.

Weight Decay

Perhaps the simplest case to understand is the "weight decay" term. In this case we assume that the weights are distributed normally about a zero mean. We can write this term as

$$\ln P(\mathscr{N}) = \ln \exp\left(-\frac{\Sigma_{ij}\, w_{ij}^2}{2\sigma^2}\right) = -\frac{1}{2\sigma^2} \sum_{ij} w_{ij}^2.$$

This amounts to a penalty for large weights. The term σ determines how important the small weight constraint is. If σ is large, the penalty term will not be very important. If it is small, than the penalty term will be heavily weighted. The derivative then is given by

$$\frac{\partial \mathscr{C}}{\partial w_{ij}} \propto -\frac{1}{\sigma^2} w_{ij}.$$

Thus, every time we see a new pattern the weights should be modified in two ways; first, they should be modified so as to reduce the overall error (as in the first time of Equation 1); then they should be moved toward zero by an amount proportional to the magnitude of the weight. The term σ determines the amount of movement that should take place.

Why should we think that the weights should be small and centered around zero? Of course, this could be a bad assumption, but it is one way of limiting the space of possible functions that the network can explore. All things being equal, the network will select a solution with small weights rather than large ones. In linear problems this is often a useful strategy. The addition of this penalty term is known as "ridge regression," a kind of "regularization" term which limits the space of possible solutions to those with smaller weights. This is an important strategy for dealing with the overfitting problem. Weight decay was first proposed for connectionist networks by Geoffrey Hinton.

Weight Elimination

A general strategy for dealing with overfitting involves a simple application of Occam's Razor—that is, of all the networks which will fit the training data, find the simplest. The idea is to use the *prior* term to measure the complexity of the network and "prefer" simpler networks to more complex ones. But how do we measure the complexity of the network? The basic idea, due to Kolmogorov (cf. Kolmogorov, 1991), is that the complexity of a function is measured by the number of bits required to communicate the function. This is, in general, difficult to measure, but it is possible to find a set of variables which vary monotonically with the complexity of a network. For example, the more weights a network has the more complex it is—each weight has to be described. The more hidden units a network has, the greater the complexity of the network; the more bits per weight, the more complex is the network; the more symmetries there are among the weights, the simpler the network is, and so on.

Weigend et al. (1990) proposed a set of priors each of which led to a reduction in network complexity: for several priors, the weight elimination procedure has been the most useful. The idea is that the weights are not drawn from a single distribution around zero, as in weight decay, but we assume that they are drawn either from a normal distribution centered at zero or from a uniform distribution between, say, ± 20. It is possible to express this prior roughly as

$$P(\mathcal{N}) = \exp\left[-\sum_{ij} \frac{(w_{ij}/\sigma_1)^2}{1 + (w_{ij}/\sigma_2)^2} \right],$$

or, taking the log and multiplying through by the sigmas, as

$$\ln P(\mathcal{N}) = -\frac{\sigma_2^2}{\sigma_1^2} \sum_{ij} \frac{w_{ij}^2}{\sigma_2^2 + w_{ij}^2}.$$

The derivative is

$$\frac{\partial \mathcal{C}}{\partial w_{ij}} \propto -\frac{\sigma_2^2}{\sigma_1^2} \frac{w_{ij}}{(\sigma_2^2 + w_{ij}^2)^2}.$$

Note that this has the property that for small weights (weights in which w_{ij} is small relative to σ_2), the denominator is approximately constant and the change in weights is simply proportional to the numerator w_{ij}, as in weight decay. For large weights (w_{ij} is large relative to σ_2) the change is proportional to $1/w^3$—in other words, very little change occurs. Thus, this penalty function causes small weight to move toward zero, *eliminates them* and leaves large weights alone. This has the effect of removing unneeded weights. In the nonlinear case, there is reason to believe that the weight elimination strategy is a more useful prior than weight decay since large weights are required to establish the nonlinearities. A number of successful experiments have been carried out using the strategy (cf. Weigend, Hubberman, & Rumelhart, 1990 and Weigend, Rumelhart, & Hubberman, 1991).

Although similar strategies have been suggested for eliminating unneeded hidden units and for reducing the information content of weights, these have been studied very little. Perhaps the most successful paradigm, however, is a generalization of the weight elimination paradigm to impose important weight symmetries. This work has been done by Nowlan (1991) and is described here.

Weight Symmetries

In weight decay the idea was to have a prior such that the weight distribution has a zero mean and is normally distributed. The weight elimination paradigm is more general in that it distinguishes two classes of weights, of which one is, like the weight decay case, centered on zero and normally distributed, and the other is uniformly distributed. In weight symmetries there is a small set of normally distributed weight clusters. The problem is to simultaneously estimate the mean of the priors and the weights themselves. In this case the priors are

$$P(\mathcal{N}) = \prod_i \sum_k \exp\left[-\frac{(w_i - \mu_k)^2}{2\sigma_k^2} \right] P(c_k),$$

where $P(c_k)$ is the probability of the kth weight cluster and μ_k is its center. To determine how the weights are to be changed, we must compute the derivative of the log of this probability. We get

$$\frac{\partial \mathcal{C}}{\partial w_i} \propto \sum_k \frac{\exp[(w_i - \mu_k)^2 \, P(c_k)/2\sigma_k^2]}{\Sigma_j \exp[(w_i - \mu_j)^2 \, P(c_j)/2\sigma_j^2]} \frac{(\mu_k - w_i)}{\sigma_k^2}.$$

We can similarly estimate μ_k, σ_k, and $P(c_k)$ by gradient methods as well. For example, we write the derivative of the error with respect to μ_k:

$$\frac{\partial \mathcal{C}}{\partial \mu_k} \propto \sum_j \frac{\exp[-(w_j - \mu_k)^2 \, P(c_k)/2\sigma_k^2]}{\Sigma_i \exp[-(w_j - \mu_i)^2 \, P(c_i)/2\sigma_i^2]} \frac{(w_j - \mu_k)}{\sigma_k^2}.$$

By similar methods, it is possible to estimate the other parameters of the network. Nowlan (1991) have shown that these priors go far toward solving the overfitting problem.

Elastic Network and the Traveling Salesman Problem

Earlier we showed how one could develop a clustering algorithm by using Gaussian hidden units and optimizing the log-likelihood of the data given the network. It turns out that by adding priors to the cost function we can put constraints on the clusters. Imagine that we are trying to solve the traveling salesman problem in which we are to find the shortest path through a set of cities. In this case, we represent the cities in terms of their $\langle x, y \rangle$ coordinate values so that there is a two-dimensional input vector for each city. The method is the same as that proposed by Durbin and Willshaw (1987). There is a set of clusters, each cluster located at some point in a two-dimensional space. We want to move the means of the clusters toward the cities until there is one cluster for each city and adjacent clusters are as close to one another as possible. This provides for the following cost function:

$$\mathscr{C} = \sum_i \ln \sum_j \exp\left[\, [-(x_i - \mu_{x,j})^2 - y_i + \mu_{d,j})^2]/2\sigma^2\right]$$

$$+ \ln \prod_j \exp\left[\, [-(\mu_{x,j} - \mu_{d,j+1})^2 - (\mu_{d,j} - \mu_{d,j+1})^2]/\lambda\right]$$

$$= \sum_i \ln \sum_j \exp\left[\, [-(x_i - \mu_{x,j})^2 - (y_i + \mu_{d,j})^2]/2\sigma^2\right]$$

$$+ \sum_j \frac{-(\mu_{x,j} - \mu_{x,j+1})^2 - (\mu_{d,j} - \mu_{d,j+1})^2}{\lambda}.$$

Note that the constraint concerning the distance between successive cities is encoded in the prior term by the assumption that adjacent cluster means are near one another.

We next must compute the derivative of the likelihood function with respect to the parameters $\mu_{x,j}$ and $\mu_{d,j}$, by now this should be a familiar form. We can write

$$\frac{\partial \mathscr{C}}{\partial \mu_{x,k}} \propto \sum_i \frac{\exp[[-(x_i - \mu_{x,k})^2 - (d_i + \mu_{d,k})^2]/2\sigma^2]}{\sum_j \exp[[-(x_i - \mu_{x,j})^2 - (d_i + \mu_{d,j})^2/2\sigma^2]} \frac{(x_i - \mu_{x,k})}{\sigma^2}$$

$$+ \frac{1}{\lambda}(\mu_{x,k+1} \quad \mu_{x,k-1}).$$

In order to make this work, we must imagine that the clusters form a ring so that the cluster before the cluster -1 is the last cluster and the cluster $n + 1$ (where we have n clusters) is the same as cluster 0. Now we proceed to solve the traveling salesman problem in the following way. We start out with a rather large value of σ. The cities are presented to the network one at a time, and the weights (i.e, the means $\mu_{x,k}$ and $\mu_{d,k}$) are adjusted until the network stabilizes. At this point it is likely that none of the cluster centers are located at any of the cities. We then decrease σ and present the cities again until it stabilizes. Then σ is decreased again. This process is repeated until there is a cluster mean located at each city. At this point we can simply follow the cluster means in order and read off the solution to the problem.

Concluding Comments

In this section we showed how knowledge and constraints can be added to the network with well-chosen priors. So far the priors have been of two types. (1) We have used priors to constrain the set of networks explored by the learning algorithm. By adding such "regularization" terms we have been able to design networks which provide much better generalization. (2) We have been able to add further constraints among the network parameter relationships. These constraints allow us to force the network to a particular set of possible solutions, such as those which minimize the tour in the traveling salesman problem.

Although not discussed here, it is possible to add knowledge to the network in another way by expressing priors about the behavior of different parts of the network. It is possible to formulate priors that, for example, constrain the output of units on successive presentations to be as similar or as dissimilar as possible to one another. The general procedure can dramatically affect the solution the network achieves.

HIDDEN UNITS

Thus far, we have focused our attention on log-likelihood cost functions, appropriate interpretation of the output units, and methods of introducing additional constraints in the network. The final section focuses on the hidden units of the network.[8] There are at least four distinct ways of viewing hidden units.

1. Sigmoidal hidden units can be viewed as approximations to linear threshold functions which divide the space into regions which can then be combined to approximate the desired function.
2. Hidden units may be viewed as a set of *basis functions*, linear combinations of which can be used to approximate the desired output function.
3. Sigmoidal hidden units can be viewed probabilistically as representing the probability that certain "hidden features" are present in the input.

---

[8]As an historical note, the term "hidden unit" is used to refer to those units lying between the input and output layers. The name was coined by Geoffrey Hinton, inspired by the notion of "hidden states" in hidden Markov models.

4. Layers of hidden units can be viewed as a mechanism for transforming stimuli from one representation to another from layer to layer until those stimuli which are functionally similar are near one another in hidden-unit space.

In the following sections we treat each of these conceptions.

Sigmoidal Units as Continuous Approximations to Linear Threshold Functions

Perhaps the simplest way to view sigmoidal hidden units is as continuous approximations to the linear threshold function. The best way to understand this is in terms of a two-dimensional stimulus space populated by stimuli which are labeled as members of class A or class B. Figure 8 illustrates such a space. We can imagine a single output unit which is to classify the input vectors (stimuli) as being in one or the other of these classes. A simple perceptron will be able to solve this problem if the stimuli are *linearly separable;* that is, we can draw a line which puts all of the A stimuli on one side of the line and all of the B stimuli on the other side. This is illustrated in part (a) of Figure 8. In part (b) we see that replacing the sharp line of the threshold function with a "fuzzy" line of the sigmoid causes little trouble. It tends to lead to a condition in which stimuli near the border as classified less certainly than those far from the border. This may not be a bad thing since stimuli near the border may be more ambiguous.

When the stimuli are not linearly separable (as illustrated in panel (c) of the figure), the problem is more difficult and hidden units are required. In this case, each hidden unit can be seen as putting down a dividing line segmenting the input field into regions. Ideally each region will contain stimuli of the same kind. Then the weights from the hidden-unit layer to the output units are used to combine the regions which go together to form the final classification. If the stimuli are binary, or more generally if the regions in which they lie are *convex* (as they are in panel (c)), a single layer of hidden threshold units will always be sufficient. If the space is concave, as illustrated in panel (d), then two layers of threshold units may be necessary so that the right regions can be combined. It is nevertheless possible to "approximate" the regions arbitrarily closely with a single hidden layer if enough hidden units are employed. Figure 9 shows how the problem illustrated can be solved exactly with two hidden units in the two-layer case and be approximated arbitrarily closely by many hidden units.

Hidden Units as Basis Functions for Function Approximation

It is also possible to see the hidden layers as forming a set of "basis functions" and see the output units as approximating the function through a linear combina-

(a)

(b)

(c)

(d)

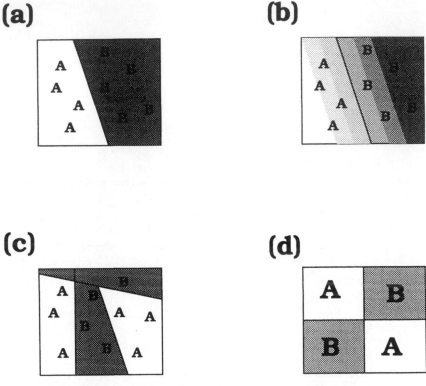

Figure 8.   (a) A simple example of a linearly separable set of points. Perceptrons are capable of classifying such data sets. (b) How the same data would be classified by a sigmoid. The density of the dots indicates the magnitude of the sigmoid. If the problem is really linearly separable, the weights on the sigmoid can grow and it can act just like a perceptron. (c) A set of lines can be used to segregate a convex region. The hidden units put down a set of lines and make space that is originally not linearly separable into one that is. (d) In a concave space it might not be possible to find a set of lines which divide the two regions. In such a case two hidden layers are sometimes convenient.

tion of the hidden units. This is a view espoused by Pogio and Girosi (1989) and others employing the "radial basis function" approach. Typically, this approach involves simply substituting a Gaussian or similar radially symmetric function for the conventional sigmoidal hidden units. Of course, there is no limit to the kind of transfer function the hidden units might employ. The only real constraint (as far as back propagation is concerned) is that the functions are differentiable in their inputs and parameters. So long as this is true any hidden-unit type is possible. Certain unit types may have advantages over others, however. Among the important considerations are the problems of local minima.

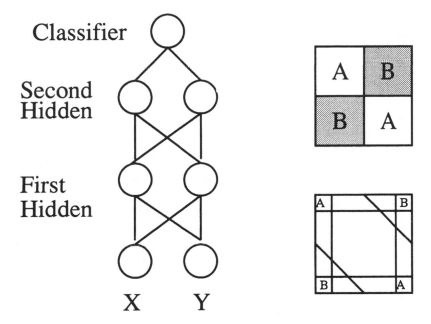

Figure 9.   The first layer works by putting in the vertical and horizontal lines and moving the points to the corners of the region. This means that at the second level the problem is convex and two further hidden units divide the space and make it linearly separable.

As we will see, sigmoidal units are somewhat better behaved than many others with respect to the smoothness of the error surface. Durbin and Rumelhart (1989), for example, have found that, although "product units" $(\mathcal{F}_j(\vec{x}_i|\vec{w}_{ij}) = \Pi_i x_i^{w_{ij}})$ are much more powerful than conventional sigmoidal units (in that fewer parameters were required to represent more functions), it was a much more difficult space to search and there were more problems with local minima.

Another important consideration is the nature of the extrapolation to data points outside the local region from which the data were collected. Radial basis functions have the advantage that they go to zero as you extend beyond the region where the data were collected. Polynomial units $\mathcal{F}_j(\eta_j) = \eta_k^p$ are very ill behaved outside of the training region and for that reason are not especially good choices. Sigmoids are well behaved outside of their local region in that they saturate and are constant at 0 or 1 outside of the training region.

Sigmoidal Hidden Units as Representing Hidden Feature Probabilities

The sigmoidal hidden unit has turned out to be a serendipitous choice. It has a number of nice properties and interpretations which make it rather useful. The first property has to do with the learning process itself. As noted from Figure 10, the sigmoidal unit is roughly linear for small weights (a net input near zero) and gets increasingly nonlinear in its response as it approaches its points of maximum curvature on either side of the midpoint. Thus, at the beginning of learning, when the weights are small, the system is mainly in its linear range and is seeking an essentially linear solution. As the weights grow, the network becomes increasing nonlinear and begins to move toward the nonlinear solution to the problem. This property of initial linearity makes the units rather robust and allows the network to reliably attain the same solution.

Sigmoidal hidden units have a useful interpretation as the posterior probability of the presence of some feature given the input. To see this, think of a sigmoidal hidden unit connected directly to the input units. Suppose that the input vectors are random variables drawn from one of two probability distributions and that the job of the hidden unit is to determine which of the two distributions is being observed. The role of the hidden unit is to give an output value equal to the probability that the input vector was drawn from distribution 1 rather than distribution 2. If drawn from distribution 1 we say that some "hidden feature" was present; otherwise we say it was absent. Denoting the hidden feature for the jth hidden unit as f_j we have

$$P(f_j = 1|\vec{x}) = \frac{P(\vec{x}|f_j = 1)P(f_j = 1)}{P(\vec{x}|f_j = 1)P(f_j = 1) + P(\vec{x}|f_j = 0)P(f_j = 0)}.$$

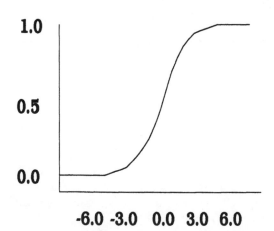

Logistic Sigmoid Function

Figure 10.   The logistic sigmoid is roughly linear near the middle of its range and reaches its maximum curvature.

Now, on the assumption that the x's are *conditionally independent* (i.e., if we know which distribution they were drawn from, there is a fixed probability for each input element that it will occur), we can write

$$P(\vec{x}|f_j = 1) = \Pi_i\, P(x_i|f_j = 1) \qquad \text{and} \qquad P(\vec{x}|f_j = 0) = \Pi_i P(x_i|f_j = 0).$$

Now, on the further assumption that the x's are binomially distributed we get

$$P(\vec{x}|f_j = 1) = \prod_i p_{ij}^{x_i}(1 - p_{ij})^{(1-x_i)},$$

$$P(\vec{x}|f_j = 0) = \prod_i q_{ij}^{x_i}(1 - q_{ij})^{(1-x_i)}.$$

So we finally have

$$P(f_j = 1|\vec{x}) = \frac{\Pi_i p_{ij}^{x_i}(1 - p_{ij})^{(1-x_i)}P(f_j = 1)}{\Pi_i p_{ij}^{x_i}(1 - p_{ij})^{(1-x_i)}P(f_j = 1) + \Pi_i q_{ij}^{x_i}(1 - q_{ij})^{(1-x_i)}P(f_j = 0)}.$$

Taking logs and exponentiating give

$P(f_j = 1|\vec{x})$

$$= \frac{\exp\left\{\sum_i (x_i \ln p_{ij} + (1 - x_i)\ln(1 - p_{ij})) + \ln P(f_j = 1)\right\}}{\exp\left\{\sum_i (x_i \ln p_{ij} + (1 - x_i)\ln(1 - p_{ij})) + \ln P(f_j = 1)\right\} + \exp\left\{\sum_i (x_i \ln q_{ij} + (1 - x_i)\ln(1 - q_{ij})) + \ln P(f_j = 0)\right\}}$$

$$= \frac{\exp\left\{\sum_i \left(x_i \ln \frac{p_{ij}}{1 - p_{ij}} + \sum_i \ln(1 - p_{ij})\right) + \ln P(f_j = 1)\right\}}{\exp\left\{\sum_i \left(x_i \ln \frac{p_{ij}}{1 - p_{ij}} + \sum_i \ln(1 - p_{ij})\right) + \ln P(f_j = 1)\right\} + \exp\left\{\sum_i \left(x_i \ln \frac{q_{ij}}{1 - q_{ij}} + \sum_i \ln(1 - q_{ij})\right) + \ln P(f_j = 0)\right\}}$$

$$= \frac{1}{1 + \exp\left\{-\sum_i \ln \frac{p_{ij}(1 - q_{ij})}{(1 - p_{ij})q_{ij}} + \sum_i \ln \frac{1 - p_{ij}}{1 - q_{ij}} + \ln \frac{P(f_j = 1)}{P(f_j = 0)}\right\}}.$$

Now, it is possible to interpret the exponent as representing η_j, the net input to the unit. If we let

$$\beta_j = \sum_i \ln \frac{1 - p_{ij}}{1 - q_{ij}} + \ln \frac{P(f_j = 1)}{P(f_j = 0)}$$

and

$$w_{ij} = \ln \frac{p_{ij}(1 - q_{ij})}{(1 - p_{ij})q_{ij}},$$

we can see the similarity. We can thus see that the sigmoid is properly understood as representing the posterior probability that some hidden feature is present given the input. Note that, as before, the binomial assumption is not necessary. It is possible to assume that the underlying input vectors are members of any of the exponential family of probability distributions. It is easy to ,write the general form

$$P(f_j = 1|\vec{x}) = \frac{\exp\left\{ \sum_i \frac{(x_i\theta_i - B(\theta_i)) + C(\vec{x},\phi)}{a(\phi)} + \ln P(f_j = 1) \right\}}{\exp\left\{ \sum_i \frac{(x_i\theta_i - B(\theta_i)) + C(\vec{x}\phi)}{a(\phi)} + \ln P(f_j = 1) \right\} + \exp\left\{ \sum_i \frac{(x_i\theta_i^* - B(\theta_i^*) + C(\vec{x},\phi))}{a(\phi)} \right\} + \ln P(f_j = 0)}.$$

By rearranging terms and dividing through by the numerator, we obtain the simple form

$$P(f_j = 1|\vec{x}) = \left(1 + \exp\left\{ -\left(\sum_i x_i \frac{\theta_i - \theta_i^*}{a(\phi)} + \sum_i \frac{B(\theta_i) - B(\theta_i^*)}{a(\phi)} + \ln \frac{P(f_j = 1)}{P(f_j = 0)} \right) \right\}\right)^{-1}$$

$$= \frac{1}{1 + \exp\left[\left(\sum_i x_i w_i + \beta_i \right) \right]}$$

Thus, under the assumption that the input variables are drawn from some member of the exponential family and differ only in their means (represented by θ_i), the sigmoidal hidden unit can be interpreted as the probability that the hidden feature is present. Note the very same form is derived whether the underlying distributions are Gaussian, binomial, or any member of the exponential family. It can readily be seen that, whereas the sigmoid represents the two-alternative case, the normalized exponential clearly represents the multialternative case. Thus, we derive the normalized exponential in exactly the same way as we derive the sigmoid:

$$P(c_j = 1|\vec{x}) = \frac{\exp\{\sum_i[(x_{ij}\theta_i - B(\theta_{ij})) + C(\vec{x}\phi)]/a(\phi) + \ln P(c_j = 1)\}}{\sum_k \exp\{\sum_i[(x_i\theta_{ik} - B(\theta_{ik})) + C(\vec{x}\phi)]/a(\phi) + \ln P(c_k = 1)\}}$$

$$= \frac{\exp\{\sum_i x_{ij}\,\theta_i/a(\phi) - \sum_i B(\theta_{ij})/a(\phi) + \ln P(c_j = 1)\}}{\sum_k \exp\{\sum_i x_i\,\theta_{ik}/a(\phi) - B(\theta_{ik})/a(\phi) + \ln P(c_k = 1)\}}$$

$$= \frac{e^{\sum_i x_{ij} w_{ij} + \beta_j}}{\sum_k e^{\sum_i x_i w_{ik} + \beta_k}}.$$

Hidden-Unit Layers as Representations of the Input Stimuli

Figure 11 illustrates a very simple connectionist network consisting of two layers of units, the input units and output units, connected by a set of weights. As a result of the particular connectivity and weights of this network, each pattern of activation presented at the input units will induce another specific pattern of activation at the output units. This simple architecture is useful in various ways. If the input and output patterns all use distributed representations (i.e., can all be

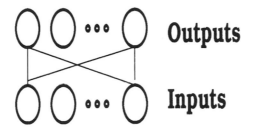

**Similar Inputs Lead
to Similar Outputs**

Figure 11.   Similar inputs produce similar outputs.

described as sets of microfeatures), then this network will exhibit the property that "similar inputs yield similar outputs," along with the accompanying generalization and transfer of learning. Two-layer networks behave this way because the activation of an output unit is given by a relatively smooth function of the weighted sum of its inputs. Thus, a slight change in the value of an input unit will generally yield a similarly slight change in the values of the output units.

Although this similarity-based processing is mostly useful, it does not always yield the correct generalizations. In particular, in a simple two-layer network, the similarity metric employed is determined by the nature of the inputs themselves. And the "physical similarity" we are likely to have at the inputs (based on the structure of stimuli from the physical world) may not be the best measure of the "functional" or "psychological" similarity we would like to employ at the output (to group appropriate similar responses). For example, it is probably true that a lowercase *a* is physically less similar to an uppercase *A* than to a lowercase *o*, but functionally and psychologically a *a* and *A* are more similar to one another than are the two lowercase letters. Thus, physical relatedness is an inadequate similarity metric for modeling human responses to letter-shaped visual inputs. It is therefore necessary to transform these input patterns from their initial physically derived format into another representational form in which patterns requiring similar (output) responses are indeed similar to one another. This involves learning new representations.

Figure 12 illustrates a layered feedforward network in which information (activation) flows up from the input units at the bottom through successive layers of hidden units, to create the final response at the layer of output units on top. Such a network is useful for illustrating how an appropriate psychological or functional representation can be created. If we think of each input vector as a point in some multidimensional space, we can think of the similarity between

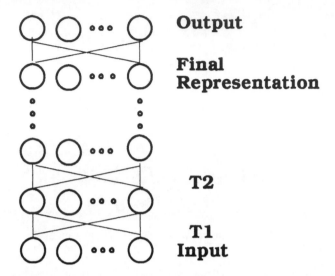

Figure 12.   We can think of multilayer networks as transforming the input through a series of successive transformations so as to create a representation in which "functionally" similar stimuli are near one another when viewed as points in a multidimensional space.

two such vectors as the distance between their two corresponding points. Furthermore, we can think of the weighted connections from one layer of units to the next as implementing a transformation that maps each original input vector into some new vector. This transformation can create a new vector space in which the relative distances among the points corresponding to the input vectors are different from those in the original vector space, essentially rearranging the points. And if we use a sequence of such transformations, each involving certain non-linearities, by "stacking" them between successive layers in the network, we can entirely rearrange the similarity relations among the original input vectors.

Thus, a layered network can be viewed simply as a mechanism for transforming the original set of input stimuli into a new similarity space with a new set of distances among the input points. For example, it is possible to move the initially distant "physical" input representations of *a* and *A* so that they are very close to one another in a transformed "psychological" output representation space, and simultaneously transform the distance between *a* and *o* output representations so that they are rather distant from one another. (Generally, we seek to attain a representation in the second-to-last layer which is sufficiently transformed that we can rely on the principle that similar patterns yield similar outputs at the final layer.) The problem is to find an appropriate sequence of transformations that accomplish the desired input-to-output change in similarity structures.

The back-propagation learning algorithm can be viewed, then, as a procedure for discovering such a sequence of transformations. In fact, we can see the role of learning in general as a mechanism for constructing the transformations which will convert the original physically based configuration of the input vectors into an appropriate functional or psychological space, with the proper similarity relationships between concepts for making generalizations and transfer of learning occur automatically and correctly.

CONCLUSION

In this chapter we have tried to provide a kind of overview and rationale for the design and understanding of networks. Although it is possible to design and use interesting networks without any of the ideas presented here, it is, in our experience, very valuable to understand networks in terms of these probabilistic interpretations. The value is primarily in providing an understanding of the networks and their behavior so that one can craft an appropriate network for an appropriate problem. Although it has been commonplace to view networks as kinds of black boxes, this leads to inappropriate applications which may fail not because such networks cannot work but because the issues are not well understood.

REFERENCES

Cover, T. H. (1965). Geometrical and statistical properties of systems of linear inequalities with applications in pattern recognition. *IEEE Transactions on Electronic Computers, 14*. pp. 326–334

Durbin, R., & Rumelhart, D. E. (1989). Product units: A computationally powerful and biologically lausible extension to backpropagation networks. *Neural Computation, 1*, 133–142.

Durbin, R., & Willshaw, D. (1987). An analogue approach to the travelling salesman problem using an elastic net method. *Nature, 326*, 689–691.

Hornik, K., Stinchcombe, M., & White, H. (1989). Multilayer Feed-forward Networks are Universal Approximators, *Neural Networks, 2*, pp. 359–366.

Jacobs, R. A., Jordan, M. I., Nowlan, S. J., & Hinton, G. E. (1991). Adaptive mixtures of local experts. *Neural Computation, 3*(1).

Jordan, M. I., & Rumelhart, D. E. (1992). Forward models: Supervised learning with a distal teacher. *Cognitive Science, 16*, pp. 307–354.

Keeler, J. D., Rumelhart, D. E., & Loew, W. (1991). Integrated segmentation and recognition of hand-printed numerals. In R. P. Lippmann, J. E. Moody, and D. S. Touretzky (Eds.), *Neural information processing systems* (Vol. 3). San Mateo, CA: Morgan Kaufmann.

Kolmogorov, A. N. (1991). *Selected Works of A. N. Kolmogorov*, Dordrecht; Boston; Kluwer Academic.

Le Cun, Y., Boser, Y. B., Denke, J. S., Henderson, R. D., Howard, R. E., Hubbard, W., & Jackel, L. D. (1990). In D. S. Touretzky (Ed.), *Handwritten digit recognition with a back-propagation network* (Vol. 2). San Mateo, CA: Morgan Kaufmann.

McCullagh, P. & Nelder, J. A. (1989). *Generalized linear models*. London: Chapman and Hall.

Mitchison, G. J., & Durbin, R. M. (1989). Bounds on the learning capacity of some multi-layer networks. *Biological Cybernetics, 60*, 345–356.

Nowlan, S. J. (1991). *Soft Competitive Adaptation: Neural Network Learning Algorithm based on*

Fitting Statistical Mixtures. Ph.D. thesis, School of Computer Science, Carnegie Mellon University, Pittsburgh, PA.

Parker, D. B. (1982). *Learning-logic* (Invention Report S81-64, File 1). Stanford, CA: Office of Technology Licensing, Stanford University.

Pogio, T., & Girosi, F. (1989). *A theory of networks for approximation and learning*. A. I. Memo No. 1140, Artificial Intelligence Laboratory, Massachusetts Institute of Technology.

Rosenblatt, F. (1962). *Principles of neurodynamics*. New York: Spartan.

Rumelhart, D. E. (1990). Brain style computation: Learning and generalization. In S. F. Zornetzer, J. L. Davis, and C. Lau (Eds.), *An introduction to neural and electronic networks*. San Diego: Academic Press.

Rumelhart, D. E., Hinton, G. E., & Williams, R. J. (1986). Learning internal representations by error propagation. In D. E. Rumelhart and J. L. McClelland (Eds.), *Parallel Distributed Processing: Explorations in the Microstructure of Cognition* (Vol. 1). Cambridge, MA: Bradford Books.

Waibel, A., Hanazawa, T., Hinton, G., Shikano, K., & Lang, K. (1989). Phoneme recognition using time-delay neural networks. *IEEE Transactions on Acoustics, Speech and Signal Processing. 37*, 328–338.

Weigend, A. S., Huberman, B. A., & Rumelhart, D. E. (1990). Predicting the future: A connectionist approach. *International Journal of Neural Systems, 1*, 193–209.

Weigend, A. S., Rumelhart, D. E., & Huberman, B. (1991). Generalization by weight-elimination with application to forecasting. In R. P. Lippman, J. Moody, and D. S. Touretsky (Eds.), *Advances in neural information processing* (Vol. 3, pp. 875–882). San Mateo, CA: Morgan Kaufman.

Werbos, P. (1974). *Beyond regression: New tools for prediction and analysis in the behavioral sciences*. Unpublished dissertation, Harvard University.

2 Phoneme Recognition Using Time-Delay Neural Networks*

Alexander Waibel
Computer Science Department, Carnegie Mellon University

Toshiyuki Hanazawa
ATR Interpreting Telephony Research Laboratories, Osaka, Japan

Geoffrey Hinton
University of Toronto

Kiyohiro Shikano
ATR Interpreting Telephony Research Laboratories, Osaka, Japan

Kevin J. Lang
Carnegie Mellon University

ABSTRACT

In this paper we present a Time-Delay Neural Network (TDNN) approach to phoneme recognition which is characterized by two important properties. 1) Using a 3 layer arrangement of simple computing units, a hierarchy can be constructed that allows for the formation of arbitrary nonlinear decision surfaces. The TDNN learns these decision surfaces automatically using error backpropagation [1]. 2) The time-delay arrangement enables the network to discover acoustic-phonetic features and the temporal relationships between them independent of position in time and hence not blurred by temporal shifts in the input.

As a recognition task, the speaker-dependent recognition of the phonemes "B," "D," and "G" in varying phonetic contexts was chosen. For comparison, several discrete Hidden Markov Models (HMM) were trained to perform the same task. Performance evaluation over 1946 testing tokens from three speakers showed that the TDNN achieves a recognition rate of 98.5 percent correct while the rate ob-

*Reprinted from IEEE TRANSACTIONS ON ACOUSTICS, SPEECH AND SIGNAL PRO-CESSING Vol. 37, No. 3, March 1989.

tained by the best of our HMM's was only 93.7 percent. Closer inspection reveals that the network "invented" well-known acoustic–phonetic features (e.g., F2-rise, F2-fall, vowel-onset) as useful abstractions. It also developed alternate internal representations to link different acoustic realizations to the same concept.

I. INTRODUCTION

In recent years, the advent of new learning procedures and the availability of high speed parallel supercomputers have given rise to a renewed interest in connectionist models of intelligence [1]. Sometimes also referred to as artificial neural networks or parallel distributed processing models, these models are particularly interesting for cognitive tasks that require massive constraint satisfaction, i.e., the parallel evaluation of many clues and facts and their interpretation in the light of numerous interrelated constraints. Cognitive tasks, such as vision, speech, language processing, and motor control, are also characterized by a high degree of uncertainty and variability and it has proved difficult to achieve good performance for these tasks using standard serial programming methods. Complex networks composed of simple computing units are attractive for these tasks not only because of their "brain-like" appeal[1] but because they offer ways for automatically designing systems that can make use of multiple interacting constraints. In general, such constraints are too complex to be easily programmed and require the use of automatic learning strategies. Such learning algorithms now exist (for an excellent review, see Lippman [2]) and have been demonstrated to discover interesting internal abstractions in their attempts to solve a given problem [1], [3]–[5]. Learning is most effective, however, when used in an architecture that is appropriate for the task. Indeed, applying one's prior knowledge of a task domain and its properties to the design of a suitable neural network model might well prove to be a key element in the successful development of connectionist systems.

Naturally, these techniques will have far-reaching implications for the design of automatic speech recognition systems, if proven successful in comparison to already-existing techniques. Lippmann [6] has compared several kinds of neural networks to other classifiers and evaluated their ability to create complex decision surfaces. Other studies have investigated actual speech recognition tasks and compared them to psychological evidence in speech perception [7] or to existing speech recognition techniques [8], [9]. Speech recognition experiments using neural nets have so far mostly been aimed at isolated word recognition (mostly the digit recognition task) [10]–[13] or phonetic recognition with predefined constant [14], [15] or variable phonetic contexts [16], [14], [17].

A number of these studies report very encouraging recognition performance

---

[1]The uninitiated reader should be cautioned not to overinterpret the now-popular term "neural network." Although these networks appear to mimic certain properties of neural cells, no claim can be made that present exploratory attempts simulate the complexities of the human brain.

[16], but only few comparisons to existing recognition methods exist. Some of these comparisons found performance similar to existing methods [9], [11], but others found that networks perform worse than other techniques [8]. One might argue that this state of affairs is encouraging considering the amount of fine-tuning that has gone into optimizing the more popular, established techniques. Nevertheless, better comparative performance figures are needed before neural networks can be considered as a viable alternative for speech recognition systems.

One possible explanation for the mixed performance results obtained so far may be limitations in computing resources leading to shortcuts that limit performance. Another more serious limitation, however, is the inability of most neural network architectures to deal properly with the dynamic nature of speech. Two important aspects of this are for a network to represent temporal relationships between acoustic events, while at the same time providing for invariance under translation in time. The specific movement of a formant in time, for example, is an important cue to determining the identity of a voiced stop, but it is irrelevant whether the same set of events occurs a little sooner or later in the course of time. Without translation invariance, a neural net requires precise segmentation to align the input pattern properly. Since this is not always possible in practice, learned features tend to get blurred (in order to accommodate slight misalignments) and their performance deteriorates. In general, shift invariance has been recognized as a critically important property for connectionist systems and a number of promising models have been proposed for speech and other domains [18]–[21], [14], [17], [22].

In the present paper, we describe a Time-Delay Neural Network (TDNN) which addresses both of these aspects of speech and demonstrate through extensive performance evaluation that superior recognition results can be achieved using this approach. In the following section, we begin by introducing the architecture and learning strategy of a TDNN aimed at phoneme recognition. Next, we compare the performance of our TDNN's to one of the more popular current recognition techniques: Hidden Markov Models (HMM). In Section III, we start by describing an HMM, under development at ATR [23], [24]. Both techniques, the TDNN and the HMM, are then evaluated over a testing database and we report the results. We show that substantially higher recognition performance is achieved by the TDNN than by the best of our HMM's. In Section IV, we then take a closer look at the internal representation that the TDNN learns for this task. It discovers a number of interesting linguistic abstractions which we show by way of examples. The implications of these results are then discussed and summarized in the final section of this paper.

II. TIME-DELAY NEURAL NETWORKS (TDNN)

To be useful for speech recognition, a layered feedforward neural network must have a number of properties. First, it should have multiple layers and sufficient interconnections between units in each of these layers. This is to ensure that the network will have the ability to learn complex nonlinear decision surfaces [2], [6]. Second, the network should have the ability to represent relationships between events in time. These events could be spectral coefficients, but might also be the output of higher level feature detectors. Third, the actual features or abstractions learned by the network should be invariant under translation in time. Fourth, the learning procedure should not require precise temporal alignment of the labels that are to be learned. Fifth, the number of weights in the network should be sufficiently small compared to the amount of training data so that the network is forced to encode the training data by extracting regularity. In the following, we describe a TDNN architecture that satisfies all of these criteria and is designed explicitly for the recognition of phonemes, in particular, the voiced stops "B," "D," and "G."

A. A TDNN Architecture for Phoneme Recognition

The basic unit used in many neural networks computes the weighted sum of its inputs and then passes this sum through a nonlinear function, most commonly a threshold or sigmoid function [2], [1]. In our TDNN, this basic unit is modified by introducing delays D_1 through D_N as shown in Fig. 1. The J inputs of such a unit now will be multiplied by several weights, one for each delay and one for the undelayed input. For $N = 2$, and $J = 16$, for example, 48 weights will be needed to compute the weighted sum of the 16 inputs, with each input now measured at three different points in time. In this way, a TDNN unit has the ability to relate and compare current input to the past history of events. The sigmoid function was chosen as the nonlinear output function F due to its convenient mathematical properties [18], [5].

For the recognition of phonemes, a three layer net is constructed.[2] Its overall architecture and a typical set of activities in the units are shown in Fig. 2.

At the lowest level, 16 normalized melscale spectral coefficients serve as input to the network. Input speech, sampled at 12 kHz, was Hamming windowed and a 256-point FFT computed every 5 ms. Melscale coefficients were computed from the power spectrum by computing log energies in each melscale energy band [25], where adjacent coefficients in frequency overlap by one spectral sample and are smoothed by reducing the shared sample by 50 percent [25].[3]

---

[2]Lippmann [2], [6] demonstrated recently that three layers can encode arbitrary pattern recognition decision surfaces. We believe that complex nonlinear decision surfaces are necessary to properly perform classification in the light of considerable acoustic variability as reported in the experiments below.

[3]Naturally, a number of alternative signal representations could be used as input, but have not been tried in this study. Filterbank coefficients were chosen as they are simple to compute and readily interpretable in the light of acoustic-phonetics. The melscale is a physiologically motivated frequency scale that provides better relative frequency resolution for lower frequency bands. Our implementation resulted in coefficients with a band-width of approximately 190 Hz up to 1400 Hz, and with increasing band-widths thereafter.

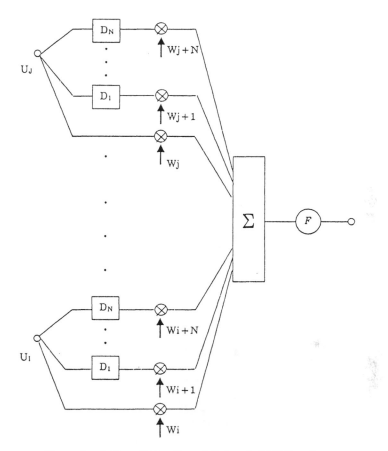

Figure 1.   A Time-Delay Neural Network (TDNN) unit.

Adjacent coefficients in time were collapsed for further data reduction resulting in an overall 10 ms frame rate. All coefficients of an input token (in this case, 15 frames of speech centered around the hand-labeled vowel onset) were then normalized. This was accomplished by subtracting from each coefficient the average coefficient energy computed over all 15 frames of an input token and then normalizing each coefficient to lie between -1 and $+1$. All tokens in our database were preprocessed in the same fashion. Fig. 2 shows the resulting coefficients for the speech token "BA" as input to the network, where positive values are shown as black squares and negative values as gray squares.

This input layer is then fully interconnected to a layer of 8 time-delay hidden units, where $J = 16$ and $N = 2$ (i.e., 16 coefficients over 3 frames with time delay 0, 1, and 2). An alternative way of seeing this is depicted in Fig. 2. It shows the inputs to these time-delay units expanded out spatially into a 3 frame window, which is passed over the input spectrogram. Each unit in the first hidden

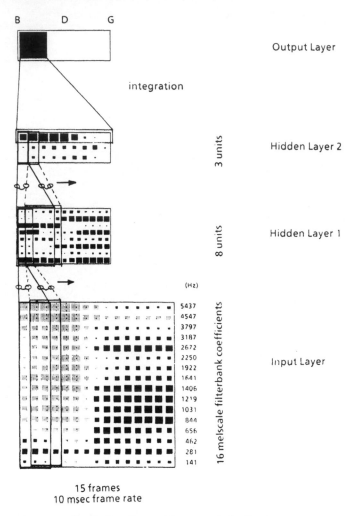

Figure 2.   The architecture of the TDNN.

layer now receives input (via 48 weighted connections) from the coefficients in the 3 frame window. The particular choice of 3 frames (30 ms) was motivated by earlier studies [26]–[29] that suggest that a 30 ms window might be sufficient to represent low level acoustic–zphonetic events for stop consonant recognition. It was also the optimal choice among a number of alternative designs evaluated by Lang [21] on a similar task.

In the second hidden layer, each of 3 TDNN units looks at a 5 frame window of activity levels in hidden layer 1 (i.e., $J = 8$, $N = 4$). The choice of a larger 5 frame window in this layer was motivated by the intuition that higher level units should learn to make decisions over a wider range in time based on more local abstractions at lower levels.

Finally, the output is obtained by integrating (summing) the evidence from each of the 3 units in hidden layer 2 over time and connecting it to its pertinent output unit (shown in Fig. 2 over 9 frames for the "B" output unit). In practice, this summation is implemented simply as another nonlinear (sigmoid function is applied here as well) TDNN unit which has fixed equal weights to a row of unit findings over time in hidden layer 2.[4]

When the TDNN has learned its internal representation, it performs recognition by passing input speech over the TDNN units. In terms of the illustration of Fig. 2, this is equivalent to passing the time-delay windows over the lower level units' firing patterns.[5] At the lowest level, these firing patterns simply consist of the sensory input, i.e., the spectral coefficients.

Each TDNN unit outlined in this section has the ability to encode temporal relationships within the range of the N delays. Higher layers can attend to larger time spans, so local short duration features will be formed at the lower layer and more complex longer duration features at the higher layer. The learning procedure ensures that each of the units in each layer has its weights adjusted in a way that improves the network's overall performance.

B. Learning in a TDNN

Several learning techniques exist for optimization of neural networks [1], [2], [30]. For the present network, we adopt the Backpropagation Learning Procedure [18], [5]. Mathematically, backpropagation is gradient descent of the mean-squared error as a function of the weights. The procedure performs two passes through the network. During the forward pass, an input pattern is applied to the network with its current connection strengths (initially small random weights). The outputs of all the units at each level are computed starting at the input layer and working forward to the output layer. The output is then compared to the desired output and its error calculated. During the backward pass, the derivative of this error is then propagated back through the network, and all the weights are adjusted so as to decrease the error [18], [5]. This is repeated many times for all the training tokens until the network converges to producing the desired output.

In the previous section, we described a method of expressing temporal structure in a TDNN and contrasted this method to training a network on a static input

---

[4]Note, however, that as for all units in this network (except the input units), the output units are also connected to a permanently active threshold unit. In this way, both an output unit's one shared connection to a row in hidden layer 2 and its dc-bias are learned and can be adjusted for optimal classification.

[5]Thus, 13 frames of activations in hidden layer 1 are generated when scanning the 15 frames of input speech with a 3 frame time delay window. Similarly, 9 frames are produced in hidden layer 2 from the 13 frames of activation in the layer below.

pattern (spectrogram), which results in shift sensitive networks (i.e., poor performance for slightly misaligned input patterns) as well as less crisp decision making in the units of the network (caused by misaligned tokens during training).

To achieve the desired learning behavior, we need to ensure that the network is exposed to *sequences* of patterns and that it is allowed (or encouraged) to learn about the most powerful cues and sequences of cues among them. Conceptually, the backpropagation procedure is applied to speech patterns that are stepped through in time. An equivalent way of achieving this result is to use a spatially expanded input pattern, i.e., a spectrogram plus some constraints on the weights. Each collection of TDNN units described above is duplicated for each one frame shift in time. In this way, the whole history of activities is available at once. Since the shifted copies of the TDNN units are mere duplicates and are to look for the same acoustic event, the weights of the corresponding connections in the time shifted copies must be constrained to be the same. To implement this, we first apply the regular backpropagation forward and backward pass to all time-shifted copies as if they were separate events. This yields different error derivatives for corresponding (time shifted) connections. Rather than changing the weights on time-shifted connections separately, however, we actually update each weight on corresponding connections by the same value, namely by *the average* of all corresponding time-delayed weight changes.[6] Fig. 2 illustrates this by showing in each layer only two connections that are linked to (constrained to have the same value as) their time-shifted neighbors. Of course, this applies to all connections and all time shifts. In this way, the network is forced to discover useful acoustic-phonetic features in the input, regardless of when in time they actually occurred. This is an important property, as it makes the network independent of error-prone preprocessing algorithms that otherwise would be needed for time alignment and/or segmentation. In Section IV-C, we will show examples of grossly misaligned patterns that are properly recognized due to this property.

The procedure described here is computationally rather expensive, due to the many iterations necessary for learning a complex multidimensional weight space and the number of learning samples. In our case, about 800 learning samples were used, and between 20 000 and 50 000 iterations of the backpropagation loop were run over all training samples. Two steps were taken to perform learning within reasonable time. First, we have implemented our learning procedure in C and Fortran on a 4 processor Alliant supercomputer. The speed of learning can be improved considerably by computing the forward and backward sweeps for several different training samples in parallel on different processors. Further improvements can be gained by vectorizing operations and possibly assembly coding the innermost loop. Our present implementation achieves about a factor

---

[6]Note that in the experiments reported below, these weight changes were actually carried out each time the error derivatives from all training samples had been computed [5].

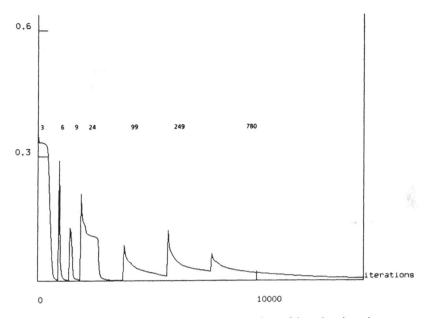

Figure 3. TDNN output error versus number of learning iterations (increasing training set size).

of 9 speedup over a VAX 8600, but still leaves room for further improvements (Lang [21], for example, reports a speedup of a factor of 120 over a VAX11/780 for an implementation running on a Convex supercomputer). The second step taken toward improving learning time is given by a staged learning strategy. In this approach, we start optimizing the network based on 3 prototypical training tokens only.[7] In this case, convergence is achieved rapidly, but the network will have learned a representation that generalizes poorly to new and different patterns. Once convergence is achieved, the network is presented with approximately twice the number of tokens and learning continues until convergence.

Fig. 3 shows the progress during a typical learning run. The measured error is $1/2$ the squared error of all the output units, normalized for the number of training tokens. In this run, the number of training tokens used were 3, 6, 9, 24, 99, 249, and 780. As can be seen from Fig. 3, the error briefly jumps up every time more variability is introduced by way of more training data. The network is then forced to improve its representation to discover clues that generalize better and to deemphasize those that turn out to be merely irrelevant idiosyncrasies of a limited sample set. Using the full training set of 780 tokens, this particular run

---

[7]Note that for optimal learning, the training data are presented by always alternating tokens for each class. Hence, we start the network off by presenting 3 tokens, one for each class.

was continued until iteration 35 000 (Fig. 3 shows the learning curve only up to 15 000 iterations). With this full training set, small learning steps have to be taken and learning progresses slowly. In this case, a step size of 0.002 and a momentum [5] of 0.1 was used. The staged learning approach was found to be useful to move the weights of the network rapidly into the neighborhood of a reasonable solution, before the rather slow fine tuning over all training tokens begins.

Despite these speedups, learning runs still take in the order of several days. A number of programming tricks [21] as well as modifications to the learning procedure [31] are not implemented yet and could yield another factor of 10 or more in learning time reduction. It is important to note, however, that the amount of computation considered here is necessary *only for learning* of a TDNN and *not for recognition*. Recognition can easily be performed in better than real time on a workstation or personal computer. The simple structure makes TDNN's also well suited for standardized VLSI implementation. The detailed knowledge could be learned "off-line" using substantial computing power and then downloaded in the form of weights onto a real-time production network.

III. RECOGNITION EXPERIMENTS

We now turn to an experimental evaluation of the TDNN's recognition performance. In particular, we would like to compare the TDNN's performance to the performance of the currently most popular recognition method: Hidden Markov Models (HMM). For the performance evaluation reported here, we have chosen the best of a number of HMM's developed in our laboratory. Several other HMM-based variations and models have been tried in an effort to optimize our HMM, but we make no claim that an exhaustive evaluation of all HMM-based techniques was accomplished. We should also point out that the experiments reported here were aimed at evaluating two different *recognition philosophies.* Each recognition method was therefore implemented and optimized using its preferred representation of the speech signal, i.e., a representation that is well suited and most commonly used for the method evaluated. Evaluation of both methods was of course carried out using the same speech input data, but we caution the reader that due to the differences in representation, the exact contribution to overall performance of the recognition strategy as opposed to its signal representation is not known. It is conceivable that improved front end processing might lead to further performance improvements for either technique. In the following sections, we will start by introducing the best of our Hidden Markov Models. We then describe the experimental conditions and the database used for performance evaluation and conclude with the performance results achieved by our TDNN and HMM.

A. A Hidden Markov Model (HMM)
for Phoneme Recognition

HMM's are currently the most successful and promising approach [32]–[34] in speech recognition as they have been successfully applied to the whole range of recognition tasks. Excellent performance was achieved at all levels from the phonemic level [35]–[38] to word recognition [39], [34] and to continuous speech recognition [40]. The success of HMM's is partially due to their ability to cope with the variability in speech by means of stochastic modeling. In this section, we describe an HMM developed in our laboratory that was aimed at phoneme recognition, more specifically the voiced stops "B," "D," and "G." The model described was the best of a number of alternate designs developed in our laboratory [23], [24].

The acoustic front end for Hidden Markov's Modeling is typically a vector quantizer that classifies sequences of short-time spectra. Such a representation was chosen as it is highly effective for HMM-based recognizers [40].

Input speech was sampled at 12 kHz, preemphasized by $(1 - 0.97\ z^{-1})$, and windowed using a 256-point Hamming window every 3 ms. Then a 12-order LPC analysis was carried out. A codebook of 256 LPC spectrum envelopes was generated from 216 phonetically balanced words. The Weighted Likelihood Ratio [41], [42] augmented with power values (PWLR) [43], [42] was used as LPC distance measure for vector quantization.

A fairly standard HMM was adopted in this paper as shown in Fig. 4. It has four states and six transitions and was found to be the best of a series of alternate models tried in our laboratory. These included models with two, three, four, and five states and with tied arcs and null arcs [23], [24].

The HMM probability values were trained using vector sequences of phonemes according to the forward-backward algorithm [32]. The vector sequences for "B," "D," and "G" include a consonant part and five frames of the following vowel. This is to model important transient information, such as formant movement, and has lead to improvements over context insensitive models [23], [24]. Again, variations on these parameters have been tried for the discrimination of these three voiced stop consonants. In particular, we have used 10 and 15 frames (i.e., 30 and 45 ms) of the following vowel in a 5 state HMM, but no performance improvements over the model described were obtained.

The HMM was trained using about 250 phoneme tokens of vector sequences

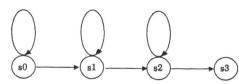

Figure 4. Hidden Markov Model.

per speaker and phoneme (see details of the training database below). Fig. 5 shows for a typical training run the average log probability normalized by the number of frames. Training was continued until the increase of the average log probability between iterations became less than $2 * 10^{-3}$.

Typically, about 10–20 learning iterations are required for 256 tokens. A training run takes about 1 h on a VAX 8700. Floor values[8] were set on the output probabilities to avoid errors caused by zero probabilities. We have experimented with composite models, which were trained using a combination of context-independent and context-dependent probability values as suggested by Schwartz et al. [35], [36]. In our case, no significant improvements were attained.

B. Experimental Conditions

For performance evaluation, we have used a large vocabulary database of 5240 common Japanese words [44]. These words were uttered in isolation by three male native Japanese speakers (MAU, MHT, and MNM, all professional announcers) in the order they appear in a Japanese dictionary. All utterances were recorded in a sound-proof booth and digitized at a 12 kHz sampling rate. The database was then split into a training set (the even numbered files as derived from the recording order) and a testing set (the odd numbered files). A given speaker's training and testing data, therefore, consisted of 2620 utterances each, from which the actual phonetic tokens were extracted.

The phoneme recognition task chosen for this experiment was the recognition of the voiced stops, i.e., the phonemes "B," "D," and "G." The actual tokens were extracted from the utterances using manually selected acoustic–phonetic labels provided with the database [44]. For speaker MAU, for example, a total of 219 "B's," 203 "D's," and 260 "G's" were extracted from the training and 227 "B's," 179 "D's," and 252 "G's," from the testing data. Both recognition schemes, the TDNN's and the HMM's, were trained and tested speaker dependently. Thus, in both cases, separate networks were trained for each speaker.

In our database, no preselection of tokens was performed. All tokens labeled as one of the three voiced stops were included. It is important to note that since the consonant tokens were extracted from entire utterances and *not* read in isolation, a significant amount of phonetic variability exists. Foremost, there is the variability introduced by the phonetic context out of which a token is extracted. The actual signal of a "BA" will therefore look significantly different from a "BI" and so on. Second, the position of a phonemic token within the utterance introduces additional variability. In Japanese, for example, a "G" is nasalized, when it occurs embedded in an utterance, but not in utterance initial position. Both of our recognition algorithms are only given the phonemic identity of a token and must find their own ways of representing the fine variations of speech.

---

[8]Here, once again, the optimal value out of a number of alternative choices was selected.

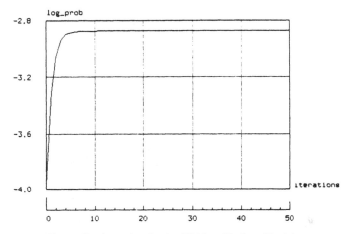

Figure 5.   Learning in the Hidden Markov Model.

C. Results

Table I shows the results from the recognition experiments described above as obtained from the *testing data*. As can be seen, for all three speakers, the TDNN yields considerably higher performance than our HMM. Averaged over all three speakers, the error rate is reduced from 6.3 to 1.5 percent—a more than fourfold reduction in error.

While it is particularly important here to base performance evaluation on testing data,[9] a few observations can be made from recognition runs over the training data. For the training data set, recognition error rates were: 99.6 percent (MAU), 99.7 percent (MHT), and 99.7 percent (MNM) for the TDNN, and 96.9 percent (MAU), 99.1 percent (MHT), and 95.7 percent (MNM) for the HMM. Comparison of these results to those from the testing data in Table I indicates that both methods achieved good generalization from the training set to unknown data. The data also suggest that better classification rather than better generalization might be the cause of the TDNN's better performance shown in Table I.

Figs. 6–11 show scatter plots of the recognition outcome for the test data for speaker MAU, using the HMM and the TDNN. For the HMM (see Figs. 6–8), the log probability of the next best matching *incorrect* token is plotted against the log probability[10] of the correct token, e.g., "B," "D," and "G." In Figs. 9–11, the activation levels from the TDNN's output units are plotted in the same fashion. Note that these plots are not easily comparable, as the two recognition methods have been trained in quite different ways. They do, however, represent the numerical values that each method's decision rule uses to determine the

---

[9]If the training data are insufficient, neural networks can in principle learn to *memorize* training patterns rather than finding generalization of speech.

[10]Normalized by number of frames.

TABLE 1
Recognition Results for Three Speakers Over Test Data
Using TDNN and HMM

speaker	number of tokens	number of errors	recognition rate	TDNN	number of errors	recognition rate	HMM
MAU	b(227)	4	98.2		18	92.1	
	d(179)	3	98.3	98.8	6	96.7	92.9
	g(252)	1	99.6		23	90.9	
MHT	b(208)	2	99.0		8	96.2	
	d(170)	0	100	99.1	3	98.2	97.2
	g(254)	4	98.4		7	97.2	
MNM	b(216)	11	94.9		27	87.5	
	d(178)	1	99.4	97.5	13	92.7	90.9
	g(256)	4	98.4		19	92.6	

recognition outcome. We present these plots here to show some interesting properties of the two techniques. The most striking observation that can be made from these plots is that the output units of a TDNN have a tendency to fire with high confidence as can be seen from the cluster of dots in the lower right-hand corner of the scatter plots. Most output units tend to fire strongly for the correct phonemic class and not all for any other, a property that is encouraged by the

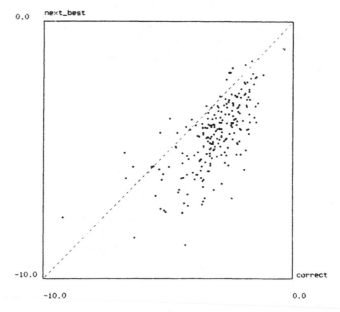

Figure 6.   Scatter plot showing log probabilities for the best matching incorrect case versus the correctly recognized "B's" using an HMM.

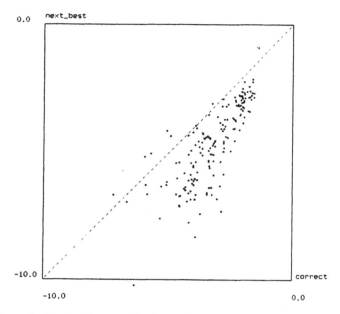

Figure 7. Scatter plot showing log probabilities for the best matching incorrect case versus the correctly recognized "D's" using an HMM.

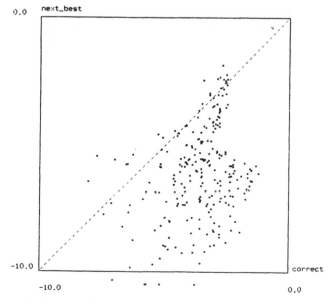

Figure 8. Scatter plot showing log probabilities for the best matching incorrect case versus the correctly recognized "G's" using an HMM.

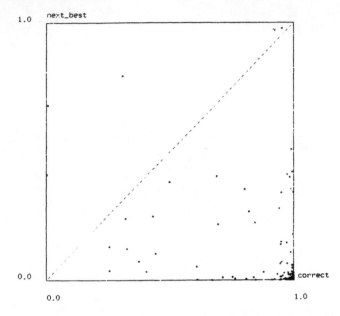

Figure 9.   Scatter plot showing activation levels for the best matching incorrect case versus the correctly recognized "B's" using a TDNN.

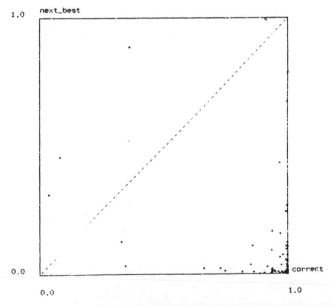

Figure 10.   Scatter plot showing activation levels for the best matching incorrect case versus the correctly recognized "D's" using a TDNN.

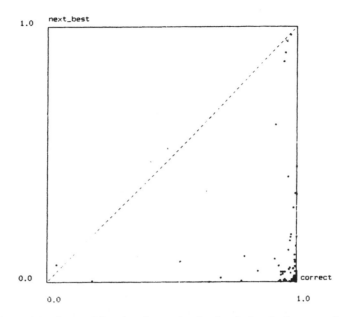

Figure 11. Scatter plot showing activation levels for the best matching incorrect case versus the correctly recognized "G's" using a TDNN.

learning procedure. One possible consequence of this is that rejection thresholds
could be introduced to improve recognition performance. If one were to eliminate among speaker MAU's tokens all those whose highest activation level is less
than 0.5 and those which result in two or more closely competing activations
(i.e., are near the diagonal in the scatter plots), 2.6 percent of all tokens would be
rejected, while the remaining substitution error rate would be less than 0.46
percent.

IV. THE LEARNED INTERNAL REPRESENTATIONS OF A TDNN

Given the encouraging performance of our TDNN's, a close look at the learned
internal representation of the network is warranted. What are the properties or
abstractions that the network has learned that appear to yield a very powerful
description of voiced stops? Figs. 12 and 13 show two typical instances of a "D"
out of two different phonetic contexts ("DA" and "DO," respectively). In both
cases, only the correct unit, the "D-output unit," fires strongly, despite the fact
that the two input spectrograms differ considerably from each other. If we study
the internal firings in these two cases, we can see that the network has learned to

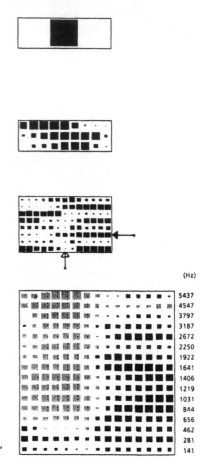

Figure 12.   TDNN activation patterns for "DA."

use alternate internal representations to link variations in the sensory input to the same higher level concepts. A good example is given by the firings of the third and fourth hidden unit in the first layer above the input layer. As can be seen from Fig. 13, the fourth hidden unit fires particularly strongly after vowel onset in the case of "DO," while the third unit shows stronger activation after vowel onset in the case of "DA."

Fig. 14 shows the significance of these different firing patterns. Here the connection strengths for the eight moving TDNN units are shown, where white and black blobs represent positive and negative weights, respectively, and the magnitude of a weight is indicated by the size of the blob. In this figure, the time delays are displayed spatially as a 3 frame window of 16 spectral coefficients. Conceptually, the weights in this window form a moving acoustic–phonetic feature detector that fires when the pattern for which it is specialized is encoun-

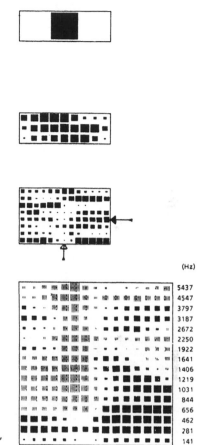

Figure 13.   TDNN activation patterns for "DO."

tered in the input speech. In our example, we can see that hidden unit number 4 (which was activated for "DO") has learned to fire when a falling (or rising) second formant starting at around 1600 Hz is found in the input (see filled arrow in Fig. 14). As can be seen in Fig. 13, this is the case for "DO" and hence the firing of hidden unit 4 after voicing onset (see row pointed to by the filled arrow in Fig. 13). In the case of "DA" (see Fig. 12), in turn, the second formant does not fall significantly, and hidden unit 3 (pointed to by the filled arrow) fires instead. From Fig. 14 we can verify that TDNN unit 3 has learned to look for a steady (or only slightly falling) second formant starting at about 1800 Hz. The connections in the second and third layer then link the different firing patterns observed in the first hidden layer into one and the same decision.

Another interesting feature can be seen in the bottom hidden unit in hidden layer number 1 (see Figs. 12 and 13, and compare them to the weights of hidden

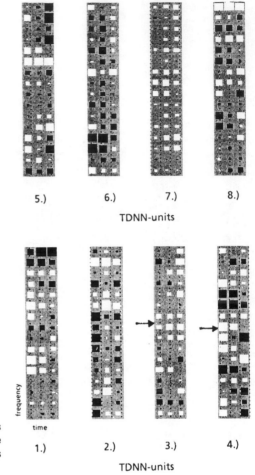

5.)   6.)   7.)   8.)

TDNN-units

Figure 14. Weights on connections from 16 coefficients over 3 time frames to each of the 8 hidden units in the first layer.

frequency

time

1.)   2.)   3.)   4.)

TDNN-units

unit 1 displayed in Fig. 14). This unit has learned to take on the role of finding the segment boundary of the voiced stop. It does so in reverse polarity, i.e., it is always on *except* when the vowel onset of the voiced stop is encountered (see unfilled arrow in Figs. 13 and 12). Indeed, the higher layer TDNN units subsequently use this "segmenter" to base the final decision on the occurrence of the right lower features at the right point in time.

In the previous example, we have seen that the TDNN can account for variations in phonetic context. Figs. 15 and 16 show examples of variability caused by the relative position of a phoneme within a word. In Japanese, a "G" embedded in a word tends to be nasalized as seen in the spectrum of a "GA" in Fig. 15. Fig. 16 shows a word initial "GA." Despite the striking differences between these two

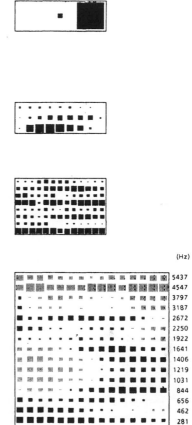

Figure 15.   TDNN activation patterns for "GA" embedded in an utterance.

input spectrograms, the network's internal alternate representations manage to produce in both cases crisp output firings for the right category.

Figs. 17 and 18, finally, demonstrate the shift invariance of the network. They show the same token "DO" of Fig. 13, misaligned by +30 ms and −30 ms, respectively. Despite the gross misalignment (note that significant transitional information is lost by the misalignment in Fig. 18), the correct result was obtained reliably. A close look at the internal activation patterns reveals that the hidden units' feature detectors do indeed fire according to the events in the input speech, and are not negatively affected by the relative shift with respect to the input units. Naturally, error rates will gradually increase when the tokens are artificially shifted to an extent that important features begin to fall outside the 15 frame data window considered here. We have observed, for example, a 2.6

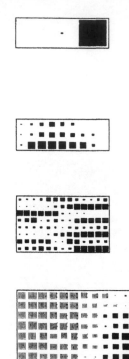

(Hz)

Figure 16.   TDNN activation patterns for "GA" in utterance initial position.

percent increase in error rate when all tokens from the training data were artificially shifted by 20 ms. Such residual time-shift sensitivities are due to the edge effects at the token boundaries and can probably be removed by training the TDNN using randomly shifted training tokens.[11] We also consider the formation of shift-invariant *internal* features to be the important desirable property we observe in the TDNN. Such internal features could be incorporated into larger speech recognition systems using more sophisticated search techniques or a syllable or word level TDNN, and hence could replace the simple integration layer we have used here for training and evaluation.

Three important properties of the TDNN's have been observed. First, our TDNN was able to learn, without human interference, meaningful linguistic

[11]We gratefully acknowledge one of the reviewers for suggesting this idea.

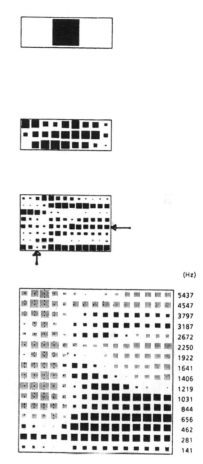

Figure 17. TDNN activation patterns for "DO" misaligned by +30 ms.

abstractions such as formant tracking and segmentation. Second, we have demonstrated that it has learned to form alternate representations linking different acoustic events with the same higher level concept. In this fashion, it can implement trading relations between lower level acoustic events leading to robust recognition performance. Third, we have seen that the network is shift invariant and does not rely on precise alignment or segmentation of the input.

V. CONCLUSION AND SUMMARY

In this paper we have presented a Time-Delay Neural Network (TDNN) approach to phoneme recognition. We have shown that this TDNN has two desirable properties related to the dynamic structure of speech. First, it can learn the

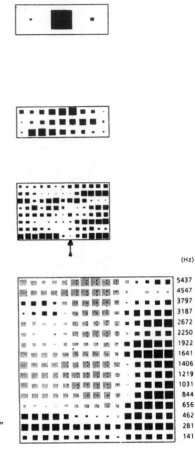

Figure 18.   TDNN activation patterns for "DO" misaligned by −30 ms.

temporal structure of acoustic events and the temporal relationships between such events. Second, it is translation invariant, that is, the features learned by the network are insensitive to shifts in time. Examples demonstrate that the network was indeed able to learn acoustic-phonetic features, such as formant movements and segmentation, and use them effectively as internal abstractions of speech.

The TDNN presented here has two hidden layers and has the ability to learn complex nonlinear decision surfaces. This could be seen from the network's ability to use alternate internal representations and trading relations among lower level acoustic-phonetic features, in order to arrive robustly at the correct final decision. Such alternate representations have been particularly useful for representing tokens that vary considerably from each other due to their different phonetic environment or their position within the original speech utterance.

Finally, we have evaluated the TDNN on the recognition of three acoustically similar phonemes, the voiced stops "B," "D," and "G." In extensive performance evaluation over testing data from three speakers, the TDNN achieved an average recognition score of 98.5 percent. For comparison, we have applied various Hidden Markov Models to the same task and only been able to recognize 93.7 percent of the tokens correctly. We would like to note that many variations of HMM's have been attempted, and many more variations of both HMM's and TDNN's are conceivable. Some of these variations could potentially lead to significant improvements over the results reported in this study. Our goal here is to present TDNN's as a new and successful approach for speech recognition. Their power lies in their ability to develop shift-invariant internal abstractions of speech and to use them in trading relations for making optimal decisions. This holds significant promise for speech recognition in general, as it could help overcome the representational weaknesses of speech recognition systems faced with the uncertainty and variability in real-life signals.

ACKNOWLEDGMENT

The authors would like to express their gratitude to Dr. A. Kurematsu, President of ATR Interpreting Telephony Research Laboratories, for his enthusiastic encouragement and support which made this research possible. We are also indebted to the members of the Speech Processing Department at ATR and Mr. Fukuda at Apollo Computer, Tokyo, Japan, for programming assistance in the various stages of this research.

REFERENCES

[1] D. E. Rumelhart and J. L. McClelland, *Parallel Distributed Processing: Explorations in the Microstructure of Cognition*, Vol. I and II. Cambridge, MA: M.I.T. Press, 1986.

[2] R. P. Lippmann, "An introduction to computing with neural nets," *IEEE ASSP Mag.*, vol. 4, Apr. 1987.

[3] D. C. Plaut, S. J. Nowlan, and G. E. Hinton, "Experiments on learning by back propagation," Tech. Rep. CMU-CS-86-126, Carnegie-Mellon Univ., June 1986.

[4] T. J. Sejnowski and C. R. Rosenberg, "NETtalk: A parallel network that learns to read aloud," Tech. Rep. JHU/EECS-86/01, Johns Hopkins Univ., June 1986.

[5] D. E. Rumelhart, G. E. Hinton, and R. J. Williams, "Learning representations by back-propagating errors," *Nature*, vol. 323, pp. 533–536, Oct. 1986.

[6] W. Y. Huang and R. P. Lippmann, "Comparison between neural net and conventional classifiers," in *Proc. IEEE Int. Conf. Neural Networks*, June 1987.

[7] J. L. McClelland and J. L. Elman, *Interactive Processes in Speech Perception: The TRACE Model*. Cambridge, MA: M.I.T. Press, 1986, ch. 15, pp. 58–121.

[8] S. M. Peeling, R. K. Moore, and M. J. Tomlinson, "The multi-layer perceptron as a tool for speech pattern processing research," in *Proc. IoA Autumn Conf. Speech Hearing*, 1986.

[9] H. Bourlard and C. J. Wellekens, "Multilayer perceptrons and automatic speech recognition," in *Proc. IEEE Int. Conf. Neural Networks*, June 1987.

[10] B. Gold, R. P. Lippmann, and M. L. Malpass, "Some neural net recognition results on isolated words," in *Proc. IEEE Int. Conf. Neural Networks*, June 1987.

[11] R. P. Lippmann and B. Gold, "Neural-net classifiers useful for speech recognition," in *Proc. IEEE Int. Conf. Neural Networks*, June 1987.

[12] D. J. Burr, "A neural network digit recognizer," in *Proc. IEEE Int. Conf. Syst., Man, Cybern.*, Oct. 1986.

[13] D. Lubensky, "Learning spectral-temporal dependencies using connectionist networks," in *Proc. IEEE Int. Conf. Acoust., Speech, Signal Processing*, Apr. 1988.

[14] R. L. Watrous and L. Shastri, "Learning phonetic features using connectionist networks: An experiment in speech recognition," in *Proc. IEEE Int. Conf. Neural Networks*, June 1987.

[15] R. W. Prager, T. D. Harrison, and F. Fallside, "Boltzmann machines for speech recognition," *Comput., Speech, Language*, vol. 3, no. 27, Mar. 1986.

[16] J. L. Elman and D. Zipser, "Learning the hidden structure of speech," Tech. Rep., Univ. Calif., San Diego, Feb. 1987.

[17] R. L. Watrous, L. Shastri, and A. H. Waibel, "Learned phonetic discrimination using connectionist networks," in *Proc. Euro. Conf. Speech Technol.*, Edinburgh, Sept. 1987, pp. 377–380.

[18] D. E. Rumelhart, G. E. Hinton, and R. J. Williams, *Learning Internal Representations by Error Propagation*. Cambridge, MA: M.I.T. Press, 1986, ch. 8, pp. 318–362.

[19] J. S. Bridle and R. K. Moore, "Boltzmann machines for speech pattern processing," in *Proc. Inst. Acoust. 1984*, 1984, 315–322.

[20] D. W. Tank and J. J. Hopfield, "Neural computation by concentrating information in time," in *Proc. Nat. Academy Sci.*, Apr. 1987, pp. 1896–1900.

[21] K. Lang, "Connectionist speech recognition," Ph.D. dissertation proposal, Carnegie-Mellon Univ., Pittsburgh, PA.

[22] K. Fukushima, S. Miyake, and T. Ito, "Neocognitron: A neural network model for a mechanism of visual pattern recognition," *IEEE Trans. Syst., Man, Cybern.*, vol. SMC-13, pp. 826–834, Sept./Oct. 1983.

[23] T. Hanazawa, T., Kawabata, and K. Shikano, "Discrimination of Japanese voiced stops using Hidden Markov Model," in *Proc. Conf. Acoust. Soc. Japan*, Oct. 1987, pp. 19–20 (in Japanese).

[24] ———, "Recognition of Japanese voiced stops using Hidden Markov Models," IEICE Tech. Rep., Dec. 1987 (in Japanese).

[25] A. Waibel and B. Yegnanarayana, "Comparative study of nonlinear time warping techniques in isolated word speech recognition systems," Tech. Rep., Carnegie-Mellon Univ., June 1981.

[26] S. Makino and K. Kido, "Phoneme recognition using time spectrum pattern," *Speech Commun.*, pp. 225–237, June 1986.

[27] S. E. Blumenstein and K. N. Stevens, "Acoustic invariance in speech production: Evidence from measurements of the spectral characteristics of stop consonants," *J. Acoust. Soc. Amer.*, vol. 66, pp. 1001–1017, 1979.

[28] ———, "Perceptual invariance and onset spectra for stop consonants in different vowel environments," *J. Acoust. Soc. Amer.*, vol. 67, pp. 648–662, 1980.

[29] D. Kewley-Port, "Time varying features as correlates of place of articulation in stop consonants," *J. Acoust. Soc. Amer.*, vol. 73, pp. 322–335, 1983.

[30] G. E. Hinton, "Connectionist learning procedures," *Artificial Intelligence*, 1987.

[31] M. A. Franzini, "Speech recognition with back propagation," in *Proc. 9th Annu. Conf. IEEE/Eng. Med. Biol. Soc.*, Nov. 1987.

[32] F. Jelinek, "Continuous speech recognition by statistical methods," *Proc. IEEE*, vol. 64, pp. 532–556, Apr. 1976.

[33] J. K. Baker, "Stochastic modeling as a means of automatic speech recognition," Ph.D. dissertation, Carnegie-Mellon Univ., Apr. 1975.

[34] L. R. Bahl, S. K. Das, P. V. de Souza, F. Jelinek, S. Katz, R. L. Mercer, and M. A. Picheny, "Some experiments with large-vocabulary isolated-word sentence recognition," in *Proc. IEEE Int. Conf. Acoust., Speech, Signal Processing*, Apr. 1984.

[35] R. Schwartz, Y. Chow, O. Kimball, S. Roucos, M. Krasner, and J. Makhoul, "Context-dependent modeling for acoustic-honetic recognition of continuous speech," in *Proc. IEEE Int. Conf. Acoust., Speech, Signal Processing,* Apr. 1985.

[36] A.-M. Derouault, "Context-dependent phonetic Markov models for large vocabulary speech recognition," in *Proc. IEEE Int. Conf. Acoust., Speech, Signal Processing,* Apr. 1987, pp. 360–363.

[37] K. F. Lee and H. W. Hon, "Speaker-independent phoneme recognition using hidden Markov models," Tech. Rep. CMU-CS-88-121, Carnegie-Mellon Univ., Pittsburgh, PA, Mar. 1988.

[38] P. Brown, "The acoustic-modeling problem in automatic speech recognition," Ph.D. dissertation, Carnegie-Mellon Univ., May 1987.

[39] L. R. Rabiner, B. H. Juang, S. E. Levinson, and M. M. Sondhi, "Recognition of isolated digits using hidden Markov models with continuous mixture densities," *AT&T Tech. J.,* vol. 64, no. 6, pp. 1211–1233, July–Aug. 1985.

[40] Y. L. Chow, M. O. Dunham, O. A. Kimball, M. A. Krasner, G. F. Kubala, J. Makhoul, S. Roucos, and R. M. Schwartz, "BYBLOS: The BBN continuous speech recognition system," in *Proc. IEEE Int. Conf. Acoust., Speech, Signal Processing,* Apr. 1987, pp. 89–92.

[41] M. Sugiyama and K. Shikano, "LPC peak weighted spectral matching measures," Inst. Elec. Commun. Eng. Japan, vol. 64-A, no. 5, pp. 409–416, 1981 (in Japanese).

[42] K. Shikano, "Evaluation of LPC spectral matching measures for phonetic unit recognition," Tech. Rep., Carnegie-Mellon Univ., May 1985.

[43] K. Aikawa and K. Shikano, "Spoken word recognition using vector quantization in power-spectrum vector space," Inst. Elec. Commun. Eng. Japan, vol. 68-D, no. 3, Mar. 1985 (in Japanese).

[44] Y. Sagisaka, K. Takeda, S. Katagiri, and H. Kuwabara, "Japanese speech database with fine acoustic-phonetic transcriptions," Tech. Rep., ATR Interpreting Telephony Res. Lab., May 1987.

3 Automated Aircraft Flare and Touchdown Control Using Neural Networks

Charles Schley
Yves Chauvin
Van Henkle
Thomson-CSF, Inc., Palo Alto Research Operation

ABSTRACT

We present a general-purpose neural network architecture capable of controlling nonlinear plants. The network is composed of dynamic, parallel, linear maps gated by nonlinear switches. Using a recurrent form of the back-propagation algorithm, we achieve control by optimizing the linear gains and the nonlinear switch parameters. A mean quadratic cost function computed across a nominal plant trajectory is minimized along with performance constraint penalties. The approach is demonstrated for a control task consisting of landing a commercial aircraft from a position on the glideslope to the ground position in difficult wind conditions. We show that the network learns how to control the aircraft in extreme wind conditions, yielding performance comparable to or better than that of a "traditional" autoland system while remaining within acceptable response characteristics constraints. Furthermore, we show that this performance is achieved not only through learning of control gains in the linear maps but also through learning of task-adapted gain schedules in the nonlinear switches.

INTRODUCTION

This chapter illustrates how a recurrent back-propagation neural network algorithm (Rumelhart, Hinton, & Williams, 1986) may be exploited as a procedure for controlling complex systems. In particular, a general-purpose task-adapted network architecture was devised for the control of nonlinear systems. To apply the technique, a simplified mathematical model of aircraft landing in the presence of severe wind gusts was developed and simulated. A recurrent back-

propagation neural network architecture was then designed to numerically estimate the parameters of an optimal nonlinear control law for landing the aircraft.
The performance of the network was then evaluated and compared to "more
traditional" methods of designing control laws.

We have exploited a general neural network approach that might be used
successfully in a variety of control system applications. For this reason, we
present in this section the general problem of controlling a physical system and
our approach to its solution. In the next section we describe the basic neural
controller architecture we devised and explain its unique features. The third
section develops the aircraft model along with a conventional control system.
The fourth section describes the recurrent implementation of the plant, the controller, and the performance indices to be minimized with performance constraints. The fifth section presents and evaluates simulation statistics. The last
section reviews our basic findings, discusses their applicability to other types of
control problems, and considers some possible extensions of this research.

A Typical Control System

A typical control system consists of a controller and a process to be controlled, as
illustrated in Figure 1. The controller's function is to accept task inputs along
with process outputs and to determine control signals tailored to the response
characteristics of the process. Frequently, it is desired that the process outputs
closely follow the task inputs. The physical process to be controlled (enclosed
within the shaded box of Figure 1) can be electromechanical, aerodynamic,
chemical, or other. It generally has well-defined behavior following physical
principles such as Newton's laws or laws of thermodynamics. The process states
are physical variables such as acceleration, velocity or temperature. Their dynamics are usually expressed in the form of differential equations relating their
interdependence and their dependence on time, position, and other quantities.

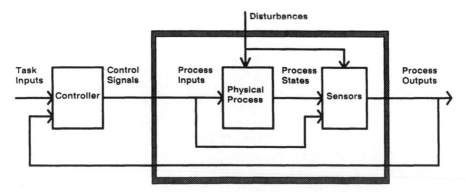

Figure 1.   Typical control system.

The process is observed through a set of sensors. Finally, the process is subjected to disturbances from its external operating environment.

Controller Design

What is the best method of designing a control law? Two types of methods, often called classical and modern methods, are described in the literature. Classical methods look at linearized versions of the plant to be controlled and some loosely defined response specifications such as bandwidth (i.e., speed of response) and phase margin (i.e., degree of stability). These methods make use of time-domain or frequency-domain mathematical tools such as root-loci methods or Bode plots.

Modern methods generally assume that a performance index for the process is specified and provide controllers that optimize this performance index. Optimal control theory attempts to find the parameters of the controller such that the performance measure (possibly with added performance constraint penalties) is minimized. In many standard optimal control problems, the controller network is linear, the plant is linear, and the performance measure is quadratic. In this case and when the process operation is over infinite time, the parameters of the controller may be explicitly derived. In general, however, if either the controller is nonlinear, the plant is nonlinear, or the performance measure is not quadratic, closed-form solutions for the controller's parameters are not available. Nevertheless, numerical methods may be used to compute an optimal control law. Modern methods make use of sophisticated mathematical tools such as the calculus of variations, Pontryagin's maximum principle, or dynamic programming.

Although modern methods are more universal, classical methods are widely used in practice, even with sophisticated control problems (McRuer, Ashkenas, & Graham, 1973). We feel that the differences between classical and modern methods can be summarized as follows:

- Classical techniques use ad hoc methods based on engineering judgement that is usually aimed at system robustness. No explicit unified performance index is optimized.
- Modern techniques use principled methods based on optimizing a performance index. However, the choice of a performance index is often somewhat ad hoc.

Narendra and Parthasarathy (1990) and others have noted that recurrent back-propagation networks implement gradient descent algorithms that may be used to optimize the performance index of a plant. The essence of such methods is to propagate performance errors back through the process and then back through the controller to give error signals for updating the controller parameters. Figure 2 provides an overview of the interaction of a neural control law with a complex system and possible performance indices for evaluating various control laws.

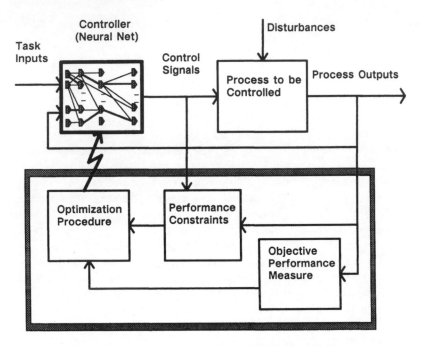

Figure 2.   Neural network controller design. At the top, the process to be controlled is the same as Figure 1 with controller replaced by a neural net.

The functional components needed to train the controller are shown within the shaded box of Figure 2. The objective performance measure contains factors that are written mathematically and usually represent terms such as weighted square error or other quantifiable measures. The performance constraints are often more subjective in nature and can be formulated as reward or penalty functions on categories such as "good" or "bad." The controller training function illustrated in Figure 2 also contains an optimization procedure used to adjust the parameters of the controller.

The network controller may be interpreted as a "neural" network when its architecture and the techniques employed during control and parameter change resemble techniques inspired from brain-style computations (e.g., Rumelhart & McClelland, 1986). In the present case, these techniques are (i) parallel computations (ii) local computations during control and learning and (iii) use of "neural" network learning algorithms. Narendra and Parthasarathy (1990) provide a more extensive review of the common properties between neural networks and control theories.

A GENERAL-PURPOSE NONLINEAR
CONTROL ARCHITECTURE

The Switching Principle

Many complex systems are in fact nonlinear or "multimodal." That is, their behavior changes in fundamental ways as a function of their position in the state-space. In practice, controllers are often designed for such systems by treating them as a collection of linear systems, each of which is linearized about a "set point" in state-space. A linear controller can then be determined separately for each of these system "modes." These observations suggest that a reasonable approach for controlling nonlinear or multimodal systems would be to design a multimodal control law.

The architecture of our proposed general nonlinear control law for multimodal plants is shown in Figure 3. Task inputs and process outputs are entered into multiple basic controller blocks (shown within the shaded box of Figure 3). Each basic controller block first determines a weighted sum of the task inputs and process outputs (multiplication by weights W). Then, the degree to which the weighted sum passes through the block is modified by means of a saturating switch and multiplier. The input to the switch is itself another weighted sum of the task inputs and process outputs (multiplication by weights V). If the input to the saturating switch is large, its output is unity and the weighted sum (weighted by W) is passed through unchanged. At the other extreme, if the saturating

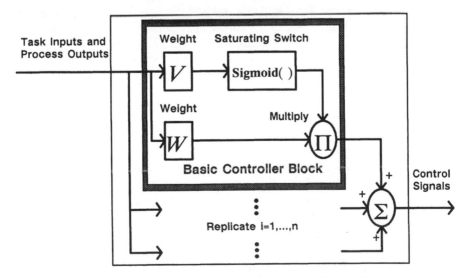

Figure 3. Architecture of the neural network controller.

switch has zero output, the weighted sum of task inputs and process outputs does not appear in the output. When these basic controller blocks are replicated and their outputs are added, control signals then consist of weighted sums of the controller inputs. Moreover, these weighted sums can be selected and/or blended by the saturating switches to yield the control signals. The overall effect is a prototypical feedahead and feedback controller with selectable gains and multiple pathways where the overall equivalent gains are a function of the task and process outputs. The resulting architecture yields a *sigma-pi* processing unit in the final controller (Rumelhart, Hinton, & Williams, 1986).

Note that the controller of Figure 3 is composed of multiple parallel computation paths and can thus be implemented with parallel hardware to facilitate fast computation. Also, should one or more of the parallel paths fail, some level of performance would remain, providing a degree of fault tolerance. In addition, since the controller can select one or more weighted mappings, it can operate in multiple modes depending on conditions within the process to be controlled or upon environmental conditions. This property can result in a controller finely tuned to a process having several different regimes of behavior (nonlinear process).

Modeling Dynamic Mappings

The weights shown in Figure 3 may be constant and represent a static relationship between input and control. However, further controller functionality is obtained by considering the weights V and W as implementing dynamic mappings. For example, proportional plus integral plus derivative (PID) feedback may be used to ensure that process outputs follow task inputs with adequate steady-state error and transient damping. A PID relationship can be expressed as a Laplace transform of the ratio $y(s)/x(s) = K_p + K_i(1/s) + K_d s$, where K_p, K_i, and K_d are the actual weights to be adjusted during controller design. Thus, the weights express differential equations in the time domain or transfer functions in the frequency domain. Standard first- and second-order filters can be combined to yield a wide variety of functionality. In general, the complexity of the dynamics of the controller depends on the complexity of the control task and on the dynamics of the plant. Therefore, the design of the architecture of the network requires knowledge of the physics of the plant and of the control requirements. In Section 4, we explain how this dynamic control is implemented in a neural network architecture for the application of aircraft landing.

AIRCRAFT AUTOLAND SYSTEM

Presented here is the development of a model for the glideslope tracking and flare phases of aircraft flight immediately prior to landing. The model is in the form of incremental equations of motion in aircraft stability axes along with typical control loops. These equations are suitable for a simulation that can be used to obtain incremental trajectory data just prior to landing. Their presentation assumes some familiarity with control systems. They are intended to specify a well-behaved aircraft plant that, although simple, responds in a realistic way to environment and control parameters. Linearized longitudinal/vertical perturbation equations of motion are used for the aircraft which is assumed to be initially trimmed in wings level flight at low altitude. Data and control system designs provide a realistic representation of a large commercial transport aircraft. High-frequency hardware and actuator dynamics are neglected. However, simplifications retain the overall quality of system response.

During aircraft landing, the final two phases of a landing trajectory consist of a "glideslope" phase and a "flare" phase. Figure 4 shows these two phases. Flare occurs at about 45 feet. Glideslope is characterized by a linear downward slope; flare by a negative exponential. When the aircraft reaches flare, its response characteristics are changed to make it more sensitive to the pilot's actions, making the process nonlinear over the whole trajectory.

In addition to linearized equations of motion for the bare airframe, the baseline system has the following components:

1. Stability augmentation control systems for the bare airframe to provide adequate damping and speed of response concerning principal aircraft dynamics (speed, phugoid, short period)
2. Glideslope tracking and flare controllers to produce commands in response to desired positions during descent

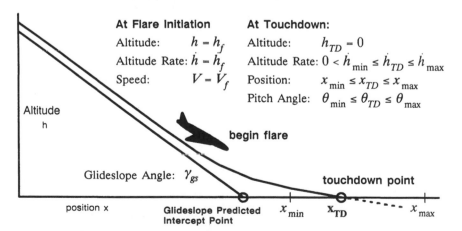

Figure 4.   Glideslope and flare geometry. The pitch angle is the angle between the aircraft body and the ground measured in the vertical plane.

3. Desired position commands based on instrument landing system (ILS) tracking and an adaptive ground speed exponential flare law to provide a smooth descent

4. Altitude wind shear and turbulent gusts modeled using a Dryden distribution (frozen field model for generating gusty winds)

Vehicle Equations of Motion

The vehicle equations of motion are derived in a general sense from Newtonian mechanics. Two preliminary assumptions are made. Only rigid-body mechanics are used and the earth is fixed in space. This means that vehicle motion may be described as translation of and rotation about the vehicle center of mass and that the vehicle inertial frame is fixed at or moves at constant velocity with respect to the earth.

Newton's law is then phrased so that the sum of forces (torques) acting on a body is equal to the time rate of change in inertial space of the body's linear (angular) momentum.

$$\frac{d}{dt}(m\mathbf{V}) = \mathbf{F}, \qquad \frac{d}{dt}(\mathbf{I}\Omega) = \mathbf{M}, \tag{1}$$

where m = vehicle mass
$\mathbf{V}$ = inertial velocity vector
$\mathbf{F}$ = externally applied force vector
$\mathbf{I}$ = moment of inertia dyad
Ω = angular velocity vector
$\mathbf{M}$ = applied torque vector

Two coordinate frames of reference are important. The first is chosen to be body fixed with its origin at the vehicle center of mass. This is the frame in which thrust and aerodynamic forces and torques exist. Figure 5 illustrates the body-fixed frame with the components of the vehicle translation and rotation velocities.

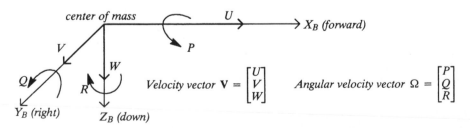

Figure 5.   Body-fixed coordinate frame (stability axes).

The second coordinate frame of interest is the inertial or earth-fixed frame in which the gravity force and the vehicle kinematics (navigation or location variables) exist. Figure 6 illustrates the inertial frame and its relationship with the body-fixed frame.

Two assumptions are made at this point. Vehicle mass and mass distribution are constant (i.e., rates of change of mass and moments of inertia are zero). Also, the X_B, Y_B plane of Figure 5 is a plane of symmetry. This means that the left side of the aircraft is the same as the right side and the cross moments of inertia I_{xy}, I_{yz} are zero.

It is noted that the body-fixed frame is rotating with respect to the inertial frame which gives rise to centripetal terms. Accounting for these along with gravitational acceleration and the expansion of the angular momentum terms, the following equations describe vehicle dynamics in the body-fixed frame:

$$ma_x = m(\dot{U} + QW - RV + g \sin \Theta) = X_F,$$

$$ma_y = m(\dot{V} + RU - PW - g \cos \Theta \sin \Phi) = Y_F,$$

$$ma_z = m(\dot{W} + PV - QU - g \cos \Theta \cos \Phi) = Z_F,$$

$$I_{xx}\dot{P} - I_{xz}\dot{R} + (I_{zz} - I_{yy})QR - I_{xz}PQ = L,$$

$$I_{yy}\dot{Q} + (I_{xx} - I_{zz})PR - I_{xz}R^2 + I_{xz}P^2 = M,$$

$$I_{zz}\dot{R} - I_{xz}\dot{P} + (I_{yy} - I_{xx})PQ + I_{xz}QR = N, \tag{2}$$

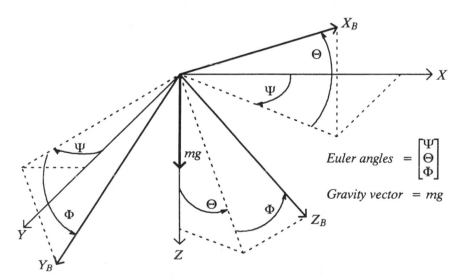

Figure 6.   Inertial coordinate frame and transformation to body fixed.

where a_x, a_y, a_z = vehicle acceleration components in body-fixed frame
U, V, W = vehicle velocity components in body-fixed frame
P, Q, R = vehicle angular velocity components in body-fixed frame
Ψ, Θ, Φ = Euler transformation angles from inertial to body-fixed frames
X_F, Y_F, Z_F = thrust and aerodynamic forces applied to vehicle
$I_{xx}, I_{xz}, I_{yy}, I_{zz}$ = moment of inertia components
L, M, N = thrust and aerodynamic torques applied to vehicle
m, g = vehicle mass, gravitational acceleration

Projecting the vehicle translational and angular velocities onto the inertial frame, the following equations are obtained describing the Euler angles and vehicle kinematics:

$$\dot{\Psi} = \frac{Q \sin \Phi + R \cos \Phi}{\cos \Theta},$$

$$\dot{\Theta} = Q \cos \Phi - R \sin \Phi,$$

$$\dot{\Phi} = P + Q \tan \Theta \sin \Phi + R \tan \Theta \cos \Phi,$$

$$\begin{bmatrix} \dot{X} \\ \dot{Y} \\ \dot{Z} \end{bmatrix} = \begin{bmatrix} \cos \Psi & -\sin \Psi & 0 \\ \sin \Psi & \cos \Psi & 0 \\ 0 & 0 & 1 \end{bmatrix} \begin{bmatrix} \cos \Theta & 0 & \sin \Theta \\ 0 & 1 & 0 \\ -\sin \Theta & 0 & \cos \Theta \end{bmatrix} \begin{bmatrix} 1 & 0 & 0 \\ 0 & \cos \Phi & -\sin \Phi \\ 0 & \sin \Phi & \cos \Phi \end{bmatrix} \begin{bmatrix} U \\ V \\ W \end{bmatrix},$$

$$(3)$$

where X, Y, Z = vehicle position components in inertial frame.

Linearized Aircraft Equations of Motion

The full 6-degree-of-freedom equations of motion, (2) and (3), are highly nonlinear and depend on complex aerodynamic effects. In order to perform analysis and stability designs efficiently, the relations are linearized. From here on, we confine our attention to the longitudinal/vertical plane of motion; that is, the X_B, Z_B plane of Figure 5 and the X, Z plane of Figure 6.

The linearized equations of motion define incremental aircraft dynamics in the longitudinal/vertical plane. They constitute the bare airframe velocity components, the pitch rate and angle along with the aircraft position. They are developed by first assuming that the aircraft is flying in a trimmed condition (i.e., zero translational and rotational accelerations). This gives rise to mean velocities for the motion values (i.e., U_0, W_0, Q_0). Small perturbations u, w, q about the mean values are considered and the equations of motion are expanded to first order. For the purposes at hand, the trim condition is assumed to consist of straight, wings-level flight. Thus, the following additional assumptions are invoked. Perturbations are small enough so that small angle approximations are valid (i.e., $\sin A = A$ and $\cos A = 1$). Also, products and squares of terms are negligible. Cross perturbation effects (lateral to longitudinal, and vice versa) are ignored. Trim values are assumed as constant true airspeed V_{tas} with $U_0 = V_{tas}$, $W_0 = 0$. Angular velocity is $Q_0 = 0$; angular position is $\Theta_0 = \Gamma_0$ where Γ_0 is the trim flight path angle. The body-fixed coordinate frame thus consists of the aircraft stability axes. Since the aircraft is trimmed at constant speed, the aircraft nose (or wing chord) direction is actually elevated with respect to the body-fixed x axis. Additionally, there is no rotation of the vertical relative to the inertial frame (i.e., no hypervelocity orbital flights). Then, the linearized equations are obtained as follows:

$$m[\dot{u} + (g \cos \Theta_0)\theta] = dX_F,$$

$$m[\dot{w} - U_0q + (g \sin \Theta_0)\theta] = dZ_F,$$

$$I_{yy}\dot{q} = dM \qquad \theta = q,$$

$$\dot{x} = (U_0 + u) \cos \Theta_0 + (w - U_0\theta) \sin \Theta_0,$$

$$\dot{h} = -\dot{z} = (U_0 + u) \sin \Theta_0 - (w - U_0\theta) \cos \Theta_0, \qquad (4)$$

where u, w, q, θ, x, z = incremental aircraft dynamic and kinematic values
$\qquad dX_F, dZ_F, dM$ = incremental aerodynamic forces and moments
$\qquad\qquad U_0, \Theta_0, g$ = nominal speeds, pitch angle, gravity

The aerodynamic forces and moments are typically functions of airspeed, air density, and various aircraft parameters (e.g., lift and drag coefficients, surface area, etc.). The following two assumptions are made at this time. Air-mass flow is assumed quasisteady. This means that the aerodynamic forces and moments depend only on the velocities of the vehicle and not on the rates of change of the velocities. Also, atmospheric properties are constant and there are no Mach number or altitude dependencies.

Then, the aerodynamic forces and moments can be expanded to first order by considering partial derivatives with respect to each principal variable. In addition, since the airmass flow is also a function of wind gusts, these latter are introduced into the force and moment expansions as follows:

$$dX_F = \frac{\partial X_F}{\partial U} (u - u_g) + \frac{\partial X_F}{\partial W} (w - w_g) + \frac{\partial X_F}{\partial \dot{W}} (\dot{w} - \dot{w}_g)$$

$$+ \frac{\partial X_F}{\partial Q} (q - q_g) + \frac{\partial X_F}{\partial \Delta} \delta,$$

$$dZ_F = \frac{\partial Z_F}{\partial U} (u - u_g) + \frac{\partial Z_F}{\partial W} (w - w_g) + \frac{\partial Z_F}{\partial \dot{W}} (\dot{w} - \dot{w}_g)$$

$$+ \frac{\partial Z_F}{\partial Q} (q - q_g) + \frac{\partial Z_F}{\partial \Delta} \delta,$$

$$dM = \frac{\partial M}{\partial U} (u - u_g) + \frac{\partial M}{\partial W} (w - w_g) + \frac{\partial M}{\partial \dot{W}} (\dot{w} - \dot{w}_g)$$

$$+ \frac{\partial M}{\partial Q} (q - q_g) + \frac{\partial M}{\partial \Delta} \delta, \tag{5}$$

where u_g, w_g, $\dot{w}_g$, q_g = wind gust components
Δ, δ = terms due to control inputs

The pitch gust disturbance q_g depends on spatial distributions of the wind speeds around the aircraft. This can be simplified to

$$q_g = -\frac{\partial w_g}{\partial x} = -\frac{\partial w_g / \partial t}{\partial x / \partial t} \approx -\frac{1}{V_{tas}} \dot{w}_g, \tag{6}$$

where q_g = spatial distribution of wind gusts in pitch direction.

The force equations can be divided by mass and the moment equation by the moment of inertia. Neglecting the q_g term and the velocity derivative terms, collecting other terms, and simplifying yields the complete longitudinal linearized equations in terms of stability derivatives. Note that the angle of attack a has been introduced, where $a = (180/\pi)(w/V_{tas})$. Also, note that the initial flight path angle Γ_0 is assumed to be 0, implying a true straight and level trim condition.

$$\dot{u} = X_u u + \frac{V_{tas}\pi}{180} X_w a + \frac{\pi}{180} X_q q - \frac{\pi}{180} g\theta$$

$$+ X_E \delta_E + X_T \delta_T - X_u u_g - X_w w_g,$$

$$\dot{a} = \frac{180}{V_{tas}\pi} Z_u u + Z_w a + \frac{1}{V_{tas}} (V_{tas} + Z_q)q$$

$$+ \frac{180}{V_{tas}\pi} (Z_E \delta_E + Z_T \delta_T - Z_u u_g - Z_w w_g),$$

$$\dot{q} = \frac{180}{\pi} M_u u + V_{tas} M_w a + M_q q$$

$$+ \frac{180}{\pi} (M_E \delta_E + M_T \delta_T - M_u u_g - M_w w_g),$$

$$\theta = q,$$

$$\dot{x} = (V_{tas} + u)\cos\theta + \frac{V_{tas}\pi}{180} a \sin\theta \approx V_{tas} + u,$$

$$h = (V_{tas} + u)\sin\theta - \frac{V_{tas}\pi}{180} a \cos\theta \approx -\frac{V_{tas}\pi}{180} a + \frac{V_{tas}\pi}{180} \theta, \tag{7}$$

where u, a, q, θ = incremental speed (ft/sec), angle of attack (deg), pitch rate (deg/sec), pitch angle (deg)

x, h = aircraft position (ft) along ground, altitude

u_g, w_g = wind gust velocity components (ft/sec)

δ_E, δ_T = incremental elevator, throttle settings

$X_u, X_w, X_q, Z_u, Z_w, Z_q, M_u, M_w, M_q$ = stability derivatives of aircraft at trim condition

$X_E, X_T, Z_E, Z_T, M_E, M_T$ = control derivatives of aircraft at trim condition

$V_{\text{tas}}\, g$ = nominal speed (ft/sec), gravity (ft/sec/sec)

Relations 7 provide the time behavior of speed (u), angle of attack (a), pitch rate (q), pitch angle (θ), and positions (x and h) in response to elevator and thrust commands (δ_E and δ_T), and horizontal and vertical wind gust speeds u_g and w_g. The parameter values listed provide specific values typical of a large commercial transport in a configuration just before landing.

$V_{\text{tas}} = 235.6$ ft/sec	$g = 32.2$ ft/sec/sec			
$X_u = -.03829$	$X_w = .051342$	$X_q = .08709$	$X_E = -.00005$	$X_T = .15781$
$Z_u = -.31338$	$Z_w = -.60538$	$Z_q = 2.34657$	$Z_E = -.14643$	$Z_T = -.030963$
$M_u = -.00036861$	$M_w = -.0027481$	$M_q = -.61162$	$M_E = -.0080083$	$M_T = .00094824$

Stability Augmentation Systems

The transient response characteristics of the longitudinal equations are typical of standard bare airframe behavior. There are two types of responses noticeable: a low-frequency, very lightly damped phugoid response and a higher-frequency, well-damped short period response. This response pattern is entirely too oscillatory to apply glideslope and flare control laws. Hence, the longitudinal aircraft dynamics are provided with a stability augmentation system (pitch control system and autothrottle).

The function of the pitch augmentation system is to significantly damp the oscillatory phugoid behavior while providing reasonably fast pitch response to commands. The pitch stability augmentation system consists of proportional plus rate feedback combined with a pitch command to develop the aircraft elevator angle as shown in Figure 7.

The function of the autothrottle as shown in Figure 8 is to maintain constant airspeed. The aircraft throttle setting δ_T is based on proportional plus integral feedback of the airspeed error. The result is that the incremental speed u is

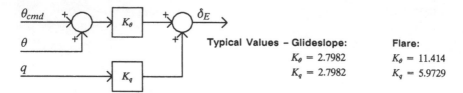

Figure 7.   Pitch stability augmentation system.

commanded to be equal to the constant component of the horizontal wind u_{gc} cos (ψ_{wind}) (see Equation 14 and Figure 8).

Relations 8 provide the equations representing the functions of the longitudinal/vertical stability augmentation system. These equations implement the diagrams of Figures 7 and 8.

$$\dot{x}_{VS1} = -u + u_{gc} \cos(\psi_{wind}),$$

$$\delta_E = K_q q + K_\theta \theta + K_\theta \theta_{cmd},$$

$$\delta_T = K_T \omega_T x_{VS1} - K_T u + K_T u_{gc} \cos(\psi_{wind}), \qquad (8)$$

where x_{VS1} = autothrottle integrator
    δ_E, δ_T = incremental elevator, throttle settings
    u, q, θ = incremental speed (ft/sec), pitch rate (deg/sec), pitch angle (deg)
    u_{gc} = constant component of the horizontal wind (ft/sec)
    θ_{cmd} = incremental pitch angle command (deg)

Control Laws

Longitudinal controllers must be specified for both the glideslope tracking and the flare modes. This involves determination of the pitch command value (θ_{cmd}) referenced in Figure 7. Other than parameter values and an open-loop pitchup command for flare, both of these controllers are constructed similarly. Figure 9 illustrates the architecture of the PID controller for both glideslope tracking and flare.

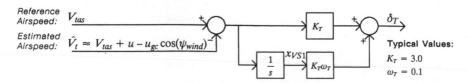

Figure 8.   Autothrottle.

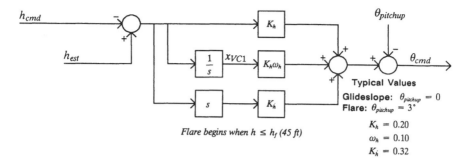

Figure 9.   Glideslope and flare controller architecture.

Relations 9 comprise the equations representing the function of the glideslope and flare controller. They implement the diagram of Figure 9.

$$\dot{x}_{VC1} = h_{est} - h_{cmd},$$

$$\theta_{cmd} = K_h \omega_h x_{VC1} + K_h h_{est} + K_{\dot{h}} \dot{h}_{est} - K_h h_{cmd} - K_{\dot{h}} \dot{h}_{cmd} + \theta_{pitchup}, \quad (9)$$

where
$\quad x_{VC1}$ = glideslope and flare controller integrator
θ_{cmd} = incremental pitch angle command (deg)
$h_{cmd}, \dot{h}_{cmd}$ = altitude (ft) and altitude rate (ft/sec) commands
$h_{est}, \dot{h}_{est}$ = altitude (ft) and altitude rate (ft/sec) estimates obtained from compl. filter
$\theta_{pitchup}$ = open-loop pitchup command (deg) for flare

As shown in Figure 9, controller inputs consist of altitude commands along with aircraft altitude and altitude rate estimates. These estimates are obtained by complementary filtering of sensor data (accelerometer, altimeter, etc.). During glideslope tracking a third-order complementary filter is used while a second-order filter is applied during flare. Figure 10 illustrates the complementary filter used during glideslope tracking. The functions of the glideslope complementary filter are implemented via Equations 10.

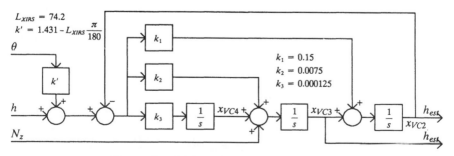

Figure 10.   Glideslope complementary filter.

$$\dot{x}_{VC2} = -k_1 x_{VC2} + x_{VC3} + k_1 k'\theta + k_1 h,$$

$$\dot{x}_{VC3} = -k_2 x_{VC2} + x_{VC4} + k_2 k'\theta + k_2 h + N_z,$$

$$\dot{x}_{VC4} = -k_3 x_{VC2} + k_w k'\theta + k_3 h,$$

$$N_z = \frac{V_{\text{tas}}\pi}{180}(-\dot{a} + \dot{\theta}) = -Z_u u - \frac{\pi}{180}(V_{\text{tas}}Z_w a + Z_q q)$$

$$- Z_E \delta_E - Z_T \delta_T + Z_u u_g + Z_w w_g,$$

$$h_{\text{est}} = x_{VC2}, \qquad \dot{h}_{\text{est}} = x_{VC3}. \tag{10}$$

where $x_{VC2}, x_{VC3}, x_{VC4}$ = glideslope complementary filter integrators
N_z = incremental vertical acceleration (ft/sec/sec)
$h_{\text{est}}, \dot{h}_{\text{est}}$ = altitude (ft) and altitude rate (ft/sec) estimates
θ, h = incremental pitch angle (deg), altitude (ft)
u, a, q = incremental speed (ft/sec), angle of attack (deg), pitch rate (deg/sec)
δ_E, δ_T = incremental elevator, throttle settings
u_g, w_g = longitudinal and vertical wind gust velocities (ft/sec)

Figure 11 shows the complementary filter used for flare. Its functions are implemented by means of Equations 11.

$$\dot{x}_{VC2} = -k_1 x_{VC2} + x_{VC3} + k_1 h,$$

$$\dot{x}_{VC3} = -k_2 x_{VC2} + k_2 h + N_z,$$

$$N_z = \frac{V_{\text{tas}}\pi}{180}(-\dot{a} + \dot{\theta}) = -Z_u u - \frac{\pi}{180}(V_{\text{tas}}Z_w a + Z_q q)$$

$$- Z_E \delta_E - Z_T \delta_T + Z_u u_g + Z_w w_g,$$

$$h_{\text{est}} = x_{VC2}, \qquad \dot{h}_{\text{est}} = x_{VC3}, \tag{11}$$

where $x_{VC2}, x_{VC3}, x_{VC4}$ = glideslope complementary filter integrators
N_z = incremental vertical acceleration (ft/sec/sec)
$h_{\text{est}}, \dot{h}_{\text{est}}$ = altitude (ft) and altitude rate (ft/sec) estimates
θ, h = incremental pitch angle (deg), altitude (ft)
u, a, q = incremental speed (ft/sec), angle of attack (deg), pitch rate (deg/sec)

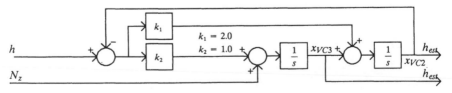

Figure 11.   Flare complementary filter.

δ_E, δ_T = incremental elevator, throttle settings

u_g, w_g = longitudinal and vertical wind gust velocities (ft/sec)

The value of the altitude command (h_{cmd}) for the glideslope and flare controller of Figure 9 must also be determined. The glideslope command is developed so that a constant descent will be commanded along an ILS path assumed fixed in space. Commanded altitude is thus a function of ground distance which is defined as the distance to the glideslope predicted intercept point on the ground. The flare command consists of an adaptive ground speed exponential law (fixed in space rather than in time). Equations 12 and 13 show the glideslope and flare altitude command computation.

Glideslope (for $x \leq x_f = -h_f/\tan \gamma_{gs}$),

$$h_{cmd} = -x \tan \gamma_{gs}, \quad x(t_{gs}) = x_{gs} = -h_{gs}/\tan \gamma_{gs},$$

$$\dot{h}_{cmd} = -\dot{x} \tan \gamma_{gs} = -(V_{tas} + u) \tan \gamma_{gs} \tag{12}$$

where h_{cmd}, $\dot{h}_{cmd}$ = altitude (ft), altitude rate (ft/sec) commands, glideslope begins at $t_{gs} = 0$

x = negative of the ground range to the GPIP (ft)

γ_{gs} = desired glideslope angle, $\gamma_{gs} \approx 2.75°$

h_{gs} = altitude at beginning of the glideslope, $h_{gs} \approx 300$ ft

x_{gs} = x distance at beginning of glideslope, $x_{gs} \approx 6245.65$ ft

Note: Values for h and x at beginning of glideslope are for simulation purposes only. Glideslope actually begins at about 1500 ft altitude.

Flare (for $x > x_f = -h_f/\tan \gamma_{gs}$)

$$h_{cmd} = \frac{h_f}{V_{tas} \tan \gamma_{gs} + \dot{h}_{TD}} [V_{tas} \tan \gamma_{gs} e^{-(x-x_f)/\tau_x} + \dot{h}_{TD}],$$

$$\dot{h}_{cmd} = -\dot{x} \tan \gamma_{gs} e^{-(x-x_f)\tau_x} = -(V_{tas} + u)\tan \gamma_{gs} e^{-(x-x_f)/\tau_x},$$

$$x_f = -h_f/\tan \gamma_{gs}, \quad \tau_x = \frac{h_f V_{tas}}{V_{tas} \tan \gamma_{gs} + \dot{h}_{TD}},$$

When $h_{cmd}(t_{TD}) = 0$, $x(t_{TD}) = x_f - \tau_x \log_e(-\dot{h}_{TD}/V_{tas} \tan \gamma_{gs})$ and $\dot{h}_{cmd}(t_{TD}) - \frac{\dot{x}(t_{TD})}{V_{tas}} \dot{h}_{TD} \approx \dot{h}_{TD}$,

where h_{cmd}, $\dot{h}_{cmd}$ = altitude (ft), altitude rate (ft/sec) commands, flare begins at $t = t_f$

h_f = altitude at beginning of flare (ft), $h_f \approx 45$ ft

$\dot{h}_{TD}$ = altitude rate (ft/sec) at touchdown time t_{TD}, $\dot{h}_{TD} \approx -1.5$ ft/sec

x = negative of the ground range to the GPIP (ft)
x_f = x distance at beginning of glideslope

Wind Disturbances

The environment influences the process through wind disturbances represented by constant-velocity and turbulence components. They are confined to wind disturbances having two components: constant velocity and turbulence. The magnitude of the constant-velocity component is a function of altitude (wind shear). Turbulence is more complex and is a temporal and spatial function as an aircraft flies through an airspace region. The constant velocity wind component exists only in the horizontal plane (i.e., combination of headwind and crosswind) and its value is given in Equation 14 as a logarithmic variation with altitude. The quantity H is a value representing the constant wind component at an altitude of 510 ft. A typical value of H is 20 ft/sec. In the next section we explain that the network was trained with a distribution of constant wind components from $H = -10$ ft/sec to $H = 40$ ft/sec. Note that a wind model with $H = 40$ represents a very strong turbulent wind.

$$u_{gc} = -H \left[1 + \frac{\log_e(h/510)}{\log_e(51)} \right], \tag{14}$$

where u_{gc} = constant (altitude shear) component of u_g, zero at 10-ft altitude
H = wind speed at 510-ft altitude (typical value = 20 ft/sec)
h = aircraft altitude

For the horizontal and vertical wind turbulence velocities, the Dryden spectra (Neuman and Foster, 1970) for spatial turbulence distribution are assumed. These spectra involve a wind disturbance model frozen in time. This is not seriously limiting since the aircraft moves in time through the wind field and thus experiences temporal wind variation. The Dryden spectra are also amenable to simulation and show reasonable agreement with measured data. The generation of turbulence velocities is effected by the application of Gaussian white noise to coloring filters. This provides the proper correlation to match the desired spectra. Figures 12 and 13 summarize turbulence calculations, while Equations 15 implement them.

$$\dot{x}_{\text{dry}_1} = -a_u x_{\text{dry}_1} + a_u \left[\sigma_u \sqrt{\frac{2}{a_u \Delta t}} \right] N(0, 1),$$

$$\dot{x}_{\text{dry}_2} = -a_w x_{\text{dry}_2} + a_w x_{\text{dry}_3} + a_w \left(\frac{a_w}{b_w} \right) \left[\sigma_w b_w \sqrt{\frac{3}{a_w^3 \Delta t}} \right] N(0, 1),$$

$$\dot{x}_{\text{dry}_3} = -a_w x_{\text{dry}_3} + a_w \left(1 + \frac{a_w}{b_w} \right) \left[\sigma_w b_w \sqrt{\frac{3}{a_w^3 \Delta t}} \right] N(0, 1),$$

$$u_g = u_{gc} + x_{\text{dry}_1}, \qquad w_g = x_{\text{dry}_2}, \tag{15}$$

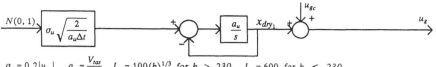

$\sigma_u = 0.2|u_{gc}|, \quad a_u = \dfrac{V_{tas}}{L_u}, \quad L_u = 100(h)^{1/3} \ for \ h > 230, \quad L_u = 600 \ for \ h \leq 230$

where: V_{tas}, h, Δt = nominal aircraft speed (ft/sec), aircraft altitude (ft), simulation time step

L_u, σ_u = scale length (ft), turbulence standard deviation (ft/sec)

$N(0, 1)$ = Gaussian white noise with zero mean and unity standard deviation

Figure 12.   Horizontal plane wind disturbance.

where x_{dry_1}, x_{dry_2}, x_{dry_3} = Dryden wind disturbance integrators
u_g, v_g, w_g = turbulent wind speed components (ft/sec)
$N(0, 1)$ = Gaussian white noise with zero mean and unity standard deviation
ψ_{wind} = direction of the constant wind
u_{gc} = constant wind speed (ft/sec)
Δt = simulation time step (sec)

Initial Conditions

In order to begin a simulation of the flight of the aircraft, all dynamic variables must have initial conditions specified. For the longitudinal/vertical equations of motion (Equations 7) for the bare airframe, initial conditions are specified by placing the aircraft on the glideslope in a steady-state condition. This means that initial values for the u, a, q, θ, x, and h variables of Relations 7 are obtained according to the following assumptions: $u_0 = u_{g_0}$, $\dot{u}_0 = 0$, $\dot{a}_0 = 0$, $\dot{q}_0 = 0$, $\theta_0 = 0$, and $\dot{h}_0 = -\dot{x}_0 \tan \gamma_{gs}$, where u_{g_0} is the initial longitudinal constant wind speed and γ_{gs} is the glideslope angle. Substituting these conditions into Relations 7

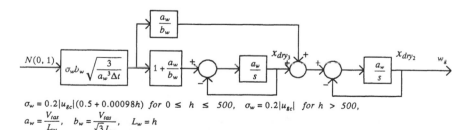

$\sigma_w = 0.2|u_{gc}|(0.5 + 0.00098h) \ for \ 0 \leq h \leq 500, \quad \sigma_w = 0.2|u_{gc}| \ for \ h > 500,$

$a_w = \dfrac{V_{tas}}{L_w}, \quad b_w = \dfrac{V_{tas}}{\sqrt{3}\,L_w}, \quad L_w = h$

where: V_{tas}, h, Δt = nominal aircraft speed (ft/sec), aircraft altitude (ft), simulation time step

L_w, σ_w = scale length (ft), turbulence standard deviation (ft/sec)

$N(0, 1)$ = Gaussian white noise with zero mean and unity standard deviation

Figure 13.   Vertical plane wind disturbance.

provides the results of Relations 16 whose solution determines the initial conditions for the variables u_0, a_0, q_0, θ_0, x_0, h_0, δ_{E_0}, and δ_{T_0}.

Initial Conditions for Longitudinal/Vertical Aircraft Variables

$$
\begin{bmatrix} u_0 \\ q_0 \\ x_0 \\ h_0 \end{bmatrix} = \begin{bmatrix} u_{g_0} \\ 0 \\ -h(t_0)/\tan \gamma_{gs} \\ h(t_0) \end{bmatrix},
$$

$$
\begin{bmatrix} \dfrac{V_{tas}\pi}{180} X_w & -\dfrac{g\pi}{180} & X_E & X_T \\[2ex] Z_w & 0 & \dfrac{180}{V_{tas}\pi} Z_E & \dfrac{180}{V_{tas}\pi} Z_T \\[2ex] V_{tas}M_w & 0 & \dfrac{180}{\pi} M_E & \dfrac{180}{\pi} M_T \\[2ex] -\dfrac{V_{tas}\pi}{180} & \dfrac{V_{tas}\pi}{180} & 0 & 0 \end{bmatrix} \begin{bmatrix} a_0 \\ \theta_0 \\ \delta_{E_0} \\ \delta_{T_0} \end{bmatrix} = \begin{bmatrix} 0 \\ 0 \\ 0 \\ -(V_{tas} + u_{g_0})\tan \gamma_{gs} \end{bmatrix},
$$

(16)

where $u_{g_0} = u_{g_c}(h_0)$ = longitudinal constant wind speed (ft/sec).

Simulation

To simulate the flight of the aircraft, the aircraft states (i.e., u, a, q, θ, x, and h) given in Equations 7 must be solved by means of some method for solution of differential equations (e.g., Runge-Kutta). The values for elevator, throttle, rudder, and aileron angles for equations [7] (i.e., δ_E and δ_T) are obtained by implementing Equations 8. These are implied by the stability augmentation diagrams of Figures 7 and 8. Here, the symbol s indicates the Laplace operator (derivative with respect to time). Input to the pitch stability augmentation system (θ_{cmd}) is calculated by implementing the controller shown in Figure 9 where flare takes place at about 45 ft of altitude. Inputs to the glideslope and flare controller (h_{est} and $\dot{h}_{est}$) are determined by means of the glideslope and flare complementary filters given by Equations 10 and 11. The h_{cmd} input to the glideslope and flare controller is provided by Equations 12 and 13. Finally, the wind disturbance functions for Equations 7 (i.e., u_g and w_g) are generated by means of the average horizontal speed given by Equation 14 and the Dryden spectra turbulence calculations of Equations 15.

A sample scenario for the generation of a trajectory involves a descent along a glideslope from an initial altitude of 300 ft followed by flare at 45 ft altitude and then touchdown. Both nominal (disturbance-free) conditions and logarithmic altitude shear turbulent conditions should be considered for completeness.

NEURAL NETWORK LEARNING IMPLEMENTATION

In this section, we present our approach for developing control laws for the aircraft model described in the preceding section and relate it to classical and modern control theories. We confine our attention to the glideslope and flare and do not consider the lateral control system. Additionally, we do not model the complementary filters and assume that their function is perfect. At any rate, in the classical approach, controllers are often specified as PID devices for both the glideslope and flare modes. Other than parameter values and an open loop pitchup command for flare, both of these controllers are constructed similarly. Recall that Figure 9 illustrates the conventional controller architecture for both glideslope and flare.

As previously noted, modern control theory suggests that a performance index for evaluating control laws should first be constructed, and then the control law should be computed to optimize the performance index. When closed form solutions are not available, numerical methods for estimating the parameters of a control law may be developed. Neural network algorithms can actually be seen as constituting such numerical methods (Narendra and Parthasarathy, 1990; Bryson and Ho, 1969; Le Cun, 1989). We present here an implementation of a neural network algorithm to address the aircraft landing problem.

Difference Equations

The state of the aircraft (including stability augmentation and autothrottle) can be represented by the following eight-dimensional vector:

$$X_t = [u_t \quad a_t \quad q_t \quad \theta_t \quad \dot{h}_t \quad h_t \quad x7_t \quad x8_t]^T. \tag{17}$$

State variables u_t, a_t, q_t, θ_t, $\dot{h}_t$, and h_t correspond to the aircraft state variables per se. Variable $x7_t$ originates from the autothrottle. Variable $x8_t$ computes the integral of the difference between actual altitude h and desired altitude h_{cmd} over the entire trajectory. Alternatively, the state variables $\dot{h}_t$ and $x8_t$ can be considered as being internal to the network controller (see below). The difference equations describing the dynamics of the controlled plant can be written as

$$X_{t+1} = A_t X_t + B_t U_t + CD_t + N_t, \tag{18}$$

$$A_t = Z_t A^{gs} + (1 - Z_t)A^{fl}, \tag{19}$$

$$B_t = Z_t B^{gs} + (1 - Z_t)B^{fl}, \tag{20}$$

$$Z_t = S((h_t - h_f)\sigma_f), \tag{21}$$

$$S(x) = 1/(1 + \exp(-x)), \tag{22}$$

where A represents the plant dynamics and B represents the aircraft response to the control U. The matrix C is used to compute $x8$ from the desired state D_t

containing desired altitude, desired altitude rate, and desired ground position, as obtained from nominal glideslope and flare trajectories. N is the additive noise computed from the wind model. The matrices A^{gs}, A^{fl}, B^{gs}, and B^{fl} are constant. The variable Z_t generates a smooth transition between glideslope and flare dynamics and makes the cost function J differentiable over the whole trajectory.

The switching controller described in Section 2 can be written as

$$U_t = P_t^T L_t \quad \text{where } P_t = S([VX_t + q]\sigma) \quad \text{and} \quad L_t = W[X_t - RD_t] + r, \tag{23}$$

where the function $S(x)$ is the logistic function $1/(1 + \exp(-x))$ taken over each element of the vector x and σ is an associated slope parameter. The weight matrix V links actual altitude h to each switch unit in P_t (the switch is static). The weight matrix W links altitude error, altitude rate error, and altitude integral error to each linear unit in L_t.

Figure 14 shows a network implementation of the equations where each unit

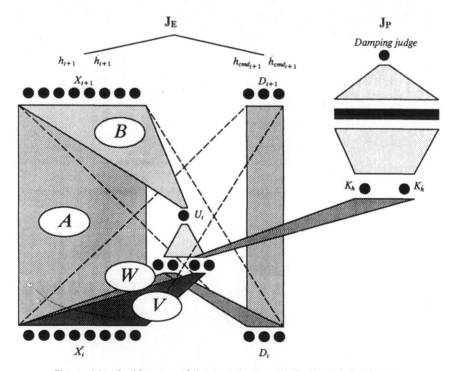

Figure 14. Architecture of the neural network. On the left, implementation of the plant dynamics and controller. In the center, the desired trajectory. On the right, implementation of the performance constraints. Connections A, B, V, and W are explained in the text along with other connections.

computes a linear mapping of $h_t - h_{cmd_t}$, $x8_t$, and $\dot{h}_t - \dot{h}_{cmd_t}$. Thus, the network controller forms a PID dynamic weighting of the altitude error $h_t - h_{cmd_t}$. Initially, we chose two basic controller blocks (see Figure 3) to represent glideslope and flare. The sigmoidal selection for each block is based on altitude alone. In this sense, we use our a priori knowledge of the physics of the plant to adapt the complexity of the network controller to the control task. The task of the network is then to learn the state-dependent PID controller gains that optimize a cost function in given environmental conditions.

Performance Index Optimization

The main optimization problem is now stated. Given an initial state X_1 and initial desired state $D_1 = [h_{cmd_1} \quad \dot{h}_{cmd_1}]^T$, minimize the expected value

$$E[J] = \int J \, p(X_1 \cdots X_T) \, dX_1 \cdots dX_T,$$

$$\text{with } J = J_E = \sum_{t=1}^{T} a_h [h_{cmd} - h_t]^2 + a_{\dot{h}} [\dot{h}_{cmd_t} - \dot{h}_t]^2 \qquad (24)$$

with respect to V, r, W, and q. Note that the cost function $E[J]$ assigns a cost to a particular control law parameterized by V, r, W, and q using knowledge of the stochastic plant model described by the distribution $p(X_1 \cdots X_T)$. Note that the quadratic cost function J is parametrized by an arbitrary choice of the parameters a_h, $a_{\dot{h}}$ (we used $a_h = a_{\dot{h}} = 1$).

When σ is large, the slope of the sigmoid S in Equation 23 becomes large and the associated switching response of the units P becomes sharp. This solution is equivalent to dividing the entire trajectory into a set of linear plants and finding the optimal linear control law for each individual linear plant. If σ is of moderate magnitude (e.g., $\sigma \approx 1$), nonlinear switching and blending of linear control laws via the sigmoidal switching unit is a priori permitted by the architecture. One of the main points of our approach resides in this switching/blending solution (through learning of V and q) as a possible minimum of the optimized cost function.

Equations 18 and 23 describing plant and controller dynamics can be represented in a network, as well as the desired trajectory dynamics (see Figure 14). Note that the resulting network is composed of six learnable weights for each basic controller block: three PID weights plus one bias weight (W weights) and two switch unit weights (V weights). Actual and desired state vectors at time $t + 1$ are fed back to the input layers. Thus, with recurrent connections between output and input layers, the network generates entire trajectories and can be seen as a recurrent back-propagation network (Rumelhart, Hinton & Williams, 1986; Nguyen & Widrow, 1990; Jordan & Jacobs, 1990). The network is then trained using the back-propagation algorithm given wind distributions.

Performance Constraints

As previously noted, the optimization procedure can also depend on performance constraints. The example we use involves relative stability constraints. As will be seen in the fifth section, the unconstrained solution shows lightly damped aircraft responses during glideslope. Here, a penalty on "bad" damping is formulated.

In order to perform a stability analysis, the controlled autoland system is structured as shown in Figure 15. The aircraft altitude responds to values of θ_{cmd} which are generated by the controller. The controller, whether conventional or neural network, can be represented as a PID operation.

The aircraft response denoted in Figure 15 (h in response to θ_{cmd}) consists of the dynamics and kinematics of the airframe along with the pitch stability augmentation system and the autothrottle. This response can be represented as a set of differential equations or, more conveniently, as a Laplace transform transfer function. Equations 25 and 26 provide the transfer functions during glideslope and flare.

Glideslope

$$F(s) = \frac{0.409736(s + 3.054256)(s - 2.288485)(s + 0.299794)(s + 0.154471)}{s(s^2 + 2.216836s + 2.407746)(s^2 + 0.673172s + 0.114482)(s + 0.091075)}, \quad (25)$$

Flare

$$F(s) = \frac{1.671273(s + 3.049899)(s - 2.294112)(s + 0.561642)(s + 0.123544)}{s(s^2 + 3.498162s + 6.184131)(s^2 + 1.057216s + 0.280124)(s + 0.103319)}. \quad (26)$$

In Equations 25 and 26, note the appearance of the short period and the damped phugoid responses (the two quadratic terms in the denominators of the transfer functions). Note also that there is a real positive term in the numerators, leading to stability concerns since the closed-loop roots (eigenvalues) could have positive real parts for some gain values. A positive eigenvalue means instability.

A schematic of a two-unit neural network controller is shown in Figure 16. In function, the network can be viewed to perform as a PID operation on the altitude

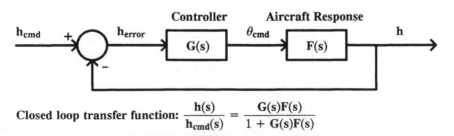

Figure 15. Closed-loop autoland system.

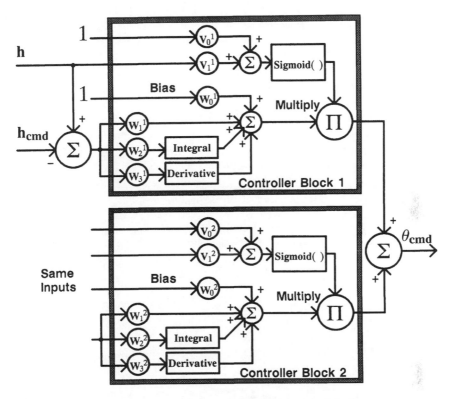

Figure 16.   Two-unit neural network autoland controller.

error $h_{\text{cmd}} - h$. However, the gains on each term are determined by altitude through the sigmoidal switch. Thus, for a particular frozen altitude point along the aircraft flight trajectory, the controller can be represented by the transfer function of Equation 27. Equation 27 also represents the function of the conventional controller.

$$G(s) = \frac{\theta_{\text{cmd}}(s)}{h(s) - h_{\text{cmd}}(s)} = K_h + K_{Ih}\frac{1}{s} + K_{\dot{h}}s = \frac{K_{\dot{h}}s^2 + K_h s + K_{Ih}}{s}. \qquad (27)$$

Taking account of the piecewise linear plant and assuming for the moment constant weights, the aircraft can have transient oscillatory responses of the form $e^{-\zeta\omega t}\cos(\sqrt{1-\zeta^2}\,\omega t + \phi)$, where ζ is a damping factor, ω is a frequency, and ϕ is a phase angle. The damping factor ζ is of particular importance since a small value will give rise to oscillations that persist in time. An analysis of the smallest damping factor was performed by probing the plant with a range of values for controller weight parameters. This data was then used to train a standard feedforward net to catagorize "good" and "bad" damping. A value of ζ greater than 0.4 was regarded as "good" for these purposes. Figure 17 illustrates the response of this "damping judge" network as a function of the proportional (K_h) and derivative ($K_{\dot{h}}$) weights. The integral weight does not have much effect on the transient response. The lower flat portion is a region of poor damping while the higher plateau represents good damping.

A penalty function was constructed using the response of the "damping judge" network shown in Figure 17. First, as shown in Figure 14, additional units were added to the network to compute the equivalent K_h and $K_{\dot{h}}$ values. These were input to the "damping judge" network to yield a ζ_{judge} value. The penalty function is then specified as follows in Equation 28 and added to the performance index for use in the minimization of Equation 24.

$$J_P = \sum_{t=1}^{T} \text{Max}(0, \zeta_{\text{judge}} - \zeta^*_{\text{judge}})(\zeta_{\text{judge}} - \zeta^*_{\text{judge}}) \quad \text{and}$$

$$J = J_E + J_p, \tag{28}$$

where ζ^*_{judge} is some arbitrary value (e.g., 0.8). Note that when $\zeta_{\text{judge}} \leq \zeta^*_{\text{judge}}$, there is no penalty and otherwise, the penalty is quadratic. The expectation is that the minimization procedure will cause the K_h and $K_{\dot{h}}$ values to remain within the "good" damping zone.

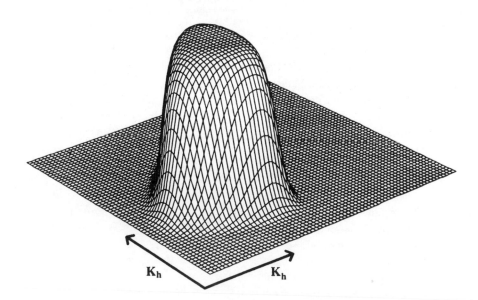

Figure 17.   Response of the damping constraint network.

SIMULATION EXPERIMENTS

We now describe our simulations. First, we introduce our training procedure. We then present the results of flight simulations for individual landings and averaged over 1000 landings for each wind condition. Finally, we discuss the control laws learned by the unconstrained and constrained networks and compare them with conventional controller laws.

Training Procedure

Unconstrained and constrained networks were initialized in the following way. The linear control gains W were set to zero. Switch weights V were either random or represented an a priori switch, inspired from the known piecewise linearity of the plant to be controlled. Simulations show that learning dynamics and learned switch weights depend on weight initialization but that the resulting gain schedules (and therefore performance) do not. The results presented were obtained with weights V initialized in various ways.

The network was trained with a selected wind parameter H distribution consisting of 15 landings (1 at $H = -10$, 4 at $H = 0$, 4 at $H = 10$, 3 at $H = 20$, 2 at $H = 30$ and 1 at $H = 40$). Several learning strategies were tested. With the first strategy, the network was trained over the complete trajectory for the entire training period. With the second strategy, the network was trained with successively increasing portions of the trajectory, starting at 200 ft. With the third strategy, the network was trained on increasing portions of the entire trajectory around flare point at 45 ft (see Nguyen & Widrow, 1990, for similar training strategies). These strategies change the way the network is exposed to the various response characteristics of the plant. The exact form of the learned switch weights V (but not much the resulting gain schedules) then depends on these strategies. The detailed results presented were obtained using the first strategy.

Typical Landings

Figure 18 represents typical landing trajectories for the conventional, the unconstrained and the constrained network controller with a headwind parameter H equal to 40. We also show the accumulated sum squared error and the altitude rate variable $\dot{h}$ during the entire trajectory as a function of ground position.

Statistical Results

After training, the performance of the network controller was tested for different wind conditions. The following statistics were computed:

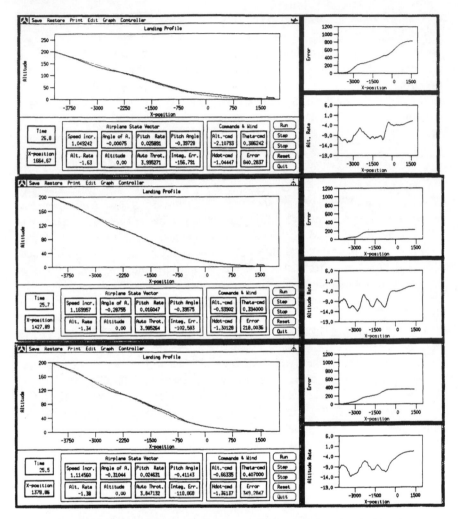

Figure 18.   On top, a nominal trajectory (dotted line) and typical land-ing trajectory (solid line) generated by the conventional controller. The values of landing time, ground position, aircraft states, and commands are indicated below the trajectory. On the right, accumulated cost J and altitude rate along the trajectory. Note the effect of "pitchup" at flare point. In the middle, curves for the unconstrained network con-troller. Note the lightly damped response during glideslope. At the bottom, curves for the zeta-constrained controller.

- Measures of overall performance: quadratic cost J per time step, landing time T
- Measures of trajectory performance for both glideslope and flare: quadratic cost J on altitude h and on altitude rate $\dot{h}$
- Measures of landing performance: ground position at touchdown x_{TD}, pitch angle at touchdown θ_{TD}, altitude rate at touchdown $\dot{h}_{TD}$.

Table 1 shows the means and standard deviations of these variables computed over 1000 landings for five wind conditions for conventional, unconstrained, and zeta-constrained neural network controllers. The goal of minimizing the performance index over the whole trajectory seems to have been reached for the unconstrained network controller. (The quadratic cost during flare is high for the conventional controller due to pitchup at the flarepoint.) Conventional controller pitchup also generates longer landing times and larger ground positions at touchdown. Altitude rates at touchdown remain within nominal range for the three controllers. However, standard deviations on x_{TD} and $\dot{h}_{TD}$ are smaller for the network controllers. We will come back to these results in the final section.

Control Laws Learned

Table 2 shows the weights learned by the networks. From these weights, Equation 23 yields the gains of an "equivalent" controller over the entire trajectory: the "gain schedules." Figure 19 presents gain schedules and evolutions of the switch unit activations (for $H = 0$) during a complete trajectory as a function of altitude. These gain schedules represent *optimality* with respect to a given performance index J. The switch builds a *smooth* transition between glideslope and flare, and provides the network controller with a *nonlinear distributed* control law over the entire trajectory.

Table 2 and Figure 19 show that the unconstrained network learned much larger control gains than those corresponding to the conventional controller. As alluded to above, although these weights do optimize the objective performance index, they control the plant at the limit of stability and would not be appropriate in a realistic aircraft implementation. The augmented performance index and its optimization within the augmented network architecture (see Figure 14) were used to provide a solution to this problem. Figure 20 shows both the unconstrained and the constrained network gain schedules in stability space (with altitude and altitude rate gains as dimensions). From this figure, we can see how the augmented network architecture forces the control weights to remain within the acceptable stability region.

Multiple-Block Controllers

Recall that the bulk of the results already presented concern two basic controller blocks (see Figure 16). As a means of investigating the effect of more basic

TABLE 1
Landing Statistics for the Conventional, Unconstrained,
and Constrained Controller: 1000 Landings and Five Wind Speeds
(std. deviations in parentheses)

Wind	Overall		Glide Slope		Flare		Touchdown		
	J/T	T	$J : h_{gs}$	$J : \dot{h}_{gs}$	$J : h_{fl}$	$J : \dot{h}_{fl}$	x_{TD}	θ_{TD}	$\dot{h}_{TD}$
Conventional Controller									
H=-10	10.00	23.9	19.5	4.60	177	38.8	1560	0.068	-1.70
	(1.9)	(0.24)	(16)	(3.2)	(38)	(4.9)	(55)	(0.0052)	(0.075)
H=0	9.15	24.4	0.0	0.00	187	36.2	1590	-0.030	-1.64
	(0.0)	(0.00)	(0)	(0.0)	(0)	(0.0)	(0)	(0.0000)	(0.000)
H=10	10.90	25.1	20.3	4.84	213	36.8	1640	-0.125	-1.57
	(1.8)	(0.23)	(17)	(3.2)	(43)	(5.0)	(53)	(0.0036)	(0.060)
H=20	15.50	25.7	94.5	21.40	244	39.7	1680	-0.220	-1.53
	(5.1)	(0.48)	(79)	(15.0)	(95)	(11.0)	(110)	(0.0079)	(0.110)
H=30	22.60	26.4	211.0	50.30	290	45.1	1710	-0.311	-1.49
	(9.6)	(0.65)	(180)	(37.0)	(140)	(20.0)	(150)	(0.0130)	(0.140)
H=40	32.20	27.1	383.0	89.80	348	52.9	1750	-0.401	-1.48
	(16.0)	(0.90)	(310)	(60.0)	(210)	(28.0)	(210)	(0.0230)	(0.190)
Unconstrained Network									
H=-10	0.981	21.7	8.280	4.220	5.58	3.24	1060	0.0809	-2.05
	(0.38)	(0.050)	(6.0)	(2.6)	(2.5)	(1.3)	(11)	(0.0075)	(0.049)
H=0	0.220	22.4	0.166	0.163	2.21	2.39	1130	-0.0090	-1.86
	(0.00)	(0.000)	(0.0)	(0.0)	(0.0)	(0.0)	(0)	(0.0000)	(0.000)
H=10	0.804	23.1	9.060	4.650	2.50	2.38	1190	-0.1070	-1.71
	(0.37)	(0.048)	(5.9)	(2.9)	(1.4)	(1.2)	(11)	(0.0099)	(0.031)
H=20	2.910	23.9	39.300	19.600	7.02	3.57	1260	-0.2050	-1.57
	(1.50)	(0.095)	(27.0)	(11.0)	(5.9)	(2.6)	(23)	(0.0200)	(0.044)
H=30	6.190	24.7	87.600	43.900	15.90	5.58	1340	-0.3040	-1.46
	(3.10)	(0.140)	(56.0)	(28.0)	(14.0)	(4.6)	(35)	(0.0290)	(0.053)
H=40	11.000	25.6	160.000	82.400	29.60	8.93	1420	-0.4010	-1.38
	(5.80)	(0.190)	(100.0)	(52.0)	(25.0)	(7.4)	(47)	(0.0340)	(0.065)
Constrained Network									
H=-10	1.34	21.6	13.500	4.230	8.50	2.67	1030	0.0473	-2.15
	(0.56)	(0.047)	(9.8)	(2.6)	(4.4)	(1.2)	(11)	(0.0039)	(0.052)
H=0	0.27	22.2	0.603	0.209	3.31	1.86	1080	-0.0400	-1.98
	(0.00)	(0.000)	(0.0)	(0.0)	(0.0)	(0.0)	(0)	(0.0000)	(0.000)
H=10	0.96	23.0	12.500	4.390	3.17	2.01	1160	-0.1260	-1.79
	(0.53)	(0.052)	(9.2)	(2.6)	(2.2)	(1.1)	(12)	(0.0046)	(0.040)
H=20	3.56	23.8	54.000	18.500	8.65	3.43	1230	-0.2170	-1.64
	(2.10)	(0.100)	(38.0)	(11.0)	(8.2)	(2.7)	(24)	(0.0100)	(0.061)
H=30	8.03	24.6	130.000	43.200	19.20	5.73	1310	-0.3110	-1.50
	(4.70)	(0.160)	(91.0)	(25.0)	(19.0)	(4.7)	(39)	(0.0170)	(0.076)
H=40	13.40	25.5	219.000	76.200	37.00	9.24	1400	-0.4030	-1.39
	(7.80)	(0.220)	(150.0)	(46.0)	(36.0)	(8.0)	(54)	(0.0230)	(0.083)

TABLE 2
PID Controller Gains W and Switch Gains V for a Conventional
Controller, the Unconstrained Network Controller, and the Zeta-
Constrained Network Controller (b stands for bias)

Controller	W								V			
	Glideslope				Flare				Unit 0		Unit 1	
	P	I	D	b	P	I	D	b	h	b	h	b
Conventional	.2	−.02	.32	0	.2	−.02	.32	−3	N.A.			
Unconstrained Net	.22	−.02	.79	.08	.22	.0	.26	.01	.092	−4.5	−.093	4.51
Constrained Net	.24	−.02	.50	.06	.19	.0	.28	.01	.094	−4.5	−.099	4.5

controller blocks, runs were made with an assumption of three controller blocks. This assumption allows more complex types of controller responses and effective gain scheduling.

The zeta constrained case is considered here. Table 3 shows the means and standard deviations of the trajectory and landing performance variables for the three-unit controller. Note that the results are very comparable to the constrained network results for the two-unit controller shown in Table 1. Performance both during the flight (see values of the performance index J) and at touchdown are very close.

Figure 21 shows the equivalent gain schedules and switch activations for the three-unit controller. The behavior of the switching units is qualitatively different here. Recall that this depends on weight initialization. For the three-unit case, switching is accomplished by having all three units activated during glideslope. Then, as flare approaches, the units turn off at different rates. As mentioned, this has similar effects to the case where some units are on and others are off during the flight. At any rate, the gain schedule behavior shown in Figure 21, although comparable in value to the two-unit case, shows somewhat more complex behavior. Gain values do not change monotonically during the flight as is true for the two-unit case.

Finally, Figure 22 illustrates the network gain schedules in stability space (with altitude and altitude rate gains as dimensions). Note that this augmented network architecture also forces the control weights to remain within the acceptable stability region. In addition, the complexity of the trace is greater in comparison with that for the two-unit case (see Figure 20). In the three-unit case, the trace has a tendency to follow the edges of the good stability region.

94   SCHLEY, CHAUVIN, VAN HENKLE

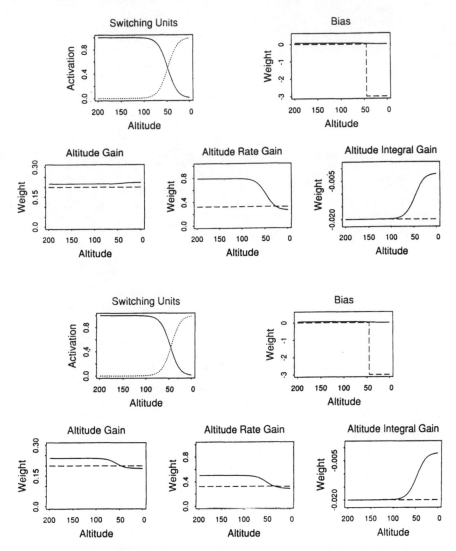

Figure 19.   Activations of switching units during a windless trajectory and associated gain schedules: (top) the unconstrained controller; (bottom) the zeta-constrained controller. The conventional controller gains are shown in dotted lines.

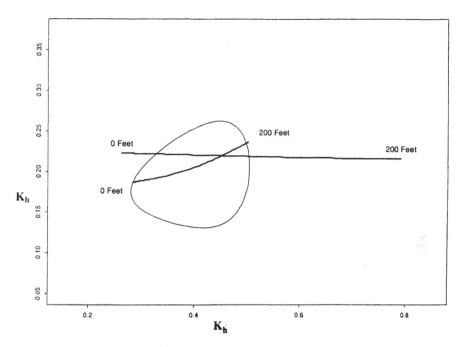

Figure 20. Gain schedules in stability space. The long curve represents the gain schedules for the unconstrained network controller, the short curve the zeta-constrained network controller. The egg-shaped region in the center of the figure represents the stability region where damping is greater than 0.4.

TABLE 3
Landing Statistics for the Three-Unit Controller: 1000 Landings
and Five Wind Speeds (std. deviations in parentheses)

Constrained Network with 3 Controller Blocks								
	Overall Performance		Glide Slope Mean Squared Error		Flare Mean Squared Error		Touchdown Performance		
Wind	J/T	T	$J : h_{gs}$	$J : \dot{h}_{gs}$	$J : h_{fl}$	$J : \dot{h}_{fl}$	x_{TD}	θ_{TD}	$\dot{h}_{TD}$
H=−10	1.300	21.9	13.60	4.16	6.71	3.95	1100	−0.0541	−2.11
	(0.55)	(0.023)	(10)	(2.3)	(3.4)	(1.8)	(5.3)	(0.0053)	(0.022)
H=0	0.367	22.6	1.64	0.47	3.01	3.17	1170	−0.1240	−1.92
	(0.00)	(0.000)	(0)	(0.0)	(0.0)	(0.0)	(0.0)	(0.0000)	(0.000)
H=10	1.100	23.3	14.20	4.60	3.23	3.65	1230	−0.1980	−1.77
	(0.58)	(0.020)	(10)	(2.5)	(1.8)	(1.6)	(4.5)	(0.0046)	(0.019)
H=20	3.520	24.1	54.60	17.60	7.37	5.33	1310	−0.2740	−1.61
	(2.00)	(0.052)	(39)	(9.6)	(5.4)	(3.8)	(12)	(0.0083)	(0.038)
H=30	7.890	25.0	131.00	42.00	16.20	7.58	1400	−0.3530	−1.46
	(4.70)	(0.081)	(92)	(24.0)	(13.0)	(6.2)	(20)	(0.0130)	(0.056)
H=40	13.900	25.9	241.00	78.40	29.00	12.20	1500	−0.4320	−1.33
	(8.10)	(0.110)	(170.0)	(44.0)	(22.0)	(10.0)	(29.0)	(0.0180)	(0.067)

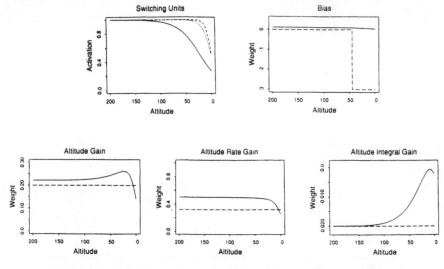

Figure 21.   Activations of switching units and associated gain schedules for a three-unit controller during a windless trajectory. The conventional controller gains are shown in dotted lines.

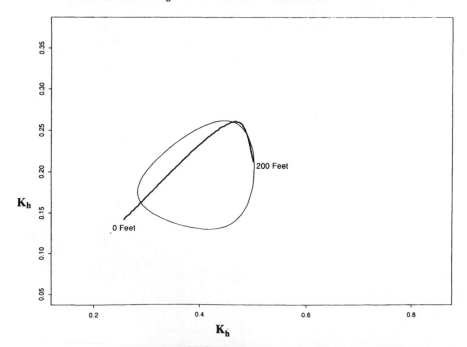

Figure 22.   Gain schedules in stability space for the three-unit case. Note how the curve follows the egg-shaped region in the center of the figure, which represents the stability region where damping is greater than 0.4.

DISCUSSION AND FUTURE DIRECTIONS

Conventional Controllers

A typical conventional controller has weights as shown in Table 2. Real-world controllers (autoland systems) actually implemented on aircraft are much more sophisticated than the conventional controller described in this chapter. For example, they attempt to smooth the transition between glideslope and flare. Our conventional controller can be seen simply as a baseline controller.

Interestingly, conventional automatic controllers do perform significantly better than human controllers during normal operations. It is only during problematic situations that human controllers can use other forms of knowledge about the environment and the plant to outperform autoland systems. It remains to be seen if network controllers might extend the range of usability of existing autoland systems.

Neural Net Controllers

The architecture we propose integrates a priori knowledge of real plants within the structure of the neural network. Previous attempts showed that approaches with less structured (but perhaps computationally more powerful) networks were not particularly successful. The knowledge of the physics of the system and its representation in the network were part of the solution. Such a priori knowledge structures are not only useful for finding control solutions, but also allow interpretations of network dynamics in term of standard control theory. By observing the weights learned by the network, we can compute gain schedules and understand how the network controls the plant. We believe this approach to be generalizable to a number of nonlinear control problems.

The augmented architecture allows us to control damping. In general, integrating optimal control performance indices with constraints on plant response characteristics is not an easy task. The neural network approach and backpropagation learning represent an interesting and elegant solution to this problem. Furthermore, as explained earlier, we simply show the feasibility of the approach. Other constraints on states or response characteristics could also be implemented with similar architectures. In the present case, the control gains were obtained to minimize the objective performance index while the plant remains within a desired stability region. The effect of this approach provided good damping and control gain schedules that make the plant robust to disturbances (Table 1).

Finally, it must be said that meaningful comparisons of performance between realistic conventional controllers and network controllers would require thorough examination of the distributions of the state variables at landing as a function of the stochastic wind process (Neuman & Foster, 1970). Such considerations are beyond the scope of this chapter.

97

ACKNOWLEDGMENTS

This research was supported by the Boeing High Technology Center. The help of Anil Phatak of Analytical Mechanics Associates was decisive for the realization of this study. We would also like to thank Richard Golden for his help during the early stages of this project and Yoshiro Miyata for letting us use his neural network simulator X-Net.

REFERENCES

Bryson, A. E., & Ho, Y. C. (1969). *Applied optimal control*. Blaisdel.

Jordan, M. I., & Jacobs, R. A. (1990). Learning to control an unstable system with forward modeling. In D. S. Touretzky (Ed.), *Neural information processing systems* 2. San Mateo, CA: Morgan Kaufman.

Le Cun, Y. (1989). A theoretical framework for back-propagation. In D. Touretzky, G. Hinton, & T. Sejnowski (Eds.), *Proceedings of the 1988 Connectionist Models Summer School*. San Mateo, CA: Morgan Kaufman.

McRuer, D., Ashkenas, I., & Graham, D. (1973). *Aircraft dynamics and automated control*. Princeton, NJ: Princeton University Press.

Narendra, K. S., & Parthasarathy, K. (1990). Identification and control of dynamical systems using neural networks. *IEEE Transactions on Neural Networks, 1,* 4–26.

Neuman, F., & Foster, J. D. (1970). *Investigation of a digital automatic aircraft landing system in turbulence* (NASA Technical Note TN D-6066). Moffett Field, CA: NASA-Ames Research Center.

Nguyen, D. H., & Widrow, B. (1990). Neural networks for self-learning control systems. *IEEE Control Systems Magazine, April,* 18–23.

Rumelhart, D. E., Hinton, G. E., & Williams, R. J. (1986). Learning internal representations by error propagation. In D. E. Rumelhart & J. L. McClelland (Eds.) *Parallel distributed processing: Explorations in the microstructures of cognition* (Vol. I). Cambridge, MA: MIT Press.

Rumelhart, D. E., & McClelland, J. L. (1986). *Parallel distributed processing: Explorations in the microstructures of cognition* (Vols. I & II). Cambridge, MA: MIT Press.

4 Recurrent Backpropagation Networks

Fernando J. Pineda
The Johns Hopkins University, Applied Physics Laboratory

ABSTRACT

This chapter reviews the theory, implementation and application of the recurrent back-propagation (RBP) algorithm for convergent dynamical systems. The additive model is used as the canonical example, although general expressions for arbitrary convergent dynamical systems are given in the appendix. Forcing techniques for creating fixed points are discussed from a dynamical point of view. The general features of a physical implementation of a collective dynamical system that performs the RBP algorithm are discussed. The results of three simulations are presented. The first shows how learning curves exhibit discontinuities as fixed points are introduced. The second shows how recurrent networks can be trained to perform error correction and autoassociative recall. The last shows how RBP has been used to solve the correspondence problem in random-dot stereograms.

INTRODUCTION

Relaxation is a powerful paradigm for computation. To use the technique it is necessary to embed problem constraints in a convergent dynamical systems. When such a dynamical system is allowed to evolve, it eventually converges to a final state that satisfies all the constraints simultaneously according to some heuristically defined measure. Dynamical systems can be *programmed* by modifying internal parameters (e.g., weights). Data can be input by modifying external parameters (*parametric input*) or setting initial states (*initial-state input*). These two kinds of input have different properties and are discussed in more detail in the next section. Algorithms that exploit relaxation techniques are ubiquitous. For example, in computer vision, the Marr-Poggio (1976) algorithm solves the correspondence problem in random-dot stereograms by embedding two constraints in a *discrete-time* dynamical system. First it embeds the constraint that along a line of sight there is only one unique surface and second, it embeds the constraint that surfaces are typically smooth and continuous. Data about the image is used to set the initial state of the network. The network is then allowed to relax to a representation of depth in a visual field. Associative memory is another application where relaxation is useful. In the discrete-time model discussed by Hopfield (1982), memories are stored by using a Hebb rule that modifies the weights in the network. The memories are subsequently recalled by relaxing the system from a fixed initial state while a subset of the processing units are clamped to input values. These input values represent partial memory cues. Another useful network is discussed by Hopfield and Tank (1985). In their network, single-visit and minimum-path-length constraints are embedded in a *continuous-time* dynamical system that solves (in an approximate sense) the traveling salesman problem. Data concerning the distances between cities is used to program the weights. The network is then allowed to relax from a fixed initial state to a representation of the best path. There is no parametric input.

In the stereo problem and in the traveling salesman problem, the dynamical parameters are hand-crafted so as to embed the problem constraints. Such an approach assumes that the constraints are known and that they can be easily represented in the dynamical system. This state of affairs, however, is certainly the exception rather than the rule; thus it is useful to have techniques for extracting constraints from examples and embedding them in convergent dynamical systems. The Hebb rule is one rule for doing this. The purpose of this chapter is to describe a gradient technique for extracting information from examples and for embedding it in convergent dynamical systems. Before going into the details, however, it is useful to review some basic notions.

For many purposes, the difference between discrete-time and continuous-time systems is not important and the formulation one uses is largely a matter of taste. In this chapter the continuous-time formulation is used unless otherwise stated. Discrete-time algorithms and continuous time algorithms can often be related by starting with a continuous-time algorithm and discretizing it. Nevertheless, there can be dramatic differences in the behavior of the two. As a trivial example, consider the continuous one-dimensional dynamical system

$$\frac{du}{dt} = -u + wu. \tag{1}$$

with a nonzero initial state. The corresponding discrete Euler approximation is obtained by replacing du/dt with $\Delta u/\Delta t$ so that (1) becomes

$$u(t + \Delta t) = (1 - \Delta t) u(t) + \Delta t w u(t). \tag{2}$$

Equation (2) describes a family of dynamical systems parametrized by Δt. In the limit $\Delta t \to 0$ the dynamics is the same as the continuous-time system. The continuous system converges to the value $u = 0$ provided $w < 1$. Notice that no oscillation is possible. In the limit $\Delta t \to 1$, on the other hand, a new behavior is found: the system oscillates forever between two states if $w = -1$. One concludes that some care must be exercised when going back and forth between discrete and continuous systems.

Many of the features of convergent dynamics that are important for computation are model independent. Therefore it is useful to introduce an abstract set of activation equations with a minimal set of properties that can stand in for any convergent neural network model. In this chapter we will use a continuous-time formulation. (Discrete versions of the algorithms are required for numerical simulation and will be discussed where appropriate.) Consider a general system of coupled nonlinear differential equations:

$$du/dt = \mathbf{G}(\mathbf{w},\mathbf{I},\mathbf{u}). \tag{3}$$

The vector $\mathbf{u} = \{u_1, \ldots, u_n\}$ represents the state of the system. The system evolves in an n-dimensional state-space. The "vector" $\mathbf{w} = \{\ldots, w_\alpha, \ldots\}$ represents a set of "internal" parameters (e.g., weights, gains, or time scales). This "vector" can actually be a scalar, matrix or tensor, in which case the "subscript" α refers to the appropriate set of indices. Similarly, the vector $\mathbf{I} = \{\ldots, I_\alpha, \ldots\}$ represents a set of "external" parameters (e.g., external biases or inputs). Assume that $\mathbf{G}$ is at least continuously differentiable. The set of trajectories that are solutions of (3) is determined by the parameters $\mathbf{w}$ and $\mathbf{I}$. Formally, a dynamical system is defined by a set of trajectories; hence, one says that each choice of $\mathbf{w}$ and $\mathbf{I}$ defines a different dynamical system. A set of trajectories for a given $\mathbf{w}$ and $\mathbf{I}$ is also called a flow. The flow is convergent if the trajectories converge to one or many equilibrium states. These equilibrium states are also known as fixed points. Henceforth, such equilibrium states will be designated by the superscript f: $\mathbf{u}^f$. The equilibrium states of convergent dynamical systems are implicit functions of $\mathbf{I}$ and $\mathbf{w}$. In general, a flow can have many equilibrium points. Accordingly, where the system converges depends on the choice of initial state. Informally, the set of all initial states that are on trajectories that converge to a given equilibrium point is the "basin of attraction" of that fixed point. In Figure 1 three fixed points and their basins are schematically illustrated.

Most of the discussion in this chapter applies to general convergent systems. For clarity, however, it is useful to particularize some of the statements to the usual additive nonlinear model for an interacting system of N units. This simple dynamical system is well studied and is the basis of much neural network research (Amari, 1972; Aplevich, 1968; Cowan, 1967; Grossberg, 1969; Hopfield, 1984; Malsburg, 1973; Sejnowski, 1977). The internal states of the model are

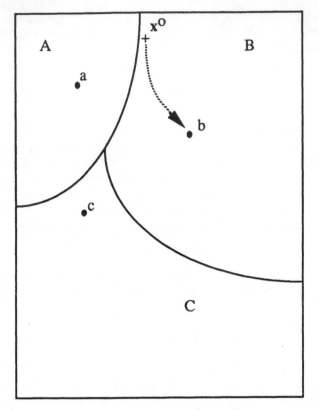

Figure 1. Schematic diagram of three fixed points and their basin boundaries. For dynamical systems with energy functions the basin boundaries correspond to ridges on the energy surface.

described by the vector $\mathbf{u} = (u_1, \ldots, u_N)$, while the outputs of the units are described by the vector $\mathbf{V} = (V_1, \ldots, V_N)$. The vectors $\mathbf{V}$ and $\mathbf{u}$ are related by $V_i = f(u_i)$ where the nonlinear function $f(\cdot)$ is commonly taken to be a hyperbolic tangent or logistic function. The additive model ignores propagation time delays between units and is specified by

$$\frac{du_i}{dt} = -u_i + \sum_j w_{ij}V_j + I_i. \tag{4}$$

The weights w_{ij} represent the synaptic strengths of the connections between the units and the biases I_i represent external inputs. Under the affine transformation

$$\mathbf{u} = \mathbf{w}\,\mathbf{v} + \mathbf{I} \tag{5}$$

Equation 4 is equivalent to

$$\frac{dv_i}{dt} = -v_i + f\left(\sum_j w_{ij}v_j + I_i\right) \qquad (6)$$

provided $\mathbf{w}$ is nonsingular and provided $\mathbf{I}$ is a constant. Equation (6) is the continuum limit of the discrete model usually associated with back propagation. To see this, simply make the discrete approximation and take the limit $\Delta t \rightarrow 1$. This results in

$$v_i(t + 1) = f\left(\sum_j w_{ij}v_j(t + 1) + I_i\right). \qquad (7)$$

If the network is feedforward with no self connections, then $\mathbf{w}$ is lower triangular and each time step corresponds to a propagation from one layer to the next, just as in ordinary back-propagation networks.

Thus far we have not precisely defined the conditions guaranteeing that the trajectory of every (or almost every) initial state converges to an equilibrium. To do so properly is beyond the scope of this chapter. The interested reader is referred to the discussion by Hirsh (1989) for a thorough treatment. For our purposes it suffices only to mention that the additive model (4) is convergent under the following conditions. First, if the weight matrix is lower triangular or if it can be converted to a lower triangular matrix by row and column exchanges. This is the case when the network has no recurrent loops. Hence, it is just a feedforward network and the dynamics is trivially convergent. Second, if the weight matrix is symmetric, the system possesses a Lyapunov function and it is convergent (Cohen and Grossberg, 1983; Hopfield, 1984). Third, Almeida (1987) has shown that the system possess a Liapunov function if it satisfies *detailed balance*. That is, if

$$w_{ij}f(u_j) = w_{ji}f(u_i). \qquad (8)$$

Detailed balance is a more general symmetry condition than symmetry of the weight matrix. In addition, if the norm of the weight matrix is sufficiently small, as is typically the case in an untrained network, the initial network can be guaranteed to have a unique and stable fixed point. This is because for sufficiently small weights the network can be made to approximate a convergent linear network arbitrarily closely. Such a network will also have no unstable fixed points. In particular, Atiya (1988) shows that a network (not necessarily symmetric) satisfying

$$\sum_i \sum_j w_{ij}^2 < \frac{1}{\max_i f'(u_i)} \qquad (9)$$

(where $f'(u) = df(u)/du$) exhibits no other behavior except going to a unique equilibrium for a given input. Finally, it is worthwhile to point out that *cascades* of convergent systems can sometimes be proved to be convergent (Hirsh, 1989).

Two dynamically distinct learning tasks shall be considered. One task is that of moving about already existing fixed points, while the second task is that of introducing new fixed points into the system. The former requires nothing more than minimizing a cost function, whereas a systematic method for the latter makes use of a second technique called *forcing* to overcome dynamical barriers that can block learning. *Teacher forcing,* as described by Williams and Zipser (1991), is a special case of the general forcing technique. The concept of forcing is described in more detail in the fourth section.

The basic idea behind training is to minimize a cost function that measures the network performance. Following the convention in this book we use C to denote such a cost function. One of the simplest cost functions is the *least mean square* (LMS) cost function, C^{lms}. It measures the Euclidean distance between the actual location of an equilibrium and the desired location of that equilibrium. It is given by

$$C^{lms} = \frac{1}{2} \sum_{i \in O} (d_i - f(u_i^f))^2, \qquad (10)$$

where the sum is over the subset O of the state variables that we wish to determine. These state variables are associated with *visible* or *output* units. The training set T consists of m input/output pattern vectors $T = \{(\mathbf{d}^1, \mathbf{x}^1), \ldots, (\mathbf{d}^m, \mathbf{x}^m)\}$. An input pattern vector $\mathbf{x}^q$ is generally used to set either the parameter vector $\mathbf{I}$ or the initial state $\mathbf{u}^o$, depending on which mode of computation one is performing. One can also input data through $\mathbf{I}$ and $\mathbf{u}^o$ simultaneously. Most algorithms that minimize cost functions are variations of gradient descent. The simplest such algorithm is to update a parameter w by the negative gradient of the cost function.

$$\Delta w_\alpha = -\eta \, \frac{\partial C}{\partial w_\alpha}. \qquad (11)$$

In this chapter there will be no discussion of more sophisticated techniques such as momentum, conjugate gradient, or Newton methods because the well-known techniques that speed up ordinary back propagation apply equally well to recurrent networks.

Recurrent back propagation (Almeida, 1987; Pineda, 1987) is a method for calculating the gradient. The RBP equations for the additive model are described in the third section, while the general equations are given in the appendix. RBP is an efficient method for obtaining a fast approximation for the gradient. RBP has the characteristic feature that for most neural network dynamical systems the gradient takes the form of an outer product of two equilibrium states. One of these equilibrium states comes from the activation dynamics, while the second one comes from an associated linear (*adjoint*) system. In analogy to the feedforward case, the activation dynamics is referred to as the forward dynamics, while the linear equations are referred to as the *backward* dynamical system. RBP is similar to the classical multistage gradient descent procedures developed independently, for optimal control, by Kelley (1960), who used adjoint methods, and by Bryson (1962), who used Lagrange multipliers. Variations of these techniques were discovered independently in the context of neural networks by Werbos (1977), Parker (1982), and Rumelhart, Hinton, and Williams (1986), to name a few. To my knowledge, Dreyfus (1962) was the first to use a recursive procedure to derive these algorithms. The "lineage" of back propagation and its recurrent generalizations are described by Le Cun (1989) and Dreyfus (1990). Unlike the numerical multistage methods, RBP lends itself to implementation in a collective physical system such as analog VLSI or optics. The outlines of a physical implementation are given in the fifth section.

Finally, in the last section there are numerical simulations that show the behavior and application of the RBP algorithm. The first example illustrates the discontinuous learning behavior that manifests itself when fixed points are introduced into the dynamics during the learning process. The second example illustrates a simple network that performs error correction and associative recall. The final example shows how to apply the algorithm to extract disparity information from random-dot stereograms.

PARAMETRIC AND INITIAL-STATE INPUT

Pineda (1988b) and Hirsh (1989) have stressed that the phenomenology of convergent dynamical systems can be exploited in two ways to perform computation. These two ways are distinguished by how one inputs data into the network. To run a net—to integrate the dynamical equations for a fixed set of weights—one must specify both the initial state u^o and the external parameters $\mathbf{I}$. This provides two ways of feeding data into the network. Specifying $\mathbf{I}$ is denoted *parametric input,* while specifying u^o is denoted *initial-state input.* The former lends itself naturally to performing continuous transformations, whereas the latter lends itself to performing associative recall or error correction. The salient features of these two modes of computation are the subject of this section.

Parametric Input

Suppose the initial state is the same for all relaxations. Then the computation performed by the dynamical system is a map from the parametric input to the final state; that is, $\mathbf{M}: \mathbf{I} \rightarrow u^f$. The essential feature of this map is that, in general, it is predominantly smooth. A small change in $\mathbf{I}$ produces a small change in u^f.

This kind of map is useful for robotics tasks and for tasks that require generalization. To be more precise, in the neighborhood of points where the Jacobian $|\partial G/\partial u|_{u=u^f}|$ does not vanish the equilibrium state u^f is an implicit function of w and I. In these neighborhoods the function $u^f(w, I)$ is differentiable and continuous. The inverse function theorem assures us that the map M is one-to-one and onto in some neighborhood of I, provided the Jacobian $|\partial G/\partial I|$ does not vanish.

The function $u^f(w, I)$ defines a manifold in the space of activations. The parametric inputs define coordinates on the manifold, while the shape of the manifold is determined by w. This is shown schematically in Figure 2 for a simple dynamical system with a three-dimensional state-space. The maps computed by purely feedforward networks are also smooth functions of their inputs (provided the squashing functions are smooth and provided there are no self-connections). The main difference between the maps computed by feedforward networks and the maps computed by recurrent networks with parametric input is that in the former the maps are explicit functions of the inputs, whereas in the latter the maps are implicit functions. This purely mathematical distinction would seem to give recurrent networks little advantage over ordinary feedforward networks. Nevertheless, recurrent networks with nonlinear squashing func-

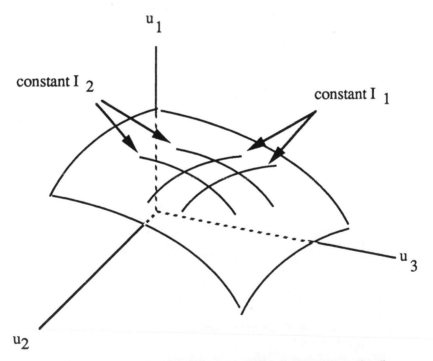

Figure 2.   A schematic diagram of a solution manifold for $u^f(w, I)$. Here we assume that the state space is three dimensional and that there are only two nonzero parametric inputs, I_1 and I_2.

tions differ from purely feedforward networks because they admit dynamics with multiple equilibrium points. Consequently, different initial states, for fixed **w** and **I,** can result in completely different maps. In principle, this gives recurrent networks additional flexibility and computational power.

Initial-State Input

The potential multiplicity of equilibrium points in nonlinear dynamical systems can be exploited for computation. In particular, suppose the parametric input **I** is the same for all relaxations and that the input data is used to determine the initial state u^o. When the input vector **x** has a smaller dimensionality than the state vector **u,** one must choose a subset of the state variables to be inputs while the remaining state variables are set to fixed or random values, say $u_i^o = x_i$ for $i = 1, \ldots, k$ and $u_i^o = 0$ for $i = k + 1, \ldots, n$, where there are k inputs. The computation performed by the dynamical system is a map from the initial state to the final state, **M**: $u^o \rightarrow u^f$. The essential features of this map are that, in general, it is many-to-one and that for initial states not near basin boundaries, a small change in the input produces no change in the output.

Computation with this map is useful for associative recall and/or error correction because any deformation or degradation of a stored pattern can be thought of as a perturbation of the initial state away from the correct equilibrium point. If this perturbation is sufficiently small, the initial state will remain in the basin of the correct equilibrium point and the network will "associate" the input with the correct output.

Two difficulties with using dynamical systems as associative memories is that at the present time there is no general way of directly controlling the details of the basin structure and second, there are often undesirable equilibria (spurious memories) that do not correspond to any stored patterns.

GRADIENT DESCENT LEARNING

This section describes the RBP algorithm for the additive model. It includes the learning equations, an analysis of the complexity and a discussion of stability considerations. The presentation is in the context of a parametric input task. For simplicity assume that the initial state is a fixed constant vector $u^o = c$ that is independent of the input. The learning rule is a special case of the general results derived in Appendix A.

RBP Equations for the Additive Model

Recall that the dynamical equations for the additive model are of the form

$$\frac{du_i}{dt} = -u_i + \sum_j w_{ij} V_j + I_i. \tag{12}$$

Let the input be **x** and let a subset **A** of the units be *input* units; that is, let $I_i = x_i$ for $i \in$ **A** and $I_i = 0$ for $i \notin$ **M**. Let the corresponding target be **d** and let a subset **O** of the units be *output* units. Then the desired values for the output units are $V_i^f = d_i$ for $i \in$ **O**. On the other hand for $i \notin$ **O** the output units have no target values. Finally, let the cost function be an LMS cost function of the form

$$C^{\mathrm{lms}} = \frac{1}{2} \sum_{i \in \mathbf{O}} (d_i - V_i^f)^2. \tag{13}$$

Now by applying the general results in Appendix A to the additive system with this LMS cost function it can be shown that the gradient takes the form

$$\frac{\partial C^{\mathrm{lms}}}{\partial w_{ij}} = z_i^f V_j^f. \tag{14}$$

The quantity z_i^f is the steady-state solution of

$$\frac{dz_i}{dt} = -z_i + f'(u_i^f) \sum_i (\mathbf{w}^T)_{ij} z_j + J^{\mathrm{lms}}{}_i, \tag{15}$$

where $f'(\cdot)$ is the derivative of $f(\cdot)$ and $\mathbf{w}^T$ is the transpose of $\mathbf{w}$: $(\mathbf{w}^T)_{ij} = w_{ji}$. The transpose appearing in Equation 15 is the signature of backwards signal propagation since it exchanges the roles of pre- and postsynaptic indices. The external error signal $J^{\mathrm{lms}}{}_i$ is

$$J^{\mathrm{lms}}{}_i = \begin{cases} d_i - V_i^f) & \text{if } i \in \mathbf{O}, \\ 0 & \text{if } i \notin \mathbf{O}. \end{cases} \tag{16}$$

The quantity z_i^f is the recurrent generalization of the error signal δ_i used in the δ-rule.

To see this, assume that **w** is a lower triangular matrix; that is, it is pure feedforward. Hence, for output units the equilibrium solution of Equation 15 is $z_i = (d_i - V_i^f)$. Next, observe that for nonoutput units, Equation 15 simplifies to

$$\frac{dz_i}{dt} = -z_i + f'(u_i^f) \sum_j (\mathbf{w}^T)_{ij} z_j \tag{17}$$

Now, in the discrete approximation ($dz_i/dt \approx \Delta z_i/\Delta t$ and $\Delta t = 1$) Equation 17 becomes

$$z_i = f'(u_i^f) \sum_j (\mathbf{w}^T)_{ij} z_j. \tag{18}$$

This is just the familiar back-propagation form except for the extra indices usually used to indicate layers. The "missing" layer index is implicit in the foregoing indexing scheme because each unit has a unique index. Equations 18 are equivalent to those given by Almeida (1987).

Complexity

The algorithms discussed in this chapter are typically implemented on digital computers, therefore it is of interest to estimate the complexity of the simulations. For this purpose, it suffices to consider the additive model in the limit of very many neurons and connections, with the fan-in/fan-out of the units assumed proportional to the number of units, n. Therefore, the number of weights, N, is proportional to n^2. The notation $O(n^2)$ means that in the large-n limit the number of operations is bounded by kn^2, where k is a constant. It is also useful to simplify the complexity calculation by assuming that the relaxations are performed using first-order Euler integration and that all the operations are performed with a fixed precision. Addition, multiplication, subtraction, and division are treated on an equal footing. The evaluation of the squashing function $f(\cdot)$ is assumed to require a fixed number of operations, independently of its argument.

Relaxations are basic to the algorithm, so it is useful to estimate their complexity. The number of operations required to relax the n Equations (4) is proportional to the number of time steps, n_t in the Euler integration. In general, the number of iterations required to converge is not predicable, since the nonlinear dynamics can lead to quite complicated trajectories. In practice, however, it seems that for typical problems the trajectories are not complicated and spend most of their time converging like decaying exponentials to the equilibrium points, as required by the Lipschitz condition. To relax the equations to machine precision can be very expensive since one must perform many iterations. In practice, one sets a tolerance ϵ such that the relaxation is halted when $|\Delta u| < \epsilon$. Since the total number of iterations is typically dominated by the asymptotic approach to equilibrium, it follows that $n_t \sim -\log(\epsilon)$ is a reasonable estimate for how n_t scales with tolerance. For the backward propagation equations (17) this scaling is exact because their analytic solutions have exponential forms. Each iteration of the $2n$ equations (4 and 17) scales like $O(n^2)$. This is because the number of operations on the right-hand sides of Equations 4 and 17 are eventually dominated by the $O(n^2)$ matrix-times-vector multiplies represented by the summations. All the other operations, including the evaluations of $f(\cdot)$ and the calculation of error signals, scale like $O(n)$. Accordingly, one concludes that the relaxation of x scales approximately like $O(-n^2 \log(\epsilon))$, while the relaxation of z scales exactly like $O(-n^2 \log(\epsilon))$. It is not necessary to use the same convergence tolerance for the forward and backward propagations. At least one group (Simard, Ottaway, & Ballard, 1988) has reported success with only one to four iterations of the backward equations. Presumably this corresponds to using a relatively large ϵ for the backward propagations.

After the equilibrium values u^f and z^f are obtained, the actual evaluation of the gradient requires only one multiplication per weight. These additional n^2 calculations are a small addition to the $O(-n^2 \log(\epsilon))$ calculations already required for the relaxation, provided ϵ is small. Thus a single gradient evaluation requires approximately $O(-n^2 \log(\epsilon))$ operations.

It is interesting to compare the gradient evaluation by RBP with other numerical schemes. In particular, to evaluate the gradient numerically requires that n^2 differences of the cost function of the form $C(\mathbf{w} + \Delta\mathbf{w}) - C(\mathbf{w})$. Each evaluation of the cost function requires a relaxation of $\mathbf{u}$. Hence, the complexity of the numerical gradient is approximately $O(-n^4 \log (\epsilon))$. Another numerical scheme is to evaluate $\mathbf{z}$ by matrix inversion (see Equation A5) rather than by relaxation and then use Equation 14 to calculate the gradient. This results requires a relaxation of $\mathbf{u}$ followed by $O(n^3)$ operations to perform a matrix inversion. The complexity of this scheme is approximately $O(An^3 - Bn^2 \log (\epsilon))$, where A and B are constants that depend on the details of the implementation. These results are summarized in Table 1.

Stability Considerations

There are a few subtleties associated with the robustness of the gradient evaluation and the continued stability of the activation dynamics as the weights slowly evolve. Some of these subtleties arise from the local properties of the fixed points, while others arise from the global properties of the basin boundaries. First we consider the local properties of the fixed points and then we consider the global properties of the fixed points and their basin boundaries.

Eigenvalue Analysis

Simard, Ottaway, and Ballard (1988) have analyzed the stability properties of recurrent networks with the aforementioned learning rule. They argue that any squashing function can introduce unstable fixed points, and they have pointed out that this can cause difficulties with the learning algorithm. They note that unstable fixed points do not turn out to be a problem in practice and they are unlikely to be present in a network with a reasonable set of initial weights, say a weight matrix with a small norm. In fact, the mere existence of unstable fixed points should not be a cause for concern since trajectories in the activation space are

TABLE 1
Comparison of the Complexity of Recurrent Back
Propagation with Other Gradient Evaluation Methods
Assuming the Additive Model and the LMS Cost Function

Numerical Gradient Evaluation Algorithm	Complexity
Numerical differentiation	$O(-n^4 \log (\epsilon))$
Matrix inversion (e.g., Gaussian elimination)	$O(An^3 - Bn^2 \log (\epsilon))$
RBP	$O(-n^2 \log (\epsilon))$

pushed away from such points. It is the possible absence of any stable fixed points that should cause concern since it is then impossible for the network to converge and it could go into oscillation. In practice oscillations are rarely a problem. Most cases where the network goes into oscillations arise when the learning rate is too large or when Δt is too large.

Almeida (1987) has observed that the local stability of the forward propagation equations is a sufficient condition for the local stability of the backward propagation equations. This follows because if the flows about the fixed points $\mathbf{u}^f$ and $\mathbf{z}^f$ are linearized, the corresponding Jacobian matrices have the same eigenvalues in the forward and backward systems. This is explained, in general, in Appendix B.

Symmetry

The learning rule given in the first subsection of this section does not depend on the symmetry of the weight matrix. In principle, this can cause problems because the weight matrix could evolve into a region where the activation dynamics is no longer convergent. In practice, this does not seem to be a problem. Nevertheless, it may be useful to use an algorithm that starts with a symmetric weight matrix and continues to preserve this symmetry during learning. Such an algorithm is guaranteed to have activation dynamics that is always globally asymptotically stable. This is most easily done by symmetrize the gradient. It corresponds to imposing the constraint $w_{ij} = w_{ji}$. With this constraint the weight update rule becomes

$$\Delta w_{ij} = -\eta \begin{cases} \dfrac{\partial C}{\partial w_{ij}} + \dfrac{\partial C}{\partial w_{ji}} & \text{if } i \neq j, \\[2mm] \dfrac{\partial C}{\partial w_{ii}} & \text{if } i = j. \end{cases} \tag{19}$$

Basin Boundaries

The interaction of the initial state with basin boundaries can cause discontinuities in the learning. These discontinuities arise either in symmetric or asymmetric networks and manifest themselves as jumps in the learning curve. The problem arises because changes in the weights not only change the locations of fixed points but also change the locations of basin boundaries. Hence, for an initial set of weights, an initial state can be in one basin, but for an updated set of weights the initial state can be in another basin. This means that the final state of the network suddenly jumps from one fixed point to another fixed point. Figure 3 schematically illustrates this problem.

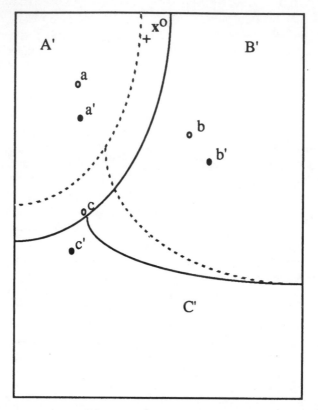

Figure 3.   Fixed points without primes and basin boundaries marked as dotted lines are before a weight update. Fixed points with primes and basin boundaries marked as solid lines are after a weight update. Most of the initial states that formerly converged to *b* now converge to *b'*. The exceptional points are those initial states that were formerly in *B* but are now not in *B'*. The point denoted by u° is such a point. A small change in a weight matrix from **w** to **w'** results in a discontinuous change in the final state of the system from *a* to *b'*. Note that the same is true for a small change in I from I to I'.

FIXED-POINT CREATION

Thus far the entire discussion has focused on how one moves around fixed points or more precisely how one sculpts the manifold determined by the map from parametric input **I** to final state $\mathbf{u}^f$. For initial state input, however, one must not only move around fixed points one may also be required to introduce new fixed points if there are fewer fixed points than patterns to be stored. For this purpose the simple gradient descent approach already discussed may not always work. To see why this is the case it suffices to examine a simple example in which the goal is to install two fixed points located at $\mathbf{d}^1$ and $\mathbf{d}^2$ respectively. Consider the general dynamical system given in Equation 1. Suppose no parametric input is used; hence, $\mathbf{I} = \mathbf{c}$, where $\mathbf{c}$ is a constant vector that does not depend on the patterns to be learned. Accordingly, the system to be trained has the general form

$$\frac{d\mathbf{u}}{dt} = \mathbf{G(w,c,u)}. \qquad (20)$$

As before, assume this system is convergent and, for the sake of argument, that the dynamics of the untrained network possesses a single stable fixed point. (This is the typical case in the additive model when the initial weights are sufficiently small.) Suppose we start each relaxation at the location of a desired fixed point (i.e., $\mathbf{u}^\circ = \mathbf{d}^\alpha$, where $\alpha = 1$ or 2). Since there is a unique stable fixed point, all the trajectories converge to the same final state $\mathbf{u}^f$ independently of the initial state. Thus, all information concerning the distinct target patterns is lost during the relaxations. The corresponding cumulative LMS cost function would be

$$C_{\text{tot}} = \tfrac{1}{2}[(\mathbf{d}^1 - \mathbf{u}^f)^2 + (\mathbf{d}^2 - \mathbf{u}^f)^2].$$

Now, since gradient descent adjusts the weights so as to move the unique fixed point in a direction that minimizes the cost function, it is clear that unless a new fixed point is introduced (by having the dynamics undergo a bifurcation) the minimum of the cost function will occur when the fixed point is at the mean pattern, namely when $\mathbf{u}^f = (\mathbf{d}^1 + \mathbf{d}^2)/2$. In other words, the system will learn a single "average" memory instead of the two distinct memories. Of course it is possible that such a bifurcation could occur by accident, but this investigator has never encountered such a fortuitous accident. It is therefore useful to add a mechanism into the learning algorithm that *systematically* introduces bifurcations.

Forcing

There are several related ways of modifying the dynamics during training so as to systematically introduce fixed points. These techniques convert the initial-state input problem into the parametric input problem. The unmodified dynamics is denoted the "free" dynamics, whereas the modified dynamics is denoted the "forced" dynamics. The basic approach is to modify the free dynamical equations by a term that depends on a target but that vanishes as the weights converge to their completely trained values. The training is performed on the forced system but the free system is used for computation. As the weights are adjusted in the forced system, fixed points are introduced into the free system and gradually move toward their respective targets. To be more explicit, consider the following modification of the free dynamical equations:

$$\frac{d\mathbf{u}}{dt} = \mathbf{G(w,c,u)} + \mathbf{F(d, u)}, \qquad (21)$$

where $\mathbf{F}$ is an arbitrary differentiable function that satisfies $\mathbf{F}(\mathbf{y}, \mathbf{y}) = 0$ for all vectors $\mathbf{y}$. This system is trained so that $\mathbf{d} = \mathbf{u}^f$. Accordingly, the equilibrium solution of Equation 21 satisfies

$$0 = \mathbf{G}(\mathbf{w}^f, \mathbf{c}, \mathbf{u}^f). \tag{22}$$

But this is just the fixed-point equation corresponding to Equation 20. We conclude that the target fixed points of equation 21 are also fixed points of Equation 20. Hence, by training equation 21 we are effectively training equation 20. Equation 21 is just a dynamical system with parametric input $\mathbf{d}$, and we already know how to train a system with parametric input.

The foregoing construction does not guarantee that the fixed points in the free and forced systems are in one-to-one correspondence. In general, the forced system can have spurious fixed points that the free system does not possess, and vice versa. Furthermore, all forcing (and clamping) techniques suffer from a potential problem. The free and forced systems do not necessarily have the same stability properties. For example, consider the free dynamical Equations 20. The stability of a fixed point $\mathbf{u}^f$ in the free system is determined by the eigenvalues of the matrix $\mathbf{L}^{\text{free}}$ whose elements are

$$L_{ij}^{\text{free}} = \left[\frac{\partial G_i}{\partial u_j} \right]_{\mathbf{u}=\mathbf{u}^f}. \tag{23}$$

On the other hand, the stability of a fixed point in the modified system depends on the eigenvalues of the matrix $\mathbf{L}^{\text{forced}}$ whose matrix elements are

$$L_{ij}^{\text{forced}} = \left[\frac{\partial G_i}{\partial u_j} + \frac{\partial F_i}{\partial u_j} \right]_{\mathbf{u}=\mathbf{u}^f}. \tag{24}$$

Obviously these two matrices are not the same and do not necessarily have the same eigenvalues. Thus, it can occur that a fixed point is stable in the forced system, while the corresponding fixed point is unstable in the free system. Note that the converse is not possible since if a fixed point is unstable in the forced system, its position cannot be adjusted in the first place.

Examples

Teacher Forcing

Teacher forcing as discussed by Williams and Zipser (1991) is a special case of generalized forcing. To see this, consider the additive model so that G_i has the form

$$G_i = -u_i + \sum_j w_{ij} f(u_j). \tag{25}$$

Consider a forcing term

$$F_i = \sum_{j \in \mathbf{O}} w_{ij}(f(d_j) - f(u_j)). \tag{26}$$

After some simple algebra one finds that the forced dynamical equation is

$$\frac{du_i}{dt} = -u_i + \sum_j w_{ij} V_i^{\text{forced}}, \tag{27}$$

where

$$V_i^{\text{forced}} = \begin{cases} f(d_i) & \text{if } j \in O, \\ f(u_i) & \text{if } j \notin O. \end{cases}$$

This is just the usual form for teacher forcing. Notice that one may think of the output units in the forced system as having two "outputs." One "output" is the clamped firing rate $f(d_i)$ that is fed back as an activation into the network, while the second "output" is the relaxed firing rate $f(u_i^f)$ that is used to calculate the cost function and the error signal that is fed back into the network.

Soft and Hard Clamping

Consider the additive model with a forcing term of the form

$$F_i = \gamma_i(d_i - f(u_i)), \tag{28}$$

where $\gamma_i = \gamma$ if $i \in O$ and $\gamma_i = 0$ otherwise. In the limit $\gamma \to +\infty$ the equilibrium solution of the output units is $f(u_i) = d_i$. If the initial values of the output units are just their target values, their activations do not evolve. In other words, the output units are clamped. In digital simulations the clamping approach has computational advantages over other approaches because it does not require the relaxation of output units. On the other hand, for finite values of γ the output units do not equilibrate to their target values until the network has been trained. The parameter γ may be thought of as parametrizing a family of algorithms with $\gamma = 0$ corresponding to no forcing or clamping, $\gamma = +\infty$ corresponding to *hard* clamping, and all other values of γ corresponding to *soft* clamping.

Terminal Attractors

Barhen, Gulati, and Zak (1989) use the additive model and RBP with a forcing term of the form

$$F_i = \gamma_i(d_i - f(u_i))^{1/3}. \tag{29}$$

If the network is fully trained, the target equilibria of the corresponding forced activation equations violate the Lipschitz condition and are called *terminal attractors* (Zak, 1989). Terminal attractors have the interesting mathematical properties that they are infinitely stable and they converge in finite rather than in logarithmic time. They evidently have some of the features of hard clamping and some of the features of soft clamping. The interested reader is referred to the aforementioned references for more details.

IMPLEMENTATION AS A COLLECTIVE
PHYSICAL SYSTEM[1]

This section outlines an approach for implementing the RBP algorithm as a physical collective dynamical system, for example as a subthreshold analog VLSI circuit. The basic idea behind realizing RBP as a physical model is to express the algorithm as a set of coupled nonautonomous ordinary differential equations that describe the dynamics of a physical system with coupled slow and fast degrees of freedom. For the case of the additive model with an LMS cost function the equations of the physical model are

$$\tau_u \frac{du_i}{dt} = -u_i + \sum_j w_{ij} V_j + I_i \left(\frac{t}{\tau_p} \right), \tag{30}$$

$$\tau_z \frac{dz_i}{dt} = -z_i + f'_i(u_i) \sum_j (\mathbf{w}^T)_{ij} z_j + J_i, \tag{31}$$

where

$$J_i = \begin{cases} d_i(t/\tau_p) - V_i & \text{if } i \in O, \\ 0 & \text{if } i \notin O, \end{cases} \tag{32}$$

$$\tau_w \frac{dw_{ij}}{dt} = z_i V_j. \tag{33}$$

The four time scales in the system are τ_u, τ_z, τ_p, and τ_w. The scales τ_u and τ_z determine how fast the activations and errors relax, τ_p determines how fast the patterns change, while τ_w determines the learning rate. In the error-propagation Equation 31 the usual steady-state activations $\mathbf{u}^f$ have been replaced by the instantaneous activations $\mathbf{u}(t)$. It is easy to see that if Equations 30 and 31 are integrated simultaneously until they equilibrate, the two systems will converge to the same fixed points that one would get if one first integrated Equation 30 until it equilibrated and then used the equilibrium state $\mathbf{u}^f$ in Equation 31. This works because Equation 31 is linear and therefore has a unique equilibrium. By replacing $\mathbf{u}^f$ with $\mathbf{u}(t)$, we change the transient behavior of the error signal $\mathbf{z}$ but not its equilibrium value.

This *dynamical* algorithm yields a good approximation to the gradient whenever $\mathbf{u}(t) \cong \mathbf{u}^f$ and $\mathbf{z}(t) \cong \mathbf{z}^f$. these conditions hold if (1) the time scales τ_u and τ_z are fast compared to all other time scales in the system so that the activations are always nearly at steady state or if (2) the time-dependent patterns change suddenly but infrequently. The latter means that $\mathbf{u}(t)$ and $\mathbf{z}(t)$ depart from their steady-state values only during the transient after a sudden change. The rest of

---

[1]This section was written in collaboration with Ron Benson. Further work can be found in (Benson, 1994).

the time $\mathbf{u}(t)$ and $\mathbf{z}(t)$ are at their steady-state values. Thus, $z_i(t)V_j(t)$ will be a good approximation for the ijth component of the gradient except immediately after a training pattern changes. The characteristic time scale over which the patterns change is τ_p; hence, the preceding arguments imply $\tau_p \gg \tau_u$ and $\tau_p \gg \tau_z$.

The complete system is capable of learning a single pattern so long as the relaxation time of the forward and backward propagations (τ_u and τ_z) is much slower than the relaxation time of the weights, τ_w. To learn multiple patterns, the patterns must be switched slowly compared to the settling time of the forward and backward equations, but rapidly compared to τ_w ($\tau_w > \tau_p$). With this condition the weights are adjusted in response to the entire training set. Without this condition the weights may simply track the most recently presented patterns.

Figure 4 shows the general features of a physical RBP model. The model is a sandwich consisting an activation layer that calculates Equation 30, a weight layer that calculates Equation 33, and an error-propagation layer that calculates Equations 31. When viewed from above, the sandwich appears as a square lattice. Lattice sites along the main diagonal are associated with neurons, whereas off-diagonal lattice sites are associated with weights. The nonlinear neurons in the activation layer are shown as black triangles, whereas the linear neurons in the error-propagation layer are shown as white triangles. The sharing of weights between the activation and error-propagation layers is indicated via vertical dotted lines at off-diagonal lattice sites. The transport of $f'(\cdot)$ from the activation layer to the error-propagation layer is indicated by a vertical dotted line. Notice how the transpose of the weights is achieved naturally by physically transposing the connections of the linear neurons relative to the nonlinear neurons. When viewed in 3-D, this arrangement has a regular columnar structure.

Figure 5 shows a neuron site and a weight site in more detail. The cross section shows the ijth weight and the linear and nonlinear neurons associated with the jth site along the main diagonal. A neuron in the nonlinear activation network sums its inputs and in the manner of a leaky integrator. It then squashes its output via a sigmoid function $V_j = f(u_j)$ and distributes this output to other neurons in the activation layer. A linear neuron in the error-propagation layer sums its inputs in the same manner, but it also multiplies the result of the summation by the derivative of the sigmoid function $f'(\cdot)$. This derivative is obtained from the activation neuron via a vertical connection. The weights project their values vertically into the activation and error layers. In this way the weights are shared by the forward and backward systems. The weight w_{ij} is updated by integrating the product of the output V_i from the ith activation unit with the error z_j of the jth linear unit. To obey Equation 33 this update must be performed continuously by a nonleaky integrator. In practice, it may be easier to use a leaky integrator or some other method that is more suited to the particular implementation technology.

In the physical model of RBP, there is no need for a clock to strobe the activations from one "layer" to the next. Instead the forward and backward

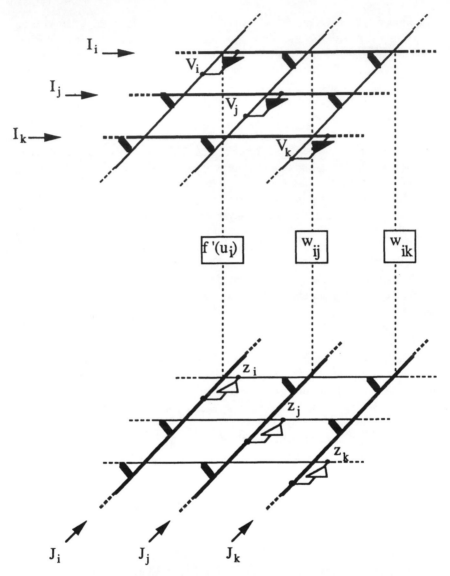

Figure 4.   This figure shows the general features of a physical RBP model. Nonlinear neurons are shown as black triangles. Linear neurons are shown as white triangles. Vertical connections are schematic and are not intended to show detailed connections at a node. When viewed from above the model has a lattice structure with neurons along the main diagonal and weights at off-diagonal sites.

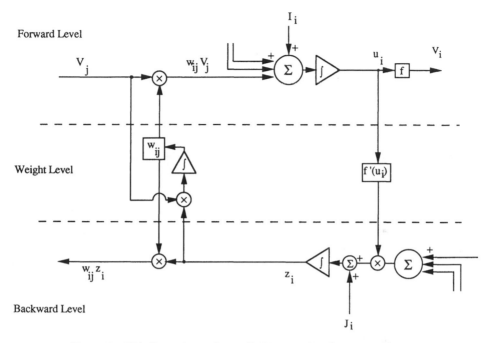

Figure 5. This figure is a schematic diagram showing connections at a neuron lattice site and at a weight lattice site. The forward-propagation network is shown on top and the error-propagation network is shown below. Integrators are shown as triangles.

propagations are accomplished by relaxing forward and backward dynamical systems while continuously updating the weights. Each unit in the network evolves its activation and error signal in response to the *instantaneous* activations and error signals of all the other units to which it is connected. Each unit eventually settles down to the correct value of the activation and the error signal, provided that the forward dynamics is convergent.

The adaptive equations presented in this section assume that there is no time delay between units. Analog VLSI systems have propagation delays due to capacitance in wires. This can cause difficulties if the circuit is driven too quickly. Marcus and Westervelt (1989) have investigated the role of time delays in analog additive systems and have shown experimentally that time delays can lead to chaos. They have also shown that these problems can be avoided by operating the system slowly enough or in suitable regions of the parameter space.

CASE STUDIES

In this section we present three case studies that illustrate the behavior and application of recurrent back-propagation networks.

Learning with Initial-State Input

In the fourth section a general method for introducing fixed points was discussed. In this section, the method is applied to the additive model and it is shown how discontinuities in learning curves arise as natural manifestation of the introduction of fixed points. To this end consider the two-layer recurrent network shown in Figure 6. The bottom layer of the network consists of visible units and is trained to reproduce the four patterns that make up the exclusive-OR (XOR). These patterns are shown in Table 2. There d_1 is the XOR of d_2 and d_3.

The free dynamics of the network is governed by Equation 4 with $V_j = \tanh(u_j)$ and with $I_i = 0$ for all i. As usual, let $\mathbf{V}^f$ denote the fixed point of Equation 4. The forced dynamics is governed by

$$\frac{du_i}{dt} = -u_i + \sum_j w_{ij}V_j + I_i + \gamma_i(T_i - V_i). \tag{34}$$

Let $\mathbf{V}^t$ denote the equilibrium of Equation 34. The learning is driven by the gradient of the forced cost function

$$C^{\text{forced}} = \frac{1}{2} \sum_i (d_i - V_i^t)^2 \tag{35}$$

Multiple patterns are dealt with in the usual way by accumulating the gradient over patterns or by performing stochastic gradient descent. The actual performance of the system on the task is measured by the free cost function, which is

$$C^{\text{free}} = \frac{1}{2} \sum_i (d_i - V_i^f)^2. \tag{36}$$

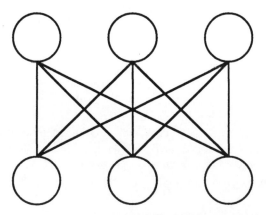

Figure 6.   Recurrent network with three visible units (bottom) and three hidden units (top). All connections are bidirectional with different weights in each direction; thus, there are a total of 18 weights.

TABLE 2
XOR Training Set

Pattern	d_1	d_2	d_3
a	−1	−1	−1
b	1	−1	1
c	1	1	−1
d	−1	1	1

As described in the fourth section all training is performed on the forced system. The corresponding gradient has the usual outer product form $\partial C^{\text{forced}}/\partial w_{ij} = -z_i^t V_j^t$, where z^t is the fixed point of the forced back-propagation equation given by

$$\frac{dz_i}{dt} = -(1 + \gamma_i)z_i + f_i'(u_i^t) \sum_j w_{ji}z_j + J_i, \tag{37}$$

where J_i^t is given by

$$J_i = \begin{cases} d_i - V_i^t & \text{if } i \in \text{visible units,} \\ 0 & \text{if } i \notin \text{visible units.} \end{cases} \tag{38}$$

The initial weights are small so that the free and forced systems both have a single fixed point. The initial states are reset before each relaxation according to

$$u_i(0) = \begin{cases} f^{-1}(d_i) & \text{if } i \in \text{visible units,} \\ 0 & \text{if } i \notin \text{visible units.} \end{cases} \tag{39}$$

Figure 7 shows learning curves obtained from this simulation. Cumulative gradient descent is used, so one epoch corresponds to one weight update. As expected from gradient descent, the forced cost function decreases monotonically and smoothly. The free cost function, on the other hand, is discontinuous. At least four discontinuities are evident in Figure 7 at epochs $t = 31$, $t = 35$, $t = 62$, and $t = 68$ respectively.

The trajectories of the fixed points in the subspace of output units are shown for each of the four initial states (patterns) in Figure 8. The beginning and end of each branch of the trajectory is labeled with the corresponding epoch. It is evident by comparing Figures 7 and 8 that each discontinuity in the free cost function is associated with a discontinuity in the trajectory of a fixed point. It is also evident from the trajectories that initial states $(-1, -1, -1)$ and $(-1, 1, 1)$, labeled (a) and (d) respectively, initially converge to the same fixed point until a jump occurs at $t = 31$. Similarly, the initial states $(1, -1, 1)$ and $(1, 1, -1)$, labeled (b) and (c) respectively, converge to another fixed point until $t = 35$, whereupon a jump occurs. These discontinuities are due to *basin hopping* in the

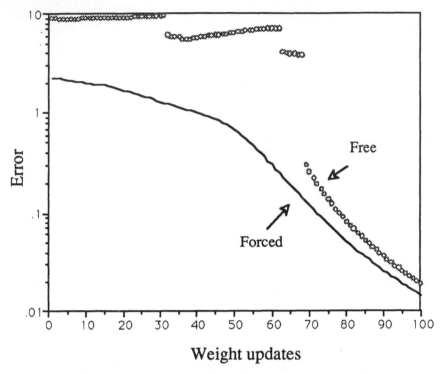

Figure 7. Forced and free cost functions as a function of epochs
(weight updates). All the dynamical equations were relaxed using Euler integration with $\Delta t = 0.25$. Cumulative gradient descent with momentum was used ($\eta = 0.1$ and $\alpha = 0.7$).

free dynamics some time after the occurrence of a bifurcation. This phenomenon
is discussed in more detail in Pineda (1988b). Intuitively it is clear that jumps
must occur in the free dynamics since, by construction, the free system has only
one fixed point initially, but, after training, the system has at least four fixed
points. Hence, there must be some discontinuities as the fixed points come into
being.

Although XOR is a useful task for debugging code and for illustrating learning dynamics, it is not a particularly interesting task. An associative memory for
visual images has large continuously valued patterns and is a more interesting
task. The next section discusses an associative memory that uses images as fixed
points.

Associative Memory with Initial State Input

A recurrent network with initial-state input can be used as an autoassociative
memory. The initial state of the visible units corresponds to memory cues, while

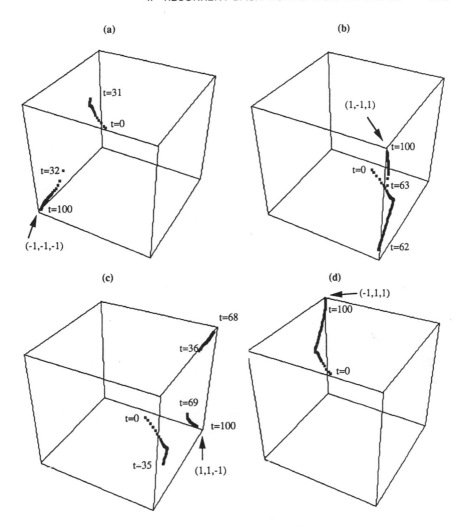

Figure 8.   This figure shows the trajectories of fixed points undergoing training in the free dynamical system. The trajectories are parametrized by epoch. Each figure corresponds to a different pattern in the
training set. This pattern is also used as the initial condition. The location of each initial condition (training pattern) is labeled by an arrow.
Each cube encloses a volume bounded by $(V_1, V_2, V_3) = (\pm 1, \pm 1, \pm 1)$.

the final state corresponds to the recalled image. In this example a network with
pure initial state input will be considered. In situations where the activations of
some of the visible units are known a priori, it is useful to clamp the activations
of visible units. In may problems of interest, however, the correct value of no
visible unit is known a priori. For example, in a memory cue that has noise added

to it, the initial values of all the units may be incorrect. For such problems clamping is inappropriate and pure initial-state input is desirable. More details of this simulation have been published elsewhere (Pineda, 1988). In this section we seek only to point out the salient characteristics of the autoassociative network.

Consider the problem of memorizing a set of faces where the images consist of 55×24 gray level pixels. The images are normalized to have the same mean pixel intensity (0.5) and contrast (standard deviation = 0.2). This task is accomplished with the recurrent network shown in Figure 9. It contains 1370 units: a visible layer with 1320 (24×55) units and a hidden layer with 50 units. The layers are randomly connected in both directions with a density of connections of approximately 20%. Symmetry of the weight matrix is not enforced and there are no connections within a layer. There are 25,406 connections. The free activation dynamics is given by Equation 4, with $\mathbf{I} = 0$. The recurrent back-propagation equations are derived using the forcing term given in the fourth section under "Teacher Forcing."

Three images were stored in this example. Figures 10a and b show the trajectories of the visible units during recall after the network has been fully trained. Each figure corresponds to a different initial state. In Figure 10b, part of the image is known and the task is to reconstruct the missing parts. In this case one could have clamped the part of the memory cue that was known and thereby enhanced the robustness of the recall. In Figure 10a, on the other hand, there is no unit whose value is correct (except by accident). The fact that no visible units

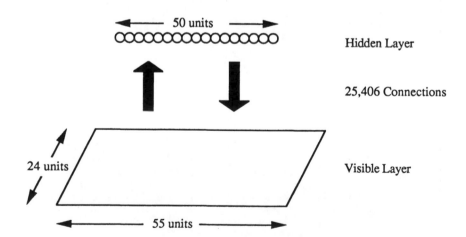

Figure 9. Recurrent architecture for autoassociative memory. There are 1320 units in the visible layer and 50 units in the hidden layer. The memory cue is used to set the initial states of the visible layer. The hidden units are initially set to zero.

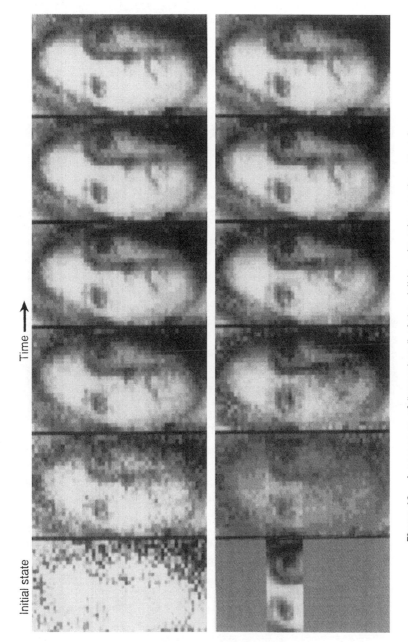

Time →

Initial state

Figure 10. A sequence of "snapshots" of the visible units taken as the network relaxes. The initial state in the top sequence is a stored memory with noise added. The initial state in the lower sequence is a partially memory. Convergence is typically obtained in approximately 20 iterations.

125

are clamped means that the system is free to adjust all the visible units so as to find the correct memory. Consequently, this system is capable of recalling memories that have been significantly degraded or deformed.

Any deformation or degradation of a stored pattern can be described as a displacement of the initial state away from the correct fixed point. If this displacement is sufficiently small, the initial state will remain in the basin of the correct fixed point and the associative memory filter will converge to the proper stored pattern. The amount of allowed displacement is difficult to quantify since it depends on the detailed shape of the basin boundaries. Nevertheless these displacements are visually significant, as can be seen from Figures 10a and 10b. From the previous discussion it is clear that the system will recall robustly in the presence of all small perturbations including translations, rotations, and scale changes.

The associative memory will disambiguate two highly correlated patterns presented simultaneously. This latter feature is a direct consequence of the nonlinearity introduced by the squashing function $f(\cdot)$. The role of nonlinearity becomes clear when one compares the behavior of this associative memory with a linear associative memory (i.e., the matrix memory described by Kohonen, 1972, and Anderson, 1972). Consider the case where the memory cue consists of a linear combination of two stored memories. In this case the nonlinear memory converges to the dominant memory provided the contribution from the secondary memory is sufficiently small. More precisely any linear combination of two memories can be represented as a point on a line joining the two memories in the state-space. If the basins are not overly convoluted the dominant memory will be recalled reliably. If the basins are overly convoluted, the dominant memory will be recalled only if the contribution from the secondary memory is sufficiently small. On the other hand, the matrix associative memory cannot separate the two images because the recall is based on a projection operator. This linear operator simply projects the memory cue onto the subspace S space spanned by the stored memories. In particular, if the initial state is the sum of a stored memory $\mathbf{u}_S$ plus a perturbation $\mathbf{e}$ (i.e., $\mathbf{u} = \mathbf{u}_S + \mathbf{e}$), the projection operator will be able to retrieve the "correct" memory, provided that $\mathbf{e}$ is contained in the space orthogonal to S. On the other hand, if $\mathbf{e}$ is contained in S the projection operator simply performs the identity operation.

Finally, it is worthwhile to make three observations. (1) The networks discussed here are quite sparsely connected. If these networks were fully connected, they would have nearly 2 million connections. (2) From the reflection symmetry of the dynamical equations it is clear that there are at least three more fixed points corresponding to negative images. These were not encountered because the perturbations that were applied to the images did not take the initial states into the basins of the negative images. (3) Only three images were stored in this network. Attempts to store more than three images usually resulted in one or more images being stored as unstable fixed points. Unstable fixed points cannot be recalled by relaxation so for all practical purposes they are not stored.[2]

Application to Binocular Depth Perception

The recovery of depth from a pair of images requires the solution of a *correspondence problem*. This requires that proper matches be made between features in the left and right images. For a given feature in the left image there may be one or more compatible features in the right image. Only one of these compatible features is the correct match. Most humans can extract stereo information without recognizing or identifying specific features (Julesz, 1960). A random-dot stereogram consists of a uniform field of random dots and hence has no recognizable features. The left and right images are identical except that a square in the central region of one of the images is shifted to the left or the right by a fixed amount. This shift, or *disparity*, is the cue that causes the central area to be perceived as a square floating above or below a uniform background of random dots. Figure 11 is an example of a random-dot stereogram.

The correspondence problem for a random-dot stereogram can be posed as a relaxation computation with a recurrent network of processing units (Marr and Poggio, 1976). The connectivity of the network enforces two physical constraints. First it enforces the continuity of surfaces, and second it enforces the uniqueness of surfaces along lines of sight. These two constraints are known as the continuity and uniqueness constraints respectively. The final stage of the network keeps only those matches that satisfy the physical constraints. Marr and Poggio enforced the constraints by determining the connection strengths of their network by hand. Qian and Sejnowski (1989) have shown that these constraints can be learned automatically. In this section we summarize the salient features of their approach with an emphasis on the dynamical aspects.

To understand how depth is extracted from stereo and how the constraints can be learned automatically, it is first necessary to understand the representation used by the networks. Let the $n \times n$ binary-valued matrices denoted by $\mathbf{L}$ and $\mathbf{R}$ represent the left and right images respectively. A *compatibility map* is a three-dimensional array that represents all possible matches between the left and right images. The third dimension is the disparity, d. One may define a match to be two pixels that have the same intensity (i.e., both black or both white), or one may define a match to be two pixels that are both black. The former defines the *dense* compatibility map $\mathbf{C}^D$, while the latter defines the *sparse* compatibility map $\mathbf{C}^S$. More formally one has

$$C_{ijd}^{\text{dense}} = \begin{cases} 1 & \text{if } L_{ij} = R_{i+d,j}, \\ 0 & \text{otherwise,} \end{cases}$$

[2]In principle, unstable fixed points can be recalled using Newton methods.

Figure 11.   When the two images in this random-dot stereogram are fused a 20 × 20 pixel floating square is seen in the center of a uniform background of random dots.

$$C_{ijd}^{\text{sparse}} = \begin{cases} 1 & \text{if } L_{ij} = R_{i+d,j} = 1, \\ 0 & \text{otherwise.} \end{cases}$$

A *disparity map* **D** is a three-dimensional array that represents the correct (dense or sparse) matches between the two images. Solving the correspondence problem in the domain of random-dot stereograms means extracting the disparity map **D** from a compatibility map **C**.

The architecture of the Marr-Poggio network accomplishes this goal by using a compatibility map as the initial state of a system whose dynamics enforces the uniqueness and continuity constraints. The final state of the dynamics is the network's best guess for the disparity map. In theory the network topology consists of one processor per element of the compatibility map. Processors on planes of constant disparity (constant d) are connected by excitatory connections. Processors along lines of sight are connected with inhibitory connections. These connections are inhibitory since, to satisfy the uniqueness constraint, there can only be one processing unit turned on along a line of sight. Figure 12 shows a cross section of the network for constant j.

The network is capable of solving the correspondence problem from dense compatibility matrices only. The network works by taking a dense compatibility map as an initial state and relaxing it until it satisfies the continuity and uniqueness constraints. The resulting final state is the network's best guess of the disparity map. Qian and Sejnowski use recurrent back propagation to train a network with the same topology as shown in Figure 12. Their units take continuous values. The activation dynamics is determined by Equation 4. To train the

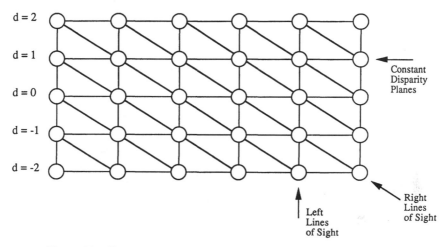

Figure 12.   Cross section of the Marr-Poggio network topology. The plane of zero disparity is the plane of fixation. Left and right lines of sight should be symmetric about the vertical axis but the indexing scheme is easier if the network is tilted.

network they use a modified parametric input approach with the correct disparity pattern as the target. They modified the parametric input approach by setting both the initial state and the parametric inputs of the visible units to an appropriate compatibility map. This lets them shape the fixed-point manifold whose coordinates are given by I and it gives them some control over the size of the shape of the basins. This will be discussed in more detail.

Qian and Sejnowski use 30×30 random-dot stereograms with three levels of disparity. A complete network therefore requires 2700 connections. Translational symmetry, however, dramatically reduces the number of weights and speeds up the learning. If each unit is connected only to its nearest neighbors there are 27 independent weights. Furthermore, if all the line-of-sight weights are constrained to be the same, all the horizontal weights are constrained to be the same and all the biases are constrained to be the same, there are only three independent weights and the system learns very rapidly. On the other hand, if additional irrelevant connections are included in the network, the learning is slowed down and sometimes gets stuck in local minima.

Qian and Sejnowski report two interesting results: first, that their network learns to extract sparse disparity, and second that their network is apparently able to store a vast quantity of redundant information. The ability to extract sparse disparity maps means that the network is able to solve transparent random-dot stereograms. Such stereograms are perceived as transparent planes of random dots floating above a random background. The Marr-Poggio network creates dense disparity maps as output and is unable to solve transparent random-dot stereograms. Dense disparity maps are created because units in regions where the density of compatible matches is high tend to turn on, whereas units in regions where the density is low tend to turn off. On the other hand, in sparse disparity maps only those units that represent actual matches are turned on in high-density regions. As Qian and Sejnowski point out, this is a harder task for two reasons. First, the density difference between solution and nonsolution areas of the sparse compatibility map is smaller than for the nontransparent case, and second only a small proportion of the black dots in the solution area of the compatibility map are correct matches. Simply weakening the strength of the connections enforcing the continuity constraint does not result in sparse disparity maps since the units then do not receive enough input and their activity decays to zero. Instead Qian and Sejnowski choose to bias each unit with the compatibility pattern to prevent decay. This is simply accomplished by setting the inputs I_i equal to the compatibility pattern. The network is trained with sparse disparity maps as targets. The performance on a test set was not as good as for dense disparity, but it still achieved a respectable 97.7% correct performance level.

For the networks that calculated sparse disparity, Qian and Sejnowski observe that the total number of stored local minima is very large. They suggest that all the local minima follow "certain inherent rules and the information is redundant" and that "this suggests that the capacity of a given network for correlated patterns can be enormous." This observation is consistent with our understanding of the nature of parametric input. Recall that training recurrent networks with parametric input can be viewed as the task of shaping a manifold of fixed points. The parametric inputs can be viewed as coordinates on this manifold. The redundant information is stored as the shape of the surface. Since each different parametric input corresponds to a different point on this manifold, the number of different fixed points that can be obtained is, in fact, infinite.

ACKNOWLEDGMENTS

The author thanks Pierre Baldi for several critical readings and for many valuable discussions. Ron Benson helped write a section and participated in several useful discussions. This work was supported by a contract from the AFOSR (AFOSR-ISSA-91-0017 and AFOSR-ISSA-90-0027).

APPENDIX A. GRADIENT EVALUATION

In this appendix we apply the method previously used in Pineda (1987, 1988a, 1988b) to a general convergent dynamical system. The result may be specialized to specific neural networks. In this appendix, the f superscript is suppressed when referring to equilibrium activations because the entire calculation is performed at an equilibrium of the activation dynamics. The cost function $C =$

$C(\mathbf{u}(\mathbf{w}, \mathbf{x}, \mathbf{d}))$, where $\mathbf{x}$ and $\mathbf{d}$ are inputs and targets, is assumed to have no explicit dependence on the internal parameters. The inclusion of an explicit dependence adds trivial terms to the gradient expressions derived below. Matrix equations are shown in component form.

Differentiating a cost function C with respect to one of the internal parameters w_α immediately yields

$$\frac{\partial C}{\partial w_\alpha} = \sum_k J_k P_{k\alpha}, \tag{A.1}$$

where $J_k \equiv -\partial C/\partial u_k$ and $P_{k\alpha} \equiv -\partial u_k/\partial w_\alpha$. To obtain an expression for $P_{k\alpha}$, one notes that $G_i(\mathbf{u}, \mathbf{w}, \mathbf{I}) = 0$ and that $\mathbf{u}$ is an implicit function of w_α. Thus, differentiating G_i with respect to w_α, we obtain

$$\left(\frac{\partial G_i}{\partial w_\alpha}\right)_e + \sum_j L_{ij} P_{j\alpha} = 0, \tag{A.2}$$

where the subscript e denotes differentiation with respect to the explicit dependence of G_i on w_α and $L_{ij} \equiv \partial G_i/\partial u_j$ is the Jacobian matrix.

Equation A.2 is simply the matrix equation $(\partial \mathbf{G}/\partial \mathbf{w})_e - \mathbf{LP} = 0$. It has the solution $\mathbf{P} = \mathbf{L}^{-1}(\partial \mathbf{G}/\partial \mathbf{w})_e$, which in component form is

$$P_{k\alpha} = \sum_i (\mathbf{L}^{-1})_{ki} \left(\frac{\partial G_i}{\partial w_\alpha}\right)_e. \tag{A.3}$$

Upon substituting this expression back into Equation A.1 and after changing the order of the resulting two summations, we obtain

$$\frac{\partial C}{\partial w_\alpha} = -\sum_i z_i^f \left(\frac{\partial G_i}{\partial w_\alpha}\right)_e, \tag{A.4}$$

where

$$z_i^f = \sum_k J_k(\mathbf{L}^{-1})_{ki}. \tag{A.5}$$

This expression is not yet the basis for a local neural network algorithm for the evaluation of the gradient for two reasons. First, to calculate the error vector $\mathbf{z}$ requires that we invert the Jacobian matrix $\mathbf{L}$. This inversion is possible provided the forward propagation converges to a stable equilibrium (cf. Appendix B). Matrix inversions cannot be performed without a considerably more complex architecture. Second, to evaluate the expression for a single parameter, w_α, requires a summation over all the dimensions in the state-space. This is highly nonlocal and expensive. Fortunately each of these problems is solvable. First, we note that $\mathbf{z}^f$ can be calculated without a matrix inversion. To see this, observe that if Equation A.5 is multiplied on both sides by L_{ij} and summed over i, we obtain (after renaming indices)

$$\sum_{j} L_{ji}z_{j}^{f} + J_{i} = 0. \qquad (A.6)$$

This matrix equation is just the fixed-point equation of the linear matrix equation given b:

$$\frac{dy_{i}}{dt} = \sum_{j} L_{ji}z_{j} + J_{i}. \qquad (A.7)$$

This is a general back-propagation equation. This equation differs from an adjoint equation (e.g., Pearlmutter, 1989) by a minus sign on the left-hand side. This is because adjoint equations are propagated backward in time. They appear naturally when considering time-dependent dynamical systems. When implemented off-line on digital computers the time direction is not important, but when one considers implementation as a physical system one must perform this relaxation forward in time.

The summation appearing in Equation A.4 leads to nonlocalities, since information from all processors is used to update the αth internal parameter. To solve this nonlocality requires an appeal to the special tensor structure of neural network dynamical equations. For example, the internal parameters in neural networks are generally weights coupled multiplicatively with the state variables. For example, in the additive model, the weights and state variables are coupled through a term of the form $\sum_{j} w_{ij}f(u_{j})$. Accordingly $(\partial G_{i}/\partial w_{jk})_{e} = \delta_{ij}f(u_{k})$, where δ_{ij} is the Kroneker δ function. More generally if the parameters and the state variables are coupled such that

$$\frac{\partial G_{i}}{\partial w_{\{\alpha_{i},\dots,j,\dots,\alpha_{m}\}}} = \delta_{ij}F_{\{\alpha_{1},\dots,j,\dots,\alpha_{m}\}}, \qquad (A.8)$$

where F_{α} is some (perhaps constant) function, it follows that only one term is nonzero in the summation in Equation A.4. Hence, Equation A.4 has the simple outer product form

$$\frac{\partial C}{\partial w_{\{\alpha_{1},\dots,j,\dots,\alpha_{m}\}}} = z_{j}^{f}F_{\{\alpha_{1},\dots,j,\dots,\alpha_{m}\}}. \qquad (A.8)$$

This is the simple Cartesian product form that is typical of algorithms based on back propagation.

APPENDIX B. STABILITY OF ERROR BACK-PROPAGATION EQUATION

To calculate the gradient in Equation A.8 it is necessary for the activation (3) and the back-propagation Equation A.7 to converge to steady states. The conditions under which the activation equations converge depend on the details of the dynamics. For the additive model, some of these conditions have already been discussed. The situation is much simpler for the back-propagation equations, as pointed out by Almeida (1987). He has observed that the local stability of a forward-propagation equation is a sufficient condition for the stability of a backward-propagation equation. To see why this must be the case in general, it suffices to linearize Equation 3 about a point attractor, $\mathbf{u} = \mathbf{u}^f + \epsilon$, where ϵ is a small perturbation. The resulting linear equation for the perturbation has the form

$$\frac{d\epsilon}{dt} = \mathbf{L}^T\epsilon, \tag{B.1}$$

where $\mathbf{L}^T$ is the transpose of the $\mathbf{L}$ matrix defined in Appendix A. It follows that the local stability of a fixed point of Equation B.1 depends on the eigenvalues of the matrix $\mathbf{L}^T$. These eigenvalues all have negative real parts since, by hypothesis, (3) is a convergent system. On the other hand, from Equation A.7 it is clear that the local stability of the backward-propagation equation depends on the eigenvalues of $\mathbf{L}$. But both $\mathbf{L}$ and its transpose $\mathbf{L}^T$ have the same eigenvalues. Hence, if a fixed point of the general activation Equation 3, is stable, it must be true that the corresponding fixed point of the back-propagation equation (A.7) is also stable.

APPENDIX C. PSEUDOCODE

A pseudocode that summarizes the gradient evaluation is given. This implementation is intended to be illustrative rather than efficient. For a description of a parallel implementation on a connection machine the reader is referred to Deprit (1989).

To use pure initial-state input, $c[i]$ is the input value to the ith unit and $x[i] = 0$ for all units. To use pure parametric input, $x[i]$ is the input value to the ith unit and $c[i] = 0$ for all units. Soft clamping is used in the forward propagation. It can be turned off by setting $\gamma = 0$. If the ith unit is an output unit, omask[i] = 1; otherwise, omask[i] = 0. Similarly, if the jth unit is connected to the ith unit, cmask[i][j] = 1; otherwise, cmask[i][j] = 0.

```
/*FORWARD PROPAGATE*/
For (i = 1 to n) {
    u[i] = c[i]
    V[i] = f(u[i])
    I[i] = x[i] + γ* omask[i]* (d[i] − V[i])
}
Relax_u()
/*BACKWARD PROPAGATE*/
For (i = 1 to n) {
```

```
    z[i] = 0
    J[i] = omask[i]* (d[i] − V[i])
}
Relax_z()
/*CALCULATE GRADIENT*/
For (i = 1 to n) For (j = 1 to n){ grad[i][j] = −cmask[i][j]*z[i]*V[j] }
```

It is not necessary to use sophisticated numerical integration algorithms such as Runge-Kutta in the relaxation routines. This is because the fixed-point equation of the discrete and of the continuous system are identical—only the basins of attraction will differ (provided the discretized equations are convergent). Since, simple Euler integration suffices, the relaxation routines are almost as easy to implement as forward and backward propagations in a feedforward network.

REFERENCES

Almeida, L. B. (1987). A learning rule for asynchronous perceptrons with feedback in a combinatorial environment. In M. Caudil & C. Butler (Eds.), *Proceedings of the IEEE First Annual International Conference on Neural Networks* (pp. 609–618). San Diego, CA: IEEE.

Amari, Shun-Ichi. (1972). Characteristics of random nets of analog neuron-like elements. *IEEE Transactions on Systems, Man and Cybernetics, 2,* 643–657.

Anderson, James A. (1972). A simple neural network generating an interactive memory. *Mathematical Biosciences, 14,* 197–220.

Aplevich, J. D. (1968). Models of certain nonlinear systems. In E. R. Caianiello (Ed.), *Neural networks* (pp. 110–115). Berlin: Springer-Verlag.

Atiya, A. (1988). Learning on a general network. In Dana Z. Anderson (Ed.), *Neural information processing systems* (pp. 22–30). New York: AIP.

Barhen, J., Gulati, S., & Zak, M. (1989). Neural learning of constrained nonlinear transformations. *IEEE Computer,* 67–76.

Benson, R. G. (1994). *Analog VLSI supervised learning system.* Dissertation submitted to Dept. of Engineering and Applied Sciences, CNS program. California Institute of Technology, Pasadena, CA.

Bryson, A. E., & Denham, W. (1962). A steepest-ascent method for solving optimum programming problems. *Journal of Applied Mechanics, 29,* 247–257.

Cohen, M. A., & Grossberg, S. (1983). Absolute stability of global pattern formation and parallel memory storage by competitive neural networks. *IEEE Transactions on Systems, Man and Cybernetics, 13,* 815–826.

Cowan, J. D. (1967). *A mathematical theory of central nervous activity.* Unpublished doctoral dissertation, Imperial College, University of London.

Deprit, E. (1989). Implementing recurrent back-propagation on the connection machine. *Neural Networks, 2,* 295–314.

Dreyfus, S. E. (1962). Numerical solution of variational problems. *Mathematical Analysis and Applications, 5,* 30–45.

Dreyfus, S. E. (1990). Artificial neural networks, back-propagation, and the Kelley-Bryson gradient procedure. *Journal of Guidance and Control, 15,* 926–928.

Grossberg, S. (1969). On learning and energy-entropy dependence in recurrent and nonrecurrent signed networks. *Journal of Statistical Physics, 1,* 319–350.

Hirsh, M. W. (1989). Convergent activation dynamics in continuous time networks. *Neural Networks, 2,* 331–349.

Hopfield, J. J. (1982). Neural networks and physical systems with emergent collective computational abilities. *Proceedings of the National Academy of Sciences USA, Bioscience, 79,* 2554.

Hopfield, J. J. (1984). Neurons with graded response have collective computational properties like those of two-state neurons. *Proceedings of the National Academy of Sciences USA, Bioscience, 81,* 3088–3092.

Hopfield, J. J., & Tank, D. W. (1985). Neural computation of decisions in optimization problems. *Biological Cybernetics, 52,* 141–152.

Julesz, B. (1971). *Foundations of cyclopean perception.* Chicago: University of Chicago Press.

Kelley, H. J. (1960). Gradient theory of optimal flight paths. *ARS Journal, 30,* 947–954.

Kohonen, K. (1972). Correlation matrix memories. *IEEE Transactions on Computers, 21,* 353–359.

Le Cun, Y. (1989). A theoretical framework for back-propagation. In D. Touretzcky, G. Hinton, & T. Sejnowski (Eds.), *Proceedings of the 1988 Connectionist Models Summer School.* San Mateo, CA: Morgan Kaufman.

Malsburg, C. van der (1973). Self-organizatin of orientation sensitive cells in striate cortex. *Kybernetic, 14,* 85–100.

Marcus, C. M., & Westervelt, M. R. (1989). Dynamics of analog neural networks with time delay. In D. Touretzky (Ed.), *Advances in information processing systems* (Vol. 1, pp. 568–576). San Mateo, CA: Morgan Kaufmann.

Marr, D., & Poggio, T. (1976). Cooperative computation of stereo disparity. *Science, 194,* 283–387.

Parker, David B. (1982). *Learning-logic* (Invention Report, S81-64, File 1). Stanford, CA: Stanford University Office of Technology Licensing.

Pearlmutter, B. (1989). Learning state space trajectories in recurrent neural networks. *Neural Computation, 1,* 263–269.

Pineda, F. J. (1987). Generalization of back-propagation to recurrent neural networks. *Physics Review Letters, 18,* 2229–2232.

Pineda, F. J. (1988a). Generalization of back-propagation to recurrent and higher order networks. In Dana Z. Anderson (Ed.). *Neural information processing systems* (pp. 602–611). New York: AIP.

Pineda, F. J. (1988b). Dynamics and architecture for neural computation. *Journal of Complexity, 4,* 216–245.

Qian, N., & Sejnowski, T. J. (1989). Learning to solve random-dot stereograms of dense and transparent surfaces with recurrent back-propagation. In D. Touretzky, G. Hinton and Terrence Sejnowski (Eds.), *Proceedings of the 1988 Connectionist Models Summer School* (pp. 435–443). San Mateo, CA: Morgan Kaufman.

Rumelhart, D. E., Hinton, G. E., & Williams, R. J. (1986). Learning internal representations by error propagation. In D. E. Rumelhart & J. L. McClelland (Eds.), *Parallel distributed processing* (pp. 318–362). Cambridge: M.I.T. Press.

Sejnowski, T. J. (1977). Storing covariance with nonlinearly interacting neurons. *Journal of Mathematical Biology, 4,* 303–321.

Simard, P. Y., Ottaway, M. B., & Ballard, Dana H. (1988). *Analysis of Recurrent back-propagation* (Technical Report 253). Rochester, NY: University of Rochester Computer Science Department.

Werbos, P. (1974). *Beyond regression: New tools for prediction and analysis in the behavior sciences.* Unpublished doctoral dissertation, Harvard University, Cambridge, MA.

Williams, R., & Zipser, D. (1991). Gradient-based learning algorithms for recurrent networks and their computational complexity. Chapter 13 this volume.

Zak, M. (1989). Terminal attractors in neural networks. *Neural Networks, 2,* 259–274.

5

A Focused Backpropagation
Algorithm for Temporal
Pattern Recognition

Michael C. Mozer
Department of Computer Science, University of Colorado

ABSTRACT

Time is at the heart of many pattern recognition tasks (e.g., speech recognition). However, connectionist learning algorithms to date are not well-suited for dealing with time-varying input patterns. This chapter introduces a specialized connectionist architecture and corresponding specialization of the back-propagation learning algorithm that operates efficiently, both in computational time and space requirements, on temporal sequences. The key feature of the architecture is a layer of self-connected hidden units that integrate their current value with the new input at each time step to construct a static representation of the temporal input sequence. This architecture avoids two deficiencies found in the back-propagation unfolding-in-time procedure (Rumelhart, Hinton, & Williams, 1986) for handing sequence recognition tasks: first, it reduces the difficulty of temporal credit assignment by focusing the back-propagated error signal; second, it eliminates the need for a buffer to hold the input sequence and/or intermediate activity levels. The latter property is due to the fact that during the forward (activation) phase, incremental activity *traces* can be locally computed that hold all information necessary for back propagation in time. It is argued that this architecture should scale better than conventional recurrent architectures with respect to sequence length. The architecture has been used to implement a temporal version of Rumelhart and McClelland's (1986) verb past-tense model. The hidden units learn to behave something like Rumelhart and McClelland's "Wickelphones," a rich and flexible representation of temporal information.

INTRODUCTION

Connectionist models have proven successful in a variety of pattern recognition tasks (e.g., Hinton, 1987; Sejnowski & Rosenberg, 1987). In some respects, these models are amazingly powerful, more so than the human brain. For instance, take a real-world image composed of light intensities and randomly rearrange pixels in the image. Most connectionist architectures can learn to recognize the permuted image as readily as the original (Smolensky, 1983), whereas humans would no doubt have great difficulty with this task. In other respects, however, the pattern recognition abilities of connectionist models are quite primitive. While humans have little trouble processing temporal patterns—indeed, all input to the sensory systems is intrinsically temporal in nature—few connectionist models deal with time. Because time is at the essence of many pattern recognition tasks, it is important to develop better methods of incorporating time into connectionist networks.

Figure 1 depicts an abstract characterization of the temporal pattern recognition task. Time is quantized into discrete steps. A sequence of inputs is presented to the recognition system, one per time step. Each element of the sequence is represented as a vector of feature values. At each point in time, the system may be required to produce a response, also represented as a vector of feature values, contingent on the input sequence of that point. In the simplest case, shown in Figure 1, a response is required only after the entire input sequence has been presented.

Many important problems are of this class. For instance, recognizing speech involves sampling the acoustic signal at regular intervals and producing as output a representation of phonemes or words. Similarly, natural language processing consists of analyzing a sequence of words to yield a structural or semantic description. And event perception can be viewed as analyzing a sequence of snapshots of the visual world to produce a description of the ensuing event. Freyd (1987) has argued that even for some static objects, perception may be dynamic in the sense that a temporal dimension is incorporated into the perceptual analysis.

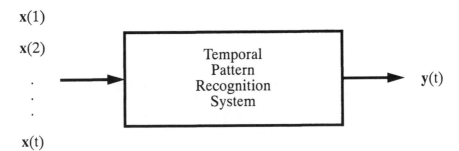

Figure 1.   Abstract characterization of the temporal pattern recognition task. $x(t)$ indicates the input pattern at time t, $y(t)$ the output pattern.

PREVIOUS CONNECTIONIST APPROACHES TO
TEMPORAL PATTERN RECOGNITION

One popular approach to temporal pattern recognition has been to construct a buffer to hold the n most recent elements of the input sequence (Elman & McClelland, 1986; Elman & Zipser, 1988; Landauer, Kamm, & Singhal, 1987; Lapedes & Farber, 1987; McClelland & Elman, 1986; Plaut, Nowlan, & Hinton, 1986; Tank & Hopfield, 1987; Waibel, Hanazawa, Hinton, Shikano, & Lang, 1987). Such a buffer can be implemented using a shift register or delay lines. The buffer turns a temporal recognition problem into a spatial recognition problem in which all relevant information for making a response is simultaneously available. Because connectionist models are relatively good at spatial recognition problems, this approach seems assured of some success.

However, the approach has four serious drawbacks. First, the buffer must be sufficient in size to accommodate the longest possible input sequence. With an n-element buffer, no sequence of duration greater than n can be recognized. Thus, the longest possible sequence—the longest interval over which context may play a role—must be known in advance. Even if a fairly large buffer can be built, say one sufficient to recognize a phoneme or demisyllable, what about higher levels of analysis—words, phrases, sentences, paragraphs? At some point, one needs to deal with the fact that not all input information can be available to the system simultaneously. A hierarchy of buffers may partially alleviate this problem, but will still require the advance specification of maximum sequence duration.

A second drawback of using a buffer is that by making a great deal of information simultaneously available, much computation is required at each time step. Essentially, all information within the buffer must be reprocessed whenever the buffer state changes. This is not a problem if one has dedicated parallel hardware, but simulations of such a connectionist system on a serial machine can be computationally expensive.

Third, when a buffer is used as input to a connectionist network, each element of the buffer must be connected to higher layers of the network. Consequently, as the buffer grows, so does the number of weights. This means that a large number of training examples must be used or else the network will not generalize well (Hinton, 1989). Another solution to this problem is to constrain the weights in some manner so as to reduce the number of free parameters (Lang, 1987; Le Cun, this volume; Waibel et al. 1987).

Fourth, the use of a buffer makes it difficult to achieve invariance under translation in time. Because the buffer turns shifts in time into shifts in space (i.e., buffer position), the representation of an input sequence occurring at one time will have little resemblance to that of an input sequence occurring at another time. Consequently, if training and test sequences are misaligned, the sequences will likely not be recognized as the same. One way of minimizing this problem is to shift inputs continuously across the buffer to ensure that each sequence is presented in each position, both during training and testing. However, this solution introduces noise into the training phase and additional computation into the testing phase.

These deficiencies of the buffer model argue that the spatial metaphor for time is not viable; a richer, more flexible representation of time is needed. Similar arguments have been raised elsewhere (Elman, 1990; Stornetta, Hogg, & Huberman, 1987; Watrous & Shastri, 1987). Despite its drawbacks, the buffer model has two properties in common with any model of temporal pattern recognition. First, some memory of the input history is required. Second, a function must be specified to combine the current memory (or *temporal context*) and the current input to form a new temporal context:

$$\mathbf{c}(t + 1) = f(\mathbf{c}(t), \mathbf{x}(t)),$$

where $\mathbf{c}(t)$ is a vector representing the context at time t, $\mathbf{x}(t)$ is the input at time t, and f is the mapping function. The buffer model is a simple scheme, where the temporal context consists of the n most recent sequence elements, and f is implemented by the shift-register operation of the buffer. Given the inadequacy of the buffer model, one would like to discover ways of representing temporal context that avoid turning intrinsically temporal information into spatial information.

One idea is based on the fact that, in a connectionist network, the connections from one set of units to another implement a mapping. Thus, by representing the input $\mathbf{x}(t)$ and context $\mathbf{c}(t)$ as patterns of activity on two sets of units, the weights connecting the input units to the context units and the context units to themselves specify a mapping function f. Jordan (1987) and Stornetta et al. (1987) have explored this approach using fixed weights that do not change with experience. In the Stornetta et al. work, there is one context unit per input unit, and each context unit is connected to itself and its corresponding input unit. In other words, the mapping function is

$$f(\mathbf{c},\mathbf{x}) = k_1\mathbf{c} + k_2\mathbf{x},$$

where k_1 and k_2 are fixed constants.

This type of network has no spatial representation of time. Consequently, the architecture does not require replicated input units, in contrast to the buffer model which requires n copies of the input units for an n-element buffer. Further, this architecture does not place a rigid upper bound on the amount of temporal context that can be considered, whereas the buffer model can remember only the n most recent sequence elements. Nonetheless, this approach is rather inflexible in that the mapping function used to construct the temporal context is predetermined and fixed. As a result, the representation of temporal context must be sufficiently rich that it can accommodate a wide variety of tasks; it cannot afford to discard too much information. The alternative to this general, task-independent representation is one suited to the task being performed, wherein only the input information relevant to the task need be retained.

Connectionist learning algorithms provide a means of adaptively constructing internal representations. However, the most promising and popular algorithm, back propagation (Rumelhart et al. 1986), is designed for feedforward networks. In order to represent temporal context, recurrent networks are required because the current context must depend on the previous. Back propagation can be used to train recurrent networks if the network is "unfolded in time" (Rumelhart et al., 1986; see also chapters in this volume by Bachrach and Mozer, Nguyen and Widrow, Servan-Schreiber et al., and Williams and Zipser). The basic trick can be seen by comparing the recurrent network in Figure 2a to the equivalent unfolded network in Figure 2b. The network in Figure 2a consists of four layers: input, context, hidden, and output. The input pattern is integrated with the current context to form a new context. The context is then mapped, by way of the hidden layer, to an output. In Figure 2b, the same functionality is achieved by replicating the input and context layers for each element of the input sequence and by constraining the weights such that the input-to-context connections and context-to-context connections are equal across time. Rather than having four pools of units, the unfolded network contains $2 + 2t$ pools, where t is the number of elements in the input sequence. Because the unfolded network is feedforward, the back-propagation algorithm can be applied to adjust the connection strengths so that a given input sequence will yield a target output.[1] The weight constraints are enforced by maintaining only one set of input-to-context and context-to-context weights. During the back-propagation phase, the changes prescribed for each weight at each level are summed to give a net weight change.

Training a network using the unfolding procedure has two significant drawbacks, however. First, part of the architecture must be replicated for each time step of the input sequence. In implementing the unfolding procedure, it is not actually necessary to replicate processing units; units need be instantiated only once if each unit remembers its activity level at each point in time—that is, maintains a stack of activity levels. During forward propagation, values are pushed on to this stack, and during back propagation values are popped in reverse temporal order.[2]

Second, the unfolding procedure creates a deeply layered network through which error signals must be propagated. This is bad not only because the time to perform back propagation is proportional to the depth of the network, but also

---

[1]Intermediate output values could readily be trained by replicating the hidden and output units at intermediate time steps, and injecting an additional error signal into the network via the output units.

[2]Almeida (1987) and Pineda (1987) have proposed a variation of the back-propagation algorithm for recurrent networks that does not need an activity-level history. However, the algorithm assumes a fixed input, and hence is suitable for pattern completion and other relaxation problems, not for analyzing a time-varying input pattern.

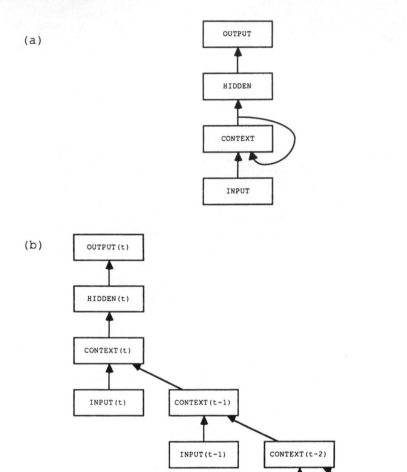

Figure 2. (a) A four-layered recurrent network consisting of input, context, hidden, and output units. Each labeled box indicates a set of processing units. The arrows indicate complete connectivity from one layer to another; that is, each unit in one layer is connected to each unit in the other. (b) The same network unfolded in time. The input and context layers are replicated for each element of the sequence. The weights are constrained so that the input-context connections are equal across time, as are the context-context connections.

because the further back an error signal is propagated, the more dispersed it becomes. To explain what I mean by "dispersed," consider that the purpose of back propagation is to assign blame to each unit for its contribution to the error. However, the assignment of blame to a given unit is meaningful only in the context of the response properties of units higher in the network. If the present responses of these units do not resemble their eventual responses, then the lower-layer unit cannot obtain an independently informative measure of its contribution to the error; back propagation through the upper layers will effectively redistribute the error signal in some random fashion. Thus, in deep networks, especially where the relevant input signal is found in the lower layers, learning can be very slow. This argument is born out by empirical comparisons of learning speed using temporal versus spatial patterns made by myself and by Steven Nowlan (personal communication).

CONSTRAINTS ON NETWORK ARCHITECTURE

Given the inherent difficulties in using back propagation to train a recurrent network to recognize temporal sequences, one useful tack is to look for constraints on solutions the network might discover that could simplify the learning problem. This strategy of building a priori structural knowledge into the network directly can often speed learning and improve generalization (Hinton, 1989).

Consider the sort of representation one might like to obtain in the context layer of the network in Figure 2a. This representation should satisfy four criteria. First, it must be a static encoding of the temporal input pattern, one that holds on to whichever features of the input are needed to produce the desired response. Second, it must be capable of encoding sequences of varying lengths with a fixed number of units. Third, it must be capable of encoding relationships between events. And fourth, it should provide a natural basis for generalization.

Wickelgren (1969) has suggested a representational scheme that seems to satisfy these criteria and has been applied successfully in several connectionist models (Mozer, 1991; Rumelhart & McClelland, 1986; Seidenberg, 1990). The basic idea is to encode each element of a sequence with respect to its local context. For example, consider the phonetic encoding of a word. Wickelgren proposed context-sensitive phoneme units, each responding to a particular phoneme in the context of a particular predecessor and successor. I will call these units *Wickelphones,* after the terminology of Rumelhart and McClelland. If the word *explain* had the phonetic spelling /eksplAn/, it would be composed of the Wickelphones $_-e_k$, $_ek_s$, $_ks_p$, $_sP_l$, $_pl_A$, $_lA_n$, and $_An_-$ (where the dash indicates a word boundary). Assuming one Wickelphone unit for each possible phoneme triple, activation of a word would correspond to a distributed pattern of activity over the Wickelphone units.

With a fixed number of Wickelphone units, it is possible to represent uniquely arbitrary strings of varying length. This means that the unordered set of Wickelphones is sufficient to allow for the unambiguous reconstruction of the ordered string. There are difficulties if the string contains repeated substrings (e.g., *Mississippi*), but these difficulties can be overcome (Mozer, 1990). The Wickelphone representation can be generalized to arbitrary sequences by substituting sequence elements for phonemes. In the general case, I call the context-sensitive encoding a *Wickelement* representation.

The trouble with Wickelements is that there are too many of them. Rumelhart and McClelland reduced the number of Wickelphones by devising a more compact and distributed encoding that depended on features of phonemes rather than the phonemes themselves. The number of units can also be reduced on the grounds that not all Wickelements are needed for every task. For instance, a $_p k_t$ Wickelphone is unnecessary for representing English words. Thus, it would be desirable to learn only the task-relevant Wickelements.

How might the network in Figure 2a be modified to learn an internal representation in the context layer that resembled Wickelements? First, to obtain local context-sensitive codes, the sequence might be presented in local "chunks." This can be achieved by turning the input layer into a small buffer, so that at time t the input pattern consists of the sequence elements at, say, times $t - 2, t - 1$, and t. Then the context units can detect conjunctions of sequence elements, or conjunctions of features of sequence elements. Once activated by a pattern in the input, the context units should remain on. Thus, it seems sensible to have self-connected context units, but not to connect each context unit to each other, say an activation function like

$$c_i(t + 1) = d_i c_i(t) + s[net_i(t)], \qquad (1)$$

where $c_i(t)$ is the activity level of context unit i at time t, d_i is a decay weight associated with the unit, s is a sigmoid squashing function, and $net_i(t)$ is the net input to the unit:

$$net_i(t) \equiv \sum_j w_{ji} x_j(t),$$

$x_j(t)$ being the activity of input unit j at time t, w_{ji} the connection strength from input unit j to context unit i. Thus, a context unit adds its current activity, weighted by the decay factor, to the new input at each time. The decay factor allows old information to fade over time if $d_i < 1$. Such decay connections have proven useful in other work (Jordan, 1987; Miyata, 1988; Stornetta et al., 1987; Watrous & Shastri, 1987).

To summarize, a recurrent network with this architecture, which I call the *focused* architecture for reasons that will become clear shortly, differs from a *full* recurrent architecture in three respects: (1) the input layer consists of a small temporal buffer holding several elements of the input sequence; (2) connectivity in the context layer is restricted to one-to-one recurrent connections; and (3) integration over time in the context layer is linear.[3]

THE FOCUSED BACK-PROPAGATION ALGORITHM

It turns out that the focused architecture has properties that overcome the two major limitations discussed earlier of a full recurrent architecture and the unfolding-in-time training procedure. First, back propagation is "focused": the error signal does not disperse as it propagates back in time. Second, to adjust the weights, back propagation in time—and saving an activity history stack—is unnecessary.

To get an intuition as to why these two statements are true, consider the weight update procedure when a t-element sequence is presented to a focused recurrent network. Following the sequence, at time t, the network is shown a target output vector. Comparing this vector to the actual output vector yields an error signal, E. To adjust weights according to the back propagation gradient descent procedure, it is necessary to compute

$$\delta_i(\tau) \equiv \frac{\partial E}{\partial c_i(\tau)}$$

for $\tau = 1, \ldots , t$. This can be achieved by back propagating in time, from the context layer at time t to $t - 1$ to $t - 2$ and so forth. However, from Equation 1 it is clear that

$$\frac{\partial c_i(\tau)}{\partial c_i(\tau - 1)} = d_i.$$

Consequently,

$$\delta_i(\tau - 1) \equiv \frac{\partial E}{\partial c_i(\tau - 1)} = \frac{\partial c_i(\tau)}{\partial c_i(\tau - 1)} \frac{\partial E}{\partial c_i(\tau)} = d_i \delta_i(\tau). \qquad (2)$$

The error signal, $\delta_i(\tau)$, changes just by a constant multiplicative factor, d_i, as it is propagated back in time. Thus, there is a simple relationship between the δ_i's at various points in time.

---

[3]The simple recurrent network (SRN) architecture described by Elman (1990) and Servan-Schreiber et al. (this volume) has some superficial similarity with the focused architecture. In particular, there is a set of feedback connections in the SRN which are both one-to-one and linear. However, these connections do not correspond to the recurrent connections in the focused architecture. The SRN is simply a generic three-layer architecture with complete recurrent connectivity in the hidden layer. This is not always clear because the SRN is usually drawn with two copies of the hidden layer, one representing the activities at the current time step and the other (often called the context) representing the activities at the previous time step. The one-to-one linear connections serve only to preserve the previous hidden activity for one time step.

Because of Equation 2, whatever error is propagated back to the context unit at time t stays within that unit as the error is passed further back in time, in contrast to a full recurrent network where the error is redistributed among the context units with each backwards pass due to cross connections between units. Error propagation with this focused architecture is therefore focused and should not disperse in time—an apparent limitation of the full recurrent architecture.

Error propagation with the focused architecture is also superior in a second respect. Because of the simple relationship described by Equation 2, it is not necessary to explicitly back-propagate in time to compute $\delta_i(\tau)$ from $\delta_i(t)$. Instead, if each connection has associated with it an *activity history trace* that is incrementally updated during the forward (activation) pass, these traces can be used to exactly achieve the effects of back propagation in time.

The appendix derives formulas for $\partial E/\partial d_i$ and $\partial E/\partial c_i(t)$ in terms of the activity traces, which yield the following weight update rules. For the recurrent connections, d_i, the rule is

$$\Delta d_i = -\epsilon\delta_i(t)\alpha_i(t),$$

where $\alpha_i(0) = 0$ and

$$\alpha_i(\tau) = c_i(\tau - 1) + d_i\alpha_i(\tau - 1).$$

Similarly, the weight update rule for the input-context connections, w_{ji}, is

$$\Delta w_{ji} = -\epsilon\delta_i(t)\beta_{ji}(t),$$

where $\beta_{ji}(0) = 0$ and

$$\beta_{ji}(\tau) = s'[net_i(\tau)]x_j(\tau) + d_i\beta_{ji}(\tau - 1).$$

These weight update rules are not just heuristics or approximations; they are *computationally equivalent* to performing the back propagation in time.

Choosing a Squashing Function for the Context Units

An interesting issue arises in the choice of a squashing function, $s[u]$, for the context units. If we indeed hope that the context units learn to behave as Wickelement detectors, we would like the squashing function to have range 0–1, in order that the response is 0.0 if the input pattern does not match the Wickelement or 1.0 if it does. But to the extent that the unit is not a perfect Wickelement detector (as will be the case initially), it will produce small positive responses on each time step. Consequently, the activity level of the context unit will grow in proportion to the number of sequence elements, an undesirable property that could result in unstable learning behavior and poor generalization. One remedy is to use a zero-mean squashing function, say with the range -0.5 to $+0.5$. Because positive and negative values will cancel when summed over time, the activity of a context unit should be independent of sequence length (at least initially, when the weights are uncorrelated with the inputs). However, the context unit will be unable to respond to Wickelements in the manner described: it is impossible to set the weights so that the zero-mean squashing function yields a positive value if the input pattern matches the Wickelement or 0.0 otherwise. To summarize, a squashing function with the range -0.5 to $+0.5$ seems appropriate initially, when weights are untrained and the output of a unit is more-or-less random, but the range 0.0 to 1.0 seems necessary to perform binary discriminations in which one of the desired output levels is 0.0.

Although one solution might be to manually adjust the range of this function as the network learns, I have opted for a different approach: to allow the network to *learn* the zero point of the function. For each context unit, I have introduced an additional parameter, z_i, the zero point, and defined the squashing function for unit i to be

$$s_i[u] \equiv \frac{1}{1 + e^{-u}} + z_i.$$

If z_i is 0.0, the range of the function is 0.0 to 1.0; if z_i is $-.5$, the range is -0.5 to $+0.5$.

As with the other parameters in the network, z_i can be adjusted by gradient descent. The update rule, derived as those for d_i and w_{ji}, is

$$\Delta z_i = -\epsilon \delta_i(t) \gamma_i(t),$$

where $\gamma_i(0) = 0$ and

$$\gamma_i(\tau) = 1.0 + d_i \gamma_i(\tau - 1).$$

Related Work

Several researchers have independently discovered the idea of computing an activity trace during the forward pass as an alternative to back propagation in time. Williams and Zipser (1989, this volume) report on a generalization to arbitrary recurrent network architectures; this generalization is of questionable practical use, however, because the number of traces grows with the cube of the number of units. Bachrach (1988), Gori, Bengio, and De Mori (1989), and Yoshiro Miyata (personal communication) have studied a version of the current architecture with a more complex context-unit activation function in which the recurrent input is contained inside the squashing function:

$$c_i(t + 1) = s[net_i(t)], \tag{3}$$

where

$$net_i(t) \equiv d_i c_i(t) + \sum_j w_{ji} x_j(t).$$

In this case, the weight update rules are as before with

$$\alpha_i(\tau) = (c_i(\tau - 1) + d_i\alpha_i(\tau - 1)) \, s'[net_i(t)]$$

and

$$\beta_{ji}(\tau) = (x_j(\tau) + d_i\beta_{ji}(\tau - 1)) \, s'[net_i(t)].$$

In practice, Miyata and I have found Equation 1 to work better than Equation 3 because squashing the recurrent input tends to cause the context units to forget their values over time. Bachrach (1988) has analyzed the nature of this forgetting more formally.

SIMULATION RESULTS

Implementation Details

The simulations reported in the following sections used an architecture like that shown in Figure 2, except that the hidden layer was not needed; the context layer mapped directly to the output layer.

The initial input-context and context-output connection strengths were randomly picked from a zero-mean Gaussian distribution and were normalized so that the L1 norm of the fan-in (incoming) weight vector was 2.0. The z_i were initially set to -0.5, and the initial d_i were picked at random from a uniform distribution over the interval 0.99–1.01.

A "batch" updating procedure was used during training; that is, the weights were updated only after a complete presentation of the training set (an *epoch*). Momentum was not used. Learning rates were determined individually for each set of connections: input-context, decay, zero points, and context-output. The learning rates were set dynamically after each epoch according to the following heuristic:

$$\epsilon_k = mse^\mu \rho \, \min\left(\omega, \frac{W_k}{\nabla_k}\right),$$

where ϵ_k is the learning rate for connections of type k, *mse* is the mean-square error across output units and patterns for the previous epoch, W_k is the mean L1 norm of the fan-in weight vector for connections of type k, ∇_k is the *mean* L1 norm of the fan-in gradient vector for input-context and context-output connections and the *maximum* magnitude for the decay and zero-point connections, and μ, ρ, and ω are constants. The *mse* term serves to decrease the learning rate as the error becomes smaller; μ is a discounting factor for this term (set to values in the neighborhood of 0.75–1.0). The second term defines a "nominal" learning rate which is set so that, on average, weight updates change each unit's fan-in weight vector by a fixed proportion (ρ, generally 0.02) of its current magnitude. The parameter ω specifies an upper limit on the step size when ∇_k becomes extremely small. This rule produces learning rates for the decay and zero-point terms that are about one-tenth of the other learning rates; this relatively small step size seems necessary to ensure stability of the network.

Although I had hoped to devise a rule for automatically adjusting the learning rates that was architecture and problem independent, the foregoing rule does not satisfy this requirement. The parameters μ, ρ, and ω had to be fine tuned for most applications to give optimal performance. However, the rule did work much better than fixed learning rates and other variants that I experimented with.

Learning Wickelements

Starting with a simple example, the network was trained to identify four sequences: _DEAR_, _DEAN_, _BEAR_, and _BEAN_. Each symbol corresponds to a single sequence element and was represented by a binary activity pattern over three units (Table 1). The input layer was a two-element buffer through which the sequence was passed. For _DEAR_, the input on successive time steps consisted of _D, DE, EA, AR, R_. The input layer had six units, the context layer two, and the output layer four. The network's task was to associate each sequence with a corresponding output unit. To perform this task, the network must learn to discriminate **D** from **B** in the first letter position and **N** from **R** in the fourth letter position. This can be achieved if the context units learn to behave as Wickelement detectors. For example, a context unit that responds to the Wickelements _D or DE serves as a **B-D** discriminator; a unit that responds to **R_** or **AR** serves as an **N-R** discriminator. Thus, a solution can be obtained with two context units.

Fifty replications of the simulation were run with different initial weight configurations. The task was learned in a median of 488 training epochs, the criterion for a correct response being that the output unit with the largest value was the appropriate one. Figure 3 shows the result of one run. The weights appear in the upper half of the figure, and activity levels for each input sequence in the lower half. The weights are grouped by connection type, with the input-

TABLE 1
Symbol Encoding

Symbol	Activity Pattern		
A	0	0	0
B	0	0	1
E	0	1	0
D	0	1	1
N	1	0	0
R	1	0	1
—	1	1	0

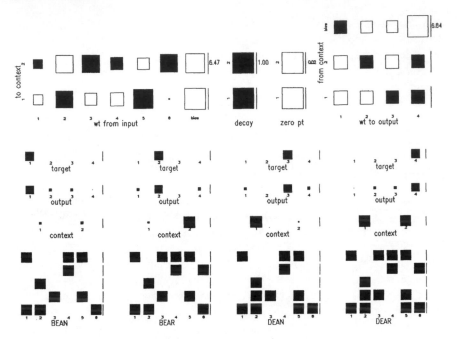

Figure 3.   The **DEAR/DEAN/BEAR/BEAN** problem. The upper half of the figure shows learned weights in the network; the lower half activity levels in response to each of the four input sequences.

context connections in the upper-left array, followed by the decay connections (d_i), zero points (z_i), and context-output connections. Each connection is depicted as a square whose *area* indicates the relative weight magnitude, and shading the weight sign—black is positive, white is negative. The sizes of the squares are normalized within each array such that the largest square has sides whose length is equal to that of the vertical bars on the right edge of the array. The absolute magnitude of the largest weight is indicated by the number in the upper-right corner. Among the input-context connections, the largest weight magnitude is 6.47, among the decay values 1.00, the zero points 0.02, and the context-output connections 6.84. Because normalization is performed within each array, weight magnitudes of different connection types must be compared with references to the normalization factors.

The units within each layer are numbered. The weights feeding into and out of context unit 1 have been arranged along a single row, and the weights of context unit 2 in the row above. Bias terms (i.e., weight lines with a fixed input of 1.0) are also shown for the context and output units.

For the activity levels in the lower half of the figure, there are four columns of values, one for each sequence. The input pattern itself is shown in the lowest array. Time is represented along the vertical dimension, with the first time step at the bottom and each succeeding one above the previous. The input at each time reflects the buffer contents. Because the buffer holds two sequence elements, note that the second element in the buffer at one time step (the activity pattern in input units 4–6) is the same as the first element of the buffer at the next (input units 1–3).

Above the input pattern are, respectively, the context unit activity levels after presentation of the final sequence element, the output unit activity levels at this time, and the target output values. The activity level of a unit is proportional to the area of its corresponding square. If a unit has an activity level of 0.0, its square has no area—an empty space. The squares are normalized such that a "unit square"—a square whose edge is the length of one of the vertical bars— corresponds to an activity level of 1.0. While the input, output, and target activity levels range from 0.0 to 1.0, the context activity levels can lie outside these bounds and are, in fact, occasionally greater than 1.0.

With these preliminaries out of the way, consider what the network has learned. At the completion of each sequence, the context unit activity pattern is essentially binary. Context unit 1 is off for _BEAN_ and _BEAR_, and on for _DEAN_ and _DEAR_; thus, it discriminates B and D. Context unit 2 is off for _BEAN_ and _DEAN_, and on for _BEAR_ and _DEAR_; thus it discriminates N and R. However, the context units do not behave in a straightforward way as Wickelements. If context unit 1 ware sharply tuned to, say, _D, the input-context weights should serve as a matched filter to the input pattern _D. This is not the case: the weights have signs $- + - - + -$ but the _D input pattern is 110011. Nor is context unit 1 tuned to the DE, whose input pattern is 011010. Instead, the unit appears to be tuned equally to both patterns. By examining the activity of the unit over time, it can be determined that the unit is activated partly by _D and partly by DE but by no other input pattern. This makes sense: _D and DE are equally valid cues to the sequence identity, and as such, evidence from each should contribute to the response. To get a feel for why the detector responds as it does, note that _D (110011) is distinguished from _B (110001) by activity in unit 5; DE (011010) from BE (001010) by activity in unit 2. The weights from inputs 2 and 5 to context unit 1 are positive, allowing the unit to detect D in either context. The other weights are set so as to prevent the unit from responding to other possible inputs. Thus, the unit selects out key features of the Wickelements _D and DE that are not found in other Wickelements. As such, it behaves as a _DE Wickelement detector, and context unit 2 similarly as a AR_ detector.

Generalization testing supports the notion that the context units have become sensitive to these Wickelements. If the input elements are permuted to produce sequences like AR_BE, which preserves the Wickelements AR_ and _BE, context unit responses are similar to those of the original sequences. However, with permutations like _RB_, _DAER_, and DEAR (without the end delimiters), which destroy the Wickelements AR_ and _BE, context unit responses are not contingent upon the **D, B, N,** and **R.** Thus, the context units are responding to these key letters, but in a context-dependent manner.

I must admit that the example in Figure 3 is fairly easy to interpret in part because the d_i and z_i were initially set to values near 1.0 and 0.0, respectively, and the learning rate for these parameters was turned down, forcing final solutions with values close to these initial ones. This encouraged the context units to produce a more sharply tuned "all-or-none" response to each sequence element.[4] Without biasing the d_i and z_i in this manner, the network was still able to discover solutions; in fact, the solutions were arrived at even more rapidly. These alternative solutions were qualitatively similar to the one described but were somewhat more difficult to interpret.

Learning the Regularities of Verb Past Tense

In English, the past tense of many verbs is formed according to a simple rule. Examples of these *regular verbs* are shown in Table 2. Each string denotes the phonetic encoding of the verb in italics, and each symbol a single phoneme. The notation of phonemes is the same as that used by Rumelhart and McClelland (1986), from whom the examples were borrowed. Regular verbs can be divided into three classes, depending on whether the past tense is formed by adding /ˆd/ (an "ud" sound, examples of which are shown in the first column in Table 2), /t/ (the second column), or /d/ (the third column). The rule for determining the class of a regular verb is as follows.

If the final phoneme is dental (/d/ or /t/), add /ˆd/;

else if the final phoneme is an unvoiced consonant, add /t/;

else (the final phoneme is voiced), add /d/.

A network was trained to classify the 60 examples in Table 2. Each phoneme was encoded by a set of four trinary acoustic features (see Rumelhart & McClelland, 1986, Table 5). The input layer of the network was a two-element buffer, so a verb like /kamp/ appeared in the buffer over time as **_k, ka, am, mp, p_.** The underscore is a delimiter symbol placed at the beginning and end of each string.

The network had eight input units (two time slices each consisting of four features), two context units, and three output units, one for each verb class. For comparison, both focused and full network architectures were studied. The full architecture was the same as the focused except it had complete connectivity in the context layer and an activation function like Equation 3 instead of Equation

---

[4]With d_i closer to 0.0, a context unit's activity depends primarily on recent sequence elements, allowing it to be sloppy with its response to earlier elements; likewise, with d_i much larger than 1.0, activity depends primarily on the early sequence elements, and the unit may be sloppy with respect to recent elements. With z_i closer to -0.5, all-or-none responses are not necessary because the effect of spurious activity can be canceled over time.

TABLE 2
Examples of Regular Verbs

+ /ˆd/	+ /t/	+ /d/
/dEpend/ (*depend*)	/ˆprOC/ (*approach*)	/Tretˆn/ (*threaten*)
/gId/ (*guide*)	/bles/ (*bless*)	/Ser/ (*share*)
/inklUd/ (*include*)	/diskˆs/ (*discuss*)	/ansˆr/ (*answer*)
/kˆmand/ (*command*)	/embarˆs/ (*embarrass*)	/dEskrIb/ (*describe*)
/mOld/ (*mold*)	/fAs/ (*face*)	/drI/ (*dry*)
/plEd/ (*plead*)	/help/ (*help*)	/fAr/ (*fare*)
/prOvId/ (*provide*)	/kamp/ (*camp*)	/frItˆn/ (*frighten*)
/rEgord/ (*regard*)	/kuk/ (*cook*)	/kUI/ (*cool*)
/sˆrWnd/ (*surround*)	/mark/ (*mark*)	/kˆntAn/ (*contain*)
/trAd/ (*trade*)	/nˆrs/ (*nurse*)	/krI/ (*cry*)
/SWt/ (*shout*)	/pˆrCˆs/ (*purchase*)	/Iˆv/ (*love*)
/ˆtempt/ (*attempt*)	/pas/ (*pass*)	/mIn/ (*mine*)
/dEvOt/ (*devote*)	/pik/ (*pick*)	/prOgram/ (*program*)
/ekspekt/ (*expect*)	/prOdUs/ (*produce*)	/rEfuz/ (*refuse*)
/kˆnsist/ (*consist*)	/puS/ (*push*)	/rEvU/ (*review*)
/nOt/ (*note*)	/rEC/ (*reach*)	/sˆpII/ (*supply*)
/prEzent/ (*present*)	/rok/ (*rock*)	/stˆdE/ (*study*)
/reprEzent/ (*represent*)	/skraC/ (*scratch*)	/trembˆI/ (*tremble*)
/trEt/ (*treat*)	/trAs/ (*trace*)	/yUz/ (*use*)
/want/ (*want*)	/woS/ (*wash*)	/prEvAI/ (*prevail*)

1. The number of connections in each architecture was the same: the focused network requires six connections within the context layer, two for the d_i, two for the z_i, and two for the biases; the full network also requires six, four to connect each unit to each other and two for the biases. Learning rate parameters were adjusted to yield the best possible performance for each architecture.

Figure 4 shows performance on the training set for the two architectures, averaged over 15 runs with different initial random weights. A verb is considered to have been categorized correctly if the most active output unit specifies the verb's class. Both focused and full networks are able to learn the task, although the full network learns somewhat more quickly. Both networks have learned the underlying rule, as indicated by their excellent generalization performance on novel sequences (data points on far right of Figure 4).

Typical weights learned by the focused network are presented in Figure 5, along with the output levels of the two context units in response to 20 verbs. These verbs, though not part of the training set, were all classified correctly.

The response of the context units is straightforward. Context unit 1 has a positive activity level if the final phoneme is a dental (/d/ or /t/), negative otherwise. Context unit 2 has positive activity if the final phoneme is unvoiced, near zero otherwise. These are precisely the features required to discriminate among the three regular verb classes. In fact, the classification rule for regular

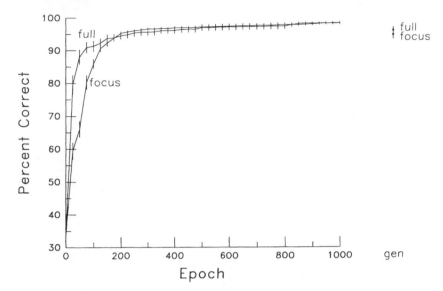

Figure 4.   Mean performance on the regular verb task as a function of learning epoch for the focused and full recurrent architectures. The bars indicate one standard error of the mean in each direction. Data points for generalization performance are shown on the far right.

verbs can be observed in the context-output weights (the rightmost weight matrix in Figure 5). Connections are such that output unit 1, which represents the "add /^d/" class, is activated by a final dental phoneme; output unit 2, which represents the "add /t/" class, is activated by a final nondental unvoiced phoneme; and output unit 3, which represents "add /d/" class, is activated by a final nondental voiced phoneme.

Note that the decay weights in this simulation are small in magnitude; the largest is 0.02. Consequently, context units retain no history of past events, which is quite sensible because only the final phoneme determines the verb class. This fact makes verb classification a simple task: it is not necessary for the context units to hold on to information over time.

Consider now the opposite problem. Suppose the network is given the same verb classification task, but the order of phonemes is reversed; instead of /eksplAn/, /nAlpske/ is presented. In this problem, the relevant information comes at the start of the sequence and must be retained until the sequence is completed. Figure 6 shows performance on reversed regular verbs, averaged over 15 runs. The focused network is able to learn this task, with two context units, although the number of training epochs required is higher than for unreversed verbs. Generalization is as good for reversed as unreversed verbs. The full network, however, does not succeed with reversed verbs. In exploring a wide

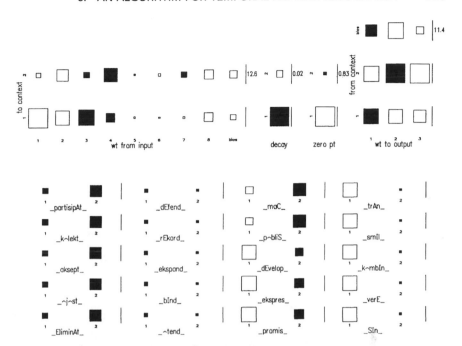

Figure 5.   The regular verb problem. The upper half shows learned
weights in the network, the lower half shows the final activity levels of
the context units in response to a variety of verbs. Verbs in the first
column all end with /t/, in the second column with /d/, in the third
column with an unvoiced consonant, and the fourth column with a
voiced consonant or vowel.

range of learning rate parameters, the highest single-run performance I was able
to obtain was 75%. The difference between reversed and unreversed verbs is that
the critical information for classification comes at the beginning of the sequence
for reversed verbs but at the end of unreversed. In terms of the unfolded architecture of Figure 2b, this corresponds to a low layer of reversed but a high layer for
unreversed. These results thus suggest that error signals are lost as they propagate back through the deeply layered full network. I return to this issue after
describing several other simulations.

Learning to Reproduce a Sequence

In this task, the network is presented with a three-element input sequence, and
then, following a fixed delay, must play back the sequence in time. The training
sequences consisted of all permutations of three elements, **A**, **B**, and **C**, resulting
in a total of six sequences; **ABC, ACB, BAC, BCA, CAB,** and **CBA.** An
element was encoded by a binary activity pattern; **A** was 100, **B** 010, and **C** 001.

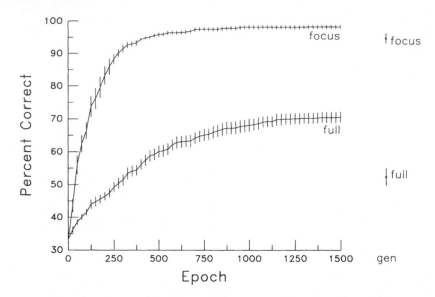

Figure 6. Mean performance on the reversed regular verb task as a function of learning epoch for the focused and full recurrent architectures. The bars indicate one standard error of the mean in each direction. Data points for generalization performance are shown on the far right.

The input layer contained three units on which the sequence was presented, one element per time step. At subsequent times, all inputs were zero. The order of events for **ABC** is presented in Table 3. In this example, there is a one time-step delay between the final element of the input sequence and the start of playback on the output units. Note that the target output levels are zero until playback commences.

The recurrent connections in the context layer allow the network to keep track of the input sequence. To help the network keep track of its position in the output sequence during playback, a set of one-to-one recurrent connections was added from the output units to three additional input units. These three units represented the output at the previous time step (an architecture suggested by Jordan, 1987). During training, these units were set to the *target* output values; for the example in Table 3, these inputs would be zero from times 1–5, 100 at time 6 and 010 at time 7. During testing, the true output values from the previous time step were "quantized" and copied back to the input. Quantization entailed setting all output levels greater than 0.5 to 1.0 and others to 0.0.

The network was made up of six input units, three for the current sequence element and three for the previous output state, three context units, and three

TABLE 3
Sequence of Input and Target
Output Patterns for ABC

Time Step	Input	Target Output
1	100 (A)	000
2	010 (B)	000
3	001 (C)	000
4	000	000
5	000	100 (A)
6	000	010 (B)
7	000	001 (C)

output units. The task of the context units was to learn a static representation of the sequence that could be used in regenerating the sequence.

Fifteen replications of the simulation were run with random initial weights for both focused and full network architectures. The focused network had two-thirds as many adjustable parameters within the context layer as the full, six instead of nine.

Performance was judged using the quantized outputs. The task was successfully learned on all runs. The mean number of training epochs required for perfect performance was 767 for the focused network and 620 for the full network. Although the focused network took a bit longer to learn, this difference was not statistically reliable ($t(28) = 0.958$, $p > 0.3$). Figure 7 shows a typical weight configuration obtained by the focused network and its response to **ABC**. The weights are quite interesting. It appears that each context unit handles a particular symbol. For example, context unit 3 (the top row of the weight arrays) is excited by both **A** in the input and **A** as the previous output, and it has the effect of inhibiting **A** on the output. Similarly, context unit 2 is tuned to **C** and unit 1 to **B**.

The sequence reproduction task becomes more difficult to learn as the delay between input and playback is increased. In the above example, the delay was one time step. Simulations were also run at a four-time-step delay. Training continued until performance was perfect, up to a maximum of 15,000 epochs. The focused network was able to learn the task perfectly on 12 of 15 runs, the full network on only 2 of 15. Mean performance over all runs following training was 98.5% for the focused network, but only 72.9% for the full. This difference was significant ($t(28) = 8.42$, $p < 0.001$).

Increasing the playback delay increases the time lag between the critical input information and the start of the response. The full network appears able to learn only when the critical input shortly precedes the response, whereas the focused network is able to learn with extended time lags. This conclusion was also suggested by the regular verb results.

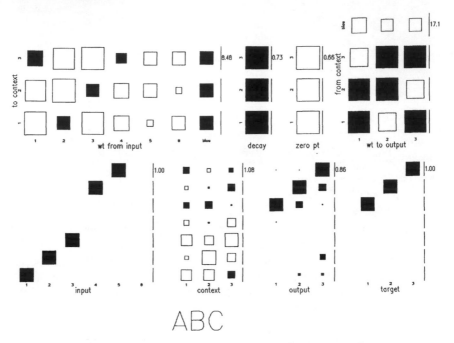

Figure 7. The sequence reproduction problem. The upper half of the figure shows learned weights in the focused network, the lower half shows input, context, output, and target activity over time for the sequence **ABC**. The sequence-to-be-reproduced is encoded on input units 1–3; the quantized output from the previous time step is encoded on input units 4–6.

Large Verb Simulation

To study a more difficult task, the regular-verb categorization problem was extended to a larger corpus of verbs. As before, the task was to classify each verb according to the manner in which its past tense is formed. The complexity of the task was increased by including both regular and irregular verbs, 136 training instances altogether, and a total of 13 response categories, 3 for regular forms and 10 for irregular. The response categories and number of training instances in each category are listed in Table 4. The categories are based loosely on a set suggested by Bybee and Slobin (1982).

The corpus of verbs was borrowed from a psychological model of Rumelhart and McClelland (1986) designed to account for children's acquisition of verb past tenses. This model would produce the past tense of a verb given its infinitive form as input. The representation used as both input and output from the model is a Wickelement encoding of the verb, each Wickelement encoding a particular

TABLE 4
Verb Classification

Category Number	Instances in Category	Examples	Category (How Past Tense is Formed)
1	20	explain (explained) cry (cried)	regular verb, add /d/
2	20	dance (danced) pack (packed)	regular verb, add /t/
3	20	reflect (reflected) guide (guided)	regular verb, add /^d/
4	7	beat (beat) put (put)	no change
5	3	send (sent) build (built)	change a final /d/ to /t/
6	8	deal (dealt) mean (meant)	internal vowel change and add a final /t/
7	6	do (did) sell (sold)	internal vowel change and add a final /d/
8	5	bring (brought) teach (taught)	internal vowel change, delete final consonant, and add a final /t/
9	5	have (had) make (made)	internal vowel change, delete final consonant, and add a final /d/
10	4	swim (swam) ring (rang)	internal vowel change of /i/ to /a/
11	17	feed (fed) get (got)	internal vowel change and stem ends in a dental
12	20	begin (begun) break (broke)	other internal vowel change
13	1	go (went)	go in a category by itself

phonetic feature in the context of two neighboring phonetic features. Because this static representation is built into the model, the model did not require temporal dynamics. My interest in studying this problem was to see whether the focused recurrent network could, given time-varying inputs, learn the task. Because the focused architecture is tailored to learning Wickelement representations, if it is able to learn the task then it must have learned a static representation somewhat like the Wickelement representation presupposed by Rumelhart and McClelland's model.

The task is difficult. The verb classes contain some internal regularities, but these regularities are too weak to be used to uniquely classify a verb. For instance, all verbs in category 3 end in a /d/ or /t/, but so do verbs in categories 4, 5, and 11. Whether a verb ending in /d/ or /t/ belongs in category 3 or one of the other categories depends on whether it is regular, but there are no simple features signaling this fact. Further, fine discriminations are necessary because two outwardly similar verbs can be classified into different categories. *Swim* and *sing* belong to category 10, but *swing* to category 12; *ring* belongs to category 10, but *bring* to category 8; *set* belongs to category 4, but *get* to category 11. Finally, the task is difficult because some verbs belong in multiple response categories; for example, *sit* could go in either category 10 or 11. The lowest category number was chosen in these cases.

Because the category to which a verb belongs is somewhat arbitrary, the network must memorize a large number of special cases. (Indeed, an earlier version of these simulations were run in which the target responses were incorrect for about 15% of the items. The network learned the task just as well, if not a bit faster than in the simulations reported here.)

The network architecture was similar to that used in the regular verb example. The input layer was a two-phoneme buffer, and the encoding of phonemes was the same as before. The output layer consisted of 13 units, one for each verb class. Both focused and full network architectures were simulated. To match the two networks on number of connections, 25 context units were used in the focused network, 16 in the full; this resulted in 613 weights for the focused network and 621 for the full network.

Figure 8 shows performance on the training set for the two architectures,

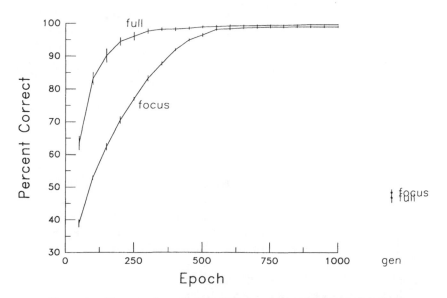

Figure 8.   Mean performance on the large verb problem as a function of learning epoch for the focused and full recurrent architectures. The bars indicate one standard error of the mean in each direction. Data points for generalization performance are shown on the far right.

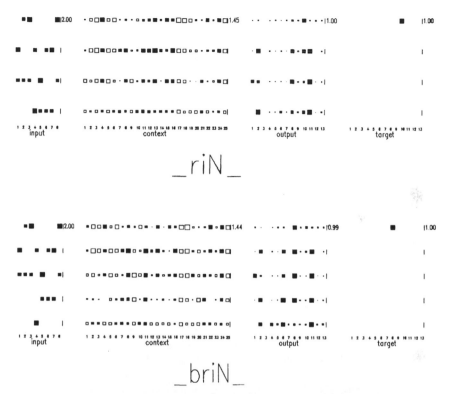

Figure 9.   The large verb task. The upper portion of the figure shows input, context, output, and target activity over time for the sequence _riN_ (*ring*), the lower portion for the sequence _briN_ (*bring*).

averaged over 10 runs with different initial random weights. A verb is considered to have been categorized correctly if the most active output unit specifies the verb's class. Both focused and full networks are able to learn the task, although the full network learns somewhat more quickly. Errors observed during training seemed quite reasonable. Verbs are sometimes "overregularized," as when *eat* becomes *eated*. Overgeneralization occurs in other respects, as when *sit* was misclassified in category 4—verbs whose past tense is the same as the root— presumably by analogy to *hit* and *fit* and *set*. Surprisingly, neither the full nor focused net had difficulty learning category 13, although it contained only a single verb—*go*.

Generalization performance on novel sequences is poor for both networks (data points on far right of Figure 8), but this is readily explained. The corpus provided by Rumelhart and McClelland had 420 verbs altogether. To normalize across categories, at most 20 verbs from each category were used in the training set. Consequently, the regular verb classes were approximately the same size as the irregular classes, eliminating any a priori bias toward classifying an unfamiliar verb as regular. The verbs from the corpus not used in training were used for generalization testing; these verbs were almost exclusively from the three regular verb categories. Thus, the network attempted to classify the unfamiliar regular verbs without any expectation that the verbs would be regular. Most all errors involved mistaking the verbs to be irregular.

Typical responses of the network are presented in Figure 9. The two sequences shown, _riN_ (*ring*) and _briN_ (*bring*), have quite similar input patterns yet produce different outputs: _riN_ belongs in category 10 and _briN_ in category 8. Due to the size of the network, interpreting the behavior of individual context units and how they serve to distinguish two inputs like _riN_ and _briN_ is extremely difficult.

EVALUATION OF THE FOCUSED ARCHITECTURE

The simulations reported above are typical of results I have obtained with the full and focused architectures. For both architectures, learning becomes more difficult as the delay between the critical input and the response is increased. This was observed in two simulations: the regular verbs and the sequence reproduction task. While this difficulty is manifested in slowed learning for the focused architecture, its effect on the full architecture is far more devastating. The full architecture is simply unable to learn tasks that involve long intervals between critical input and response. Not all tasks are of this nature, however. For tasks in which the information contained in the input is more evenly distributed across time (e.g., the large verb simulation), the full network appears to learn in fewer training cycles when full and focused networks are matched on total number of connections.

Nonetheless, the focused architecture shows advantages over two competing approaches: the back propagation unfolding-in-time procedure and the real-time recurrent learning (RTRL) algorithm of Williams and Zipser (1989, this volume). Learning in the focused architecture is less computation intensive than the unfolding-in-time procedure because back propagation of the error signal in time is avoided. The focused architecture requires about two-thirds as many floating-point operations per training cycle as the unfolding-in-time procedure. This savings is achieved whether the network is implemented in serial or parallel hardware. Although the focused architecture turns out to be a special case of the RTRL algorithm, the space requirements of the more general RTRL algorithm are far worse. In RTRL, the number of internal state variables grows with the cube of the number of units, whereas in the focused architecture the number of internal state variables grows with only the product of the numbers of input and context units.

Scaling Properties

A critical question to be asked of any network architecture is how well its performance will scale as the problem size increases. The focused architecture promises to scale better than the full architecture with respect to the sequence length. The reasoning is as follows. As I discussed previously, any recurrent architecture (e.g., Figure 2a) can be unfolded in time to obtain a computationally equivalent feedforward network (Figure 2b). The *depth* of this unfolded network increases with sequence length. However, an unfolded version of the focused architecture can be constructed with a fixed depth and a *breadth* that increases with sequence length (Figure 10). The input units and context units are replicated for each time step of the sequence. Each set of context units is activated solely by the input at the corresponding time step. In the third layer of the network, the net activity of context unit i is computed by taking a weighted sum of unit i's activity at each time τ from $\tau - 1, \ldots, t$. This simple summation is possible because the integration of context unit activity over time is linear. That is, the context unit activation equation

$$c_i(t) = d_i c_i(t - 1) + s[net_i(t)] \qquad (1)$$

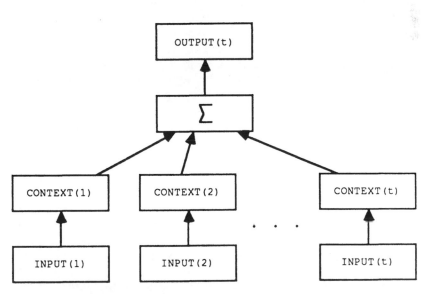

Figure 10. An unfolded version of the focused architecture having four layers. Input and context units are replicated for each time step of the input sequence. The activity of each context unit is summed over time in the third layer, weighted by a time-dependent decay factor.

can be rewritten in closed form as

$$c_i(t) = \sum_{\tau=1}^{t} d_i^{t-\tau} s[net_i(\tau)].$$

Each set of units in the second layer of Figure 10 computes $s[net_i(\tau)]$. The third layer then sums the $s[net_i(\tau)]$ across τ, weighted by the decay factor $d_i^{t-\tau}$, to obtain $c_i(t)$.

Consider the situation when all d_i are near 1.0, as they are set at the start of a simulation. Information from all times will be integrated with equal weight; no matter when in time an input appears, it will be treated uniformly. If the desired response of the network depends on a critical input at a particular time, it will not matter when in time this input occurs. Further, increasing the length of a sequence serves only to add background noise against which the critical input must be detected.[5]

To recap, longer sequences translate to a greater effective depth of the full architecture, but a greater effective breadth of the focused architecture. As I argued earlier, one has reason to suspect that deep and narrow networks are more troublesome for back propagation than shallow and wide ones. If so, the focused network should scale better with respect to sequence length.

Indeed, comparisons of the full and focused architectures reported here can be interpreted as support for this claim. Consider the regular verb example. When the verbs are presented unreversed, only the final sequence element is critical for classification. Thus, although the unfolded full network may have as many layers as sequence elements, the *effective* depth to which the network must attend is quite shallow. Reversing the verbs increases the effective depth. The comparison of unreversed and reversed verbs in the full network is therefore a test of scaling as the effective depth increases; the same comparison in the focused network is a test of scaling as the effective breadth increases. In this case, greater depth is clearly more detrimental than greater breadth.

The focused and full networks differ along two dimensions. The focused network has 1-1 connections in the context layer and the context unit activation function is linear; the full network has complete connectivity in the context layer and a nonlinear context unit integration function (one in which the recurrent connections are contained within the squashing function). The depth-versus-breadth result is contingent on linear integration, not on 1-1 connections within the context layer. As discussed earlier, several researchers have examined a third architecture with 1-1 connections and nonlinear integration. This architecture does not seem to perform well, as one might predict on the basis of the nonlinear

---

[5]Note that if the decay terms become much less or greater than 1.0, there becomes a bias toward recent or distant information, respectively. It is thus important to start the system with initial decay terms near 1.0 and to change them slowly.

integration function. Note that we have not yet explored a fourth and potentially promising architecture, one with complete connectivity in the context layer and a linear integration function.

Problems with the Approach

Despite reasonable success with the focused architecture, some difficulties should be pointed out. First, instability problems arise if the decay values become larger than 1.0 because such values allow a unit's activity to grow exponentially over time. In practice, this is not a serious problem as long as learning rates for the decay connections are kept small. Nonetheless, the final activity levels of the context units can become ridiculously large, particularly on generalization testing if the novel patterns are longer than the training patterns. For example, in the reversed regular verb problem, generalization testing occasionally produced context unit activity levels above 25. One possible solution is to constrain the allowed values of the decay connections. I have tried restricting the allowed values to the interval 0–1. Generally, this restriction increases the number of learning trials required, but does improve stability and generalization performance.

A second criticism of the focused architecture is that it uses an input buffer. This buffer was motivated by the desire to train context units to respond to Wickelements, but is not strictly necessary. Without a buffer, though, the context units are unable to obtain nonlinear interactions across time. For instance, a single unit cannot be tuned to respond sharply to input **A** followed by input **B** but not to either **A** or **B** in isolation. No matter, the buffer used in the focused architecture is altogether different from that required by the naive buffer model presented in the introduction. The buffer in the buffer model specifies a temporal window over which information integration can occur, whereas the focused architecture's buffer specifies a temporal window over which nonlinear interactions can occur. The focused architecture will generally not need as large a buffer as the buffer model. For example, the past-tense network had only a two-slot buffer, whereas a buffer model would likely require as many slots as there are phonemes in the longest verb.

A final difficulty with the focused architecture is that, while it may be appropriate for relatively short sequences, it is unclear how well the approach will work on long sequences in which very little information is contained in a single sequence element, such as a speech recognition task with the time-domain waveform as input. Of course, this sort of problem is difficult for the full architecture as well. One solution is to extend the buffer size to capture significant segments of the input. It would seem a more promising solution, however, to preprocess the input in some manner, perhaps using unsupervised learning mechanisms, to obtain higher-order features which could then be fed into the recognition system.

APPENDIX: DERIVATION OF THE FOCUSED BACK-PROPAGATION ALGORITHM

Assume the following situation: a t-time-step sequence has been presented and at time t a desired output is specified that allows for the computation of an error signal. The problem is to determine two quantities: the error gradient with respect to the recurrent connections ($\partial E/\partial d_i$) and with respect to the input-context connections ($\partial E/\partial w_{ji}$).

Beginning with the recurrent connections, the chain rule can be used to expand $\partial E/\partial d_i$:

$$\frac{\partial E}{\partial d_i} = \frac{\partial E}{\partial c_i(t)} \frac{\partial c_i(t)}{\partial d_i},$$

and $\partial E/\partial c_i(t)$ can be computed directly by back-propagating from the output layer to the context layer at time t. Thus, the problem is to determine $\partial c_i(t)/\partial d_i$. Given that

$$c_i(t) = d_i c_i(t - 1) + s[net_i(t)] \tag{A.1}$$

and

$$net_i(\tau) \equiv \sum_k w_{ki} x_k(\tau) \tag{A.2}$$

(Equation 1 from the main text), and assuming the initial condition $c_i(0) = 0$, the difference equation (A.1) can be rewritten in closed form as

$$c_i(t) = \sum_{\tau=1}^{t} d_i^{t-\tau} s[net_i(\tau)]. \tag{A.3}$$

Defining

$$\alpha_i(t) \equiv \frac{\partial c_i(t)}{\partial d_i}.$$

by substituting $c_i(t)$ from Equation A.3 and computing the partial derivative, we obtain

$$\alpha_i(t) = \frac{\partial}{\partial d_i} \left[\sum_{\tau=1}^{t} d_i^{t-\tau} s[net_i(\tau)] \right]$$

$$= \sum_{\tau=1}^{t-1} (t - \tau) d_i^{t-\tau-1} s[net_i(\tau)]. \tag{A.4}$$

Regrouping the terms gives

$$\alpha_i(t) = \sum_{k=1}^{t-1} \sum_{\tau=1}^{k} d_i^{t-\tau-1} s(net_i(\tau))]$$

$$= \sum_{k=1}^{t-1} d_i^{t-k-1} \sum_{\tau=1}^{k} d_i^{k-\tau} s[net_i(\tau)]. \tag{A.5}$$

Combining Equations A.3 and A.5, we have

$$\alpha_i(t) = \sum_{k=1}^{t-1} d_i^{t-k-1} c_i(k).$$

Removing the $k = t - 1$ term from the summation and factoring out d_i, we obtain

$$\alpha_i(t) = c_i(t - 1) + d_i \sum_{k=1}^{t-2} d_i^{t-k-2} c_i(k). \tag{A.6}$$

From Equation A.4, the summation in Equation A.6 can be replaced by $\alpha_i(t - 1)$ to yield the incremental expression:

$$\alpha_i(t) = c_i(t - 1) + d_i\alpha_i(t - 1).$$

Following a similar derivation for the input-context connections, we can expand $\partial E/\partial w_{ji}$:

$$\frac{\partial E}{\partial w_{ji}} = \frac{\partial E}{\partial c_i(t)} \frac{\partial c_i(t)}{\partial w_{ji}}.$$

As stated, $\partial E/\partial c_i(t)$ can be computed directly by back-propagating from the output layer to the context layer at time t. Thus, the problem is to determine $\partial c_i(t)/\partial w_{ji}$. Defining

$$\beta_{ji}(t) \equiv \frac{\partial c_i(t)}{\partial w_{ji}},$$

by substituting $c_i(t)$ from Equation A.3 and computing the partial derivative, we obtain

$$\beta_{ji}(t) = \frac{\partial}{\partial w_{ji}} \left[\sum_{\tau=1}^{t} d_i^{t-\tau} s[net_i(\tau)] \right].$$

Using Equation A.2 to compute the derivative of $s[net_i(\tau)]$ gives

$$\beta_{ji}(t) = \sum_{\tau=1}^{t} d_i^{t-\tau} s'[net_i(\tau)]x_j(\tau). \tag{A.7}$$

Removing the $\tau = t$ term from the summation and factoring out d_i, we obtain

$$\beta_{ji}(t) = s'[net_i(t)]x_j(t) + d_i \sum_{\tau=1}^{t-1} d_i^{t-\tau-1} s'[net_i(\tau)]x_j(\tau). \qquad (A.8)$$

From Equation A.7, the summation in Equation A.8 can be replaced by $\beta_{ji}(t - 1)$ to yield the incremental expression

$$\beta_{ji}(t) = s'[net_i(t)]x_j(t) + d_i\beta_{ji}(t - 1).$$

ACKNOWLEDGMENTS

Thanks to Jeff Elman, Yoshiro Miyata, Yves Chauvin, and Geoff Hinton for their insightful comments and assistance. The graphical displays of network states are due to Yoshiro's code. Dave Rumelhart and Jay McClelland were kind enough to provide me with the phonological encoding and classification of verbs from their simulation work. This research was supported by NSF Presidential Young Investigator award IRI-9058450 and grant 90-21 from the James S. McDonnell Foundation, as well as grant 87-2-36 from the Alfred P. Sloan Foundation to Geoffrey Hinton.

REFERENCES

Almeida, L. (1987). A learning rule for asynchronous perceptions with feedback in a combinatorial environment. In M. Caudill & C. Butler (Eds.), *Proceedings of the IEEE First Annual International Conference on Neural Networks* (Vol. 2, pp. 609–618). San Diego, CA: IEEE Publishing Services.

Bachrach, J. (1988). *Learning to represent time.* Unpublished master's thesis, University of Massachusetts, Amherst.

Bybee, J. L., & Slobin, D. I. (1982). Rules and schemas in the development and use of the English past tense. *Language, 58,* 265–289.

Elman, J. L. (1990). Finding structure in time. *Cognitive Science, 14,* 179–212.

Elman, J. L., & McClelland, J. L. (1986). Exploiting lawful variability in the speech wave. In J. S. Perkell & D. H. Klatt (Eds.), *Invariance and variability in speech processes* (pp. 360–380). Hillsdale, NJ: Lawrence Erlbaum Associates.

Elman, J. L., & Zipser, D. (1988). Learning the hidden structure of speech. *Journal of the Acoustical Society of America, 83,* 1615–1625.

Freyd, J. (1987). Dynamic mental representations. *Psychological Review, 94,* 427–438.

Gori, M., Bengio, Y., & Mori, R. de (1989). BPS: A learning algorithm for capturing the dynamic nature of speech. In *Proceedings of the First International Joint Conference on Neural Networks* (Vol. 2, pp. 417–423).

Hinton, G. (1987). Learning distributed representations of concepts. In *Proceedings of the Eighth Annual Conference of the Cognitive Science Society* (pp. 1–12). Hillsdale, NJ: Lawrence Erlbaum Associates.

Hinton, G. (1989). Connectionist learning procedures. *Artificial Intelligence, 40,* 185–234.

Jordan, M. I. (1987). Attractor dynamics and parallelism in a connectionist sequential machine. In *Proceedings of the Eighth Annual Conference of the Cognitive Science Society* (pp. 531–546). Hillsdale, NJ: Lawrence Erlbaum Associates.

Landauer, T. K., Kamm, C. A., & Singhal, S. (1987). Teaching a minimally structured back propagation network to recognize speech. In *Proceedings of the Ninth Annual Conference of the Cognitive Science Society* (pp. 531–536). Hillsdale, NJ: Lawrence Erlbaum Associates.

Lang, K. (1987). *Connectionist speech recognition*. Unpublished Ph.D. thesis proposal, Carnegie-Mellon University, Pittsburgh, PA.

Lapedes, A., & Farber, R. (1987). *Nonlinear signal processing using neural networks* (Report No. LA-UR-87-2662). Los Alamos, NM.

McClelland, J. L., & Elman, J. L. (1986). Interactive processes in speech perception: The TRACE model. In J. L. McClelland & D. E. Rumelhart (Eds.), *Parallel distributed processing: Explorations in the microstructure of cognition. Volume II: Psychological and biological models* (pp. 58–121). Cambridge, MA: MIT Press.

Miyata, Y. (1988). *The learning and planning of actions* (ICS Technical Report 8802). La Jolla, CA: University of California, San Diego, Institute for Cognitive Science.

Mozer, M. C. (1990). Discovering faithful "Wickelfeature" representations in a connectionist network. In *Proceedings of the 12th Annual Conference of the Cognitive Science Society* (pp. 356–363). Hillsdale, NJ: Lawrence Erlbaum Associates.

Mozer, M. C. (1991). *The perception of multiple objects: A connectionist approach*. Cambridge, MA: MIT Press/Bradford Books.

Pineda, F. (1987). Generalization of back propagation to recurrent neural networks. *Physical Review Letters, 19,* 2229–2232.

Plaut, D. C., Nowlan, S., & Hinton, G. E. (1986). *Experiments on learning by back propagation* (Technical report CMU-CS-86-126). Pittsburgh, PA: Carnegie-Mellon University, Department of Computer Science.

Rumelhart, D. E., Hinton, G. E., & Williams, R. J. (1986). Learning internal representations by error propagation. In D. E. Rumelhart & J. L. McClelland (Eds.), *Parallel distributed processing: Explorations in the microstructure of cognition. Volume I: Foundations* (pp. 318–362). Cambridge, MA: MIT Press/Bradford Books.

Rumelhart, D. E., & McClelland, J. L. (1986). On learning the past tenses of English verbs. In J. L. McClelland & D. E. Rumelhart (Eds.), *Parallel distributed processing: Explorations in the microstructure of cognition. Volume II: Psychological and biological models* (pp. 216–271). Cambridge, MA: MIT Press/Bradford Books.

Seidenberg, M. S. (1990). Word recognition and naming: A computational model and its implications. In W. D. Marslen-Wilson (Ed.), *Lexical representation and process.* Cambridge, MA: MIT Press.

Sejnowski, T. J., & Rosenberg, C. R. (1987). Parallel networks that learn to pronounce English text. *Complex Systems, 1,* 145–168.

Smolensky, P. (1983). Schema selection and stochastic inference in modular environments. In *Proceedings of the Sixth Annual Conference on Artificial Intelligence AAAI-83* (pp. 109–113).

Stornetta, W. S., Hogg, T., & Huberman, B. A. (1987). A dynamical approach to temporal pattern processing. In *Proceedings of the IEEE Conference on Neural Information Processing Systems.*

Tank, D., & Hopfield, J. (1987). *Proceedings of the National Academy of Sciences, 84,* 1896.

Waibel, A., Hanazawa, T., Hinton, G., Shikano, K., & Lang, K. (1987). *Phoneme recognition using time-delay neural networks* (Technical report TR-1-0006). Japan: ATR Interpreting Telephony Research Labs.

Watrous, R. L., & Shastri, L. (1987). Learning acoustic features from speech data using connectionist networks. In *Proceedings of the Ninth Annual Conference of the Cognitive Science Society* (pp. 518–530). Hillsdale, NJ: Lawrence Erlbaum Associates.

Wickelgren, W. (1969). Context-sensitive coding, associative memory, and serial order in (speech) behavior. *Psychological Review, 76,* 1–15.

Williams, R. J., & Zipser, D. (1989). A learning algorithm for continually running fully recurrent neural networks. *Neural Computation, 1,* 270–280.

6 Nonlinear Control with Neural Networks

Derrick H. Nguyen
and Bernard Widrow
Department of Electrical Engineering, Stanford University

ABSTRACT

Neural networks can be used to solve highly nonlinear control problems. This chapter shows how a neural network can learn of its own accord to control a nonlinear dynamic system. An emulator, a multilayered neural network, learns to identify the system's dynamic characteristics. The controller, another multilayered neural network, next learns to control the emulator. The self-trained controller is then used to control the actual dynamic system. The learning process continues as the emulator and controller improve and track the physical process. Two examples are given to illustrate these ideas. A neural network is trained to control an inverted pendulum on a cart. This is a self-learning "broom-balancer." The "truck backer-upper," a neural network controller steering a trailer truck while backing up to a loading dock, is also demonstrated. The controller is able to guide the truck to the dock from almost any initial position. The technique explored here should be applicable to a wide variety of nonlinear control problems.

INTRODUCTION

Layered neural networks adapted by means of the back propagation algorithm discovered by Rumelhart, Hinton, and Williams (1986), Parker (1985), and Werbos (1974) are powerful tools for pattern recognition, associative memory, and adaptive filtering. In this chapter, adaptive neural networks will be used to solve nonlinear adaptive control problems that are very difficult to solve with conventional methods. The methodology shows promise for application to control problems that are so complex that analytical design techniques do not exist

171

and may not exist for some time to come. Neural networks can be used to implement highly nonlinear controllers with weights or internal parameters that can be determined by a self-learning process.

THE CONTROL PROBLEM

The standard representation of a finite-dimensional discrete-time plant is shown in Figure 1. The vector u_k represents the inputs to the plant at time k and the vector z_k represents the state of the plant at time k. The function $A(z_k, u_k)$ maps the current inputs and state into the next state. When the plant is linear, the usual state equation holds, where F and G are matrices:

$$z_{k+1} = A(z_k, u_k) = Fz_k + Gu_k. \tag{1}$$

The function $A(z_k, u_k)$ would be nonlinear for a nonlinear plant.

A common problem in control is to provide the correct input vector to drive a nonlinear plant from an initial state to a subsequent desired state z_d. The typical approach used in solving this problem involves linearizing the plant around a number of operating points, building linear state-space models of the plant at these operating points, and then building a controller which employs state feed-back to control the plant. Another approach involves open-loop optimal control as described by Bryson and Ho (1975). In this approach, an objective function measuring the performance of the system is defined, and the set of u_k that minimizes this function is analytically computed. These approaches are usually computationally intensive and requires considerable design effort.

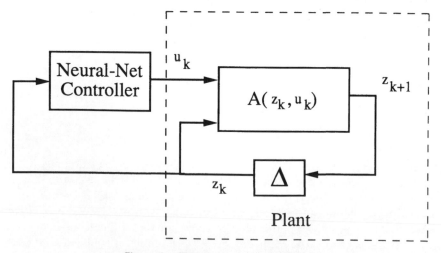

Figure 1. The plant and the controller.

In this presentation, the objective is to train a controller, in this case a neural network, to produce the correct signal u_k to drive the plant to the desired state z_d given the current state of the plant z_k (Figure 1). Each value of u_k over time plays a part in determining the state of the plant. Knowing the desired state, however, does not easily yield information about the values of u_k that would be required to achieve it.

A number of different approaches for training a controller have been described in the literature. They include reinforcement learning, which has been explored by Widrow, Gupta, and Maitra (1973), by Barto, Sutton, and Anderson (1983), and by Anderson (1989), inverse control, which has been explored by Widrow (1986) and by Psaltis, Sideris, and Yamamura (1988), and optimal control, which has been explored by Psaltis et al. (1988) and by Jordan (1988). The architecture and training algorithms presented in this chapter are novel in that they require little guidance from the designer to solve the control problem. This approach uses neural networks in optimal control by training the controller to maximize a performance function. The approach is different from Psaltis et al. (1988) in that the plant can be an unknown plant and plant identification is a part of the algorithm. A similar approach has been used by Widrow and Stearns (1985), Widrow (1986), and Jordan (1988).

SINGLE-STAGE CONTROLLERS

Given that the plant is in state z_k and that the objective is to drive it to the desired state z_d, it is simplest to train the controller to produce u_k so that the plant's next state z_{k+1} will be close to z_d. Therefore, we would like to minimize the error function C, where $E(\cdot)$ denotes an average and C is averaged over the set of possible starting states z_k:

$$C = E(\|z_d - z_{k+1}\|^2) \qquad (2)$$

A controller trained in this fashion is called a single-stage controller since it tries to make the next state z_{k+1} as close as possible to the desired state. The fact that the controller's output u_k will also affect the state of the plant after time $k + 1$ is ignored by the algorithm.

Plant Identification—Training the Plant Emulator

Before training the neural net controller, it is useful to train a separate neural net to behave like the plant. Specifically, the neural net is trained to emulate $A(z_k, u_k)$. The purpose of training this emulator will be explained later. Training the emulator is similar to plant identification in control theory, except that the plant identification here (Figure 2) is done automatically by a neural network capable of modeling nonlinear plants.

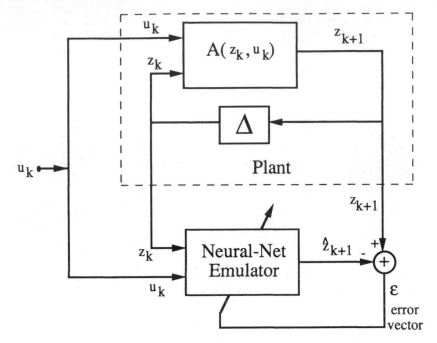

Figure 2.   Training the neural net plant emulator.

In this chapter we assume that the states of the plant are directly observable without noise. A neural net with as many outputs as there are states, and as many inputs as there are states plus plant inputs, is created. The number of layers in the neural net and the number of nodes in each layer are presently determined empirically since they depend on the degree of nonlinearity of the plant.

In Figure 2, the training process begins with the plant in an initial state. The plant inputs are randomly generated. At time k, the input of the neural net is set equal to the current state of the plant z_k and the plant input u_k. The neural net is trained by back propagation to predict the next state of the plant, with the value of the next state of the plant z_{k+1} used as the desired response during training. This process is roughly analogous to the steps that would be taken by a human designer to identify the plant. In this case, however, the plant identification is done automatically by a neural network. The neural network emulator is pre-sented here is analogous to the mental model of Rumelhart and the forward model of Jordan (1988).

Training the Neural Network Controller

After the plant emulator has been trained, we use it for the purpose of training the controller. The training process starts with the plant and the neural net plant emulator in a state z_k. The initially untrained controller will output a control signal u_k to the plant, and the plant moves to the next state z_{k+1}. To train the controller, we need to know the error in the controller output u_k. Unfortunately, only the error in the plant state, $z_d - z_{k+1}$, is available. However, since the controller and the emulator are connected in series, they may be considered to be a single network. Therefore, the plant error $z_d - z_{k+1}$ may be propagated through the plant emulator (while keeping the weights of the emulator fixed) to get an error for the controller. This error is then used to update the weights of the controller by using the back-propagation algorithm. The emulator in a sense translates the error in the final plant state to the error in the controller output. The real plant cannot be used here because the error cannot be propagated through it. This is why the neural network emulator is needed.

An Example: The Inverted Pendulum (the Broom-Balancer)

The inverted pendulum on a cart problem (Figure 3) is used here to illustrate the approach. This is a standard problem that has been used by many researchers in the field of neural control in the past. In this problem, the goal is to design a controller to move a cart so that an inverted pendulum mounted on the cart stays vertical. For now, to keep the problem simple, the position of the cart is not controlled. To make the problem nonlinear, a "bang-bang" controller is used. The controller is only allowed to push the cart with maximum force to the left or to the right. This is accomplished by placing a hard quantizer between the

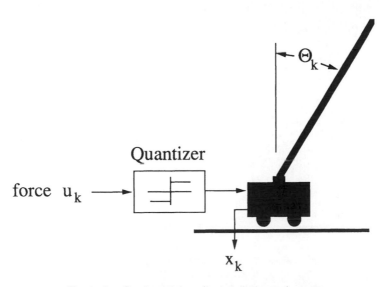

Figure 3. Cart/pendulum (broom-balancer) system.

controller and the cart/pendulum system. This quantizer is considered to be part of the plant in the algorithm described earlier. A linear controller is also possible. We have trained such a controller with the algorithm, and it learned much more quickly than the bang-bang controller.

For this example, the cart/pendulum system is simulated on a digital computer. The mass of the cart and of the pendulum are 1.0 kg and 0.1 kg, respectively, and the length of the pendulum is 1.0 m. The frictional force due the motion of the cart is proportional to its velocity with a proportional constant of 0.0005 N-s/m. The controller is allowed to push on the cart with a force of 10 N to either the left or the right. The cart position x is constrained to be between -1.4 and 1.4 m. A trial is started by placing the cart at the center of the track and the pendulum vertical, and a crash occurs when the magnitude of the pendulum angle θ exceeds 40° or when the cart runs out of track ($|x| \geq 1.4$). When a crash occurs, the trial is stopped, the cart and the pendulum are reset to their initial positions, and the next trial is initiated. The controller neural net is given the current state and it computes a new control signal every 0.03 sec.

In this problem, the state vector z_k consists of four variables: the position of the cart x, the velocity of the cart $\dot{x}$, the angular position of the pendulum θ, and the angular velocity of the pendulum $\dot{\theta}$. The values of these variables completely describe the state of the system at any moment in time. The cart position x is measured from the center of the track, and the pendulum θ is measured from

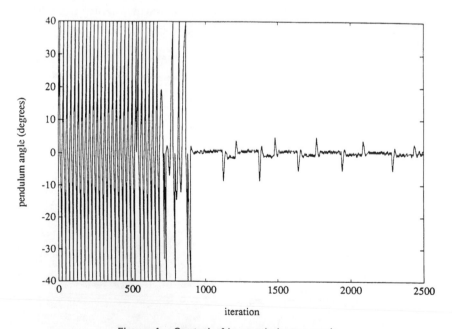

Figure 4.   Control of broom-balancer angle.

vertical. The state variables and the force input to the plant are all scaled so that they are roughly between -1 and 1 before being fed into the neural networks.

The plant-emulator neural net has five inputs and it contains two layers of adaptive weights, six units in the hidden layer, and four units in the output layer. It is trained for about 40,000 iterations to emulate the real plant as described before. During this training process, the force input to the plant is generated randomly and uniformly between -10 and 10 N.

After the emulator has been trained, its weights are fixed and the controller neural net is trained to keep the pendulum vertical, that is, to keep its angle as close as possible to zero. The controller is a single adaptive unit with four inputs. Figure 4 shows the pendulum angle θ as functions of time during training. Note that the pendulum angle stays closer to zero as training time increases. The lengths of the trials remain relatively short, however, even after large training time, because the cart eventually runs into the ends of the track and the trial is stopped. Recall that the position of the cart x is not controlled.

THE MULTISTAGE NEURAL NETWORK CONTROLLER

For the cart/pendulum experiment the neural network controller was trained to keep the pendulum as vertical as possible ($\theta_{desired} = 0$), but not to control the other three state variables, the cart position and the velocities. Because of this, the cart wanders away from center of the track and eventually crashes into the ends.

One may expect that incorporating the desired response $x_{desired} = 0$ into the training process would improve performance since the controller would try to keep the cart near the center and the pendulum vertical, and the system would never crash. Unfortunately this does not work. The controller will never learn to do this even after long training.

The problem is that we are trying to drive two state variables, x_{k+1} and θ_{k+1}, to their desired values by adjusting the parameter u_k. However, in general it is impossible to control x_{k+1} and θ_{k+1} by choosing a single parameter u_k because there are not enough degrees of freedom to satisfy the requirements.

To circumvent this problem, we need to train the controller to look farther ahead. It will control x_{k+2} and θ_{k+2} by adjusting u_k and u_{k+1}. Note that x_{k+1} and θ_{k+1} take on values as they will as we control x_{k+2} and θ_{k+2}. (We may think of this as training the network to be more "farsighted." It may make a move that is bad in the near term but good in the long run.)

In general, if a plant has M state variables of which K are to be controlled, then it will take at least K time steps to bring them to their desired values if the plant is linear. If nonlinearities exist, more time steps may be required. The training algorithm will need to adjust the controller to outputs a series of K control signals u_k and to sense only the plant state at the end to compute the final plant state error. It then uses this error to adjust the weights of the controller. A controller trained in this fashion is called a multistage controller after Bryson and Ho (1975).

Training the Neural Network Controller

Before training the controller, we train a neural network to emulate the plant we have described. Given that the emulator closely matches the plant dynamics, we use it for the purpose of training the controller. The controller learns to drive the plant emulator from an initial state z_0 to the desired state z_d in K time steps. Learning takes place during many trials or runs, each starting from an initial state and terminating at a final state z_K. The objective of the learning process is to find a set of controller weights which minimizes the error function C, where C is averaged over the set of initial states z_0:

$$C = E(\|z_d - z_K|^2),\tag{3}$$

The training process for the controller is illustrated in Figure 5. The training process starts with the neural net plant emulator set in a random initial state z_0. Because the neural net controller is initially untrained, it will output an erroneous control signal u_0 to the plant emulator and to the plant itself. The plant emulator will then move to the next state z_1, and this process continues for K time steps. At this point the plant is in the state z_K (Note that the number of time steps K is problem dependent and needs to be determined by the designer.)

We now would like to modify the weights in the controller network so that the square error $(z_d - z_K)^2$ will be less at the end of the next run. To train the controller, we need to know the error in the controller output u_k for each time step

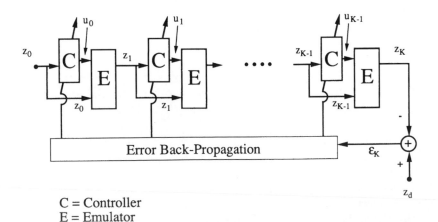

C = Controller
E = Emulator

Figure 5.   Training the controller.

k. Unfortunately, only the error in the final plant state, $z_d - z_K$, is available. Just as in the case of the single-stage controller, we can back-propagate the final plant error $z_d - z_K$ through the plant emulator to get an equivalent error for the controller in the Kth stage and use this error to train the controller. We then continue to back propagate the error through all K stages of the run, and the controller's weight change is computed for each stage. The weight changes from all the stages obtained from the back-propagation algorithm are added together and then added to the controller's weights. This completes the training for one run. (This method of breaking the feedback and unfolding the network in time has been explored for noncontrol applications by Rumelhart et al. (1986). See also the chapter in this book by Williams and Zipser.)

The algorithm described would require saving all the weight changes so that they can be added to the original weights at the end of the run. In practice, for simplicity's sake, the weight changes are added immediately to the weights as they are computed. This does not significantly affect the final result, since the weight changes are small and do not affect the controller's weights very much after one run. It is their accumulated effects over a large number of runs that improve the controller's performance.

Figure 5 represents the controller training process. For reasons of clarity, the details of error back propagation are not illustrated there, but are described above. Because the training algorithm is essentially an implementation of gradient descent, local minima in the error function may yield suboptimal results. In practice, however, a good solution is almost always achieved by using a large number of adaptive units in the hidden layers of the neural networks.

We will show two examples to illustrate the approach: a neural truck backer-upper and a broom-balancer that centers the cart as well as keeps the pendulum vertical.

An Example: The Truck Backer-Upper

The first example involves training a neural network to steer a truck while it backs up to a loading dock. Backing a trailer truck to a loading dock is a difficult exercise for all but the most skilled truck drivers. Anyone who has tried to back up a house trailer or a boat trailer will realize this. Normal driving instincts lead to erroneous movements, and a great deal of practice is required to develop the requisite skills.

When watching a truck driver backing toward a loading dock, one often observes the driver backing and then going forward and repeating this several times until finally backing to the desired position along the dock. The forward and backward movements help to position the trailer for successful backing up to the dock. A more difficult backing-up sequence would only allow backing with no forward movements permitted. The specific problem treated in this example is that of the design by self-learning of a nonlinear controller to control the steering of a trailer truck while backing up to a loading dock from any initial position. Only backing up is allowed. Computer simulation of the truck and its controller has demonstrated that the algorithm described can train a controller to control the truck very well. An experimental neural controller consisting of two layers of adaptive weights with 25 adaptive neural units in the hidden layer and one unit in the output layer has exhibited excellent backing-up control. The trailer truck can be straight or initially jackknifed and aimed in many different directions, toward and away from the dock, but as long as there is sufficient clearance the controller appears to be capable of finding a solution.

Figure 6 shows a computer-screen image of the truck, the trailer, and the loading dock. The state vector representing the position of the truck consists of the following elements: θ_{cab}, the angle of the cab, $\theta_{trailer}$, the angle of the trailer, and $x_{trailer}$ and $y_{trailer}$, the Cartesian position of the rear of the center of the trailer. The definition of the state variables is illustrated in Figure 6.

The truck is placed at some initial position and is backed up while being steered by the controller. The run ends when the truck comes to the dock. The goal is to cause the back of the trailer to be parallel to the loading dock, that is, to make $\theta_{trailer}$ go to zero, and to have the point $(x_{trailer}, y_{trailer})$ be aligned as closely as possible with the point (x_{dock}, y_{dock}). The final cab angle does not matter. The controller will learn to achieve these objectives by adapting its weights to minimize the objective function C, where C is averaged over all training runs:

$$C = E(\alpha_1(x_{dock} - x_{trailer})^2 + \alpha_2(y_{dock} - y_{trailer})^2 \\ + \alpha^3(0 - \theta_{trailer})^2). \tag{4}$$

The constants α_1, α_2, and α_3 are chosen by the designer to weight the importance of each error component.

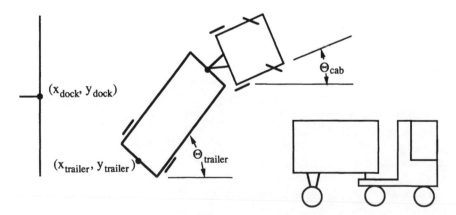

Figure 6.   Truck, trailer, and loading dock.

Training

As described in the previous section, the learning process for the truck backer-upper controller involves two stages. The first stage trains a neural network to be an emulator of the truck and trailer kinematics. The second stage enables the neural network controller to learn to control the truck by using the emulator as a guide. The control process consists of feeding the state vector z_k to the controller, which in turn provides a steering signal u_k between -1 (hard right) and $+1$ (hard left) to the truck (k is the time index). Each time step, the truck backs up by a fixed small distance. The next state is determined by the present state and the steering signal, which is fixed during the time step.

The process used to train the emulator is shown in Figure 2. The emulator used in this example is a network consisting of two layers of adaptive weights with 25 units in the hidden layer and 4 units in the output layer. A suitable architecture for this network was determined by experiment. Experience shows that the choice of network architecture is important but a range of variation is permissible (See the chapters in this book on the theory of feedforward networks for discussions on network architecture.) The emulator network has five inputs corresponding to the four state variables x_k and the steering signal u_k, and four outputs corresponding to the four next state variables z_{k+1}.

During training, the truck backs up randomly, going through many cycles with randomly selected steering signals. The emulator learns to generate the next positional state vector when given the present state vector and the steering signal. This is done for a wide variety of positional states and steering angles. The emulator is adapted by means of the back propagation algorithm. By this process, the emulator "gets the feel" of how the trailer and truck behave. Once the emulator is trained, it can then be used to train the controller.

Refer to Figure 5. The identical blocks labeled C represent the controller net. The identical blocks labeled E represent the truck and trailer emulator. Let the weights of C be chosen at random initially. Let the truck back up. The initial state vector z_0 is fed to C whose output sets the steering angle of the truck. The backing-up cycle proceeds with the truck backing a small fixed distance so that the truck and trailer soon arrive at the next state z_1. With C remaining fixed, a new steering angle is computed for state z_1, and the truck backs up a small fixed distance once again. The backing-up sequence continues until the truck hits something and stops. The final state z_K is compared with the desired final state (the rear of the trailer parallel to the dock with proper positional alignment) to obtain the final state error vector ϵ_K. (Note that in reality there is only one controller C. Figure 5 shows multiple copies of C for the purpose of explanation.) The error vector contains four elements which are the errors of interest in x_{trailer}, y_{trailer}, θ_{trailer}, and θ_{cab} and are used to adapt the controller C. The final angle of the cab θ_{cab} does not matter, so the element of the error vector due to

θ_{cab} is set to 0. Each element of the error vector is also weighted by the corresponding α_i of Equation 4.

The method of adapting the controller C is illustrated in Figure 5. The final state error vector ϵ_K is used to adapt the blocks labeled C, which are maintained identical to each other throughout the adaptive process. The controller C is a neural network with two layers of adaptive weights. The hidden layer has the six state variables as inputs and contains 25 adaptive units. The output layer has one adaptive unit and produces the steering signal as its output.

The controller C is adapted as described in the previous section. The weights of C are chosen initially at random. The initial position of the truck is chosen at random. The truck backs up, undergoing many individual back-up moves, until it comes to the dock. The final error is then computed and used by back propagation to adapt the controller. The error is used to update the weights as it is back-propagated through the network. This way, the controller is adapted to minimize the sum of the squares of the components of the error vector. The entire process is repeated by placing the truck and trailer in another initial position and allowing it to back up until it stops. Once again, the controller weights are adapted, and so on.

The controller and the emulator are neural networks with two layers of adaptive weights, each containing 25 hidden units. Thus, each stage of Figure 5 amounts to four layers of adaptive weights. The entire process of going from an initial state to the final state can be seen from Figure 5 to be analogous to a neural network having a number of layers of adaptive weights equal to four times the number of backing-up steps when going from the initial state to the final state. The number of steps K varies of course with initial position of the truck and trailer relative to the position of the target, the loading dock. In this experiment, we use initials positions of the truck that require from as few as four time steps to as many as 50 time steps.

The diagram of Figure 5 was simplified for clarity of presentation. The output error actually back propagates through the E blocks and C blocks. Thus, the error used to adapt each of the C blocks does originate from the output error ϵ_K, but travels through the proper back-propagation paths. For purposes of back propagation of the error, the E blocks are the truck emulator. But the actual truck kinematics are used when sensing the error ϵ_K itself.

The training of the controller was divided into several "lessons." In the beginning, the controller was trained with the truck initially set to points very near the dock and the trailer pointing at the dock. Once the controller was proficient at working with these initial positions, the problem was made harder by starting the truck farther away from the dock and at increasingly difficult angles. This way, the controller learned to do easy problems first and more difficult problems after it mastered the easy ones. There were 16 lessons in all. In the easiest lesson the trailer was set about half a truck length from the dock in the

x direction pointing at the dock, and the cab at a random angle between $\pm 30°$. In the last and most difficult lesson the rear of the trailer was set randomly between one and two truck lengths from the dock in the x direction and ± 1 truck length from the dock in the y direction. The cab and trailer angle was set to be the same, at a random angle between $\pm 90°$. (Note that uniform distributions were used to generate the random parameters.) The controller was trained for about 1000 truck backups per lesson during the early lessons, and 2000 truck backups per lesson during the last few. It took altogether about 20,000 backups to train the controller.

Results

The controller learned to control the truck very well with the above training process. Near the end of the last lesson, the root-mean-square error of y_{trailer} was about 3% of a truck length. The root-mean-square error of θ_{trailer} was about $7°$. There is no error in x_{trailer} since a truck backup is stopped when $x_{\text{trailer}} = x_{\text{dock}}$. One may, of course, trade off the error in y_{trailer} with the error in θ_{trailer} by giving them different weights in the objective function during training.

After training, the controller's weights were fixed. The truck and trailer were placed in a variety of initial positions, and backing up was successfully done in each case. A backup run when using the trained controller is demonstrated in Figure 7. Initial and final states are shown on the computer screen displays, and the backing up trajectory is illustrated by the time-lapse plot. The trained controller was capable of controlling the truck from initial positions it had never seen. For example, the controller was trained with the cab and trailer placed at angles between $\pm 90°$, but was capable of backing up the truck with cab and trailer placed at any angle provided that there was enough distance between the truck and the dock.

A More Sophisticated Objective Function

The truck controller was trained to minimize only the final state error. One can also train it to minimize total path length or control energy in addition to the final state error. For example, the objective function to minimize control energy is the following, with C averaged over all training trials.

$$C = E\left[\alpha_1(x_{\text{dock}} - x_{\text{trailer}})^2 + \alpha_2(y_{\text{dock}} - y_{\text{trailer}})^2 \right.$$
$$\left. + \alpha_3(\theta_{\text{dock}} - \theta_{\text{trailer}})^2 + \alpha_e \sum_{k=0}^{K-1} u_k^2 \right]. \tag{5}$$

A simple change is made to the algorithm to minimize this objective function. In the original algorithm, the equivalent error for the controller at each time step k is

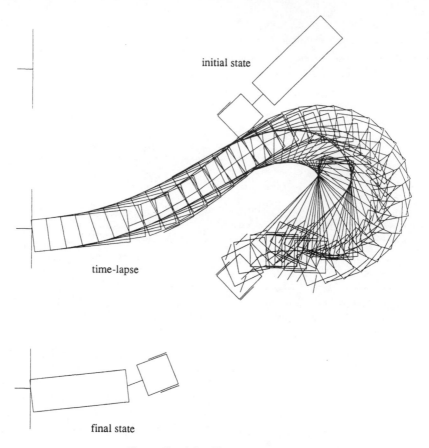

initial state

time-lapse

final state

Figure 7.   A backing-up example.

computed during the backward pass of the back-propagation algorithm. It is easy to show that control energy can be minimized by adding $-\alpha_4 u_k$ to the equivalent error of the controller at each time step. The modified equivalent error is then back-propagated through the controller to update the controller's weights just as before. This change makes sense, since using $-\alpha_4 u_k$ as an error in u_k causes the controller to learn to make u_k smaller in magnitude.

Training the controller to minimize control energy would cause it to drive the truck to the dock with as little steering as possible. An example with the controller trained in this manner is shown in Figure 8. This example uses the same truck and trailer initial position as with the example of Figure 7. Note that the path of the truck controlled by the new controller contains fewer sharp turns. Of course, the final state error increases somewhat because of the new control objective.

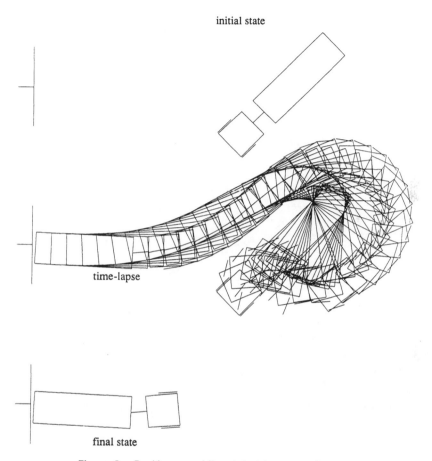

initial state

time-lapse

final state

Figure 8.   Backing up while minimizing control energy.

The Broom-Balancer Revisited

The algorithm described, which was used to successfully train a controller for the trailer truck, was used to train a controller for the cart/pendulum system to keep the cart near the center of the track and the pendulum vertical at the same time. The overall picture was the same as before (Figure 3). In this case however, the multistage training algorithm was used with the objective of all four state variables equaling zero. The system was run for 15 time steps or until it crashed, whichever came first; then the weights of the controller were updated using the multistage training algorithm. The system was then run for 15 more time steps and training repeated, and so on. The training process for the controller required

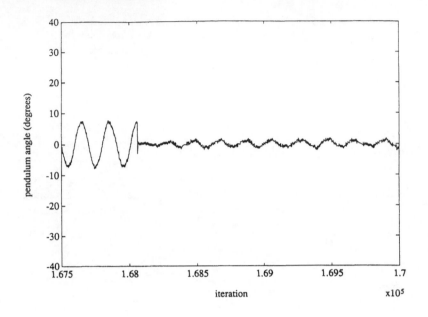

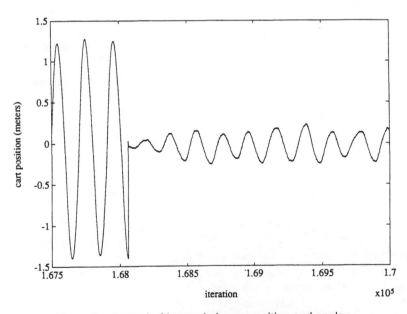

Figure 9.   Control of broom-balancer position and angle.

about 200,000 time steps. Figure 9 shows the cart position and pendulum angle as a function of time near the end of training. It can be seen that after training, the controller established a limit cycle, keeping the pendulum from falling and the cart near $x = 0$ indefinitely.

SUMMARY

The multistage training algorithm for neural network controllers is a very powerful algorithm. It presents us with a way of controlling nonlinear systems that are difficult to work with using other methods. The truck emulator in the form of a neural network was able to represent the trailer and truck when jackknifed, in line, or in any condition in between. Nonlinearity in the emulator was essential for accurate modeling of the kinematics. The angle between truck and trailer was not small, and thus $\sin \theta$ could not be represented approximately as θ. Controlling the nonlinear kinematics of the truck and trailer required a nonlinear controller, implemented by another neural network. Self-learning processes were used to determine the parameters of both the emulator and the controller. Thousands of backups were required to train these networks, requiring an hour or so on a workstation. Without the learning process, however, substantial amounts of human effort and design time would have been required to devise the controller.

The multistage controller learns to solve sequential decision problems. The control decisions made early in the control process have substantial effects upon final results. Early moves may not always be in a direction to reduce error, but they position the plant for ultimate success. In many respects, the truck backer-upper learns a control strategy that is like a dynamic programming problem solution. The learning is done in a layered neural network. Connecting signals from one layer to another corresponds to the idea that the final state of a given backing-up cycle is the same as the initial state of the next backing-up cycle.

Future research will be concerned with

- Determination of complexity of emulator as related to complexity of the system being controlled
- Determination of complexity of controller as related to complexity of emulator
- Determination of convergence and rate of learning for emulator and controller
- Proof of robustness of control scheme
- Analytic derivation of nonlinear controller for truck backer-upper, and comparison with self-learned controller
- Relearning in the presence of movable obstacles
- Exploration of other areas of application of self-learning neural networks

ACKNOWLEDGMENTS

This research was sponsored by SDIO Innovative Science and Technology Office and managed by ONR under contract #N00014-86-K-0718, by the Department of the Army Belvoir R D & E Center under Contract #DAAK70-89-K-0001, by NASA Ames under Contract #NCA2-389, by Rome Air Development Center under Subcontract #E-21-T22-S1 with the Georgia Institute of Technology, and by grants from the Thomson CSF Company and the Lockheed Missiles and Space Company.

This material is based on work supported under a National Science Foundation Graduate Fellowship. Any opinions, findings, conclusions, or recommendations expressed in this publication are those of the authors and do not necessarily reflect the views of the National Science Foundation.

REFERENCES

Anderson, C. W. (1989). Learning to control an inverted pendulum using neural networks. *IEEE Control Systems Magazine, 3,* 31–37.

Barto, A. G., Sutton, R. S., & Anderson, C. W. (1983). Neuronlike adaptive elements that can solve difficult learning control problems. *IEEE Transactions on Systems, Man, and Cybernetics, 5,* 834–846.

Bryson, A. E., & Ho, Y. (1975). *Applied optimal control.* Washington, DC: Hemisphere.

Jordan, M. I. (1988). *Supervised learning and systems with excess degrees of freedom* (COINS Report 88-27). Cambridge, MA: Massachusetts Institute of Technology.

Parker, D. B. (1985). *Learning logic* (Technical Report TR-47). Cambridge, MA: Massachusetts Institute of Technology, Center for Computational Research in Economics and Management Science.

Psaltis, D., Sideris, A., & Yamamura, A. A. (1988). A multilayered neural network controller. *IEEE Control Systems Magazine, 3,* 17–21.

Rumelhart, D. E., Hinton, G. E., & Williams, R. J. (1986). Learning internal representations by error propagation. In D. E. Rumelhart & J. L. McClelland (Eds.), *Parallel distributed processing: Explorations in the microstructure of cognition. Volume 1: Foundations.* Cambridge, MA: MIT Press.

Werbos, P. J. (1974). *Beyond regression: New tools for prediction and analysis in the behavioral sciences.* Unpublished doctoral dissertation. Cambridge, MA: Harvard University.

Widrow, B. (1986). Adaptive inverse control. *Proceedings of the 2nd International Federation of Automatic Control.*

Widrow, B., Gupta, N. K., & Maitra, S. (1973). Punish/reward: Learning with a critic in adaptive threshold systems. *IEEE Transactions on Systems, Man, and Cybernetics, 5,* 455–465.

Widrow, B., & Stearns, S. D. (1985). *Adaptive signal processing.* Englewood Cliffs, NJ: Prentice-Hall.

7

Forward Models: Supervised Learning with a Distal Teacher

Michael I. Jordan
Department of Brain and Cognitive Sciences
Massachusetts Institute of Technology

David E. Rumelhart
Department of Psychology, Stanford University

ABSTRACT

Internal models of the environment have an important role to play in adaptive systems in general and are of particular importance for the supervised learning paradigm. In this chapter we demonstrate that certain classical problems associated with the notion of the "teacher" in supervised learning can be solved by judicious use of learned internal models as components of the adaptive system. In particular, we show how supervised learning algorithms can be utilized in cases in which an unknown dynamical system intervenes between actions and desired outcomes. Our approach applies to any supervised learning algorithm that is capable of learning in multilayer networks.

Recent work on learning algorithms for connectionist networks has seen a progressive weakening of the assumptions made about the relationship between the learner and the environment. Classical supervised learning algorithms such as the perceptron (Rosenblatt, 1962) and the LMS algorithm (Widrow & Hoff, 1960) made two strong assumptions: (1) the output units are the only adaptive units in the network; and (2) there is a "teacher" that provides desired states for all of the output units. Early in the development of such algorithms it was recognized that more powerful supervised learning algorithms could be realized by weakening the first assumption and incorporating internal units that adaptively recode the input representation provided by the environment (Rosenblatt, 1962). The subsequent development of algorithms such as Boltzmann learning (Hinton & Sejnowski, 1986) and back propagation (LeCun, 1985; Parker, 1985; Rumelhart, Hinton, & Williams, 1986; Werbos, 1974) have provided the means for training networks with adaptive nonlinear internal units. The second assumption has also

189

been weakened—learning algorithms that require no explicit teacher have been developed (Becker & Hinton, 1989; Grossberg, 1987; Kohonen, 1982; Linsker, 1988; Rumelhart & Zipser, 1986). Such "unsupervised" learning algorithms generally perform some sort of clustering or feature extraction on the input data and are based on assumptions about the statistical or topological properties of the input ensemble.

In this paper we examine in some detail the notion of the "teacher" in the supervised learning paradigm. We argue that the teacher is less of a liability than has commonly been assumed and that the assumption that the environment provides desired states for the output of the network can be weakened significantly without abandoning the supervised learning paradigm altogether. Indeed, we feel that an appropriate interpretation of the role of the teacher is crucial in appreciating the range of problems to which the paradigm can be applied.

The issue that we wish to address is best illustrated by way of an example. Consider a skill-learning task such as that faced by a basketball player learning to shoot baskets. The problem for the learner is to find the appropriate muscle commands to propel the ball toward the goal. Different commands are appropriate for different locations of the goal in the visual scene; thus, a mapping from visual scenes to muscle commands is required. What learning algorithm might underlie the acquisition of such a mapping? Clearly, clustering or feature extraction on the visual inputs is not sufficient. Moreover, it is difficult to see how to apply classical supervised algorithms to this problem, because there is no teacher to provide muscle commands as targets to the learner. The only target information provided to the learner is in terms of the outcome of the movement—that is, the sights and sounds of a ball passing through the goal.

The general scenario suggested by the example is shown in Figure 1. *Intentions* are provided as inputs to the learning system. The learner transforms intentions into *actions,* which are transformed by the environment into *outcomes.* Actions are *proximal* variables—that is, variables that the learner controls directly —while outcomes are *distal* variables—variables that the learner controls indirectly through the intermediary of the proximal variables. During the learning process, target values are assumed to be available for the distal variables but not for the proximal variables. Therefore, from a point of view outside the learning system, a "distal supervised learning task" is a mapping from intentions to

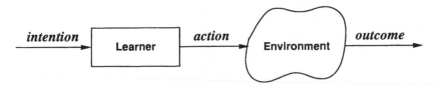

Figure 1.   The distal supervised learning problem. Target values are available for the distal variables (the "outcomes") but not for the proximal variables (the "actions").

desired outcomes. From the point of view of the learner, however, the problem is to find a mapping from intentions to actions that can be composed with the environment to yield desired distal outcomes. The learner must discover how to vary the components of the proximal action vector so as to minimize the components of the distal error.

The distal supervised learning problem also has a temporal component. In many environments the effects of actions are not punctate and instantaneous, but rather linger on and mix with the effects of other actions. Thus the outcome at any point in time is influenced by any of a number of previous actions. Even if there exists a set of variables that have a static relationship to desired outcomes, the learner often does not have direct control over those variables. Consider again the example of the basketball player. Although the flight of the ball depends only on the velocity of the arm at the moment of release—a static relationship—it is unlikely that the motor control system is able to control release velocity directly. Rather, the system outputs forces or torques, and these variables do not have a static relationship to the distal outcome.

In the remainder of the chapter we describe a general approach to solving the distal supervised learning problem. The approach is based on the idea that supervised learning in its most general form is a two-phase procedure. In the first phase the learner forms a predictive internal model (a forward model) of the transformation from actions to distal outcomes. Because such transformations are often not known a priori, the internal model must generally be learned by exploring the outcomes associated with particular choices of actions. This auxiliary learning problem is itself a supervised learning problem, based on the error between internal, predicted outcomes and actual outcomes. Once the internal model has been at least partially learned, it can be used in an indirect manner to solve for the mapping from intentions to actions.

The idea of using an internal model to augment the capabilities of supervised learning algorithms has also been proposed by Werbos (1987), although his perspective differs in certain respects from our town. There have been a number of further developments of the idea (Kawato, 1990; Miyata, 1988; Munro, 1987; Nguyen & Widrow, 1989; Robinson & Fallside, 1989; Schmidhuber, 1990), based either on the work of Werbos or our own unpublished work (Jordan, 1983; Rumelhart, 1986). There are also close ties between our approach and techniques in optimal control theory (Kirk, 1970) and adaptive control theory (Goodwin & Sin, 1984; Narendra & Parthasarathy, 1990). We discuss several of these relationships, although we do not attempt to be comprehensive.

DISTAL SUPERVISED LEARNING
AND FORWARD MODELS

This section and the following section present a general approach to solving distal supervised learning problems. We begin by describing our assumptions about the environment and the learner.

We assume that the environment can be characterized by a next-state function f and an output function g. At time step $n - 1$ the learner produces an *action* $\mathbf{u}[n - 1]$. In conjunction with the state of the environment $\mathbf{x}[n - 1]$ the action determines the next state $\mathbf{x}[n]$:

$$\mathbf{x}[n] = f(\mathbf{x}[n - 1], \mathbf{u}[n - 1]). \tag{1}$$

Corresponding to each state $\mathbf{x}[n]$ there is also a *sensation* $\mathbf{y}[n]$:

$$\mathbf{y}[n] = g(\mathbf{x}[n]). \tag{2}$$

(Note that sensations are output vectors in the current formalism—"outcomes" in the language of the introductory section.) The next-state function and the output function together determine a state-dependent mapping from actions to sensations.

We assume that the learner has access to the state of the environment; we do not address issues relating to state representation and state estimation. State representations might involve delayed values of previous actions and sensations (Ljung & Söderström, 1986), or they might involve internal state variables that are induced as part of the learning procedure (Mozer & Bachrach, 1990). Given the state $\mathbf{x}[n - 1]$ and given the *input* $\mathbf{p}[n - 1]$, the learner produces an action $\mathbf{u}[n - 1]$:

$$\mathbf{u}[n - 1] = h(\mathbf{x}[n - 1], \mathbf{p}[n - 1]).[1] \tag{3}$$

The goal of the learning procedure is to make appropriate adjustments to the input-to-action mapping h based on data obtained from interacting with the environment.

A *distal supervised learning problem* is a set of training pairs $\{\mathbf{p}_i[n - 1], \mathbf{y}_i^*[n]\}$, where $\mathbf{p}_i[n - 1]$ are the input vectors and $\mathbf{y}_i^*[n]$ are the corresponding desired sensations. For example, in the basketball problem, the input might be a high-level intention of shooting a basket, and a desired sensation would be the corresponding visual representation of a successful outcome. Note that the distal supervised learning problem makes no mention of the actions that the learner must acquire; only inputs and desired sensations are specified. From a point of view outside the learning system the training data specify desired input/output behavior across the *composite performance system* consisting of the learner and the environment (see Figure 2). From the point of view of the learner, however, the problem is to find a mapping from inputs $\mathbf{p}[n - 1]$ to actions $\mathbf{u}[n - 1]$ such that the resulting distal sensations $\mathbf{y}[n]$ are the target values $\mathbf{y}^*[n]$. That is, the learner must find a mapping from inputs to actions that can be placed in series with the environment so as to yield the desired pairing of inputs and sensations. Note that there may be more than one action that yields a given desired sensation

---

[1] The choice of time indices in Equations 1, 2, and 3 is based on our focus on the output at time n. In our framework a learning algorithm alters $\mathbf{y}[n]$ based on previous values of the states, inputs, and actions.

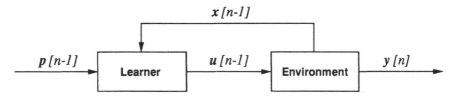

Figure 2. The composite performance system consisting of the learner and the environment. This system is a mapping from inputs $p[n - 1]$ to sensations $y[n]$. The training data $\{p_i[n - 1], y_i^*[n]\}$ specify desired input/output behavior across the composite system. Note that there is an implicit loop within the environment such that the output at time n depends on the state at time $n - 1$ (cf. Equation 1).

from any given state; that is, the distal supervised learning problem may be underdetermined. Thus, in the basketball example, there may be a variety of patterns of motor commands that yield the same desired sensation of seeing the ball pass through the goal.

Forward Models

The learner is assumed to be able to observe states, actions, and sensations and can therefore model the mapping between actions and sensations. A *forward model* is an internal model that produces a predicted sensation $\hat{y}[n]$ based on the state $x[n - 1]$ and the action $u[n - 1]$. That is, a forward model predicts the consequences of a given action in the context of a given state vector. As shown in Figure 3, the forward model can be learned by comparing predicted sensations to

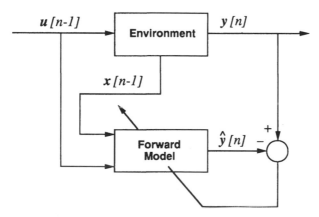

Figure 3. Learning the forward model using the prediction error $y[n] - \hat{y}[n]$.

actual sensations and using the resulting *prediction error* to adjust the parameters of the model. Learning the forward model is a classical supervised learning problem in which the teacher provides target values directly in the output coordinate system of the learner.[2]

Distal Supervised Learning

We now describe a general approach to solving the distal supervised learning problem. Consider the system shown in Figure 4, in which the learner is placed in series with a forward model of the environment. This *composite learning system* is a state-dependent mapping from inputs to predicted sensations. Suppose that the forward model has been trained previously and is a perfect model of the environment; that is, the predicted sensation equals the actual sensation for all actions and all states. We now treat the composite learning system as a single supervised learning system and train it to map from inputs to desired sensations according to the data in the training set. That is, the desired sensations y_i^* are treated as targets for the composite system. Any supervised learning algorithm can be used for this training process; however, the algorithm must be constrained so that it does not alter the forward model while the composite system is being trained. By fixing the forward model, we require the system to find an optimal composite mapping by varying only the mapping from inputs to actions. If the forward model is perfect, and if the learning algorithm finds the globally optimal solution, then the resulting (state-dependent) input-to-action mapping must also be perfect in the sense that it yields the desired composite input/output behavior when placed in series with the environment.

Consider now the case of an imperfect forward model. Clearly an imperfect forward model will yield an imperfect input-to-action map if the composite system is trained in the obvious way, using the difference between the desired sensation and the predicted sensation as the error term. This difference, the *predicted performance error* $y^* - \hat{y}$, is readily available at the output of the composite system, but it is an unreliable guide to the true performance of the learner. Suppose instead that we ignore the output of the composite system and substitute the *performance error* $y^* - y$ as the error term for training the composite system (see Figure 5). If the performance error goes to zero the system has found a correct input-to-action map, regardless of the inaccuracy of the forward model. The inaccuracy in the forward model manifests itself as a bias during the learning process, but need not prevent the performance error from going to zero. Consider, for example, algorithms based on steepest descent. If the forward model is not too inaccurate the system can still move downhill and

---

[2]In the engineering literature, this learning process is referred to as "system identification" (Ljung & Söderström, 1986).

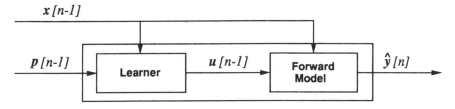

Figure 4. The composite learning system. This composite system maps from inputs **p**[n] to predicted sensations $\hat{\mathbf{y}}$[n] in the context of a given state vector.

thereby reach the solution region, even though the movement is not in the direction of steepest descent.

To summarize, we propose to solve the distal supervised learning problem by training a composite learning system consisting of the learner and a forward model of the environment. This procedure solves implicitly for an input-to-action map by training the composite system to map from inputs to distal targets. The training of the forward model must precede the training of the composite system, but the forward model need not be perfect, nor need it be pretrained throughout all of the state-space. The ability of the system to utilize an inaccurate forward model is important, it implies that it may be possible to interleave the training of the forward model and the composite system.

We will discuss the issues of interleaved training, inaccuracy in the forward model, and the choice of the error term in more detail. We first turn to an interesting special case of the general distal supervised learning problem—that of learning an inverse model of the environment.

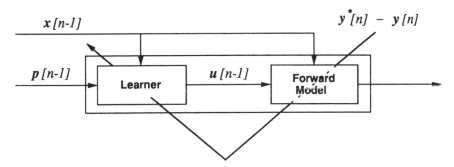

Figure 5. The composite system is trained using the performance error. The forward model is held fixed while the composite system is being trained.

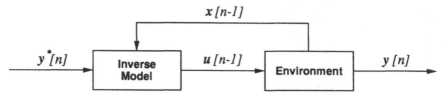

Figure 6. An inverse model as a controller.

Inverse Models

An *inverse model* is an internal model that produces an action $\mathbf{u}[n - 1]$ as a function of the current state $\mathbf{x}[n - 1]$ and the desired sensation $\mathbf{y}^*[n]$. Inverse models are defined by the condition that they yield the identity mapping when placed in series with the environment.

Inverse models are important in a variety of domains. For example, if the environment is viewed as a communications channel over which a message is to be transmitted, then it may be desirable to undo the distorting effects of the environment by placing it in series with an inverse model (Carlson, 1986). A second example, shown in Figure 6, arises in control system design. A controller receives the desired sensation $\mathbf{y}^*[n]$ as input and must find actions that cause actual sensations to be as close as possible to desired sensations; that is, the controller must invert the transformation from actions to sensations.[3] One approach to achieving this objective is to utilize an explicit inverse model of the environment as a controller.

Whereas forward models are uniquely determined by the environment, inverse models are generally not. If the environment is characterized by a many-to-one mapping from actions to sensations then there are generally an infinite number of possible inverse models. It is also worth noting that inverses do not always exist—it is not always possible to achieve a particular desired sensation from any given state. As we shall discuss, these issues of existence and uniqueness have important implications for the problem of learning an inverse model.

There are two general approaches to learning inverse models using supervised learning algorithms: the distal learning approach presented above and an alternative approach that we refer to as "direct inverse modeling" (cf. Jordan & Rosenbaum, 1989). We begin by describing the latter approach.

Direct Inverse Modeling

Direct inverse modeling treats the problem of learning an inverse model as a classical supervised learning problem (Widrow & Stearns, 1985). As shown in

[3]Control system design normally involves a number of additional constraints involving stability and robustness; thus, the goal is generally to invert the environment as nearly as possible subject to these additional constraints.

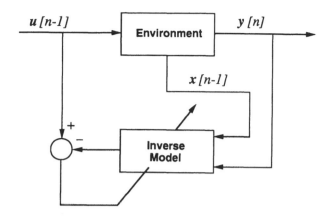

Figure 7. The direct inverse modeling approach to learning an inverse model.

Figure 7, the idea is to observe the input/output behavior of the environment and to train an inverse model directly by reversing the roles of the inputs and outputs. Data are provided to the algorithm by sampling in action space and observing the results in sensation space.

Although direct inverse modeling has been shown to be a viable technique in a number of domains (Atkeson & Reinkensmeyer, 1988; Kuperstein, 1988; Miller, 1987), it has two drawbacks that limit its usefulness. First, if the environment is characterized by a many-to-one mapping from actions to sensations, then the direct inverse modeling technique may be unable to find an inverse. The difficulty is that nonlinear many-to-one mappings can yield nonconvex inverse images, which are problematic for direct inverse modeling.[4] Consider the situation shown in Figure 8. The nonconvex region on the left is the inverse image of a point in sensation space. Suppose that the points labeled by X's are sampled during the learning process. Three of these points correspond to the same sensation; thus, the training data as seen by the direct inverse modeling procedure are one-to-many—one input is paired with many targets. Supervised learning algorithms resolve one-to-many inconsistencies by averaging across the multiple targets (the form of the averaging depends on the particular cost function that is used). As is shown in the figure, however, the average of points lying in a nonconvex set does not necessarily lie in the set. Thus the globally optimal (minimum-cost) solution found by the direct inverse modeling approach is not necessarily a correct inverse model. (We present an example of such behavior in a following section).

The second drawback with direct inverse modeling is that it is not "goal directed." The algorithm samples in action space without regard to particular

[4]A set is *convex* if for every pair of points in the set all points on the line between the points also lie in the set.

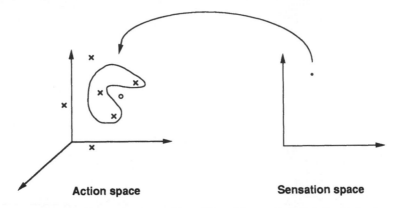

Action space   **Sensation space**

Figure 8.   The convexity problem. The region on the left is the inverse image of the point on the right. The arrow represents the direction in which the mapping is learned by direct inverse modeling. The three points lying inside the inverse image are averaged by the learning procedure, yielding the vector represented by the small circle. This point is not a solution, because the inverse image is not convex.

targets or errors in sensation space. That is, there is no direct way to find an action that corresponds to a particular desired sensation. To obtain particular solutions the learner must sample over a sufficiently wide range of actions and rely on interpolation.

Finally, it is also important to emphasize that direct inverse modeling is restricted to the learning of inverse models—it is *not* applicable to the general distal supervised learning problem.

The Distal Learning Approach to Learning an Inverse Model

The methods described earlier in this section are directly applicable to the problem of learning an inverse model. The problem of learning an inverse model can be treated as a special case of the distal supervised learning problem in which the input vector and the desired sensation are the same (that is, $\mathbf{p}[n-1]$ is equal to $\mathbf{y}^*[n]$ in Equation 3). Thus, an inverse model is learned by placing the learner and the forward model in series and learning an identity mapping across the composite system.[5]

A fundamental difference between the distal learning approach and direct

[5]An interesting analogy can be drawn between the distal learning approach and indirect techniques for solving systems of linear equations. In numerical linear algebra, rather than solving explicitly for a generalized inverse of the coefficient matrix, solutions are generally found indirectly (e.g., by applying Gaussian elimination to both sides of the equation $GA = I$, where I is the identity matrix).

inverse modeling approach is that rather than averaging over regions in action space, the distal learning approach finds particular solutions in action space. The globally optimal solution for distal learning is a set of vectors $\{\mathbf{u}_i\}$ such that the performance errors $\{\mathbf{y}_i^* - \mathbf{y}_i\}$ are zero. This is true irrespective of the shapes of the inverse images of the targets $\mathbf{y}_i^*$. Vectors lying outside of an inverse image, such as the average vector shown in Figure 8, do not yield zero performance error and are therefore not globally optimal. Thus nonconvex inverse images do not present the same fundamental difficulties for the distal learning framework as they do for direct inverse modeling.

It is also true that the distal learning approach is fundamentally goal directed. The system works to minimize the performance error; thus, it works directly to find solutions that correspond to the particular goals at hand.

In cases in which the forward mapping is many-to-one, the distal learning procedure finds a particular inverse model. Without additional information about the particular structure of the input-to-action mapping there is no way of predicting which of the possibly infinite set of inverse models the procedure will find. As is discussed later, however, the procedure can also be constrained to find particular inverse models with certain desired properties.

DISTAL LEARNING AND BACK PROPAGATION

In this section we describe an implementation of the distal learning approach that utilizes the machinery of the back-propagation algorithm. It is important to emphasize at the outset, however, that back propagation is not the only algorithm that can be used to implement the distal learning approach. Any supervised learning algorithm can be used as long as it is capable of learning a mapping across a composite network that includes a previously trained subnetwork; in particular, Boltzmann learning is applicable (Jordan, 1983).

We begin by introducing a useful shorthand for describing back propagation in layered networks. A layered network can be described as a parameterized mapping from an input vector $\mathbf{x}$ to an output vector $\mathbf{y}$:

$$\mathbf{y} = \phi(\mathbf{x}, \mathbf{w}), \tag{4}$$

where $\mathbf{w}$ is a vector of parameters (weights). In the classical paradigm, the procedure for changing the weights is based on the discrepancy between a target vector $\mathbf{y}^*$ and the actual output vector $\mathbf{y}$. The magnitude of this discrepancy is measured by a cost functional of the form

$$J = \tfrac{1}{2}(\mathbf{y}^* - \mathbf{y})^T(\mathbf{y}^* - \mathbf{y}) \tag{5}$$

(J is the sum of squared error at the output units of the network). It is generally desired to minimize this cost.

Back propagation is an algorithm for computing gradients of the cost functional. The details of the algorithm can be found elsewhere (e.g., Rumelhart, Hinton, & Williams, 1986); our intention here is to develop a simple notation that hides the details. This is achieved formally by using the chain rule to differentiate J with respect to the weight vector $\mathbf{w}$:

$$\nabla_{\mathbf{w}} J = -\frac{\partial \mathbf{y}^T}{\partial \mathbf{w}} (\mathbf{y}^* - \mathbf{y}). \tag{6}$$

This equation shows that any algorithm that computes the gradient of J effectively multiplies the error vector $\mathbf{y}^* - \mathbf{y}$ by the transpose Jacobian matrix $(\partial \mathbf{y}/\partial \mathbf{w})^T$.[6] Although the back-propagation algorithm never forms this matrix explicitly (back propagation is essentially a factorization of the matrix; Jordan, 1988), Equation 6 nonetheless describes the results of the computation performed by back propagation.[7]

Back propagation also computes the gradient of the cost functional with respect to the activations of the units in the network. In particular, the cost functional J can be differentiated with respect to the activations of the input units to yield

$$\nabla_{\mathbf{x}} J = -\frac{\partial \mathbf{y}^T}{\partial \mathbf{x}} (\mathbf{y}^* - \mathbf{y}). \tag{7}$$

We refer to Equation 6 as "back propagation-to-weights" and Equation 7 as "back propagation-to-activation." Both computations are carried out in one pass of the algorithm; indeed, back propagation-to-activation is needed as an intermediate step in the back-propagation-to-weights computation.

In the remainder of this section we formulate two broad categories of learning problems that lie within the scope of the distal learning approach and derive expressions for the gradients that arise. For simplicity it is assumed in both of these derivations that the task is to learn an inverse model (that is, the inputs and the distal targets are assumed to be identical). The two formulations of the distal learning framework focus on different aspects of the distal learning problem and have different strengths and weaknesses. The first approach, the "local optimization" formulation, focuses on the local dynamical structure of the environment. Because it assumes that the learner is able to predict state transitions based on in-

---

[6]The Jacobian matrix of a vector function is simply its first derivative—it is a matrix of first partial derivatives. That is, the entries of the matrix $(\partial \mathbf{y}/\partial \mathbf{w})$ are the partial derivatives of each of the output activations with respect to each of the weights in the network.

[7]To gain some insight into why a transpose matrix arises in back propagation, consider a single-layer linear network described by $\mathbf{y} = W\mathbf{x}$, where W is the weight matrix. The rows of W are the incoming weight vectors for the output units of the network, and the columns of W are the outgoing weight vectors for the input units of the network. Passing a vector forward in the network involves taking the inner product of the vector with each of the incoming weight vectors. This operation corresponds to multiplication by W. Passing a vector backward in the network corresponds to taking the inner product of the vector with each of the outgoing weight vectors. This operation corresponds to multiplication by W^T, because the rows of W^T are the columns of W.

formation that is available locally in time, it depends on prior knowledge of an adequate set of state variables for describing the environment. It is most naturally applied to problems in which target values are provided at each moment in time, although it can be extended to problems in which target values are provided intermittently (as we demonstrate in a following section). All of the computations needed for the local optimization formulation can be performed in feedforward networks, thus there is no problem with stability. The second approach, the "optimization-along-trajectories" formulation, focuses on global temporal dependencies along particular target trajectories. The computation needed to obtain these dependencies is more complex than the computation needed for the local optimization formulation, but it is more flexible. It can be éxtended to cases in which a set of state variables is not known a priori, and it is naturally applied to problems in which target values are provided intermittently in time. There is potentially a problem with stability, however, because the computations for obtaining the gradient involve a dynamical process.

Local Optimization

The first problem formulation that we discuss is a local optimization problem. We assume that the process that generates target vectors is stationary and consider the general cost functional

$$J = \tfrac{1}{2}E\{(\mathbf{y}^* - \mathbf{y})^T(\mathbf{y}^* - \mathbf{y})\}, \tag{8}$$

where $\mathbf{y}$ is an unknown function of the state $\mathbf{x}$ and the action $\mathbf{u}$. The action $\mathbf{u}$ is the output of a parameterized inverse model of the form

$$\mathbf{u} = h(\mathbf{x}, \mathbf{y}^*, \mathbf{w}),$$

where $\mathbf{w}$ is a weight vector.

Rather than optimizing J directly, by collecting statistics over the ensemble of states and actions, we utilize an on-line learning rule (cf. Widrow & Stearns, 1985) that makes incremental changes to the weights based on the instantaneous value of the cost functional:

$$J_n = \tfrac{1}{2}(\mathbf{y}^*[n] - \mathbf{y}[n])^T(\mathbf{y}^*[n] - \mathbf{y}[n]). \tag{9}$$

An on-line learning algorithm changes the weights at each time step based on the stochastic gradient of J—that is, the gradient of J_n:

$$\mathbf{w}[n + 1] = \mathbf{w}[n] - \eta \nabla_{\mathbf{w}} J_n,$$

where η is a step size. To compute this gradient, we apply the chain rule to Equation 9:

$$\nabla_{\mathbf{w}} J_n = -\left(\frac{\partial \mathbf{u}}{\partial \mathbf{w}}\right)^T \left(\frac{\partial \mathbf{y}}{\partial \mathbf{u}}\right)^T (\mathbf{y}^*[n] - \mathbf{y}[n]), \tag{10}$$

where the Jacobian matrices $(\partial\mathbf{y}/\partial\mathbf{u})$ and $(\partial\mathbf{u}/\partial\mathbf{w})$ are evaluated at time $n - 1$. The first and the third factors in this expression are easily computed: The first factor describes the propagation of derivatives from the output units of the inverse model (the "action units") to the weights of the inverse model, and the third factor is the distal error. The origin of the second factor is problematic, however, because the dependence of $\mathbf{y}$ on $\mathbf{u}$ is assumed to be unknown a priori. Our approach to obtaining an estimate of this factor has two parts: first, the system acquires a parameterized forward model over an appropriate subdomain of the state space. This model is of the form

$$\hat{\mathbf{y}} = \hat{f}(\mathbf{x}, \mathbf{u}, \mathbf{v}), \tag{11}$$

where $\mathbf{v}$ is a vector of weights and $\hat{\mathbf{y}}$ is the predicted sensation. Second, the distal error is propagated backward through the forward model; this effectively multiplies the distal error by an estimate of the transpose Jacobian matrix $(\partial\mathbf{y}/\partial\mathbf{u})$.

Putting these pieces together, the algorithm for learning the inverse model is based on the estimated stochastic gradient

$$\hat{\nabla}_{\mathbf{w}}J_n = - \left(\frac{\partial\mathbf{u}}{\partial\mathbf{w}}\right)^T \left(\frac{\partial\hat{\mathbf{y}}}{\partial\mathbf{u}}\right)^T (\mathbf{y}^*[n] - \mathbf{y}[n]). \tag{12}$$

This expression describes the propagation of the distal error $(\mathbf{y}^*[n] - \mathbf{y}[n])$ backward through the forward model and down into the inverse model where the weights are changed.[8] The network architecture in which these computations take place is shown in Figure 9. This network is a straightforward realization of the block diagram in Figure 5. It is composed of an inverse model, which links the state units and the input units to the action units, and a forward model, which links the state units and the action units to the predicted-sensation units.

Learning the Forward Model

The learning of the forward model can itself be formulated as an optimization problem based on the cost functional

$$L = \tfrac{1}{2}E\{(\mathbf{y} - \hat{\mathbf{y}})^T(\mathbf{y} - \hat{\mathbf{y}})\},$$

where $\hat{\mathbf{y}}$ is of the form given in Equation 11. Although the choice of procedure for finding a set of weights $\mathbf{v}$ to minimize this cost is entirely independent of the choice of procedure for optimizing J in Equation 8, it is convenient to base the learning of the forward model on a stochastic gradient as before:

$$\nabla_{\mathbf{v}}L_n = - \left(\frac{\partial\hat{\mathbf{y}}}{\partial\mathbf{v}}\right)^T (\mathbf{y}[n] - \hat{\mathbf{y}}[n]), \tag{13}$$

---

[8]Note that the error term $(\mathbf{y}^*[n] - \mathbf{y}[n])$ is not a function of the output of the forward model; nonetheless, activation must flow forward in the model because the estimated Jacobian matrix $(\partial\hat{\mathbf{y}}/\partial\mathbf{u})$ varies as a function of the activations of the hidden units and the output units of the model.

| Inverse Model | Forward Model |

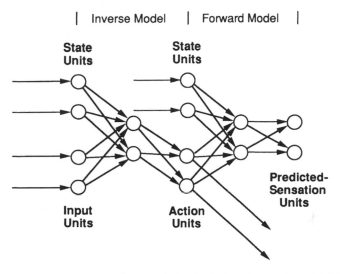

Figure 9.   A feedforward network that includes a forward model. The action units are the output units of the system.

where the Jacobian matrix $(\partial\hat{\mathbf{y}}/\partial\mathbf{v})$ is evaluated at time $n - 1$. This gradient can be computed by the propagation of derivatives within the forward model and therefore requires no additional hardware beyond that already required for learning the inverse model.

The Error Signals

It is important to clarify the meanings of the error signals used in Equations 12 and 13. As shown in Table 1, there are three error signals that can be formed from the variables $\mathbf{y}$, $\hat{\mathbf{y}}$, and $\mathbf{y}^*$: *the prediction error* $\mathbf{y} - \hat{\mathbf{y}}$, the *performance error* $\mathbf{y}^* - \mathbf{y}$, and the *predicted performance error* $\mathbf{y}^* - \hat{\mathbf{y}}$. All three of these error signals are available to the learner because each of the signals $\mathbf{y}^*$, $\mathbf{y}$ and $\hat{\mathbf{y}}$ are available individually; the target $\mathbf{y}^*$ and the actual sensation $\mathbf{y}$ are provided by the environment, whereas the predicted sensation $\hat{\mathbf{y}}$ is available internally.

TABLE 1
The Error Signals and Their Sources

	Name	*Source*
$\mathbf{y}^* - \mathbf{y}$	Performance error	Environment, environment
$\mathbf{y} - \hat{\mathbf{y}}$	Prediction error	Environment, model
$\mathbf{y}^* - \hat{\mathbf{y}}$	Predicted performance error	Environment, model

For learning the forward model, the prediction error is clearly the appropriate error signal. The learning of the inverse model, however, can be based on either the performance error or the predicted performance error. Using the performance error (see Equation 12) has the advantage that the system can learn an exact inverse model even though the forward model is only approximate. There are two reasons for this: first, Equation 12 preserves the minima of the cost functional in Equation 9—they are zeros of the estimated gradient. That is, an inaccurate Jacobian matrix cannot remove zeros of the estimated gradient (points at which $\mathbf{y}^* - \mathbf{y}$ is zero), although it can introduce additional zeros (spurious local minima). Second, if the estimated gradients obtained with the approximate forward model have positive inner product with the stochastic gradient in Equation 10, then the expected step of the algorithm is downhill in the cost. Thus the algorithm can in principle find an exact inverse model even though the forward model is only approximate.

There may also be advantages to using the predicted performance error. In particular, it may be easier in some situations to obtain learning trials using the internal model rather than the external environment (Rumelhart, Smolensky, McClelland, & Hinton, 1986; Sutton, 1990). Such internal trials can be thought of as a form of "mental practice" (in the case of back propagation-to-weights) or "planning" (in the case of back propagation-to-activation). These procedures lead to improved performance if the forward model is sufficiently accurate. (Exact solutions cannot be found with such procedures, however, unless the forward model is exact.)

Modularity

In many cases the unknown mapping from actions to sensations can be decomposed into a series of simpler mappings, each of which can be modeled independently. For example, it may often be preferable to model the next-state function and the output function separately rather than modeling them as a single composite function. In such cases, the Jacobian matrix $(\partial \hat{\mathbf{y}} / \partial \mathbf{u})$ can be factored using the chain rule to yield the estimated stochastic gradient

$$\hat{\nabla}_{\mathbf{w}} J_n = - \left(\frac{\partial \mathbf{u}}{\partial \mathbf{w}} \right)^T \left(\frac{\partial \hat{\mathbf{x}}}{\partial \mathbf{u}} \right)^T \left(\frac{\partial \hat{\mathbf{y}}}{\partial \mathbf{x}} \right)^T (\mathbf{y}^*[n] - \mathbf{y}[n]). \tag{14}$$

The estimated Jacobian matrices in this expression are obtained by propagating derivatives backward through the corresponding forward models, each of which is learned separately.

Optimization along Trajectories[9]

A complete inverse model allows the learner to synthesize the actions that are needed to follow any desired trajectory. In the local optimization formulation we

---

[9]This section is included for completeness and is not needed for the remainder of the chapter.

effectively assume that the learning of an inverse model is of primary concern and the learning of particular target trajectories is secondary. The learning rule given by Equation 12 finds actions that invert the dynamics of the environment at the current point in state-space, regardless of whether that point is on a desired trajectory or not. In terms of network architectures, this approach leads to using feedforward networks to model the local forward and inverse state transition structure (see Figure 9).

In the current section we consider a more specialized problem formulation in which the focus is on particular classes of target trajectories. This formulation is based on variational calculus and is closely allied with methods in optimal control theory (Kirk, 1970; LeCun, 1987). The algorithm that results is a form of "back propagation-in-time" (Rumelhart, Hinton, & Williams, 1986) in a recurrent network that incorporates a learned forward model. The algorithm differs from the algorithm presented before in that it not only inverts the relationship between actions and sensations at the current point in state-space but also moves the current state toward the desired trajectory.

We consider an ensemble of target trajectories $\{y_\alpha^*[n]\}$ and define the cost functional

$$J = \frac{1}{2} E \left\{ \sum_{n=1}^{N_\alpha} (y_\alpha^*[n] - y_\alpha[n])^T (y_\alpha^*[n] - y_\alpha[n]) \right\}, \tag{15}$$

where α is an index across target trajectories and y_α is an unknown function of the state x_α and the action u_α. The action u_α is a parameterized function of the state x_α and the target y_α^*:

$$u_\alpha = h(x_\alpha, y_\alpha^*, w).$$

As in the previous formulation, we base the learning rule on the stochastic gradient of J, that is, the gradient evaluated along a particular sample trajectory y_α:

$$J_\alpha = \frac{1}{2} \sum_{n=1}^{N_\alpha} (y_\alpha^*[n] - y_\alpha[n])^T (y_\alpha^*[n] - y_\alpha[n]). \tag{16}$$

The gradient of this cost functional can be obtained using the calculus of variations (see also LeCun, 1987, Narendra & Parthasarathy, 1990). Letting $\Psi[n]$ represent the vector of partial derivatives of J_α with respect to $x_\alpha[n]$, and letting $\Phi[n]$ represent the vector of partial derivatives of J_α with respect to $u_\alpha[n]$, Appendix A shows that the gradient of J_α is given by the recurrence relations

$$\Phi[n-1] = \left(\frac{\partial z_\alpha}{\partial x_\alpha}\right)^T \Phi[n] + \left(\frac{\partial u_\alpha}{\partial x_\alpha}\right)^T \Psi[n] - \left(\frac{\partial y_\alpha}{\partial x_\alpha}\right)^T (y_\alpha^*[n] - y_\alpha[n]), \tag{17}$$

$$\Psi[n] = \left(\frac{\partial z_\alpha}{\partial u_\alpha}\right)^T \Phi[n], \tag{18}$$

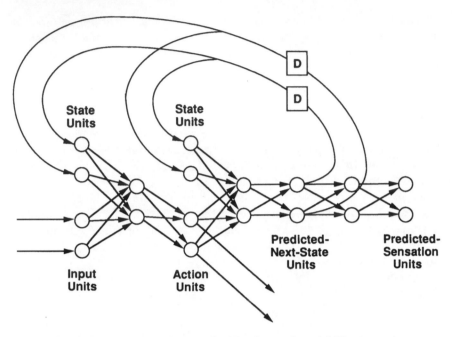

Figure 10.   A recurrent network with a forward model. The boxes labeled by D's are unit delay elements.

and

$$\nabla_{\mathbf{w}} J_\alpha[n] = \left(\frac{\partial \mathbf{u}_\alpha}{\partial \mathbf{w}}\right)^T \Psi[n], \tag{19}$$

where the Jacobian matrices are all evaluated at time step n and $\mathbf{z}_\alpha$ stands for $\mathbf{x}_\alpha[n + 1]$ (thus, the Jacobian matrices $(\partial \mathbf{z}_\alpha/\partial \mathbf{x}_\alpha)$ and $(\partial \mathbf{z}_\alpha/\partial \mathbf{u}_\alpha)$ are the derivatives of the next-state function). This expression describes back propagation-in-time in a recurrent network that incorporates a forward model of the next-state function and the output function. As shown in Figure 10, the recurrent network is essentially the same as the network in Figure 9, except that there are explicit connections with unit delay elements between the next-state and the current state.[10] Back propagation-in-time propagates derivatives backward through these recurrent connections as described by the recurrence relations in Equations 17 and 18.

As in the local optimization case, the equations for computing the gradient involve the multiplication of the performance error $\mathbf{y}^* - \mathbf{y}$ by a series of transposed Jacobian matrices, several of which are unknown a priori. Our approach to

---

[10]Alternatively, Figure 9 can be thought of as a special case of Figure 10 in which the back-propagated error signals stop at the state units (cf. Jordan, 1986).

estimating the unknown factors is once again to learn forward models of the underlying mappings and to propagate signals backward through the models. Thus the Jacobian matrices $(\partial \mathbf{z}_\alpha / \partial \mathbf{u}_\alpha)$, $(\partial \mathbf{z}_\alpha / \partial \mathbf{x}_\alpha)$, and $(\partial \mathbf{y}_\alpha / \partial \mathbf{x}_\alpha)$ in Equations 17, 18, and 19 are all replaced by estimated quantities in computing the estimated stochastic gradient of J.

In the following two sections, we pursue the presentation of the distal learning approach in the context of two problem domains. The first section describes learning in a static environment, whereas the second section describes learning in a dynamic environment. In both sections, we utilize the local optimization formulation of distal learning.

STATIC ENVIRONMENTS

An environment is said to be *static* if the effect of any given action is independent of the history of previous actions. In static environments the mapping from actions to sensations can be characterized without reference to a set of state variables. Such environments provide a simplified domain in which to study the learning of inverse mappings. In this section, we present an illustrative static environment and focus on two issues: (1) the effects of nonconvex inverse images in the transformation from sensations to actions and (2) the problem of goal-directed learning.

The problem that we consider is that of learning the forward and inverse kinematics of a three-joint planar arm. As shown in Figure 11 and Figure 12 the

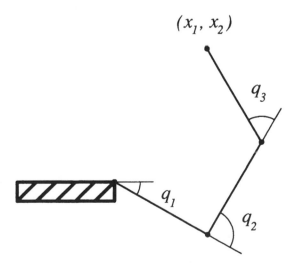

Figure 11. A three-joint planar arm.

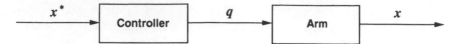

Figure 12.   The forward and inverse mappings associated with arm kinematics.

configuration of the arm is characterized by the three joint angles q_1, q_2, and q_3, and the corresponding pair of Cartesian variables x_1 and x_2. The function that relates these variables is the *forward kinematic* function $\mathbf{x} = g(\mathbf{q})$. It is obtained in closed form using elementary trigonometry:

$$\begin{bmatrix} x_1 \\ x_2 \end{bmatrix} = \begin{bmatrix} l_1 \cos(q_1) + l_2 \cos(q_1 + q_2) + l_3 \cos(q_1 + q_2 + q_3) \\ l_1 \sin(q_1) + l_2 \sin(q_1 + q_2) + l_3 \sin(q_1 + q_2 + q_3) \end{bmatrix}, \quad (20)$$

where l_1, l_2, and l_3 are the link lengths.

The forward kinematic function $g(\mathbf{q})$ is a many-to-one mapping; that is, for every Cartesian position that is inside the boundary of the workspace, there are an infinite number of joint-angle configurations to achieve that position. This implies that the *inverse kinematic* relation $g^{-1}(\mathbf{x})$ is not a function; rather, there are an infinite number of inverse kinematic functions corresponding to particular choices of points $\mathbf{q}$ in the inverse images of each of the Cartesian positions. The problem of learning an inverse kinematic controller for the arm is that of finding a particular inverse among the many possible inverse mappings.

Simulations

In the simulations reported below, the joint-angle configurations of the arm were presented using the vector $[\cos(q_1 - \pi/2), \cos(q_2), \cos(q_3)]^T$ rather than the vector of joint angles. This effectively restricts the motion of the joints to the intervals $[-\pi/2, \pi/2]$, $[0, \pi]$, and $[0, \pi]$, respectively, assuming that each component of the joint-angle configuration vector is allowed to range over the interval $[-1, 1]$. The Cartesian variables x_1 and x_2 were represented as real numbers ranging over $[-1, 1]$. In all of the simulations, these variables were represented directly as real-valued activations of units in the network. Thus, three units were used to represent joint-angle configurations and two units were used to represent Cartesian positions. Further details on the simulations are provided in Appendix B.

The Nonconvexity Problem

One approach to learning an inverse mapping is to provide training pairs to the learner by observing the input/output behavior of the environment and reversing the role of the inputs and outputs. This approach, which we referred to earlier as "direct inverse modeling," has been proposed in the domain of inverse kinematics by Kuperstein (1988). Kuperstein's idea is to randomly sample points $\mathbf{q}'$ in joint space and to use the real arm to evaluate the forward kinematic function $\mathbf{x} = g(\mathbf{q}')$, thereby obtaining training pairs $(\mathbf{x}, \mathbf{q}')$ for learning the controller. The controller is learned by optimization of the cost functional

$$J = \tfrac{1}{2}E\{(\mathbf{q}' - \mathbf{q})^T(\mathbf{q}' - \mathbf{q})\}, \tag{21}$$

where $\mathbf{q} = h(\mathbf{x}^*)$ is the output of the controller.

As we discussed earlier, a difficulty with the direct inverse modeling approach is that the optimization of the cost functional in Equation 21 does not necessarily yield an inverse kinematic function. The problem arises because of the many-to-one nature of the forward kinematic function (cf. Figure 8). In particular, if two or more of the randomly sampled points $\mathbf{q}'$ happen to map to the same endpoint, then the training data that are provided to the controller is one-to-many. The particular manner in which the inconsistency is resolved depends on the form of the cost functional; use of the sum-of-squared error given in Equation 21 yields an arithmetic average over points that map to the same endpoint. An average in joint space, however, does not necessarily yield a correct result in Cartesian space, because the inverse images of nonlinear transformations are not necessarily convex. This implies that the output of the controller may be in error even though the system has converged to the minimum of the cost functional.

In Figure 13 we demonstrate that the inverse kinematics of the three-joint arm is not convex. To see if this nonconvexity has the expected effect on the direct inverse modeling procedure we conducted a simulation in which a feedforward network with one hidden layer was used to learn the inverse kinematics of the three-joint arm. The simulation provided target vectors to the network by sampling randomly from a uniform distribution in joint space. Input vectors were

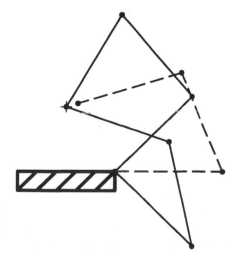

Figure 13.   The nonconvexity of inverse kinematics. The dotted configuration is an average in joint space of the two solid configurations.

obtained by mapping the target vectors into Cartesian space according to Equation 20. The initial value of the root-mean-square (RMS) joint-space error was 1.41, filtered over the first 500 trials. After 50,000 learning trials the filtered error reached asymptote at a value of 0.43. A vector field was then plotted by providing desired Cartesian vectors as inputs to the network, obtaining the joint-angle outputs, and mapping these outputs into Cartesian space using Equation 20. The resulting vector field is shown in Figure 14. As can be seen, there is substantial error at many positions of the workspace, even though the learning algorithm has converged. If training is continued, the loci of the errors continue to shift, but the RMS error remains approximately constant. Although this error is partially due to the finite learning rate and the random sampling procedure ("misadjustment," see Widrow & Stearns, 1985), the error remains above 0.4 even when the learning rate is taken to zero. Thus, misadjustment cannot account for the error, which must be due to the nonconvexity of the inverse kinematic relation. Note, for example, that the error observed in Figure 13 is reproduced in the lower left portion of Figure 14.

In Figure 15, we demonstrate that the distal learning approach can find a particular inverse kinematic mapping. We performed a simulation that was initialized with the incorrect controller obtained from direct inverse modeling. The simulation utilized a forward model that had been trained previously (the forward

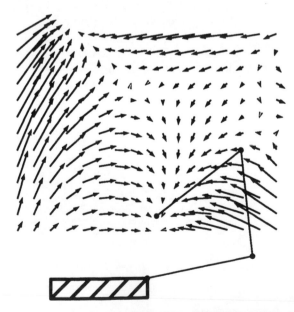

Figure 14.   Near-asymptotic performance of direct inverse modeling. Each vector represents the error at a particular position in the workspace.

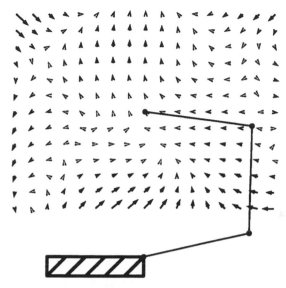

Figure 15.   Near-asymptotic performance of distal learning.

model was trained during the direct inverse modeling trials). A grid of 285 evenly spaced positions in Cartesian space was used to provide targets during the second phase of the distal learning procedure.[11] On each trial the error in Cartesian space was passed backward through the forward model and used to change the weights of the controller. After 28,500 such learning trials (100 passes through the grid of targets), the resulting vector field was plotted. As shown in the figure, the vector error decreases toward zero throughout the workspace; thus, the controller is converging toward a particular inverse kinematic function.

Additional Constraints

A further virtue of the distal learning approach is the ease with which it is possible to incorporate additional constraints in the learning procedure and thereby bias the choice of a particular inverse function. For example, a minimum-norm constraint can be realized by adding a penalty term of the form $-\lambda x$ to the propagated errors at the output of the controller. Temporal smoothness constraints can be realized by incorporating additional error terms of the form $\lambda(x[n] - x[n-1])$. Such constraints can be defined at other sites in the network as well, including the output units or hidden units of the forward model. It is also possible to provide additional contextual inputs to the controller and thereby learn multiple, contextually appropriate inverse functions. These aspects of the distal learning approach are discussed in more detail in Jordan (1988, 1990).

[11]The use of a grid is not necessary; the procedure also works if Cartesian positions are sampled randomly on each trial.

Goal-Directed Learning

Direct inverse modeling does not learn in a goal-directed manner. To learn a specific Cartesian target, the procedure must sample over a sufficiently large region of joint space and rely on interpolation. Heuristics may be available to restrict the search to certain regions of joint space, but such heuristics are essentially prior knowledge about the nature of the inverse mapping and can equally well be incorporated into the distal learning procedure.

Distal learning is fundamentally goal directed. It is based on the performance error for a specific Cartesian target and is capable of finding an exact solution for a particular target in a small number of trials. This is demonstrated by the simulation shown in Figure 16. Starting from the controller shown in Figure 14, a particular Cartesian target was presented for 10 successive trials. As shown in Figure 16, the network reorganizes itself so that the error is small in the vicinity of the target. After 10 additional trials, the error at the target is zero within the floating-point resolution of the simulation.

Approximate Forward Models

We conducted an additional simulation to study the effects of inaccuracy in the forward model. The simulation varied the number of trials allocated to the learning

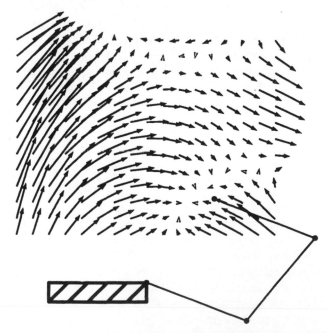

Figure 16.   Goal-directed learning. A Cartesian target in the lower right portion of the figure was presented for 10 successive trials. The error vectors are close to zero in the vicinity of the target.

of the forward model from 50 to 5000. The controller was trained to an RMS criterion of 0.001 at the three target positions $(-0.25, 0.25)$, $(0.25, 0.25)$, and $(0.0, 0.65)$. As shown in Figure 17, the results demonstrated that an accurate controller can be found with an inaccurate forward model. Fewer trials are needed to learn the target positions to criterion with the most accurate forward model; however, the dropoff in learning rate with less accurate forward models is relatively slight. Reasonably rapid learning is obtained even when the forward model is trained for only 50 trials, even though the average RMS error in the forward model is 0.34 after 50 trials, compared to 0.11 after 5000 trials.

Further Comparisons with Direct Inverse Modeling

In problems with many output variables it is often unrealistic to acquire an inverse model over the entire workspace. In such cases the goal-directed nature of distal learning is particularly important because it allows the system to obtain inverse images for a restricted set of locations. However, the forward model must also be learned over a restricted region of action space, and there is no general a priori method of determining the appropriate region of the space in which to sample. That is, although distal learning is goal directed in its acquisition of the inverse model, it is not inherently goal directed in its acquisition of the forward model.

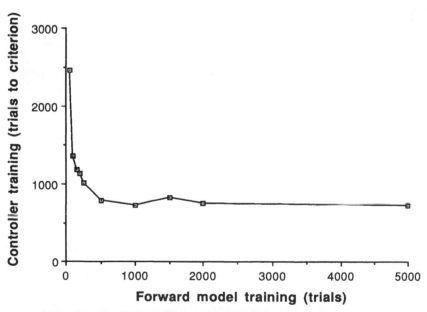

Figure 17.   Number of trials required to train the controller to an RMS criterion of 0.001 as a function of the number of trials allocated to training the forward model. Each point is an average over three runs.

Because neither direct inverse modeling nor distal learning is entirely goal directed, in any given problem it is important to consider whether it is more reasonable to acquire the inverse model or the forward model in non-goal-directed manner. This issue is problem dependent, depending on the nature of the function being learned, the nature of the class of functions that can be represented by the learner, and the nature of the learning algorithm. There is, however, an inherent trade-off in complexity between the inverse model and the forward model, due to the fact that their composition is the identity mapping. This trade-off suggests a complementarity between the classes of problems for which direct inverse modeling and distal learning are appropriate. We believe that distal learning is more generally useful, however, because an inaccurate forward model is generally acceptable, whereas an inaccurate inverse model is not. In many cases, it may be preferable to learn an inaccurate forward model that is specifically inverted at a desired set of locations rather than learning an inaccurate inverse model directly and relying on interpolation.

DYNAMIC ENVIRONMENTS: ONE-STEP DYNAMIC MODELS

To illustrate the application of distal learning to problems in which the environment has state, we consider the problem of learning to control a two-joint robot arm. Controlling a dynamic robot arm involves finding the appropriate torques to cause the arm to follow desired trajectories. The problem is difficult because of the nonlinear couplings between the motions of the two links and because of the fictitious torques due to the rotating coordinate systems.

The arm that we consider is the two-link version of the arm shown in Figure 11. Its configuration at each point in time is described by the joint angles $q_1(t)$ and $q_2(t)$), and by the Cartesian variables $x_1(t)$ and $x_2(t)$. The kinematic function $\mathbf{x}(t) = g(\mathbf{q(t)})$ that relates joint angles to Cartesian variables can be obtained by letting l_3 equal zero in Equation 20:

$$\begin{bmatrix} x_1(t) \\ x_2(t) \end{bmatrix} = \begin{bmatrix} l_1 \cos(q_1(t)) + l_2 \cos(q_1(t) + q_2(t)) \\ l_1 \sin(q_1(t)) + l_2 \sin(q_1(t) + q_2(t)) \end{bmatrix},$$

where l_1 and l_2 are the link lengths. The state space for the arm is the four-dimensional space of positions and velocities of the links.

The essence of robot arm dynamics is a mapping between the torques applied at the joints and the resulting angular accelerations of the links. This mapping is dependent on the state variables of angle and angular velocity. Let $\mathbf{q}$, $\dot{\mathbf{q}}$, and $\ddot{\mathbf{q}}$ represent the vector of joint angles, angular velocities, and angular accelerations, respectively, and let $\boldsymbol{\tau}$ represent the torques. In the terminology of earlier sections, $\mathbf{q}$ and $\dot{\mathbf{q}}$ together constitute the "state" and $\boldsymbol{\tau}$ is the "action." For convenience, we take $\ddot{\mathbf{q}}$ to represent the "next state" (see the discussion following). To obtain an analog of the next-state function in Equation 1, the following differential equation can be derived for the angular motion of the links, using standard Newtonian or Lagrangian dynamical formulations (Craig, 1986):

$$M(\mathbf{q})\ddot{\mathbf{q}} + C(\mathbf{q}, \dot{\mathbf{q}})\dot{\mathbf{q}} + G(\mathbf{q}) = \boldsymbol{\tau}, \tag{22}$$

where $M(\mathbf{q})$ is an inertia matrix, $C(\mathbf{q}, \dot{\mathbf{q}})$ is a matrix of Coriolis and centripetal terms, and $G(\mathbf{q})$ is the vector of torque due to gravity. Our interest is not in the physics behind these equations per se, but in the functional relationships that they define. In particular, to obtain a "next-state function," we rewrite Equation 22 by solving for the accelerations to yield

$$\ddot{\mathbf{q}} = M^{-1}(\mathbf{q})[\boldsymbol{\tau} - C(\mathbf{q}, \dot{\mathbf{q}})\dot{\mathbf{q}} - G(\mathbf{q})], \tag{23}$$

where the existence of $M^{-1}(\mathbf{q})$ is always assured (Craig, 1986). Equation 23 expressed the state-dependent relationship between torques and accelerations at each moment in time: given the state variables $\mathbf{q}(t)$ and $\dot{\mathbf{q}}(t)$, and given the torque $\boldsymbol{\tau}(t)$, the acceleration $\ddot{\mathbf{q}}(t)$ can be computed by substitution in Equation 23. We refer to this computation as the *forward dynamics* of the arm.

An inverse mapping between torques and accelerations can be obtained by interpreting Equation 22 in the proper manner. Given the state variables $\mathbf{q}(t)$ and $\dot{\mathbf{q}}(t)$, and given the acceleration $\ddot{\mathbf{q}}(t)$, substitution in Equation 22 yields the corresponding torques. This (algebraic) computation is referred to as *inverse dynamics*. It should be clear that inverse dynamics and forward dynamics are complementary computations: Substitution of $\boldsymbol{\tau}$ from Equation 22 into Equation 23 yields the requisite identity mapping.

These relationships between torques, accelerations, and states are summarized in Figure 18. It is useful to compare this figure with the kinematic example shown in Figure 12. In both the kinematic case and the dynamic case, the forward and inverse mappings that must be learned are fixed functions of the instantaneous values of the relevant variables. In the dynamic case, this is due to the fact that the structural terms of the dynamical equations (the terms M, C, and G) are explicit functions of state rather than time. The dynamic case can be thought of as a generalization of the kinematic case in which additional contextual (state) variables are needed to index the mappings that must be learned.[12]

Figure 18 is an instantiation of Figure 6, with the acceleration playing the role of the "next state." In general, for systems described by differential equations, it is convenient to define the notion of next state in terms of the time derivative of one or more of the state variables (e.g., accelerations in the case of arm dynamics). This definition is entirely consistent with the development in preceding sections; indeed, if the differential equations in Equation 22 are simulated in discrete time on a computer, then the numerical algorithm must compute the

---

[12]This perspective is essentially that underlying the local optimization formulation of distal learning.

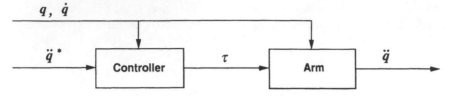

$q, \dot{q}$

$\ddot{q}^{\,*}$ → **Controller** → τ → **Arm** → $\ddot{q}$

Figure 18. The forward and inverse mappings associated with arm dynamics.

accelerations defined by Equation 23 to convert the positions and velocities at the current time step into the positions and velocities at the next time step.[13]

Learning a Dynamic Forward Model

A forward model of arm dynamics is a network that learns a prediction $\hat{\ddot{\mathbf{q}}}$ of the acceleration $\ddot{\mathbf{q}}$, given the position $\mathbf{q}$, the velocity $\dot{\mathbf{q}}$, and the torque $\boldsymbol{\tau}$. The appropriate teaching signal for such a network is the actual acceleration $\ddot{\mathbf{q}}$, yielding the cost functional

$$L = \tfrac{1}{2}E\{(\ddot{\mathbf{q}} - \hat{\ddot{\mathbf{q}}})^T(\ddot{\mathbf{q}} - \hat{\ddot{\mathbf{q}}})\}. \tag{24}$$

The prediction $\hat{\ddot{\mathbf{q}}}$ is a function of the position, the velocity, the torque, and the weights:

$$\hat{\ddot{\mathbf{q}}} = \hat{f}(\mathbf{q}, \dot{\mathbf{q}}, \boldsymbol{\tau}, \mathbf{w}).$$

For an appropriate ensemble of control trajectories, this cost functional is minimized when a set of weights is found such that $\hat{f}(\cdot, \mathbf{w})$ best approximates the forward dynamical function given by Equation 23.

An important difference between kinematic problems and dynamic problems is that it is generally infeasible to produce arbitrary random control signals in dynamical environments, because of considerations of stability. For example, if $\boldsymbol{\tau}(t)$ in Equation 22 is allowed to be a stationary white-noise stochastic process, then the variance of $\mathbf{q}(t)$ approaches infinity (much like a random walk). This yields data that is of little use for learning a model. We have used two closely related approaches to overcome this problem. The first approach is to produce random *equilibrium* positions for the arm rather than random torques. That is, we define a new control signal $\mathbf{u}(t)$ such that the augmented arm dynamics are given by

$$M(\mathbf{q})\ddot{\mathbf{q}} + C(\mathbf{q}, \dot{\mathbf{q}})\dot{\mathbf{q}} + G(\mathbf{q}) = k_v(\dot{\mathbf{q}} - \dot{\mathbf{u}}) + k_p(\mathbf{q} - \mathbf{u}), \tag{25}$$

---

[13]Because of the amplification of noise in differentiated signals, however, most realistic implementations of forward dynamical models would utilize positions and velocities rather than accelerations. In such cases the numerical integration of Equation 23 would be incorporated as part of the forward model.

for fixed constants k_p and k_v. The random control signal **u** in this equation acts as a "virtual" equilibrium position for the arm (Hogan, 1984) and the augmented dynamics can be used to generate training data for learning the forward model. The second approach also utilizes Equation 25 and differs from the first approach only in the choice of the control signal $\mathbf{u}(t)$. Rather than using random controls, the target trajectories themselves are used as controls (that is, the trajectories utilized in the second phase of learning are also used to train the forward model). This approach is equivalent to using a simple fixed-gain proportional-derivative (PD) feedback controller to stabilize the system along a set of reference trajectories and thereby generate training data.[14] Such use of an auxiliary feedback controller is similar to its use in the feedback-error learning (Kawato et al., 1987) and direct inverse modeling (Atkeson & Reinkensmeyer, 1988; Miller, 1987) approaches. As is discussed later, the second approach has the advantage that it does not require the forward model to be learned in a separate phase.

Composite Control System

The composite system for controlling the arm is shown in Figure 19. The control signal in this diagram is the torque $\boldsymbol{\tau}$, which is the sum of two components:

$$\boldsymbol{\tau} = \boldsymbol{\tau}_{ff} + \boldsymbol{\tau}_{fb},$$

where $\boldsymbol{\tau}_{ff}$ is a feedforward torque and $\boldsymbol{\tau}_{fb}$ is the (optional) feedback torque produced by the auxiliary feedback controller. The feedforward controller is the learning controller that converges toward a model of the inverse dynamics of the arm. In the early phases of learning, the feedforward controller produces small random torques, thus the major source of control is provided by the error-correcting feedback controller.[15] When the feedforward controller begins to be learned it produces torques that allow the system to follow desired trajectories with smaller error, thus the role of the feedback controller is diminished. Indeed, in the limit where the feedforward controller converges to a perfect inverse model, the feedforward torque causes the system to follow a desired trajectory without error and the feedback controller is therefore silent (assuming no disturbances). Thus the system shifts automatically from feedback-dominated control to feedforward-dominated control over the course of learning (see also Atkeson & Reinkensmeyer, 1988; Kawato et al., 1987; Miller, 1987).

There are two error signals utilized in learning inverse dynamics: the prediction error $\ddot{\mathbf{q}} - \hat{\ddot{\mathbf{q}}}$ and the performance error $\ddot{\mathbf{q}}^* - \ddot{\mathbf{q}}$.[16] The prediction error is used

[14]A PD controller is a device whose output is a weighted sum of position errors and velocity errors. The position errors and the velocity errors are multiplied by fixed numbers (gains) before being summed.

[15]As discussed later, this statement is not entirely accurate. The learning algorithm itself provides a form of error-correcting feedback control.

[16]As noted above, it is also possible to include the numerical integration of $\hat{\ddot{\mathbf{q}}}$ as part of the forward model and learn a mapping whose output is the predicted next-state $(\dot{\mathbf{q}}[n], \mathbf{q}[n])$. This approach may be preferred for systems in which differentiation of noisy signals is a concern.

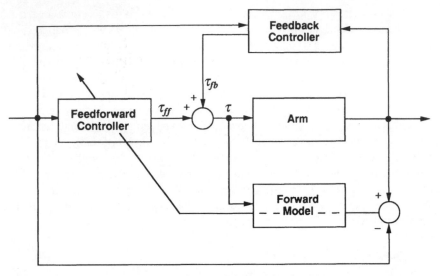

Figure 19.   The composite control system.

to train the forward model as discussed in the previous section. Once the forward model is at least partially learned, the performance error can be used in training the inverse model. The error is propagated backward through the forward model and down into the feedforward controller where the weights are changed. This process minimizes the distal cost functional:

$$J = \tfrac{1}{2}E\{(\ddot{\mathbf{q}}^* - \ddot{\mathbf{q}})^T(\ddot{\mathbf{q}}^* - \ddot{\mathbf{q}})\}. \tag{26}$$

Simulations

The arm was modeled using rigid-body dynamics assuming the mass to be uniformly distributed along the links. The links were modeled as thin cylinders. Details on the physical constants are provided in Appendix C. The simulation of the forward dynamics of the arm was carried out using a fourth-order Runge-Kutta algorithm with a sampling frequency of 200 Hz. The control signals provided by the networks were sampled at 100 Hz.

Standard feedforward connectionist networks were used in all of the simulations. There were two feedforward networks in each simulation—a controller and a forward model—with overall connectivity as shown in Figure 18 (with the box labeled "Arm" being replaced by a forward model). Both the controller and the forward model were feedforward networks with a single layer of logistic hidden units. In all of the simulations, the state variables, torques, and accelerations were represented directly as real-valued activations in the network. Details of the networks used in the simulations are provided in Appendix B.

In all but the final simulation reported later, the learning of the forward model

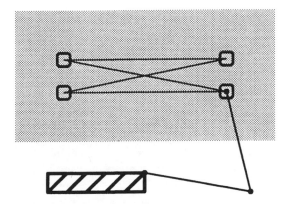

Figure 20. The workspace (the gray region) and four target paths.
The trajectories move from left to right along the paths shown.

and the learning of an inverse model were carried out in separate phases. The
forward model was learned in an initial phase by using a random process to drive
the augmented dynamics given in Equation 25. The random process was a white
noise position signal chosen uniformly within the workspace shown in Figure 20.
The learning of the forward model was terminated when the filtered RMS prediction error reached 0.75 rad/sec^2.

Learning with an Auxiliary Feedback Controller

After learning the forward model, the system learned to control the arm along
the four paths shown in Figure 20. The target trajectories were minimum-jerk
trajectories of 1 sec duration each. An auxiliary PD feedback controller was
used, with position gains of 1.0 N·m/rad and velocity gains of 0.2 N·m·sec/rad.
Figure 21 shows the performance on a particular trajectory before learning (with

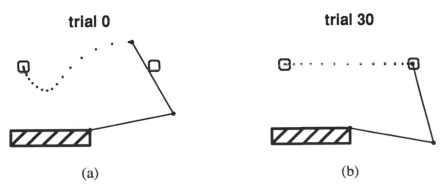

Figure 21. Performance on one of the four learned trajectories:
(a) before learning; (b) after 30 learning trials.

the PD controller alone) and during the thirtieth learning trial. The corresponding waveforms are shown in Figure 22 and Figure 23. The middle graphs in these figures show the feedback torques (dashed lines) and the feedforward torques (solid lines). As can be seen, in the early phases of learning the torques are generated principally by the feedback controller and in later phases the torques are generated principally by the feedforward controller.

Learning without an Auxiliary Feedback Controller

An interesting consequence of the goal-directed nature of the forward modeling approach is that it is possible to learn an inverse dynamic model without using an auxiliary feedback controller. To see why this is the case, first note that minimum-jerk reference trajectories (and other "smooth" reference trajectories) change slowly in time. This implies that successive time steps are essentially repeated learning trials on the same input vector; thus, the controller converges rapidly to a "solution" for a local region of state space. As the trajectory evolves, the solution tracks the input; thus, the controller produces reasonably good torques prior to any "learning." Put another way, the distal learning approach is itself a form of error-correcting feedback control in the parameter space of the controller. Such error correction must eventually give way to convergence of the weights if the system is to learn an inverse model; nonetheless, it is a useful feature of the algorithm that it tends to stabilize the arm during learning.

This behavior is demonstrated by the simulations shown in Figure 24. The figure shows performance on the first learning trial as a function of the learning rate. The results demonstrate that changing the learning rate essentially changes the gain of the error-correcting behavior of the algorithm. When the learning rate is set to 0.5, the system produces nearly perfect performance on the first learning trial. This feature of the algorithm makes it important to clarify the meaning of the learning curves obtained with the distal learning approach. Figure 25 shows two such learning curves. The lower curve is the RMS error that is obtained with a learning rate of 0.1. The upper curve is the RMS error that is obtained when the learning rate is temporarily set to zero after each learning trial. Setting the learning rate to zero allows the effects of learning to be evaluated separately from the error-correcting behavior. The curves clearly reveal that on the early trials the main contributor to performance is error correction rather than learning.

Combining Forward Dynamics and Forward Kinematics

Combining the forward dynamic models of this section with the forward kinematic models of the preceding section makes it possible to train the controller using Cartesian target trajectories. Given that the dynamic model and the kinematic model can be learned in parallel, there is essentially no performance decrement associated with using the combined system. In our simulations, we

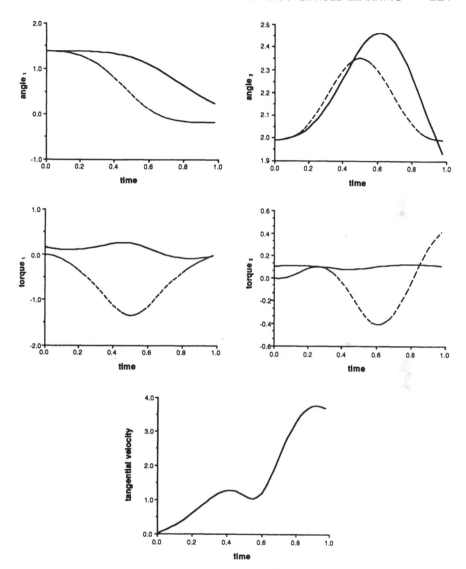

Figure 22   Before learning. In the top graphs, the dotted line is the reference angle and the solid line is the actual angle. In the middle graphs, the dotted line is the feedback torque and the solid line is the feedforward torque.

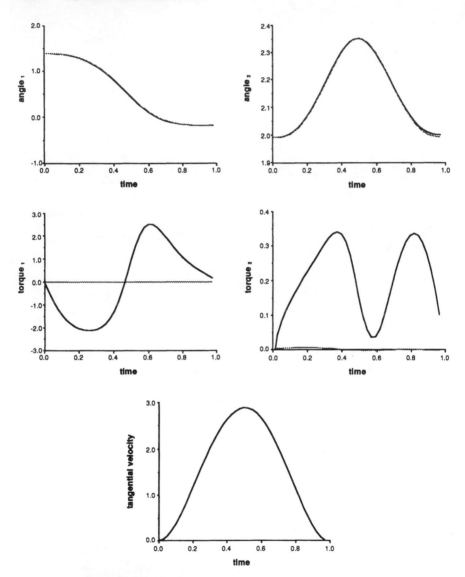

Figure 23.   After learning. In the top graphs, the dotted line is the reference angle and the solid line is the actual angle. In the middle graphs, the dotted line is the feedback torque and the solid line is the feedforward torque.

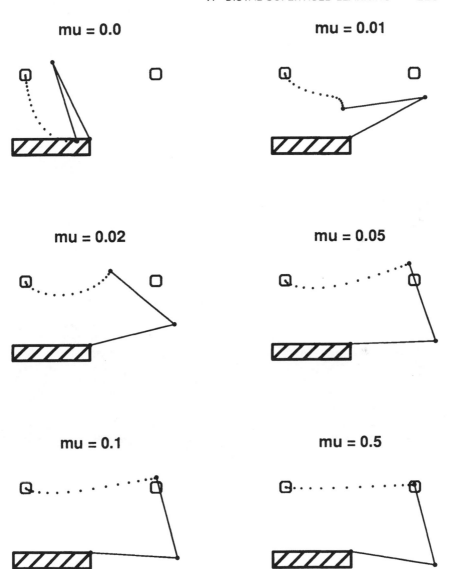

Figure 24. Performance on the first learning trial as a function of the learning rate.

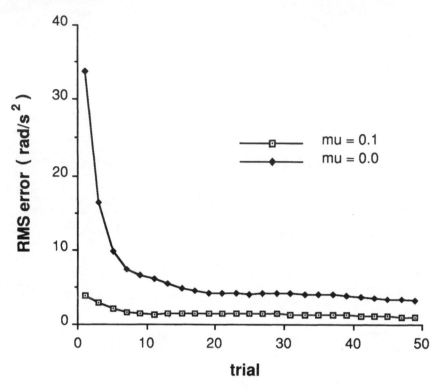

Figure 25.   RMS error for zero and nonzero learning rates.

find that learning times increase by approximately 8% when using Cartesian targets rather than joint-angle targets.

Learning the Forward Model and the Controller Simultaneously

The distal learning approach involves using a forward model to train the controller; thus, learning of the forward model must precede the learning of the controller. It is not necessary, however, to learn the forward model over the entire state space before learning the controller—a *local* forward model is generally sufficient. Moreover, as we have discussed, the distal learning approach does not require an exact forward model—approximate forward models often suffice. These two facts, in conjunction with the use of smooth reference trajectories, imply that it should be possible to learn the forward model and the controller simultaneously. An auxiliary feedback controller is needed to stabilize the system initially; however, once the forward model begins to be learned, the learning algorithm itself tends to stabilize the system. Moreover, as the controller begins to be learned, the errors decrease and the effects of the feedback controller diminish automatically. Thus the system bootstraps itself toward an inverse model.

The simulation shown in Figure 26 demonstrates the feasibility of this approach. Using the same architecture as in previous experiments the system learned four target trajectories starting with small random weights in both the controller and the forward model. On each time step two passes of the backpropagation algorithm were required—one pass with the prediction error $\ddot{q} - \hat{\ddot{q}}$ to change the weights of the forward model, and a second pass with the performance error $\ddot{q}^* - \ddot{q}$ to change the weights of the controller. An auxiliary PD feedback controller was used, with position gains of 1.0 N·m/rad and velocity gains of 0.2 N·m·sec/rad. As shown in the figure, the system converges to an acceptable level of performance after 30 learning trials.

Although the simultaneous learning procedure requires more presentations of the target trajectories to achieve a level of performance comparable to that of the two-phase learning procedure, the simultaneous procedure is in fact more efficient than two-phase learning because it dispenses with the initial phase of learning the forward model. This advantage must be weighed against certain disadvantages; in particular, the possibility of instability is enhanced because of the error in the gradients obtained from the partially learned forward model. In practice we find that it is often necessary to use smaller step sizes in the simultaneous learning approach than in the two-phase learning approach. Preliminary experiments have also shown that is worthwhile to choose specialized representations than enhance the speed with which the forward model converges. This can be done separately for the state variable input and the torque input.

trial 0   **trial 30**

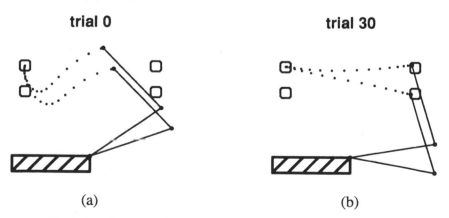

(a)   (b)

Figure 26. Learning the forward model and the controller simultaneously: (a) performance before learning on two of the target trajectories; (b) performance after 30 learning trials.

DYNAMIC ENVIRONMENTS: SIMPLIFIED MODELS

In the previous section we demonstrated how the temporal component of the distal supervised learning problem can be addressed by knowledge of a set of state variables for the environment. Assuming prior knowledge of a set of state variables is tantamount to assuming that the learner has prior knowledge of the maximum delay between the time at which an action is issued and the time at which an effect is observed in the sensation vector. In the current section we present preliminary results that aim to broaden the scope of the distal learning approach to address problems in which the maximum delay is not known (see also Werbos, 1987).

A simple example of such a problem is one in which a robot arm is required to be in a certain configuration at time T, where T is unknown, and where the trajectory in the open interval from 0 to T is unconstrained.[17] One approach to solving such problems is to learn a one-step forward model of the arm dynamics and then to use back propagation-in-time in a recurrent network that includes the forward model and a controller (Jordan, 1990; Kawato, 1990).[18] In many problems involving delayed temporal consequences, however, it is neither feasible nor desirable to learn a dynamic forward model of the environment, either because the environment is too complex or because solving the task at hand does not require knowledge of the evolution of all of the state variables. Consider, for example, the problem of predicting the height of a splash of water when stones of varying size are dropped into a pond. It is unlikely that a useful one-step dynamic model could be learned for the fluid dynamics of the pond. Moreover, if the control problem is to produce splashes of particular desired heights, it may not be necessary to model fluid dynamics in detail. A simple forward model that predicts an integrated quantity—splash height as a function of the size of the stone—may suffice.

Jordan and Jacobs (1990) illustrated this approach by using distal learning to solve the problem of learning to balance an inverted pendulum on a moving cart. This problem is generally posed as an avoidance control problem in which the only corrective information provided by the environment is a signal to indicate that failure has occurred (Barto, Sutton, & Anderson, 1983). The delay between actions (forces applied to the cart) and the failure signal is unknown and indeed can be arbitrarily large. In the spirit of the foregoing discussion, Jordan and

[17]A unique trajectory may be specified by enforcing additional constraints on the temporal evolution of the actions; however, the only explicit target information is assumed to be that provided at the final time step.

[18]In Kawato's work, back propagation-in-time is implemented in a spatially unrolled network and the gradients are used to change activations rather than weights; however, the idea of using a one-step forward dynamic model is the same. See also Nguyen and Widrow (1989) for an application to a kinematic problem.

Jacobs also assumed that it is undesirable to model the dynamics of the cart-pole system; thus, the controller cannot be learned by using back propagation-in-time in a recurrent network that includes a one-step dynamic model of the plant.

The approach adopted by Jordan and Jacobs involves learning a forward model whose output is an integrated quantity—an estimate of the inverse of the time until failure. This estimate is learned using temporal difference techniques (Sutton, 1988). At time steps on which failure occurs, the target value for the forward model is unity:

$$e(t) = 1 - \hat{z}(t),$$

where $\hat{z}(t)$ is the output of the forward model, and $e(t)$ is the error term used to change the weights. On all other time steps, the following temporal difference error term is used:

$$e(t) = \frac{1}{1 + \hat{z}^{-1}(t + 1)} - \hat{z}(t),$$

which yields an increasing arithmetic series along any trajectory that leads to failure. Once learned, the output of the forward model is used to provide a gradient for learning the controller. In particular, because the desired outcome of balancing the pole can be described as the goal of maximizing the time until failure, the algorithm learns the controller by using zero minus the output of the forward model as the distal error signal.[19]

The forward model used by Jordan and Jacobs differs in an important way from the other forward models described in this chapter. Because the time-until-failure depends on future actions of the controller, the mapping that the forward model must learn depends not only on fixed properties of the environment but also on the controller. When the controller is changed by the learning algorithm, the mapping that the forward model must learn also changes. Thus the forward model must be updated continuously during the learning of the controller. In general, for problems in which the forward model learns to estimate an integral of the closed-loop dynamics, the learning of the forward model and the controller *must* proceed in parallel.

Temporal difference techniques provide the distal learning approach with enhanced functionality. They make it possible to learn to make long-term predictions and thereby adjust controllers on the basis on quantities that are distal in time. They can also be used to learn multi-step forward models. In conjunction with backpropagation-in-time, they provide a flexible set of techniques for learning actions on the basis of temporally-extended consequences.

---

[19]This technique can be considered as an example of using supervised learning algorithms to solve a reinforcement learning problem.

DISCUSSION

In this chapter we have argued that the supervised learning paradigm is broader than is commonly assumed. The distal supervised learning framework extends supervised learning to problems in which desired values are available only for the distal consequences of a learner's actions and not for the actions themselves. This is a significant weakening of the classical notion of the "teacher" in the supervised learning paradigm. In this section we provide further discussion of the class of problems that can be treated within the distal supervised learning framework. We discuss possible sources of training data and we contrast distal supervised learning with reinforcement learning.

How Are Training Data Obtained?

To provide support for our argument that distal supervised learning is more realistic than classical supervised learning it is necessary to consider possible sources of training data for distal supervised learning. We discuss two such sources, which we refer to as *imitation* and *envisioning*.

One of the most common ways for humans to acquire skills is through imitation. Skills such as dance or athletics are often learned by observing another person performing the skill and attempting to replicate their behavior. Although in some cases a teacher may be available to suggest particular patterns of limb motion, such direct instruction does not appear to be a necessary component of skill acquisition. A case in point is speech acquisition—children acquire speech by hearing speech sounds, not by receiving instruction on how to move their articulators.

Our conception of a distal supervised learning problem involves a set of (intention, desired outcome) training pairs. Learning by imitation clearly makes desired outcomes available to the learner. With regard to intentions, there are three possibilities. First, the learner may know or be able to infer the intentions of the person serving as a model. Alternatively, an idiosyncratic internal encoding of intentions is viable as long as the encoding is consistent. For example, a child acquiring speech may have an intention to drink, may observe another person obtaining water by uttering the form "water," and may utilize the acoustic representation of "water" as a distal target for learning the articulatory movements for expressing a desire to drink, even thought he other person uses the water to douse a fire. Finally, when the learner is acquiring an inverse model, as in the simulations reported in the paper, the intention is obviously available because it is the same as desired outcome.

Our conception of distal supervised learning problem as a set of training pairs is of course an abstraction that must be elaborated when dealing with complex tasks. In a complex task such as a dance, it is presumably not easy to determine the choice of sensory data to be used as distal targets for the learning procedure. Indeed, the learner may alter the choice of targets once he or she has achieved a modicum of skill. The learner may also need to decompose the task into simpler tasks and to set intermediate goals. We suspect that the role of external "teachers" is to help with these representational issues rather than to provide proximal targets directly to the learner.

Another source of data for the distal supervised learning paradigm is a process that we refer to as "envisioning." Envisioning is a general process of converting abstract goals into their corresponding sensory realization, without regard to the actions needed to achieve the goals. Envisioning involves deciding what it would "look like" or "feel like" to perform some task. This process presumably involves general deductive and inductive reasoning abilities as well as experience with similar tasks. The point that we want to emphasize is that envisioning need not refer to the actions that are needed to actually carry out a task; that is the problem solved by the distal learning procedure.

Comparisons with Reinforcement Learning

An alternative approach to solving the class of problems that we have discussed in this paper is to use reinforcement learning algorithms (Barto, 1989; Sutton, 1984). Reinforcement learning algorithms are based on the assumption that the environment provides an *evaluation* of the actions produced by the learner. Because the evaluation can be an arbitrary function, the approach is in principle applicable to the general problem of learning on the basis of distal signals.

Reinforcement learning algorithms work by updating the probabilities of emitting particular actions. The updating procedure is based on the evaluations received from the environment. If the evaluation of an action is favorable, then the probability associated with that action is increased and the probabilities associated with all other actions are decreased. Conversely, if the evaluation is unfavorable, then the probability of the given action is decreased and the probabilities associated with all other actions are increased. These characteristic features of reinforcement learning algorithms differ in important ways from the corresponding features of supervised learning algorithms. Supervised learning algorithms are based on the existence of a signed error vector rather than an evaluation. The signed error vector is generally, although not always, obtained by comparing the actual output vector to a target vector. If the signed error vector is small, corresponding to a favorable evaluation, the algorithm initiates no changes. If the signed error vector is large, corresponding to an unfavorable evaluation, the algorithm corrects the current action in favor of a particular alternative action. Supervised learning algorithms do not simply increase the probabilities of all alternative actions; rather, they choose particular alternatives based on the directionality of the signed error vector.[20]

---

[20]As pointed out by Barto, Sutton, and Anderson (1983), this distinction between reinforcement learning and supervised learning is significant only if the learner has a repertoire of more than two actions.

It is important to distinguish between learning *paradigms* and learning *algorithms*. Because the same learning algorithm can often be utilized in a variety of learning paradigms, a failure to distinguish between paradigms and algorithms can lead to misunderstanding. This is particularly true of reinforcement learning tasks and supervised learning tasks because of the close relationships between evaluative signals and signed error vectors. A signed error vector can always be converted into an evaluative signal (any bounded monotonic function of the norm of the signed error vector suffices); thus, reinforcement learning algorithms can always be used for supervised learning problems. Conversely, an evaluative signal can always be converted into a signed error vector (using the machinery that we have discussed; see also Munro, 1987); thus, supervised learning algorithms can always be used for reinforcement learning problems. The definition of a learning paradigm, however, has more to do with the manner in which a problem is naturally posed than with the algorithm used to solve the problem. In the case of the basketball player, for example, assuming that the environment provides directional information such as "too far to the left," "too long," or "too short," is very different from assuming that the environment provides evaluative information of the form "good," "better," or "best." Furthermore, learning algorithms differ in algorithmic complexity when applied across paradigms: using a reinforcement learning algorithm to solve a supervised learning problem is likely to be inefficient because such algorithms do not take advantage of directional information. Conversely, using supervised learning algorithms to solve reinforcement learning problems is likely to be inefficient because of the extra machinery that is required to induce a signed error vector.

In summary, although it has been suggested that the difference between reinforcement learning and supervised learning is the latter's reliance on a "teacher," we feel that this argument is mistaken. The distinction between the supervised learning paradigm and the reinforcement learning paradigm lies in the interpretation of environmental feedback as an error signal or as an evaluative signal, not the coordinate system in which such signals are provided. Many problems involving distal credit assignment may be better conceived of as supervised learning problems rather than reinforcement learning problems if the distal feedback signal can be interpreted as a performance error.

CONCLUSIONS

There are a number of difficulties with the classical distinctions between "unsupervised," "reinforcement," and "supervised" learning. Supervised learning is generally said to be dependent on a "teacher" to provide target values for the output units of a network. This is viewed as a limitation because in many domains there is no such teacher. Nevertheless, the environment often does provide sensory information about the consequences of an action which can be employed in making internal modifications just as if a teacher had provided the information to the learner directly. The idea is that the learner first acquires an internal model that allows prediction of the consequences of actions. The internal model can be used as a mechanism for transforming distal sensory information about the consequences of actions into proximal information for making internal modifications. This two-phase procedure extends the scope of the supervised learning paradigm to include a broad range of problems in which actions are transformed by an unknown dynamical process before being compared to desired outcomes.

We first illustrated this approach in the case of learning an inverse model of a simple "static" environment. We showed that our method of utilizing a forward model of the environment has a number of important advantages over the alternative method of building the inverse model directly. These advantages are especially apparent in cases where there is no unique inverse model. We also showed that this idea can be extended usefully to the case of a dynamic environment. In this case, we simply elaborate both the forward model and the learner (i.e., controller) so they take into account the current state of the environment. Finally, we showed how this approach can be combined with temporal difference techniques to build a system capable of learning from sensory feedback that is subject to an unknown delay.

We also suggest that comparative work in the study of learning can be facilitated by making a distinction between learning algorithms and learning paradigms. A variety of learning algorithms can often be applied to a particular instance of a learning paradigm; thus, it is important to characterize not only the paradigmatic aspects of any given learning problem, such as the nature of the interaction between the learner and the environment and the nature of the quantities to be optimized, but also the trade-offs in algorithmic complexity that arise when different classes of learning algorithms are applied to the problem. Further research is needed to delineate the natural classes at the levels of paradigms and algorithms and to clarify the relationships between levels. We believe that such research will begin to provide a theoretical basis for making distinctions between candidate hypotheses in the empirical study of human learning.

ACKNOWLEDGMENTS

This chapter originally appeared in *Cognitive Science*, 1992, *16*, 307–354. Copyright 1992 by Ablex Publishing. Reprinted by permission.

We wish to thank Michael Mozer, Andrew Barto, Robert Jacobs, Eric Loeb, and James McClelland for helpful comments on the manuscript. This project was supported in part by BRSG 2 S07 RR07047-23 awarded by the Biomedical Research Support Grant Program, Division of Research Resources, National Institutes of Health, by a grant from ATR Auditory and Visual Perception Research Laboratories, by a grant from Siemens Corporation, by a grant from the Human Frontier Science Program, and by grant N00014-90-J-1942 awarded by the Office of Naval Research.

REFERENCES

Atkeson, C. G., & Reinkensmeyer, D. J. (1988). Using associative content-addressable memories to control robots. *IEEE Conference on Decision and Control.* San Francisco, CA.

Barto, A. G. (1989). From chemotaxis to cooperativity: Abstract exercises in neuronal learning strategies. In R. M. Durbin, R. C. Maill, & G. J. Mitchison (Eds.), *The computing neurone.* Reading, MA: Addison-Wesley.

Barto, A. G., Sutton, R. S., & Anderson, C. W. (1983). Neuronlike adaptive elements that can solve difficult learning control problems. *IEEE Transactions on Systems, Man, and Cybernetics, SMC-13,* 834–846.

Becker, S., & Hinton, G. E. (1989). *Spatial coherence as an internal teacher for a neural network.* (Technical Report CRG-TR-89-7). Toronto: University of Toronto.

Carlson, A. B. (1986). *Communication systems.* New York: McGraw-Hill.

Craig, J. J. (1986). *Introduction to robotics.* Reading, MA: Addison-Wesley.

Gelfand, I. M., & Fomin, S. V. (1963). *Calculus of variations.* Englewood Cliffs, NJ: Prentice-Hall.

Goodwin, G. C., & Sin, K. S. (1984). *Adaptive filtering prediction and control.* Englewood Cliffs, NJ: Prentice-Hall.

Grossberg, S. (1987). Competitive learning: From interactive activation to adaptive resonance. *Cognitive Science, 11,* 23–63.

Hinton, G. E., & Sejnowski, T. J. (1986). Learning and relearning in Boltzmann machines. In D. E. Rumelhart and J. L. McClelland (Eds.), *Parallel distributed processing* (Vol. 1, pp. 282–317). Cambridge, MA: MIT Press.

Hogan, N. (1984). An organising principle for a class of voluntary movements. *Journal of Neuroscience, 4,* 2745–2754.

Jordan, M. I. (1983). *Mental practice.* Unpublished dissertation proposal. San Diego: Center for Human Information Processing, University of California.

Jordan, M. I. (1986). *Serial order: A parallel, distributed processing approach* (Technical Report 8604). La Jolla, CA: University of California, San Diego.

Jordan, M. I. (1988). *Supervised learning and systems with excess degrees of freedom* (COINS Technical Report 88-27). Amherst, MA: University of Massachusetts, Computer and Information Sciences.

Jordan, M. I. (1990). Motor learning and the degrees of freedom problem. In M. Jeannerod (Ed.), *Attention and performance, XIII.* Hillsdale, NJ: Lawrence Erlbaum Associates.

Jordan, M. I., & Jacobs, R. A. (1990). Learning to control an unstable system with forward modeling. In D. Touretsky (Ed.), *Advances in neural information processing systems 2.* San Mateo, CA: Morgan Kaufmann.

Jordan, M. I., & Rosenbaum, D. A. (1989). Action. In M. I. Posner (Ed.), *Foundations of cognitive science.* Cambridge, MA: MIT Press.

Kawato, M. (1990). Computational schemes and neural network models for formation and control of multijoint arm trajectory. In W. T. Miller III, R. S. Sutton, & P. J. Werbos (Eds.), *Neural networks for control.* Cambridge: MIT Press.

Kawato, M., Furukawa, K., & Suzuki, R. (1987). A hierarchical neural-network model for control and learning of voluntary movement. *Biological Cybernetics, 57,* 169–185.

Kirk, D. E. (1970). *Optimal control theory.* Englewood Cliffs, NJ: Prentice-Hall.

Kohonen, T. (1982). Self-organized formation of topologically correct feature maps. *Biological Cybernetics, 43,* 56–69.

Kuperstein, M. (1988). Neural model of adaptive hand-eye coordination for single postures. *Science, 239,* 1308–1311.

LeCun, Y. (1985). A learning scheme for asymmetric threshold networks. *Proceedings of Cognitiva 85.* Paris, France.

LeCun, Y. (1985). *Modèles connexionnistes de l'apprentissage.* Unpublished doctoral dissertation, Université de Paris, VI.

Linsker, R. (1988). Self-organization in a perceptual network. *Computer, 21,* 105–117.

Ljung, L., & Söderström, T. (1986). *Theory and practice of recursive identification.* Cambridge: MIT Press.

Miller, W. T. (1987). Sensor-based control of robotic manipulators using a general learning algorithm. *IEEE Journal of Robotics and Automation, 3,* 157–165.

Miyata, Y. (1988). An unsupervised PDP learning model for action planning. *Proceedings of the Tenth Annual Conference of the Cognitive Science Society.* Hillsdale, NJ: Lawrence Erlbaum Associates.

Mozer, M. C., & Bachrach, J. (1990). Discovering the structure of a reactive environment by exploration. In D. Touretzky (Ed.), *Advances in neural information processing systems 2.* San Mateo, CA: Morgan Kaufmann.

Munro, P. (1987). A dual back-propagation scheme for scalar reward learning. *Proceedings of the Ninth Annual Conference of the Cognitive Science Society.* Hillsdale, NJ: Lawrence Erlbaum Associates.

Narendra, K. S., & Parthasarathy, K. (1990). Identification and control of dynamical systems using neural networks. *IEEE Transactions on Neural Networks, 1,* 4–27.

Nguyen, D., & Widrow, B. (1989). The truck backer-upper: An example of self-learning in neural networks. *Proceedings of the International Joint Conference on Neural Networks, 2* (pp. 357–363). Piscataway, NJ: IEEE press.

Parker, D. (1985). *Learning-logic* (Technical Report TR-47). Cambridge, MA: MIT Sloan School of Management.

Robinson, A. J., & Fallside, F. (1989). Dynamic reinforcement driven error propagation networks with application to game playing. *Proceedings of Neural Information Systems.* American Institute of Physics.

Rosenblatt, F. (1962). *Principles of neurodynamics.* New York: Spartan.

Rumelhart, D. E. (1986). Learning sensorimotor programs in parallel distributed processing systems. *US-Japan Joint Seminar on Competition and Cooperation in Neural Nets, II.* Unpublished presentation.

Rumelhart, D. E., Hinton, G. E., & Williams, R. J. (1986). Learning internal representations by error propagation. In D. E. Rumelhart & J. L. McClelland (Eds.), *Parallel distributed processing* (Vol. 1, pp. 318–363). Cambridge, MA: MIT Press

Rumelhart, D. E., Smolensky, P., McClelland, J. L., & Hinton, G. E. (1986). Schemata and sequential thought processes in PDP models. In D. E. Rumelhart & J. L. McClelland (Eds.), *Parallel distributed processing* (Vol. 2, pp. 7–57). Cambridge, MA: MIT Press.

Rumelhart, D. E., & Zipser, D. (1986). Feature discovery by competitive learning. In D. E. Rumelhart & J. L. McClelland (Eds.), *Parallel distributed processing* (Vol. 1, pp. 151–193). Cambridge, MA: MIT Press.

Schmidhuber, J. H. (1990). An on-line algorithm for dynamic reinforcement learning and planning in reactive environments. *Proceedings of the International Joint Conference on Neural Networks, 2* (pp. 253–258). Piscataway, NJ: IEEE Press.

Sutton, R. S. (1984). *Temporal credit assignment in reinforcement learning.* (COINS Technical Report 84-02). Amherst, MA: University of Massachusetts, Computer and Information Sciences.

Sutton, R. S. (1988). Learning to predict by the methods of temporal differences. *Machine Learning, 3,* 9–44.

Sutton, R. S. (1990). Integrated architectures for learning, planning, and reacting based on approximating dynamic programming. *Proceedings of the Seventh International Conference on Machine Learning.*

Werbos, P. (1974). *Beyond regression: New tools for prediction and analysis in the behavioral sciences.* Unpublished doctoral dissertation, Harvard University.

Werbos, P. (1987). Building and understanding adaptive systems: A statistical/numerical approach to factory automation and brain research. *IEEE Transactions on Systems, Man, and Cybernetics,* *17*, 7–20.

Widrow, B., & Hoff, M. E. (1960). Adaptive switching circuits. *Institute of Radio Engineers, Western Electronic Show and Convention, Convention Record, Part 4,* pp. 96–104.

Widrow, B., & Stearns, S. D. (1985). *Adaptive signal processing.* Englewood Cliffs, NJ: Prentice-Hall.

APPENDIX A

To obtain an expression for the gradient of Equation 16, we utilize a continuous-time analog, derive a necessary condition, and then convert the result into discrete time. To simplify the exposition we compute partial derivatives with respect to the actions $\mathbf{u}$ instead of the weights $\mathbf{w}$. The resulting equations are converted into gradients for the weights by premultiplying by the transpose of the Jacobian matrix $(\partial \mathbf{u}/\partial \mathbf{w})$.

Let $\mathbf{u}(t)$ represent an action trajectory, and let $\mathbf{y}(t)$ represent a sensation trajectory. These trajectories are linked in the forward direction by the dynamical equations

$$\dot{\mathbf{x}} = f(\mathbf{x}, \mathbf{u}) \qquad \text{and} \qquad \mathbf{y} = g(\mathbf{x}).$$

The action vector $\mathbf{u}$ is assumed to depend on the current state and the target vector:

$$\mathbf{u} = h(\mathbf{x}, \mathbf{y}^*).$$

The functional to be minimized is given by the integral

$$J = \frac{1}{2} \int_0^T (\mathbf{y}^* - \mathbf{y})^T (\mathbf{y}^* - \mathbf{y})\, dt,$$

which is the continuous-time analog of Equation 16 (we have suppressed the subscript α to simplify the notation).

Let $\Phi(t)$ and $\Psi(t)$ represent vectors of time-varying Lagrange multipliers and define the Lagrangian:

$$L(t) = \tfrac{1}{2}(\mathbf{y}^* - \mathbf{y})^T(\mathbf{y}^* - \mathbf{y}) + [f(\mathbf{x}, \mathbf{u}) - \dot{\mathbf{x}}]^T\Phi + [h(\mathbf{x}, \mathbf{y}^*) - \mathbf{u}]^T\Psi.$$

The Lagrange multipliers have an interpretation as sensitivities of the cost with respect to variations in $\dot{\mathbf{x}}$ and $\mathbf{y}$, respectively. Because these sensitivities become partial derivatives when the problem is converted to discrete time, we are interested in solving for $\Psi(t)$.

A necessary condition for an optimizing solution is that it satisfy the Euler-Lagrange equations (Gelfand & Fomin, 1963):

$$\frac{\partial L}{\partial \mathbf{x}} - \frac{d}{dt}\frac{\partial L}{\partial \dot{\mathbf{x}}} = 0 \quad \text{and} \quad \frac{\partial L}{\partial \mathbf{u}} - \frac{d}{dt}\frac{\partial L}{\partial \dot{\mathbf{u}}} = 0$$

at each moment in time. These equations are the equivalent in function space of the familiar procedure of setting the partial derivatives equal to zero.

Substituting for $L(t)$ and simplifying, we obtain

$$\dot{\Phi} = -\left(\frac{\partial f}{\partial \mathbf{x}}\right)^T \Phi - \left(\frac{\partial k}{\partial \mathbf{x}}\right)^T \Psi + \left(\frac{\partial g}{\partial \mathbf{x}}\right)^T (\mathbf{y}^* - \mathbf{y})$$

and

$$\Psi = \left(\frac{\partial f}{\partial \mathbf{u}}\right)^T \Phi.$$

Using an Euler approximation, we can rewrite these equations in discrete time as recurrence relations:

$$\Phi[n-1] = \Phi[n] + \tau \left(\frac{\partial f}{\partial \mathbf{x}}\right)^T \Phi[n] + \tau \left(\frac{\partial k}{\partial \mathbf{x}}\right)^T \Psi[n]$$

$$- \tau \left(\frac{\partial g}{\partial \mathbf{x}}\right)^T (\mathbf{y}^*[n] - \mathbf{y}[n]) \tag{A.1}$$

and

$$\Psi[n] = \left(\frac{\partial f}{\partial \mathbf{u}}\right)^T \Phi[n], \tag{A.2}$$

where τ is the sampling period of the discrete approximation. To utilize these recurrence relations in a discrete-time network, the sampling period τ is absorbed in the network approximations of the continuous-time mappings. The network approximation of f must also include an identity feedforward component to account for the initial autoregressive term in Equation A.1. Premultiplication of Equation A.2 by the transpose of the Jacobian matrix $(\partial \mathbf{u}/\partial \mathbf{w})$ then yields Equations 17, 18, and 19.

APPENDIX B

The networks used in all of the simulations were standard feedforward connectionist networks (see Rumelhart, Hinton, & Williams, 1986).

Activation functions: The input units and the output units of all networks were linear and the hidden units were logistic with asymptotes of -1 and 1.

Input and target values: In the kinematic arm simulations, the joint angles were represented using the vector $[\cos(q_1 - \pi/2), \cos(q_2), \cos(q_3)]^T$. The Cartesian targets were scaled to lie between -1 and 1 and fed directly into the network.

In the dynamic arm simulations, all variables—joint angles, angular velocities, angular accelerations, and torques—were scaled and fed directly into the network. The scaling factors were chosen such that the scaled variables ranged approximately from -1 to 1.

Initial weights: Initial weights were chosen randomly from a uniform distribution on the interval $[-0.5, 0.5]$.

Hidden units: A single layer of 50 hidden units was used in all networks. No attempt was made to optimize the number of the hidden units or their connectivity.

Parameter values: A learning rate of 0.1 was used in all of the kinematic arm simulations. The momentum was set to 0.5.

In the dynamic arm simulations, a learning rate of 0.1 was used in all cases, except for the simulation shown in Figure 24, in which the learning rate was manipulated explicitly. No momentum was used in the dynamic arm simulations.

APPENDIX C

The dynamic arm was modeled using rigid-body mechanics. The link lengths were 0.33 m for the proximal link and 0.32 m for the distal link. The masses of the links were 2.52 kg and 1.3 kg.

The mass was assumed to be distributed uniformly along the links. The moments of inertia of the links about their centers of mass were therefore given by $I_i = m_i l_i^2 / 12$, yielding 0.023 kg·m² and 0.012 kg·m² for the proximal and distal links, respectively.

8 Backpropagation: Some Comments and Variations

Stephen José Hanson
Siemens Corporate Research, Princeton, New Jersey

> *The art of model-building is the exclusion of real but irrelevant parts of the problem, and entails hazards for the builder and the reader. The builder may leave out something genuinely relevant; the reader, armed with too sophisticated an experimental probe or too accurate a computation, may take literally a schematized model whose main aim is to be a demonstration of possibility.*
> —P. W. Anderson (from Nobel acceptance speech, 1977)

INTRODUCTION

For the last ten years a simple algorithm called back propagation has held an important place in creating, catalyzing, and spreading what will at least be seen as a minor revolution in the cognitive and brain sciences. At the same time, this relatively simple algorithm has polarized large segments of the research community developing and studying neural-like algorithms. Many kinds of complaints arise:

1. It is nothing new.
2. It is too complex to be in the brain.
3. Its learning method is NP-complete.
4. It is *just* regression.
5. It is too simple to solve complex engineering problems.

It is rather remarkable that such diverse dissension has arisen based on what appears to be simple properties of this one algorithm. How could that be? What

237

caused all this? Why should this particular algorithm be the focus of such debate and disagreement?

As unlikely as it may seem, one event which crystallized much of the interest in neural nets was a single simple back-propagation application which learned to map text to sound: NETtalk. Amazingly enough this model was a nexus for interest, excitement, and activity concerning neural networks and in particular back propagation. I want to beg the reader's patience for a moment to recount a short historical note about this period of time, which provides motivation and perspective for much of technical and conceptual work to follow.

I remember this period quite well as Charlie Rosenberg was part of the Princeton Cognitive Science Lab at that time and both George Miller and I were acting as his thesis advisors. Near the summer of 1985, Charlie had expressed interest in working on some sort of neural computation, and we had both read the Boltzmann machine paper and talked about doing some similar research. As summer drew closer, Charlie had formed a plan to gain practical experience by going to a relevant lab for part of the summer where such work was being done and then coming back well grounded in connectionist research early in the next semester. Charlie had seen Terry Sejnowski give a talk on Boltzmann machines at Princeton and eventually called him about the possibility of working through the summer. Terry agreed that having Charlie come to the lab for the summer would be no problem. Charlie packed up and we agreed to stay in touch and to have him visit Princeton throughout the summer. Well, all was quiet for a month or so, and then I began receiving electronic mail that indicated Charlie was quite excited about something and " . . . would George and I be around this weekend so he could show us something?" As it turned out, both George and I were in the lab on Sunday afternoon, and Charlie showed up with very broad grin and a demo.

Well, or course, what Charlie showed us looked to be an amazing performance after only an evening of training, about 10 hours. His and Terry's little network of 309 units was doing 85% correct phoneme prediction on a new corpus of data after moderate training on 11,000 words from a dictionary. I was quite surprised, and George sat back and observed, "hmmm. .this is all very interesting, but of course you've lost all the rules haven't you?" Well, indeed it seemed as though the network was some sort of "trapdoor" and the rules of production were no longer accessible. We all became intensely interested in the way the information was represented by the network. Charlie was interested in understanding the nature of the performance errors and perhaps this would help him understand some of the representational principles underlying NETtalk's knowledge. He wondered if he could borrow a DECTALK I had lying around at the time so he could hear some of the performance errors. By the next week, he had NETtalk expressing its behavior through the DECTALK. Throughout the next semester, "Nah rum na rum ba . . ." could be heard down the hall as this precocious network mastered vowels and consonants and their combinations. Early in that semester, Mike Gazzaniga, who was then at Cornell Medical College in New York, was visiting George and got to hear the now famous NETtalk/DECTALK demo. Upon returning to New York the next day, he happened to have lunch with NBC science editor Robert Bazell, to whom he happened to mention a remarkable performance of a "neural net." Well, soon thereafter the *Today Show* ran a minute-and-half spot on NETtalk. The AP news wire picked it up, and within a few weeks the *New York Times, Business Week,* radio programs (I heard it on NPR!), everything but the *National Enquirer* (as far as I know), seemed to have a story about NETtalk. Incredibly, neural networks were quickly becoming part of standard grocery line and coffee table chatter.

I suspect that most of the criticisms of back propagation can be traced back to NETtalk and the particular mythologies that seemed to surround it. But as this historical footnote suggests, much of the interest and focus on NETtalk was quite accidental. In particular, back propagation, like any technology put to a given use cannot be credited with the successes or failures of a particular application. In retrospect, the importance of the NETtalk was nothing more than a demonstration of possibility, of learning from *tabula rasa,* a complex behavior. Its implications for phonology, expert systems, knowledge representation, learnability theory, speech synthesis, rule learning, and complex skill learning all hovered like some clouds prior to a downpour. No one wanted to get wet, but no one wanted to go inside either.

BACK PROPAGATION AS A FRAMEWORK FOR THINKING ABOUT NEURAL NETWORKS

In the following years, after NETtalk, there have been many more demonstrations of the use of back propagation in applied domains, some controversial some less. The issues concerning the nature of representation and learning have become more polarized and somewhat more confused. In this chapter I would like to discuss some of the issues that still seem to "hover" about back propagation, and some enduring misconceptions about the algorithm and its genesis as well as its place in the vast sea of more normative statistical and modeling methods.

Back propagation can be seen as representing a specific case of a more general way to think about and ask questions about neural computation. Hopfield networks, Boltzmann machines, and the like all share with back propagation a number of very simple innovations. Nonetheless, these innovations, I claim, make such models unique, complementary, and productive.

In the past years, at workshops, conferences, and in print a number of innuendoes, claims, and platitudes have been put forth concerning back propagation. I would like to discuss some of these briefly. Actually, I think one of the first claims I heard about back propagation was that it was just "statistics."

Statistics

It's true. It is just statistics. And we're all just made out of atoms and so are tables. I mean—really—observations like this are just too general to be very useful.[1] But I have heard more specific comments. too. It is just *regression*. It is just nonlinear regression. It is just multivariate, nonlinear stochastic approximation (we're getting closer!). It is just multivariate, nonlinear, nonparametric,[2] stochastic approximation. Finally, it is just multivariate, nonlinear, nonparametric, stochastic approximation with dynamic feature extraction/selection. Whew! Yup, this is it. And it does have a place in standard regression/model specification literature (cf. Werbos, 1974; Draper & Smith, 1975; Barron, 1989) and apparently a place in approximation and regularization theory (Poggio & Girosi, 1989). That is, considering back propagation as representing a *class* of statistical models it is not new. Nonetheless, as a *particular* model using non-linearities (in the parameters), stochastic approximation, and dynamic feature extraction/selection it is quite unique and novel. And of course, logical varia-tions on aspects of the model are also novel. I think its pretty ungenerous of working statisticians who know how hard it is to come by models not to credit Rumelhart, Hinton, and Williams (RHW) with coming up with a rather interest-ing composite-variable, nonlinear regression model. What seems to cause the confusion here is that RHW were not interested in space vehicle landing trajecto-ries, wheat yields in South Dakota, or the multitude of fascinating specific applications that arise for the processional statistician working in the real world. Rather, they outlined a number of *general* considerations for how a model that had some abstract brainlike properties might look. These general considerations, however, do not at the same time make the model general. Instead they lead to a pretty interesting model that can do principal components (cf. Baldi, this vol-ume), nonlinear regression, composite-variable extraction, sigmoidal function approximation, and nonconvex discriminant analysis. Whether any of this has to do with the brain or not depends on how plausible those general considerations are about the simplified brainlike assumptions that RHW posited. I still think it is rather interesting that various well-known statistical methods can "pop out" of a model motivated from rather general, abstract, and, no doubt, cartoonlike prop-erties of the brain. Frankly, this still seems to me to be the a remarkable aspect of back propagation.

Notwithstanding these sort of coincidences, connectionists seem to have cho-sen a rather arcane and difficult set of problems. What they seem to have in common is that they are *nonnormative* and typically unexplored in terms of algorithm space. It is as though neural network people have thrown a dart in the

---

[1]Recently similar comments like "it just optimization" have been heard and are just like the "just statistics" observations and thus suffer from the similar problem.

[2]Nonparametric is used to refer to models where neither the functional form of the mean function nor the error distribution is prespecified.

middle of the region of the algorithm space that represents approaches that are nonlinear, nonparametric, dynamic, and high dimensional—areas statisticians (and other sensible people) try to avoid. And yet even superficial, or perhaps especially superficial, views of the brain suggest that it is a computational device that is nonlinear, nonparametric, dynamic, and very high dimensional which seems to work quite well. What the exact connection is between neural networks and biological networks remains to be seen (but see Hanson & Olson, 1990; Gluck & Rumelhart, 1990).

Another platitude that seems to be popular these days is the claim that . . . " . . . if you don't design in what you know learning is hopeless." This claim is made in many forms and consequently results in many misconceptions about the relationship between learning and evolution or, more precisely, the complex interplay between the ontogeny (the developmental history) and phlogeny (the species history) of the biological system and its relationship with its niche.

Nature versus Nurture

Actually this complaint is really an attack on learning, not just unstructured networks using back propagation. It also seems to be validated by much of the recent work showing that learning in multilayer networks is NP-complete (Judd, 1988; Blum & Rivest, 1988). There are a number of issues here, so let me try to separate them a bit. First the "nature versus nurture" polarization is a very old one, and has been often articulated in the area of "intelligence testing" and the nature of intelligence. The entanglement of genetic endowment and experience is not a simple one to unravel. Many decades of research with identical and fraternal twins reared together or separated from birth has led to many confusing sorts of results; some suggesting that aspects of intelligence might be inherited, while others suggest aspects might be due to experience. The vast majority of such analyses usually suggest the worst outcome: it's a bit of both. Intelligence, like many other complex biological traits, is both learned and preconditioned. It is naive to assume that complex traits are somehow prewired and immutable.

But the complaint is usually more mundane than this. It usually just involves the relationship between engineering and adaptation. It goes like this: "look, we know that we have retinas, we know we have basilar membranes, so let's build those right and then start learning." Well, no one of course would disagree with the idea that starting with inputs that might make the problem easier or more biologically relevant is good one. This is a strawman. What is really at issue is, what can we actually assume is the functional design of the retina, optic tract, LGN, and other waystations to visual cortex? What is the necessary level of detail? What can be ignored? What can't? Besides waiting for neuroscientists to answer these questions, modelers can propose hypothetical structure in networks that learn and ask what would happen if . . . ? And yes, even unstructured networks could be useful in trying to understand the nature of various structures that might be apparent in the brain but not obvious in terms of their particular function (cf. Lehky & Sejnowski, 1988; Hanson & Kegl, 1987). Furthermore, structures like retinas, wings, and brains themselves all evolved, which of course could be seen as "learning" on just a longer time scale. Such analyses can be quite informative in determining how such traits may have evolved or on shorter time scales how such traits like feature analyzers in the brain may have developed (cf. Linsker, 1990).

Recently, this has all gotten entwined with complexity or abstract learnability theory. It has been shown a number of times how learning even in very simple networks is NP-complete. At the risk of oversimplifying a subtle and rather complex idea, roughly what this means for learning is that as either the network or the number examples to process increases, the time for "learning" becomes unreasonably big (exponential), in fact intractable. So, the conclusion might be don't try to do learning because it won't work.

Three facts put such results in some perspective. First these are "worst-case" results. We don't know what average, or typical, case results might be. Furthermore the conditions under which such proofs are done can be weakened in terms of the sort of information that is available in the learner's environment which may be more biologically plausible or reflect "pedagogy." And finally, the scale of interest that learning models might operate may be well within reasonable time scales for certain types of skill learning or function computation. So networks even of size 10^4 or 10^5 may be biologically relevant (in terms of circuits, or even nuclei) and computationally tractable.

In fact, what such results conclusively rule out is hooking up 10^{11} neurons and back-propagating the network until it's intelligent. This won't work. Nonetheless, traveling salesmen still get around much more than I like, and I have absolutely no fear that I will ever get lost in even very large grocery stores for an exponential amount of time. Moreover, learning is a *fact* about biological systems, not a theorem requiring proof.

Perhaps one the cutest comments I have heard about back propagation involves hidden units: "Got a hard problem?—the Fairy Dust approach—Just sprinkle with hidden units."

Controlling the Resources

Actually the point here is also not endemic to back propagation, but underscores a critical relationship between learning and representations which might support learning, one of controlling the degrees of freedom inherent in the resources of the learning system. This is a crucial problem which for some reason seemed to come into clearer focus within the context of back propagation. It is important to realize that the relationship between the number of hidden units and its ability to solve and correctly generalize is a central learning problem.

Of course, it is flip to say just add more hidden units. In general, this won't necessarily either solve the problem of interest or produce significant generalization. This is really an enduring problem of how to relate the dimensionality of problem to the dimensionality of the learning system. No one has a decent or complete response to this problem, and "hidden units" in connectionist networks are but one way to characterize the degrees of freedom of the learning system. Hidden units are interesting for other reasons as well (e.g., data reduction and hidden unit interpretability; cf. Hanson & Burr, 1990; Saund, 1989).

One way to characterize the degrees of freedom in a learning system is to use the discrete nature of hidden units represented in feature space as dichotomies (cf. Cover, 1965). The linear threshold unit "quantizes" the feature space leading to a precipitous relationship between the dimensionality of the space (n) and the parameters (k) in the learning system. Learning is guaranteed to occur if

$$\frac{k-1}{n} \geq \frac{1}{2}. \tag{1}$$

If the ratio of the adjustable parameters of learning system relative to the dimensionality of the problem is less than $1/2$, learning is unlikely. On the other hand, if this ratio exceeds $1/2$, the learning probability increases rapidly to 1.0, with a concomitant increase in the number of possible solutions to a given categorization problem. Thus, there appears to be a critical match between having "enough" dimensionality in the system without exceeding the critical dimensionality of the problem (cf. Baum & Haussler, 1989; Tisby & Sompolinsky, 1990). Unfortunately, for threshold systems this dimensionality "breakpoint" becomes very narrow in higher dimensions. This means that matching the degrees of freedom of the learning system to a given problem requires some intelligence in our search strategies.

For example the learning algorithm might dynamically alter the dimensionality in order to approach a critical dimensionality. Adding or delcting hidden units during learning may provide such an approach to this problem. We consider one such model, for example, the meiosis network, toward the end of the chapter.

I would like to consider a number of simple variations of back propagation I have studied in the past few years. Each variation I believe to be dependent on the neural metaphor each in its own way. At least part of my strategy in thinking about back propagation is to consider what if one were to complicate what seems to be a "normative" assumptions in the model. These include the nature of signal transmission, type of error signals, cell death, presence of local noises, and a simple model of cell growth and variation.[3] Each of these variations could be

---

[3]One other obvious variation includes feedback or recurrence among cells. This sort of variation can seriously complicate the learning and representational problems and will of course alter any of the simpler variations I consider here. Nonetheless, any of the variations I consider could easily be combined with recurrence properties.

said to try and take the biophysics and detail of the brain process more seriously, but not too seriously.

TAKING BIOPHYSICS SOMEWHAT MORE SERIOUSLY

Part of the unarticulated strategy of many connectionists is that the brain metaphor for building models is a guideline or rough set of constraints within which to work. I don't believe anyone stands by a principle like: "whatever you do, don't take the brain seriously!" On the other hand, it just isn't clear what we should take seriously. One can say with some justification: "heavens to Betsy, neurons don't do dot products and don't just squash their outputs!" Well, they probably don't. On the other hand, neurons do integrate information, and they do have thresholds and rate-limiting mechanisms. It may have been obvious to neuroscientists studying the biophysical properties of neurons that a single layer of sigmoidal units connecting inputs and outputs can do efficient function approximation (Cybenko, 1989; Sontag, 1989), but I don't think so. The point here is that *network* properties may provide emergent behavior that just won't be obvious at the single cell level. This isn't to say the single cell information is not useful; it is to say its a *different* problem. Moreover, I don't think anyone stands by the belief that information from the cell level won't interact with network properties—of course they will! All such analyses take time, and as more of the detail of cell biology, or circuit biology, or sensory function, or whatever are included at the network level, the story will certainly become richer and even more interesting. What is important *not* to do at this point is to polarize this issue, assuming either there is only one way to characterize neural computation or, worse, that the details won't matter.

DENDRITES AND SYNAPES: NONLINEARITY
IN THE INPUT

Consider a simple variation in the integration or fan-in of a neural unit. Suppose instead of dot product we assume some more complex terms in the integration of inputs to a unit. Dave Burr and I had (Hanson & Burr, 1987) suggested several variations on input integration, one of which has become popular in recent models in order to cluster the input data (Moody & Darken, 1989; Kruschke, 1990; Kanerva, 1984; Albus, 1975; Poggio & Giorsi, 1989), prior to constructing the generalization surface, do local interpolation through constraint satisfaction (Nowlan, 1990), or do general function approximation by estimating (through gradient descent, for example) both the centers and radii of the spherical units (Hanson & Burr, 1987; Niranjan & Fallside, 1988). this is a special case of using general volumes as decision boundaries within a feature space and is an old idea in pattern recognition (Cooper, 1962). We felt it was clearer to keep the decision boundary separate from the activation function as each of these choices affect the nature of the categorization and generalization that the network might accomplish. Thus we considered

$$x_j = \sigma_j \sum_i (x_i - w_{ij})^2. \tag{2}$$

It is possible to define any number of activation functions, for example, any distribution function, that is, assuming the output of our units to be some sort of probability of firing or "firing rate" function. Possibilities reminiscent of neural firing rate or likelihood could include any number of distribution functions like logistic, normal, Cauchy, and Weibull, for example. It would seem that the necessary features of such a function is just that it be increasing monotonically with net input.

Nonetheless, almost all approaches using spherical regions in feature space define an activation function which are exponentially decreasing. Now if one

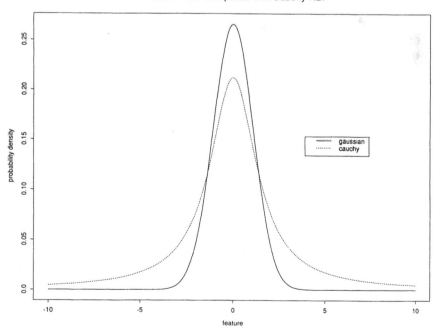

Figure 1. Comparison of Cauchy radial basis units and Gaussian radial basis units. The Cauchy has heavier tails proceeding out from the center.

assumes the standard logistic, the spherical regions *increase* from their center rather than decrease. This is similar to radial basis functions with an increasing cone of acceptance. The logistic-spherical unit would have an increasing cone of *rejection*. The usual exponential assumption leads to a compact Gaussian region of acceptance with maximal classification at the center of the spherical region. One sort of problem with "Gaussian units" is that they so are highly compact. They fall off so fast that almost 70% of the mass is within one standard deviation of its center. This means in higher dimensions, the locality of the Gaussian units becomes more exaggerated, and thus many more of them are required for coverage in the feature space. Some researchers (Poggio & Girosi, 1989; Krushke, 1990) have added parameters to stretch or shrink one of the principle axes to increase the global extent of each unit. Although this sort of tack will probably work for some cases, it calls into question either the use of the radial shape or the activation function.

Assuming for the moment that the radial shape is a reasonable property, one can consider other activation functions which lead to much more global extent in the feature space. For example, one possibility Burr and I had considered was a simple rectangular hyperbolic distribution. The hyperbolic activation-spherical unit assumptions leads to a familiar distribution function—the Cauchy—which,

spherical unit solution

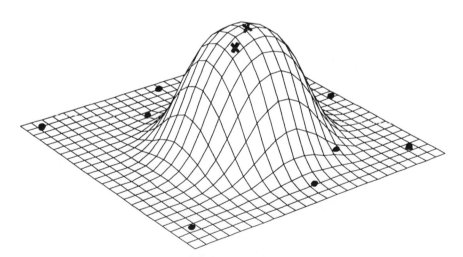

Figure 2.   Spherical unit performing an arbitrary pattern recognition. The response surface of a spherical unit performing an arbitrary categorization task of separating x's from o's. Note that a linear solution of this problem would require at least three units.

like the compact Gaussian units, are symmetric and have local receptive field properties and a monotonic increasing rate function. Does this matter? Well maybe not for engineering purposes, since perhaps one spherically defined region is much like another no matter how ad hoc the motivation was that resulted in them. But then the main distinction to focus on is between algorithms that use dichotomies to ones that use volumes; other distinctions probably won't matter.

Nonetheless, two properties are affected by such choices. First, is the global extent of the mass centered at the spherical kernel, and the other is learning. For example, the Cauchy units shown along with the Gaussian units in Figure 1 have much heavier tails, and, consequently, much greater effect in feature space, and cause significantly more competition during learning (Hanson & Gluck, 1990). Also affected by these arcane choices is the learning function. The gradients (if one chooses to do learning by gradient descent) of our approach and others with different activation functions will be quite different. Although my intention is not to attempt exhaustively characterize the interaction between the learning gradients and the decision boundary, this will obviously be a critical task. In passing we show a simple nonconvex discrimination problem solved by a single hidden unit employing a spherical decision region and a hyperbolic activation function (see Figure 2).

SUPERVISED LEARNING: WHAT DO NEURONS KNOW?

In supervised learning it is assumed that there will be some sort of labeling or target information available due to a omniscient and benevolent teacher. In the real world this may seem unlikely, but there may be sneaky ways to get labeling by using the physics of the "god-given" system and some hardwiring to explore the world ("forward maps"; Rumelhart, 1987; Jordan & Rumelhart, 1990). Worse, teachers can't label everything, and of course if they did then we would never need to learn anything. So most target information must in principle be considered as a sample from a population.

It has been pointed out that back propagation actually requires more hardware than just a feedforward network. It does require some sort of target memory and some way to compute error and then some way to send the error back through the network without using the same lines for forward propagation as this would be not happen with real axons. Consequently, there might be hypothesized some other circuit nearby that provides error signals. Several proposals involve extra neural hardware (Tesauro, 1990; Zipser, 1990). Such signals might be quite complex and not necessarily statistically normative. In fact, there may be very good reasons to assume errors are weighted or biased based on input. Given the nonlinearity in most networks and in most interesting problems it is probably reasonable to assume that least squares may not be the best way to approach minimizing the error (also see, Baum & Wilczek, 1988). Two cases are considered: one involving a generalization of the error metric, and another involving adding bias terms to the standard error metric. Both have reasonably simple neural interpretation; the first involves the notion that the interaction between sets of networks—one providing error signals for the other—is possibly very complex. The second sort of error biasing involves the notion that synapses or cells die.

Least Squares

The simplest and statistically normative way to assume error information is used in any system is to compute some sort of least-squares average. This idea is very old and dates back to at least Gauss and Legendre in the seventeenth century. In fact, the standard back propagation is derived by minimizing least-squares error as a function of connection weights within a completely connected layered network. The error for the Euclidean case is (for a single input-output pair)

$$E = \frac{1}{2} \sum_i (\hat{y}_i - y_i)^2, \tag{3}$$

where $\hat{y}$ is the activation of a unit and y represents an independent teacher signal. Now, although sums of squares has some theoretically important properties, other sorts of error functions may have some advantages. Moreover, it may be unreasonable or at least presumptive to assume that "neural error correction" is likely to be least squares because it is optimal or "simple" in some statistical sense. A generalization of least squares are the Minkowski-r metrics or norms (Hanson & Burr, 1988), which are parametrized for city block ($r = 1$), least-squares ($r = 2$), and L_∞ norms ($r \rightarrow \infty$).

Minkowski-r Back Propagation

Standard back propagation is laid out clearly in other chapters in this volume and won't be repeated here. Recall the three-term differential for a starting point to see how we result in a form for the Minkowski-r back propagation:

$$\frac{\partial E}{\partial w_{hi}} = \frac{\partial E}{\partial y_i} \frac{\partial y_i}{\partial x_i} \frac{\partial x_i}{\partial w_{hi}}, \tag{4}$$

which from the equations before turns out to be

$$\frac{\partial E}{\partial w_{hi}} = (y_i - \hat{y}_i)y_i(1 - y_i)y_h. \tag{5}$$

Generalizing the error for Minkowski-r power metrics, we get

$$E = \frac{1}{r} \sum_i (y_i - \hat{y}_i)^r. \tag{6}$$

Using Equation 4 with Equation 6 we can easily find an expression for the gradient in the general Minkowski-r case:

$$\frac{\partial E}{\partial w_{hi}} = (y_i - \hat{y}_i)^{r-1} y_i (1 - y_i) y_h. \tag{7}$$

This gradient is used in the weight update rule proposed by Rumelhart et al. (1986):

$$w_{hi}(n + 1) = \eta \frac{\partial E}{\partial w_{hi}} + w_{hi}(n). \tag{8}$$

Since the gradient computed for the hidden layer is a function of the gradient for the output, the hidden layer weight updating proceeds in the same way as in the Euclidean case, simply substituting this new Minkowski-r gradient.

Variations in r

Various r values may be useful for various aspects of representing information in the feature domain. Changing r basically results in a reweighting of errors from output variables. Small r's give less weight for large deviations and tend to reduce the influence of outlier points in the feature space during learning. It can be shown that if the distributions of feature vectors are non-Gaussian then the $r = 2$ case will not be a maximum likelihood estimator of the weights (Mosteller & Tukey, 1980). The city block case, $r = 1$, arises if the underlying conditional probability distributions are *Laplace*. More generally, though, r's less than 2 will tend to model non-Gaussian distributions where the tails of the distributions are more pronounced than in the Gaussian. Better estimators can be shown to exist for general noise reduction and have been studied in the area of *robust estimation* procedures of which the Minkowski-r metric is only one possible case to consider. It is generally recommended that an $r = 1.5$ may be optimal for many noise reduction problems (Tukey, 1987).

Large r's tend to weight large deviations. When noise is not possible in the learning task or where token clusters are compact, then better generalization surfaces may be created with larger r values. For example, in the simple XOR problem, the main effect of increasing r is to pull the decision boundaries closer into the nonzero targets.

Another case also involving a nonlinear separable pattern recognition problem like XOR is when two clusters are "meshed." Typical solutions for $r = 2$ in this case tend to use a large number of hidden units to separate the two sets of exemplars. For example, in Figure 3a notice that a typical (based on several runs) Euclidean back prop has found a solution involving five decision boundaries (lines shown in the plane also representing hidden units), while the $r = 3$ case used only three decision boundaries and placed a number of other boundaries redundantly near the center of maximum uncertainty of the meshed region (see Figure 3b).

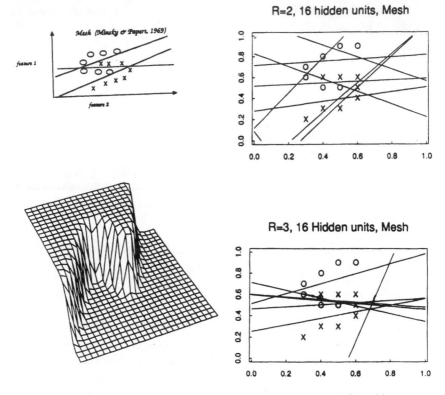

Figure 3. A nonlinearly separable problem, the "mesh" problem solved: (a) typical back-propagation solution (b) and Minkowski-r solution with $r = 3$.

SYNAPSE DEATH

Rumelhart (1987) has proposed a way to increase the generalization capabilities of learning networks that use gradient descent methods and to automatically control the resources learning networks use—for example, in terms of "hidden" units. His hypothesis concerns the nature of the representation in the network: " . . . the simplest most robust network which accounts for a data set will, on average, lead to the best generalization to the population from which the training set has been drawn."

The basic approach involves adding penalty terms to the usual error function in order to constrain the search and cause weights to decay differentially. This is similar to many proposals in statistical regression where a "simplicity" measure is minimized along with the error term and is sometimes referred to as "biased" regression (Rawlings, 1988). Basically, the statistical concept of biased regression derives from parameter estimation approaches that attempt to achieve a best linear unbiased estimator (BLUE; see Rawlings, 1988). By definition an unbiased estimator is one with the lowest possible variance, and theoretically, unless there is significant collinearity[4] or nonlinearity among the variables, a least-squares estimator (LSE) also can be shown to be a BLUE. If, on the other hand, input variables are correlated or nonlinear with the output variables (as is the case in back propagation) then there is no guarantee that the LSE will also be unbiased. Consequently, introducing a bias may actually reduce the variance of the estimator below the theoretically unbiased estimator.

Since back propagation is a special case of multivariate nonlinear regression methods, we must immediately give up on achieving a BLUE. Worse yet, the input variables are also very likely to be collinear in that input data are typically expected to be used for feature extraction. Consequently, the neural network framework leads naturally to the exploration of biased regression techniques; unfortunately, it is not obvious (from neural networks or statistics) what sorts of biases ought to be introduced and whether they may be problem dependent. Furthermore, the choice of particular biases probably determines the particular representation that is chosen and its nature in terms of size, structure, and "simplicity." This representation bias may in turn induce generalization behavior which is greater in accuracy with larger coverage over the domain. Nonetheless, since there is no particular motivation for minimizing a least-squares estimator it is important to begin exploring possible biases that would lead to lower variance and more robust estimators.

We explore two general types of bias that introduce explicit constraints on the hidden units (see also Hanson & Pratt, 1989; Chauvin, 1989). We discuss the standard back-propagation method, various past methods of biasing, which have been called "weight decay"; the properties of our biases; and finally some simple benchmark tests using parity.

Past work[5] using biases have generally been based on ad hoc arguments that weights should differentially decay allowing large weights to persist and small weights to tend toward zero sooner. Apparently, this would tend to concentrate more of the input into a smaller number of weights. Generally, the intuitive notion is to somehow reduce the complexity of the network as defined by the number of connections and number of hidden units. A simple but inefficient way of doing this is to include a weight decay term in the usual delta updating rule causing all weights to decay on each learning step (where $w = w_{ij}$ throughout):

---

[4]For example, *ridge regression* is a special case of biased regression which attempts to make a singular correlation matrix nonsingular by adding a small arbitrary constant to the diagonal of the matrix. This increase in the diagonal may lower the impact of the off-diagonal elements and thus reduce the effects of collinearity.

[5]Most of the work discussed here has not been previously published but nonetheless has entered into general use in many connectionist models and was recently summarized on the *Connectionist Bulletin Board* by John Kruschke.

$$w_{n+1} = \alpha \left(-\frac{\partial E}{\partial w_{ij}} \right)_n + \beta w_n. \tag{9}$$

Solving this difference equation shows that for $0.0 < \beta < 1.0$ weights are decaying exponentially over steps toward zero:

$$w_n = \alpha \sum_{i=1}^{n} \beta^{n-i} \left(-\frac{\partial E}{\partial w_{ij}} \right)_i + \beta^n w_0. \tag{10}$$

This approach introduces the decay term in the derivative itself, causing error terms to also decrease over learning steps, which may not be desirable.

Bias per Synapse

The sort of weight decay just discussed can also be derived from general consideration of "costs" on weights. For example, it is possible to consider E with a bias term that in the simple decay case is quadratic with weight value (i.e., w^2).

We now combine this bias with E producing an objective function that includes both the error term and this bias function:

$$O = E + B, \tag{11}$$

where we now want to minimize

$$\frac{\partial O}{\partial w_{ij}} = \frac{\partial E}{\partial w_{ij}} + \frac{\partial B}{\partial w_{ij}}. \tag{12}$$

In the quadratic case the updating rule becomes

$$w_{n+1} = \alpha \left(\left(-\frac{\partial E}{\partial w_{ij}} \right)_n - 2w_n \right) + w_n. \tag{13}$$

Solving this difference equation derives the updating rule from Equation 4:

$$w_n = \alpha \sum_{i=1}^{n} (1 - 2\alpha)^{n-i} \left(-\frac{\partial E}{\partial w_{ij}} \right)_i + (1 - 2\alpha)^n w_0. \tag{14}$$

In this case, however, without introduction of other parameters, α is both the learning rate and related to the decay term and must be $< \frac{1}{2}$ for weight decay.

Uniform weight decay has a disadvantage in that large weights decay at the same rate as small weights. It is possible to design biases that influence weights only when they are relatively small or even in a particular range of values. For example, Rumelhart has entertained a number of biases; one form in particular that we will also explore is based on a rectangular hyperbolic function,

$$B = \frac{w^2}{1 + w^2}. \tag{15}$$

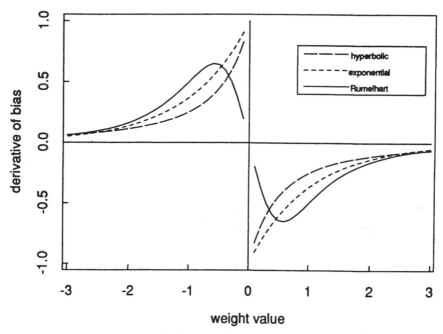

Figure 4.   Derivative of the bias function of Rumelhart's bias, hyperbolic, and exponential.

It is informative to examine the derivative associated with this function in order to understand its effect on the weight updates:

$$-\frac{\partial B}{\partial w_{ij}} = -\frac{2w}{(1 + w^2)^2}. \tag{16}$$

This derivative is plotted in Figure 4 (indicated as Rumelhart) and is non-monotonic, showing a strong differential effect on small weights ($+$ or $-$), pushing them toward zero, while near-zero and large weight values are not significantly affected.

CELL DEATH

It is possible to consider bias on each hidden-unit weight group. This has the potentially desirable effect of isolating weight changes to hidden-unit weight groups and could be used with a threshold to eliminate hidden units. Consequently, the hidden units are directly determining the bias. In order to do this, first define

$$w_i = \sum_j |w_{ij}|, \qquad (17)$$

where i is the ith hidden unit.

Hyperbolic Bias per Cell

Now consider a function similar to Rumelhart's, but this time with w_i, the ith hidden group as the variable:

$$B = \frac{w_i}{1 + \lambda w_i}. \qquad (18)$$

The new gradient includes the term from the bias, which is

$$-\frac{\partial B}{\partial w_{ij}} = -\frac{\text{sgn}(w_{ij})}{(1 + \lambda w_i)^2}. \qquad (19)$$

Exponential Bias per Cell

A similar kind of bias would be to consider the negative exponential:

$$B = (1 - e^{-\lambda w_i}). \qquad (20)$$

This bias is similar to the hyperbolic bias term as above but involves the exponential, which potentially produces more uniform and gradual rate changes toward zero:

$$-\frac{\partial B}{\partial w_{ij}} = -\frac{\lambda \text{sgn}(w_{ij})}{e^{\lambda w_i}}. \qquad (21)$$

The behavior of these two biases (hyperbolic, exponential) are shown as functions of weight magnitudes in Figure 4. Notice that the exponential bias term is more similar in slope change to Rumelhart's (even though his is nonmonotonic) than the hyperbolic as weight magnitude to a hidden unit increases.

Obviously there are many more kinds of bias that one can consider. These two were chosen in order to provide a systematic test of varying biases and to explore their differential effectiveness in minimizing network complexity.

We tested each of the biases on 100 runs each of exclusive-OR and 4-bit parity. The number of hidden units used per run is reported at first separation. In both cases, as shown in Figures 5a and 5b, are the histograms of the number of

---

Figure 5. (*facing page*) (a) Distributions of XOR runs for back-propagation, hyperbolic, and exponential bias. Note how hyperbolic and exponential skew distributions toward smaller number of hidden units. (b) Distributions of 4-bit parity runs for back-propagation, hyperbolic, and exponential bias.

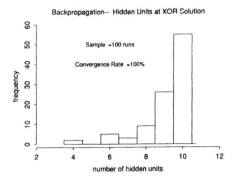

Backpropagation-- Hidden Units at XOR Solution

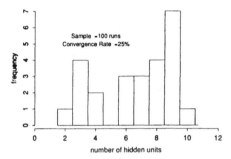

Hyperbolic Constraint-- Hidden Units at XOR Solution

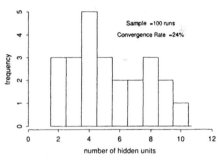

Exponential Constraint-- Hidden Units at XOR Solution

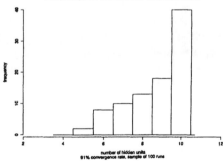

backpropagation--Hidden units at 4 bit parity solution

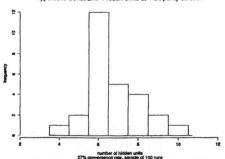

Hyperbolic Constraint--Hidden units at 4 bit parity solution

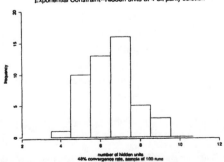

Exponential Constraint--Hidden units at 4 bit parity solution

hidden units actually used at solution. Included in the margin of the each graph are the number of runs that converged. Notice that the skew is greater the 4-bit minimum is larger for the exponential bias than for the hyperbolic bias, while both are considerably better than unbiased back propagation. Nonetheless as the number of constraints increase it is clear from the convergence rate in the biased cases that search becomes critical, since less than $1/4$ of the runs actually converge (we did not anneal learning parameters, which has been reported to increase convergence; Rumelhart, this volume). As either the dimensionality of the problem or the constraints and structure of the network increases, it becomes obvious that the balance between learning and generalization depends on search strategies.

NOISE IN TRANSMISSION: HEURISTIC SEARCH?

Actual neural systems involve noise. Responses from the same individual unit (in isolated cortex) due to cyclically repeated identical stimuli will never result in identical bursts (Burns, 1968; Tompko & Crapper, 1974). Transmission of excitation through neural networks in living systems is essentially stochastic in nature. The activation function, typically a smooth monotonically increasing function used in neural network/connectionist models must reflect an integration over some time interval of what neurons actually produce: discrete randomly distributed pulses of finite duration. In fact, the typical activation function used in connectionist models must be assumed to be an average over many such intervals. This suggests that a particular neural signal in time may be modeled by a *distribution* of synaptic values rather than a single value. Further this sort of representation provides a natural way to affect the synaptic efficacy in time. In order to introduce noise adaptively, we require that the synaptic modification be a random increment or decrement proportional in size to the present error signal. Consequently, the weight delta or gradient itself becomes a random variable based on prediction performance. Thus, the noise that seems ubiquitous and apparently useless throughout the nervous system can be turned to at least three advantages, in that it provides the system with mechanisms for (1) entertaining multiple-response hypotheses given a single input (which can be useful for local search),

(2) maintaining a coarse prediction history (as in a distribution of potential weight changes) that is local, recent, and cheap, thus providing more informed credit assignment opportunities, and (3) revoking parameterizations that are easy to reach, locally stable, but distant from a solution. Thus, introducing noise locally, under constrained conditions, may provide the system with greater search efficiency.[6]

[6]In the early 1960s several methods for random search were introduced dubbed "random creep," which basically were hill-climbing variations which did parameter perturbation and subsequently saved improvements. These methods scale very poorly. Unlike these past methods, notice in the present approach that the noise is introduced within the constraints of a *directed* search process.

The Stochastic Delta Rule

The present algorithm (see Hanson, 1990) was implemented by assuming a connection strength to be represented as a distribution of weights with a finite mean and variance (see Figure 6). A forward activation or recognition pass consists of randomly sampling a weight from the existing distribution and then calculating the dot product producing an output for that pass:

$$x_i = \sum_j w_{ij}^* y_j, \tag{22}$$

where the sample is found from

$$S(w_{ij} = w_{ij}^*) = \mu_{w_{ij}} + \sigma_{w_{ij}} \phi_{w_{ij}}. \tag{23}$$

Consequently $S(w_{ij} = w_{ij}^*)$ is a random variable constructed from a finite mean $\mu_{w_{ij}}$ and standard deviation $\sigma_{w_{ij}}$ based on a normal random variate (ϕ) with mean zero and standard deviation of unity. Forward recognition passes are therefore one-to-many mappings, each sampling producing a different weight depending on the mean and standard deviation of the particular connection, while the system remains stochastic.

In the present implementation there are actually three equations for learning. First, the mean of the weight distribution is modified as a function of the usual gradient based upon the error. Note that the random sample point is retained for this gradient calculation and is used to update the mean of the distribution for that synapse:

$$\mu_{w_{ij}}(n + 1) = \alpha \left(-\frac{\partial E}{\partial w_{ij}^*} \right) + \mu_{w_{ij}}(n). \tag{24}$$

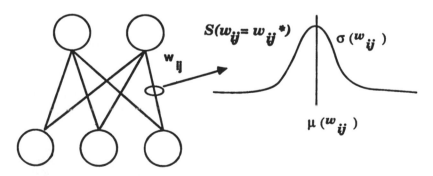

Figure 6. Portion of a network showing the representation of a single connection in the present algorithm. Each weight is conceived of as a distribution of values with a finite mean and variance. Recognition passes are determined by randomly sampling from the distribution, and learning consists of both updating the mean and variance based on prediction error.

Second, the standard deviation of the weight distribution is modified as a function of the gradient; however, the sign of the gradient is ignored and the update can only increase the variance if an error results. Thus, errors immediately increase the variance of the synapse to which they may be attributed.

$$\sigma_{w_{ij}}(n + 1) = \beta \left| \frac{\partial E}{\partial w_{ij}^*} \right| + \sigma_{w_{ij}}(n). \tag{25}$$

A third and final learning rule determines the decay of the variance of synapses in the network:

$$\sigma_{w_{ij}}(n + 1) = \zeta \sigma_{w_{ij}}(n), \qquad 0 < \zeta < 1. \tag{26}$$

As the system evolves for $\zeta < 1$, the last equation of this set guarantees that the variances of all synapses approach zero (assuming the error approaches zero) and that the system itself becomes deterministic prior to solution. For small ζ the system evolves very rapidly to being deterministic, while larger ζ's allow the system to revisit chaotic states as needed during convergence. Another way to derive this algorithm involves just the gradient itself as a random variable (which would involve both a separate increment and decrement rule); however, this approach confounds the growth in variance of the weight distribution with the decay and makes parametric studies more complicated to construct.

There are several properties of this algorithm that we have touched on implicitly in this discussion that are worth making explicit:

1. Adaptive noise injection early in learning is tantamount to starting in parallel many different networks and selecting one that reduces error the quickest, thus primarily dissociating initial random starting point from eventual search path.
2. Noise injections are local and accumulate to parts of the network primarily responsible for poor predictions. This allows the network to maintain a cheap prediction history concerning the consequences of various response hypotheses.
3. Given enough time in local minima (this is determined by both the gradient and ζ), a single synapses can accumulate enough noise to perpetuate variance increase throughout the entire network, thus inducing a "chaotic episode."
4. On average, the network will follow the gradient as in a "drunkard's walk." This allows synapses of the network with greater certainty (lower variance) to follow the gradient exactly, while synapses of less certainty to explore other parts of weight space.
5. Finally, local (as opposed to global) synaptic noise injection introduces noise indirectly into the unit activation, output predictions, and, thus, er-

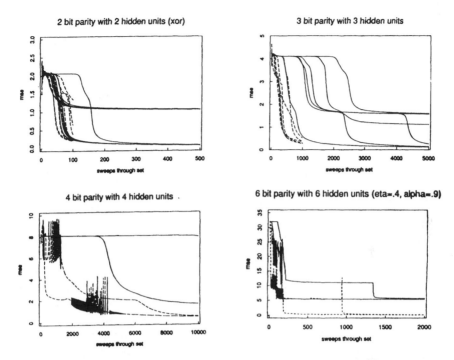

Figure 7. Learning curves from four different cases of the parity predicate with back propagation (solid lines) paired on random starting value with stochastic delta rule (dashed line). Note that in the XOR (2-bit parity case) only 3 of the 10 runs of back propagation converged with the 500 sweeps, while all but one of the stochastic delta rule runs converged within 100 sweeps. In the 3-bit parity case three of the six runs converged within 5000 sweeps; however, all six runs of the stochastic delta rule converged within 1000 sweeps. In the 4-bit parity case, neither back-propagation run converged in 10,000 sweeps, while noise is actually regenerated during late phases of convergence in one of the stochastic delta rule runs soon followed by attaining a global minimum. Finally, shown in the 6-bit parity run with a lowered learning rate are two back-propagation runs that do not converge in 2000 sweeps. While the stochastic delta rule runs both converge within 1000 sweeps, one produces a single chaotic episode near sweep 995, which apparently "shakes" it loose and convergence soon follows on sweep 998.

rors, and on average implements a local, learning-dependent, simulated annealing process (cf. Kirkpatrick, Gelatt, & Vecchi, 1983).[7]

[7]Many of the beneficial effects seen in the next section could be due to averaging effects from considering the algorithm as a distribution of networks in parallel that are smoothing ravines and gullies bounded by plateaus rather than due to a sampling process that might "fortuitously jump" out of a local minima. Experiments are being done in order to test these possible accounts. Nonetheless, both sorts of effects may be responsible for speed improvements. I thank Geoff Hinton for pointing this out to me.

Parity

We have tested this algorithm in a number of domains, although in the following we again show results in an arbitrary but topologically bad domain of parity (Boolean counting). In Figure 7 we show typical results using a parity predicate in which the input of the network is the number of bits to count and the output is a single bit signaling the even (1) or odd (0) determination. Shown are paired runs with random starting points from standard gradient descent back-propagation runs (solid lines) and from the stochastic delta rule runs (dashed lines). All tests were run with the minimal number of hidden units to solve the problem (n-bit parity requires n hidden units, but see Sontag, 1989), high learning rates ($\eta \approx$ 0.9–2.0), and slow variance decay ($\zeta \approx$ 0.9–0.999). The number of sweeps through the set increases with input dimension and the number of test cases are fewer with higher parity (10 @ 2-bit, 6 @ 3-bit, and 2 @ 4-bit and 6-bit). The size of these networks ranges from 9 to 49 weights. In the 6-bit case the learning rate was lowered (>0.6) to examine interaction of variance parameters on learning rate. Note that the main effect in small-parity cases is to produce a good random starting point which seems uniformly to guarantee as well as speed up convergence. In the 4-bit and 6-bit cases, noise regeneration late in convergence is apparently associated with local minima. Examination of the paired back-propagation run seems to indicate that chaotic episodes co-occur with very long resolution phases of learning and tend to be followed relatively soon by attaining the global minimum.

CELL GROWTH

An alternative to cell death or minimizing the complexity of an oversized network is to attempt to grow the network to the proper size as it learns. Recall that runs with the stochastic delta rule were all fixed with the minimum number of hidden units for solution. This made the search problem particularly difficult. Perhaps another way to ease the search problem is to start with a small network, one that is inadequate for the problem and allow it to "account for" cases until some point where it can no longer accommodate new data, thus forcing it to generalize. This seemingly has many advantages, first it may allow the network learning to be more efficient, in that early in learning fewer wasted cycles are due to updating weights unnecessary for task solution. Second, the network may be able to incrementally detect the complexity of the problem. Finally, since the solution found would be minimal in terms of degrees of freedom, the network might be expected to provide a high level of correct generalization to new examples.

There are several ways one can implement such a mechanism in neural networks. The approach we have taken is built upon the work from the last section, using the stochastic delta rule, which uses the variance measures in the network to promote growth from prediction errors. The principle governing growth is that prediction errors lead to variance increase in the network. Hidden units connected to features with large prediction errors should be associated with large uncertainty. As the variance of the cell increases beyond the signal (weight) the cell receives, the cell splits into two cells each copying half the variance from the original cell. Although presently there are other ways to add units to a net (cf. Ash, 1989; Gallant, 1986; Fahlman & Lebiere, 1990; Frean, 1990; Mezard & Nadal, 1989; Hanson, 1990b), the approach advocated here was motivated by the noise and cell growth metaphors and builds directly on the stochastic delta rule as a starting point for the cell-splitting algorithm.

This network growth literature is itself growing quickly, and there seem to be two general trends. From an extreme point of view there are either nets that focus on breadth (b-nets, Hanson, Ash) or ones that focus on depth (d-nets, everyone else). The d-nets are themselves of two kinds, either ones that pass a single bit information about the orientation of the decision surface relative to a feature space region, in which case it is nothing more than a decision tree (CART-like), or it sends activation from that part of feature space (e.g., Cascade-correlation). This second type of d-net can build higher-order relations on lower-order local regions in feature space. Roughly, depth nets favor locality in feature space, while breadth nets favor competition and global sensitivity in feature space. Conventional wisdom about such tendencies is summarized in the Table 1.

Meiosis

The meiosis network uses the same architectural variation that was described before; weights are treated as sampling distributions. Furthermore, the learning rules are identical for both the mean and the standard deviation of the weights. What differs is the way the network responds to error. Initially the network is configured with a single hidden unit. Weight means and variances are randomized as usual. Then, as learning proceeds, measures are taken at the input and output of the hidden unit to determine the relationship of the mean to the variance, the coefficient of variation. As the weight variance in both the input and output increases beyond the weight mean value or, equivalently, as the coefficient of variation exceeds 100%, the node splits.

TABLE 1
d-Nets versus b-Nets

Construction	Learning	Recognition	Generalization
Depth	Slow	Fast	Good
Breadth	Fast	Slow	Poor

$$\frac{\sigma}{\mu} \times 100 \geq 100\%. \tag{27}$$

Basically a meiosis net is using the prediction history implicit in the weights of the stochastic delta rule model to help configure the network. The configuration of the meiosis net involves both the signal and noise arising from weights: if the "signal" or mean value is dominated by the variability or noise arising from the weights then more degrees of freedom may be necessary for task solution.

Meiosis proceeds as follows (see Figure 8):

1. A forward stochastic pass is made, producing an output.
2. Output is compared to target-producing errors which are then used to update the mean and variance of weight.
3. The composite input and output variance and means are computed for each hidden unit.
4. For those hidden units whose composite C.V.s are $>100\%$, node splitting occurs; half the variance is assigned to each new node with a mean centered at the old mean.
5. Old hidden units are queried last. New hidden units are queried first. Consequently, oldest splits persist.

MEIOSIS

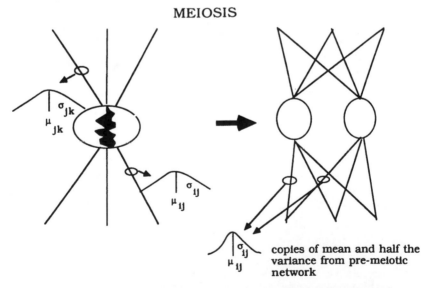

copies of mean and half the variance from pre-meiotic network

Figure 8. Portion of network showing how meiosis proceeds. Note that as the variance exceeds the mean strength of the weight the unit "splits" into two units, each new unit copying the mean half the variance of the parent weight.

5. There are no independent stopping criteria outside this algorithm. The network stops creating nodes based on the prediction error and noise level (β, ζ).

In sum, the unit splits into two units and each new unit is initialized with half the variance from the parent unit and a mean value randomly perturbed from the parent mean (with a Gaussian centered on the parent mean weight). In the next section we test the algorithm on four sets of data which vary systematically on the complexity of their decision surface.

Detection of Decision Surface Complexity

One useful test of growth nets is to see if, given the opportunity, they are sensitive to the complexity of a decision surface. Over many runs with different starting points, what was the distribution of units that were created in order to solve the problem? We examine four data sets with known decision surface complexity. This allows a systematic test of the model's ability to detect the underlying complexity of the decision surface.

Michalski Soybean Disease Data

A classic case from the AI/machine learning literature due to Michalski (1978), is the soybean disease classification problem. Originally this problem was touted as hard, but turns out to be linearly separable, as shown by a stepwise linear-discriminant analysis. In Figure 9 are plotted the 35-dimensional, 258-feature (coloration, dryness, root-rot, etc.), 4-class problem (the 14 class problem representing ass 14 diseases is 96% correctly classified in a jackknife test) in the first two discriminant variables. Notice the data almost separates on one linear combination! Meiosis nets were run 10 times on all the data starting at different starting points. The number of hidden units were noted after all the data were correctly classified and the simulation stopped. In this case all runs ended up with either one or two hidden units.

Fisher Iris Data

A classical case from the statistics literature is Fisher's iris data in which petal and sepal measurements are taken from three species of iris flowers. These data, although usually claimed to be linearly separable, are actually almost linearly separable. As shown in Figure 10, the first two discriminant variables or projections are shown for the 4-variable, 3-class, 150-token case. Notice classes 2 and 3 have at least three tokens which cross the line separating them. Meiosis nets were run 10 times on all the data staring at different starting points. The number of hidden units were noted after the data were correctly classified and the simulation stopped. Runs were distributed fairly evenly between two to three hidden units.

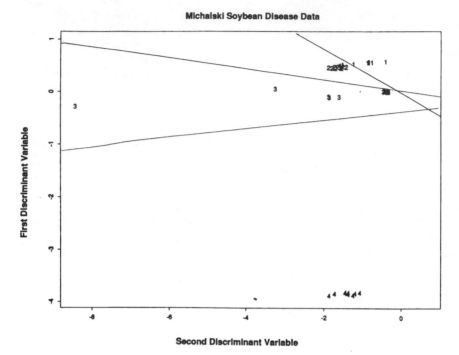

Figure 9. Michalski's soybean data (35 dimensions, 4 classes, 258 tokens) projected into the first two discriminant variables from a step-wise linear discriminant analysis.

Parity-2 and Parity-3

Parity problems were used for 500 runs each of the meiosis net at different starting points. Shown in Figures 11a and 11b are the two distributions of hidden-unit numbers that were found for each of the parity problems. Note that the modes and medians of these two distribution are equal to the parity number. Note that for parity 3 some parity 2 solutions are also found.

Siemens Blood Disease Data

The final data set consists of 10 continuous kinds of blood measurements, in-cluding total lipid content, cholesterol (mg/dl), high-density lipids, low-density lipids, and triglycerides, as well as some NMR measures. There are 238 tokens which group into two classes, 146 normal and 92 disease. Shown in Figure 12 are data projected into the first two discriminant variables from a stepwise linear-discriminant analysis. Notice the rough nonlinear envelope which surrounds the

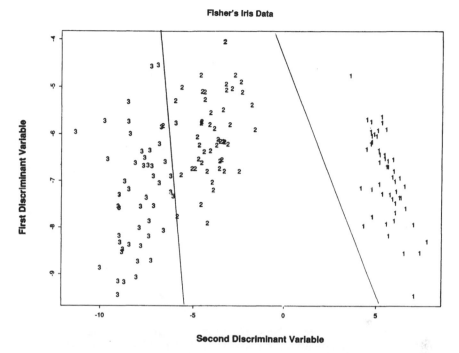

Figure 10.   Fisher's iris data (4 dimensions, 3 classes, 150 tokens) projected into the first two discriminant variables from a stepwise linear discriminant analysis.

normal class of subjects. Although the linear projections are likely to distort the decision surface, its complexity is apparent. Data were split in half for training and generalization. In this case back propagation was run on the data with 2, 3, 4, 5, 6, 7, and 20 hidden units. Meiosis nets were run 10 separate times. Shown in Table 2 are the generalization results comparing the seven hidden solutions of meiosis to all runs of back propagation, including the seven hidden solutions. Note that meiosis reduces the error by 7–8% more than the back-propagation solution with the same number of hidden units.

In Table 3 we summarize all results on all data sets. This table indicates that meiosis networks systematically increase their number of hidden units based on the underlying complexity of the decision surface.

Summary

The key property of the present scheme is the integration of representational aspects that are sensitive to network prediction and at the same time control the

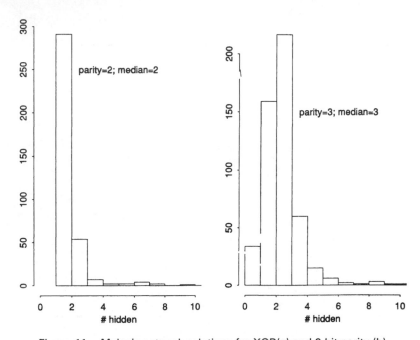

Figure 11.   Meiosis network solutions for XOR(a) and 3-bit parity (b). Small-parity problems were used to explore sensitivity of the noise parameters on node splitting and to benchmark the method. All runs were with fixed learning rate (η = 0.5) and momentum (α - 0.75). Low values of ζ (<0.7) produce minimal or no node splitting, while higher values (>0.99) seem to produce continuous node splitting without regard to the problem type. ζ was fixed (0.98) and β, the noise per step parameter, was varied between 0.1 and 0.5. The following runs were unaffected by varying β between these two values. Shown are 500 runs of exclusive-OR (a) and 500 runs of 3-bit parity (b). Histograms show for exclusive-OR that almost all runs (>95%) ended up with two hidden units, while for the 3-bit parity case most runs produce three hidden units, although with considerably more variance, some ending with 2 while a few runs ended with as many 10 hidden units.

architectural resources of the network. Consequently, with meiosis networks it is possible to dynamically and opportunistically control network complexity and, therefore, indirectly its learning efficiency and generalization capacity.

SIMPLE MODELS AND COMPLEX VARIATIONS: THE BRAIN?

So what does this all have to do with the brain? Maybe nothing. Clearly, variations on simple models which were not initially meant to model specific parts of

Siemens Blood Disease Data

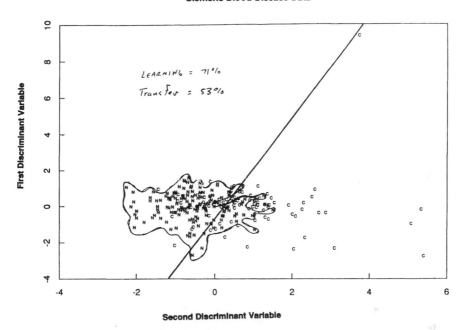

Figure 12. Siemens blood measurement data (10 dimensions, 2 classes, 238 tokens) projected into the first two discriminant variables from a stepwise linear discriminant analysis.

TABLE 2
Median Transfer Error Rate Based
on 10 Runs

Method/#hids	Backprop	Meiosis
0	49%	—
2	38%	—
3	39%	—
4	38%	—
5	38.5%	—
6	37.6%	—
7	37.5%	30%
20	38%	—

TABLE 3
Summary of Results

Dataset Separability	Mean	# Hidden
Michalski soybean	Linear	1–3
Fisher iris	Near linear	2–3
Parity-2	Nonlinear	2
Parity-3	Nonlinear	3
SMS-Blood	Nonlinear-complex	7–9

cortex are not accidentally going to converge on the complexity of the brain. We won't end up with exact cortical circuits of various sensory systems by modeling with homogeneous computing elements connected in acyclic graphs. But we might be in the ball park. This is the really exciting part of all of this and perhaps the most contentious. One could argue that it's an awfully big ball park and therefore getting into it is easy and not very informative. Actually, I think it isn't so big. And I think it does matter how you get into it.

There are really two issues here:

- Who's the competition? What are the other approaches for modeling the mind? How big is the ball park?
- Where do constraints for modeling come from? How much detail from such constraints are really necessary? How do we get into the ball park?

First, the logical competition to connectionist modeling has always been artificial intelligence (AI). It is true that neural modeling approaches could be seen to be a special case of AI; however, there are some important differences that begin to clarify the tensions between the "child" and the "parent" and hopefully this discussion. Historically, of course, connectionism and AI were distinct disciplines both competing in very similar territory. Frank Rosenblatt, as a main proponent of neural modeling in the 1950s and 1960s, was well aware of the differences between AI and neural computation.[8] In the preface to his book *Neurodynamics,* he wrote

There seems to have been at least three main reasons for the negative reaction to the program (neural modelling). First, was the admitted lack of mathematical rigor in preliminary reports. Second, was the handling of the first public announcement of the program in 1958 by the popular press, which fell to the task with the exuberance and sense of discretion of a pack of happy bloodhounds. Such headlines as 'Frankenstein Monster Designed by Navy Robot that Thinks' were hardly designed to inspire scientific confidence. Third, and perhaps most significant, there has been a

[8]Interestingly, this is well before Minsky and Papert's book and well before the "death" of neural networks. The relationship between neural models and AI is a complex one historically and can only be touched upon here.

failure to comprehend the different in motivation between perceptron program and the various engineering projects concerned with automatic pattern recognition, 'artificial intelligence' and advanced computers.

The difference between AI and neural computation (perceptrons) that Rosenblatt alludes to I think revolves around three main tensions:

1. Logic versus heuristics
2. Constraints arising from the brain and their relation to perception and cognition
3. Learning versus design

The first tension has been greatly diluted over the years, as the majority of AI can be seen today as embracing the heuristic approach and those adhering to logic as a central tenet of AI are in the minority. However tensions 2 and 3 remain today as major differences in philosophy. Point 2 reflects the sorts of degrees of freedom available in the modeling language. It seems as though AI researchers strive to get more and more degrees of freedom in their modeling languages, while connectionists have (begrudgingly) given up most of them. Point 3 reflects the sorts of tensions that arise in enduring arguments between empiricists and nativists. Learning has been a contentious battle ground in psychology for some time. People like Skinner and his followers managed to polarize the issues while not providing convincing demonstrations that representation within the brain was not critical to understand—that is, what learning affected was the representations not the behavior. At the other extreme, AI researchers have avoided learning partly because the design issues seemed so complex and partly because the learning (from the neural net debacle of the 1950s) seemed intractable.

Well, these days learning is not intractable (though it is still hard), and it is clear that it interacts in important ways with design problems (Hanson & Burr, 1990). Moreover, AI has been slow, if not halted completely, in producing some impressive design results that would not at the same time look ad hoc and unrelated. It is still early for connectionism, but as results appear it is clear there is a strong family resemblance between the principles and approaches that made each model successful. The multidisciplinary nature of connectionism is at least a testimony to the success of the modeling language that has been evolving and the way it reflects the power of the approach to utilize simple homogeneous techniques, like back propagation, for modeling complex behavior.

REFERENCES

Albus, J. S. (1975). A new approach to manipulator control: The cerebellar model articulation controller (CMAC). *American Society of Engineers, Transactions G (Journal of Dynamic Systems, Measurement and Control)*, 97(3), 220–227.

Ash, T. (1989). *Dynamic node creation in backpropagation networks.* (Cognitive Science Technical Report.)

Barron, A. (1989). Statistical properties of artificial·neural networks. *Conference on Decision and Control.*

Baum, E., & Haussler, D. (1989). What size net gives a valid generalization? In D. S. Touretzky (Ed.), *Advances in neural information processing systems 1* (pp. 81–90). San Mateo, CA: Morgan Kaufmann.

Baum, E., & Wilczek, F. (1988). Supervised learning of probability distributions by neural networks. Neural Information Processing Systems, American Institute of Physics.

Blum, A., & Rivest, R. (1989). Training a 3-node neural network is NP-complete. In D. Touretzky (Ed.), *Advances in neural information processing systems 1* (pp. 494–502). San Mateo, CA: Morgan Kaufmann.

Burns, B. D. (1968). *The uncertain nervous system.* London: Edward Arnold.

Chauvin, Y. (1989). A back-propagation algorithm with optimal use of hidden units. In D. S. Touretzky (Ed.), *Advances in neural information processing systems 2* (pp. 519–526). San Mateo, CA: Morgan Kaufmann.

Cooper, P. (1962). The hypersphere in pattern recognition. *Information and Control, 5,* 324–346.

Cover, T. M. (1965). Geometrical and statistical properties of systems of linear inequalities with applications to pattern recognition. *IEEE Transactions on Electronic Computers, EC-14(3),* 326–334.

Cybenko (1989). Approximation by superposition of a sigmoidal function. *Mathematical Control Systems Signals,* Math. Control, Signals & Systems 2, 1989, p. 303–314.

Draper, N. R., & Smith, H. (1975). *Applied regression analysis.* New York: Wiley.

Fahlman, S., Lebiere, C. L. (1990). The cascade-correlation learning architecture. In D. S. Touretzky (Ed.), *Advances in neural information processing systems 2* (p. 524). San Mateo, CA: Morgan Kaufmann.

Frean, M. (1990). The upstart algorithm: A method for constructing and training feed forward neural networks. *Neural Computation, 2(2).*

Gallant, S. I. (1986). Three constructive algorithms for network learning. *Procedures of the 8th Annual Conference of Cognitive Science Society* (pp. 652–660).

Gluck, M., & Rumelhart, D. (1990). *Connectionism and neuroscience.* Hillsdale, NJ: Erlbaum.

Hanson, S. J. (1990a). A stochastic version of the delta rule. *Physica D.,* 265–272.

Hanson, S. J. (1990). Meiosis networks. In D. S. Touretzky (Ed.), *Advances in neural information processing systems 2* (p. 533). San Mateo, CA: Morgan Kaufmann.

Hanson, S. J., & Burr, D. J. (1987). *Knowledge representation in connectionist networks* (Technical Report). Bellcore.

Hanson, S. J., & Burr, D. J. (1988). Minkowski back-propagation: Learning in connectionist models with non-euclidean error signals. Neural Information Processing Systems, American Institute of Physics.

Hanson, S. J., & Burr, D. J. (1990). What connectionist models learn: Learning and representation in connectionist models. *Behavioral and Brain Sciences, 13(3),* 471.

Hanson, S. J., & Gluck, M. A. (1990). Spherical units and their implications for human learning and generalization. NIPS, Denver, Colorado.

Hanson, S. J., & Kegl, J. (1987). Parsnip: A connectionist model that learns natural language grammar from exposure to natural language sentences. *Ninth Annual Cognitive Science Conference.* Seattle.

Hanson, S. J., & Olson, C. R. (1990). *Connectionist modeling and brain function: The developing interface.* Cambridge: MIT Press/Bradford.

Jordan, M. (1986). Sequential behavior. (ICS Technical Report 8604).

Judd, J. S. (1988). *The complexity of learning in neural networks.* Cambridge, MA: MIT Press.

Kanerva, P. (1984). *Self propagating search: A unified theory of memory.* Unpublished doctoral dissertation, Stanford University.

Kirkpatrick, S., Gelatt, C. D., & Vecchi, M. P. (1983). Optimization by simulated annealing. *Science, 220,* 671–680.

Kruschke, J. (1990). *A connectionist model of category learning.* Unpublished doctoral dissertation, University of California, Berkeley.

Lehky, S., & Sejnowski, T. J. (1988). Network model of shape-from-shading: Neural function arises from both receptive and projective fields. *Nature, 333,* 452–454.

Linsker, R. (1990). Self organization in a perceptual system: How network models and information theory may shed light on neural organization. In S. Hanson & C. Olson (Eds.), *Connectionist modeling and brain function: The developing interface.* Cambridge: MIT Press/Bradford.

Mezard, M., & Nadal, J. P. (1989). Learning in feed forward layered networks: The tiling algorithm. *Journal of Physics A, 22,* 2129.

Michalski, R. S., & Stepp, R. E. (1983). Learning from observation: Conceptual clustering. In R. S. Michalski, J. G. Carbonell, & T. M. Mitchell (Eds.), *Machine learning: An artificial intelligence approach* (pp. 331–363). Palo Alto, CA: Tioga.

Moody, J., & Darken, C. (1989). Learning with localized receptive fields. *Neural Computation.*

Mosteller, F., & Tukey, J. (1980). *Robust estimation procedures.* Reading, MA: Addison-Wesley.

Niranjan, M., & Fallside, F. (1988). *Neural implications of radial basis functions* (Engineering Technical Report). Cambridge, England: Cambridge University.

Nowlan, S. (1990). *Max likelihood competition in RBF networks* (Technical Report CRG-TR-90-2). University of Toronto.

Poggio, T., & Girosi, F. (1989). *A theory of networks for approximation and learning* (A.I. Memo No. 1140). MIT.

Rawlings, J. O. (1988). *Applied regression analysis.* Wadsworth & Brooks/Cole.

Rumelhart, D. E. (1987). Personal communication. Princeton.

Rumelhart, D. E., Hinton, G. E., & Williams, R. (1986). Learning internal representations by error propagation. *Nature.*

Saund, E. (1989). Dimensionality-reduction using connectionist networks. *IEEE Transactions on Pattern Analysis and Machine Intelligence, 2*(3), 304–314.

Sontag, E. (1989). Sigmoids distinguish more efficiently than heavisides (SYCON Technical Report). Rutgers, Mathematics Department.

Tesauro, G. (1990). Neural models of classical conditioning: A theoretical viewpoint. In S. Hanson & C. Olson (Eds.), *Connectionist modeling and brain function: The developing interface.* Cambridge: MIT Press/Bradford.

Tishby, N., & Sompolinsky, H. (1990). *Statistical thermodynamics and learning.* Siemens CLNL workshop, Princeton, NJ.

Tomko, G. J., & Crapper, D. R. (1974). Neural variability: Non-stationary response to identical visual stimuli. *Brain Research, 79,* 405–418.

Tukey, J. (1987). Personal communication.

Werbos, P. J. (1974). *Beyond regression: New tools for prediction and analysis in the behavioral sciences.* Unpublished doctoral dissertation, Harvard University.

Zipser, D. (1990). Neural models of backpropagation. In M. Gluck and D. Rumelhart (Eds.), *Neuroscience and connectionism.* Hillsdale, NJ: Erlbaum.

9

Graded State Machines: The Representation of Temporal Contingencies in Feedback Networks

Axel Cleeremans
Department of Psychology, Carnegie-Mellon University

David Servan-Schreiber
School of Computer Science, Carnegie-Mellon University

James L. McClelland
Department of Psychology, Carnegie-Mellon University

ABSTRACT

We explore a network architecture introduced by Elman (1988, 1990) for predicting successive elements of a sequence. The network uses the pattern of activation over a set of hidden units from time step $t - 1$, together with element t, to predict element $t + 1$. When the network is trained with strings from a particular finite state grammar, it can learn to be a perfect finite state recognizer for the grammar. When the network has a minimal number of hidden units, patterns on the hidden units come to correspond to the nodes of the grammar; however, this correspondence is not necessary for the network to act as a perfect finite state recognizer. Next, we provide a detailed analysis of how the network acquires its internal representations. We show that the network progressively encodes more and more temporal context by means of a probability analysis. Finally, we explore the conditions under which the network can carry information about distant sequential contingencies across intervening elements to distant elements. Such information is maintained with relative ease if it is relevant at each intermediate step; it tends to be lost when intervening elements do not depend on it. At first glance this may suggest that such networks are not relevant to natural language, in which dependencies may span indefinite distances. However, embeddings in natural language are not completely independent of earlier information. The final simulation shows that long distance sequential contingencies can be encoded by the network even if only subtle statistical properties of embedded strings depend on the early information. The network encodes long-distance dependencies by *shading* internal representations that are responsible for processing common embeddings in otherwise different sequences. This ability to represent simultaneously similarities and differences between several sequences relies on the graded nature of representations used by the network, which contrast with the finite states of traditional automata. For this reason, the network and other similar architectures may be called *graded state machines*.

INTRODUCTION

As language abundantly illustrates, the meaning of individual events in a stream, such as words in a sentence, is often determined by preceding events in the sequence which provide a context. The word "ball" is interpreted differently in "The countess threw the ball" and in "The pitcher threw the ball." Similarly, goal-directed behavior and planning are characterized by coordination of behaviors over long sequences of input-output pairings, during which goals and plans act as a context for the interpretation and generation of individual events.

The similarity-based style of processing in connectionist models provides natural primitives to implement the role of context in the selection of meaning and actions. However, until recently, most connectionist models of sequence processing have used a spatial metaphor to represent time. In these early models, all cues of a sequence are presented in parallel, and there is often an assumption that the sequence of relevant elements is of a fixed length (e.g., Cottrell, 1985; Fanty, 1985; Sejnowski & Rosenberg, 1987; Hanson and Kegl, 1987). Typically, these models used a pool of input units for the event present at time t, another pool for event $t + 1$, and so on, in what is often called a "moving window" paradigm. As Elman (1990) points out, such implementations are not psychologically satisfying, and they are also computationally wasteful since some unused pools of units must be kept available for the rare occasions when the longest sequences are presented.

Recent work by a number of researchers, however, has specifically addressed the problems of learning and of representing the information contained in sequences in more powerful and elegant ways, and there is now a wide variety of algorithms in which past input or output history is allowed to modulate processing of current events by means of modifications to the learning rule or by the use of delay lines (see Williams and Zipser, this volume, for a review). Our purpose in initiating the research described in this chapter was to explore the computational characteristics of the simplest models of this type. One such model was described by Jordan (1986). In this network, the output associated to each state was fed back and blended with the input representing the next state over a set of "state units" (Figure 1).

After several steps of processing, the pattern present on the input units is characteristic of the particular sequence of states that the network has traversed.

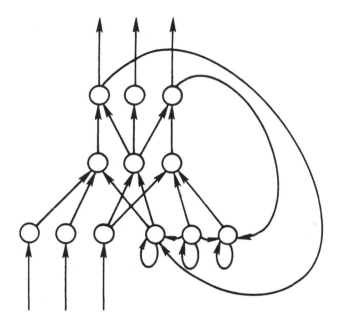

Figure 1.   The Jordan (1986) sequential network.

With sequences of increasing length, the network has more difficulty discriminating on the basis of the first cues presented, but the architecture does not rigidly constrain the length of input sequences. However, while such a network learns *how to use* the representation of successive states, it does not discover a representation for the sequence.

In 1988, Elman (1988, 1990) introduced an architecture, which we call the simple recurrent network (SRN), that has the potential to master an infinite corpus of sequences with the limited means of a learning procedure that is *completely local in time* (Figure 2). In the SRN, the hidden-unit layer is allowed to feed back on itself, so that the intermediate results of processing at time $t - 1$ can influence the intermediate results of processing at time t. In practice, the simple recurrent network is implemented by copying the pattern of activation on the hidden units onto a set of "context units," which feed into the hidden layer along with the input units. These context units are comparable to Jordan's state units.

In Elman's simple recurrent networks, the set of context units provides the system with memory in the form of a trace of processing at the previous time slice. As Rumelhart, Hinton, and Williams (1986) have pointed out, the pattern of activation on the hidden units corresponds to an "encoding" or "internal representation" of the input pattern. By the nature of back propagation, such representations correspond to the input pattern partially processed into features

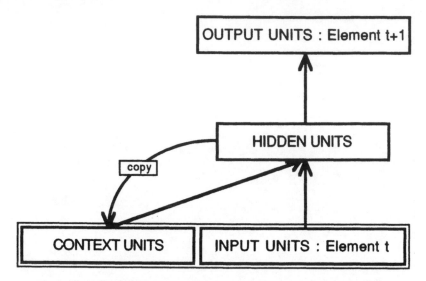

Figure 2.   The simple recurrent network. Each box represents a pool of units, and each forward arrow represents a complete set of trainable connections from each sending unit to each receiving unit in the next pool. The backward arrow from the hidden layer to the context layer denotes a copy operation.

relevant to the task (e.g. Hinton, McClelland, & Rumelhart, 1986). In recurrent networks, internal representations encode not only the prior event but also relevant aspects of the representation that was constructed in predicting the prior event from its predecessor. When fed back as input, these representations could provide information that allows the network to maintain prediction-relevant features of an entire sequence. It can easily be induced from the architecture of the SRN (Figure 2) that it has the potential of doing so. Consider first the class of computational objects called finite state automata (FSA). Simply put, FSAs are capable of maintaining information about sequences of previous inputs. They do so by using a different state for each sequence of previous inputs, and by producing a different response for each of these states. The following equations (adapted from Minsky, 1967) subsume these mechanisms, and constitute the definition of an FSA:

$$H(t + 1) = G(H(t), S(t)), \qquad (1)$$

$$R(t + 1) = F(H(t + 1)). \qquad (2)$$

Equation 1 says that the state H of the machine at time $t + 1$ is a function G of its state at time t and of the input S at time t. Equation 2 says that the response R of the machine at time $t + 1$ is a function F of its state at time $t + 1$. Could SRNs mimic the behavior of such machines? Consider again the network illustrated in Figure 2. The activation pattern of the hidden units at any time (i.e., the internal state of the network) is a function of the previous pattern of activation (now represented on the context units) and of the current input. In turn, the activation pattern of the output units on the same time slice—that is, the response of the network—is a function of the new activation pattern now prevailing on the hidden units. In other words, the SRN architecture seems to provide, prima facie, the means of implementing an FSA. Indeed, one could manually set the weights in the network to provide the appropriate transfer functions between each pool of units so as to have the SRN mimic any FSA. Mozer and Bachrach (this volume), for instance, show how it is possible to hand-wire a simple linear network to behave as an update graph, another way of representing an FSA. The problem we were most interested in when initiating this research was to determine if SRNs could *learn* to behave like specific FSAs. In the following, we show that the SRN can indeed learn to mimic closely an FSA, both in its behavior and in its state representations. In addition, we show that SRNs can learn to process an *infinite* corpus of strings based on experience with a *finite* set of training exemplars. We then explore the capacity of this architecture to recognize and use nonlocal contingencies between elements of a sequence that cannot be represented easily in a traditional FSA. We show that the SRN encodes such long-distance dependencies by *shading* internal representations that are responsible for processing common embeddings in otherwise different sequences. This ability to represent simultaneously similarities and differences between sequences in the same state of activation relies on the graded nature of representations used by the network, which contrast with the discrete states on which traditional automata rely. For this reason, we suggest that the SRN and other similar architectures may be exemplars of a new class of automata, one that we may call *graded state machines*.

In contrast with other research represented in this book (see for instance Bachrach & Mozer, or Williams & Zipser; this volume), our approach is distinctly psychological. We were more interested in documenting the characteristics of learning and representation in these simple networks than in identifying the most powerful architecture suitable to perform temporal tasks. For example, because we were concerned about the psychological plausibility of such networks, we limited our investigation to simple training conditions and valid sequences of exemplars. This perspective has led some of us to extend the research described in this chapter to explore how well the SRN may account for the processes underlying human learning of sequential material (see Cleeremans & McClelland, 1991).

LEARNING A FINITE STATE GRAMMAR

Material and Task

As in all of the following explorations, the network is assigned the task of *predicting* successive elements of a sequence. The stimulus set should exhibit

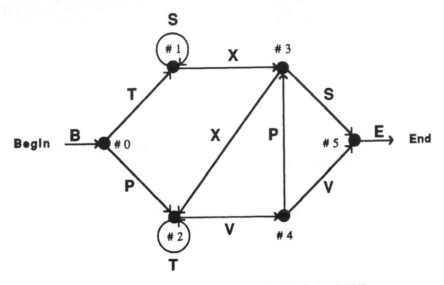

Figure 3.   The finite state grammar used by Reber (1976).

various interesting features with regard to the potentialities of the architecture (i.e., the sequences must be of different lengths, their elements should be more or less predictable in different contexts, loops and subloops should be allowed, etc.). In our first experiment, we asked whether the network could learn the contingencies implied by a small finite state grammar. Reber (1976) used a small finite state grammar in an artificial grammar learning experiment that is well suited to our purposes (Figure 3). Finite state grammars consist of nodes connected by labeled arcs. A grammatical string is generated by entering the network through the "start" node and by moving from node to node until the "end" node is reached. Each transition from one node to another produces the letter corresponding to the label of the arc linking these two nodes. Examples of strings that can be generated by the above grammar are: "TXS," "PTVV," "TSX-XTVPS."

This task is interesting because it allows us to examine precisely how the network extracts information about whole sequences without actually seeing more than two elements at a time. In addition, it is possible to manipulate precisely the nature of these sequences by constructing different training and testing sets of strings that require integration of more-or-less temporal information.

The difficulty in mastering the prediction task when letters of a string are presented individually is that two instances of the same letter may lead to different nodes and therefore entail different predictions about its successors. For instance, an S at node 1 may be followed by itself or by an X, whereas an S at node 3 may only be followed by E, the end symbol. Thus, in order to perform the task adequately, it is necessary for the network to encode more than just the identity of the current letter. This task should still be relatively simple, however, since no more than two letters of context are ever needed to achieve perfect predictions (strictly speaking, all the network needs to do in order to perform this first task accurately is to develop six different internal representations, one for each node of the grammar).

Network Architecture

As illustrated in Figure 4, the network has a three-layer architecture. The input layer consists of two pools of units. The first pool is called the context pool, and its units are used to represent the temporal context by holding a copy of the hidden units' activation level at the previous time slice. Note that the ensemble of connections to and from the context pool is strictly equivalent to a fully connected feedback loop on the hidden layer. The second pool of input units represents the current element of the string. On each trial, the network is presented with an element of the string, and is trained to produce the next element on the output layer. In both the input and the output layers, letters are represented by the activation of a single unit. Five units therefore code for the five possible letters in each of these two layers. In addition, two units code for *begin* and *end* symbols. These two symbols are needed so that the network can be trained to predict the first element and the end of a string (although only one *transition* symbol is strictly necessary). In this first experiment, the number of hidden units was set to

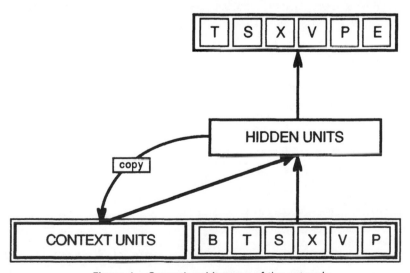

Figure 4. General architecture of the network.

3. Assuming that hidden units take on binary values, this should be just enough resources for the network to develop the minimal representations needed to perform the prediction task accurately. Indeed, 3 units taking on binary activations could represent eight different states, two more than are actually needed to represent the states of the grammar, which contain all the information necessary to achieve optimal predictions about the identity of the next element. Other values for the number of hidden units will be reported as appropriate.

Coding of the Strings

A string of n letters is coded as a series of $n + 1$ training patterns. Each pattern consists of two input vectors and one target vector. The target vector is a 7-bit vector representing element $t + 1$ of the string. The two input vectors are

- A 3-bit vector representing the activation of the hidden units at time $t - 1$
- A 7-bit vector representing element t of the string

Training

On each of the 60,000 string presentations, a string was generated from the grammar, starting with the B. Successive arcs were then selected randomly from the two possible continuations, with a probability of 0.5. Each letter was then presented sequentially to the network. The activations of the context units were reset to 0 at the beginning of each string. After each letter, the error between the network's prediction and the *actual successor* specified by the string was computed and back-propagated. The 60,000 randomly generated strings ranged from 3 to 30 letters (mean: 7, sd: 3.3).[1]

Performance

Figure 5 shows the state of activation of all the units in the network, after training, when the start symbol is presented (here the letter B for begin). Activation of the output units indicate that the network is predicting two possible successors, the letters P and T. Note that the best possible prediction always activates two letters on the output layer except when the end of the string is predicted. Since during training P and T followed the start symbol equally often, each is activated partially in order to minimize error.[2] Figure 6 shows the state of

---

[1]Slightly modified versions of the BP program from McClelland and Rumelhart (1988) were used for this and all subsequent simulations reported in this chapter. The weights in the network were initially set to random values between -0.5 and $+0.5$. Values of η and α were chosen sufficiently small to avoid large oscillations and were generally in the range of 0.01 to 0.02 for η and 0.5 to 0.9 for α.

[2]This is a simple consequence of error minimization. For any single output unit, given that targets are binary, and assuming a fixed input pattern for all training exemplars, the error can be expressed as

String	**B** t x x v v						
	B	T	S	P	X	V	E
Output	00	53	00	38	01	02	00
Hidden		01	00	10			
Context		00	00	00			
	B	T	S	P	X	V	E
Input	100	00	00	00	00	00	00

Figure 5.   State of the network after presentation of the Begin symbol (following training). Activation values are internally in the range 0 to 1.0 and are displayed on a scale from 0 to 100. The capitalized bold letter indicates which letter is currently being presented on the input layer.

the network at the next time step in the string "BTXXVV." The pattern of activation on the context units is now a copy of the pattern generated previously on the hidden layer. The two successors predicted are X and S.

The next two figures illustrate how the network is able to generate different predictions when presented with two instances of the same letter on the input layer in different contexts. In Figure 7a, when the letter X immediately follows T, the network predicts again S and X appropriately. However, as Figure 7b shows, when a second X follows, the prediction changes radically as the network now expects T or V. Note that if the network were not provided with a copy of the previous pattern of activation on the hidden layer, it would activate the four possible successors of the letter X in both cases.

In order to test whether the network would generate similarly good predictions after every letter of any grammatical string, we tested its behavior on 20,000 strings derived randomly from the grammar. A prediction was considered accurate if, for every letter in a given string, activation of its successor was above 0.3. If this criterion was not met, presentation of the string was stopped and the string was considered "rejected." With this criterion, the network correctly "accepted" all of the 20,000 strings presented.

We also verified that the network did not accept ungrammatical strings. We presented the network with 130,000 strings generated from the same pool of letters but in a random manner—that is, mostly "nongrammatical." During this

---

$C = (1 - y)^2 + (1 - p)y^2$, where p is the probability that the unit should be on, and y is the activation of the unit. The first term applies when the desired value is 1, the second when the desired value is 0. Back propagation tends to minimize the derivative of this expression, which is simply $2y - 2p$. The minimum is attained when $y = p$, in other words, when the activation of the unit is equal to its probability of being on in the training set (Rumelhart, personal communication, 1989).

```
String        b T x x v v
              B   T   S   P   X   V   E
Output       00  01  39  00  56  00  00
Hidden               84  00  28
Context              01  00  10
              B   T   S   P   X   V   E
Input        00 100 00  00  00  00  00
```

Figure 6.   State of the network after presentation of an initial T. Note that the activation pattern on the context layer is identical to the activation pattern on the hidden layer at the previous time step.

test, the network is first presented with the B and one of the five letters or E is then selected at random as a successor. If that letter is predicted by the network as a legal successor (i.e., activation is about 0.3 for the corresponding unit), it is then presented to the input layer on the next time step, and another letter is drawn at random as its successor. This procedure is repeated as long as each letter is predicted as a legal successor until E is selected as the next letter. The procedure is interrupted as soon as the actual successor generated by the random procedure is *not* predicted by the network, and the string of letters is then considered "rejected." As in the previous test, the string is considered "accepted" if all its letters have been predicted as possible continuations up to E. Of the 130,000 strings, 0.2% (260) happened to be grammatical, and 99.8% were nongrammatical. The network performed flawlessly, accepting all the grammatical strings and rejecting all the others. In other words, for all nongrammatical strings, when the first nongrammatical letter was presented to the network its activation on the output layer at the previous step was less than 0.3 (i.e., it was *not* predicted as a successor of the previous, grammatically acceptable, letter).

Finally, we presented the network with several extremely long strings such as

"BTSSSSSSSSSSSSSSSSSSSSSSSSXXVPXVPXVPXVPXVPX
VPXVPXVPXVPXVPXTTTTTTTTTTTTTTTTTT
TTTTTTTTTTTTTTTTVPXVPXVPXVPXVPXVPXVPS"

and observed that, at every step, the network correctly predicted both legal successors and no others.

Note that it is possible for a network with more hidden units to reach this performance criterion with much less training. For example, a network with 15 hidden units reached criterion after 20,000 strings were presented. However, activation values on the output layer are not as clearly contrasted when training is less extensive. Also, the selection of a threshold of 0.3 is not completely arbi-

String	b t **X** x v v						
	B	T	S	P	X	V	E
Output	00	04	44	00	37	07	00
Hidden			74	00	93		
Context			84	00	28		
	B	T	S	P	X	V	E
Input	00	00	00	00	100	00	00

a

String	b t x **X** v v						
	B	T	S	P	X	V	E
Output	00	50	01	01	00	55	00
Hidden			06	09	99		
Context			74	00	93		
	B	T	S	P	X	V	E
Input	00	00	00	00	100	00	00

b

Figure 7.   (a) State of the network after presentation of the first X. (b) State of the network after presentation of the second X.

trary. The activation of output units is related to the frequency with which a particular letter appears as the successor of a given sequence. In the training set used here, this probability is 0.5. As discussed earlier, the activation of a legal successor would then be expected to be 0.5. However, because of the use of a momentum term in the back-propagation learning procedure, the activation of correct output units following training was occasionally below 0.5, sometimes as low as 0.3.

Analysis of Internal Representations

Obviously, in order to perform accurately, the network takes advantage of the representations that have developed on the hidden units which are copied back onto the context layer. At any point in the sequence, these patterns must somehow encode the position of the current input in the grammar on which the network was trained. One approach to understanding how the network uses these patterns of activation is to perform a cluster analysis. We recorded the patterns of activation on the hidden units following the presentation of each letter in a small random set of grammatical strings. The matrix of Euclidean distances between each pair of vectors of activation served as input to a cluster analysis program.[3] The graphical result of this analysis is presented in Figure 8. Each leaf in the tree corresponds to a particular string, and the capitalized letter in that string indicates which letter has just been presented. For example, if the leaf is identified as "pvPs," P is the current letter and its predecessors were P and V (the correct prediction would thus be X or S).

From the figure, it is clear that activation patterns are grouped according to the different nodes in the finite state grammar: all the patterns that produce a similar prediction are grouped together, independently of the current letter. For example, the bottom cluster groups patterns that result in the activation of the End unit (i.e., following the last V or last S in a string). Therefore, when one of the hidden layer patterns is copied back onto the context layer, the network is provided with information about the *current node*. That information is combined with input representing the *current letter* to produce a pattern on the hidden layer that is a representation of the *next node* (see the FSA equations). To a degree of approximation, the recurrent network behaves exactly like the finite state automaton defined by the grammar. It does not use a stack or registers to provide contextual information but relies instead on simple state transitions, just like a finite state machine. Indeed, the network's perfect performance on randomly generated grammatical and nongrammatical strings shows that it can be used as a finite state recognizer.

However, a closer look at the cluster analysis reveals that within a cluster corresponding to a particular node, patterns are further divided according to the path traversed before that node. For example, looking again at the bottom cluster, patterns produced by a "VV," "PS," and "SXS" ending of the string are grouped

---

[3]Cluster analysis is a method that finds the optimal partition of a set of vectors according to some measure of similarity (here the Euclidean distance). On the graphical representation of the obtained clusters, the contrast between two groups is indicated by the length of the vertical links. The length of horizontal links is not meaningful.

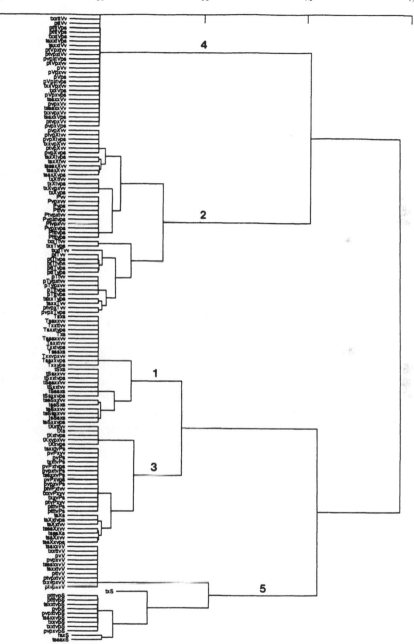

Figure 8. Hierarchical cluster analysis of the hidden unit activation
patterns after 60,000 presentations of strings generated at random
from the Reber grammar (3 hidden units). A small set of strings was
used to test the network. The single uppercase letter in each string
shown in the figure corresponds to the letter actually presented to the
network on that trial.

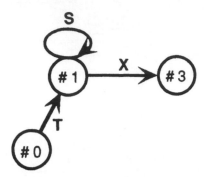

Figure 9. A transition network corresponding to the upper-left part of Reber's finite state grammar.

separately by the analysis: they are more similar to each other than to the abstract prototypical pattern that would characterize the corresponding "node."[4] We can illustrate the behavior of the network with a specific example. When the first letter of the string "BTX" is presented, the initial pattern on context units corresponds to node 0. This pattern together with the letter T generates a hidden layer pattern corresponding to node 1. When that pattern is copied onto the context layer and the letter X is presented, a new pattern corresponding to node 3 is produced on the hidden layer, and this pattern is in turn copied on the context units. If the network behaved *exactly* like a finite state automaton, the exact same patterns would be used during processing of the other strings "BTSX" and "BTSSX." That behavior would be adequately captured by the transition network shown in Figure 9. However, since the cluster analysis shows that slightly different patterns are produced by the substrings "BT," "BTS," and "BTSS," Figure 10 is a more accurate description of the network's state transitions. As states 1, 1', and 1", on the other hand, and 3, 3', and 3", on the other, are nevertheless very similar to each other, the finite state machine that the network implements can be said to approximate the idealization of a finite state automaton corresponding exactly to the grammar underlying the exemplars on which it has been trained. With more training, the approximation would tend to become even better.

However, we should point out that the close correspondence between representations and function obtained for the recurrent network with three hidden units is rather the exception than the rule. With only three hidden units, representation-

---

[4]This fact may seem surprising at first, since the learning algorithm does not apply pressure on the weights to generate different representations for different paths to the same node. Preserving that kind of information about the path does not contribute in itself to reducing error in the prediction task. We must therefore conclude that this differentiation is a direct consequence of the recurrent nature of the architecture rather than a consequence of back propagation. Indeed, in Servan-Schreiber, Cleeremans, and McClelland (1988), we showed that some amount of information about the path is encoded in the hidden-layer patterns when a succession of letters is presented, even in the absence of any training.

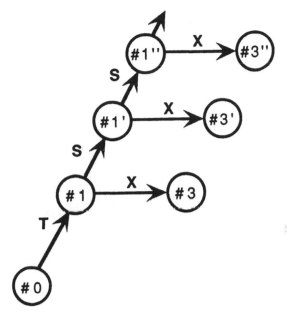

Figure 10. A transition network illustrating the network's true behavior.

al resources are so scarce that back-propagation forces the network to develop representations that yield a prediction on the basis of the current node alone, ignoring contributions from the path. This situation precludes the development of different—redundant—representations for a particular node that typically occurs with larger numbers of hidden units. When redundant representations do develop, the network's behavior still converges to the theoretical finite state automaton—in the sense that it can still be used as a perfect finite state recognizer for strings generated from the corresponding grammar—but internal representations do not correspond to that idealization. Figure 11 shows the cluster analysis obtained from a network with 15 hidden units after training on the same task. Only nodes 4 and 5 of the grammar seem to be represented by a unique "prototype" on the hidden layer. Clusters corresponding to nodes 1, 2, and 3 are divided according to the preceding arc. Information about arcs is not relevant to the prediction task and the different clusters corresponding to a single node play a redundant role.

Finally, preventing the development of redundant representations may also produce adverse effects. For example, in the Reber grammar, predictions following nodes 1 and 3 are identical (X or S). With some random sets of weights and training sequences, networks with only three hidden units occasionally develop

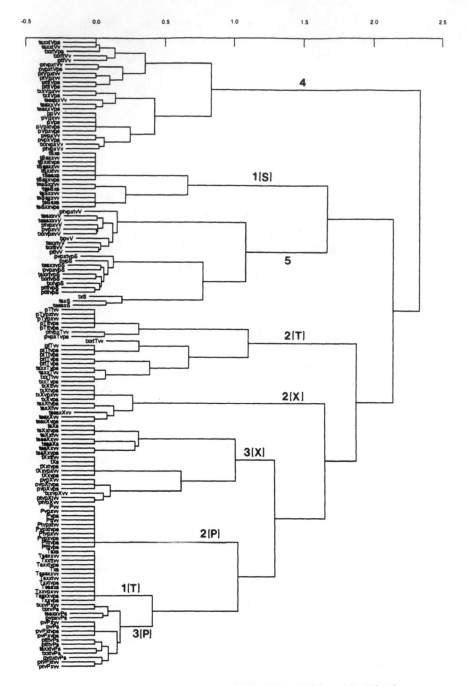

Figure 11.   Hierarchical cluster analysis of the hidden-unit activation patterns after 60,000 presentations of strings generated at random from the Reber grammar (15 hidden units).

almost identical representations for nodes 1 and 3, and are therefore unable to differentiate the first from the second X in a string.

In the next section we examine a different type of training environment, one in which information about the path traversed becomes relevant to the prediction task.

DISCOVERING AND USING PATH INFORMATION

The previous section has shown that simple recurrent networks can learn to encode the nodes of the grammar used to generate strings in the training set. However, this training material does not require information about arcs or sequences of arcs—the "path"—to be maintained. How does the network's performance adjust as the training material involves more complex and subtle temporal contingencies? We examine this question in the following section, using a training set that places many additional constraints on the prediction task.

Material

The set of strings that can be generated from the grammar is finite for a given length. For lengths 3 to 8, this amounts to 43 grammatical strings. The 21 strings shown in Figure 12 were selected and served as training set. The remaining 22 strings can be used to test generalization.

The selected set of strings has a number of interesting properties with regard to exploring the network's performance on subtle temporal contingencies:

- As in the previous task, identical letters occur at different points in each string, and lead to different predictions about the identity of the successor. No stable prediction is therefore associated with any particular letter, and it is thus necessary to encode the position or the node of the grammar.
- In this limited training set, length places additional constraints on the encoding because the possible predictions associated with a particular node in the grammar are dependent on the length of the sequence. The set of possible letters that follow a particular node depends on how many letters have already been presented. For example, following the sequence "TXX" both T and V are legal successors. However, following the sequence "TXXVPX," X is the sixth letter and only V would be a legal successor. This information must therefore also be somehow represented during processing.
- Subpatterns occurring in the strings are not all associated with their possible successors equally often. Accurate predictions therefore require that information about the identity of the letters that have already been presented be

290 CLEEREMANS, SERVAN-SCHREIBER, McCLELLAND

TSXS	TXS	TSSSXS
TSSXXVV	TSSSXXVV	TXXVPXVV
TXXTTVV	TSXXTVV	TSSXXVPS
TSXXTVPS	TXXTVPS	TXXVPS
PVV	PTTVV	PTVPXVV
PVPXVV	PTVPXTVV	PVPXVPS
PTVPS	PVPXTVPS	PTTTVPS

Figure 12.   The 21 grammatical strings of length 3 to 8.

maintained in the system; that is, the system must be sensitive to the frequency distribution of subpatterns in the training set. This amounts to encoding the full path that has been traversed in the grammar.

These features of the limited training set obviously make the prediction task much more complex than in the previous simulation. One way to measure this additional complexity consists of rewriting the finite state grammar augmented by the length constraints into a distinct but equivalent grammar in which additional states are used to represent the length constraints. This analysis revealed that this equivalent grammar contains 64 different states, considerably more than the original 6. This problem is therefore obviously much more difficult than the first one.

Network Architecture

The same general network architecture was used for this set of simulations. The number of hidden units was arbitrarily set to 15. Note that this is more than is actually required to encode the 64 states of the length-constrained grammar (six hidden units with binary encoding would suffice).

Performance

The network was trained on the 21 different sequences (a total of 130 patterns) until the total sum-squared error (*tss*) reached a plateau with no further improvements. This point was reached after 2000 epochs and *tss* was 50. Note that *tss* cannot be driven much below this value, since most partial sequences of letters are compatible with 2 different successors. At this point, the network correctly predicts the possible successors of each letter, and distinguishes between different occurrences of the same letter, as it did in the simulation described previously. However, the network's performance makes it obvious that many additional constraints specific to the limited training set have been encoded. Figure 13a shows that the network expects a T or a V after a first presentation of the second X in the grammar.

String	b t x **X** v p x v v												
	B	T	S	P	X	V	E							
Output	00	49	00	00	00	50	00							
Hidden	27	89	02	16	99	43	01	06	04	18	99	81	95	18	01
Context| 01	18	00	41	95	01	60	59	05	06	84	99	19	05	00
	B	T	S	P	X	V	E							
Input	00	00	00	00	100	00	00							

a

String	b t x x v p **X** v v												
	B	T	S	P	X	V	E							
Output	00	03	00	00	00	95	00							
Hidden	00	85	03	85	31	00	72	19	31	03	93	99	61	05	00
Context| 01	07	05	90	93	04	00	10	71	40	99	16	90	05	82
	B	T	S	P	X	V	E							
Input	00	00	00	00	100	00	00							

b

Figure 13. (a) State of the network after presentation of the second X.
(b) State of the network after a second presentation of the second X.

Contrast these predictions with those illustrated in Figure 13b, which shows the state of the network after a *second* presentation of the second X: although the same node in the grammar has been reached, and T and V are again possible alternatives, the network now predicts only V.

Thus, the network has successfully learned than an X occurring late in the sequence is never followed by a T, a fact which derives directly from the maximum-length constraint of eight letters.

It could be argued that the network simply learned that when X is preceded by P it cannot be followed by T, and thus relies only on the preceding letter to make that distinction. However, the story is more complicated than this.

In the following two cases, the network is presented with the first occurrence of the letter V. In the first case, V is preceded by the sequence "tssxx," while in

String	b t s s x x **V** v													
	B	T	S	P	X	V	E							
Output	00	00	00	54	00	48	00							
Hidden	44	98	30	84	99	82	00	47	00	09	41	98	13	02	00
Context	89	90	01	01	99	70	01	03	02	10	99	95	85	21	00
	B	T	S	P	X	V	E							
Input	00	00	00	00	00	100	00							

a

String	b t s s s x x **V** v													
	B	T	S	P	X	V	E							
Output	00	00	00	02	00	97	00							
Hidden	56	99	48	93	99	85	00	22	00	10	77	97	30	03	00
Context	54	67	01	04	99	59	07	09	01	06	98	97	72	16	00
	B	T	S	P	X	V	E							
Input	00	00	00	00	00	100	00							

b

Figure 14. Two presentations of the first V, with slightly different paths.

the second case it is preceded by "tsssxx." The difference of a single S in the sequence, which occurred five presentations before, results in markedly different predictions when V is presented (Figures 14a and 14b).

The difference in predictions can be traced again to the length constraint imposed on the strings in the limited training set. In the second case, the string spans a total of seven letters when V is presented, and the only alternative compatible with the length constraint is a second V and the end of the string. This is not true in the first case, in which both "VV" and "VPS" are possible endings.

Thus, it seems that the representation developed on the context units encodes more than the immediate context—the pattern of activation could include a full representation of the path traversed so far. Alternatively, it could be hypothesized that the context units encode only the preceding letter and a counter of how many letters have been presented.

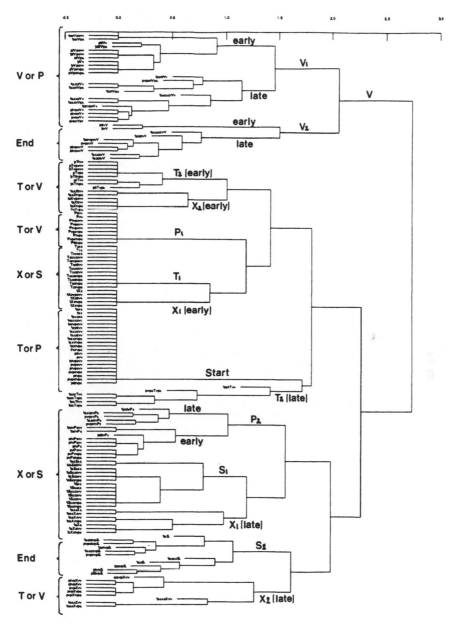

Figure 15. Hierarchical cluster analysis of the hidden-unit activation patterns after 2000 epochs of training on the set of 21 strings (15 hidden units).

In order to understand better the kind of representations that encode sequential context we performed a cluster analysis on all the hidden-unit patterns evoked by each letter in each sequence.

The resulting analysis is shown in Figure 15. We labeled the arcs according to the letter being presented (the "current letter") and its position in the Reber grammar. Thus V_1 refers to the first V in the grammar and V_2 to the second V, which immediately precedes the end of the string. "Early" and "Late" refer to whether the letter occurred early or late in the sequence (for example, in "PT . . ." T_2 occurs early; in "PVPXT . . ." it occurs late). Finally, in the left margin we indicated what predictions the corresponding patterns yield on the output layer (e.g., the hidden unit pattern generated by B predicts T or P).

From the figure, it can be seen that the patterns are grouped according to three distinct principles: (1) according to similar predictions, (2) according to similar letters presented on the input units, and (3) according to similar paths. These factors do not necessarily overlap since several occurrences of the same letter in a sequence usually implies different predictions and since similar paths also lead to different predictions depending on the current letter.

For example, the top cluster in the figure corresponds to all occurrences of the letter V and is further subdivided among V_1 and V_2. The V_1 cluster is itself further divided between groups where V_1 occurs early in the sequence (e.g., "pV . . .") and groups where it occurs later (e.g., "tssxxV . . ." and "pvpxV . . ."). Note that the division according to the path does not necessarily correspond to different predictions. For example, V_2 always predicts END and always with maximum certainty. Nevertheless, sequences up to V_2 are divided according to the path traversed.

Without going into the details of the organization of the remaining clusters, it can be seen that they are predominantly grouped according to the predictions associated with the corresponding portion of the sequence and then further divided according to the path traversed up to that point. For example, T_2, X_2, and P_1 all predict T or V, T_1 and X_1 both predict X or S, and so on.

Overall, the hidden units patterns developed by the network reflect two influences: a top-down pressure to produce the correct output, and a bottom-up pressure from the successive letters in the path which modifies the activation pattern independently of the output to be generated.

The top-down force derives directly from the back-propagation learning rule. Similar patterns on the output units tend to be associated with similar patterns on the hidden units. Thus, when two different letters yield the same prediction (e.g., T_1 and X_1), they tend to produce similar hidden layer patterns. The bottom-up force comes from the fact that, nevertheless, each letter presented with a particular context can produce a characteristic mark or *shading* on the hidden unit pattern (see Pollack, 1989, for a further discussion of error-driven and recurrence-driven influences on the development of hidden-unit patterns in recurrent networks). The hidden-unit patterns are not truly an "encoding" of the input, as is often suggested, but rather an encoding of the *association* between a particular input and the relevant prediction. It really reflects an influence from both sides.

Finally, the specific internal representations acquired by the network are nonetheless sufficiently abstract to ensure good generalization. We tested the network on the remaining untrained 22 strings of length 3 to 8 that can be generated by the grammar. Over the 165 predictions of successors in these strings, the network made an incorrect prediction (activation of an incorrect successor > 0.05) in only 10 cases, and it failed to predict one of two continuations consistent with the grammar and length constraints in 10 other cases.

Finite State Automata and Graded State Machines

In the previous sections, we have examined how the recurrent network encodes and uses information about meaningful subsequences of events, giving it the capacity to yield different outputs according to some specific traversed path or to the length of strings. However, the network does not use a separate and explicit representation for nonlocal properties of the strings such as length. It only learns to associate different predictions to a subset of states; those that are associated with a more restricted choice of successors. Again there are no stacks or registers, and each different prediction is associated to a specific state on the context units. In that sense, the recurrent network that has learned to master this task still behaves like a finite state machine, although the training set involves nonlocal constraints that could only be encoded in a very cumbersome way in a finite state *grammar.*

We usually do not think of finite state automata as capable of encoding nonlocal information such as length of a sequence. Yet, finite state machines have in principle the same computational power as a Turing machine with a finite tape and they can be designed to respond adequately to nonlocal constraints. Recursive or augmented transition networks and other Turing-equivalent automata are preferable to finite state machines because they spare memory and are modular and therefore easier to design and modify. However, the finite state machines that the recurrent network seems to implement have properties that set them apart from their traditional counterparts:

- At least in the simple cases we have examined so far, and for tasks with an appropriate structure, recurrent networks develop their own state transition diagram, sparing this burden to the designer.
- The large amount of memory required to develop different representations for every state needed is provided by the representational power of hidden-layer patterns. For example, 15 hidden units with four possible values (e.g., 0, .25, .75, 1) can support more than 1 billion different patterns ($4^{15} =$ 107,374,1824).

- The network implementation remains capable of performing similarity-based processing, making it somewhat noise tolerant (the machine does not "jam" if it encounters an undefined state transition and it can recover as the sequence of inputs continues), and it remains able to generalize to sequences that were not part of the training set.

Because of its inherent ability to use *graded* rather than discrete states, the SRN is definitely not a finite state machine of the usual kind. As mentioned, we have come to consider it as an exemplar of a new class of automata that we call *graded state machines.*

In the next section, we examine how the SRN comes to develop appropriate internal representations of the temporal context.

LEARNING

We have seen that the SRN develops and learns to use compact and effective representations of the sequences presented. These representations are sufficient to disambiguate identical cues in the presence of context, to code for length constraints and to react appropriately to atypical cases.[5] How are these representations discovered?

As noted, in an SRN the hidden layer is presented with information about the current letter and, on the context layer, with an encoding of the relevant features of the previous letter. Thus, a given hidden-layer pattern can come to encode information about the relevant features of two consecutive letters. When this pattern is fed back on the context layer, the new pattern of activation over the hidden units can come to encode information about three consecutive letters, and so on. In this manner, the context layer patterns can allow the network to maintain prediction-relevant features of an entire sequence.

As discussed elsewhere in more detail (Servan-Schreiber et al., 1988, 1989), learning progresses through three qualitatively different phases. During a first phase, the network tends to ignore the context information. This is a direct consequence of the fact that the patterns of activation on the hidden layer, and hence the context layer, are continuously changing from one epoch to the next as the weights from the input units (the letters) to the hidden layer are modified. Consequently, adjustments made to the weights from the context layer to the hidden layer are inconsistent from epoch to epoch and cancel each other. In contrast, the network is able to pick up the stable association between each *letter* and all its possible successors. For example, after only 100 epochs of training, the response pattern generated by S_1 and the corresponding output are almost

---

[5]In fact, length constraints are treated exactly as atypical cases since there is no representation of the length of the string as such.

Epoch	100													
String	b **S** s x x v p s													
	B	T	S	P	X	V	E							
Output	00	00	36	00	33	16	17							
Hidden	45	24	47	26	36	23	55	22	22	26	22	23	30	30	33
Context	44	22	56	21	36	22	64	16	13	23	20	16	25	21	40
	B	T	S	P	X	V	E							
Input	00	00	100	00	00	00	00							

a

Epoch	100													
String	b s s x x v p **S**													
	B	T	S	P	X	V	E							
Output	00	00	37	00	33	16	17							
Hidden	45	24	47	25	36	23	56	22	21	25	21	22	29	30	32
Context	42	29	53	24	32	27	61	25	16	33	25	23	28	27	41
	B	T	S	P	X	V	E							
Input	00	00	100	00	00	00	00							

b

Figure 16. (a) State of the network after presentation of the first S in a sequence, after 100 epochs of training. (b) State of the network after presentation of the second S in a sequence, after 100 epochs of training.

identical to the pattern generated by S_2, as Figures 16a and 16b demonstrate. At the end of this phase, the network thus predicts all the successors of each letter in the grammar, independently of the *arc* to which each letter corresponds.

In a second phase, patterns copied on the context layer are now represented by a unique code designating which letter preceded the current letter, and the network can exploit this stability of the context information to start distinguishing between different occurrences of the same letter—different arcs in the grammar.

Thus, to continue with the above example, the response elicited by the presentation of an S_1 would progressively become different from that elicited by an S_2.

Finally, in a third phase, small differences in the context information that reflect the occurrence of previous elements can be used to differentiate position-dependent predictions resulting from length constraints. For example, the network learns to differentiate between "tssxxV," which predicts either P or V, and "tsssxxV," which predicts only V, although both occurrences of V correspond to the same arc in the grammar. In order to make this distinction, the pattern of activation on the context layer must be a representation of the entire path rather than simply an encoding of the previous letter.

Naturally, these three phases do not reflect sharp changes in the network's behavior over training. Rather, they are simply particular points in what is essentially a continuous process, during which the network progressively encodes increasing amounts of temporal context information to refine its predictions. It is possible to analyze this smooth progression toward better predictions by noting that these predictions converge toward the optimal conditional probabilities of observing a particular successor to the sequence presented up to that point. Ultimately, given sufficient training, the SRN's responses *would become* these optimal conditional probabilities (that is, the minima in the error function are located at those points in weight space where the activations equal the optimal conditional probabilities). This observation gives us a tool for analyzing how the predictions change over time. Indeed, the conditional probability of observing a particular letter at any point in a sequence of inputs varies according to the number of preceding elements that have been encoded. For instance, since all letters occur twice in the grammar, a system basing its predictions on only the current element of the sequence will predict all the successors of the current letter, independently of the arc to which that element corresponds. If two elements of the sequence are encoded, the uncertainty about the next event is much reduced, since in many cases, subsequences of two letters are unique, and thus provide an unambiguous cue to its possible successors. In some other cases, subtle dependencies such as those resulting from length constraints require as much as six elements of temporal context to be optimally predictable.

Thus, by generating a large number of strings that have exactly the same statistical properties of those used during training, it is possible to estimate the conditional probabilities of observing each letter as the successor to each possible path of a given length. The *average* conditional probability (ACP) of observing a particular letter at every node of the grammar, after a given amount of temporal context (i.e., over all paths of a given length) can then be obtained easily by weighting each individual term by its frequency. This analysis can be conducted for paths of any length, thus yielding a set of ACPs for each order considered.[6]

---

[6]*For each order,* the analysis consisted of three steps: First, we estimated the conditional probabilities of observing each letter after each possible path through the grammar (e.g., the probabilities

Each set of ACPs can then be used as the predictor variable in a regression analysis against the network's responses, averaged in a similar way. We would expect the ACPs based on short paths to be better predictors of the SRN's behavior early in training, and the ACPs based on longer paths to be better predictors of the SRN's behavior late in training, thus revealing the fact that, during training, the network learns to base its predictions on increasingly larger amounts of temporal context.

An SRN with 15 hidden units was trained on the 43 strings of length 3 to 8 from the Reber grammar, in exactly the same conditions as described earlier. The network was trained for 1000 epochs, and its performance tested once before training, and every 50 epochs thereafter, for a total of 21 tests. Each test consisted of (1) freezing the connections, (2) presenting the network with the entire set of strings (a total of 329 patterns) once, and (3) recording its response to each individual input pattern. Next, the average activation of each response unit (i.e., each letter in the grammar) given six elements of temporal context was computed (i.e., after all paths of length 6 that are followed by that letter).

In a separate analysis, seven sets of ACPs (from order 0 to order 6) were estimated in the manner described. Each of these seven sets of ACPs was then used as the predictor variable in a regression analysis on each set of average activations produced by the network. These data are represented in Figure 17. Each point represents the percentage of variance explained in the network's behavior on a particular test by the ACPs of a particular order. Points corresponding to the same set of ACPs are linked together, for a total of seven curves, each corresponding to the ACPs of a particular order.

What the figure reveals is that the network's responses are approximating the conditional probabilities of increasingly higher orders. Thus, before training, the performance of the network is best explained by the zeroth order ACPs (i.e., the frequency of each letter in the training set). This is due to the fact that before training, the activations of the response units tend to be almost uniform, as do the zeroth-order ACPs. In the next two tests (i.e., at epoch 50 and epoch 100), the network's performance is best explained by the first-order ACPs. In other words, the network's predictions during these two tests were essentially based on paths of length 1. This point in training corresponds to the first phase of learning identified earlier, during which the network's responses do not distinguish between different occurrences of the same letter.

---

of observing each of the seven letters given the sequence "TSS"). Second, we computed the probabilities that each of the above paths leads to each node of the grammar (e.g., the probabilities that the path "TSS" finishes at node 1, node 2, etc.). Third, we obtained the average conditional probabilities (ACP) of observing each letter at each node of the grammar by summing the products of the terms obtained in steps 1 and 2 over the set of possible paths. Finally, all the ACPs that corresponded to letters that could *not* appear at a particular node (e.g., a V at node 0, etc.) were eliminated from the analysis. Thus, for each statistical order, we obtained a set of 11 ACPs (one for each occurrence of the five letters, and one for E, which can only appear at node 6. B is never predicted).

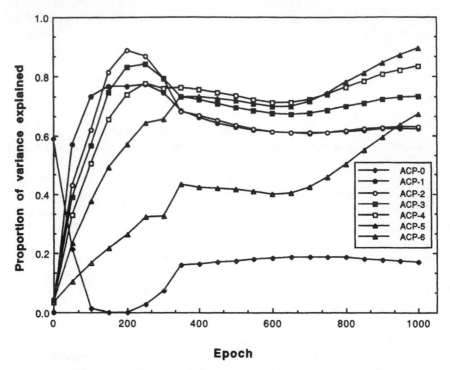

Epoch

Figure 17.   A graphic representation of the percentage of variance in the network's performance explained by average conditional probabilities of increasing order (from 0 to 6). Each point represents the R^2 of a regression analysis using a particular set of average conditional probabilities as the predictor variable, and average activations produced by the network at a particular point in training as the dependent variable.

Soon, however, the network's performance comes to be better explained by ACPs of higher orders. One can see the curves corresponding to the ACPs of order 2 and 3 progressively take over, thus indicating that the network is essentially basing its predictions on paths of length 2, then of length 3. At this point, the network has entered the second phase of learning, during which it now distinguishes between different occurrences of the same letter. Later in training, the network's behavior can be seen to be better captured by ACPs based on even longer paths, first of length 4, and finally, of length 5. Note that the network remains at that stage for a much longer period of time than for shorter ACPs. This reflects the fact that encoding longer paths is more difficult. At this point, the network has started to become sensitive to subtler dependencies such as length constraints, which require an encoding of the full path traversed so far. Finally, the curve corresponding to the ACPs of order 6 can be seen to raise steadily toward increasingly better fits, only to be achieved considerably later in training.

There is a large amount of overlap between the percentage of variance explained by the different sets of ACPs. This is not surprising, since most of the sets of ACPs are partially correlated with each other. Even so, we see the successive correspondence to longer and longer temporal contingencies with more and more training.

In all the learning problems we examined so far, contingencies between elements of the sequence were relevant at each processing step. In the next section, we propose a detailed analysis of the constraints guiding the learning of more complex contingencies, for which information about distant elements of the sequence have to be maintained for several processing steps before they become useful.

ENCODING NONLOCAL CONTEXT

Processing Loops

Consider the general problem of learning two arbitrary sequences of the same length and ending by two different letters. Under what conditions will the network be able to make a correct prediction about the nature of the last letter when presented with the penultimate letter? Obviously, the *necessary and sufficient condition* is that the internal representations associated with the penultimate letter are different (indeed, the hidden units patterns *have* to be different if different outputs are to be generated). Let us consider several different prototypical cases and verify if this condition holds:

$$PABC \ X \quad \text{and} \quad PABC \ V \tag{4}$$

$$PABC \ X \quad \text{and} \quad TDEF \ V \tag{5}$$

Clearly, problem 4 is impossible: as the two sequences are identical up to the last letter, there is simply no way for the network to make a different prediction when presented with the penultimate letter (C in the above example). The internal representations induced by the successive elements of the sequences will be strictly identical in both cases. Problem 5, on the other hand, is trivial, as the last letter is contingent on the penultimate letter (X is contingent on C; V on F). There is no need here to maintain information available for several processing steps, and the different contexts set by the penultimate letters are sufficient to ensure that different predictions can be made for the last letter. Consider now problem 6:

$$PSSS \ P \quad \text{and} \quad TSSS \ T \tag{6}$$

As can be seen, the presence of a final T is contingent on the presence of an initial T; a final P on the presence of an initial P. The shared Ss do not supply any relevant information for disambiguating the last letter. Moreover, the predictions the network is required to make in the course of processing are identical in both sequences up to the last letter.

Obviously, the only way for the network to solve this problem is to develop *different internal representations* for *every* letter in the two sequences. Consider the fact that the network is required to make different predictions when presented with the last S. As stated earlier, this will only be possible if the input presented at the penultimate time step produces different internal representations in the two sequences. However, this necessary difference can not be due to the last S itself, as it is presented in both sequences. Rather, the only way for different internal representations to arise when the last S is presented is when the context pool holds different patterns of activation. As the context pool holds a copy of the internal representations of the previous step, these representations must themselves be different. Recursively, we can apply the same reasoning up to the first letter. The network must therefore develop a different representation for all the letters in the sequence. Are initial different letters a sufficient condition to ensure that each letter in the sequences will be associated with different internal representations? The answer is twofold.

First, note that developing a different internal representation for each letter (including the different instances of the letter S) is provided *automatically* by the recurrent nature of the architecture, even without any training. Successive presentations of identical elements to a recurrent network generate different internal representations at each step because the context pool holds different patterns of activity at each step. In the preceding example, the first letters will generate different internal representations. On the following step, these patterns of activity will be fed back to the network, and induce different internal representations again. This process will repeat itself up to the last S, and the network will therefore find itself in a state in which it is potentially able to correctly predict the last letter of the two sequences of problem 6. Now, there is an important caveat to this observation. Another fundamental property of recurrent networks (and of FSAs as well; see Minsky, 1967) is convergence toward an attractor state when a long sequence of identical elements are presented. Even though, initially, different patterns of activation are produced on the hidden layer for each S in a sequence of S's, eventually the network converges toward a stable state in which every new presentation of the same input produces the same pattern of activation on the hidden layer. The number of iterations required for the network to converge depends on the number of hidden units. With more degrees of freedom, it takes more iterations for the network to settle. Thus, increasing the number of hidden units provides the network with an increased *architectural* capacity of maintaining differences in its internal representations when the input elements are identical.[7]

---

[7]For example, with three hidden units, the network converges to a stable state after an average of three iterations when presented with identical inputs (with a precision of two decimal points for each unit). A network with 15 hidden units converges after an average of 8 iterations. These results were obtained with random weights in the range [−0.5, +0.5].

Second, consider the way back propagation interacts with this natural process of maintaining information about the first letter. In problem 6, the predictions in each sequence are identical up to the last letter. As similar outputs are required on each time step, the weight adjustment procedure pushes the network into developing *identical* internal representations at each time step and for the two sequences, therefore going in the opposite direction than is required. This "homogenizing" process can strongly hinder learning, as will be illustrated below. Note that if the network were trained to predict a successor only at the end of a sequence, its ability to master such sequences may be improved (see Jordan & Rumelhart, this volume). This is a matter for further research.

From the foregoing reasoning, we can infer that optimal learning conditions exist when both contexts and predictions are different in each sequence. If the sequences share identical sequences of predictions—as in problem 6—the process of maintaining the differences between the internal representations generated by an (initial) letter can be disrupted by back propagation itself. The very process of learning to predict correctly the intermediate shared elements of the sequence can even cause the total error to rise sharply in some cases after an initial decrease. Indeed, the more training the network gets on these intermediate elements, the more likely it is that their internal representations will become identical, thereby completely eliminating initial slight differences that could potentially be used to disambiguate the last element. Further training can only worsen this situation.[8] Note that in this sense back propagation in the recurrent network is not guaranteed to implement gradient descent. Presumably, the ability of the network to resist the homogenization induced by the learning algorithm will depend on its representational power—the number of hidden units available for processing. With more hidden units, there is also less pressure on each unit to take on specified activation levels. Small but crucial differences in activation levels will therefore be allowed to survive at each time step, until they finally become useful at the penultimate step.

To illustrate this point, a network with 15 hidden units was trained on the two sequences of problem 6. The network is able to solve this problem very accurately after approximately 10,000 epochs of training on the two patterns. Learning proceeds smoothly until a very long plateau in the error is reached. This plateau corresponds to a learning phase during which the weights are adjusted so that the network can take advantage of the small differences that remain in the representations induced by the last S in the two strings in order to make accurate predictions about the identity of the last letter. These slight differences are of course due to the different context generated after presentation of the first letter of the string.

To understand further the relation between network size and problem size,

---

[8]Generally, small values for the ν and α, as well as many hidden units, help to minimize this problem.

four different networks (with 7, 15, 30, or 120 hidden units) were trained on each of four different versions of problem 6 (with 2, 4, 6, or 12 intermediate elements). As predicted, learning was faster when the number of hidden units was larger. There was an interaction between the size of the network and the size of the problem: adding more hidden units was of little influence when the problem was small, but had a much larger impact for larger numbers of intervening S's. We also observed that the relation between the size of the problem and the number of epochs to reach a learning criterion was exponential for all network sizes. These results suggest that for relatively short embedded sequences of identical letters, the difficulties encountered by the simple recurrent network can be alleviated by increasing the number of hidden units. However, beyond a certain range, maintaining different representations across the embedded sequence becomes exponentially difficult (see also Allen, 1988, 1990, for a discussion of how recurrent networks hold information across embedded sequences).

An altogether different approach to the question can also be taken. In the next section, we argue that some sequential problems may be less difficult than problem 6. More precisely, we will show how very slight adjustments to the predictions the network is required to make in otherwise identical sequences can greatly enhance performance.

Spanning Embedded Sequences

The previous example is a limited test of the network's ability to preserve information during processing of an embedded sequence in several respects. Relevant information for making a prediction about the nature of the last letter is at a constant distance across all patterns and elements inside the embedded sequence are all identical. To evaluate the performance of the SRN on a task that is more closely related to natural language situations, we tested its ability to maintain information about long-distance dependencies on strings generated by the grammar shown in Figure 18.

If the first letter encountered in the string is a T, the last letter of the string is also a T. Conversely, if the first letter is a P, the last letter is also a P. In between these matching letters, we interposed almost the same finite state grammar that we had been using in previous experiments (Reber's) to play the role of an embedded sentence. We modified Reber's grammar by eliminating the S loop and the T loop in order to shorten the average length of strings.

In a first experiment we trained the network on strings generated from the finite state grammar with the same probabilities attached to corresponding arcs in the bottom and top version of Reber's grammar. This version was called the "symmetrical grammar": contingencies inside the subgrammar are the same independently of the first letter of the string, and all arcs had a probability of 0.5. The average length of strings was 6.5 (sd = 2.1).

After training, the performance of the network was evaluated in the following

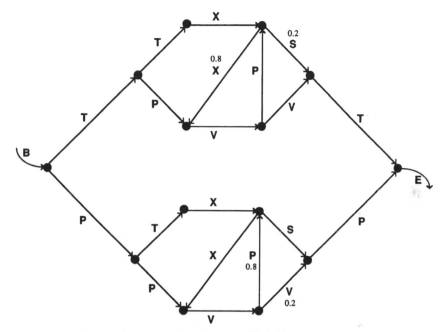

Figure 18. A complex finite state grammar involving an embedded clause. The last letter is contingent on the first one, and the intermediate structure is shared by the two branches of the grammar. Some arcs in the asymmetrical version have different transitional probabilities in the top and bottom substructure as explained in the text.

way: 20,000 strings generated from the symmetrical grammar were presented and for each string we looked at the relative activation of the predictions of T and P upon exit from the subgrammar. If the Luce ratio for the prediction with the highest activation was below 0.6, the trial was treated as a "miss" (i.e., failure to predict one or the other distinctively).[9] If the Luce ratio was greater or equal to 0.6 and the network predicted the correct alternative, a "hit" was recorded. If the incorrect alternative was predicted, the trial was treated as an "error." Following training on 900,000 exemplars, performance consisted of 75% hits, 6.3% errors, and 18.7% misses. Performance was best for shorter embeddings (i.e., three to four letters) and deteriorated as the length of the embedding increased (see Figure 19).

---

[9]The Luce ratio is the ratio of the highest activation on the output layer to the sum of all activations on that layer. This measure is commonly applied in psychology to model the strength of a response tendency among a finite set of alternatives (Luce, 1963). In this simulation, a Luce ratio of 0.5 often corresponded to a situation where T and P were equally activated and all other alternatives were set to zero.

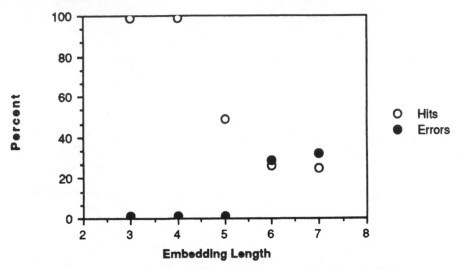

Figure 19.   Percentage of hits and errors as a function of embedding length. All the cases with seven or more letters in the embedding were grouped.

However, the fact that contingencies inside the embedded sequences are similar for both subgrammars greatly raises the difficulty of the task and does not necessarily reflect the nature of natural language. Consider a problem of number agreement illustrated by the following two sentences:

The **dog** *that chased the cat* **is** very playful

The **dogs** *that chased the cat* **are** very playful

We would contend that expectations about concepts and words forthcoming in the embedded sentence are different for the singular and plural forms. For example, the embedded clauses require different agreement morphemes—chases vs. chase—when the clause is in the present tense, etc. Furthermore, even after the same word has been encountered in both cases (e.g., "chased"), expectations about possible successors for that word would remain different. (e.g., a single dog and a pack of dogs are likely to be chasing different things). As we have seen, if such differences in predictions do exist the network is more likely to maintain information relevant to non-local context since that information is relevant at several intermediate steps.

To illustrate this point, in a second experiment, the same network—with 15 hidden units—was trained on a variant of the grammar shown in Figure 18. In this "asymmetrical" version, the second X arc has a 0.8 probability of being selected during training, whereas in the bottom subgrammar, the second P arc had a probability of 0.8 of being selected. Arcs stemming from all other nodes had the same probability attached to them in both subgrammars. The mean length of strings generated from this asymmetrical version was 5.8 letters (sd = 1.3).

Following training on the asymmetrical version of the grammar the network was tested with strings generated from the *symmetrical* version. Its performance level rose to 100% hits. It is important to note that performance of this network cannot be attributed to a difference in statistical properties of the test strings between the top and bottom subgrammars—such as the difference present during training—since the testing set came from the *symmetrical* grammar. Therefore, this experiment demonstrates that the network is better able to preserve information about the predecessor of the embedded sequence across identical embeddings as long as the ensemble of *potential* pathways is differentiated during training. Furthermore, differences in potential pathways may be only statistical and, even then, rather small. We would expect even greater improvements in performance if the two subgrammars included a set of nonoverlapping sequences in addition to a set of sequences that are identical in both.

It is interesting to compare the behavior of the SRN on this embedding task with the corresponding FSA that could process the same strings. The FSA would have the structure of Figure 18. It would only be able to process the strings successfully by having two distinct copies of all the states between the initial letter in the string and the final letter. One copy is used after an initial P, the other is used after an initial T. This is inefficient since the embedded material is the same in both cases. To capture this similarity in a simple and elegant way, it is necessary to use a more powerful machine such as a recursive transition network. In this case, the embedding is treated as a subroutine which can be "called" from different places. A return from the call ensures that the grammar can correctly predict whether a T or a P will follow. This ability to handle long-distance dependencies without duplication of the representation of intervening material lies at the heart of the arguments that have lead to the use of recursive formalisms to represent linguistic knowledge.

But the graded characteristics of the SRN allows the processing of embedded material as well as the material that comes after the embedding, without duplicating the representation of intervening material, and without actually making a subroutine call. The states of the SRN can be used *simultaneously* to indicate where the network is inside the embedding and to indicate the history of processing prior to the embedding. The identity of the initial letter simply *shades* the representation of states inside the embedding, so that corresponding nodes have similar representations, and are processed using overlapping portions of the knowledge encoded in the connection weights. Yet the shading that the initial letter provides allows the network to carry information about the early part of the string through the embedding, thereby allowing the network to exploit long-distance dependencies. This property of the internal representations used by the SRN is illustrated in Figure 20. We recorded some patterns of activation over the hidden units following the presentation of each letter inside the embeddings.

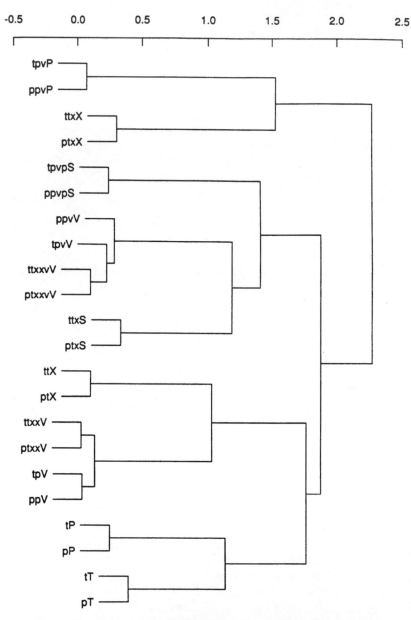

Figure 20. Cluster analysis of hidden unit activation patterns follow-ing the presentation of identical sequences in each of the two sub-grammars. Labels starting with the letter t come from the top sub-grammars; labels starting with the letter p come from the bottom subgrammar.

The first letter of the string label in the figure (t or p) indicates whether the string corresponds to the upper or lower subgrammar. The figure shows that the patterns of activation generated by identical embeddings in the two different subgrammars are more similar to each other (e.g., "tpvP" and "ppvP") than to patterns of activation generated by different embeddings in the same subgrammar (e.g., "tpvP" and "tpV"). This indicates that the network is sensitive to the similarity of the corresponding nodes in each subgrammar, while retaining information about what preceded entry into the subgrammar.

DISCUSSION

In this study, we attempted to understand better how the simple recurrent network could learn to represent and use contextual information when presented with structured sequences of inputs. Following the first experiment, we concluded that copying the state of activation on the hidden layer at the previous time step provided the network with the basic equipment of a finite state machine. When the set of exemplars that the network is trained on comes from a finite state grammar, the network can be used as a recognizer with respect to that grammar. When the representational resources are severely constrained, internal representations actually converge on the nodes of the grammar. Interestingly, though, this representational convergence is not a necessary condition for functional convergence: networks with more than enough structure to handle the prediction task, sometimes represent the same node of the grammar using two quite different patterns, corresponding to different paths into the same node. This divergence of representations does not upset the network's ability to serve as a recognizer for well-formed sequences derived from the grammar.

We also showed that the mere presence of recurrent connections pushed the network to develop hidden-layer patterns that capture information about sequences of inputs, even in the absence of training. The second experiment showed that back propagation can be used to take advantage of this natural tendency when information about the path traversed is relevant to the task at hand. This was illustrated with predictions that were specific to particular subsequences in the training set or that took into account constraints on the length of sequences. Encoding of sequential structure depends on the fact that back propagation causes hidden layers to encode task-relevant information. In the simple recurrent network, internal representations encode not only the prior event but also relevant aspects of the representation that was constructed in predicting the prior event from its predecessor. When fed back as input, these representations provide information that allows the network to maintain prediction-relevant features of an entire sequence. We illustrated this with cluster analyses of the hidden-layer patterns.

Our description of the stages of learning suggested that the network initially learns to distinguish between events independently of the temporal context (e.g., simply distinguish between different letters). The information contained in the context layer is ignored at this point. At the end of this stage, each event is associated to a specific pattern on the hidden layer that identifies it for the following event. In the next phase, thanks to this new information, different occurrences of the same event (e.g., two occurrences of the same letter) are distinguished on the basis of immediately preceding events—the simplest form of a time tag. This stage corresponds to the recognition of the different "arcs" in the particular finite state grammar used in the experiments. Finally, as the representation of each event progressively acquires a time tag, subsequences of events come to yield characteristic hidden-layer patterns that can form the basis of further discriminations (e.g., between an early and late T_2 in the Reber grammar). In this manner, and under appropriate conditions, the hidden-unit patterns achieve an encoding of the entire sequence of events presented.

We do not mean to suggest that simple recurrent networks can learn to recognize *any* finite state language. Indeed, we were able to predict two conditions under which performance of the simple recurrent network will deteriorate (1) when different sequences may contain identical embedded sequences involving *exactly* the same predictions and (2) when the number of hidden units is restricted and cannot support redundant representations of similar predictions, so that identical predictions following different events tend to be associated with very similar hidden unit patterns thereby erasing information about the initial path. We also noted that when recurrent connections are added to a three-layer feedforward network, back propagation is no longer guaranteed to perform gradient descent in the error space. Additional training, by improving performance on shared components of otherwise differing sequences, can eliminate information necessary to "span" an embedded sequence and result in a sudden rise in the total error. It follows from these limitations that the simple recurrent network could not be expected to learn sequences with a moderately complex recursive structure—such as context-free grammars—if contingencies inside the embedded structures do not depend on relevant information preceding the embeddings.

What is the relevance of this work with regard to language processing? The ability to exploit long-distance dependencies is an inherent aspect of human language processing capabilities, and it lies at the heart of the general belief that a recursive computational machine is necessary for processing natural language. The experiments we have done with SRNs suggest another possibility: It may be that long-distance dependencies can be processed by machines that are simpler than fully recursive machines, as long as they make use of *graded* state information. This is particularly true if the probability structure of the grammar defining the material to be learned reflects, even very slightly, the information that needs to be maintained. As we noted previously, natural linguistic stimuli may show this property. Of course, true natural language is far more complex than the simple strings that can be generated by the machine shown in Figure 18, so we cannot claim to have shown that graded state machines will be able to process all aspects of natural language. However, our experiments indicate already that they are more powerful in interesting ways than traditional finite state automata (see also the work of Allen and Riecksen, 1989; Elman, in press; and Pollack, 1990). Certainly, the SRN should be seen as a new entry into the taxonomy of computational machines. Whether the SRN, or rather some other instance of the broader class of graded state machines of which the SRN is one of the simplest, will ultimately turn out to prove sufficient for natural language processing remains to be explored by further research.

ACKNOWLEDGMENT

We gratefully acknowledge the insightful comments of David Rumelhart and Yves Chauvin. Jordan Pollack and an anonymous reviewer also contributed numerous useful remarks on an earlier version of this chapter. David Servan-Schreiber was supported by NIMH Individual Fellow Award MH-09696-01. Axel Cleeremans was supported by a grant from the National Fund for Scientific Research (Belgium). James L. McClelland was supported by NIMH Research Scientist Career Development Award MH-00385. Support for computational resources was provided by NSF(BNS-86-09729) and ONR(N00014-86-G-0146). Most of the text of this chapter has previously appeared in Servan-Schreiber, Cleeremans, and McClelland (1989), and in Cleeremans, Servan-Schreiber, and McClelland (1990). Since most of the changes are relatively minor edits this article should be viewed as a simple merger of these earlier publications. Axel Cleeremans is at the Department of Psychology, Free University of Brussels, Belgium. David Servan-Schreiber is at the Western Psychiatric Institute and Clinic, School of Medicine, University of Pittsburgh. James L. McClelland is at the Department of Psychology, Carnegie Mellon University.

REFERENCES

Allen, R. B. (1988). Sequential connectionist networks for answering simple questions about a microworld. *Proceedings of the Tenth Annual Conference of the Cognitive Science Society,* Hillsdale, NJ: Erlbaum.

Allen, R. B. (1990). *Connectionist language users* (TR-AR-90-402). Morristown, NJ: Bell Communications Research.

Allen, R. B., & Riecksen, M. E. (1989). Reference in connectionist language users. In R. Pfeifer, Z. Schreter, F. Fogelman-Soulié, & L. Steels (Eds.), *Connectionism in perspective* (pp. 301–308). Amsterdam: North-Holland.

Bachrach, J., & Mozer, M. C. (this volume). Connectionist modeling and control of finite state systems given partial state information.

Cleeremans, A., & McClelland, J. L. (1991). Learning the structure of event sequences. *Journal of Experimental Psychology: General, 120,* 3, 235–253.

Cleeremans, A., Servan-Schreiber, D., & McClelland, J. L. (1989). Finite state automata and simple recurrent networks. *Neural Computation, 1,* 372–381.

Cottrell, G. W. (1985). Connectionist parsing. *Proceedings of the Seventh Annual Conference of the Cognitive Science Society.* Hillsdale, NJ: Erlbaum.

Elman, J. L. (1989). Finding structure in time (CRL Technical Report 8801). San Diego: Center for Research in Language, University of California.

Elman, J. L. (1990). Finding structure in time. *Cognitive Science, 14,* 179–211.

Elman, J. L. (1990). Representation and structure in connectionist models. In G. Altmann (Ed.), *Cognitive models of speech processing.* MIT Press: Cambridge, MA (pp. 345–382).

Fanty, M. (1985). *Context-free parsing in connectionist networks* (TR174), Rochester: University of Rochester, Computer Science Department.

Hanson, S., & Kegl, J. (1987). PARSNIP: A connectionist network that learns natural language from exposure to natural language sentences. *Proceedings of the Ninth Annual Conference of the Cognitive Science Society.* Hillsdale, NJ: Erlbaum.

Hinton, G., McClelland, J. L., & Rumelhart, D. E. (1986). Distributed representations. In D. E. Rumlehart & J. L. McClelland (Eds.), *Parallel Distributed Processing. I: Foundations.* Cambridge, MA: MIT Press.

Jordan, M. I. (1986). Attractor dynamics and parallelism in a connectionist sequential machine. *Proceedings of the Eighth Annual Conference of the Cognitive Science Society.* Hillsdale, NJ: Erlbaum.

Jordan, M. I., & Rumelhart, D. E. (this volume). Forward models: Supervised learning with a distal teacher.

Luce, R. D. (1963). Detection and recognition. In R. D. Luce, R. R. Bush, & E. Galanter (Eds.), *Handbook of mathematical psychology* (Vol. 1). New York: Wiley.

McClelland, J. L., & Rumelhart, D. E. (1988). *Explorations in parallel distributed processing: A handbook of models, programs and exercises.* Cambridge, MA: MIT Press.

Minsky, M. (1967). *Computation: Finite and infinite machines.* Englewood Cliffs, NJ: Prentice-Hall.

Pollack, J. (1989). Implication of recursive distributed representations. In D. S. Touretzky (Ed.), *Advances in neural informaton processing systems 1.* San Mateo, CA: Morgan Kauffman. [Collected papers of the IEEE Conference on Neural Information Processing Systems—Natural and Synthetic, Denver, Nov. 28–Dec. 1, 1988]

Pollack, J. (1990). RAAM: Recursive distributed representations. *Artificial Intelligence, 46,* 77–105.

Reber, A. S. (1976). Implicit learning of synthetic languages: The role of the instructional set. *Journal of Experimental Psychology: Human Learning and Memory, 2,* 88–94.

Rumelhart, D. E., Hinton, G., & Williams, R. J. (1986). Learning internal representations by error propagation. In D. E. Rumelhart & J. L. McClelland (Eds.), *Parallel distributed processing. I: Foundations.* Cambridge, MA: MIT Press.

Sejnowski, T. J., & Rosenberg, C. (1987). Parallel networks that learn to pronounce English text. *Complex Systems, 1,* 145–168.

Servan-Schreiber, D., Cleeremans, A., & McClelland, J. L. (1988). *Encoding sequential structure in simple recurrent networks* (Technical Report CMU-CS-183). Pittsburgh: School of Computer Science, Carnegie Mellon University.

Servan-Schreiber, D., Cleeremans, A., & McClelland, J. L. (1989). Learning sequential structure in simple recurrent networks. In D. S. Touretzky (Ed.), *Advances in neural information processing systems 1.* San Mateo, CA: Morgan Kauffman. [Collected papers of the IEEE Conference on Neural Information Processing Systems—Natural and Synthetic, Denver, Nov. 28–Dec. 1, 1988]

Williams, R. J., & Zipser, D. (this volume). Gradient-based learning algorithms for recurrent networks and their computational complexity.

10 Spatial Coherence as an Internal Teacher for a Neural Network

Suzanna Becker
Department of Psychology, McMaster University

Geoffrey E. Hinton
Department of Computer Science, University of Toronto

ABSTRACT

Supervised learning procedures for neural networks have recently met with considerable success in learning difficult mappings. So far, however, they have been limited by their poor scaling behavior, particularly for networks with many hidden layers. A promising alternative is to develop unsupervised learning algorithms by defining objective functions that characterize the quality of an internal representation without requiring knowledge of the desired outputs of the system. Our major goal is to build self-organizing network modules which capture important regularities in the environment in a simple form. A layered hierarchy of such modules should be able to learn in a time roughly linear in the number of layers. We propose that a good objective for perceptual learning is to extract higher-order features that exhibit simple coherence across time or space. This can be done by transforming the input representation into an underlying representation in which the mutual information between adjacent patches of the input can be expressed in a simple way. We have applied this basic idea to develop several interesting learning algorithms for discovering spatially coherent features in images. Our simulations show that a network can discover depth of surfaces when trained on binary random-dot stereograms with discrete global shifts, as well as on real-valued stereograms of surfaces with continuously varying disparities. Once a module of depth-tuned units has developed, we show that units in a higher layer can discover a simple form of surface interpolation of curved surfaces by learning to predict the depth of one image region based on depth measurements in surrounding regions.

313

INTRODUCTION

The mammalian perceptual system can recognize complex stimuli with remarkable speed and robustness. So far, the performance of computational models of perceptual skills such as the recognition of continuous speech and complex scenes has fallen far short of the performance level of humans on these tasks. How does the brain achieve such remarkable pattern recognition abilities? A partial explanation may be that the brain undergoes substantial self-organization as the young animal gradually learns to find regularities in the complex patterns of stimuli which it encounters. By examining the ways in which the brain employs self-organizing principles, we can gain some insight as to how we should design efficient, and biologically plausible computational models of learning.

Evidence of Activity-Driven Self-Organization in the Brain

There is substantial evidence that brain development and perceptual functioning are markedly affected by exposure to structured environmental input. In this section, we briefly review some of the neurophysiological evidence for these claims. For a more extensive review, see Miller, 1990.

Much of the evidence comes from single-cell recordings in the primary visual cortex of cats (area 17) and more recently, cell recordings in primate visual and somatosensory systems. In several mammals, visual cortical neurons have been found to be tuned to a variety of stimulus features such as orientation (i.e., some cells respond maximally to edges or bars of particular orientations), spatial frequency, velocity, direction of movement, and binocular disparity. The fine-tuning of the visual system to some of these features occurs primarily during certain "sensitive periods of development" early in life, and can be disrupted if an animal is reared in an impoverished environment.

When kittens are raised in environments containing only vertical or horizontal contours, cortical cell populations exhibit orientation selectivities which are skewed in favor of those particular contours to which the animal was exposed (Blakemore & van Sluyters, 1975; Blakemore & Cooper, 1970; Hirsch & Spinelli, 1970). However, since orientation tuning is present in visually inexperienced kittens (Hubel & Wiesel, 1963), it is unclear whether the effect of distorted environmental input is to actually alter the orientation selective response of single cells (e.g., via a competitive activity-dependent process), or to simply cause deterioration of these cells as a consequence of their disuse (Miller, 1990). Spatial-frequency tuning of feline cortical cells is also influenced by early visual experience: while no visual input is necessary for normal development of spatial-frequency selectivity during the first three weeks, the subsequent fine-tuning of frequency sensitivity which normally occurs in weeks 4–8 is blocked if the cat is deprived of patterned input (Derrington, 1984).

Another widely studied developmental phenomenon in the cat's visual cortex is the appearance of ocular dominance columns (ODCs); after normal binocular visual experience, cortical cells which receive input from both eyes eventually segregate into alternating eye-specific patches. This effect can be strongly influenced by environmental factors: when a cat is subjected to monocular deprivation, particularly during the second postnatal month, cortical cells become almost exclusively and irrecoverably responsive to input from the exposed eye (Wiesel & Hubel, 1965; Olson & Freeman, 1980). However, if *both* eyes are deprived of exposure to patterned input (e.g., in dark-reared and eyelid-sutured kittens), there is evidence that ocular dominance segregation may still occur to some degree (Stryker & Harris, 1986). It is possible that spontaneously generated, random input from retinal cells may be a factor; when retinal ganglion cell activity is completely blocked with a drug called tetrodotoxin during the period in which ocular segregation normally occurs in the cortex, ODCs fail to develop (Stryker & Harris, 1986).

There is similar evidence of activity-dependent development in primate perceptual systems. For example, monkeys with optically induced strabismus (a misalignment of the two eyes, either convergent or divergent) early in life, followed by three years of normal binocular experience, have a marked reduction in the number of cortical binocular cells (in both areas V1 and V2) and are behaviourally stereoblind (Crawford et al., 1984). Interestingly, children with esotropia (convergent strabisumus, a condition commonly referred to as "cross-eyed") in infancy, which is surgically corrected between 10–13 years of age, perform identically to the strabismic monkeys on stereopsis tasks (i.e., they are clinically stereoblind), suggesting the possibility of a similar critical period in humans for the development of binocular vision (Crawford et al., 1983).

Cortical reorganization occurs not only during sensitive periods early in development, but continues through the lifetime of an animal, as a result of changing environmental demands. For example, Merzenich and his associates (1987) have studied plasticity in the somatosensory cortex of adult owl monkeys (for a review, see Merzenich et al., 1988); neurons in this region of the brain respond to tactile input from local areas of the skin surface, forming roughly a topographic map of the body. Merzenich's group has extensively studied cells whose receptive fields correspond to regions of skin surface on the hand (in area 3B); these receptive fields change drastically when the spatiotemporal correlations of tactile stimulation are experimentally varied.

It is possible that cortical cells employ some very general, sensory modality-independent organizing principles in developing their characteristic responses to patterned input. Startling evidence for this possibility comes from an unusual study in ferrets (Sur, Garraghty, & Roe, 1988). Nerve fibers from the primary visual pathway were artificially redirected into the auditory cortex, and these visual inputs formed synaptic contacts with cells in the auditory cortex. After the ferrets were reared to adulthood, the majority of "auditory" cortical cells tested had become visually driven, some having center-surround response characteristics similar to cells in the visual cortex.

The ability to develop a set of environmentally tuned feature detectors is of clear adaptive advantage. The organism need not have a completely genetically predetermined perceptual system; rather, the primitive organization laid out by the genetic blueprint can be fine-tuned after birth, as the statistics of the environment, and even the physical properties of the organism's own sensors (e.g., the distance between the two eyes, two ears, etc.) change over time. Once an environmentally tuned set of feature detectors has been learned, important features of the world such as local variations in position and depth can be quickly extracted by individual cells or cell populations in parallel. The response of these cells can then serve as a preprocessed input to higher layers, which can in turn self-organize to form still more complex representations.

Computational Models of Learning

Motivated by the evidence of activity-dependent self-organization in the brain, described earlier, and by the poor scaling behavior of supervised learning procedures, our goal is to discover ways in which artificial systems can perform unsupervised learning. By discovering good solutions to this problem in simulated networks of neuronlike processing elements, we hope to cast light on how the brain may solve the same problem.

Much of the current research on computational models of learning in neural networks focuses on learning algorithms in which the network learns from an external teacher. The goal of the network is to learn some prespecified mapping, so that the output of the network matches the teaching signal on each case. Supervised learning algorithms have met with considerable success in solving some difficult tasks, such as subproblems of speech recognition (e.g., Lang & Hinton, 1988; Watrous & Shastri, 1987) and image understanding (e.g., the recognition of hand-drawn digits (Le Cun et al., 1989). However, these algorithms have so far been limited by their poor scaling behavior, particularly when applied to full-scale real-world problems (like continuous speech recognition) which require large networks with many hidden layers. Additionally, they tend to find problem-specific representations which may not carry over well to new situations.

One solution to these problems may be to make use of unsupervised learning, as the brain apparently does: rather than trying to solve difficult problems in one stage by training a large multilayer network, we can subdivide the problem. First we build adaptive preprocessing modules that can capture some of the interesting features in the environment, and form representations of a simpler form than the raw, unprocessed input. Modules can then be assembled hierarchically to extract features of progressively higher order. Finally, once the hierarchy of unsupervised modules has extracted the important underlying causes of the perceptual inputs, we add supervised modules on top which can quickly learn to associate responses with the causes of the perceptual input rather than the input itself.

Related Work on Unsupervised Learning

Various approaches have been taken to modeling unsupervised learning processes. In this section, we briefly review examples of two major approaches. We then discuss what type of data distributions each is best at modeling, and finally, what kind of representation should be extracted to be useful for further stages of learning.

Clustering Algorithms

An example of a fairly simple, yet impressive application of the idea of using an unsupervised preprocessing layer to speed up subsequent supervised learning is the recent work of Moody and Darken (1989). They trained an adaptive preprocessing layer of Gaussian units by a standard k-means clustering algorithm; an additional layer of units was then trained by a supervised learning procedure (mean-squared error minimization) to solve several difficult problems: phoneme recognition and chaotic time-series prediction. They report that this hybrid algorithm results in about two orders of magnitude speedup in the learning time compared to pure supervised learning with back propagation. The layer of Gaussian units speeds learning for two reasons. First, two very different input vectors will tend to activate nonoverlapping sets of Gaussian units, so there will be no interference (generalization) between these two training cases. Second, the incoming weights of Gaussian units do not depend on the outgoing weights so there is modularity of learning between these two layers of weights.

Many algorithms have been developed for unsupervised learning in artificial neural networks. Many of these are variants of statistical clustering algorithms and are generally referred to as competitive learning procedures (e.g., Grossberg, 1987; Von der Malsburg, 1973; Rumelhart & Zipser, 1986; Kohonen, 1982; Fukushima, 1975). Clustering algorithms such as k-means or competitive learning are useful when the goal is to find a limited number of prototypes in high-dimensional data. Each competitive unit or module comes to encode the center of a cluster of data points in a high-dimensional space, and considerable dimensionality reduction can be achieved, provided that the data points all lie on or near a lower-dimensional surface (Steve Nowlan, personal communication). With a more elaborate architecture employing recurrent connections, Grossberg's version of competitive learning (Grossberg, 1987; Carpenter & Grossberg, 1987) continuously adapts to new inputs, while maintaining relatively stable representations, and with some parameter tuning gives one control over the plasticity-stability trade-off. Recently, a "soft competitive learning" method has been proposed (Nowlan, 1990); rather than only allowing the winner to adapt, each unit can adapt its weights for every input case, so that as a group the units form a good multimodal model of the underlying distribution.

Principal-Components Analysis

Another major approach to unsupervised learning is based on the objective of representing the principal components of the input distribution.[1] Several researchers have developed learning algorithms which accomplish part or all of this task. Oja (1982) showed that a normalized version of the simple Hebbian learning rule allows a unit to extract the first principal component of the input. Extending this idea, Oja's subspace learning algorithm (Oja, 1989) finds a set of k weight vectors which span the same subspace as the first k principal components. The same is true of the weights learned by an auto-encoder (Baldi, Chauvin, & Hornik, chapter 12, this volume; Baldi & Hornik, 1989; Bourlard & Kamp, 1988). Sanger's generalized Hebbian algorithm (Sanger, 1989a, 1989b) allows a group of linear units to learn a full principal components decomposition of the input distribution by combining Hebbian learning with Gram-Schmidt orthogonalization. Finally, Foldiak (1990) has described a related, but more biologically plausible algorithm that uses anti-Hebbian learning.

A principal components representation has several nice optimality properties. First, it can be shown to minimize the mean-squared error in optimal linear reconstruction of the inputs (for a detailed analysis, see Sanger, 1989c). Second, Linsker (1988) has pointed out that under certain conditions the principal-component analyzing unit resulting from a Hebbian learning rule also transmits maximal information about its inputs. Hence this approach to unsupervised learning is useful if the main objective is to achieve maximal data compression, while retaining as much information as possible about the data. On the other hand, even Linsker (1989) has questioned the relevancy of accurate input reconstruction as a goal for biological perceptual systems.

How Can We Best Model the Input Distribution?

Ideally we would like to be able to capture all the "interesting features" in the data. However, it is unlikely that a single unsupervised learning method can do this in reasonable time for any arbitrary input distribution, without making some a priori assumptions about the kinds of structure in the environment. Each of the approaches we have mentioned can be expected to perform well on certain distributions, and poorly on others.

Algorithms related to principal-components analysis (PCA) learn a set of

---

[1]That is, the eigenvectors of the input correlation matrix.

linear orthogonal projections in the directions of principal variation in the input distribution, or a rotated subspace of these directions. In some cases, the principal components decomposition may coincide with features of interest in the input. Oja (1989) suggests that subspace methods are particularly useful for representing and classifying patterns such as spectra and histograms. Linsker (1986a, 1986b, 1986c) shows how interesting feature detectors similar to those found in early visual cortex can develop via a Hebbian learning mechanism in a linear network operating on spatially localized patches of random inputs. Miller, Keller, and Stryker (1989) have performed similar simulations with units having binocular inputs and local lateral excitatory connections; using a Hebbian learning rule with decay in this case leads to the formation of ocular dominance columns.

For arbitrary input distributions, there is no guarantee that a subspace method or PCA will capture the interesting structure. PCA would be expected to represent poorly parameters which vary in a highly nonlinear manner, and may in fact, depending on the distribution, obscure clusters in the data (i.e., if there are too many isotropically distributed clusters; Huber, 1985).

In situations where PCA fails to find any interesting structure in the data, competitive learning schemes may in some cases be advantageous, since they attempt to represent explicitly the locations of clusters. Each cluster may implicitly come to represent conjunctions of interesting features, which can be interpreted as describing prototypical class members. On the other hand, the effectiveness of such learning schemes is likely to be very dependent on the number and distribution of clusters in the data, hence, the architecture must be carefully chosen to suit the input distribution. Further, most competitive learning algorithms based on a hard "winner-take-all" strategy are very sensitive to the initial conditions (i.e., initial random weights) and the order of presentation of input patterns.

What Kind of Representation Is Best for Later Learning?

In designing unsupervised learning algorithms, in addition to the question of what type of representation best models the data, we must address a related question: what type of representation will be most convenient as input for further learning?

PCA has the nice property of finding a set of *uncorrelated* projections. This will typically be very helpful for a method such as back-propagation learning by steepest descent. One thing that makes supervised back-propagation learning slow is that there may be interacting effects of different weights on the error. Because of these interactions, convergence can be expected to be very slow, even with simple local accelerating procedures such as momentum (Plaut, Nowlan & Hinton, 1986) or delta-bar-delta (which employs an adaptive learning rate for each weight based on gradient information); (Jacobs, 1987). If, on the other hand, the input representation uses uncorrelated components, then the Hessian of the error function is diagonal, so simple acceleration methods will permit a considerable speedup, by scaling the learning rates appropriately along each weight axis independently. Of course, this analysis ignores the nonlinearities of a multilayer back-propagation network, but it may still provide a useful heuristic for designing good input representations even in the nonlinear case.

If later learning requires interpolating a smooth function from points in the input distribution, then any reasonable set of radial basis functions will make a good set of interpolation points (Moody & Darken, 1989; Renals & Rohwer, 1989; Poggio, 1989). However, in some situations there are disadvantages to this type of representation. We may be collapsing information about underlying features of the data within each cluster; we are thereby scattering essential information about the continuity of individual features, and about combinations of these features, across many clusters. Suppose, for example, that there is a weak correlation between the desired output and the first component of the input vector. Since the correlation is weak, a large sample is required to distinguish between the correlation and sampling error. To get a large sample it may be necessary to combine data points that differ considerably on the values of *other* components. In a system that uses narrowly tuned radial basis functions, only a few of the training cases will activate each RBF, and so the information about the weak correlation will be spread over many different RBFs and it will be hard to detect the correlation. RBF's make it easier to detect correlations between the desired output and very high-order combinations of input values, but harder to detect some of the low-order correlations that are easily detected by systems that use a less local representation.

While clustering and PCA-related algorithms may be useful forms of pre-processing for achieving data compression, noise reduction, and smoothing, we would like to take unsupervised learning much further. Our major goal is to build self-organizing network modules which capture important regularities of the environment in a simple form suitable for further perceptual processing. We would like an unsupervised learning procedure to be applicable at successive layers, so that it can extract and explicitly represent progressively higher-order features. If at one stage the algorithm could learn to explicitly represent continuous real-valued parameters such as relative depth, position, and orientation of features in an image, subsequent learning could then discover higher-order relations between these features, representing, for example, the location of object boundaries.

SPATIAL COHERENCE AS AN OBJECTIVE FUNCTION

An unprocessed pixel image of a natural scene contains a wealth of information, but this information is in a complex form; a combination of intrinsic parameters such as depth, reflectance, and surface orientation, as well as effects of noise and illumination, all contribute to the intensity of each pixel. We would like an unsupervised processing stage to learn to encode this complex information in a simpler form, by representing the underlying parameters of interest explicitly. In order to constrain the kinds of regularities that our algorithm may discover, we propose that a good objective for perceptual learning is to extract higher-order features that exhibit simple coherence across space. In other words, we would like to represent the information in one spatially localized image region in a way that makes it easy to predict the representation of information in neighboring patches.

Some unpublished results of Peter Brown suggest that a good way to implement this general idea is to try to maximize the explicit mutual information between pairs of parameters extracted from adjacent but nonoverlapping parts of the input. We derive a family of algorithms based on this principle, beginning with the simple case of binary parameters, and extending it to the case of continuously varying parameters.

The mutual information between two variables, a and b, is given by

$$I(a; b) = H(a) + H(b) - H(a, b),$$

where $H(a) = -\langle \log p(a) \rangle$ is the entropy of a, and $H(a, b) = -\langle \log p(a, b) \rangle$ is the entropy of the joint distribution of a and b. The equation shows that the mutual information between two variables can only be high if their joint distribution has low entropy, while each variable has high individual entropy. The latter requirement that each has high individual entropy is one advantage of mutual information over measures like the mean-squared error between a and b; two variables can have minimal squared error simply by taking on constant, equal values, thus conveying no information. By maximizing the mutual information between variables extracted by two modules, each module is forced to convey a lot of information about some (spatially coherent) feature of its input. Figure 1 shows how this objective function can be used to train a multilayer network.

Experiments with Binary Units

For the simple case of two binary probabilistic units, we can estimate the mutual information by discrete sampling of their activity values over a large set of input cases. Similarly, we can obtain an analytic expression for the derivative of their mutual information, as shown in Appendix A. The final expression we use for the partial derivative of the mutual information between the outputs of the ith and jth units with respect to the expected output of the ith unit on training case α, p_i^α, is

$$\frac{\partial I(y_i; y_j)}{\partial p_i^\alpha} = -P^\alpha \left[\log \frac{p_i}{p_{\bar{i}}} - p_j^\alpha \log \frac{p_{ij}}{p_{\bar{i}j}} - p_{\bar{j}}^\alpha \log \frac{p_{i\bar{j}}}{p_{\bar{i}\bar{j}}} \right] \quad (1)$$

where P^α is the probability of training case α, $p_i = \langle y_i \rangle$ is the expected value of the ith unit's output averaged over the fluctuations for each training case and also

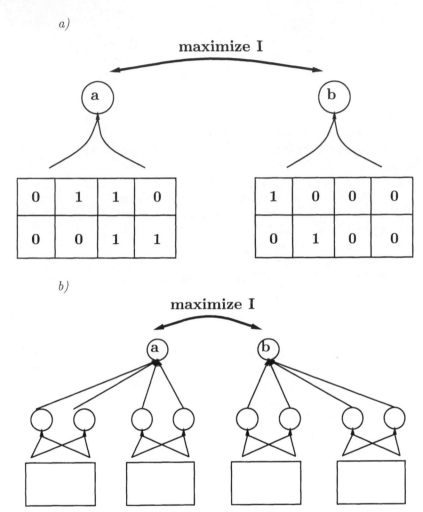

Figure 1. (a) Two units receive input from adjacent, nonoverlapping parts of the image. The learning algorithm adjusts the weights of each unit to maximize the mutual information, over the ensemble of training cases, between the states of the two units. (b) In a multilayer version of this architecture, once the first layer of weights has been trained to extract some low-order features, the next layer can hierarchically combine these noisy estimates into more accurate feature estimates.

over the whole ensemble of cases (when y_i is treated as a stochastic binary variable), $p_i^- = \langle(1 - y_i)\rangle$, and $p_{ij} = \langle y_i y_j \rangle$.

We can see from Equation 1 that in order for the ith unit to perform gradient ascent in $I(y_i; y_j)$, it needs to accumulate two ensemble-averaged statistics: the expected value that it is on, p_i, and the expected value of the joint event that it is on and the jth unit is also on, p_{ij}; from these two values the other terms in the individual and joint distributions can be derived (see Appendix A). In our simulations we use a batch version of this algorithm: we make one sweep through the input cases to accumulate these probabilities, and a second sweep to accumulate the gradients. One could, however, implement an online version of the algorithm by accumulating time-averaged estimates of these probabilities, and using these approximate statistics to compute the weight update on each case.

We have found that this method works well for the task of discovering depth in an ensemble of very simple, binary random-dot stereograms, such as those shown in the input layer in Figure 1a. Each input vector consists of a one-dimensional strip from the right image and the corresponding strip from the left image. The right image is purely random and the left image is generated from it by choosing, at random, a single global shift. So the input can be interpreted as an approximation to a one-dimensional stereogram of a fronto-parallel surface at an integer depth. The only local property that is invariant across space is the depth (i.e., the shift). Hence, if one unit looks at one area of the two images, and another unit looks at another area, the only way they can provide mutual information about each other's outputs is by representing the depth. We can measure the degree to which output units are tuned to depth by performing "simulated neurophysiology": we present the network with a number of patterns at different depths, and observe how the activity levels of units vary with depth. A useful performance measure, indicative of the extent to which the outputs are shift-tuned, is the mutual information between each output unit's activity and the degree of shift.

We used two global shifts (one pixel rightward or one pixel leftward) operating on binary image strips. Each pair of strips was divided into $n \times 2$ patches with a gap of one pixel between patches,[2] where the receptive field width n varied in different experiments. Each stochastic binary unit used the logistic nonlinearity $\sigma(s) = 1/(1 + e^{-s})$ to determine the probability of outputting a 1 as a function of its total weighted summed input s.[3] Units learned roughly by the

---

[2]With no gap between the receptive fields of two neighboring units, those units could simply learn the uninformative correlations between the upper (lower) rightmost bit of the left unit's field and the lower (upper) leftmost bit of the right unit's field, while ignoring the rest of their inputs.

[3]Rather than running stochastic simulations of probabilistic binary units, we actually used a mean-field approximation in which the output of each unit on a particular case α is taken to be its expected value $\sigma(s^\alpha)$. In practice this yields equivalent behavior, but is much faster since we can obtain good estimates of the various probability statistics required for our learning algorithm in only one sweep through the training set.

method of gradient ascent, with the modification that the step size for each weight was truncated to lie within $[-0.1, 0.1]$. We found that in practice the gradients tended to increase by many orders of magnitude as the algorithm neared a solution, and this upper limit on the step size prevented the learning from "blowing up" in this situation.

We performed a number of preliminary experiments with the algorithm, varying the architecture and the training set size. With random patterns and a small training set there is a high probability that units will learn some of the random structure in the data in addition to the shift; as the number of training cases increases, sampling error decreases and units become more tuned to shift.

We can further increase the likelihood that shift will be learned, rather than random structure, by increasing the number of receptive fields (and hence the input size), because shift is the only feature common to the inputs of all units. When we extend the architecture shown in Figure 1a to multiple receptive fields (with one unit receiving input from each receptive field) each unit now tries to maximize the sum of its pairwise mutual information with each of the other units. In this case, an interesting effect occurs as the learning proceeds: once some pair or subset of units within a layer has "caught on" to the shift feature, their mutual information gradients become very large, and convergence accelerates. This provides stronger shift-tuned signals to the other units, so that the effect rapidly spreads across the layer.

Since shift is a higher-order feature of the input (i.e., it can be predicted from the products of pairs of pixel intensities but not by any linear combination of the individual intensities), a network with a single layer of weights cannot learn to become a perfect shift detector.[4] Hence, the problem requires a multilayer (nonlinear) network, so that with each successive layer, units can combine the "votes" from several lower-level feature detectors to make more robust predictions. Using a hierarchical architecture as shown in Figure 1b, the partially shift-tuned noisy features extracted by the first layer from several patches of input can be combined by the second-layer units, thereby increasing the signal to noise ratio in the prediction of shift. At the top layer, every "output" unit maximizes the sum of its mutual information with each of the others. In the middle layer, there are m clusters of units, each cluster receiving input from a different receptive field, and each output unit receiving input from a different set of clusters.

As mentioned, the performance measure we use is the mutual information between the output units' activities and the shift, when shift is treated as a binary feature of the input pattern. For a network with two output units and four 2-unit clusters in the middle layer each with 2×5 receptive fields, the learning converged after about 300 passes through a training set of 500 patterns, and the output units learned to convey, on average (over five repetitions from different initial random weights), about 0.03 bit of information about the shift. As we

---

[4]See Minsky and Papert (1969) for a thorough treatment of the issue of what can and cannot be learned by single-layer networks.

increased the number of receptive fields, the ability of the network to learn shift increased dramatically. The most shift-tuned (and largest) network we experimented with on random shift patterns had five output units, each receiving input from two 2-unit clusters of units in the middle layer, and ten 2 × 4 receptive fields in the input layer. For this network, the learning took about 500 passes to converge on a training set of 1000 random patterns. The output units conveyed on average about 0.23 bit of information about the shift, and the most shift-tuned unit (over five runs from different initial random weights) conveyed 0.46 bit of information about the shift. Note that the maximum possible information that could be conveyed about a binary feature is 1 bit.

Using Back Propagation to Train the Hidden Layers

The multilayer algorithm described above has the nice property that layers can be trained sequentially. Once the initial layer has partly learned the shift problem, subsequent layers can take advantage of this earlier learning and quickly become even more shift-tuned. However, there is no guarantee that the shift patterns will be perfectly classified by the top layer, since units in lower layers within a cluster may learn redundant features, which only apply to a subset of the input patterns. Since we only maximized the mutual information between *pairs* of hidden units, there was nothing to prevent many pairs from learning exactly the same feature. We can improve the performance of the network by applying our objective function between units at the top layer *only*, and using back-propagated gradients to train the middle layer. The back-propagated gradients send a more global training signal to the hidden units, which is best optimized by having hidden units differentiate to detect different features. In practice, as we shall see in the next section, a combination of the sequential, layer by layer, application of the same objective (as described in the previous section) and "top-down" or back-propagation training of the hidden units, seems to result in optimal performance.

Starting from random initial weights, the back-propagated gradients from the output units initially tend to be very small, in fact many orders of magnitude smaller than those near the solution. This causes convergence problems if the step size is a fixed proportion η of the gradient. What seems like a reasonable learning rate at the beginning will cause the learning to "blow up" near the solution. A more sophisticated optimization method would employ an adaptive learning rate, or better yet, a line search. For our early experiments using back propagation, described in the remainder this section, we used what could be viewed as a very crude approximation to an adaptive learning rate, in which we empirically chose a very large value of η for the first 50 iterations, and then fixed it at a much smaller value for the remainder of learning. (Additionally, as before, the step size for each weight was truncated to lie within [−0.1, 0.1].) We found that in practice this speeded up convergence considerably.[5]

---

[5]In our subsequent experiments on real-valued units (described in a later section in this paper), we employed a simple line search to accelerate convergence.

We can remove the possibility that units may learn any of the random input structure by creating a complete set of unambiguous binary patterns. Using 2×4 receptive fields, there are $2^4 = 16$ possible left-shifted and 16 right-shifted patterns within a receptive field. We remove the eight ambiguous patterns.[6] We used two modules, and created 16-bit patterns by presenting each possible combination of pairs of the 12 unambiguous 2×4 bit left-shifted patterns, and each combination of pairs of right-shifted patterns, yielding a total training set of 288 sixteen-bit patterns.

The hierarchical architecture shown in Figure 1b was helpful in dealing with noise when we trained layers sequentially, because the output units could compute a weighted average of information from multiple receptive fields. However, when we are back-propagating derivatives to hidden units, we can deal with this problem by simply adding more hidden units for each receptive field, because the back-propagated signal from an output unit provides pressure for the hidden units to extract different features. In our experiments on the unambiguous pattern set (and in the remaining experiments reported in this chapter), instead of the hierarchical architecture used earlier, we used a modular architecture as shown in figure 2. Each 2×4 patch was used as input to a separate module that contained a layer of hidden units and one "output" unit.

Since we had removed the random aspect of the input patterns, we found we could now get by with a much smaller network having only two modules. When we trained our two-module network on this complete set of patterns (with back propagation to the hidden layers), we usually got (at least one of two) output units that were pure shift detectors within about 300 passes through the training set. The mutual information between the two output units occasionally approached the global maximum of 1 bit (corresponding also to 1 bit of information about the shift), although usually the network found only locally maximum solutions, as shown in Figure 3a.

Improving the Performance with Bootstrapping

The learning is rather slow for two reasons. First, we are not specifying desired values for the "output" units; we are only specifying that their pairwise mutual information should be high. The derivative of this objective function w.r.t. a weight depends on *three* other layers of adaptive weights—one other layer in the same module and two layers in the adjacent module. So in this respect the difficulty of learning resembles back-propagation through four layers of weights. Second, with random starting weights, the initial gradient of the objective function is very small.

---

[6]The ambiguous patterns have 1111, 0000, 1010, or 0101 in the top half. Note that the left- and right-shifted versions of each of these (using shift with wraparound within receptive fields) are indistinguishable. The use of wraparound within each receptive field makes this example differ slightly from a simple version of a stereo task.

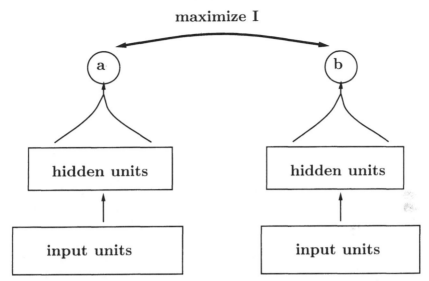

Figure 2. Two modules that receive input from adjacent receptive fields. Each module has one layer of hidden units. The learning algorithm maximizes the mutual information between the states of the two output units, and the gradients are back-propagated to hidden units.

The performance of the algorithm, in terms of both convergence speed and quality of the final solution, is greatly improved by using a "bootstrapping" method. We start by applying our objective function between pairs of units within layers (as we did when in the hierarchical version) until these units are somewhat tuned to the shift. Then the gradients of the mutual information between the output units are much bigger and the objective function can be applied at that layer *only* and the derivatives back-propagated.[7] More globally coherent information can now be provided to the hidden units that failed to find any useful features in the bootstrapping phase.

We ran simulations with three versions of the algorithm, one with bootstrapping, one with back propagation, and one combined. We compared their performance on a network with two modules, using eight hidden units and one output unit per module, on the complete, unambiguous pattern set described earlier. The three versions of the learning algorithm we used were

- **Version 1.** 50 bootstrapping learning iterations, in which each layer was trained to maximize information between pairs of units between modules, followed by 250 iterations with information maximization between the top two units and back propagation of gradients to the hidden units.

---

[7]One could alternatively apply both objectives simultaneously to the hidden units.

I(a;b) (bits)

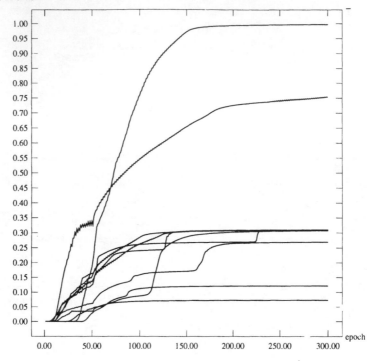

I(a;b) (bits)

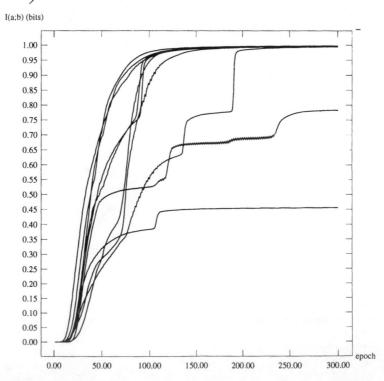

- **Version 2.** 300 iterations in which each layer was trained to maximize information between pairs of units in different modules in the same layer, without back propagation (as in the bootstrapping phase of Version 1).
- **Version 3.** 300 iterations with information maximization between the top two units and back-propagation to the hidden units (as in the back-propagation phase of Version 1).

Version 1 performed by far the best: in 48 out of 50 runs from different initial random weights, the network learned an exact solution to the shift problem, in which one or both output units predicted shift almost perfectly.[8] In Versions 2 and 3, while the top-level units nearly always became highly shift-tuned, only in 27 out of 50 and 30 out of 50 repetitions, respectively, did the network learn to perfectly separate the two classes of patterns. Figure 3 shows the learning curves for ten runs of Version 1 (bootstrapping) versus Version 3. We can see that in some cases the mutual information between the top two units asymptotically approaches the global optimum, while in other cases the procedure has become stuck in suboptimal regions of weight space.

It appears that the bootstrapping procedure increases the likelihood that the network will converge to globally optimal solutions. The reason for this may be that because we are applying two different learning procedures to the hidden units, they have more opportunities to discover useful features at each stage. During the bootstrapping stage, a given pair of hidden units attempting to achieve high mutual information cannot learn to predict shift perfectly, since the shift problem is not learnable by a single layer of weights. However, some units do learn to be partially correlated with shift at the bootstrapping stage. This makes the job of a pair of output units in adjacent modules much easier, since they now have more spatially correlated inputs, which are at least partially shift-tuned. Now when we back-propagate the information gradients to the hidden units, those hidden units which failed to learn anything useful in the bootstrapping stage are under increased pressure to become shift-tuned.

Not only does the bootstrapping procedure increase the overall quality of the solution, but on more difficult learning problems it substantially reduces the

---

[8]That is, the mutual information between the unit's output and shift was greater than or equal to 0.6 nat = about 0.86 bit. In the remaining two runs, the output units were still both highly shift-tuned, but did not meet this criterion.

Figure 3. (facing page) Mutual information between two modules versus learning epochs on 288 binary shift patterns. (a) shows learning curves using back propagation alone, for 10 runs starting from different initial random weights, and (b) shows learning curves using back propagation preceded by 50 "bootstrapping" iterations, for 10 runs starting from the same initial weights as in (a).

learning time. We find that for the continuous version of our algorithm (described in the next section), on stereograms with continuously varying depths, when the hidden units are initially trained with bootstrapping, the subsequent learning with back propagation of gradients is accelerated by roughly an order of magnitude.

MODULES WITH REAL-VALUED OUTPUTS

The binary probabilistic output units we used in our initial experiments tend to learn solutions with large weights, resulting in sharp decision boundaries. The drive toward maximal entropy causes a unit to adopt its two possible states with equal probability over the ensemble of training cases, but the drive toward minimal joint entropy causes it *on each particular case* to be either strongly on or strongly off, so that it can agree with its neighbor with high probability. This "within-case" tendency toward strongly binary behavior of the output units has some undesirable consequences. As the magnitudes of the weights increase, the unit's sigmoidal probabilistic response function sharpens into a step function. On each particular case, the unit's response is at one of the extremes of this function, where its slope is virtually zero. This means that effectively the unit can neither adapt any further, nor can its output be used to indicate its degree of uncertainty about its decision, since it has virtually become a linear threshold unit.

This binary behavior makes it difficult to represent depth in more realistic images that contain smoothly curved surfaces which have real-valued depths. In this case, we would like units to learn to encode continuous ranges of depths with real values. Ideally, we would like a group of units to form a population code for depth, in which each unit has a roughly Gaussian response to some limited range of disparities. Such a mechanism appears to be employed in biological systems (Lehky and Sejnowski, 1990), and could be achieved, for example, using the continuous interval encoding scheme proposed by Saund (1986). We are investigating the use of an alternative scheme in our current research; for now, however, let us assume that it is possible for a single unit's real-valued output to reliably encode depth, given that the input patterns have only a small range of disparities.

In the following simulations, we use random-dot stereograms of curved surfaces, as shown in Figure 4, and modules with deterministic, real-valued outputs that learn to represent real-valued depths (disparities) with subpixel accuracy. A slice of a curved surface is generated by randomly choosing a collection of control points (scaled to lie within a fixed depth range), and fitting a curve through these points using spline interpolation, as shown in Figure 4. The curve can be thought of as the depth of a gently curved surface as a function of the (horizontal) x coordinate, for a fixed y coordinate. Points are pseudorandomly scattered on the curve by dividing the x axis into a fixed number of intervals, and randomly placing a point within each interval, to create a pattern of random features.

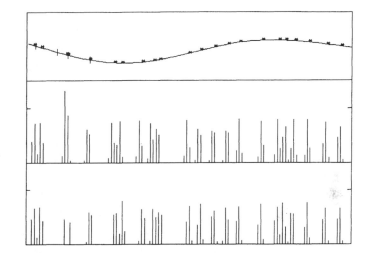

Random Spline Curve

Left Image

Right Image

Figure 4. Part of a cubic spline fitted through seven randomly chosen control points, with randomly located features scattered on it, and the "intensity" values in the two images of the surface strip. The images are made by taking two slightly different parallel projections of the feature points, filtering the projections through a Gaussian, and sampling the filtered projections at equally spaced sample points. The sample values in corresponding patches of the two images are used as the inputs to a module. The boundaries of two neighboring patches are shown on the spline.

Stereo images are formed from this pattern by taking two parallel projections from slightly different viewing angles.[9] Finally, we add Gaussian blur (using a Gaussian with standard deviation roughly equal to one image pixel) to the stereo images and integrate these blurred patterns within equally spaced intervals to create the discretized real-valued n-dimensional input vectors. The Gaussian blurring causes a single point from the random-dot pattern to spread over several pixels in the final image. The final pair of n-pixel stereo patterns is treated as a $2 \times n$ image, which is divided into smaller stereo receptive fields. The spacing of the random features is chosen so that, on average, each receptive field will contain about two features, and never less than one feature. (We discuss the problem of missing or unreliable data in the final section.)

The analytic expression for the mutual information between two real-valued variables a and b is $I(a; b) = -[\int \log p(a) + \int \log p(b) - \int \int \log p(a, b)]$. To

---

[9]The parameters of the projection (focal length, eye offset and image width) were chosen so that the maximum disparity was 6 minutes of visual arc in the "imaging system," corresponding to a final disparity of 2 image pixels.

extend our algorithm to real-valued units, we must make some simplifying assumptions about the probability distributions of the variables, in order to obtain a tractable approximation to this expression. We start by making the following very simple coherence assumption (which will be relaxed later): There is some locally detectable parameter which is approximately constant for nearby patches. So, given two modules A and B that receive input from neighboring patches, we want their outputs a and b to be approximately equal. We can think of b as a signal that we are trying to predict and a as a version of that signal that is corrupted by additive, independent, Gaussian noise. If we assume that both a and b have Gaussian distributions, the information that a provides about b is determined by the log ratio of two variances:

$$I_{a;b} = 0.5 \log \frac{V(\text{signal} + \text{noise})}{V(\text{noise})}.$$

The reader who is familiar with information theory will recognize that the above is a standard expression for the information transmission rate of a noisy channel when the signal and noise have Gaussian distributions (Shannon, 1949).

In our model, where a is a noisy estimator of b, the information rate is

$$I_{a;b} = \log \frac{V(a)}{V(a - b)}.$$

So, for a to provide a lot of information about b we need a to have high variance but $a - b$ to have low variance. For symmetry, we actually optimize the following objective function (where κ is a small constant which prevents the information measure from becoming infinitely large):

$$I_{a;b}^* = I_{a;b} + I_{b;a} = \log \frac{V(a)}{V(a - b) + \kappa} + \log \frac{V(b)}{V(a - b) + \kappa}.$$

In the foregoing model, modules A and B are actually making inconsistent assumptions about each other's output distributions (Ralph Linsker, personal communication). Theoretically, $I_{a;b}$ should be equal to $I_{b;a}$. However, each module is assuming that it is conveying a noisy version of some signal, and that the other is conveying the pure signal. Under these assumptions, A would predict its own output to have higher variance than b, while B would predict its own output to have higher variance than a. Thus, the assumptions cannot both be valid except in the limit as the variance of $a - b$ approaches zero. However, in practice this is not a problem, because each module is minimizing $V(a - b)$, so our model becomes more accurate as learning proceeds.

To avoid the asymmetry in our mutual information measure, another possibility would be to assume that both a and b are noisy versions of the same underlying signal, each with independent additive Gaussian noise. This alternative model has the advantage that modules A and B are now making consistent assumptions about each other, but the disadvantage that we cannot exactly compute the information that either of the modules alone transmits about the underlying signal. As an approximation, we could optimize the expression

$$\log \frac{V(a + b)}{V(a - b)} = \log \frac{V(\text{signal} + \text{noise}_a + \text{signal} + \text{noise}_b)}{V(\text{noise}_a - \text{noise}_b)}$$

$$= \log \frac{V(2 * \text{signal} + \text{noise}_a + \text{noise}_b)}{V(\text{noise}_a + \text{noise}_b)},$$

as suggested by Allan Jepson (personal communication). This measure tells how much information the sum $a + b$ conveys about the signal. In our simulations, we use the former model, with the preceding expression for I^* and we find that it gives good results in practice.

The derivation for the gradient of our objective function I^* is given in Appendix B. The final expression we use in our learning algorithm for the partial derivative of $I^*(y_i; y_j)$, the mutual information between the outputs of the ith and jth units with respect to the output of the ith unit on case α, y_i^α, is

$$\frac{\partial I^*(y_i; y_j)}{\partial y_i^\alpha} = \frac{2}{N} \left[\frac{y_i^\alpha - \langle y_i \rangle}{V(y_i)} - 2 \frac{(y_i^\alpha - y_j^\alpha) - \langle y_i - y_j \rangle}{V(y_i - y_j) + \kappa} \right], \qquad (2)$$

where $\langle y_i \rangle$ is the output of the ith unit averaged over the ensemble of N training cases.

The objective we have proposed for the continuous case is closely related to a statistical method called ACE (alternating conditional expectation; Hastie & Tibshirani, 1990) a nonlinear generalization of regression. ACE minimizes the squared error between a single nonlinearly transformed predictor variable y and an additive nonlinear transformation of a set of m observed variables x_i, over an ensemble of n observations:

$$E = \sum_{i=1}^{n} (f(y_i) - \sum_{j=1}^{m} \phi(x_{ij}))^2$$

subject to the constraint that $f(y)$ has unit variance. While ACEs underlying model differs from ours (we compute nonlinear transformations of *two* sets of variables—the two input patches, and we do not use an additive model, since the input components are not in general independent), both objectives are equivalent to maximizing the correlation between two nonlinearly transformed variables.

Discovering Real-Valued Depth for Fronto-Parallel Surfaces

Figure 4 shows how we generate stereo images of curved surface strips. The same technique can be applied to generate images of fronto-parallel planar surfaces. Using 1000 training cases of this simpler type of input, we trained a network that contained 10 modules each of which tried to maximize I^* with the immediately adjacent modules. Each module had a single linear output unit, and 10 nonlinear hidden units.

Each update of the weights involves two complete passes through the training set. In the first pass, we compute the mean and variance of each output value and the mean and variance of each pairwise difference between output values given the current weights (see in Appendix B). In the second pass we compute the derivatives of I^* (w.r.t. each unit's output) as shown in Equation 2 for the output units of each pair of adjacent modules. We then back-propagate these terms to the hidden layer, and for each unit, we use these derivatives to accumulate dI^*/dw for all weights. Then we update all the weights in parallel. After each weight update, we average corresponding weights in all the modules in order to enforce the constraint that every module computes exactly the same function of its input vector. (This idea of constraining the weights has been used effectively by Le Cun et al. (1989) in a supervised learning task).

Without these equality constraints among groups of weights, the algorithm does not converge; each module tries to learn some of the random structure that it finds in common with the adjacent neighbor, and this effect "swamps out" the effect of disparity. This is because it is much easier for two units to learn correlations between pairs of their input lines than it is to learn higher-order structure that would eventually lead to more globally optimal solutions. When we average weight updates among groups of units receiving input from different input patches, the effect of this low-order noise is reduced, since only the disparity is common to all input patches. (Note that we dealt with this problem differently in the binary case, by allowing each unit to maximize mutual information with *many* other units rather than just its immediate neighbors.)

To accelerate the convergence, we used a simple line search. Each learning iteration consists of two phases: (1) computation of the gradient, as described above, and (2) computation of an appropriate learning rate η. At the beginning of each iteration, η is increased by a factor of 1.05. In phase 2, we first increment the weights by a proportion η of the gradient, and then if the average amount of mutual information between adjacent output units has decreased, we repeatedly backtrack, halving η each time, until the average information is greater than or equal to its previous value.

Before applying this learning algorithm, we first trained the hidden layer only, with 100 bootstrapping learning iterations, maximizing I^* between pairs of hidden units in adjacent modules.[10] We then trained the 10 modules, as described

---

[10]As in the binary case, we do not want two hidden units within the same module to directly or indirectly optimize their mutual information (for they could learn trivial solutions). They could do so indirectly by each optimizing their mutual information with the same unit in another module. Hence we arbitrarily number the n units within the hidden layer of each module, and only allow hidden units in different modules to communicate with each other if they have been given the same number.

before, for 1400 iterations. Each module became highly tuned to disparity, as shown in Figure 5a.

Speeding the Learning Using Radial Basis Functions

We experimented with an additional method to accelerate learning, in which the first hidden layer of adaptive units in each module is replaced by a large number of nonadaptive radial basis functions (RBFs; Moody & Darken, 1989). Each radial basis unit has a "center" $\bar{x}$, that is equal to a typical input vector selected at random, and gives an output y, which is a Gaussian function of the distance between the current input vector and the unit's "center":

$$y = \frac{1}{\sqrt{2\pi}\sigma} e^{\frac{\|x-\bar{x}\|}{\sigma^2}}$$

All the Gaussians have the same variance σ^2, which is chosen by hand.[11] Each module had 8×2 input units connected to a layer of 100 nonadaptive RBFs. Every module used exactly the same set of RBFs so that we could constrain all the modules to compute the same function.

We compared the performance of the learning with a nonadaptive hidden layer of RBFs, versus the algorithm described in the previous subsection with an adaptive layer of nonlinear hidden units, on the fronto-parallel surfaces. We found that with the RBFs, the learning took only about 50 iterations to converge, a speedup of roughly an order of magnitude. However, there is some loss of precision in the solution; units still became highly depth-tuned, but had greater variance, as shown in Figure 5b.

In the remaining experiments described in this paper for discovering depth in stereo pairs of curved surface strips, we used an initial layer of RBFs, choosing to sacrifice some precision for increased learning speed.

More Complex Types of Coherence

So far, we have described a very simple model of coherence in which an underlying parameter at one location is assumed to be approximately equal to the parameter at a neighboring location. This model is fine for fronto-parallel surfaces but it is far from the best model of slanted or curved surfaces. Fortunately, we can use a far more general model of coherence in which the parameter at one location is assumed to be an unknown linear function of the parameters at nearby locations. The particular linear function that is appropriate can be learned by the network.

We used a network of the type shown in Figure 6a (but with 10 modules and

---

[11]The variance was 0.1. The input vectors had peak values of about 0.3.

a)

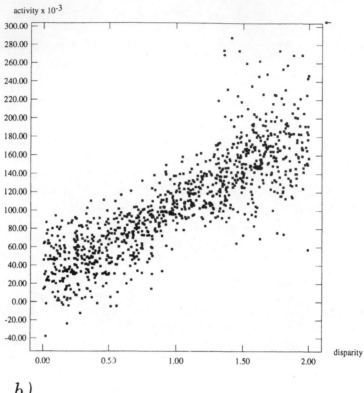

b)

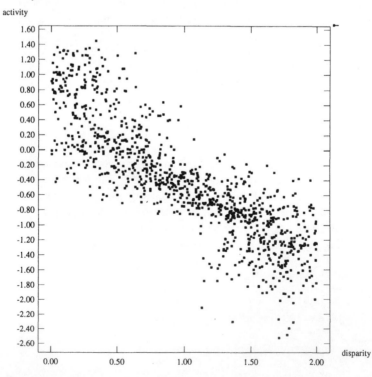

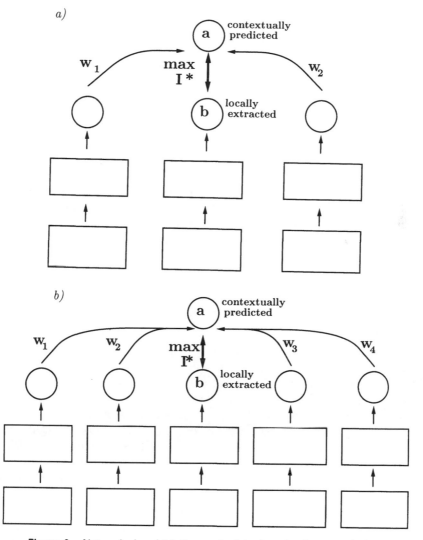

Figure 6.   Networks in which the goal of the learning is to maximize the information between the output of a local module and the contextually predicted output that is computed by using a linear function of the outputs of nearby modules. (a) The network used for planar surface interpolation. (b) The network used for curved surface interpolation.

Figure 5.   (facing page) The activity of the linear output unit of a module (vertical axis) as a function of the disparity (horizontal axis) for all 1000 test cases using planar surface strips. (a) shows the response for a network trained with 10 adaptive nonlinear hidden units per module, and (b) for a network trained with 100 nonadaptive Gaussian units per module.

with a contextual predictor unit for all modules except the two at the ends). We tried to maximize I^* between the output of each module and the contextual prediction of this output that was produced by computing a linear function of the outputs of one adjacent module on each side. We used weight averaging to constrain this interpolating function to be identical for all modules. We also back-propagated the error derivatives through the interpolating weights. Before applying this new objective function, we first used a bootstrapping stage in which we maximized I^* between adjacent pairs of modules as before, for 30 learning iterations.

After having been trained for 100 iterations on 3000 patterns, the two weights learned for the interpolating function were .55, .54. The output of these units is similar to the response profile of units trained on fronto-parallel surfaces, shown in Figure 5b, but even more finely depth-tuned. Thus, the interpolating units have learned that the depth at one patch on a planar surface can be approximated by the average of the depths of surrounding patches.

Discovering a Surface Interpolator
for Curved Surfaces

As we introduce curvature in the surfaces, the prediction of depth from neighboring patches becomes more difficult; at regions of high curvature, a simple average of the depths of two adjacent patches will under- or overestimate the true depth. In this case, a better interpolator would base its predictions on more than two local measurements of depth, thereby taking curvature into account.

We trained a network of 10 modules on 1000 of the stereograms of curved surface strips, using the same architecture and objective function as for the planar surface task, for 30 iterations. We then added an interpolating layer; this time, however, the contextual prediction of a given module was a linear function of the outputs of *two* adjacent modules on either side, as shown in Figure 6b. After 100 iterations, the four weights learned for the interpolating function were $-.04$, .64, .65, $-.04$. Positive weights are given to inputs coming from the immediately adjacent modules, and smaller negative weights are given to inputs coming from the other two neighbors. The activity of these units is well tuned to disparity, as shown in Figure 7. Given noise-free depth values, the optimal linear interpolator for the surface strips we used is approximately $-.2$, .7, .7, $-.2$. But with noisy depth estimates it is better to use an interpolator more like the one the network learned because the noise amplification is determined by the sum of the squares of the weights.

DISCUSSION

The goal of our depth interpolating unit was to discover how to predict one value from a liner combination of nearby values, by maximizing the log ratio of its

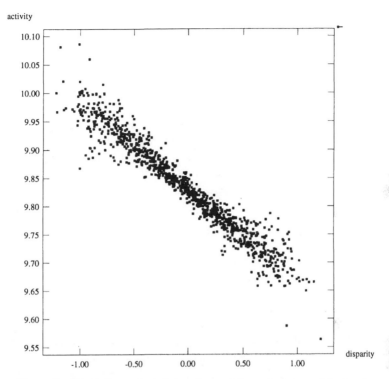

Figure 7.   The output of a unit (vertical axis) as a function of the local disparity (horizontal axis) for a test set of 1000 patterns, when trained on 1000 curved surface strips. The unit learned to predict the depth locally extracted from one module as a linear function of the outputs of the two adjacent modules on either side.

output variance to the variance of the prediction error. Another way to pose this problem is to find an invariant relation between the predicted value and the other values by learning a linear combination of *all* the values, such that the combined value always equals zero (Richard Durbin, personal communication). In this case, we would minimize the variance of the predicting unit's output about zero, while maximizing the variances of the individual inputs. This amounts to discovering invariant higher-order properties by learning invariance detectors that have low variance even though their input lines have high variances and large weights. One attractive aspect of this view is that the actual output of an invariance detector would represent the extent to which the current input violates the network's model of the regularities in the world. This is an efficient way of transmitting information about the current input. Furthermore, it has been suggested that the computation of invariant features about the world plays a fundamental role in human pattern recognition (Dodwell, 1983).

An invariance detector that minimizes the ratio of its output variance divided by the variance that would be expected if the input lines were independent Gaussian variables is a real-valued, deterministic, approximate version of the G-maximization learning procedure (Pearlmutter & Hinton, 1986) which finds regularities by maximizing the extent to which the independence assumption is incorrect in predicting the output of a unit. It also has an interesting relation to Linsker's learning procedure (Linsker, 1988). Linsker assumes the variances and covariances of the activities on the input lines to a unit are fixed (because he does not back-propagate derivatives) and he shows that, with the appropriate Gaussian assumptions, the information conveyed by the unit about its input vector is maximized by using weights which *maximize* the ratio of the output variance divided by the sum of the squares of the weights.

Learning Multidimensional Features

We have described the learning procedure for modules which each have a single real-valued output. For modules with several real-valued outputs, the natural way to generalize the objective function is to use the information rate for multi-dimensional Gaussians, where the variance is replaced by the determinant of the covariance matrix (Shannon, 1949). Zemel and Hinton (1991) have applied a version of this algorithm to explicitly extract information about the parameters of the viewing transform in images of simple two-dimensional objects.

Modeling Discontinuities

We have also ignored the ubiquitous problem of discontinuities. Images of real scenes have strong local coherence punctuated by discontinuities. We do not want our learning procedure to smear out the strong local coherence by trying to convey information across the discontinuities. We would prefer a module to make accurate predictions in continuity cases and no predictions in other cases rather than making rather inaccurate predictions in all cases.

We can achieve this by allowing a module A to use a slightly more compli-cated model to predict b, the depth of a nearby patch (or a linear combination of several nearby depths). Instead of assuming that the predicted signal b is always drawn from a Gaussian distributed identically to its own output a (plus noise), module A models b's distribution as a mixture of two Gaussians, as shown in Figure 8. For each input pattern, A assumes that b was either drawn from a normal distribution $N_1(b, \mu_1, \sigma_1^2)$ with mean $\mu_1 = a$ and small variance σ_1^2 (a continuity case) or from another less predictable distribution $N_2(b, \mu_2, \sigma_2^2)$ with much greater variance (a discontinuity case).

The posterior probability that the current case α is a continuity example can be computed by comparing the probability densities, under both the continuity and

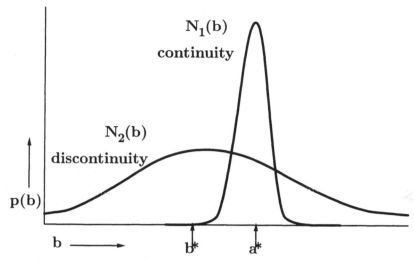

Figure 8. The probability distribution of b, p(b), is modeled as a mixture of two Gaussians: $N_1(b)$ with mean = a* and small variance, and $N_2(b)$ with large variance. Sample points for a and b, a* and b* are shown. In this case, a* and b* are far apart so b* is more likely to have been drawn from N_2.

discontinuity distributions, of the observed output of module B, as is done in the EM algorithm[12] (Dempster, Laird, & Rubin, 1977):

$$p_1(b^\alpha) = \frac{\pi_1 N_1(b,\mu_1,\sigma_1^2)}{\Sigma_{i=1}^2 \pi_i N_i(b,\mu_i,\sigma_i^2)}, \tag{3}$$

where π_i's are the mixing proportions. The proportions can be fixed, or can be estimated from the data as in the EM algorithm (e.g., $\pi_1 = \Sigma_{\alpha=1}^n p_1^\alpha/n$). We can now optimize the *average* information a transmits about b, by optimizing the product of the mixing proportion π_1 of the continuity Gaussian and the information conveyed given that we have a continuity case:

$$I^{**} = -\pi_1[\langle \log p(a) \rangle + \langle \log p_1(b) \rangle - \langle \log p_1(a, b) \rangle].$$

The contribution to the accumulated gradient is thus made proportional to the probability that the current case is a continuity example. This means that clear cases of discontinuity do not affect the weights learned by the continuity model.

One way to implement this idea is with an iterative two-phase learning proce-

---

[12]EM is an iterative optimization procedure which can be used to find a (locally) maximum likelihood model using a finite mixture of arbitrary component densities for a set of incomplete data points.

dure, in which we first adjust the weights while freezing the mixture model parameters, and then freeze the weights while optimizing the mixture model. After each sweep through the training data, we could use a gradient method to update the weights in the network, and then use several iterations of EM to reestimate the variances and mixing proportions of the continuity and discontinuity Gaussians. This only approximately follows the gradient of the foregoing objective function, since the implicit assumption is made that the weights and model parameters are independent. In practice, there are difficulties in getting this method to converge, probably due to the invalidity of the independence assumption.

A better approach would be to have a means of estimating the mixture model parameters which is independent of the weights in the stereo network. For example, an additional "expert network" could estimate the likelihood that each input pattern represents a continuity or discontinuity case, as in the competing experts model of Jacobs et al. (1991).

Population Codes for Depth

An alternative way to model discontinuities falls out naturally if we use a population code (as discussed at the beginning of the second section) to represent depth rather than using the activity of each output unit to encode the entire range of disparities. If each member of a group of units is tuned to a slightly different disparity, with a roughly Gaussian response, and each receives input from roughly the same region, we can interpret the response of each unit in this population (when normalized by the total population response) as the likelihood that it detected its preferred disparity. This population code can also be viewed as a mixture of Gaussians model for depth within a local image region. When one unit is most strongly active, its preferred disparity is, with high probability, close to the true disparity. If there are two sharp peaks in the population's depth response, this is strong evidence of a depth discontinuity within the region (assuming that we do not have two transparent surfaces).

Another problem we have not dealt with is that of missing or noisy data. When we are interpreting the activity of a unit directly as a real-valued code for depth, there is no obvious way to represent the certainty of the local estimate. The population code handles this problem in a natural way. When the local data is missing or very ambiguous, the population will have uniform low activity over all units. Thus, the entropy of the activity distribution represents uncertainty.

A simple way to ensure that the population encodes a probability distribution is to make the expected output of each unit be

$$p_i = \frac{e^{s_i/T}}{\sum_j e^{s_j/T}},$$

where s_i is the total input to the ith unit in the population. This also allows an additional way of explicitly modeling uncertainty by using a critic to compute an appropriate value of T. For example, when the relative phase of two bandpass-filtered images is used to extract disparity, there are some easily detectable situations in which the disparity estimate is unreliable (Allan Jepson, personal communication, 1989). A critic could detect these situations and set T to a high value. In principle, the critic's weights could also be learned by back propagation. It remains to be seen whether this works in practice.

Discovering Other Kinds of Coherence

In this chapter, we have described a learning procedure for discovering coherence across space in visual images, and demonstrated its effectiveness in learning about depth from stereo images. There are many other spatially coherent features which could be learned, such as illumination, texture, orientation, and curvature. There is also coherence within and between signals acquired in other sensory modalities, such as the correspondence between tactile and visual information.

Finally, in virtually every sensory modality, there is coherence across time. In the visual domain, for example, in sequences of images at successive points in time, there is temporal coherence in features such as the size and shape of moving objects. To train a network to learn temporal coherence, we could apply essentially the same learning procedure as before, by maximizing the mutual information between a network's outputs at successive time frames.

CONCLUSIONS

We have described the broad goals of unsupervised learning as twofold: first, we would like it to capture as much as possible of the interesting structure in the sensory input; second, we wish to represent that structure in a form which facilitates subsequent supervised learning. In particular, we would like the unsupervised learning to discover a transformation of the sensory input into an explicit representation of the underlying *causes* of the sensory input. The visual system, for example, transforms the patterns of light impinging on the retina into important features of the world such as object boundaries, motion, and depth.

With relatively few constraints, simple statistical methods such as clustering and principal components analysis can be applied to images to reduce noise, and represent simple low-order features. As we further constrain the learning, we can discover more specific, higher-order features and form explicit representations of important parameters of the world.

One way to constrain the learning is to find features that are spatially predictive, allowing a network to discover spatially coherent properties of visual images, such as depth, texture, and curvature. The procedure we have described has several appealing properties. First, it builds into the objective function (and the architecture) a type of prior knowledge that is strongly constraining but widely applicable to perceptual tasks. Second, using the bootstrapping approach it may be possible to train deep networks fairly rapidly, provided the domain is such that higher-order features that exhibit long-range coherence can be built out of lower-order features that exhibit shorter-range coherence. We have illustrated this idea by first training a network to discover depth in small patches of stereo images, and then training depth-interpolating units which combine depth estimates from several local patches.

ACKNOWLEDGMENTS

We thank Peter Brown, Francis Crick, Richard Durbin, Allan Jepson, Barak Pearlmutter, and Steven Nowlan for helpful discussions. This research was supported by grants from DuPont, the Ontario Information Technology Research Center, and the Canadian Natural Science and Engineering Research Council. Geoffrey Hinton is a fellow of the Canadian Institute for Advanced Research.

APPENDIX A
THE MUTUAL INFORMATION GRADIENT IN THE BINARY CASE

We assume a simple model neuron which computes a nonlinear probabilistic function σ of its real-valued total input s_i. For a particular input case α, the output of the ith unit is a binary variable $y_i \in \{0, 1\}$, which is on with probability $p_i^\alpha = \sigma(S_i^\alpha)$ and off with probability $1 - p_i^\alpha$. The total input to a unit is computed as a weighted sum of the activities on its input lines: $s_i^\alpha = \sum_k w_{ik} y_k^\alpha$.

We can compute the probability that the ith unit is on or off by averaging over the input sample distribution, with P^α being the prior probability of an input case α:

$$p_i = \sum_\alpha P^\alpha p_i^\alpha, \qquad p_{\bar{i}} = 1 - p_i.$$

Similarly, for a pair of binary units in a feedforward network which are not connected to one another (but may share the same inputs), and hence compute independent functions on a particular case, we can compute the four possible values in the joint (discrete) probability distribution of their outputs, y_i and y_j, as follows:

$$p_{ij} = \sum_\alpha P^\alpha p_i^\alpha p_j^\alpha,$$

$$p_{\bar{i}j} = p_j - p_{ij},$$

$$p_{i\bar{j}} = p_i - p_j,$$

$$p_{\bar{i}\bar{j}} = 1 - p_j - p_i + p_{ij}.$$

The partial derivatives of the (expected) individual and joint probabilities with respect to the expected output of the ith unit on case α are

$$\frac{\partial p_i}{\partial p_i^\alpha} = P^\alpha, \qquad \frac{\partial p_{\bar\imath}}{\partial p_i^\alpha} = -P^\alpha, \qquad \frac{\partial p_{ij}}{\partial p_i^\alpha} = P^\alpha p_j^\alpha, \qquad \frac{\partial p_{\bar\imath j}}{\partial p_i^\alpha} = -P^\alpha p_j^\alpha,$$

$$\frac{\partial p_{ij}}{\partial p_i^\alpha} = P^\alpha(1 - p_j^\alpha), \qquad \frac{\partial p_{\bar\imath\bar\jmath}}{\partial p_i^\alpha} = -P^\alpha(1 - p_j^\alpha).$$

The amount of information transmitted by the ith unit on case α when it is on is

$$I(y_i^\alpha = 1) = -\log p_i^\alpha.$$

If the log is base 2, the units of information are bits; for the natural log, the units are nats. From here on, we use *log* to denote the natural log. When the value of y_i^α is unknown, the average information (or equivalently the entropy or uncertainty) in y_i^α is

$$H(y_i^\alpha) = -[p_i^\alpha \log p_i^\alpha + p_{\bar\imath}^\alpha \log p_{\bar\imath}^\alpha].$$

Averaged over all input cases, the entropy of y_i is

$$H(y_i) = -\langle \log p(y_i) \rangle = -[p_i \log p_i + p_{\bar\imath} \log p_{\bar\imath}].$$

The mutual information between the outputs of the ith and jth units, y_i and y_j, is

$$I(y_i; y_j) = H(y_i) + H(y_j) - H(y_i, y_j),$$

where $H(y_i, y_j)$ is entropy of the joint distribution $p(y_i, y_j)$:

$$\begin{aligned}
H(y_i, y_j) &= -\langle \log p(y_i, y_j) \rangle \\
&= -[p_{ij} \log p_{ij} + p_{i\bar\jmath} \log p_{i\bar\jmath} + p_{\bar\imath j} \log p_{\bar\imath j} + p_{\bar\imath\bar\jmath} \log p_{\bar\imath\bar\jmath}].
\end{aligned}$$

The partial derivative of $I(y_i; y_j)$ with respect to the expected output of unit i on case α, p_i^α, can now be computed; since $H(y_j)$ does not depend on p_i^α, we need only differentiate $H(y_i)$ and $H(y_i, y_j)$.

$$\begin{aligned}
\frac{\partial H(y_i)}{\partial p_i^\alpha} &= \frac{\partial}{\partial p_i^\alpha}[-(p_i \log p_i + p_{\bar\imath} \log p_{\bar\imath})] \\[2mm]
&= -\left[\frac{\partial p_i}{\partial p_i^\alpha} \log p_i + \frac{p_i}{p_i}\frac{\partial p_i}{\partial p_i^\alpha} + \frac{\partial p_{\bar\imath}}{\partial p_i^\alpha} \log p_{\bar\imath} + \frac{p_{\bar\imath}}{p_{\bar\imath}}\frac{\partial p_{\bar\imath}}{\partial p_i^\alpha}\right] \\[2mm]
&= -\left[\frac{\partial p_i}{\partial p_i^\alpha}(\log p_i + 1) + \frac{\partial p_{\bar\imath}}{\partial p_i^\alpha}(\log p_{\bar\imath} + 1)\right] \\[2mm]
&= -[P^\alpha(\log p_i + 1) - P^\alpha(\log p_{\bar\imath} + 1)] \\[2mm]
&= -P^\alpha \log \frac{p_i}{p_{\bar\imath}},
\end{aligned}$$

$$\frac{\partial H(y_i, y_j)}{\partial p_i^{\alpha}} = \frac{\partial}{\partial p_i^{\alpha}} [-(p_{ij} \log p_{ij} + p_{i\bar{j}} \log p_{i\bar{j}} + p_{\bar{i}j} \log p_{\bar{i}j} + p_{\bar{i}\bar{j}} \log p_{\bar{i}\bar{j}})]$$

$$= - \left[\frac{\partial p_{ij}}{\partial p_i^{\alpha}} \log p_{ij} + \frac{p_{ij}}{p_{ij}} \frac{\partial p_{ij}}{\partial p_i^{\alpha}} + \frac{\partial p_{i\bar{j}}}{\partial p_i^{\alpha}} \log p_{i\bar{j}} + \frac{p_{i\bar{j}}}{p_{i\bar{j}}} \frac{\partial p_{i\bar{j}}}{\partial p_i^{\alpha}} \right.$$

$$\left. + \frac{\partial p_{\bar{i}j}}{\partial p_i^{\alpha}} \log p_{\bar{i}j} + \frac{p_{\bar{i}j}}{p_{\bar{i}j}} \frac{\partial p_{\bar{i}j}}{\partial p_i^{\alpha}} + \frac{\partial p_{\bar{i}\bar{j}}}{\partial p_i^{\alpha}} \log p_{\bar{i}\bar{j}} + \frac{p_{\bar{i}\bar{j}}}{p_{\bar{i}\bar{j}}} \frac{\partial p_{\bar{i}\bar{j}}}{\partial p_i^{\alpha}} \right]$$

$$= - \left[\frac{\partial p_{ij}}{\partial p_i^{\alpha}} (\log p_{ij} + 1) + \frac{\partial p_{i\bar{j}}}{\partial p_i^{\alpha}} (\log p_{i\bar{j}} + 1) \right.$$

$$\left. + \frac{\partial p_{\bar{i}j}}{\partial p_i^{\alpha}} (\log p_{\bar{i}j} + 1) + \frac{\partial p_{\bar{i}\bar{j}}}{\partial p_i^{\alpha}} (\log p_{\bar{i}\bar{j}} + 1) \right]$$

$$= -[P^{\alpha} p_j^{\alpha} (\log p_{ij} + 1) - P^{\alpha} p_j^{\alpha} (\log p_{\bar{i}j} + 1)$$

$$+ P\alpha (1 - p_j^{\alpha})(\log p_{i\bar{j}} + 1) - P^{\alpha} (1 - p_j^{\alpha})(\log p_{\bar{i}\bar{j}} + 1)]$$

$$= -P\alpha \left[p_j^{\alpha} \log \frac{p_{ij}}{p_{\bar{i}j}} + p_j^{\alpha} \log \frac{p_{i\bar{j}}}{p_{\bar{i}\bar{j}}} \right],$$

$$\frac{\partial I(y_i; y_j)}{\partial p_i^{\alpha}} = \frac{\partial H(y_i)}{\partial p_i^{\alpha}} - \frac{\partial H(y_i, y_j)}{\partial p_i^{\alpha}}$$

$$= -P^{\alpha} \left[\log \frac{p_i}{p_{\bar{i}}} - p_j^{\alpha} \log \frac{p_{ij}}{p_{\bar{i}j}} - p_j^{\alpha} \log \frac{p_{i\bar{j}}}{p_{\bar{i}\bar{j}}} \right].$$

APPENDIX B
THE MUTUAL INFORMATION GRADIENT IN THE CONTINUOUS CASE

In the real-valued case, we assume each unit deterministically computes its output y_i according to some (linear or nonlinear) function $y_i = \sigma(s_i)$ of its total input s_i. The total input to a unit on case α is computed as a weighted sum of the activities on its input lines: $s_i^{\alpha} = \Sigma_k w_{ik} y_k^{\alpha}$. The goal of the ith unit is to transmit as much information as possible about some underlying signal to be extracted from its input. In the simplest model, unit i assumes that its own output y_i is equal to the (Gaussian) signal plus some Gaussian noise, and that the jth output y_j is exactly that signal. Under this model, the mutual information between y_i and y_j is

$$I_{y_i; y_j} = \log \frac{V(\text{signal} + \text{noise})}{V(\text{noise})} = \log \frac{V(y_i)}{V(y_i - y_j)}.$$

For symmetry, we optimize the following approximation to the information rate:[13]

$$I^*_{y_i;y_j} = I_{y_i;y_j} + I_{y_j;y_i} = \log \frac{V(y_i)}{V(y_i - y_j)} + \log \frac{V(y_j)}{V(y_i - y_j)}.$$

For unit i to maximize the preceding information measure, it must store four statistics: its output mean $\langle y_i \rangle$ and variance $V(y_i)$, and the mean and variance of the difference of the units' outputs, $\langle y_i - y_j \rangle$ and $V(y_i - y_j)$. These statistics are computed in an initial pass through the training set:

$$\langle y_i \rangle = \frac{1}{N} \sum_{\alpha=1}^{N} y_i^\alpha,$$

$$V(y_i) = \frac{1}{N} \sum_{\alpha=1}^{N} (y_i^\alpha)^2 - \langle y_i \rangle^2,$$

$$\langle y_i - y_j \rangle = \frac{1}{N} \sum_{\alpha=1}^{N} (y_i^\alpha - y_j^\alpha),$$

$$V(y_i - y_j) = \frac{1}{N} \sum_{\alpha=1}^{N} (y_i^\alpha - y_j^\alpha)^2 - \langle y_i - y_j \rangle^2.$$

Now we can compute the partial derivative of the information the ith unit conveys about the jth unit with respect to the output of the ith unit on case α:

$$\frac{\partial I^*_{y_i;y_j}}{\partial y_i^\alpha} = \frac{\partial}{\partial y_i^\alpha} \left[\log \frac{V(y_i)}{V(y_i - y_j)} + \log \frac{V(y_i)}{V(y_i - y_j)} \right]$$

$$= \frac{\partial \log V(y_i)}{\partial y_i^\alpha} - 2 \frac{\partial \log V(y_i - y_j)}{\partial y_i^\alpha}$$

$$= \frac{1}{V(y_i)} \frac{\partial V(y_i)}{\partial y_i^\alpha} - \frac{2}{V(y_i - y_j)} \frac{\partial V(y_i - y_j)}{\partial y_i^\alpha}$$

$$= \frac{1}{V(y_i)} \left(\frac{2}{N} y_i^\alpha - \frac{2}{N} \langle y_i \rangle \right) - 2 \left[\frac{1}{V(y_i - y_j)} \left(\frac{2}{N} (y_i^\alpha - y_j^\alpha) - \frac{2}{N} \langle y_i - y_j \rangle \right) \right]$$

$$= \frac{2}{N} \left[\frac{y_i^\alpha - \langle y_i \rangle}{V(y_i)} - 2 \frac{(y_i^\alpha - y_j^\alpha) - \langle y_i - y_j \rangle}{V(y_i - y_j)} \right].$$

---

[13]Actually, we add a small constant κ to the denominator terms $V(y_i - y_j)$; this prevents the information measure from growing infinitely large and stabilizes the convergence. Thus a minor change to the above derivation is required when we add in this stabilizing term.

REFERENCES

Baldi, P., & Hornik, K. (1989). Neural networks and principal components analysis: Learning from examples without local minima. *Neural Networks, 2;* 53–58.

Blakemore, C., & Cooper, G. (1970). Development of the brain depends on the visual environment. *Nature, 228;* 477–478.

Blakemore, C., & van Sluyters, R. (1975). Innate and environmental factors in the development of the kitten's visual cortex. *Journal of Physiology, 248;* 663–716.

Bourlard, H., & Kamp, Y. (1988). Auto-association by multilayer perceptrons and singular value decomposition. *Biological Cybernetics, 59;* 291–294.

Carpenter, G., & Grossberg, S. (1987). ART 2: Self-organization of stable category recognition codes for analog input patterns. *Applied Optics, 26*(23). Special issue on neural networks.

Crawford, M., Smith, E., Harwerth, R., & von Noorden, G. (1984). Stereoblind monkeys have few binocular neurons. *Investigative Opthalmology and Visual Science, 25*(7); 779–781.

Crawford, M., von Noorden, G., Meharg, L., Rhodes, J., Harwerth, R., Smith, E., & Miller, D. (1983). Binocular neurons and binocular function in monkeys and children. *Investigative Opthalmology and Visual Science, 24*(4); 491–495.

Dempster, A. P., Laird, N. M., & Rubin, D. B. (1977). Maximum likelihood from incomplete data via the EM algorithm. *Proceedings of the Royal Statistical Society B, 39;* 1–38.

Derrington, A. (1984). Development of spatial frequency selectivity in striate cortex of vision-deprived cats. *Experimental Brain Research, 55;* 431–437.

Dodwell, P. (1983). The lie transform group model of visual perception. *Perception and Psychophysics, 34*(1); 1–16.

Minsky, M. L., & Papert, S. (1969). *Perceptrons.* Cambridge, MA: MIT Press.

Moody, J., & Darken, C. (1989). Fast learning in networks of locally-tuned processing units. *Neural Computation, 1*(2); 281–294.

Nowlan, S. J. (1990). Maximum likelihood competitive learning. In D. S. Touretzky, (Ed.) *Neural Information Processing Systems, Vol. 2,* p. 574–582. San Mateo, CA: Morgan Kaufmann.

Oja, E. (1982). A simplified neuron model as a principal component analyzer. *Journal of Mathematical Biology, 15*(3); 267–273.

Oja, E. (1989). Neural networks, principal components, and subspaces. *International Journal Of Neural Systems, 1*(1); 61–68.

Olson, C., & Freeman, R. (1980). Profile of the sensitive period for monocular deprivation in kittens. *Experimental Brain Research, 39;* 17–21.

Pearlmutter, B. A., & Hinton, G. E. (1986). G-maximization: An unsupervised learning procedure. In *Snowbird Conference on Neural Networks and Computing.*

Plaut, D. C., Nowlan, S. J., & Hinton, G. E. (1986). *Experiments on learning by back-propagation* (Technical Report CMU-CS-86-126). Pittsburgh, PA: Carnegie-Mellon University.

Poggio, T. (1989). *A theory of networks for approximation and learning.* A.I. Memo No. 1140, C.B.I.P. Paper No. 31, MIT Artificial Intelligence Laboratory, and Center for Biological Information Processing, Whitaker College.

Renals, S., & Rohwer, R. (1989). Phoneme classification experiments using radial basis functions. *IEEE International Conference on Neural Networks.*

Rumelhart, D. E., & Zipser, D. (1986). Feature discovery by competitive learning. In D. E. Rumelhart, J. L. M. & and the PDP research group, (Eds.) *Parallel distributed processing: Explorations in the microstructure of cognition,* Vol. I. Cambridge, MA: Bradford Books.

Sanger, T. (1989a). Optimal unsupervised learning in a single-layer linear feedforward neural network. *Neural Networks, 2;* 459–473.

Sanger, T. (1989b). An optimality principle for unsupervised learning. In D. Touretzky, (Ed.) *Advances in neural information processing systems,* Vol. 1, (p. 11–19). San Mateo, CA: Morgan Kaufmann.

Sanger, T. D. (1989c). *Optimal unsupervised learning in feedforward neural networks.* Unpublished master's thesis, MIT Department of Electrical Engineering and Computer Science.

Saund, E. (1986). Abstraction and representation of continuous variables in connectionist networks. *Proceedings of the Fifth National Conference on Artificial Intelligence* (p. 638–644). San Mateo, CA: Morgan Kaufmann.

Shannon, C. E. (1949). A mathematical theory of communication. III. *Bell System Technical Journal, 28,* 623–656.

Stryker, M. P., & Harris, W. A. (1986). Binocular impulse blockade prevents the formation of ocular dominance columns in cat visual cortex. *The Journal of Neuroscience, 6*(8); 2117–2133.

Sur, M., Garraghty, P., & Roe, A. (1988). Experimentally induced visual projections into auditory thalamus and cortex. *Science, 242;* 1437–1441.

Von der Malsburg, C. (1973). Self-organization of orientation sensitive cells in striate cortex. *Kybernetik, 14;* 85–100.

Watrous, R. L., & Shastri, L. (1987). Learning phonetic features using connectionist networks: An experiment in speech recognition. *IEEE International Conference on Neural Networks.*

Wiesel, T. N., & Hubel, D. H. (1965). Comparison of the effects of unilateral and bilateral eye closure on cortical unit responses in kittens. *Journal of Neurophysiology, 28;* 1029–1040.

Zemel, R. S., & Hinton, G. E. (1991). Discovering viewpoint-invariant relationships that characterize objects. In R. P. Lippmann, J. E. Moody, & D. S. Touretzky, (Eds.) *Advances in neural information processing systems 3* (p. 299–305). San Mateo, CA: Morgan Kaufmann.

11

Connectionist Modeling and Control of Finite State Systems Given Partial State Information

Jonathan R. Bachrach
Department of Computer Science,
University of Massachusetts at Amherst

Michael C. Mozer
Department of Computer Science,
University of Colorado, Boulder

ABSTRACT

Consider a robot wandering around an unfamiliar environment, performing actions, and observing the perceptual consequences. The robot's task is to construct an internal model of its environment, a model that will allow it to predict the outcome of its actions and to determine what sequences of actions to take to reach particular goal states. Rivest and Schapire (1987a, 1987b, 1988) have studied this problem and have designed a symbolic algorithm to strategically explore and infer the structure of finite-state environments. The heart of this algorithm is a clever representation of the environment called an *update graph*. We have developed a connectionist implementation of the update graph using a highly specialized network architecture. We also describe a technique for using the connectionist update graph to guide the robot from an arbitrary starting state to a goal state. This technique requires a *critic* that associates the update graph's current state with the expected time to reach the goal state. At each time step the action is chosen which minimizes the output of the critic. The control acquisition technique is demonstrated on several environments.

INTRODUCTION

Consider a robot placed in an unfamiliar environment. The robot is allowed to explore the environment by performing actions and observing the perceptual consequences. The robot's task is to construct an internal model of the environment, a model that will allow it to predict the outcome of its actions and to determine what sequences of actions to take to reach particular goal states. This

351

scenario is extremely general; it applies not only to physical environments, but also to abstract and artificial environments such as electronic devices (e.g., a VCR, phone answering machine, car radio), computer programs (e.g., a text editor), and classical AI problem-solving domains (e.g., the blocks world). Any agent—human or computer—that aims to manipulate its environment toward some desired end requires an internal representation of the environment. This is because, in any reasonably complex situation, the agent can directly perceive only a small fraction of the global environmental state at any time; the rest must be stored internally if the agent is to act effectively.

The goal of this research is to develop connectionist learning algorithms that can efficiently construct models of, and controllers for, unfamiliar finite state environments. The model is used to predict the environment's behavior, and the controller is used to determine sequences of actions that lead to desirable environmental states. The modeling task involves learning a model that mimics the behavior of the environment such that, given an identical sequence of actions, the model will yield predictions of the sensations that match those produced by the environment. Although a model cannot be constructed without carefully exploring the environment, the emphasis of this chapter is primarily on the modeling and control problems, and the most primitive exploration strategies are assumed.

The architecture of our connectionist network model is based on a representation of finite state environments developed by Rivest and Schapire (1987a, 1987b, 1988). Rivest and Schapire have also developed a symbolic algorithm to infer this representation by exploring the environment. We have taken a connectionist approach to the same problem, and we show that the connectionist approach offers complementary strengths and new insights into the problem. This chapter is composed of a modeling section followed by a control section. The focus of this chapter is on the modeling technique; the control examples are meant to demonstrate that such models can be useful in control. We begin by describing several environments of the sort we wish to model.

Environments

In each environment, the robot has a set of discrete *actions* it can execute to move from one environmental state to another. At each environmental state, a set of discrete-valued *sensations* can be detected by the robot. Descriptions of five sample environments follow, the first four of which come from Rivest and Schapire. Note that in these environments, environmental states are not distinguished by unique sensory configurations; hence, the environmental state cannot be determined from the sensations alone (Barto and Sutton, 1981; Sutton, 1990).

The Little Prince Environment

The robot resides on the surface of a 2D planet (Figure 1). There are four distinct locations on the planet: north, south, east, and west. To the east, there is

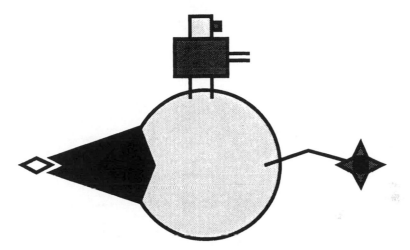

Figure 1.   The little prince environment.

a rose; to the west, a volcano. The robot has two sensations, one indicating the presence of a rose at the current location, the other a volcano. The robot has available three actions: move to the next location in the direction it is currently facing, move to the next location away from the direction it is facing, and turn its head around to face in the opposite direction.

The Car Radio Environment

The robot can fiddle with knobs on a radio that receives only three stations. It can recognize the type of music that the radio is playing as either classical, rock, or news (Figure 2). It can tune in a station with left-scan and right-scan buttons, which scan from one station to the next with wraparound. The robot can also manipulate a set of two presets, X and Y. It can save the current station in either preset, and it can recall a setting in either preset.

The n-Bit Shift Register Environment

The robot senses the value on the leftmost bit of an n-bit shift register as shown in Figure 3. It can rotate the register left or right. The robot can also flip the leftmost bit.

The n × n Grid Environment

A robot is placed in an $n \times n$ grid with wraparound as shown in Figure 4. The robot occupies a square and faces in one of four geographic directions: north, south, east, or west. It can move forward one square or rotate 90° left or right

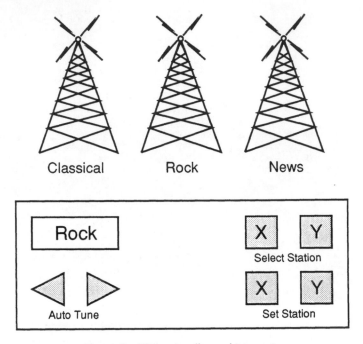

Figure 2.   The car radio environment.

with the left-turn or right-turn actions. Each square is colored either red, green, or blue and the robot has sensors that detect the color of the square it's facing. Moving forward not only changes the robot's position, but also paints the previous square the color of the square the robot now occupies.

The n × n Checkerboard Environment

The checkerboard environment consists of an $n \times n$ grid of squares as shown in Figure 5. The robot occupies a particular square and can sense the landmark in that square, if any. There are a number of unique landmarks distributed in a checkerboard pattern across the grid. These are depicted as the numbers in the

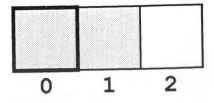

Figure 3. An example of the *n*-bit register environment. White squares indicate a bit is on, and shaded squares indicate a bit is off.

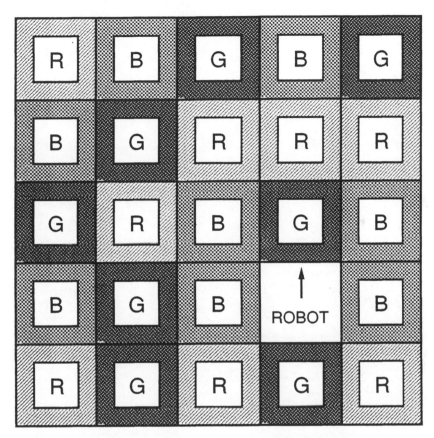

Figure 4. An example of the $n \times n$ grid environment.

squares. Half of the squares have no landmark and are indistinguishable from each other. At each time step the robot can move either up, down, left, or right one square. Movement off one edge of the grid wraps around to the other side.

MODELING

The environments we wish to consider can be modeled by finite state automata, henceforth called an FSA. Nodes of the FSA correspond to states of the environment. Labeled links connect each node of the FSA to other nodes and correspond to the actions that the robot can execute to move between environmental states. Associated with each node is a set of discrete-valued sensations that can be detected by the robot in the corresponding environmental state. Figure 6 illus-

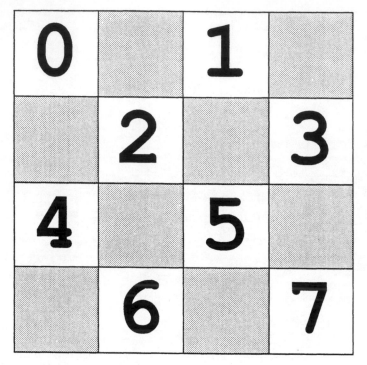

Figure 5.   An example of the $n \times n$ checkerboard environment.

trates the FSA for the 3-bit shift register environment. Each node is labeled by the corresponding environmental state, coded as the values of the bits of the shift register. There are $2^3 = 8$ states for this environment, one for each of the possible settings of the bits in the register. Associated with each node is a set of values which are the sensations corresponding to the environmental state. In the case of the 3-bit shift register environment, there is only one sensation, the value of the leftmost bit, which is depicted by the shade of the node. Links between nodes are labeled with one of the three actions: flip (F), shift left (L), or shift right (R).

An FSA is one to represent the structure of the environment. If the FSA is known, one can predict the sensory consequences of any sequence of actions. Further, the FSA can be used to determine a sequence of actions needed to obtain a certain goal state. For example, if the robot wishes to turn on all the bits in the register, it should follow a link or sequence of links in the FSA that lead to the FSA state in which all the bits are on.

Although one might try developing an algorithm to learn the FSA directly, Schapire (1988) presents several arguments against doing so. Most important is that the FSA often does not capture structure inherent in the environment. As an

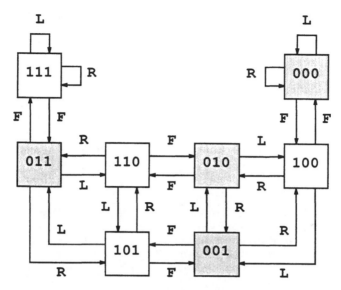

Figure 6.   The Finite State Automaton for the 3-bit shift register environment. Each box represents a state with the shade of the box coding the single sensation value for that state. A shaded square indicates that the leftmost bit is off, a light square that the leftmost bit is on. The transitions are depicted as arrows labeled with the particular action, where L is shift left, R is shift right, and F is flip the leftmost bit.

example of this point, in the n-bit shift register, the F action has the same behavior independent of the value of the nonobservable bits (i.e., the bits other than the leftmost bit), yet in the FSA of Figure 6, knowledge about F must be encoded for each bit and in the context of the particular states of the other bits. Thus, the simple semantics of an action like F are encoded repeatedly for each of the 2^n distinct states.

The Update Graph

Rather than trying to learn the FSA, Rivest and Schapire suggest learning another representation of the environment called an *update graph*. The advantage of the update graph representation is that in environments with many regularities, the number of nodes in the update graph can be much smaller than in the FSA, for example, $2n$ versus 2^n in the n-bit shift register environment.[1] Mozer and Bachrach (1991) summarize Rivest and Schapire's formal definition of the up-

---

[1]The potential disadvantage is that in degenerate, completely unstructured environments, the number of nodes of update graph can be exponentially larger than the number of nodes of the FSA.

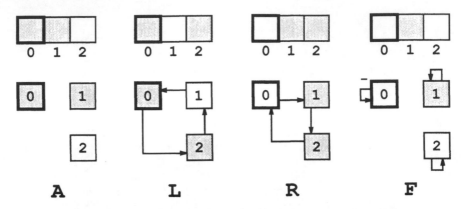

Figure 7. Panel A shows the 3-bit shift register at the top and the update graph without links at the bottom. White squares indicate a bit is on, and shaded squares indicate a bit is off. The observable leftmost bit is emphasized with a thicker box. Panels L, R, and F depict the result of performing the designated action in the shift register environment above and the corresponding computation of the update graph below.

date graph. Rivest and Schapire's definition is based on the notion of *tests* that can be performed on the environment, and the equivalence of different tests. In this section, we present an alternative, more intuitive view of the update graph that facilitates a connectionist interpretation.

Consider again the 3-bit shift register environment. To model this environment, the essential knowledge required is the values of the bits. Assume the update graph has a node for each of these environment variables, and each node has an associated value indicating whether the bit is on or off.

If we know the values of the variables in the current environmental state, what will their new values be after taking some action, say L? The new value of the leftmost bit, bit 0, becomes the previous value of bit 1; the new value of bit 1 becomes the previous value of bit 2; and the new value of bit 2 becomes the previous value of bit 0. As depicted in Figure 7L, this action thus results in shifting values among the three nodes, mimicking the intuitive behavior of a shift register. Figure 7R shows the analogous flow of information for the action R. Finally, the action F should cause the value of leftmost bit to be complemented while the values of the other bits remain unaffected (Figure 7F). In Figure 8I, the three sets of links from panels L, R, and F of Figure 7 have been superimposed and have been labeled with their associated actions.

One final detail: the Rivest and Schapire update graph formalism does not make use of the "complementation" link. To avoid it, one may split each node into two values, one representing the value of a bit and the other its complement (Figure 8C). Flipping thus involves exchanging the values of bit 0 and bit $\bar{0}$. Just as the values of bit 0, bit 1, and bit 2 must be shifted for the actions L and R, so must their complements.

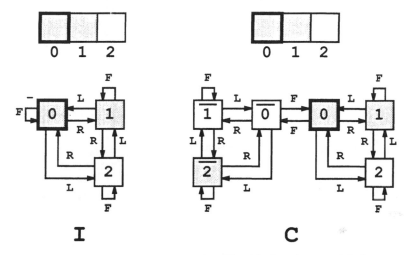

Figure 8. Panel I shows the complete "intuitive" update graph below for the 3-bit shift register environment above. Panel C shows the complete update graph (without complementation links) below for the 3-bit shift register environment above.

Given the update graph in Figure 8C and the value of each node for the current environmental state, the result of any sequence of actions can be predicted simply by shifting values around in the graph. Thus, as far as predicting the input/output behavior of the environment is concerned, the update graph serves the same purpose as the FSA.

For every FSA, there exists a corresponding update graph. In fact, the update graph in Figure 8C might even be viewed as a distributed representation of the FSA in Figure 6. In the FSA, each environmental state is represented by *one* "active" node. In the update graph, each environmental state represented by a pattern of activity across the nodes.

A defining property of the update graph is that each node has exactly one incoming link for each action. This property, which we call the *one-input-per-action property,* has no intuitive justification based on the description of the update graph we have presented, but see Mozer and Bachrach (1991) or Schapire (1988) for an explanation. The one-input-per-action property clearly holds in Figure 8C; for example, note that bit 0 gets input from bit $\bar{0}$ for the action F, from bit 1 for L, and from bit 2 for R.

In the *n*-bit shift register environment, it happens that each node has exactly one outgoing link for each action (the *one-output-per-action property*). The one-input-per-action and one-output-per-action properties jointly hold for a class of environments Rivest and Schapire call *permutation environments,* in which no information is ever lost (i.e., each action can be undone by some fixed sequence of actions). Update graphs of nonpermutation environments, such as the car radio environment, do not possess the one-output-per-action property. Thus, one must not consider the one-output-per-action property to be a defining characteristic of the update graph; to do so would restrict the set of environments one could model.

The Rivest and Schapire Learning Algorithm

Rivest and Schapire have developed a symbolic algorithm (hereafter, *the RS algorithm*) to strategically explore an environment and learn its update graph representation. They break the learning problem into two steps: (a) inferring the structure of the update graph, and (b) inferring the values of each node in the update graph. Step (b) is relatively straightforward. Step (a) involves formulating explicit hypotheses about regularities in the environment. These hypotheses are concerned with whether two action sequences are equivalent in terms of their sensory outcome. For example, two equivalent action sequences in the 3-bit register environment are LL and R because shifting left twice yields the same value on the leftmost bit as shifting right once, no matter how the bits are initially set. By conducting experiments in the environment, the RS algorithm tests each hypothesis and uses the outcome to construct the update graph.

For permutation environments (described in the previous section), a special version of the RS algorithm is guaranteed to infer the environmental structure— within an acceptable margin of error—in a number of moves polynomial in the number of update graph nodes and the number of alternative actions. The general case of the RS algorithm makes fewer assumptions about the nature of the environment, but has no proof of probable correctness.

If only one hypothesis is tested at a time, the RS algorithm is "single minded" and does not make full use of the environmental feedback obtained. Consequently, Rivest and Schapire have developed heuristics to test multiple hypotheses at once. These heuristics can improve the efficiency of the basic algorithm by several orders of magnitude (Rivest and Schapire, 1987b). Because reasonable performance is achieved only by incorporating special—and potentially problematic—heuristics to make better use of environmental feedback, it seems worthwhile to explore alternative methods whose natural properties allow them to evaluate multiple hypotheses at once. We have pursued a connectionist approach, which has shown promising results in preliminary experiments as well as suggesting a different conceptualization of the update graph representation.

Connectionist Approach to Modeling Environments

SLUG is a connectionist network that performs *subsymbolic learning of update graphs*. Before the learning process itself can be described, however, we must first consider the desired outcome of learning. That is, what should SLUG look like following training if it is to behave as an update graph? Start by assuming one unit in SLUG for each node in the update graph. The activity level of the unit represents the value associated with the update graph node. Some of these units serve as "outputs" of SLUG. For example, in the 3-bit shift register environment, the output of SLUG is the unit that represents the value of the leftmost bit. In other environments (e.g., the little prince environment), there may be several sensations in which case several output units are required.

What is the analog of the labeled links in the update graph? The labels indicate that values are to be sent down a link when a particular action occurs. In connectionist terms, the links should be *gated* by the action. To elaborate, we might include a set of units that represent the possible actions; these units act to multiplicatively gate the flow of activity between units in the update graph. Thus, when a particular action is to be performed, the corresponding action unit is turned on, and the connections that are gated by this action are enabled.

If the action units form a local representation (i.e., only one is turned on at a time), exactly one set of connections is enabled at a time. Consequently, the gated connections can be replaced by a set of weight matrices, one matrix per action (as shown in Figure 9). To predict the consequences of a particular action, say F, the weight matrix for F is simply plugged into the network and activity is allowed to propagate through the connections. In this manner, SLUG is dynamically rewired contingent on the current action. Figure 10 shows SLUG executing the action sequence LFLR.

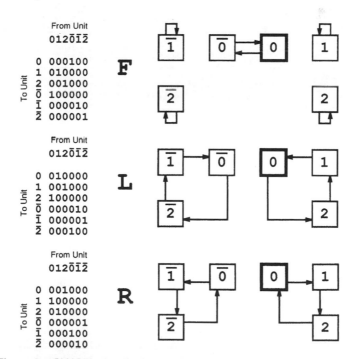

Figure 9. SLUG depicted as a separate weight matrix for each action. The left side of the figure shows the separate weight matrices, and the right side shows the connections having nonzero weights.

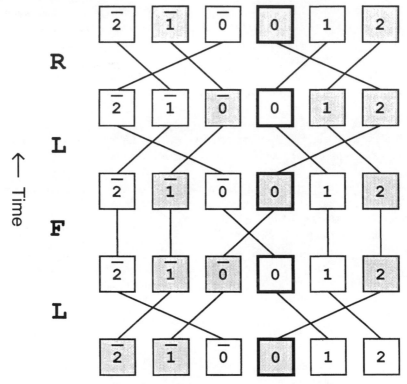

Figure 10. SLUG is dynamically rewired contingent on the current action in order to execute the action sequence LFLR.

The effect of activity propagation should be that the new activity of a unit is the previous activity of some other unit. A linear activation function is sufficient to achieve this:

$$\mathbf{x}(t) = W_{a(t)}\mathbf{x}(t - 1), \tag{1}$$

where $a(t)$ is the action selected at time t, $W_{a(t)}$ is the weight matrix associated with this action, and $\mathbf{x}(t)$ is the activity vector that results from taking action $a(t)$. Assuming weight matrices which have zeroes in each row except for one connection of strength 1, the activation rule will cause activity values to be copied around the network.

Although nonlinearities are introduced by the operation of rewiring SLUG based on the current action, the behavior of SLUG *in a single time step* is indeed linear. This is handy because it allows us to use tools of linear algebra to better understand the network's behavior. We elaborate on this point in Mozer and Bachrach (1991).

Training SLUG

We have described how SLUG could be hand-wired to behave as an update graph, and now we turn to the procedure used to *learn* the appropriate connection strengths. For expository purposes, assume that the number of units in the update graph is known in advance. (This is not necessary, as we shall show.) SLUG starts off with this many units, s of which are set aside to represent the sensations. These s units are the output units of the network; the remainder are hidden units. A set of weight matrices, $\{W_a\}$, is constructed—one matrix per action— and initialized to random values. To train SLUG, random actions are performed on the environment and the resulting sensations are compared with those predicted by SLUG. The mismatch between observed and predicted sensations provides an error measure, and the weight matrices can be adjusted to minimize this error.

This procedure in no way guarantees that the resulting weights will possess the one-input-per-action property, which is required of the update graph connectivity matrices. We can try to achieve this property by performing gradient descent not in the $\{W_a\}$ directly, but in an underlying parameter space, $\{Z_a\}$, from which the weights are derived using a normalized exponential transform:

$$w_{aij} = \frac{e^{z_{aij}/T}}{\sum_k e^{z_{aik}/T}}, \tag{2}$$

where w_{aij} is the strength of connection to unit i from unit j for action a, z_{aij} is the corresponding underlying parameter, and T is a constant. This approach[2] permits unconstrained gradient descent in $\{Z_a\}$ while constraining the w_{aij} to nonnegative values and

$$\sum_i w_{aij} = 1. \tag{3}$$

By gradually lowering T over time, the solution can be further constrained so that all but one incoming weight to a unit approaches zero. In practice, we have found that lowering T is unnecessary because solutions discovered with a fixed T essentially achieve the one-input-per-action property.

Below, we report on simulations of SLUG using this approach, which we will refer to as the version of the algorithm with *constrained weights,* and also simulations run with unconstrained weights. In the latter case,

$$w_{aij} = z_{aij}. \tag{4}$$

---

[2]This approach was suggested by the recent work of Bridle (1990), Durbin (1990), and Rumelhart (1989), who have applied the normalized exponential transform to activity vectors; in contrast, we have applied it to weight vectors.

Details of the Training Procedure

Before the start of training, initial values of the z_{aij} are randomly selected from a uniform distribution in the range $[-1, 1]$, and the $w_a n_{ij}$ are derived therefrom. The activity vector $\mathbf{x}(0)$ is reset to $\mathbf{0}$. At each time t, the following sequence of events transpires:

1. An action, $a(t)$, is selected at random.
2. The weight matrix for that action, $W_{a(t)}$, is used to compute the activities at t, $\mathbf{x}(t)$, from the previous activities $\mathbf{x}(t - 1)$.
3. The selected action is performed on the environment, and the resulting sensations are observed.
4. The observed sensations are compared with the sensations predicted by SLUG (i.e., the activities of the units chosen to represent the sensations) to compute a measure of error.
5. The back-propagation algorithm (Rumelhart et al., 1986) is used to compute the derivative of the error with respect to each weight, $\partial E / \partial w_{aij}$. Because SLUG contains recurrent connections and back propagation applies only to feedforward nets, the "unfolding-in-time" procedure of Rumelhart et al. is used. This procedure is based on the observation that any recurrent network can be transformed into a feedforward network with identical behavior, over a finite period of time. The feedforward net, shown in Figure 10, will have a layer of units corresponding to the units of SLUG at each time step: the top layer of the feedforward net represents $\mathbf{x}(t)$, the layer below represents $\mathbf{x}(t - 1)$, below that $\mathbf{x}(t - 2)$, and so on, back to a layer that represents $\mathbf{x}(t - \tau)$. (We discuss the choice of τ later.) The weights feeding into the top layer are $W_{a(t)}$, the weights feeding into the layer below that are $W_{a(t-1)}$, and so forth. Back propagation can be applied in a direct manner to this feedforward network. The error gradient for some action i, $\partial E / \partial W_i$, is computed by summing the back-propagated error derivatives over all layers l of the feedforward net in which the action corresponding to that layer, $a(l)$, is equal to i.
6. The error gradient in terms of the $\{W_a\}$ is transformed into a gradient in terms of the $\{Z_a\}$. With constrained weights (Equation 2), the relation is

$$\frac{\partial E}{\partial z_{aij}} = \frac{w_{aij}}{T} \left[\frac{\partial E}{\partial w_{aij}} - \sum_k \frac{\partial E}{\partial w_{aik}} w_{aik} \right]. \tag{5}$$

With unconstrained weights (Equation 4), the mapping is simply the identity.
7. The $\{Z_a\}$ are updated by taking a step of size η down the error gradient:

$$\Delta z_{aij} = - \eta \, \frac{\partial E}{\partial z_{aij}}. \tag{6}$$

The $\{W_a\}$ are then recomputed from the new $\{Z_a\}$.

8. The temporal record of unit activities, $\mathbf{x}(t - i)$ for $i = 0, \ldots, \tau$, which is maintained to permit back propagation in time, is updated to reflect the new weights. This involves recomputing the forward flow of activity from time $t - \tau$ to t for the hidden units. (The output units are unaffected because their values are forced, as described in the next step.)

9. The activities of the output units at time t, which represent the predicted sensations, are replaced by the observed sensations. This implements a form of *teacher forcing* (Williams and Zipser, this volume). A consequence of teacher forcing is that the error derivative for weights feeding into the output units at times $t - 1, t - 2, \ldots$, should be set to zero in Step 5; that is, error should not be back-propagated from time t to output units at earlier times. It is not sensible to adjust the response properties of output units at some earlier time i to achieve the correct response at time t because the appropriate activation levels of these units have already been established by the sensations at time i.

Steps 5 and 8 require further elaboration. One parameter of training is the amount of temporal history, τ, to consider. We have found that, for a particular problem, error propagation beyond a certain critical number of time steps does not help SLUG to discover a solution more quickly, although any fewer does indeed hamper learning. In the results to be described, we arbitrarily set τ for a particular problem to one less than the number of nodes in the update graph solution of the problem. Informal experiments manipulating τ revealed that this was a fairly conservative choice. To avoid the issue of selecting a value for τ, one could instead use the on-line recurrent network training algorithm of Williams and Zipser (1989).

To back-propagate error in time, a temporal record of unit activities is maintained. However, a problem arises with these activities following a weight update: the activities are no longer consistent with the weights; that is, Equation 1 is violated. Because the error derivatives computed by back propagation are exact only when Equation 1 is satisfied, future weight updates based on the inconsistent activities are not assured of being correct. Empirically, we have found the algorithm extremely unstable if we do not address this problem.

In most situations where back propagation is applied to temporally extended sequences, the sequences are of finite length. Consequently, it is possible to wait until the end of the sequence to update the weights, at which point consistency between activities and weights no longer matters because the system starts afresh at the beginning of the next sequence. In the present situation, however, the sequence of actions does not terminate. We were thus forced to consider alternative means of ensuring consistency. One approach we tried involved updating the weights only after every, say, 25 time steps. Immediately following the update, the weights and activities are inconsistent, but after τ time steps (when the inconsistent activities drop off the activity history record), consistency is once again achieved. A more successful approach involved updating the activities after each weight change to force consistency (step 8). To do this, we propagated the earliest activities in the temporal record, $x(t - \tau)$, forward again to time t, using the updated weight matrices.[3]

The issue of consistency arises because at no point in time is SLUG instructed as to the state of the environment. That is, instead of being given an activity vector as input, part of SLUG's learning task is to discover the appropriate activity vector. This might suggest a strategy of explicitly learning the activity vector, that is, performing gradient descent in both the weight space and activity space. However, our experiments indicate that this strategy does not improve SLUG's rate of learning. One plausible explanation is the following. If we perform gradient descent in just weight space based on the error from a single trial, and then force activity-weight consistency, the updated output unit activities are guaranteed to be closer to the target values, assuming a sufficiently small learning rate. Thus, the effect of this procedure is to reduce the error in the observable components of the activity vector, which is similar to performing gradient descent in activity space directly.

A final comment regarding the training procedure: in our simulations, learning performance was better with target activity levels of -1 and $+1$ (indicating that the leftmost bit of the shift register is *off* or *on*, respectively) rather than 0 and 1. One explanation for this is that random activations and random (nonnegative) connection strengths tend to cancel out in the $-1/+1$ case, but not in the 0/1 case. For other arguments concerning the advantages of symmetric activity levels see Stornetta and Huberman (1987).

Results

Figure 11 shows the weights in SLUG for the 3-bit shift register environment at three stages of training. The "step" refers to how many moves SLUG has taken or, equivalently, how many times the weights have been updated. The bottom

---

[3]Keeping the original value of $x(t - \tau)$ is a somewhat arbitrary choice. Consistency can be achieved by propagating *any* value of $x(t - \tau)$ forward in time, and there is no strong reason for believing $x(t - \tau)$ is the appropriate value. We thus suggest two alternative schemes, but have not yet tested them. First, we might select $x(t - \tau)$ such that the new $x(t - i)$, $i = 0, \ldots, \tau - 1$, are as close as possible to the old values. Second, we might select $x(t - \tau)$ such that the output units produce as close to the correct values as possible. Both these schemes require the computation-intensive operation of finding a least-squares solution to a set of linear equations.

Step 0

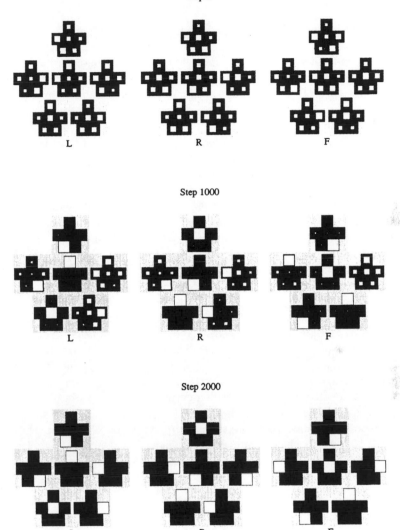

Step 1000

Step 2000

Figure 11. SLUG's weights at three stages of training for the 3-bit shift register environment. Step 0 reflects the initial random weights, step 1000 reflects the weights midway through learning, and step 2000 reflects the weights upon completion of learning. Each large diagram (with a light gray background) represents the weights corresponding to one of the three actions. Each small diagram contained within a large diagram (with a dark gray background) represents the connection strengths feeding into a particular unit for a particular action. There are six units, hence six small diagrams within each large diagram. The output unit, which indicates the state of the light in the current room, is the protruding "head" of the large diagram. A white square in a particular position of a small diagram represents the strength of connection from the unit in the homologous position in the large diagram to the unit represented by the small diagram. The area of the square is proportional to the connection strength, with the largest square having the value 1.

diagram in the figure corresponds to the update graph of Figure 8C. To explain the correspondence, think of the diagram as being in the shape of a person who has a head, left and right arms, left and right legs, and a heart. For the action L, the head—the output unit—receives input from the left leg, the left leg from the heart, and the heart from the head, thereby forming a three-unit loop. The other three units—the left arm, right leg, and right arm—form a similar loop. For the action R, the same two loops are present but in the reverse direction. These two loops also appear in Figure 8C. For the action F, the left and right arms, heart, and left leg each keep their current value, while the head and the right leg exchange values. This corresponds to the exchange of values between the bit 0 and bit $\bar{0}$ nodes of Figure 8C.

The weights depicted in Figure 11 are the w_{aij}'s. These weights are derived from the underlying parameters z_{aij}. The values of z_{aij} corresponding to the weights at Step 2000 are shown in Figure 12. The normalized exponential transform maps z_{aij} values in the range $-\infty \rightarrow +\infty$ to values in the range $0 \rightarrow 1$.

In addition to learning the update graph connectivity, SLUG has simultaneously learned the correct activity values associated with each node for the current state of the environment. Armed with this information, SLUG can predict the outcome of any sequence of actions. Indeed, the prediction error drops to zero, causing learning to cease and SLUG to become completely stable. Figure 13 shows the evolution of activity in SLUG at six consecutive time steps. At step 2000, the value of the leftmost bit is 1, as indicated by the white square in the diagram's head. When the action F is performed, the head and right leg exchange values while all other units maintain their current value. Between steps 2001 and 2005, the action sequence RLLR is executed. Because shifting left and right are complementary actions, SLUG's state at step 2005 is the same as at step 2001.

SLUG shows two advantages over other connectionist approaches to learning FSA (e.g., Elman, 1990; Pollack, 1990; Servan-Schreiber, Cleeremans, and

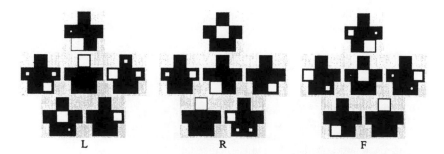

Figure 12. The underlying z_{aij} parameters corresponding to the weights in the bottom diagram of Figure 11. White squares indicate positive values, black squares negative values. The largest square represents a value of 4.5.

Action F   Action R   Action L   Action L   Action R

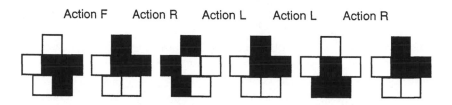

Step 2000   Step 2001   Step 2002   Step 2003   Step 2004   Step 2005

Figure 13. The pattern of activity in SLUG at six consecutive time steps. White squares indicate a unit with activity level of +1, black squares a unit with activity level −1. The arrangement of units in this figure matches the arrangement of weights in the previous two figures. Thus, the output unit is the protruding "head" of each diagram. The transition between two consecutive states arises from performing the action printed between the two states.

McClelland, 1988). First, because the ultimate weights and activities are discrete, SLUG can operate indefinitely with no degradation in its ability to predict the future. Other connectionist networks have the drawback that states are not represented discretely. Consequently, minor numerical imprecisions can accumulate, causing the networks to wander from one state to another. For example, Pollack (1990) trained a network to accept strings of the regular language 1* (i.e., any number of 1's). However, the network would accept strings containing a 0 if followed by a long enough string of 1's. The network would eventually "forget" that it was in the reject state. SLUG with constrained weights is not susceptible to this problem, as illustrated by the fact that the state at step 2001 in Figure 13 is *exactly* the same as the state at step 2005. The second advantage of SLUG over other connectionist approaches is that the network weights and activities can readily be interpreted—as an update graph. Consequently, the correctness of SLUG's solution can be assessed analytically.

To evaluate SLUG, we examined its performance as measured by the number of actions that must be executed before the outcomes of subsequent actions can be predicted, that is, before a perfect model of the environment has been constructed. One means of determining when SLUG has reached this criterion is to verify that the weights and activities indeed correspond to the correct update graph. Such a determination is not easy to automate; we instead opted for a somewhat simpler criterion: SLUG is considered to have learned a task by a given time step if the correct predictions are made for at least the next 2500 steps. In all simulation results we report in this paper, performance is measured by this criterion—the number of time steps before SLUG can correctly predict the sensations at the 2500 steps that follow. Because results vary from one run to another due to the random initial weights, we report the median performance over 25 replications of each simulation. On any replication, if SLUG was unable to converge on a solution within 100,000 steps, we stopped the simulation and counted it as a failure.

Now for the bad news: SLUG succeeded in discovering the correct update graph for the 3-bit shift register environment on only 15 of 25 runs. The median number of steps taken by SLUG before training terminated—either by reaching the performance criterion on successful runs or by reaching the maximum number of steps on failed runs—was 6428. Even on failed runs, however, SLUG does learn most of the update graph, as evidenced by the fact that after 10,000 steps SLUG correctly predicts sensations with an average accuracy of 93%.

With unconstrained weights, SLUG's performance dramatically improves: SLUG reaches the performance criterion in a median of 298 steps. From our experiments, it appears that constraints on the weights seldom help SLUG discover a solution. In the remainder of this article, we therefore describe the performance of the version of SLUG with unconstrained weights. In Mozer and Bachrach (1991), we consider why constraining the weights is harmful and possible remedies.

Comparing SLUG and Other Connectionist Approaches

With unconstrained weights, SLUG suffers from the two drawbacks common to other connectionist approaches that we described earlier. First, slight inaccuracies in the continuous-valued weights and activities can cause degeneration of SLUG's predictive abilities in the distant future. Consequently, it is essential that SLUG converge on an exact solution. To assist toward this end, we scaled down the learning rate, η, as SLUG approached a solution. (That is, η was set in proportion to the mean-squared prediction error.) The second advantage lost when weights are unconstrained is that, although SLUG learns effectively, the resulting weight matrices, which contains a collection of positive and negative weights of varying magnitudes, is not readily interpretable (see Figure 14).

The loss of these two benefits might seem to indicate that SLUG is no better than other connectionist approaches to the problem of inducing finite state environments, but comparisons of SLUG and a conventional connectionist recurrent architecture indicate that SLUG achieves far superior performance. The "conventional" architecture we tested was a three layer network consisting of *input, hidden, and output* units, with feedforward connections from input to hidden and hidden to output layers as well as recurrent connections within the hidden layer (Bachrach, 1988; Elman, 1990; Mozer, 1989; Servan-Schreiber et al., 1989). Input units represent the current sensations and an action, output units represent the sensations predicted following the action. Our experiments using the conventional architecture were spectacularly unsuccessful. We were unable to get the conventional architecture to learn the 3-bit shift register environment on even one run, despite our best efforts at varying the number of hidden units, the number of

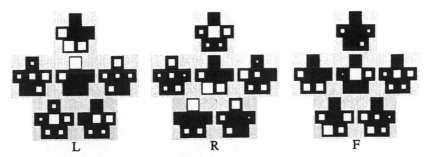

Figure 14. The 3-bit shift register environment. Weights learned by SLUG with six units and unconstrained weights. White squares indicate positive weights, black negative.

steps τ through which error was back-propagated, and learning rates in every conceivable combination. We lowered our sights somewhat and attempted to train the conventional architecture on a simpler environment, the little prince environment. The conventional architecture was able to learn this environment on 24 of 25 replications, with a median of 27,867 steps until the prediction task was mastered. In contrast, SLUG learned perfectly on every replication and in a median of 91 steps.

Besides testing the conventional architecture on the environment inference problem, we also tested SLUG on problems studied using the conventional architecture.[4] Servan-Schreiber et al. (1989) have worked on the problem of inferring regular languages from examples, which is formally identical to the environment inference problem except that an exploration strategy is unnecessary because sample strings are given to the system. They trained the conventional architecture on strings of a language. After 200,000 sample strings, the network was able to reject invalid strings. In contrast, SLUG required a mere 150 training examples on average before it mastered the acceptability judgement task.[5]

The fact that SLUG achieves considerably better performance than conventional connectionist approaches justifies its nonintuitive network architecture, dynamics, and training procedure.[6] Thus, Rivest and Schapire's update graph

---

[4]This comparison was performed in collaboration with Paul Smolensky.

[5]The training procedure was slightly different for the two architectures. Servan-Schreiber et al.'s network was shown positive examples only, and was trained to predict the next element in a sequence. SLUG was shown both positive and negative examples, and was trained to accept or reject an entire string. We see no principled reason why one task would be more difficult than the other.

[6]It remains to be seen which properties of SLUG that differ from the conventional connectionist approach are crucial for SLUG's improved performance. One key property is undoubtably the gating connections between actions and state units. See Giles et al. (1990) for a related architecture that also shares this property.

representation, which motivated the architecture of SLUG, has proven beneficial, even if what SLUG (with unconstrained weights) learns does not correspond exactly to an update graph.

Interpreting Unconstrained Solutions Discovered by SLUG

One reason why the final weights in SLUG are difficult to interpret in the case of the 3-bit shift register environment is that SLUG has discovered a solution that does not satisfy the update graph formalism; it has discovered the notion of complementation links of the sort shown in Figure 8I. With the use of complementation links, only three units are required, not six. Consequently, the three unnecessary units are either cut out of the solution or encode information redundantly. SLUG's solutions are much easier to understand when the network consists of only three units. Figure 15 depicts one such solution, which approximates the graph in Figure 8I. Ignoring the connections of small magnitude, the three units are connected in a clockwise loop for action L, a counterclockwise loop for action R, and the output unit toggles its value while the two internal units maintain their values for action F. Although a comparison of Figures 15 and 8I might seem to indicate that the connections of small magnitude in Figure 15 introduce noise, this is not so. The solution discovered by SLUG is exact—it predicts sensations accurately because the effects of these connections exactly cancel out. SLUG also discovers other solutions in which two of the three connections in the three-unit loop are negative, one negation canceling out the effect of the other. Allowing complementation links can halve the number of update graph nodes required for many environments. This is one fairly direct extension of Rivest and Schapire's update graph formalism that SLUG suggests.

Treating the update graph as matrices of connection strengths has suggested another generalization of the update graph formalism. Because SLUG is a linear

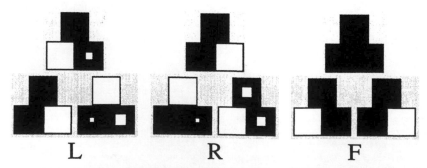

Figure 15. The 3-bit shift register environment. Weights learned by SLUG with three units and unconstrained weights.

system, any rank-preserving linear transform of the weight matrices will produce an equivalent system, but one that does not have the local connectivity of the update graph. Thus, one can view the Rivest and Schapire update graph formalism as one example of a much larger class of equivalent solutions that can be embodied in a connectionist network. While many of these solutions do not obey constraints imposed by a symbolic description (e.g., all-or-none links between nodes), they do yield equivalent behavior. By relaxing the symbolic constraints, the connectionist representation allows far greater flexibility in expressing potential solutions. See Mozer and Bachrach (1991) for a further elaboration of this point.

Comparing SLUG and the RS Algorithm

Table 1 compares the performance of the RS algorithm and SLUG for a sampling of environments.[7] In these simulations, we ran the version of SLUG with unconstrained weights. All runs of SLUG eventually converged on an adequate set of weights. The learning rates used in our simulations were adjusted dynamically every 100 steps by averaging the current learning rate with a value proportional to the mean-squared error obtained on the last 100 steps. Several runs were made to determine what initial learning rate and constant of proportionality yielded the best performance. It turned out that performance was relatively invariant under a wide range of these parameters. Including momentum in the back-propagation algorithm did not appear to help significantly.[8]

In simple environments, SLUG can outperform the RS algorithm. These results are quite surprising when considering that the action sequence used to train SLUG is generated at random, in contrast to the RS algorithm, which involves a strategy for exploring the environment. We conjecture that SLUG does as well as it does because it considers and updates many hypotheses in parallel at each time step. That is, after the outcome of a single action is observed, nearly all weights in SLUG are adjusted simultaneously. In contrast, the RS algorithm requires special-purpose heuristics that are not necessarily robust in order to test multiple hypotheses at once.

A further example of SLUG's parallelism is that it learns the update graph structure at the same time as the appropriate unit activations, whereas the RS algorithm approaches the two tasks sequentially. During learning, SLUG continually makes predictions about what sensations will result from a particular action. These predictions gradually improve with experience, and even before learning is complete, the predictions can be substantially correct. The RS algo-

---

[7]We thank Rob Schapire for providing us with the latest results from his work.

[8]Just as connectionist simulations require a bit of voodoo in setting learning rates, the RS algorithm has its own set of adjustable parameters that influence performance. One of us (JB) experimented with the RS algorithm, but, without expertise in parameter tweaking, was unable to obtain performance in the same range as the measures reported by Rivest and Schapire.

TABLE 1
Number of Steps Required to Learn Update Graph

Environment	Size of Update Graph	Median Number of Actions	
		The RS Algorithm	SLUG
Little prince	4	200	91
Car radio	6	27,695	8,167
3-bit shift register	8	408	298
4-bit shift register	9	1,388	1,509
5 × 5 grid	27	583,195	fails
32-Bit shift register	32	52,436	fails
6 × 6 checkerboard	36	96,041	8,142

rithm cannot make predictions based on its partially constructed update graph. Although the algorithm could perhaps be modified to do so, there would be an associated cost.

In complex environments—ones in which the number of nodes in the update graph is quite large and the number of distinguishing environmental sensations is relatively small—SLUG does poorly. Two examples of such, the 32-bit shift register environment and the 5 × 5 grid environment, cannot be learned by SLUG, whereas the RS algorithm succeeds. An intelligent exploration strategy seems necessary in complex environments: with a random exploration strategy, the time required to move from one state to a distant state becomes so great that links between the states cannot be established.

The 32-bit shift register environment and the 5 × 5 grid environment are extreme: all locations are identical and the available sensory information is meager. Such environments are quite unlike natural environments, which provide a relative abundance of sensory information to distinguish among environmental states. SLUG performs much better when more information about the environment can be sensed directly. For example, learning the 32-bit shift register environment is trivial if SLUG is able to sense the values of all 32 bits at once (the median number of steps to learn is only 1209). The checkerboard environment is another environment as large as the 32-bit shift register environment in terms of the number of nodes SLUG requires, but it is much easier to learn because of the rich sensory information.

Noisy Environments. The RS algorithm originally could not handle environments with unreliable sensations, although a variant of the algorithm has recently been designed to overcome this limitation (Schapire, personal comm., 1988). In contrast, SLUG, like most connectionist systems, deals naturally with noise in that SLUG's ability to predict degrades gracefully in the presence of noise. To illustrate this point, we trained SLUG on a version of the little prince environment in which sensations are registered incorrectly 10% of the time. SLUG was still able to learn the update graph. However, to train SLUG properly in noisy environments, we needed to alter the training procedure slightly, in particular, the step in which the observed sensations replace SLUG's predicted sensations. The problem is that if the observed sensations are incorrectly registered, the values of nodes in the network will be disrupted, and SLUG will require a series of noise-free steps to recover. Thus, we used a procedure in which the predicted sensations were not completely replaced by the observed sensations, but rather some average of the two was computed, according to the formula

$$(1 - \omega)p_i + \omega o_i, \tag{7}$$

where p_i and o_i are the predicted and observed values of sensation i, and ω is a weighting factor.[9] The value of ω is a function of SLUG's performance level, as measured by the mean proportion of prediction errors. If SLUG is making relatively few errors, it has learned the correct environment model and ω should be set to 0—the observed value should be ignored because it is occasionally incorrect. However, if SLUG is performing poorly, the prediction p_i should not be relied upon, and ω should have a value closer to 1. Rather than computing ω as a function of SLUG's performance, another possibility is to adjust ω via gradient descent in the overall error measure.

Prior Specification of Update Graph Size.   The RS algorithm requires an upper bound on the number of nodes in the update graph. The results presented in Table 1 are obtained when the RS algorithm knows in advance exactly how many nodes are required. The algorithm fails if it is given an upper bound less than the required number of nodes, and performance—measured as the number of steps required to discover the solution—degrades as the upper bound increases above the required number. SLUG will also fail to learn perfectly if it is given fewer units than are necessary for the task. However, performance does not appear to degrade as the number of units increases beyond the minimal number. Table 2 presents the median number of steps required to learn the 4-bit shift register environment as the number of units in SLUG (with unconstrained weights) is varied. Although performance is independent of the number of units here, extraneous units greatly *improve* performance when the weights are constrained: only 4 of 25 replications of the 4-bit shift register environment simulation with 8 units and constrained weights successfully learned the update graph, whereas 19 of 25 replications succeeded when 16 units were used.

---

[9]A more principled but computationally more expensive technique for updating the predicted sensations can be derived using Kalman filtering theory (Gelb, 1974).

TABLE 2
Number of Steps Required to Learn
Update Graph as Number of Units
in SLUG Is Varied

Units in SLUG	Median Number of Steps to Learn Update Graph
4	2028
6	1380
8	1509
10	1496
12	1484
14	1630
16	1522
18	1515
20	1565

Limitations of SLUG

The connectionist approach to the problem of inferring the structure of a finite state environment has two fundamental problems that must be overcome if it is to be considered seriously as an alternative to the symbolic approach. First, using a random exploration strategy, SLUG has no hope of scaling to complex environments. An intelligent strategy could potentially be incorporated to encourage SLUG to explore unfamiliar regions of the environment. One approach we are currently investigating, based on the work of Cohn et al. (1990), is to have SLUG select actions that result in maximal uncertainty in its predictions, where uncertainty is defined as how far a predicted sensation is from one of the discrete sensation values. Second, our greatest successes have occurred when we allowed SLUG to discover solutions that are not necessarily isomorphic to an update graph. One virtue of the update graph formalism is that it is relatively easy to interpret; the same cannot generally be said of the continuous-valued weight matrices discovered by SLUG. However, as we discuss in Mozer and Bachrach (1991), there is promise of developing methods for transforming the large class of formally equivalent solutions available to SLUG into the more localist update graph formalism to facilitate interpretation.

CONTROL ACQUISITION

Having discussed a method for learning a model of the environment, we turn to a control acquisition architecture that can use this model to determine a minimal sequence of actions to follow to reach a particular goal state. The architecture consists of a *forward model* and a *critic*. The basic architecture is shown in

Time to Goal

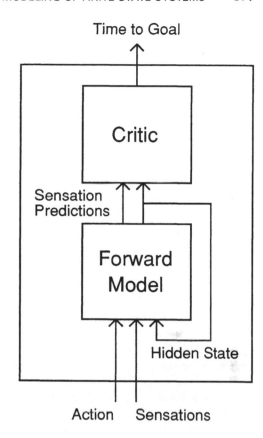

Figure 16. Connectionist control acquisition architecture.

Action   Sensations

Figure 16 and will be called the *control network*. The forward model maps its current state and the current action to the predicted next state, and the critic maps the forward model's next state to the expected time to reach the goal state. The forward model's state is composed of both sensations values and hidden state information. (This corresponds to the output and hidden units of SLUG.)

The controller is implicit in this architecture. At each time step the action is chosen which minimizes the output of the critic. More precisely, each action in turn is presented as input to the control network. The control network computes a prediction of the time to reach the goal state if that particular action were taken in the current state. The control network splits this computation into two parts: first, the forward model computes the state q that results from taking that particular action, and then the critic computes the prediction of the time to reach the goal state from state q. The action which results in the minimum prediction of time to reach the goal state is then chosen.

In our experiments, the training procedure is split into two phases. First, the forward model is trained during an exploration phase using the unconstrained version of SLUG. The weights of SLUG are then fixed. Second, the control network is trained to produce optimal trajectories from an arbitrary initial state to a particular goal state. This phase involves a series of trials commencing in the goal state and ending in the goal state. At the beginning of each trial the robot wanders for a fixed number of steps by taking actions selected at random from a uniform distribution. The number of such steps is conservatively chosen to be the number of states in the environment. This places the robot in a random initial state.[10] During the rest of the control trial, the robot chooses actions resulting in minimal predictions of the time to reach the goal state. In order to encourage exploration during control trials, the robot sometimes (with probability 0.25 in all the simulations) selects alternative actions instead of selecting the action that currently looks best. This exploration strategy is not optimal, but provides the necessary exposure to the state space. Sutton (1990) and Watkins (1989) present more sophisticated techniques for exploration. Throughout the entire control acquisition phase—during wandering and during the control trials—the forward model constantly updates itself to reflect the current state of the environment.

The critic is trained using a *temporal difference* (*TD*) method developed by Sutton (1984, 1988). A system using this method learns to predict by maintaining consistency across successive predictions and by forcing the prediction to agree with any available training signals. In the case of predicting the time to reach the goal state, the critic is trained to make successive predictions decrease by one and to make the prediction at the goal state zero. Instead of having the robot directly sense the goal state, the robot receives a reinforcement signal that indicates when it is located at the goal; the reinforcement signal is 1 when the robot is located at the goal and 0 otherwise. Finally, the critic is trained only when the robot actually selects the action that currently looks best and not when the robot takes exploratory steps.

The critic is implemented as either a one- or two-layer network with a single linear output unit. The hidden layer is unnecessary for some of the environments. The critic's optional hidden layer consists of logistic units with outputs ranging from −1 to +1.

Results

The control acquisition technique was applied to the environments listed in Table 3. In all the environments, goal states were chosen to be indistinguishable from

---

[10]There are two motivations for this wandering procedure. Firsts, in a learning situation with minimal supervision, the robot needs to get into the initial state on its own; it cannot depend on a supervisor to place it in a random initial state. Second, the forward model needs to reflect the current environmental state. If the robot is placed in a random state, substantial effort would be required to establish the environmental state. However, by starting at the goal state and wandering from there, the robot can maintain continual knowledge of the environmental state.

TABLE 3
Control Acquisition Technique Was Applied to These
Environments with Their Respective Goal States

Environment	Goal State
Little Prince	Robot on the north location facing east
Car radio	Playing classical, rock in preset X, and news in preset Y
3-bit shift register	Bit pattern 101
4-bit shift register	Bit pattern 1010
4 × 4 checkerboard	Square (1, 1)
6 × 6 checkerboard	Square (2, 2)
8 × 8 checkerboard	Square (3, 3)

other states based on only on the sensations. For example, to be considered in the goal state in the car radio environment, the robot must have the rock station stored in preset X and the news station stored in preset Y as well as be listening to the classical station. In the $n \times n$ checkerboard environment, the goal location is a particular square located in the middle of the grid that does not contain a landmark. The coordinates given in Table 3 are relative to the bottom left square (0,0).

We use the 3-bit shift register environment to illustrate the control acquisition technique. Initially an unconstrained SLUG model of this environment was constructed with the techniques described earlier. Next, using the units of SLUG as inputs to a critic network, the critic was trained to indicate the number of time steps to achieve the bit pattern 101 from any possible initial bit pattern. Once trained, the control network implicitly defines a *control law* that specifies the shortest action sequence required to achieve the goal state.

Figure 17 summarizes the resulting control law and evaluation function learned for the 3-bit shift register environment. All states of the shift register are shown, including the goal state, 101, which is at the bottom of the figure. Each state is depicted as a shift register with the corresponding bit settings, where gray denotes a value of zero, and white denotes a value of unity. The states are depicted in decreasing order from top to bottom in terms of the output of the critic for that state (i.e., expected minimum number of time steps needed to reach the goal state). This figure summarizes the implicit control law by showing the optimal transitions from state to state. For example, suppose the robot is in state 100 and is going to choose the best next action. The robot could choose action L resulting in state 001 with value 1, or action R resulting in state 010 with value 2, or action F resulting in state 000 with value 3. The best action available to the robot is L which is shown with the solid line; the suboptimal actions (F and R) are shown with dotted lines.

The robot chooses the optimal action given the current state. For example, if

Critic Output

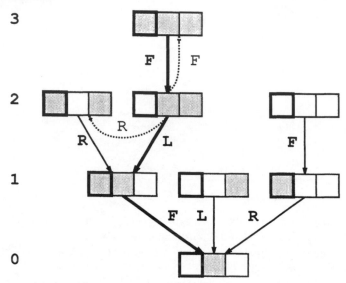

Figure 17. Summary of the control law and evaluation function for the 3-bit shift register environment. Each state is depicted as a 3-bit shift register where gray denotes a value of 0 in a particular cell, white a value of 1. Arrows indicate some of the possible transitions from one state to another. Solid arrows correspond to the optimal actions; dashed arrows correspond to suboptimal actions.

the shift register starts in state 000, the optimal action sequence is FLF. This trajectory is depicted in Figure 17 as a sequence of double thick arrows connecting state 000 to state 100 to state 001 to state 101.

As a further demonstration of the control network, we present the behavior of the network on the car radio and 8 × 8 checkerboard environments after training. In the car radio environment, the robot learns to store the proper stations in the presets and then play classical music. One example sequence of state/action pairs is shown in Table 4.

In the 8 × 8 checkerboard environment, the goal state was chosen to be square (3,3). The resulting controller is able to choose optimal actions from each square in the grid that move it one step closer to the goal position. Figure 18 shows two trajectories for this environment. Figure 19 shows the relative output of the critic in all the squares. The evaluations decrease steadily to zero at the goal square (3,3).

To evaluate the control acquisition architecture, we examined its performance as measured by the total number of actions that must be executed before the system produces optimal goal-seeking behavior. The total number of actions

TABLE 4
An Example State/Action Sequence for the Car
Radio Environment

	State		Action
Current	Preset X	Preset Y	
Classical	Classical	Classical	Scan left
News	Classical	Classical	Store in preset Y
News	Classical	News	Scan left
Rock	Classical	News	Store in preset X
Rock	Rock	News	Scan left
Classical	Rock	News	

include wandering actions, exploration actions, as well as actual control actions during which learning occurs. The system is considered to have learned a task by a given time step if optimal control actions are taken for at least the next 2500 actions. In order to judge whether a control action is optimal, a table of the minimum number of time steps needed to reach home for each state is constructed prior to training. An action that changes the environmental state from x to y is considered optimal if the minimum number of time steps needed to reach home from state y is one less than the minimum number needed from state x. For each environment, several runs were made to determine the learning rate that yielded the best performance. Because results vary from one run to another due to the random initial weights, we report the median performance over 25 replications of each simulation. On all replications, the control network was able to converge on a solution.

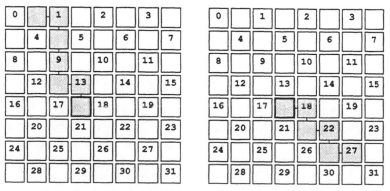

Figure 18.   Two example trajectories for the 8 × 8 checkerboard environment. Each trajectory is shown as a sequence of shaded squares connected by line segments and ending in the goal square.

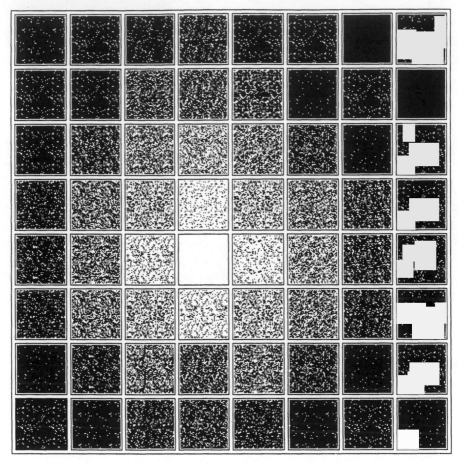

Figure 19.   The output of the critic at each of the squares in the 8 × 8 checkerboard environment. The evaluations are portrayed with white being the lowest and black the highest.

Table 5 reports the performance of the control acquisition technique for the environments listed in Table 3. Table 5 lists the number of environmental states, the number of logistic hidden units contained in the critic network (where 0 in this column means that a hidden layer was unnecessary), and the learning rate used for training the critic. Table 5 also reports the median total number of actions, number of control actions, and number of trials needed to learn to produce optimal behavior. Because the control network is only trained during control actions, the number of control actions equals the number of weight updates.

Because of the large number of wandering and exploratory actions, the ratio

TABLE 5
Performance of the Control Acquisition Technique

Environment	No. of Env. States	No. of Hidden Units	Learning Rate	Median Number Needed to Learn Optimal Behavior		
				Actions		
				All	Control	Trials
Little prince	4	0	0.100	20	8	2
3-bit shift register	8	8	0.050	4443	778	373
4-bit shift register	16	16	0.020	7662	1937	282
Car radio	27	16	0.010	12512	2199	355
4 × 4 checkerboard	16	0	0.001	6061	1114	262
6 × 6 checkerboard	36	0	0.001	57915	5692	1327
8 × 8 checkerboard	64	0	0.001	106507	8777	1446

of the number of control actions to the total number of actions is small. More sophisticated wandering and exploration procedures would substantially increase this ratio. Figure 20 shows some learning curves for the 4-bit shift register environment. The curves demonstrate that the system rapidly learns the majority of the control law and then takes significantly longer to learn the residual behavior.

Relation to Other Work

Our control acquisition architecture is strongly related to the three-net architecture, proposed by Werbos (1990) and also based on the ideas of Barto, Sutton, and Anderson (1983), Sutton (1984), Barto, Sutton, and Watkins (1990), and Jordan and Rumelhart (1990). (See also Werbos, 1987; Sutton, 1988, 1990; Barto, 1990; Watkins, 1989, for related architectures and techniques.) The basic idea is to learn an evaluation function and then train the controller by differentiating this function with respect to the controller weights. These derivatives indicate how to change the controller's weights in order to minimize or maximize the evaluation function. The three-net architecture consists of a controller, a forward model, and a critic. The controller maps states to actions, the forward model maps state/action pairs to next states, and the three-net critic maps states to evaluations.

Our control acquisition architecture is a version of a three-net architecture without an explicit controller. Instead of training a controller, our technique chooses actions based solely on the output of the critic and not based on the output of a controller. In the three-net architecture the controller and critic are intimately related: the controller must adapt in response to changes in the critic,

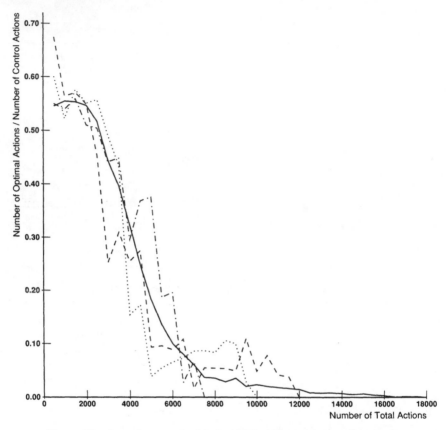

Figure 20.   Learning curves for the 4-bit shift register environment. The y axis shows the fraction of suboptimal actions chosen during the past 500 time steps. The bold line shows the average performance over time for the control network over 25 replications. The dotted, dashed, and stippled lines show the performance over time for three different individual runs.

and vice versa. In contrast, in our technique this relationship is simplified—the critic directly defines the actions. In particular, the actions are chosen according to the current evaluation function—the action with the best evaluation is chosen.

It is useful to compare our architecture to the two-net architecture proposed by Werbos (1990) and Jordan and Jacobs (1989). The two-net architecture consists of a controller and a critic. The controller maps states to actions, and the two-net critic maps state/action pairs to evaluations. It has been said that it is easier to train a two-net architecture than a three-net architecture because there is no forward model (1990). One problem with building a model is that it is not sensitive to the particular control task. Many features of the environment might be unrelated to the control task, and any technique that employs a model would have to spend a disproportionate amount of time learning parts of the environment irrelevant to the control task. With a two-net architecture, only a two-net critic is trained based on state/action input pairs. But what if a forward model already exists or even a priori knowledge exists to aid in explicit coding of a forward model? Knowledge of relations between actions and the effect of particular actions can be hardwired into the weights of the model network. In SLUG, the explicit representation of the effects of actions on the model's state as separate weight matrices eases this process. For example, symmetries in actions (such as action inverses) can be coded into the model. In the extreme case, the entire model can be hardwired. In environments where a priori knowledge exists, this can significantly speed up the overall learning process because the critic learns an evaluation function based on state only and not state/action pairs as in the two-net critic.

Our technique provides the possibility of learning a model and control law simultaneously. This would allow the robot to learn in dynamic environments and would also permit the use of a model for performing mental experiments as demonstrated by Sutton (1990). Sutton shows how a model can dramatically speed up the control acquisition process.

A variation of the control architecture can be used in difficult-to-learn environments, where training a model would be overly time consuming. All components of the architecture remain the same, but the model would no longer be required to produce predictions of the sensations. Instead of predicting the next sensation values, the model produces state information used by the critic in order to learn the evaluation function. Consequently, the model will produce only state information necessary for the control task. In this case, the combination of the critic and model form a two-net critic. Judging from the superior performance of unconstrained SLUG over a "conventional" connectionist architecture, we would expect that unconstrained SLUG used in conjunction with a critic network would outperform one large, undifferentiated connectionist architecture.

Our aim in this section is by no means to present the final word on connectionist control. There are many viable alternative architectures and training procedures. However, at some level all approaches require an understanding of the environment in order to predict the consequences of actions. An explicit environmental model is especially important in environments whose state cannot be directly perceived. Thus a flexible, powerful model like SLUG can be an essential component of a goal-seeking system operating in complex environments.

ACKNOWLEDGMENTS

Our thanks to Andy Barto, Clayton Lewis, Rob Schapire, Paul Smolensky, Rich Sutton, and the University of Massachusetts Adaptive NetWorks Group for helpful discussions. This work was supported by NSF Presidential Young Investigator award IRI-9058450 and grant 90-21 from the James S. McDonnell Foundation to Michael Mozer, grant AFOSR-89-0526 from the Air Force Office of Scientific Research, Bolling AFB, and NSF grant ECS-8912623 to Andrew Barto.

REFERENCES

Bachrach, J. R. (1988). *Learning to represent state.* Unpublished master's thesis, University of Massachusetts, Amherst, COINS Department, Amherst, MA.

Barto, A. G. (1990). Connectionist learning for control: An overview. In T. Miller, R. S. Sutton, & P. J. Werbos (Eds.), *Neural networks for control.* Cambridge, MA: MIT Press.

Barto, A. G., & Sutton, R. S. (1981). Landmark learning: An illustration of associative search. *Biological Cybernetics, 42,* 1–8.

Barto, A. G., Sutton, R. S., & Anderson, C. W. (1983). Neuronlike elements that can solve difficult learning control problems. *IEEE Transactions on Systems, Man, and Cybernetics, 13,* 835–846. Reprinted in J. A. Anderson and E. Rosenfeld (1988). *Neurocomputing: Foundations of research,* Cambridge, MA: MIT Press.

Barto, A. G., Sutton, R. S., & Watkins, C. (1990). Sequential decision problems and neural networks. In D. S. Touretzky (Ed.), *Advances in neural information processing systems 2.* San Mateo, CA: Morgan Kaufmann.

Bridle, J. (1990). Training stochastic model recognition algorithms as networks can lead to maximum mutual information estimation of parameters. In D. S. Touretzky (Ed.), *Advances in neural information processing systems 2.* San Mateo, CA: Morgan Kaufmann.

Cohn, D., Atlas, L., Ladner, R., El-sharkawi, R. M. II, Aggoune, M., & Park, D. (1990). Training connectionist networks with queries and selective sampling. In D. S. Touretzky (Ed.), *Advances in neural information processing systems 2.* San Mateo, CA: Morgan Kaufmann.

Durbin, R. (1990, April). *Principled competitive learning in both unsupervised and supervised networks.* Poster presented at the conference on neural networks for computing, Snowbird, UT.

Elman, J. L. (1990). Finding structure in time. *Cognitive Science, 14,* 179–212.

Gelb, A. (1974). *Optimal estimation.* Cambridge, MA: MIT Press.

Giles, C. L., Sun, G. Z., Chen, H. H., Lee, Y. C., & Chen, D. (1990). Higher order recurrent networks and grammatical inference. In D. S. Touretzky (Ed.), *Advances in neural information processing systems 2.* San Mateo, CA: Morgan Kaufmann.

Jordan, M. I., & Jacobs, R. (1989). Learning to control an unstable system with forward modeling. In D. S. Touretzky (Ed.), *Advances in neural information processing systems 2.* San Mateo, CA: Morgan Kaufmann.

Jordan, M. I., & Rumelhart, D. E. (1992). Forward models: Supervised learning with a distal teacher. *Cognitive Science, 16,* 307–354.

Mozer, M. C. (1989). A focused back-propagation algorithm for temporal pattern recognition. *Complex Systems, 3*(4), 349–381.

Mozer, M. C., & Bachrach, J. R. (1991). SLUG: A connectionist architecture for inferring the structure of finite-state environments. *Machine Learning, 7,* 139–160.

Pollack, J. B. (1990). Language acquisition via strange automata. *Proceedings of the Twelfth Annual Conference of the Cognitive Science Society.* Hillsdale, NJ: Erlbaum.

Rivest, R. L., & Schapire, R. E. (1987a). Diversity-based inference of finite automata. *Proceedings of the Twenty-Eighth Annual Symposium on Foundations of Computer Science* (pp. 78–87).

Rivest, R. L., & Schapire, R. E. (1987b). A new approach to unsupervised learning in deterministic environments. In P. Langley (Ed.), *Proceedings of the Fourth International Workshop on Machine Learning* (pp. 364–375).

Rumelhart, D. E. (1989, April). *Specialized architectures for back propagation learning*. Paper presented at the conference on neural networks for computing, Snowbird, UT.

Rumelhart, D. E., Hinton, G. E., & Williams, R. J. (1986). Learning internal representations by error propagation. In D. E. Rumelhart & J. L. McClelland (Eds.), *Parallel distributed processing: Explorations in the microstructure of cognition*, (Vol. 1). Cambridge, MA: Bradford Books/ MIT Press.

Schapire, R. E. Personal communication, 1988.

Schapire, R. E. (1988). *Diversity-based inference of finite automata*. Unpublished master's thesis, MIT.

Servan-Schreiber, D., Cleermans, A., & McClelland, J. L. (1988). *Encoding sequential structure in simple recurrent networks* (Report No. CMU-CS-88-183). Pittsburgh, PA: Carnegie-Mellon University, Department of Computer Science.

Servan-Schreiber, D., Cleeremans, A., & McClelland, J. L. (1989). Learning sequential structure in simple recurrent networks. In D. S. Touretzky (Ed.), *Advances in neural information processing systems 1*. San Mateo, CA: Morgan Kaufmann.

Stornetta, W. S., & Huberman, B. A. (1987). An improved three-layer back propagation algorithm. *Proceedings of the IEEE First Annual International Conference on Neural Networks* (pp. 637– 643).

Sutton, R. S. (1984). *Temporal credit assignment in reinforcement learning*. Unpublished doctoral dissertation, Department of Computer and Information Science, University of Massachusetts at Amherst.

Sutton, R. S. (1988). Learning to predict by the methods of temporal differences. *Machine Learning, 3*, 9–44.

Sutton, R. S. (1990). Integrated architectures for learning, planning, and reacting based on approximating dynamic programming. *Proceedings of the Seventh International Conference on Machine Learning* (pp. 216–224). San Mateo, CA: Morgan Kaufmann.

Watkins, C. J. C. H. (1989). *Learning from delayed rewards*. Unpublished doctoral dissertation, Cambridge University, Cambridge, England. Pending.

Werbos, P. J. (1987). Building and understanding adaptive systems: A statistical/numerical approach to factory automation and brain research. *IEEE Transactions on Systems, Man, and Cybernetics*.

Werbos, P. J. (1990). Reinforcement learning over time. In T. Miller, R. S. Sutton, & P. J. Werbos (Eds.), *Neural networks for control*. Cambridge, MA: MIT Press.

Williams, R. J., & Zipser, D. (1989). A learning algorithm for continually running fully recurrent neural networks. *Neural Computation, 1*(2), 270–280.

Williams, R. J., & Zipser, D. (in press). Gradient-based learning algorithms for recurrent connectionist networks. In Y. Chauvin & D. E. Rumelhart (Eds.), *Back-propagation: Theory, architectures and applications*. Hillsdale, NJ: Erlbaum.

12 Backpropagation and Unsupervised Learning in Linear Networks

Pierre Baldi
Jet Propulsion Laboratory and Division of Biology,
California Institute of Technology

Yves Chauvin
Net-ID, Inc., San Francisco, California

Kurt Hornik
Institut für Statistik und Wahrscheinlichkeitstheorie,
Technische Universität Wien

INTRODUCTION

This chapter addresses the problems of back-propagation learning in layered networks of linear units.* One may expect the topic to be very restricted; yet it is in fact quite rich and far from being exhausted. Since the first approximations of biological neurons using threshold gates (Mc Culloch and Pitts, 1943), the nonlinear aspects of neural computations and hardware have often been emphasized, and linear networks dismissed as uninteresting, for only being able to express linear input-output maps. Furthermore, multiple forward layers of linear units can always be collapsed by multiplying the corresponding weight matrices. Nonlinear computations are obviously extremely important, but these arguments should be considered as suspicious because, by stressing only the input-output relation, they miss the subtle problems of dynamics, structure, and self-organization that normally arise during learning and plasticity, even in simple linear systems. There are other reasons why linear networks deserve careful attention. General results in the nonlinear case are often absent or difficult to derive analytically, whereas the linear case can often be analyzed in mathematical detail. As in the theory of differential equations, the linear setting should be regarded as the first simple case to be studied. More complex situations can often be investigated by linearization,

---

*It is a slightly shortened and modified version, with permission, of Baldi and Hornik, 1994.

although this has not been attempted systematically for neural networks. In back-propagation, learning is often started with zero or small random initial weights and bias. Thus, at least during the initial phase of training, the network is operating in its linear regime. Even when training is completed, one often finds several units in the network which are operating in their linear range. From the standpoint of theoretical biology, it has been argued that at least certain classes of neurons may be operating most of the time in a linear or quasi linear regime and linear input-output relations seem to hold for certain specific biological circuits (see Robinson, 1981, for an example). Finally, a posteriori, the study of linear networks leads to new interesting questions, insights, and paradigms which could not have been guessed in advance and to new ways of looking at certain classical statistical techniques.

To begin with, we shall consider a linear feedforward network with an $n - p - m$ architecture comprising one input layer, one hidden layer, and one output layer with n, p, and m units, respectively (see Fig. 1). The more general case with, for instance, multiple hidden layers, can be reduced to this simple setting as we shall see. A will usually denote the $m \times p$ matrix of connection weights from the middle layer to the output, and B the $p \times n$ matrix connecting the input to the middle layer. Thus, for instance, a_{ij} represents the strength of the coupling between the jth hidden unit and the ith output unit (double indices are always in the post-presynaptic order). The network therefore computes the linear function $y = ABx$. In the usual learning from examples setting, we suppose that a set of n-dimensional input patterns x_t ($1 \leq t \leq T$) is given together with a corresponding set of m-dimensional target output patterns y_t ($1 \leq t \leq T$) (all vectors are assumed to be column vectors). $X = [x_1, \ldots, x_T]$ and $Y = [y_1, \ldots, y_T]$ are the $n \times T$ and $m \times T$ matrices having the patterns as their columns. Because of the need for target outputs, this form of learning will also be called supervised. For simplicity, unless otherwise stated, all the patterns are assumed to be centered (i.e., $\langle x_t \rangle = \langle y_t \rangle = 0$). The symbol "$\langle \cdot \rangle$" will be used for averages over the set of patterns or sometimes over the pattern distribution, depending on the context. The approximation of one by the other is a central problem in statistics; but is not our main concern here. The environment is supposed to be stationary but the results could be extended to a slowly varying environment to deal with plasticity issues. Throughout the chapter, learning is based on the minimization of an error function E depending on the synaptic weights, usually

$$E(A, B) = \langle \|y_t - ABx_t\|^2 \rangle, \qquad (1)$$

where $\|u\|$ represents the Euclidean norm of the vector u. When no target outputs are provided, the learning (which then must be based on criteria to be specified, such as the maximization of the output variance) is unsupervised. An important special case, which sits at the boundary between supervised and unsupervised, is the case of autoassociation, when the input is used as a teacher (i.e., $y_t = x_t$). This is also called autoencoding or identity mapping in the literature. Auto-

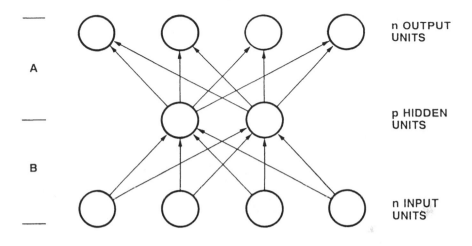

ERROR FUNCTION:

$$E\,(A,\,B)\;=\;\sum_t \left\| y_t - ABx_t \right\|^2$$

Figure 1. The basic network in the autoassociative case $(m = n)$.

association is the most simple non-trivial input/output relationship. It has the advantage of being often analytically tractable.

Learning rules are algorithms for altering the connection weights to achieve a desirable goal, such as the minimization of an error function. Often, three different versions of the same rule can be given: the "on-line"[1] version where the modification is calculated after the presentation of each pattern; the "off-line" version where the previous modifications are averaged over the cycle of all patterns; and the "continuous" (and stochastic) version, where the discrete changes induced by the "off-line" algorithm are approximated continuously by a differential equation governing the evolution of the weights in time. In some cases, the three formulations can be shown to lead essentially to the same results.

We define the covariance matrices $\Sigma_{XX} = \langle x_t x_t' \rangle$, $\Sigma_{XY} = \langle x_t y_t' \rangle$, $\Sigma_{YY} = \langle y_t y_t' \rangle$, and $\Sigma_{YX} = \langle y_t x_t' \rangle$ with the prime denoting transposition of matrices. Σ_{XX}, for instance, is a real $n \times n$ symmetric matrix, and as such all its eigenvalues are real. Since it is a covariance matrix, they are nonnegative and can be ordered as $\lambda_1 \geq \ldots \geq \lambda_n \geq 0$. For mathematical simplicity, we shall often assume that $\lambda_1 > \ldots > \lambda_n > 0$. This should not be regarded as very restrictive, since this

---

[1]Some authors use the term "stochastic" instead.

condition can always be enforced by, at worst, perturbing the data by infinitesimal amounts and attributing these perturbations to "noise." Most of the conclusions are only slightly different when some eigenvalues coincide.

Although this chapter contains many equations, it is not intended for mathematicians, and a good familiarity with linear algebra and basic calculus on the part of the reader is sufficient. All the statistical techniques required to understand some of the results are briefly reviewed in the second section. These include least-squares regression, principal-component analysis, and discriminant analysis. In the fourth section, we treat the case of supervised learning with back propagation and the corresponding autoassociative special case. We study the landscape of the error function E of Equation (1), its connections to statistical techniques, and several consequences and generalizations, including noisy and deep networks. In the fourth section, we study the problems of validation, generalization, and overfitting a simple one layer network trained, by gradient descent, to learn the identity map. Under some assumptions, we give a complete description of the evolution of the validation error as a function of training time. In the fifth section, a restricted number of unsupervised algorithms for linear networks is briefly studied. Some of the more technical proofs are deferred to the Appendix.

MATHEMATICAL BACKGROUND

Optimization of Quadratic Forms over Spheres

Let S be a symmetric $n \times n$ matrix. Then all the eigenvalues λ_i of S are real and can be ordered in the form $\lambda_1 \geq \lambda_2 \geq \ldots \geq \lambda_n$ with corresponding normalized eigenvectors $u_1, \ldots, u_n$. Consider the problem of maximizing the quadratic form $E(a) = a'Sa$ over the sphere of radius ρ and centered at the origin ($\|a\| \leq \rho$). In geometry, it is well known (for instance Apostol, 1967) that the maximum of E is then reached on the surface of the sphere in the direction of the first eigenvector, that is at the points $\pm\rho u_1$, where $E(\pm\rho u_1) = \lambda_1\rho^2$. If $\lambda_1 > \lambda_2$, these are the only two solutions. Similarly, the maximum of E over the intersection of the sphere with the linear space orthogonal to u_1 is reached at $\pm\rho u_2$, and so forth. Finally, the minimum of E over the entire sphere is obtained at $\pm\rho u_n$. All these psoperties are easily derived by decomposing a as $a = \Sigma_i \alpha_i u_i$ and noticing that $E(a) = \Sigma_i \lambda_i \alpha_i^2$.

Singular Value Decomposition

Let Z be an arbitrary $k \times l$ matrix with rank r. Then there exist numbers $\sigma_1 \geq \ldots \geq \sigma_r > 0$, the *singular values* of Z, an orthogonal $k \times k$ matrix U, and an orthogonal $l \times l$ matrix V such that $S = U'ZV$ is a $k \times l$ diagonal matrix of the form

$$S = \begin{bmatrix} D & O \\ O & O \end{bmatrix}, \tag{2}$$

where $D = \text{diag}(\sigma_1, \ldots, \sigma_r)$ is the diagonal matrix with entries $\sigma_1, \ldots, \sigma_r$. The decomposition

$$Z = USV' \tag{3}$$

is called the singular value decomposition (SVD) of Z (it is not necessarily unique). The matrices U and V in the SVD have the following meaning. Since $Z'Z = VS'U'USV' = VS'SV'$, we have $Z'ZV = VS'S = V \, \text{diag}(\sigma_1^2, \ldots, \sigma_r^2, 0 \ldots, 0)$. Hence, the columns of V are unit-length, mutually perpendicular eigenvectors of $Z'Z$, and $\sigma_1^2, \ldots, \sigma_r^2$ are the nonzero eigenvalues of $Z'Z$. Similarly, the columns of U are unit-length, mutually perpendicular eigenvectors of ZZ'. With the aid of the SVD, the pseudoinverse of Z can easily be given explicitly. If we write

$$S^+ = \begin{bmatrix} D^{-1} & O \\ O & O \end{bmatrix}, \tag{4}$$

then $Z^+ = VS^+U'$ is the pseudoinverse of Z (see, for instance, Magnus and Neudecker, 1988 and Horn and Johnson, 1985 for more details on SVD and pseudoinverses).

Orthogonal Projections

If $\mathcal{L}$ is a linear subspace, we denote by $P_{\mathcal{L}}x$ the orthogonal projection of a vector x onto $\mathcal{L}$ and by $P_{\mathcal{L}\perp}x = Q_{\mathcal{L}}x = x - P_{\mathcal{L}}x$ its projection onto the orthogonal complement of $\mathcal{L}$. If $\mathcal{L}$ has dimension l and is spanned by the independent vectors $z_1, \ldots, z_l$, then $P_{\mathcal{L}}x = P_Z x$, where $Z = [z_1, \ldots, z_l]$ and $P_Z = Z(Z'Z)^{-1}Z'$. In particular, if the vectors z_i are mutually perpendicular unit vectors, the projection of x is then simply $ZZ'x = z_1z_1'x + \ldots + z_lz_l'x$. If the matrix Z is not full rank, P_Z can still be written as

$$P_Z = ZZ^+ = u_1u_1' + \cdots + u_ru_r' \tag{5}$$

where $u_1, \ldots, u_r$ are the first r columns of the U matrix in the SVD of Z (and r is the rank of Z). Consider now the problem of finding a vector w which minimizes $F(w) = \|c - Mw\|^2$. In other words, we are looking for the vector in the image of M (the space spanned by the columns of M) which is closest to c. Clearly this is the orthogonal projection of c onto the image of M. In particular, if M is of full rank, then at the optimum we must have $M(M'M)^{-1}M'c = Mw$ or, equivalently, $w = (M'M)^{-1}M'c$. The Hessian of F is $2M'M$; hence, if M is full rank, the Hessian is positive definite and the problem is strictly convex without any other critical points.

Least-Squares Regression

The problem of linear regression is the following. Given a set of n-dimensional input vectors $x_1, \ldots, x_T$ and a corresponding set of m-dimensional output vectors $y_1, \ldots, y_T$ (as already mentioned, all patterns are assumed to be centered), find an $m \times n$ matrix A which minimizes $E(A) = \langle \|y_t - Ax_t\|^2 \rangle$. In other words, linear regression is exactly the usual learning problem in a linear network without any hidden units. Since the output units are completely uncoupled, the connection weights for each of them can be synthesized separately, and therefore one needs only to consider the case $m = 1$ (i.e., $A = a'$). In this case, the problem has a simple geometrical interpretation: find a hyperplane through the origin in $(n + 1)$-dimensional space which best fits (in the least-squares sense) a cloud of T points with coordinates $(x'_1, y_1)', \ldots, (x'_T, y_T)'$. Now

$$E(a) = \langle (y_t - a'x_t)^2 \rangle = a'\Sigma_{XX}a - 2\Sigma_{YK}a + \langle y_t^2 \rangle \tag{6}$$

and

$$\frac{\partial E}{\partial a} = 2\Sigma_{XX}a - 2\Sigma_{XY}. \tag{7}$$

E is continuous, differentiable, and bounded below by zero, and therefore it must reach its minimum for a vector a satisfying $\Sigma_{XX}a = \Sigma_{XY}$. If Σ_{XX} is positive definite, then there is a unique solution given by

$$a = \Sigma_{XX}^{-1}\Sigma_{XY}, \tag{2.7}$$

and, in addition, E is strictly convex (with Hessian $2\Sigma_{XX}$) and so without any local minima (or even without any other critical point). The landscape is therefore as simple as possible, and this remains true even if some of the connections are forced in advance to take some fixed values, typically zero in the case of "local" connectivity (this introduces linear, thus convex, restrictions on the set of possible weights). When $m > 1$, everything goes through mutatis mutandis. In the definite positive case, the unique optimal A is called the slope matrix of the regression of y on x and is given by

$$A = \Sigma_{YX}\Sigma_{XX}^{-1}, \tag{9}$$

which generalizes Equation (8), taking into account that $A = a'$ in one dimension. (Formally, to reduce the m-dimensional case it is sufficient to notice that E can be rewritten as $E(A) = \|\text{vec } Y - (X' \otimes I)\text{vec } A\|^2/T$ where $\otimes$ denotes the Kronecker product of two matrices and "vec" is an operator which transforms a matrix into a vector by stacking its columns one above the other (see Baldi and Hornik, 1989 for details). In particular, even if the connectivity between the input and the output is local, the problem remains convex and without local minima and therefore, in principle easy to learn by a gradient-descent type of mechanism. Finally, notice that if for an input x_t we approximate the corresponding output pattern y_t by its linear estimate $\hat{y}_t = \Sigma_{YX}\Sigma_{XX}^{-1}x_t$, then the covariance matrix of the estimates is $\Sigma = \langle \hat{y}_t\hat{y}'_t \rangle = \Sigma_{YX}\Sigma_{XX}^{-1}\Sigma_{XY}$.

Principal-Component Analysis

Suppose we are given a collection of T objects. For each object x_t, the measurements of the same n characteristics $x_{1,t}, \ldots, x_{n,t}$ are available, and assume it is desired to extract some "structure" or "main features" from this collection of data. For efficient classification, it is obviously useful to compress the high-dimensional input data into something low-dimensional without discarding too much relevant information. Of course, there are several different techniques for feature extraction and data compression. One of the simplest and most general-purpose ones is a statistical method known as principal component analysis (PCA).

By possibly subtracting the average $\langle x_t \rangle$, we can think of the data set $x_{i,t}$ ($1 \leq i \leq n$, $1 \leq t \leq T$) as a cloud of T points in n-dimensional Euclidean space centered around the origin. In order to capture the main features of the data set, PCA is *looking for directions along which the dispersion or variance of the point cloud is maximal*, that is, looking for subspaces $\mathscr{L}$ such that the projection of the points x_t onto $\mathscr{L}$ has a maximal variance. If $\mathscr{L}$ is the line spanned by the unit vector a, the projection $P_{\mathscr{L}}x_t$ is given by $P_a x_t = aa'x_t$ with squared length $\|P_a x_t\|^2 = (a'x_t)^2 = a'x_t x_t'a$. Hence, the average dispersion of the data set in the direction of the line is $\langle \|P_a x_t\|^2 \rangle = \langle a'x_t x_t'a \rangle = a' \langle x_t x_t' \rangle a = a'\Sigma_{XX}a$, where $\Sigma_{XX} = \langle x_t x_t' \rangle$ is the data covariance matrix. PCA looks for a unit vector a which maximizes $a'\Sigma_{XX}a$ over the set of all unit vectors. If $\lambda_1 > \ldots > \lambda_n > 0$ are the eigenvalues of Σ_{XX} with eigenvectors $u_1, \ldots, u_n$, then, by the previous result on quadratic forms, we know that $a = u_1$ (or equivalently $-u_1$) is the answer.

To sum up, PCA starts by finding the direction in which the dispersion of the cloud is maximal, which is the direction u_1 of the first eigenvector of the data covariance matrix. The first "feature" which is extracted is the *first principal component* $u_1'x_t$. The component of the data "explained" by the first principal component is the projection onto the line spanned by u_1. What remains unexplained is the dispersion of the residual $x_t - P_{u_1}x_t$ which is just the projection $Q_{u_1}x_t$ of x_t onto the orthogonal complement of u_1. In a second step, we proceed as before, but with the points x_t replaced by $Q_{u_1}x_t$. That is, we look for straight lines $\mathscr{L}$ *perpendicular to the line spanned by* u_1 such that the projections of the points $Q_{u_1}x_t$ have maximal variance. This amounts to finding a unit vector b, perpendicular to u_1, which maximizes $b'\Sigma_{XX}b$ over all unit vectors perpendicular to u_1. Again, by the previous result, we know the answer is $b = \pm u_2$, and so forth. At the kth step, we look for lines $\mathscr{L}$ perpendicular to the space spanned by $u_1, \ldots, u_{k-1}$ such that the projections of the points x_t along $\mathscr{L}$ have maximal dispersion. This is achieved by choosing $\mathscr{L}$ as the line spanned by u_k.

After the completion of p steps, we extract the first p principal components $u_1'x_t, \ldots, u_p'x_t$ and reduce x_t to its projection onto the hyperplane spanned by the first p eigenvectors. One may be interested in asking whether this is the best possible data reduction of the kind under consideration, that is, the best possible projection of the data onto a p-dimensional hyperplane $\mathscr{H}$ in the sense that the projections of the data onto $\mathscr{H}$ have maximal variance. After all, a better result might have been achieved by choosing the hyperplane in a single step. However, this is not the case.

Among all p-dimensional hyperplanes $\mathcal{H}$, the one spanned by the first p principal vectors $u_1, \ldots, u_p$ is the hyperplane such that $\langle \|P_{\mathcal{H}}x_t\|^2 \rangle$ is maximal. Equivalently, it is the hyperplane for which the average projection error $\langle \|x_t - P\mathcal{H}x_t\|^2 \rangle$ is minimal.

It is therefore possible to incrementally build the PCA feature extractor. Since $\mathcal{H}$ is the best p-dimensional hyperplane we can fit to the n-dimensional point cloud, the "flatter" the cloud the better the fit. It is worth investigating how good the fit is, that is, how much of the variance in the data set is actually explained by the first p principal components? This is easily computed, for the variance of the ith component is given by

$$\langle \|P_{u_i}x_t\|^2 \rangle = \langle (u_i'x_t)^2 \rangle = u_i' \Sigma_{XX} u_i = u_i' \lambda_i u_i = \lambda_i.$$

The total variance being equal to the sum of all the eigenvalues of Σ_{XX}, *the proportion of total variance explained by the first p principal components equals* $(\lambda_1 + \cdots + \lambda_p)/(\lambda_1 + \cdots + \lambda_n)$.

In fact, PCA performs "best data compression" among a wider class of methods. Let us write $U_p = [u_1, \ldots, u_p]$ for the matrix having the first p normalized eigenvectors of Σ_{XX} as its columns and let us stack the first p features $u_1'x_t, \ldots, u_p'x_t$ extracted by PCA into a column vector z_t. Then $z_t = U_p'x_t$ and $P_{U_p}x_t = U_pU_p'x_t = U_pz_t$. Hence, PCA is one method that linearly compresses n-dimensional inputs x_t into p-dimensional vectors z_t for some $p < n$, that is, $z = Bx$ for a suitable $p \times n$ matrix B. Linear reconstruction of the data can then be achieved by approximating x by $Az = ABx$ for some suitable $n \times p$ matrix A.

Among all $n \times p$ matrices A and $p \times n$ matrices B, optimal linear data compression, in the sense that the average reconstruction error $\langle \|x_t - ABx_t\|^2 \rangle$ is minimized, is achieved if and only if the global map $W = AB$ equals the orthogonal projection P_{U_p} onto the hyperplane spanned by the first p eigenvectors of Σ_{XX}.

Finally, if we compute the covariance of two principal components, we find that for $i \neq j$,

$$\langle (u_i'x_t)(u_j'x_t) \rangle = \langle u_i'x_tx_t'u_j \rangle = u_i' \langle x_tx_t' \rangle u_j = \lambda_j u_i'u_j = 0.$$

Thus different components are uncorrelated and we can think of the transformation of x_t into the vector of n principal components $[u_1'x_t, \ldots, u_n'x_t]'$ as an orthogonal transformation of the Euclidean space such that in the new system of coordinates the components of the points in the cloud are uncorrelated and with decreasing variance. Again, if only the first few coordinates in the new system vary significantly, we may essentially locate points by giving only these few coordinates.

PCA can also be examined from an information-theoretic standpoint and shown to be optimal, under simple assumptions, for a different measure. More precisely, consider a transmission channel (in our case, one can think of the network connecting the input units to the hidden units) with n-dimensional centered input vectors having a Gaussian distribution with covariance matrix $\Sigma_{XX} = \langle xx' \rangle$. The output of the channel are constrained to be p-dimensional vectors of the form $y = Lx$, for some $p \times n$ matrix L (and, without any loss of generality, we can assume that L has rank p, $p < n$). Hence, y is also Gaussian with covariance matrix $L\Sigma_{XX}L'$. Classically, the differential entropy of x is given by (see, for instance, Blahut, 1987 for more details)

$$H(x) = - \int p(x)\ln p(x) \, dx = \frac{1}{2} \ln[(2\pi e)^n \det\Sigma_{XX}], \qquad (10)$$

and similarly

$$H(y) = \tfrac{1}{2} \ln[(2\pi e)^p \det(L\Sigma_{XX}L')]. \qquad (11)$$

The conditional distribution of x given y (for instance Kshirsagar, 1972) is normal with mean

$$\mu_{X.Y} = \Sigma_{XY}\Sigma_{Y}^{-1}y = \Sigma L'(L\Sigma L')^{-1}y \qquad (12)$$

and covariance matrix

$$\Sigma_{XX.Y} = \Sigma_{XX} - \Sigma_{XY}\Sigma_{Y}^{-1}\Sigma_{YK} = \Sigma - \Sigma L'(L\Sigma L')^{-1}L\Sigma. \qquad (13)$$

It can be shown that $H(x/y)$, the conditional entropy of x given y (i.e., the entropy of the conditional distribution), is given by

$$H(x/y) = \tfrac{1}{2} \ln((2\pi e)^{n-p}\gamma_1 \cdots \gamma_{n-p}), \qquad (14)$$

where $\gamma_1 \geq \cdots \geq \gamma_{n-p} > 0$ are the nonzero eigenvalues of $\Sigma_{XX.Y}$. As the entropy is one way of measuring our uncertainty, it is desirable to choose L so as to minimize $H(x/y)$. It can be shown that the optimal L is of the form $L = CU$ where C is an invertible $p \times p$ matrix and $U = [u_1, \ldots, u_p]'$. In particular, this choice also maximizes the information that y conveys about x measured by the mutual information $I(x, y)$ defined to be

$$I(x, y) = H(x) - H(x/y) \qquad (15)$$

with value

$$I_{PCA}(x, y) - \tfrac{1}{2} \ln((2\pi e)^p \lambda_1 \cdots \lambda_p). \qquad (16)$$

Thus, at least in the Gaussian setting, up to trivial transformations the optimal linear map maximizing the mutual information is the principal-component analyzer. Finally, PCA can also be connected to optimal inference methods (see Linsker, 1988).

To illustrate the PCA feature extraction technique, consider the "open/closed book" data set in Mardia, Kent, and Bibby (1979 Table 1.2.1, p. 3f). The data consist of the scores of $T = 88$ students on examinations in mechanics, vectors, algebra, analysis, and statistics (i.e., $n = 5$), where the first two exams were closed book and the other three were open book. For each exam, the best possible score was 100. It is found that the average score $\langle x \rangle$ equals (39.0, 50.6, 50.6, 46.7, 42.3)' and that the eigenvalues of the covariance matrix Σ_{XX} are given by $\lambda_1 = 679.2$, $\lambda_2 = 199.8$, $\lambda_3 = 102.6$, $\lambda_4 = 83.7$, and $\lambda_5 = 31.8$. Hence, the first two principal components already explain 80% of the variance in the data (and 91% is achieved with the first three). The first two eigenvectors are $u_1 = (0.51, 0.37, 0.35, 0.45, 0.53)'$ and $u_2 = (0.75, 0.21, -0.08, -0.30, -0.55)'$. These findings can easily be interpreted: the authors conclude that ". . . the first principal component gives positive weight to all the variables and thus represents an average grade. On the other hand, the second principal component represents a contrast between the open-book and closed-book examinations. . . ." For example, the scores and first two principal components of the two best students are (77, 82, 67, 67, 81), 66.4, and 6.4, and (63, 78, 80, 70, 81), 63.7, and -6.4. Even without looking at the individual test scores, by considering only the first two principal components one would conclude that the overall performances of the two students are very similar, but the first student did better on closed-book and the second one better on open-book exams.

In conclusion, PCA is optimal in the least-mean-square sense and can serve two purposes: data compression by projecting high-dimensional data into a lower-dimensional space and feature extraction by revealing, through the principal components, relevant but unexpected structure hidden in the data (although an interpretation of the new dimensions in terms of the original variables may not always be straightforward).

Mean-Square Classifier and Discriminant Analysis

Consider now the problem where the patterns x_t must be classified into m classes $C_1, \ldots, C_m$, with, in general, $m \ll n$. Thus for every input pattern x_t, there is a binary target output pattern $y_t = (0, \ldots, 1, \ldots, 0)'$ where $y_{i,t} = 1$ if and only if x_t belongs to C_i. One possible classification method consists in finding an $m \times n$ matrix L such that $\langle \|y_t - Lx_t\|^2 \rangle$ is minimal. Needless to say, this is a special case of least squares regression, and, as we have seen, under the usual assumptions the optimal L is given by $L = \Sigma_{YX}\Sigma_{XX}^{-1}$ and is called the *mean-square classifier*.

In a lot of applications n is very large compared to m and therefore it becomes useful to first reduce the dimensionality of the input data. One is thus led to find a linear subspace of dimension p such that, when projected onto this subspace, the patterns x_t fall as much as possible into well-defined separated clusters facilitating the classification. This problem of finding an optimal projection is similar to the one encountered in PCA. However, because of the clustering, a new measure must be introduced to compare different projections. Consider a projection $z_t = C'x_t$, where C is an $n \times p$ matrix. The total dispersion (variation) in the x-sample can be decomposed into the sum of within class dispersions and between class dispersions. When the x's are centered, the total dispersion is Σ_{XX}, and the dispersion between classes can be shown to be $\Sigma_{XY}\Sigma_{YY}^{-1}\Sigma_{YX}$. Upon projecting the patterns, the corresponding total and between classes dispersions of the z_t patterns become $C'\Sigma_{XX}C$ and $C'\Sigma_{XY}\Sigma_{YY}^{-1}\Sigma_{YX}C$. A projection is optimal if the between classes variation of the z's is as large as possible relative to the total variation. Different cost functions can be introduced at this stage. If the size of a variation matrix is measured by its determinant (the determinant of a matrix measures the volume of the image of a unit cube under the corresponding linear map), then we are led to the problem of finding an $n \times p$ matrix C maximizing the ratio

$$E(C) = \frac{\det(C'\Sigma_{XY}\Sigma_{YY}^{-1}\Sigma_{YX}C)}{\det(C'\Sigma_{XX}C)}. \tag{17}$$

The solution is well known: *all optimal matrices, the so-called discriminant analysis (DA) matrices, are of the form $H_p R$, where H_p has the first p eigenvectors of $\Sigma_{XX}^{-1}\Sigma_{XY}\Sigma_{YY}^{-1}\Sigma_{YX}$ as its columns and R is an arbitrary $p \times p$ invertible matrix.*

It is not easy to see what the solutions look like in general. However there is one case where all optimal solutions can easily be described.

When $p = r = \mathrm{rank}\Sigma_{XY}$, an $n \times p$ matrix C is a DA matrix if and only if the space spanned by the columns of C coincides with the space spanned by the column of L', where $L = \Sigma_{YX}\Sigma_{XX}^{-1}$ is the mean-square classifier.

(See, for instance, Kshirsager, 1972 for more details on DA.)

BACK PROPAGATION

The Landscape Properties of *E*

We now consider the setting described in the introduction where the learning procedure is based on the minimization of the cost function $E(A, B)$. A complete description of the landscape properties of E is given in Baldi and Hornik (1989). We shall here briefly review the most salient features. E is best described in terms of its critical points, that is, the points where $\partial E/\partial a_{i,j} = \partial E/\partial b_{i,j} = 0$. It is first important to observe that if C is any $p \times p$ invertible matrix, then $E(A, B) = E(AC, C^{-1}B)$. Therefore at any point E really depends on the global map $W = AB$ rather than on A and B. For instance, there is an infinite family of pairs of matrices (A, B) corresponding to any critical point. However, unlike the simple case of linear regression, W cannot be chosen arbitrarily: the network architecture constrains W to have at most rank p.

The remarkable property of the landscape of E is the absence of local minima in spite of the fact that E is not convex (nor is the set of all matrices of rank at most p). E is characterized by a unique global minimum (up to multiplication by a matrix C). All other critical points are saddle points. The structure of the critical points can be described completely. More precisely, assume for simplicity that $p \leq m \leq n$ and that $\Sigma = \Sigma_{YX}\Sigma_{XX}^{-1}\Sigma_{XY}$, the covariance matrix of the linear estimates $\hat{y}_t$ (see the second section) is full rank with m distinct eigenvalues $\lambda_1 > \cdots > \lambda_m$ and corresponding orthonormal eigenvectors $u_1, \ldots, u_m$. If $\mathcal{J} = \{i_1, \ldots, i_p\}$ ($1 \leq i_1 < \cdots < i_p \leq m$) is any ordered p-index set, let $U_\mathcal{J}$ denote the matrix $[u_{i_1}, \ldots, u_{i_p}]$. Then two full-rank matrices A and B define a critical point of E if and only if there exist an ordered p-index set $\mathcal{J}$ and an invertible $p \times p$ matrix C such that

$$A = U_\mathcal{J}C, \tag{18}$$

$$B = C^{-1}U'_\mathcal{J}\Sigma_{YX}\Sigma_{XX}^{-1}. \tag{19}$$

For such a critical point we have

$$W = P_{U_\mathcal{J}}\Sigma_{YX}\Sigma_{XX}^{-1} \tag{20}$$

$$E(A,B) = \text{tr } \Sigma_{YY} - \sum_{i \in \mathcal{J}} \lambda_i. \tag{21}$$

Therefore a critical W of rank p is always the product of the ordinary least squares regression matrix followed by an orthogonal projection onto the subspace spanned by p eigenvectors of Σ. The critical map W associated with the index set $\{1, 2, \ldots, p\}$ is the unique local and global minimum of E. The remaining $\binom{m}{p} - 1$ p-index sets correspond to saddle points. All additional critical points defined by matrices A and B which are not of full rank are also saddle points and can be characterized in terms of orthogonal projections onto subspaces spanned by q eigenvectors, with $q < p$ (see Figure 2). In the auto-associative case, Equations (18), (19), and (20) become

$$A = U_\mathcal{J}C, \tag{22}$$

$$B = C^{-1}U'_\mathcal{J}, \tag{23}$$

$$W = P_{U_\mathcal{J}}, \tag{24}$$

and therefore the unique locally and globally optimal map W is the orthogonal projection onto the space spanned by the first p eigenvectors of Σ_{XX}.

This analysis links back propagation in linear networks to several classical statistical techniques. In particular, at the global minimum of E, if $C = I_p$ then the activities in the hidden layer are given by $u'_1\hat{y}_t, \ldots, u'_p\hat{y}_t$, the principal components of the least-squares estimators $\hat{y}_t$ (see, for instance, Kshirsagar, 1972). In the autoassociative mode, these activities are given by $u'_1 x_t, \ldots, u'_p x_t$ and correspond to the coordinates of the vector x_t along the first p eigenvectors of Σ_{XX} as in the usual PCA. In general, if the initial conditions are random, one should not expect the back-propagation algorithm to converge to an optimum satisfying $C = I_p$. In the autoassociative case, this means that the rows of the final B and $u_1, \ldots, u_p$ will span the same space but $B' \neq [u_1, \ldots, u_p]$.

THE LANDSCAPE OF E

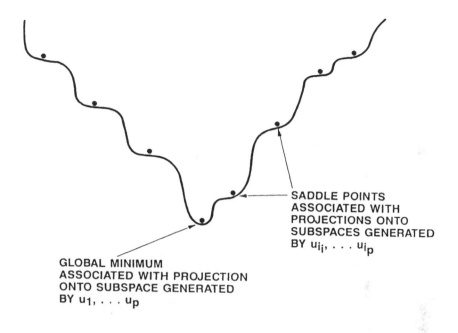

SADDLE POINTS
ASSOCIATED WITH
PROJECTIONS ONTO
SUBSPACES GENERATED
BY $u_{i_i}, \ldots u_{i_p}$

GLOBAL MINIMUM
ASSOCIATED WITH PROJECTION
ONTO SUBSPACE GENERATED
BY $u_1, \ldots u_p$

$u_1 \ldots, u_n$ ARE NORMALIZED EIGENVECTORS
CORRESPONDING TO THE EIGENVALUES
$\lambda_1 > \lambda_2 > \ldots \lambda_n > 0$ OF THE COVARIANCE MATRIX Σ

Figure 2.   The landscape of E (one caveat is that, in highly dimensional spaces, the direction of approach to and escape from a saddle point are usually distinct).

Although at first sight this may seem a drawback, it must be regarded as a property leading to more robust networks. Indeed, in a physical implementation where the compressed version of the data in the hidden layer is to be sent to further processing layers, it is not desirable that one of the units, extracting the principal component, have a variance much larger than the other units.[2] A more balanced strategy, where all the variances in the hidden layer are comparable, is by far preferable and is commonly observed in simulations.

Since the optimal solution can be expressed analytically, it can also be ob-

---

[2]It is known, for instance, that in the case of random symmetric matrices, $\lambda_2 \ll \lambda_1$ almost always (see Füredi and Komlós, 1981).

tained effectively with numerical analysis techniques without resorting to any descent procedure. However, as pointed out in the introduction, this is not the most relevant point of view here where the emphasis is on the learning behavior and emergent organizational principles of simple adaptive networks.

One of the central issues in learning from examples is the problem of generalization, that is, how does the network perform when exposed to a pattern never seen previously? In this setting, a precise quantitative answer can be given to this question. For instance, in the autoassociative case, the distortion on a new pattern is exactly given by its distance to the subspace generated by the first p eigenvectors of Σ_{XX}.

In the special case where rank(Σ_{XY}) = r = p, Gallinari, Thiria, and Fogelman Soulie (1988) have shown that if an $n - p - m$ architecture is trained to classify n-dimensional inputs into m ($m < n$) classes, then the corresponding network performs discriminant analysis in the sense that, for an optimal $W = AB$, B' is a *DA* matrix. In other words, under these assumptions, the projection realized by B' maximizes the ratio given in Equation (17). However, in this context, either $p = r = m$, in which case the architecture is $n - m - m$ and there is no bottleneck, or $r < m$ and then full classification into m categories is not supported by the available data and there is no proper data compression (only filtering out of linear dependencies). In any case, all the network ever learns is to be a mean-square classifier, and this can be achieved without any hidden layer.

Deep Networks, Local Connectivity, Nonlinearities, and Bias

In Baldi (1989), the case of deep networks with multiple hidden layers is briefly examined. It is easy to see that, in this case, the main constraint on the network comes from its bottleneck, that is, from the hidden layer with smallest size p (clearly p could be attained in more than one hidden layer). Although the expression for the critical points may now become more involved, the main features of the landscape are unchanged: a multiplicity of saddle points, an absence of local minima, and a unique optimal input/output map satisfying Equation (20) with $\mathcal{I} = \{1, \ldots, p\}$.

The bottleneck layer imposes a rank restriction on the map computed by the network. Additional important constraints can be introduced on the geometry of the connections. Often connections are assumed to be local, in the sense that a unit in one layer receives projections only from a restricted subset of elements in the previous layer, for instance according to a Gaussian distribution. These geometrical constraints play an essential role in self-organizing maps and in a number of models of "linear" cortical development (see, for instance, Linsker, 1988 and Miller, Keller, and Stryker, 1989). These topics deserve separate treatment and will not be addressed here. However, as mentioned in the previous section, in the case of a locally connected linear network without any hidden layer the landscape of the usual quadratic error is again completely devoid of local minima. Learning by descent methods should then be efficient. The landscape properties of linear locally connected multilayer networks have not been carefully studied yet, and the previous results only give lower bounds. In particular, the question of whether the landscape of the error function of a linear feed-forward network, with *local* connections, has any local minima remains open, in spite of its disarming simplicity.

In the case of nonlinear units, few analytical results are known, but certainly local minima do appear. However, an important remark has been made by Bourlard and Kamp, 1988. In the autoassociative mode, it is natural to use linear units in the output layer. Under these conditions, *nothing is to be gained by using nonlinear elements in the hidden layer.* This is basically because the network is trying to approximate a linear map: the identity function. The remark can be extended to any linear map. That is, if the set of pairs (x_t, y_t) of examples is such that, for every t, $y_t = F(x_t)$ where F is linear, then nonlinear units in the hidden layer can lead to an approximation of F which is at best equivalent to the approximation obtainable by using linear units exclusively. Reports of simulations in the literature confirm this point and sometimes seem to indicate that the solution found using nonlinear elements is "close" to PCA (Cottrell, Munro, and Zipser, 1988).

Finally, if it is not desirable to assume the existence of a preprocessing stage where the data are centered, then the theory can easily be extended to the case of linear units with bias (see, for instance, Bourlard and Kamp, 1989; Williams, 1985 for more details).

Noise Analysis

How robust are the previous results against the effects of noise? Different sorts of noise can be introduced, for instance at the level of the synaptic weights or of the activation functions. To fix the ideas, assume in our case that the activation functions in both the hidden layer and the output layer are "noisy." Hence for an input x, the output of the hidden layer is $w = Bx + e$ and the activity in the output units is $z = Aw + u = ABx + Ae + u$. Assume that the noise terms e and u have mean 0, covariance matrices Σ_{EE} and Σ_{UU} and that they are uncorrelated with each other and with the patterns x and y. It is also reasonable to assume for simplicity that Σ_{EE} is full rank. We are now interested in the problem of minimizing

$$\bar{E}(A, B) = \langle \|y_t - (ABx_t + Ae_t + u_t)\|^2 \rangle = E(A, B) + \mathrm{tr}(A\Sigma_{EE}A')$$
$$+ \mathrm{tr}\, \Sigma_{UU}. \tag{25}$$

Observe that the term $\mathrm{tr}\Sigma_{UU}$ is just an additive constant and has no influence on the variation of $\bar{E}$ with A and B. For any positive μ, $\bar{E}(A/\mu, \mu B) - \bar{E}(A, B) = \mathrm{tr}(A\Sigma_{EE}A')(1 - \mu^2)/\mu^2$. Thus, if $A \neq 0$ and $\mu > 1$, then $\bar{E}(A/\mu, \mu B) < \bar{E}(A, B)$.

As a result, without any additional constraints, there is no optimal pair (A, B). This is intuitively clear for the network will try to make B as large as possible and/or A as small as possible so that the signal dominates the noise. It is therefore necessary to constrain the entries of B, which leads to the problem of minimizing Equation (25) with A arbitrary and $B \in \mathcal{B}$, where $\mathcal{B}$ is some compact subset of the set of all $p \times n$ matrices containing the origin: for instance, a closed sphere centered at zero. Under these restrictions, the problem has a well-defined solution and an optimal B must lie on the boundary $\partial\mathcal{B}$ of $\mathcal{B}$ (if not, we could find a $\mu > 1$ such that $\mu B \in \mathcal{B}$). Now, let us write $\Sigma_{EE} = \sigma R$, where σ measures the noise level and R is some structure matrix (the simplest case is $R = I$, but if the units are physically close it may be unnatural to assume that the individual components of the noise are uncorrelated). One may intuitively predict (see also Linsker, 1988) the following:

(i) If σ is very small, the solutions of the constrained noisy problem are essentially the same as the solutions of the nonnoisy problem.

(ii) If σ is very large, the solutions of the constrained noisy problem are of maximum redundancy where all the hidden units try to do the same thing (for instance, extract the principal component in the simple autoassociative case).

To see this, we use a continuity and compactness argument. The explicit dependence of $\tilde{E}$ on σ can be taken into account by writing

$$\tilde{E}(A, B) = \tilde{E}_\sigma(A, B) = E(A, B) + \sigma\text{tr}(ARA') + \text{tr}\Sigma_{UU}. \quad (26)$$

As soon as $\sigma \leq 1$ (for example), it is straightforward to see that the solutions of the problem of minimizing $\tilde{E}$ with $B \in \mathcal{B}$ are identical to the solutions of minimizing $\tilde{E}$ with $A \in \mathcal{A}$ and $B \in \mathcal{B}$, where $\mathcal{A}$ is some fixed compact set independent of σ. By Equation (26), as $\sigma \to 0$, $\tilde{E}(A, B)$ converges uniformly to $E(A, B) + \text{tr}\Sigma_{UU}$ over the compact set $\mathcal{A} \times \mathcal{B}$. Since these two functions differ only by an additive constant, the solutions of the noisy constrained problem approach the set of all pairs of matrices (A, B) satisfying Equations (18) and (19), with, in addition, $B \in \mathcal{B}$ (this automatically forces A to be in $\mathcal{A}$ by restricting the norm of the matrix C). In other words,

$$\lim_{\sigma \to 0} \mathcal{B}_\sigma = \{B : B = CU'_p\Sigma_{YX}\Sigma_{XX}^{-1}\} \text{ with } C\ p \times p \text{ invertible}\} \cap \partial\mathcal{B}, \quad (27)$$

where $\mathcal{B}_\sigma$ is the set of all matrices $B \in \mathcal{B}$ which are optimal for noise level σ. The case of very large noise, together with a few additional remarks, is treated in the Appendix.

GENERALIZATION DYNAMICS

This section is essentially taken from Baldi and Chauvin (1991) and is included here for completeness.

Formal Setting

Generalization properties of neural networks trained from examples seem fundamental to connectionist theories but also poorly understood. In practice, the question to be answered is how should one allocate limited resources and parameters, such as network size and architecture, initial conditions, training time, and available examples, in order to optimize generalization performance? One conventional approach is to consider the problem of learning as a surface fitting problem. Accordingly, neural networks should be very constrained, with a minimal number of parameters, in order to avoid the classical "overfitting" problem. In practice, however, not too much is known about overfitting, its nature, and its onset both as a function of network parameters and training time. Furthermore, the conventional view has sometimes been challenged and may need to be revised to some extent. It may be the case, for instance, that a suitable strategy consists rather in designing networks with a little extra parameters. These larger networks must be used in conjunction with a prior distribution on the parameters in a Bayesian framework and/or must be trained for shorter times, based on a careful monitoring of the validation error (see also Wang et al. 1994).

Partial interesting results on generalization problems have been obtained in recent years in terms of VC dimension and statistical mechanics (see, for instance, Baum and Haussler, 1989; Levin, Tishby, and Solla, (1990); and Sompolinsky, Tishby, and Seung, 1990). Most of the results, however, are static in the sense that they study generalization as a function of network architecture or number of examples. Here, we propose a different and complementary approach consisting in a detailed analysis of the temporal evolution of generalization in simple feedforward linear networks. Even in this simple framework, the questions are far from trivial. Thus, we have restricted the problem even further: learning the identity map in a single-layer feedforward linear network. With suitable assumptions on the noise, this setting turns out to be insightful and to yield analytical results which are relevant to what one observes in more complicated situations. Here, we are going first to define our framework and derive the basic equations first in the noiseless case and then in the case of noisy data. The basic point is to derive an expression for the validation function in terms of the statistical properties of the population and the training and validation samples. Then we examine the main results, which consist of an analysis of the landscape of the validation error as a function of training time. Simple simulation results are also presented. Mathematical proofs are deferred to the Appendix.

We consider a simple feedforward network with n input units connected by a weight matrix W to n output linear units. The network is trained to learn the identity function (autoassociation) from a set of centered training patterns $x_1, \ldots, x_T$. The connection weights are adjusted by gradient descent on the usual LMS error function

$$E(W) = \frac{1}{T} \sum_t \|x_t - Wx_t\|^2. \tag{28}$$

The gradient of E with respect to the weights W is

$$\nabla E = (W - I)C, \tag{29}$$

where $C = C_{XX} (= \Sigma_{XX})$ is the covariance matrix of the training set (in this section we introduce several covariance matrices, some of which are different from those appearing in the other sections and therefore we have used the letter C). Thus, the gradient descent learning rule can be expressed as

$$W^{k+1} = W^k - \eta(W^k - I)C, \tag{30}$$

where W^k is the weight matrix after the kth iteration of the algorithm and η is the constant learning rate. If e_i and λ_i ($\lambda_1 \geq \cdots \geq \lambda_n > 0$) denote the eigenvectors and eigenvalues of C, then

$$W^{k+1}e_i = \eta\lambda_i e_i + (1 - \eta\lambda_i)W^k e_i. \tag{31}$$

A simple induction shows that

$$W^k = W^0(I - \eta C)^k - ((I - \eta C)^k - I), \tag{32}$$

and therefore

$$W^k e_i = (1 - (1 - \eta\lambda_i)^k)e_i + (1 - \eta\lambda_i)^k W^0 e_i. \tag{33}$$

The behavior of Equation (33) is clear: provided the learning rate is less than the inverse of the largest eigenvalue ($\eta < 1/\lambda_1$), W^k approaches the identity exponentially fast. This holds for any starting matrix W^0. The eigenvectors of C tend to become eigenvectors W^k, and the corresponding eigenvalues approach 1 at different rates depending on λ_i (larger eigenvalues are learned much faster). As a result, it is not very restrictive to assume, for ease of exposition, that the starting matrix W^0 is diagonal in the e_i basis, that is, $W^0 = \mathrm{diag}(\alpha_i^{(0)})$[3] (in addition, learning is often started with the zero matrix). In this case, Equation (32) becomes

$$W^k e_i = [1 - (1 - \eta\lambda_i)^k(1 - \alpha_i^{(0)})]e_i = \alpha_i^{(k)}e_i. \tag{34}$$

A simple calculation, shows that the corresponding error can be written as

$$E(W^k) = \sum_{i=1}^{n} \lambda_i(\alpha_i^{(k)} - 1)^2 = \sum_{i=1}^{n} \lambda_i(1 - \alpha_i^{(0)})^2(1 - \eta\lambda_i)^{2k}. \tag{35}$$

We now modify the setting so as to introduce noise. To fix the ideas, the reader may think, for instance, that we are dealing with handwritten realizations of single-digit numbers. In this case, there are 10 possible patterns but numerous possible noisy realizations. In general, we assume that there is a population

---

[3]Superscripts on the sequence α are in parentheses to avoid possible confusion with exponentiation.

of patterns of the form $x_p + n_p$, where x_p denotes the signal and n_p denotes the noise, characterized by the covariance matrices $\bar{C}_{XX}$, $\bar{C}_{NN}$, and $\bar{C}_{XN}$. Here, as everywhere else, we assume that the signal and the noise are centered. A sample $x_t + n_t$ ($1 \leq t \leq T$) from this population is used as a training set. The training sample is characterized by the covariance matrices $C = C_{XX}$, C_{NN}, and C_{XN} calculated over the sample. Similarly, a different sample $x_v + n_v$ from the population is used as a validation set. The validation sample is characterized by the covariance matrices $C' = C'_{XX}$, C'_{NN}, and C'_{XN}. To make the calculations tractable, we shall make, when necessary, several assumptions. First, $\bar{C} = C = C'$; thus there is a common basis of eigenvectors e_i and corresponding eigenvalues λ_i for the signal in the population and in the training and validation sample. Then, with respect to this basis of eigenvectors, the noise covariance matrices are diagonal: $C_{NN} = \mathrm{diag}(v_i)$ and $C'_{NN} = \mathrm{diag}(\eta'_i)$. Finally, the signal and the noise are always uncorrelated: $C_{XN} = C'_{XN} = 0$. Obviously, it also makes sense to assume that $\bar{C}_{NN} = \mathrm{diag}(\bar{v}_i)$ and $\bar{C}_{XN} = 0$, although these assumptions are not needed in the main calculation. Thus we make the simplifying assumptions that both on the training and validation patterns the covariance matrix of the signal is identical to the covariance of the signal over the entire population, that the components of the noise are uncorrelated and that the signal and the noise are uncorrelated. Yet we allow the estimates v_i and v'_i of the variance of the components of the noise to be different in the training and validation sets.

For a given W, the LMS error function over the training patterns is now

$$E(W) = \frac{1}{T} \sum_t \|x_t - W(x_p + n_t)\|^2. \tag{36}$$

Differentiating gives

$$\nabla E = W(C + C_{NX} + C_{XN} + C_{NN}) - C - C_{XN}, \tag{37}$$

and since $C_{XN} = C_{NX} = 0$, the gradient is

$$\nabla E = (W - I)C + WC_{NN}. \tag{38}$$

To compute the image of any eigenvector e_i during training, we have

$$W^{k+1}e_i = \eta\lambda_i e_i + (1 - \eta\lambda_i - \eta v_i)W^k e_i. \tag{39}$$

Thus, by induction

$$W^k = W^0 M^k - C(C + C_{NN})^{-1}(M^k - I), \tag{40}$$

where $M = I - v(C + C_{NN})$, and

$$W^k e_i = \frac{\lambda_i}{\lambda_i + v_i}[1 - (1 - \eta\lambda_i - \eta v_i)^k]e_i + (1 - \eta\lambda_i - \eta v_i)^k W^0 e_i. \tag{41}$$

Again if we assume here, as in the rest of the chapter, that the learning rate satisfies $\eta < \min[1/(\lambda_i + v_i)]$, the eigenvectors of C tend to become eigenvectors of W^k, and W^k approaches exponentially fast the diagonal matrix $\text{diag}(\lambda_i/(\lambda_i + v_i))$. Assuming that $W^0 = \text{diag}(\alpha_i^{(0)})$ in the e_i basis, we get

$$W^k e_i = \frac{\lambda_i}{\lambda_i + v_i}(1 - b_i a_i^k)e_i = \alpha_i^{(k)}e_i, \tag{42}$$

where $b_i = 1 - \alpha_i^{(0)}(\lambda_i + v_i)/\lambda_i$ and $a_i = (1 - v\lambda_i - \eta v_i)$. Notice that $0 < a_i < 1$. Since the signal and the noise are uncorrelated, the error in general can be written in the form

$$E(W) = \frac{1}{P} \sum_p x_p' x_p - x_p' W x_p - x_p' W' x_p + x_p' W' W x_p + n_p' W' W n_p. \tag{43}$$

Using the fact that $C_{NN} = \text{diag}(v_i)$ and $W^k = \text{diag}(\alpha_i^{(k)})$, we have

$$E(W^k) = \sum_{i=1}^n \lambda_i - 2\lambda_i\alpha_i^{(k)} + \lambda_i(\alpha_i^{(k)})^2 + v_i(\alpha_i^{(k)})^2, \tag{44}$$

and finally

$$E(W^k) = \sum_{i=1}^n \lambda_i(1 - \alpha_i^{(k)})^2 + v_i(\alpha_i^{(k)})^2. \tag{45}$$

It is easy to see that $E(W^k)$ is a monotonically decreasing function of k which approaches an asymptotic residual error value given by

$$E(W^\infty) = \sum_{i=1}^n \frac{\lambda q_i v_i}{\lambda_i + v_i}. \tag{46}$$

For any matrix W, we can define the validation error to be

$$E^V(W) = \frac{1}{V} \sum_v \|x_v - W(x_v + n_v)\|^2. \tag{47}$$

Using the fact that $C_{XN}' = 0$ and $C_{NN}' = \text{diag}(v_i')$, a derivation similar to Equation (45) shows that the validation error $E^V(W^k)$ is

$$E^V(W^k) = \sum_{i=1}^n \lambda_i(1 - \alpha_i^{(k)})^2 + v_i'(\alpha_i^{(k)})^2. \tag{48}$$

Clearly, as $k \to \infty$, $E^V(W^k)$ approaches its horizontal asymptote, which is independent of $\alpha_i^{(0)}$ and given by

$$E^V(W^\infty) = \sum_{i=1}^n \frac{\lambda_i(v_i^2 + v_i'\lambda_i)}{(\lambda_i + v_i)^2}. \tag{49}$$

However, it is the behavior of E^V before it reaches its asymptotic value which is of most interest to us. This behavior, as we shall see, can be fairly complicated.

Validation Analysis

Obviously, $d\alpha_i^{(k)}/dk = -(\lambda_i b_i a_i^k \log a_i)/(\lambda_i + v_i)$. Thus using Equation (48) and collecting terms yield

$$\frac{dE^V(W^k)}{dk} = \sum_{i=1}^{n} \frac{2\lambda_i^2 b_i \log a_i}{(\lambda_i + v_i)^2} a_i^k [v_i - v_i' + b_i a_i^k (\lambda_i + v_i')], \qquad (50)$$

or, in more compact form,

$$\frac{dE^V}{dk} = \sum_{i=1}^{n} A_i a_i^k + B_i a_i^{2k}, \qquad (51)$$

with

$$A_i = \frac{2\lambda_i^2 b_i}{(\lambda_i + v_i)^2} (v_i - v_i') \log a_i, \qquad (52)$$

and

$$B_i = \frac{2\lambda_i^2 b_i^2}{(\lambda_i + v_i)^2} (\lambda_i + v_i') \log a_i. \qquad (53)$$

The behavior of E^V depends on the relative size of v_i and v_i' and the initial conditions $\alpha_i^{(0)}$, which together determine the signs of b_i, A_i, and B_i. The main result we can prove is:

Assume that learning is started with the zero matrix or with a matrix with sufficiently small weights satisfying, for every i,

$$\alpha_i^{(0)} \leq \min \left(\frac{\lambda_i}{\lambda_i + v_i}, \frac{\lambda_i}{\lambda_i + v_i'} \right). \qquad (54)$$

(1) If for every i, $v_i' \leq v_i$, then the validation function E^V decreases monotonically to its asymptotic value and training should be continued as long as possible.

(2) If for every i, $v_i' > v_i$, then the validation function E^V decreases monotonically to a unique minimum and then increases monotonically to its asymptotic value.

The derivatives of all orders of E^V also have a unique zero crossing and a unique extremum. For optimal generalization, E^V should be monitored and train-

ing stopped as soon as E^V begins to increase. A simple bound on the optimal training time k^{opt} is

$$\min_i \frac{1}{\log a_i} \log \frac{-A_i}{B_i} \leq k^{opt} \leq \max_i \frac{1}{\log a_i} \log \frac{-A_i}{B_i}. \tag{55}$$

In the most general case of arbitrary initial conditions and noise, the validation function E^V can have several local minima of variable depth before converging to its asymptotic value. The number of local minima is always at most n.

The main result is a consequence of the following statements, which are proved in the Appendix.

First case. For every i, $v'_i \geq v_i$, that is, the validation noise is bigger than the training noise. Then

(a) If for every i, $\alpha_i^{(0)} \geq \lambda_i/(\lambda_i + v_i)$, then E^V decreases monotonically to its asymptotic value.

(b) If for every i, $\lambda_i/(\lambda_i + v'_i) \leq \alpha_i^{(0)} \leq \lambda_i/(\lambda_i + v_i)$, then E^V increases monotonically to its asymptotic value.

(c) If for every i, $\alpha_i^{(0)} \leq \lambda_i/(\lambda_i + v'_i)$ and $v_i \neq v'_i$, then E^V decreases monotonically to a unique global minimum and then increases monotonically to its asymptotic value. The derivatives of all orders of E^V have a unique zero crossing and a unique extremum.

Second *case.* For every i, $v'_i \leq v_i$; that is, the validation noise is smaller than the training noise. Then

(a) If for every i, $\alpha_i^{(0)} \geq \lambda_i/(\lambda_i + v'_i)$ and $v_i \neq v'_i$, then E^V decreases monotonically to a unique global minimum and then increases monotonically to its asymptotic value. The derivatives of all orders of E^V have a unique zero crossing and a unique extremum.

(b) If for every i, $\lambda_i/(\lambda_i + v_i) \leq \alpha_i^{(0)} \leq \lambda_i/(\lambda_i + v'_i)$, then E^V increases monotonically to its asymptotic value.

(c) If for every i, $\alpha_i^{(0)} \leq \lambda_i/(\lambda_i + v_i)$, then E^V decreases monotonically to its asymptotic value.

Several remarks can be made on the previous statements. First, notice that in both (b) cases, E^V increases because the initial W^0 is already too good for the given noise levels. The monotone properties of the validation function are not always strict in the sense that, for instance, at the common boundary of some of the cases E^V can be flat. These degenerate cases can be easily checked directly. The statement of the main result assumes that the initial matrix be the zero matrix or a matrix with a diagonal form in the basis of the eigenvectors e_i. A random initial non-zero matrix will not satisfy these conditions. However, E^V is continuous and even infinitely differentiable in all of its parameters. Therefore the results are true also for random sufficiently small matrices. If we use, for instance, an L^2 norm for the matrices, then the norm of a starting matrix is the same in the original or in the orthonormal e_i basis. Equation 54 yields a trivial upper-bound of $n^{1/2}$ for the initial norm which roughly corresponds to having random initial weights of order at most $n^{-1/2}$ in the original basis. Thus, heuristically, the variance of the initial random weights should be a decreasing function of the size of the network. This condition is *not* satisfied in many of the usual simulations found in the literature where initial weights are generated randomly and independently using, for instance, a centered Gaussian distribution with *fixed* standard deviation. In nonlinear networks, small initial weights are also important for not getting stuck in high local minima during training.

When more arbitrary conditions are considered, in the initial weights or in the noise, multiple local minima can appear in the validation function. As can be seen in one of the curves of the example given in Figure 3, there exist even cases where the first minimum is *not* the deepest one, although these may be rare. In addition, in this case, an indication that training should not be stopped at the first minimum is that at that point the LMS curve is still decreasing significantly. Also in this figure, better validation results seem to be obtained with smaller initial conditions. This can easily be understood, in this small-dimensional example, from some of the arguments given in the Appendix.

Another potentially interesting and relevant phenomena is illustrated in Figure 4. It is possible to have a situation where, after a certain number of training cycles, both the LMS and the validation functions appear to be flat and to have converged to their asymptotic values. If training is continued, however, one observes that these plateaux can end, and the validation function starts decreasing again. In the example, the first minimum is still optimal. Yet, it is possible to construct examples of validation functions, in higher dimensions, where long plateaux are followed by a phase of significant improvements (see Chauvin, 1991).

Finally, we have made an implicit distinction between validation and generalization throughout most of the previous sections. If generalization performance is measured by the LMS error calculated over the entire population, it is clear that our main result can be applied to the generalization error by assuming that $\bar{C}_{NN} = \mathrm{diag}(\bar{\nu}_i)$, and $\nu_i' = \bar{\nu}_i$ for every i. In particular, in the second statement of the main result, if for every i, $\bar{\nu}_i > \nu_i$, then the generalization curve has a unique minimum. Now, if a validation sample is used as a predictor of generalization performance and the ν_i's are close to the $\bar{\nu}_i$'s, then by continuity the validation and the generalization curves are close to each other. Thus, in this case, the strategy of stopping in a neighborhood of the minimum of the validation function should also lead to near-optimal generalization performance.

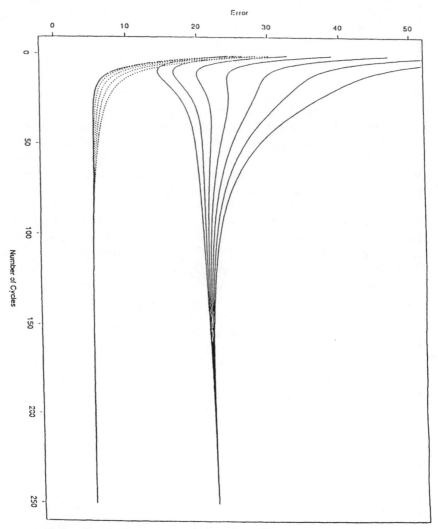

Figure 3. LMS error functions (lower curves) and corresponding validation error functions (upper curves). The parameters are $n = 3$, $\lambda_i =$ 22, .7, 2.5, $v_i = 4, 1, 3$, $v_i' = 20, 20, 20$, $\alpha_1^{(0)} = \alpha_2^{(0)} = 0$. From top to bottom, the third initial weight corresponding to $\alpha_3^{(0)}$ takes the values 0.3, 0.5, 0.7, 0.9, 1.1, 1.3, 1.5. The horizontal asymptote of the validation error functions is at 23.34. Notice, in particular, the fourth validation curve ($\alpha_3^{(0)} = 0.9$), which has two local minima, the second being deeper than the first. At the first minimum, the LMS function is still far from its horizontal asymptote. Also in this case, the validation improves as the initial conditions become closer to 0.

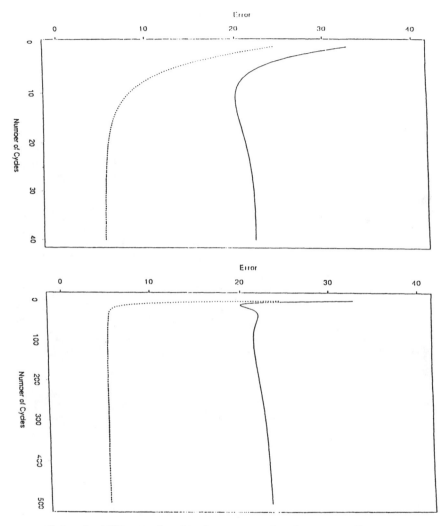

Figure 4. LMS error function (lower curves) and corresponding validation error functions (upper curves). The parameters are $n = 3$, $\lambda_i = 22, .7, 2.5$, $v_i = 4, 1, 4$, $v_i' = 20, 20, 20$, $\alpha_1^{(0)} = \alpha_2^{(0)} = 0$ and $\alpha_3^{(0)} = .7$. Notice, on the first two curves, that after 40 cycles both the LMS and the validation function appear to be flat and would suggest one stop the training. The second set of curves corresponds to 500 training cycles. Notice the existence of a second (although shallow) minimum, undetectable after 40 cycles.

Conclusion

In the framework constructed, based on linear single-layer feedforward networks, it has been possible to analytically derive interesting results on generalization. In particular, under simple noise assumption, we have given a complete description of the validation error E^V as a function of training time. It is rather remarkable that all the complex phenomena related to generalization which are observed in simulations of nonlinear networks are already present in the linear case. Although the framework is simplistic, it can lead to many nontrivial and perhaps mathematically tractable questions. This analysis is only a first step in this direction. More work is required to test the statistical significance of some of the observations (multiple local minima, plateaux effects, etc.) and their relevance for practical simulations. For instance, it seems to us that in the case of general noise and arbitrary initial conditions, the upper bound on the number of local minima is rather weak in the sense that, at least on the average, there are far fewer. It seems also that in general the first local minima of E^V is also the deepest. Thus, "pathological" cases may be somewhat rare. In the analysis conducted here, we have used uniform assumptions on the noise. In general, we can expect this not to be the case, and properties of the noise cannot be fixed a priori. It would also be of interest to study whether some of the assumptions made on the noise in the training and validation sample can be relaxed and how noise effects can be related to the finite size of the samples. Finally, other possible directions of investigation include the extension to multilayer networks and to general input/output associations.

UNSUPERVISED LEARNING

This section briefly examines a number of unsupervised learning algorithms for linear networks and their relations to the results derived in the third section, paticularly in terms of principal component extraction and absence of local minima. It should be noticed that the distinction between supervised and unsupervised learning is sometimes blurry. This is particularly obvious in the auto-associative case. Like back-propagation, a number of unsupervised algorithms are also based on gradient descent, although on error functions which do not depend on known target values. For instance, in the linear case, the usual Hebbian rule performs gradient descent over the variance of the output of the postsynaptic unit. With this in mind, we begin with algorithms defined for a single unit, by looking at variance maximization, Hebbian learning, and some of its variations. We then examine the general case with multiple units and show that several "symmetric" algorithms which have been proposed are in fact identical. The section leaves out many interesting unsupervised learning algorithms for

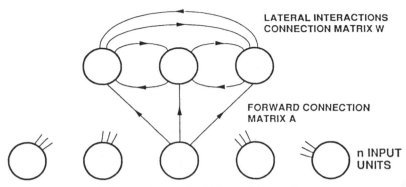

Figure 5.   Network with lateral interactions.

principal component extraction, which are beyond the scope of this chapter, that are based on a combination of Hebbian learning and lateral inhibition among competing units in the output layer as in Figure 5 (for example, Földiak, 1989, Sanger, 1989, Rubner and Tavan, 1990, Hornik and Kuan, 1991 and Xu, 1993). A more complete survey of unsupervised learning in linear networks can be found in Baldi and Hornik (1994).

One-Unit Algorithms

Assume, for now, that there is only one linear unit described by the input-output relation $y = a'x$, where a is the vector of weights to be trained, as usual, from a set of centered inputs x_t, $1 \leq t \leq T$. (It is useful, for the forthcoming extensions to many units, to notice that y can be seen as the dot product of the $n \times 1$ vectors a and x or as the matrix produt of the $1 \times n$ matrix a' and the vector x.)

Variance Maximization and Hebbian Learning

Suppose, as is often the case, that a desirable goal for the unit is to find a set of weights which differentiates the inputs as much as possible. This can be formalized by requiring that the output variance of the unit be as large as possible. In other words, we want to minimize the cost function

$$E(a) = -\langle (a'x_t)^2 \rangle = -a'\Sigma_{XX}a. \tag{56}$$

Obviously

$$\frac{\partial E}{\partial a_i} = -2 \langle x_{i,t}y_t \rangle. \tag{57}$$

In the corresponding on-line learning rule, upon presentation of a pattern x, a is modified by an amount Δa given by

$$\Delta a_i = \eta x_i y, \tag{58}$$

which is exactly Hebb's rule in its simplest form. However, it is clear that without any other restrictions, E has no minimum and by taking coefficients a_i of arbitrarily large magnitude we can easily have $E \to -\infty$. If we modify the problem so that the variance is to be maximized under the restriction that $\|a\| \leq 1$, then we already know the optimal solution by applying the general result of the second section on quadratic forms. The optimal a will be equal to $\pm u_1$, where u_1 is the normalized eigenvector of Σ_{xx} corresponding to the largest eigenvalue and, at the optimum, the network will compute the principal component of the input. In addition, the problem has no local minima. It is instructive to remark that if we try to maximize the variance under the constraint that, for every i, $|a_i| \leq 1$ (i.e., if we constrain the weights to belong to the inside of an n-dimensional scube rather than a sphere), then by a convexity argument it is easy to see that the optimum must be reached at one of the corners of the hypercube where $|a_i| = 1$ for every i (and strictly so if Σ_{xx} is positive definite). However, the determination of which corner of the hypercube realizes the maximum is an NP-complete problem (see, for instance, the matrix cover problem in Garey and Johnson, 1979, p. 282) and therefore probably computationally intractable. The previous discussion shows that it is useful to try to modify the simple Hebbian rule of Equation (58) so as to attempt to maximize the output variance while keeping the norm of the weight vector bounded.

Oja's Algorithm

Oja (1982) suggested keeping the weights normalized by having, upon presentation of pattern x,

$$a_i \leftarrow \frac{a_i + \eta y x_i}{[\Sigma_i (a_i + \eta y x_i)^2]^{1/2}}. \tag{59}$$

For η small,

$$\Delta a_i = \eta y[x_i - y a_i] + O(\eta^2), \tag{60}$$

which yields, in more compact notation, the learning rule

$$\Delta a = \eta[xy - ay^2], \tag{61}$$

comprising the usual Hebbian term and a very simple normalizing term. By summing the right-hand side of Equation (61) over all patterns, the corresponding off-line version can be expressed in the form

$$a(k + 1) = a(k) + \eta(\Sigma_{xx} a(k) - a(k) a'(k) \Sigma_{xx} a(k)). \tag{62}$$

Oja's rule cannot be interpreted in terms of a gradient of some error function because $\partial(x_i y - a_i y^2)/\partial a_j = x_i x_j - 2a_i y x_j - \delta_{i,j} y^2$, and this expression is *not* symmetric in i and j (in other words, the condition that $\partial^2 E/\partial a_i \partial a_j = \partial^2 E/\partial a_j \partial a_i$ is violated). (This does not exclude the possibility that there may exist an error function E such that the scalar product of the gradient of E with the correction vector corresponding to the learning rule remains positive. In other words, one may still be going downhill, although not along the steepest lines.)

What can we say about the convergence of Oja's algorithm? If the on-line or off-line version of the algorithm converges, then by Equation (62) (or equivalently by Equation (61) applied to each pattern)

$$\Sigma_{XX} a = a a' \Sigma_{XX} a \tag{63}$$

must be satisfied at any equilibrium point a, Reasonably $a \neq 0$, and therefore a is an eigenvector of Σ_{XX} with eigenvalue $a' \Sigma_{XX} a$ and, by multiplying the Equation (63) by a' on the left we find that $a' a = 1$. So all the possible limits of the off-line version of the algorithm are the normalized eigenvectors of Σ_{XX}. According to Oja (1982), if the distribution of the patterns x_t satisfies some not unrealistic assumptions and if $\eta \to 0$ at a suitable rate, then Equations (61) and (62) can be approximated by the differential equation

$$\frac{da(t)}{dt} = \Sigma_{XX} a - a a' \Sigma_{XX} a, \tag{64}$$

and the solution of Equation (64) will approach with probability 1 a uniformly asymptotically stable equilibrium of the differential equation. In addition, if Σ_{XX} is positive definite with the largest eigenvalue λ_1 with multiplicity 1 (and normalized eigenvector u_1) and $a(0)$ is not perpendicular to u_1, then $a(t) \to \pm u_1$ as $t \to \infty$ and $\pm u_1$ is uniformly asymptotically stable.

The case of Oja's algorithm is typical of what we have usually found concerning the relations between the three versions of a given learning algorithm. If the weight changes induced by each pattern presentation are very small, then the on-line version can be approximated by the off-line version (or vice versa). By setting the weight changes to zero in the off-line version, all the possible stable points of the algorithm are derived. The actual limits are, in general, a strict subset of these possible solutions. In the stochastic approximation framework, if the learning rate tends to zero at a suitable rate and the input environment satisfies certain assumptions, such as stationarity, then the paths of the on- or off-line version asymptotically approach the solution paths of the ordinary differential equation corresponding to the continuous version. In particular, the actual limits must be asymptotically stable equilibria of the differential equation. In general, this requirement is sufficient to show that the learning process converges to the desired value.

418 BALDI, CHAUVIN, HORNIK

Chauvin's Approach

In Chauvin (1989), a slightly different approach has been proposed based on the construction of a cost function comprising two terms: a variance term to be maximized and a term penalizing large weight vectors. More explicitly, one wants to minimize

$$E(a) = -\alpha a' \Sigma_{XX} a + \beta (a'a - 1)^2 \qquad (65)$$

where α and β are two positive real coefficients that can be varied to adjust the relative importance of the two factors. The gradient of this cost function corresponding to the presentation of one pattern x is

$$\frac{\partial E}{\partial a_i} = -2\alpha x_i y + 4\beta (a'a - 1) a_i \qquad (66)$$

with the corresponding learning rule

$$\Delta a_i = \eta(2\alpha x_i y - 4\beta (a'a - 1) a_i) \qquad (67)$$

and its averaged vector version

$$a(k + 1) = a(k) + \eta(2\alpha \Sigma_{XX} a(k) - 4\beta (a'(k)a(k) - 1)a(k)). \qquad (68)$$

Notice that, in addition to the usual Hebbian part, Equation (67) contains a normalizing term which is not very local in the sense that it depends on all the weights a_i associated with a given unit. Because of the competition between the two terms, it is clear that E has a minimum which is attained for some optimal a_{opt}. If we consider E restricted to the surface $\|a\| = \|a_{\text{opt}}\| = \rho$, the second term on the right-hand side of Equation (65) remains constant. Hence, by applying again the result on the optimization of quadratic forms over spheres, we have that a_{opt} is collinear to u_1; that is, $\Sigma_{XX} a_{\text{opt}} = \lambda_1 a_{\text{opt}}$. Since we know the direction of a_{opt}, it is now sufficient to determine its length ρ. Clearly $E(a_{\text{opt}}) = -\alpha \lambda_1 \rho^2 + \beta(\rho^2 - 1)^2$ and this is a quartic polynomial which is minimized when $dE/d\rho = 0$, that is, for $\rho = \pm(1 + \alpha\lambda_1/2\beta)^{1/2}$. So finally,

$$a_{\text{opt}} = \pm \left(1 + \frac{\alpha\lambda_1}{2\beta} \right)^{1/2} u_1. \qquad (69)$$

Notice that this analysis is to a certain extent independent of the detailed form of the term used to constrain the length of a in $E(a)$ (the term needs only to be some function of $\|a\|$). What can be said about the rest of the landscape of E? Clearly, at any equilibrium point of the algorithm, the relation

$$2\alpha \Sigma_{XX} a = 4\beta (a'a - 1)a \qquad (70)$$

must be satisfied and therefore either $a = 0$ or a is an eigenvector of Σ_{XX}. It can be shown (see Chauvin, 1989 for details) that for $a = 0$, $E(0) = \beta$, and this corresponds to a local maximum of E. If Σ_{XX} is positive definite with all eigenvalues of multiplicity 1, then all the critical points of E are of the form $a = \pm(1 + \alpha\lambda_i/2\beta)^{1/2}u_i$, with associated cost $E(a) = -\alpha\lambda_i(1 + \alpha\lambda_i/4\beta)$ ($i = 1, \ldots, n$). All these critical points are saddle points with the exception of a_{opt} (corresponding to $i = 1$), which, as we have already seen, realizes the global minimum of E. In particular, this landscape has no local minima. In the off-line version, if the starting weight vector is not orthogonal to u_1 (and this can always be assumed for practical purposes) then, provided that the learning rate satisfies

$$\eta \ll \frac{1}{2\alpha\lambda_1} \quad \text{and} \quad \eta < \frac{1}{4(2\beta + \alpha\lambda_1)}, \tag{71}$$

Equation (40) always leads to a decrease of the cost function E and therefore the algorithm must converge.

Linsker's Approach

In Linsker (1988), layered networks of units with linear biased output of the form

$$y = a'x + b \tag{72}$$

are considered together with the class of learning rules

$$\Delta a_i = \eta_1 x_i y + \eta_2 x_i + \eta_3 y + \eta_4, \tag{73}$$

that is, Hebbian rules with additional linear or constant terms. The a_i are constrained to be in an interval $[-c, c]$ and the patterns are not necessarily centered. By averaging Equation (73) over all patterns and taking its continuous approximation with the proper units, one can easily derive the system of differential equations:

$$\dot{a}_l = \sum_j \sigma_{i,j}a_j + k_1 + k_2 \sum_j a_j, \tag{74}$$

where σ_{ij} is the (i, j)th element of the covariance matrix Σ_{XX} of the input patterns, and k_1 and k_2 are two constants which can easily be calculated from Equations (72) and (73). In vector notation,

$$\dot{a} = \Sigma_{XX}a + k_1 J_{n,1} + k_2 J_{n,n}a, \tag{75}$$

where $J_{p,q}$ denotes the $p \times q$ matrix with all entries equal to 1. If we let

$$E(a) = -\frac{1}{2}a'\Sigma_{XX}a - k_1 a'J_{n,1} - \frac{k_2}{2}a'J_{n,1}J'_{n,1}a, \tag{76}$$

then $\partial E/\partial a = -\dot{a}$. Therefore the learning rule in Equation (75) tends to minimize E. Depending on the values of the constants k_1 and k_2 and the covariance matrix Σ_{XX} different mature states can be reached. Most importantly, Linsker shows how in layered systems of units satisfying Equation (72), with the proper range of parameters and where successive layers evolve in time according to Equation (75) particular feature detector cells such as center-surround or orientation selective can emerge in different layers, even with completely random external inputs to the first layer. Linsker also observes that, empirically, the learning process "does not get stuck in high lying local minima." This can be understood in several particular but important situations. Consider, for instance, a unit submitted to random inputs such that $\Sigma_{XX} = I$ and k_1 and k_2 are positive (this is automatically satisfied if all the learning rates in Equation (73) and the average $\langle x_{i,t} \rangle$ are positive). The matrix $M = I + k_2 J_{n,n}$ is positive definite as the sum of two positive matrices, one definite and the other semidefinite. By convexity, the minimum of E must therefore occur at the boundary of the cube $[-c, c]^n$. Recall that in general this point on the boundary may be very difficult to determine. Here, however, by inspection the optimum is reached at the vertex $a' = (c, \ldots, c)$. If we consider the system

$$\dot{a} = Ma + k_1 J_{n,1}, \tag{77}$$

with $a(0) = a_0$, it is clear that if the initial a_0 has all its components identical, this property will be preserved under the evolution described by Equation (77). As a result, the system will converge to its global minimum. In particular, if the initial weights are zero (or random but small), the mature a will essentially be the global minimum. We can also calculate how long it takes for the learning process to converge. If we assume for simplicity that $a_0 = 0$, then the solution of Equation (77) is

$$a(t) = e^{tM} \int_0^t e^{-uM} k_1 J_{n,1} \, du. \tag{78}$$

A simple induction on n shows that the eigenvalues of M are of two types:

(i) $\lambda_1 = 1 + nk_2$, with multiplicity 1 and normalized eigenvector $v_1 = n^{-1/2} J_{n,1}$;

(ii) $\lambda_2 = \cdots = \lambda_n = 1$ with multiplicity $n - 1$ and normalized eigenvectors $v_2, \ldots, v_n$ orthogonal to v_1 (their explicit form is not required to finish the calculation).

Let V be the matrix $[v_1, \ldots, v_n]$ and Λ the diagonal matrix $\text{diag}(\lambda_1, \ldots, \lambda_n)$ so that $VV' = I$ and $MV = V\Lambda$. Then the matrix exponentials can be computed by using the relation

$$e^{uM} = V \, \text{diag}(e^{\lambda_1 u}, \ldots, e^{\lambda_n u}) V'. \tag{79}$$

Some additional manipulations finally yield the solution

$$a(t) = \frac{k_1(e^{\lambda_1 t} - 1) J_{n,1}}{\lambda_1}, \tag{80}$$

and the cell reaches its mature state at time $t = t_c$ when

$$t_c = \frac{1}{\lambda_1} \ln \left(1 + \frac{c\lambda_1}{k_1} \right).$$ (81)

A Remark

In (b) and (c), the optimal a's are the principal eigenvectors. From the general analysis done on back propagation and especially Equations (22) and (23), there exists at least one other interesting cost function for the training of one unit given by

$$E(a) = \langle \|x_t - aa'x_t\|^2 \rangle,$$ (82)

which can be rewritten as

$$E(a) = \langle \|x_t\|^2 \rangle + (\|a\|^2 - 2)a'\Sigma_{XX}a.$$ (83)

Notice that this time E is a form of degree 4 in the coefficients a_i. It is not difficult to see that E has no local minima and that at the optimum $a = \pm u_1$, as desired. A straightforward calculation shows that the gradient can be expressed in the form

$$\frac{\partial E}{\partial a_i} = -2(2 - \|a\|^2)\langle x_{i,t}y_t \rangle + 2a_i\langle y_t^2 \rangle.$$ (84)

Although this expression is not particularly simple or local, one should notice that, when the length of a is close to 1, Equation (84) can be approximated by $-2\langle x_{i,t}y_t \rangle + 2a_i\langle y_t^2 \rangle$, which corresponds exactly to Oja's algorithm in its off-line form.

Symmetric Algorithms

Symmetric Algorithms

Baldi (1989) remarks that, in the auto-associative case, if we let $C = I$ in Equations (23) and (24), then at the optimum the matrices A and B are transposed of each other. This in turn suggests a possibly faster algorithm where at each step a gradient correction is applied only to one of the connection matrices while the other is modified in a symmetric fashion, thus avoiding the back propagation of errors in one of the layers. One possible version of this idea can be expressed as

$$A(k + 1) = A(k) - \eta\frac{\partial E}{\partial A},$$

$$B(k + 1) = A'(k + 1),$$ (85)

with $A(0)$ random and, for instance, $B(0) = A'(0)$ or, more precisely, in the averaged form

$$A(k + 1) = A(k) + \eta(I - W(k))\Sigma_{XX}A(k),$$

$$B(k + 1) = B(k) + \eta B(k)\Sigma_{XX}(I - W(k)), \tag{86}$$

where $W(k) = A(k)B(k)$. As in the case of the algorithm suggested by Chauvin, it can be seen that there exist exceptional starting points which can *in theory* prevent the algorithm from converging to the optimal solution by incorporating a projection onto a nonprincipal eigenvector. Moreover, it can be seen that a necessary condition for convergence to the optimum is that

$$\eta < \frac{1}{2\lambda_1} \tag{87}$$

(at least in the final stages of the learning process). In this algorithm, one needs only to keep track of one of the matrices. If we look at the evolution of the matrix A (or B') and specialize it to the case of one unit, we find that

$$a(k + 1) = a(k) + \eta(\Sigma_{XX}a(k) - a(k)a'(k)\Sigma_{XX}a(k)), \tag{88}$$

which is identical to Equation (62). In other words, Oja's algorithm is equivalent to a one-dimensional version of Equation (86). A similar approach for the general symmetric case can also be obtained by generalizing the previous remark and introducing the error function

$$E(A) = \langle\|x_t - AA'x_t\|^2\rangle. \tag{89}$$

Generalizing Oja's Algorithm

Conversely, one can start from Oja's algorithm and try to generalize it to the case of many units (see also Oja, 1989, and Krogh and Hertz, 1990). If we replace a by A, the *formal* generalization of Equation (61) is

$$\Delta A = \eta(xy' - Ayy'), \tag{90}$$

where $y = A'x$ and with the corresponding averaged version

$$A(k + 1) = A(k) + \eta(\Sigma_{XX}A(k) - A(k)A'(k)\Sigma_{XX}A(k)), \tag{91}$$

which is the symmetric algorithm seen before. Perhaps more convincingly, suppose that we want, in the course of the training period, to progressively modify the matrix A using a rule of the form $\Delta A = \eta(xy' + R)$, i.e. based on a Hebbian term to maximize the variance and an additional correction R to be determined. If, as we have seen, a desired objective is that at each step the connection matrix remain suborthogonal ($A'A = I$), then we must have $(A + \Delta A)'(A + \Delta A) \approx I$. If η is small, a first order approximation gives $A'(xy' + R) + (yx' + R')A = 0$ or, equivalently, $A'R + R'A = -2yy'$. This relation is true for any correction term R of the form $R = -Ayy' + C$, where C is any matrix satisfying $A'C + C'A = 0$. By taking $C = 0$, one obtains Equation (90). In any case, if we suppose that Equations (5.35) or (5.36) converges, then the limit A must satisfy

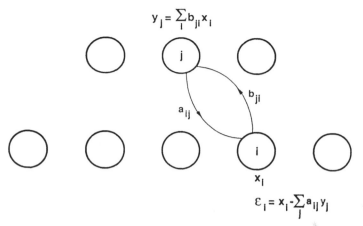

Figure 6. The SEC (symmetric error correction) network.

$$(I - AA')\Sigma_{XX}A = 0. \tag{92}$$

In the Appendix, it is shown that if Σ_{XX} is positive definite and the limit A has full rank p, then $A = U_{\delta}C$, where C is an orthogonal $p \times p$ matrix.

Williams' SEC Algorithm

In Williams (1985), the following SEC (symmetric error correction) learning algorithm is described. Consider a linear network, comprising only two layers, n input units connected to p hidden units with a connection matrix B and feedback connections from the p hidden units back to the input units through a connection matrix A (see Figure 6). A pattern x is presented and propagated forward to give $y = Bx$ and then backward to allow the computation of an error $\epsilon = x - Ay$. The weight matrix B is then corrected according to

$$\Delta b_{i,j} = \eta y_i \epsilon_j, \tag{93}$$

and A is updated symmetrically, in the sense that $\Delta a_{ji} = \Delta b_{ij}$ or $\Delta A = (\Delta B)'$. In matrix notation, Equation (5.38) is easily rewritten as

$$\Delta B = \eta Bx(x - ABx)' \tag{94}$$

or, in averaged form,

$$B(k + 1) = B(k) + \eta(B(k)\Sigma_{XX}(I - B'(k)A'(k))), \tag{95}$$

which is Equation (86), provided the algorithm is started with symmetric initial conditions; that is, $A(0) = B'(0)$. Williams shows that the only stable points of the continuous approximation of Equation (95) (given by $\dot{B} = (B\Sigma_{XX}(I - B'B))$ correspond to projections onto the space spanned by the first p principal components.

In conclusion, we see that, quite remarkably, several algorithms proposed in the literature in Oja (1982) and its generalization, in Williams (1985) and in Baldi (1989) which have been derived using slightly different heuristics, are completely identical. Parallel hardware implementation of the algorithm, probably in the formulation given by Williams (1985), is not inconceivable.

APPENDIX: SOME MATHEMATICAL PROOFS

Noise Analysis: Some Remarks and the Case of High Levels of Noise

Consider the setting of the third section. As in Baldi and Hornik (1989), one has the following two facts for $\tilde{E}$.

Fact 1. For any fixed A, the function $\tilde{E}(A, B)$ is convex in the coefficients of B and attains its minimum for any B satisfying

$$A'AB\Sigma_{XX} = A'\Sigma_{YX}. \tag{A.1}$$

If Σ_{XX} is invertible and A is full rank p, then $\tilde{E}$ is strictly convex and has a unique minimum reached when

$$B = \tilde{B}(A) = (A'A)^{-1}A'\Sigma_{YX}\Sigma_{XX}^{-1}. \tag{A.2}$$

This follows immediately since, for fixed A, the additional term $\mathrm{tr}(A\Sigma_{EE}A') + \mathrm{tr}\Sigma_{UU}$ is just an additive constant.

Fact 2. For any fixed B, the function $\tilde{E}(A, B)$ is convex in the coefficients of A and attains its minimum for any A satisfying

$$A(B\Sigma_{XX}B' + \Sigma_{EE}) = \Sigma_{YX}B'. \tag{A.3}$$

In particular, if Σ_{EE} is invertible, then $\tilde{E}$ is strictly convex and has a unique minimum reached when

$$A = \tilde{A}(B) = \Sigma_{YX}B'(B\Sigma_{XX}B' + \Sigma_{EE})^{-1}. \tag{A.4}$$

For the proof, it can be checked that the gradient of $\tilde{E}$ with respect to A is given by

$$\frac{\partial\tilde{E}(A,B)}{\partial(\mathrm{vec}A)'} = 2[((B\Sigma_{XX}B' + \Sigma_{EE}) \otimes I)\mathrm{vec}A - \mathrm{vec}(\Sigma_{YX}B')], \tag{A.5}$$

and the corresponding Hessian is

$$\frac{\partial^2 \bar{E}(A,B)}{\partial \text{vec } A \, \partial (\text{vec } A)'} = 2((B\Sigma_{XX}B' + \Sigma_{EE}) \otimes I), \qquad (A.6)$$

from which the fact follows in the usual way.

Now, if $\Sigma_{EE} = \sigma R$, then for fixed B,

$$\bar{A}_\sigma(B) = \Sigma_{YX}B'(B\Sigma_{XX}B' + \sigma R)^{-1}, \qquad (A.7)$$

and by direct calculation

$$\min_A \bar{E}_\sigma(A,B) = \bar{E}_\sigma(\bar{A}_\sigma(B),B)$$

$$= \text{tr}[\Sigma_{YY} + \Sigma_{UU} - (\Sigma_{YX}B'(B\Sigma_{XX}B' + \sigma R)^{-1}B\Sigma_{XY})].$$

Thus, if $\sigma \gg 1$, we find that

$$\min_A \bar{E}_\sigma(A,B) = \text{tr}(\Sigma_{YY} + \Sigma_{UU}) - \sigma^{-1}\text{tr}(\Sigma_{YX} B' R^{-1} B \Sigma_{XY}) + O(\sigma^{-2})$$

uniformly over $\mathcal{B}$. Let $\check{\Sigma} = \Sigma_{XY}\Sigma_{YX}$ and $\Phi(B) = \text{tr}(B\check{\Sigma}B'R^{-1})$. Hence, if σ is very large, we might expect that the solutions to the constrained noisy problem are "very close" to the set of elements of $\mathcal{B}$ which maximize $\Phi(B)$ over $\mathcal{B}$. More precisely, one has the following proposition.

Proposition 1. *Suppose we choose, for all $\sigma > 0$, matrices $B_\sigma \in \mathcal{B}_\sigma$. Then*

$$\lim_{\sigma \to \infty} \Phi(B_\sigma) = \phi = \max_{\mathcal{B}} \Phi(B). \qquad (A.8)$$

Proof. Obviously, $\lim \sup_{\sigma \to \infty} \Phi(B_\sigma) \leq \phi$. Suppose the previous inequality were strict. Then, there exists a $\gamma > 0$ and a subsequence $\sigma_k \to \infty$ as $k \to \infty$ such that, for all k, $\Phi(B_{\sigma_k}) \leq \phi - \gamma$. Pick $B \in \mathcal{B}$ such that $\Phi(B) = \phi$. Then $\bar{E}_{\sigma_k}(\bar{A}_{\sigma_k}(B_{\sigma_k}),B_{\sigma_k}) - \bar{E}_{\sigma_k}(\bar{A}_{\sigma_k}(B),B) = \sigma_k^{-1}(\Phi(B) - \Phi(B_{\sigma_k})) + O(\sigma_k^{-2}) \geq \sigma_k^{-1}\gamma + O(\sigma_k^{-2})$, implying that $\lim \inf_{k \to \infty} \sigma_k(\bar{E}_{\sigma_k}(\bar{A}_{\sigma_k}(B_{\sigma_k}),B_{\sigma_k}) - \bar{E}_{\sigma_k}(\bar{A}_{\sigma_k}(B),B)) > 0$, which is impossible.

If we write

$$\mathcal{B}_\Phi = \{B \in \partial\mathcal{B} : \Phi(B) = \phi\}, \qquad (A.9)$$

then, in the foregoing sense,

$$\lim_{\sigma \to \infty} \mathcal{B}_\sigma = \mathcal{B}_\Phi. \qquad (A.10)$$

In order to explicitly describe the optimal set $\mathcal{B}_\Phi$, we assume that

$$\mathcal{B} = \{B : \text{tr}(BSB') \leq \rho\} \qquad (A.11)$$

for some suitable symmetric and positive definite matrix S. In this case, $\mathcal{B}_\Phi$ is the set of all $p \times n$ matrices B that maximize $\Phi(B) = \text{tr}(B\check{\Sigma}B'R^{-1})$ over $\text{tr}(BSB')$

$= \rho$. Let us write $B = \sqrt{\rho}CS^{-1/2}$ such that $C = BS^{1/2}\rho^{-1/2}$. Then by simple calculation

$$\Phi(B) = \rho(\text{vec}C)'(S^{-1/2}\tilde{\Sigma}S^{-1/2} \otimes R^{-1})\text{vec}C$$

and

$$(\text{vec}C)'\text{vec}C = \text{tr}(CC') = \rho^{-1}\text{tr}(BSB') = 1.$$

As a result,

$$\mathcal{B}_\Phi = \{B:B = \sqrt{\rho}CS^{-1/2}\}, \tag{A.12}$$

where $c = \text{vec}C$ maximizes $c'(S^{-1/2}\tilde{\Sigma}S^{-1/2} \otimes R^{-1})c$ over $c'c = 1$. But again, by the result on quadratic forms reviewed in the second section, we know that c is a normalized principal eigenvector of $S^{-1/2}\tilde{\Sigma}S^{-1/2} \otimes R^{-1}$. It can be seen that all such c's are given by $c = \text{vec}(v\bar{u}')$, where $\bar{u}$ is a normalized principal eigenvector of $S^{-1/2}\tilde{\Sigma}S^{-1/2}$ and v is a normalized principal eigenvector of R^{-1}. In conclusion, we have the following proposition.

Proposition 2. *Suppose that $\mathcal{B} = \{B:\text{tr}(BSB') \leq \rho\}$. Then*

$$\mathcal{B}_\Phi = \{B:B = \sqrt{\rho}v\bar{u}'S^{-1/2}\}, \tag{A.13}$$

where $\bar{u}$ is a normalized principal eigenvector of $S^{-1/2}\tilde{\Sigma}S^{-1/2}$ and v is a normalized principal eigenvector of R^{-1}. In particular, all such B are rank 1 matrices.

Apart from multiplicative constants, all rows of optimal B matrices are identical and the network provides maximal redundancy. Several corollaries can be derived upon making more specific assumptions about the matrices $\tilde{\Sigma}$, R, and S. If $R \neq I_p$, the structure of the noise at the hidden layer is taken into account by suitable scaling of the rows of B. If $R = I_p$, we find that all p-dimensional unit-length vectors are normalized principal eigenvectors of R^{-1}, so in particular there is one optimal B with identical rows. If $S = I_n$, the corresponding $\bar{u}$ is a normalized principal eigenvector of $\tilde{\Sigma}$; in particular, in the autoassociative case, we find that $\backslash\Sigma = \Sigma_{XX}^2$ and therefore $\bar{u}$ is a principal eigenvector of Σ_{XX}. Finally, if the maximal eigenvalues of both $S^{-1/2}\tilde{\Sigma}S^{-1/2}$ and R^{-1} are simple, then the optimal B is uniquely determined.

A different class of sets $\mathcal{B}$ is considered in Linsker (1988), namely

$$\mathcal{B} = \{B = [b_1, \ldots, b_p]':\|b_i\| \leq 1\}. \tag{A.14}$$

By solving the first-order conditions associated with the Lagrangian

$$\Phi(B) + \sum_{i=1}^{p} \mu_i(b_i'b_i - 1), \tag{A.15}$$

we find that any constrained optimal B satisfies

$$R^{-1}B\tilde{\Sigma} = MB, \qquad (A.6)$$

where here $M = \text{diag}(\mu_1, \ldots, \mu_p)$ is a diagonal matrix of Lagrange multipliers. If $R = I_p$, we find that $B\tilde{\Sigma} = MB$, which means that the rows b_i' of B are left eigenvectors of $\tilde{\Sigma}$ with eigenvalue μ_i. Hence, the optimal B matrices are the ones which have normalized principal eigenvectors of $\tilde{\Sigma}$ as their rows.

Analysis of the Landscape of the Validation Function

Let us study E^V under uniform conditions. We deal only with the case $v_i' \geq v_i$ for every i (the case $v_i' \leq v_i$ is similar).

(a) If for every i, $\alpha_i^{(0)} \geq \lambda_i/(\lambda_i + v_i)$, then $b_i \leq 0$, $A_i \leq 0$, and $B_i \leq 0$. Therefore, $dE^V/dk \leq 0$ and E^V decreases to its asymptotic value.

(b) If for every i, $\lambda_i/(\lambda_i + v_i') \leq \alpha_i^{(0)} \leq \lambda_i/(\lambda_i + v_i)$, then $0 \leq b_i \leq (v_i' - v_i)/(\lambda_i + v_i')$, $A_i \geq 0$, $B_i \leq 0$, and $A_i + B_i \geq 0$. Since a_i^{2k} decays to zero faster than a_i^k, $dE^V/dk \geq 0$ and E^V increases its asymptotic value.

(c) The most interesting case is when, for every i, $\alpha_i^{(0)} \leq \lambda_i/(\lambda_i + v_i')$, that is, when $b_i \geq (v_i' - v_i)/(\lambda_i + v_i')$. Then $A_i \geq 0$, $B_i \leq 0$, and $A_i + B_i \leq 0$, so dE^V/dk is negative at the beginning and approaches zero from the positive side as $k \to \infty$. Strictly speaking, this is not satisfied if $A_i = 0$. This can occur only if $b_i = 0$ or $\lambda_i = 0$ (but then $B_i = 0$ also) or if $v_i = v_i'$. For simplicity, let us add the assumption that $v_i \neq v_i'$. A function which first increases (resp. decreases) and then decreases (resp. increases) with a unique maximum (resp. minimum) is called unimodal. We need to show that E^V is unimodal. For this, we use induction on n combined with an analysis of the unimodality properties of the derivatives of any order of E^V. We actually prove the stronger result that the derivatives of all orders of E^V are unimodal and have a unique zero crossing.

For $p = 1, 2, \ldots$, define

$$F^p(k) = \frac{d^p E^V}{dk^p}. \qquad (A.17)$$

Then

$$F^p(k) = \sum_i f_i^p(k) = \sum_i A_i^p a_i^k + B_i^p a_i^{2k}, \qquad (A.18)$$

with $A_i^1 = A_i$, $B_i^1 = B_i$, $A_i^p = A_i(\log a_i)^{p-1}$, and $B_i^p = B_i(2 \log a_i)^{p-1}$. Clearly, for any $p \geq 1$, $\text{sign}(A_i^p) = (-1)^{p+1}$, $\text{sign}(B_i^p) = (-1)^p$, and $\text{sign}(f_i^p)(0) = \text{sign}(A_i^p + B_i^p) = (-1)^p$. Therefore $\text{sign}(F^p(0)) = (-1)^p$ and, as $k \to \infty$, $F^p(k) \to 0$ as $\sum_i A_i^p a_i^k$, thus with the sign of A_i^p which is $(-1)^{p+1}$. As a result, all the continuous functions F^p must have at least one zero crossing. If F^p is unimodal, then F^p has a unique zero crossing. If F^{p+1} has a unique zero crossing, then F^p is unimodal.

Thus if for some p_0, F^{p_0} has a unique zero crossing, then all the functions $F^p(1 \leq p < p_0)$ are unimodal and have a unique zero crossing. Therefore, E^V has a unique minimum if and only if there exists an index p such that F^p has a unique zero crossing. By using induction on n, we are going to see that for p large enough this is always the case. Before we start the induction, for any continuously differentiable function f defined over $[0, \infty)$, let

$$\text{zero}(f) = \inf\{x : f(x) = 0\} \qquad (A.9)$$

and

$$\text{ext}(f) = \inf\left\{x : \frac{df}{dx}(x) = 0\right\}. \qquad (A.20)$$

Most of the time, zero and ext will be applied to functions which have a unique zero or extremum. In particular, for any i and p, it is trival to see that the functions f_i^p are unimodal and with a unique zero crossing. A simple calculation gives

$$\text{zero}(f_i^p) = \frac{1}{\log a_i} \log \frac{-A_i}{2^{p-1} B_i} = \frac{1}{\log a_i} \log \frac{v_i' - v_i}{2^{p-1} b_i(\lambda_i + v_i')} \qquad (A.21)$$

and

$$\text{ext}(f_i^p) = \text{zero}(f_i^{p+1}) = \frac{1}{\log a_i} \log \frac{-A_i}{2^p B_i}$$

$$= \frac{1}{\log a_i} \log \frac{v_i' - v_i}{2^p b_i(\lambda_i + v_i')}. \qquad (A.22)$$

Also notice that for any $p \geq 1$

$$\min_i \text{zero}(f_i^p) \leq \text{zero } F^p \leq \max_i \text{zero}(f_i^p) \qquad (A.23)$$

and

$$\min_i \text{ext}(f_i^p) \leq \text{ext } F^p \leq \max_i \text{ext}(f_i^p). \qquad (A.24)$$

Equations A.23 and A.24 are true for *any* zero crossing or extremum of F^p.

We can now begin the induction. For $n = 1$, E^V has trivially a unique minimum and all its derivatives are unimodal with a unique zero crossing. Let us suppose that this is also true of any validation error function of $n - 1$ variables. Let $\lambda_1 \geq \cdots \geq \lambda_n > 0$ and consider the corresponding ordering induced on the variables $a_i = 1 - \eta\lambda_i - \eta v_i$, $1 > a_{i_1} \geq \cdots \geq a_{i_n} \geq 0$. Let i_j be a fixed index such that $a_{i_1} \geq a_{i_j} \geq a_{i_n}$ and write, for any $p \geq 1$,

$$F^p(k) = G^p(k) + f_{i_j}^p(k) \qquad \text{with } G^p(k) = \Sigma_{i \neq i_j} f_i^p(k).$$

The function $f^p_{i_j}$ is unimodal with a unique zero crossing and so is G^p by the induction hypothesis. Now it is easy to see that F^p will have a unique zero crossing if

$$\text{zero}(G^p) \leq \text{zero}(f^p_{i_j}) \leq \text{ext}(G^p). \tag{A.25}$$

By applying Equations (A.23) and (A.24) to G^p, we see that F^p will have a unique zero crossing if

$$\max_{i \neq i_j} \text{zero}(f^p_i) \leq \text{zero}(f^p_{i_j}) \leq \min_{i \neq i_j} \text{ext}(f^p_i) \tag{A.26}$$

Substituting the values given by Equations (A.19) and (A.21), we can see that for large p, Equation (A.26) is equivalent to

$$\max_{i \neq i_j} - p \, \frac{\log 2}{\log a_i} \leq -p \, \frac{\log 2}{\log a_{i_j}} \leq \min_{i \neq i_j} - p \, \frac{\log 2}{\log a_i}, \tag{A.27}$$

and this is satisfied since $a_{i_1} \geq \cdots \geq a_{i_n}$. Therefore, using the induction hypothesis, we see that there exists an integer p_0 such that, for any $p > p_0$, F^p has a unique zero crossing. But, as we have seen, this implies that F^p has a unique zero crossing also for $1 \leq p \leq p_0$. Therefore E^V is unimodal with a unique minimum and its derivatives of all orders are unimodal with a unique zero crossing.

Notice that $F(k)$ cannot be zero if all the functions $f_i(k)$ are simultaneously negative or positive. Therefore, a simple bound on the position of the unique minimum k^{opt} is given by

$$\min_i \text{zero}(f_i) \leq \text{zero}(F) \leq \max_i \text{zero}(f_i) \tag{A.28}$$

or

$$\min_i \frac{1}{\log a_i} \log \frac{-A_i}{B_i} \leq k^{opt} \leq \max_i \frac{1}{\log a_i} \log \frac{-A_i}{B_i}. \tag{A.29}$$

[It is also possible, for instance, to study the effect of the initial $\alpha_i^{(0)}$ on the position or the value of the local minima. By differentiating the relation $F^1(k) = 0$, one gets immediately

$$F^2(k)dk = \sum_i \left(\frac{\lambda_i + \nu_i}{\lambda_i b_i} \right) (A_i a_i^k + 2B_i a_i^{2k}) \, d\alpha_i^{(0)}; \tag{A.30}$$

(see Figure 2)].

To find an upper bound on the number of local minima of E^V in the general case of arbitrary noise and initial conditions, we first order the $2n$ numbers a_i and a_i^2 into an increasing sequence c_i, $i = 1, \ldots, 2n$. This induces a corresponding ordering on the $2n$ numbers A_i and B_i yielding a second sequence C_i, $i = 1, \ldots, 2n$. Now the derivative of E^V can be written in the form

$$\frac{dE^V}{dk} = F^1(k) = \int C(a)a^k \, d\mu(a), \qquad (A.31)$$

where μ is the finite positive measure concentrated at the points a_i and a_i^2. The kernel a^k in the integral is totally positive. Thus (see, for instance, Karlin, 1968, Theorem 3.1, p. 233) the number of sign changes of $F^1(k)$ is bounded by the number of sign changes in the sequence C. Therefore the number of sign changes in F^1 is at most $2n - 1$ and the number of zeros of F^1 is at most $2n - 1$. Thus, the number of local minima of E^V is at most n.

Limits of the Symmetric Algorithms

If the on-line or off-line version of one of the symmetric algorithms converges, then

$$(I - AA')\Sigma_{XX}A = 0. \qquad (A.32)$$

Assume that Σ_{XX} is positive definite and that the limit A is of full rank p. Then, by multiplying Equation A.32 on the left by A' and using the fact that $A'\Sigma_{XX}A$ is invertible, we find that $A'A = I$. Hence, $P_A = AA'$, and Equation (A.32) can be written as $\Sigma_{XX}A = P_A\Sigma_{XX}A$. Multiplying by A' from the right, we find that $\Sigma_{XX}P_A = P_A\Sigma_{XX}P_Z$; therefore $A = U_\mathcal{F}C$, where C is an invertible $p \times p$ matrix (see the proof of Facts 3 and 4 in Baldi and Hornik, 1989). Furthermore, $I = A'A = C'U'_\mathcal{F}U_\mathcal{F}C = C'C$, so C is orthogonal.

ACKNOWLEDGMENT

Work in part supported by grants from NSF and ONR to P. B.

REFERENCES

Apostol, T. (1967). Calculus (Vol. II, 2nd ed.). New York: Wiley.

Atkinson. (1978). *An introduction to numerical analysis.* New York: Wiley.

Baldi, P., & Hornik, K. (1989). Neural networks and principal component analysis: Learning from examples without local minima. *Neural Networks, 2*(1), 53–58.

Baldi, P. (1989). Linear learning: Landscapes and algorithms. In D. S. Tourtezky (Ed.), *Advances in neural information processing systems 2.* San Mateo, CA: Morgan Kaufmann.

Baldi, P., & Chauvin, Y. (1991). Temporal evolution of generalization during learning in linear networks. *Neural Computation, 3*(4), 589–603.

Baldi, P., & Hornik, K. (1994). Learning in linear neural networks: A survey. IEEE Transactions on Neural Networks, in press.

Baum, E. B., & Haussler, D. (1989). What size net gives valid generalization? *Neural Computation, 1,* 151–160.

Blahut, R. E. (1987). *Principles and practice of information theory.* Reading, MA: Addison-Wesley.

Bourlard, H., & Kamp, Y. (1988). Auto-association by the multilayer perceptrons and singular value decomposition. *Biological Cybernetics, 59*, 291–294.

Chauvin, Y. (1989). Principal component analysis by gradient descent on a constrained linear hebbian cell. *Proceedings of the 1989 IJCNN Conference.* (pp. 373–380). Washington DC: IEEE Press.

Chauvin, Y. (1991). Generalization dynamics in LMS trained linear networks. In *Neural information processing systems 4.* San Mateo, CA: Morgan Kaufmann.

Cottrell, G. W., Munro, P. W., & Zipser, D. (1988). Image compression by back propagation: A demonstration of extensional programming. In N. E. Sharkey (Ed.), *Advances in cognitive science* (Vol. 2). Norwood, NJ: Ablex.

Földiák, P. (1989). Adaptive network for optimal linear feature extraction. *Proceedings of the 1989 IJCNN Conference,* Washington DC.

Füredi, Z., & Komlós, J. (1981). The eigenvalues of random symmetric matrices. *Combinatorica, 1*(3), 233–241.

Gallinari, P., Thiria, S., & Fogelman Soulie, F. (1988). Multilayer perceptrons and data analysis. *Proceedings of the 1988 ICNN Conference,* (pp. 391–399). San Diego.

Garey, M. R., & Johnson, D. S. (1979). *Computers and intractability.* New York: W. H. Freeman.

Horn, R. A., & Johnson, C. R. (1985). *Matrix analysis.* Cambridge: Cambridge University Press.

Hornik, K., & Kuan. (1991). Convergence analysis of local PCA algorithms. Preprint.

Karlin, S. (1968). *Total positivity.* Stanford, CA: Stanford University Press.

Krogh, A., & Hertz, J. A. (1990). Hebbian learning of principal components. In *Parallel processing in neural systems and computers.* R. Eckmiller, G. Hartman and G. Hauske (Eds.). New York: Elsevier.

Kshirsagar, A. N. (1972). *Multivariate analysis.* New York: Dekker.

Levin, E., Tishby, N., & Solla, S. A. (1990). A statistical approach to learning and generalization in layered neural networks. P-IEEE, *78*(10), 1568–1574.

Linsker, R. (1988). Self-organization in a perceptual network. *Computer, March,* 105–117.

MacKay, D. J. C., & Miller, K. D. (1990). Analysis of Linsker's simulation of Hebbian rules. *Neural Computation 2,* 173–187.

Magnus, J. R., & Neudecker, H. (1988). *Matrix differential calculus with applications in statistics and econometrics.* New York: Wiley.

Mardia, K. V., Kent, J. T., & Bibby, M. (1979). *Multivariate analysis.* New York: Academic Press.

McCulloch, W. S., & Pitts, W. (1943). A logical calculus of ideas immanent in nervous activity. *Bulletin of Mathematical Biophysics 5,* 115–133.

Miller, K. D., Keller, J. B., & Stryker, M. P. (1989). Ocular dominance column development: Analysis and simulation. *Science, 245,* 605–615.

Oja, E. (1982). A simplified neuron model as a principal component analyzer. *Journal of Mathematical Biology, 15,* 267–273.

Oja, E. (1989). Neural networks, principal components and subspaces. *International Journal of Neural Systems, 1,* 61–68.

Robinson, D. A. (1981). The use of control systems analysis in the neurophysiology of eye movement. *Annual Review of Neuroscience, 4,* 463–503.

Rubner, J., & Tavan, P. (1990). A self-organizing network for principal component analysis. Preprint.

Sanger, T. (1989). Optimal unsupervised learning in a single-layer linear feedforward neural network. *Neural Networks 2,* 459–473.

Sompolinsky, H., Tishby, N., & Seung, H. S. (1990). Learning from examples in large neural networks. *Physical Review Letters, 65,* 13, 1683–1686.

Wang, C., Judd, S., & Venkatesh, S. S. (1994). An optimal stopping and effective machine size in learning. In J. D. Cown, G. Tesauro & J. Alspector (Eds.). *Advances in Neural Information Processing Systems 6,* San Francisco, CA: Morgan Kaufmann.

Williams, R. J. (1985). Feature discovery through error-correction learning. *Institute for Cognitive Science*, Tech. Rep. No. 8501, UCSD, La Jolla, California.

Xu, L. (1993). Least mean square error reconstruction principle for self-organising neural nets. *Neural Networks 6*, 627–648.

13

Gradient-Based Learning Algorithms for Recurrent Networks and Their Computational Complexity

Ronald J. Williams
College of Computer Science, Northeastern University

David Zipser
Department of Cognitive Science, University of California, San Diego

INTRODUCTION

Learning in Recurrent Networks

Connectionist networks having feedback connections are interesting for a number of reasons. Biological neural networks are highly recurrently connected, and many authors have studied recurrent network models of various types of perceptual and memory processes. The general property making such networks interesting and potentially useful is that they manifest highly nonlinear dynamical behavior. One such type of dynamical behavior that has received much attention is that of settling to a fixed stable state, but probably of greater importance both biologically and from an engineering viewpoint are time-varying behaviors.

Here we consider algorithms for training recurrent networks to perform *temporal supervised learning tasks,* in which the specification of desired behavior is in the form of specific examples of input and desired output trajectories. One example of such a task is sequence classification, where the input is the sequence to be classified and the desired output is the correct classification, which is to be produced at the end of the sequence, as in some of the work reported by Mozer (1989; Chapter 5, this volume). Another example is sequence production, as studied by Jordan (1986), in which the input is a constant pattern and the corresponding desired output is a time-varying sequence. More generally, both the input and desired output may be time-varying, as in the prediction problems investigated by Cleeremans, Servan-Screiber, and McClelland (1989; Chapter 9, this volume) and the control problems studied by Nguyen and Widrow (Chapter 6, this volume). While limited forms of time-varying behaviors can be handled by using feedforward networks and tapped delay lines (e.g., Waibel et al., 1987),

433

recurrent networks offer a much richer set of possibilities for representing the necessary internal state. Because their internal state representation is adaptive rather than fixed, they can form delay line structures when necessary while also being able to create flip-flops or other memory structures capable of preserving a state over potentially unbounded periods of time. This point has been emphasized in (Williams, 1990) and similar arguments have been made by Mozer (1988; Chapter 5, this volume).

There are a number of possible reasons to pursue the development of learning algorithms for recurrent networks, and these may involve a variety of possible constraints on the algorithms one might be willing to consider. For example, one might be interested in understanding how biological neural networks learn to store and reproduce temporal sequences, which requires that the algorithm used be "biologically plausible," implying that the specific implementation of the algorithm map onto known neural circuitry in a reasonable way. Or, one might seek an algorithm which does not necessarily conform to known biological constraints but is at least implementable in entirely local fashion, requiring essentially no additional connectivity beyond that already present in the network to be trained. A still weaker constraint on the algorithm is that it allow a reasonable implementation in parallel hardware, even if that requires certain additional mechanisms within the overall system beyond those present in the network to be trained. These last two constraints are of some importance for attempts to create special-purpose hardware realizations of networks with on-line adaptation capabilities. Another possible constraint on the algorithm is that it be efficient when implemented in serial hardware. This constraint may be important for off-line development of networks which are useful for certain engineering applications, and it can also be important for cognitive modeling studies which are designed to examine the internal representations necessary to perform certain sequential tasks.

Overview of This Chapter

In this chapter we describe several gradient-based approaches to training a recurrent network to perform a desired sequential behavior in response to input. In characterizing these approaches as "gradient-based" we mean that at least part of the learning algorithm involves computing the gradient of some form of performance measure for the network in weight space, either exactly or approximately, with this result then used in some appropriate fashion to determine the weight changes. For the type of task investigated here, the performance measure is a simple measure of error between actual and desired output.

Because we deal here only with gradient-based learning algorithms, our primary focus will be on techniques for computing this exact or approximate gradient information. It is to be understood that there may be various alternative ways to use this gradient information in a particular learning algorithm, including simple proportional descent along the error gradient or the use of "momentum" or other more sophisticated acceleration techniques.

We discuss several approaches to performing the desired gradient computation, some based on the familiar backpropagation algorithm and some involving other ideas. Part of the intent of this chapter is to discuss the relationship between these various alternative approaches to gradient computation in recurrent networks. We begin by developing exact gradient computation algorithms, but later we note how they give rise to useful approximation strategies having more desirable computational features. For all these approaches to exact or approximate gradient computation we also provide an analysis of their computational requirements. The reader interested in performing digital computer simulation experiments of these various algorithms may find these analyses particularly helpful. In addition, we note some special architectures which readily lend themselves to specific hybrid strategies giving rise to conceptually and/or computationally simpler algorithms for exact gradient computation. Additional topics discussed are *teacher forcing,* a useful adjunct to all of the techniques discussed, and some experimental comparisons of the performance of some of the algorithms.

CONTINUAL VERSUS EPOCHWISE OPERATION

It is important to distinguish between two approaches to operating (and training) a recurrent network. In *epochwise operation* the network is run from some particular starting start until some stopping time is reached, after which the network is reset to its starting state for the next epoch. It is not essential that the state at the beginning of each epoch be the same; the important feature of this approach is that the state at the start of the new epoch is unrelated to the state at the end of the previous epoch. Because of this, an epoch boundary serves as a barrier across which "credit assignment" should not pass; erection of these barriers rules out any possibility that activity from one epoch might be relevant to producing the desired behavior for any later epoch.[1]

Note that an epoch in the sense used here is only loosely related to the corresponding notion sometimes used in the context of *batch training,* as distinguished from *incremental training,* of feedforward networks. The key issue in that case is when the weight updates are performed. In the batch approach to training a feedforward network, weight changes are performed only after a complete cycle of pattern presentations; in the incremental approach, weight

---

[1]Interestingly, these functions can be dissociated from one another. For example, one might imagine imposing no state reset at any time, while still allowing a learning algorithm to take advantage of occasional information provided by a teacher which effectively tells the learning system that no state reached prior to some particular time is relevant to producing correct performance at subsequent times.

changes are made after each pattern is presented. In the current terminology, a single epoch for the recurrent network corresponds to one training pattern for a feedforward network, so a network which operates epochwise may be trained using an incremental approach, in which weight changes are made at the end of each epoch, or a batch approach, in which weight changes are performed after several epochs.

In contrast, a network is considered to *operate continually* if neither "manual" state resets nor other such artificial credit-assignment barriers are available to a trainer of the network. The concept of a continually operating network would appear to be more appropriate for situations when on-line learning is required, although this introduces some subtleties when attempting to formalize the overall objective of learning. These subtleties are not present in the epochwise case because one can imagine that each epoch involves a potentially repeatable event, like the presentation of a single pattern to a feedforward network, with these individual events considered independent of one another. An additional subtlety in the continual operation case is due to the need to make weight changes while the network runs. Unlike the epochwise case, the continual operation case offers no convenient times at which to imagine beginning anew with different weight values.

As an example of the use of this distinction, consider the task of training a network to match the input-output behavior of a given finite state machine through observation of this behavior. A number of the training algorithms to be described in this chapter have been used for just such tasks. If one assumes that there is a distinguished start state and a set of distinguished final states in the machine to be emulated by the network, then it seems reasonable to train the network in an epochwise fashion. In this approach, whenever the machine being emulated is restarted in its start state after arriving in a final state, the network is reset to its start state as well. However, one might also consider trying to emulate finite state machines having no such distinguished states, in which case letting the network operate continually is more appropriate. In general, resetting the network to match a particular state of the machine being emulated is an additional mechanism for giving training information to the network, less informative than the extreme of giving complete state information (which would make the task easy), but more informative than giving only input-output information. In this case the training information helps learning during the time period shortly after the reset. There is also another difference between the continual operation case and the epochwise case which may be important. If transitions are added from the final states to the start state in the finite state machine emulation task, an epochwise task is turned into a continual-operation task. Note that a network trained to perform the epochwise version of the task is never required to make the transition to this distinguished state on its own, so one would not expect it to perform the same on the continual-operation version of the task as a network actually trained on that version. In particular, it may not be able to "reset itself" when appropriate.

While we include discussion of learning algorithms for networks which operate epochwise, much of our emphasis here is on algorithms especially appropriate for training continually operating networks.

FORMAL ASSUMPTIONS AND DEFINITIONS

Network Architecture and Dynamics

All the algorithms presented in this chapter are based on the assumption that the network consists entirely of semilinear units. More general formulations of these algorithms are possible, and it is straightforward to use the same approach to deriving them. Another assumption we make here is the use of discrete time. There are continuous-time analogs of all the approaches we discuss, some of which are straightforward to obtain and others of which involve more work.

Let the network have n units, with m external input lines.[2] Let $\mathbf{y}(t)$ denote the n-tuple of output of the units in the network at time t, and let $\mathbf{x}^{\text{net}}(t)$ denote the m-tuple of external input signals to the network at time t. We also define $\mathbf{x}(t)$ to be the $(m + n)$-tuple obtained by concatenating $\mathbf{x}^{\text{net}}(t)$ and $\mathbf{y}(t)$ in some convenient fashion. To distinguish the components of $\mathbf{x}$ representing unit outputs from those representing external input values where necessary, let U denote the set of indices k such that x_k, the kth component of $\mathbf{x}$, is the output of a unit in the network, and let I denote the set of indices k for which x_k is an external input. Furthermore, we assume that the indices on $\mathbf{y}$ and $\mathbf{x}^{\text{net}}$ are chosen to correspond to those of $\mathbf{x}$, so that

$$x_k(t) = \begin{cases} x_k^{\text{net}} & \text{if } k \in I \\ y_k(t) & \text{if } k \in U. \end{cases} \tag{1}$$

For example, in a computer implementation using zero-based array indexing, it is convenient to index units and input lines by integers in the range $[0, m + n)$, with indices in $[0, m)$ corresponding to input lines and indices in $[m, m + n)$ corresponding to units in the network. Note that one consequence of this notational convention is that $x_k(t)$ and $y_k(t)$ are two different names for the same quantity when $k \in U$. The general philosophy behind our use of this notation is that variables symbolized by x represent input and variables symbolized by y represent output. Since the output of a unit may also serve as input to itself and other units, we will consistently use x_k when its role as input is being emphasized and y_k when its role as output is being emphasized. Furthermore, this naming convention is intended to apply both at the level of individual units and at the level of the entire network. Thus, from the point of view of the network, its input is denoted $\mathbf{x}^{\text{net}}$ and, had it been it necessary for this exposition, we would have

---

[2]What we call *input lines* others have chosen to call *input units*. We avoid this terminology because we believe that they should not be regarded as units since they perform no computation. Another reasonable alternative might be to call them *input terminals*.

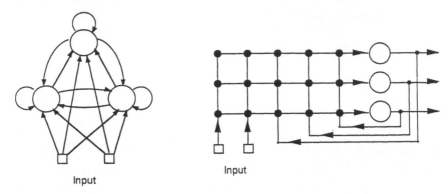

Figure 1. Two representations of a completely connected recurrent network having three units and two input lines. One input line might serve as a bias and carry the constant value 1. Any subset of these three units may serve as output units for the net, with the remaining units treated as hidden units. The 3 × 5 weight matrix for this network corresponds to the array of heavy dots in the version on the right.

denoted its output by $\mathbf{y}^{\text{net}}$ and chosen its indexing to be consistent with that of $\mathbf{y}$ and $\mathbf{x}$.

Let $\mathbf{W}$ denote the weight matrix for the network, with a unique weight between every pair of units and also from each input line to each unit. By adopting the indexing convention just described, we can incorporate all the weights into this single $n \times (m + n)$ matrix. The element w_{ij} represents the weight on the connection to the ith unit from either the jth unit, if $j \in U$, or the jth input line, if $j \in I$. Furthermore, note that to accommodate a bias for each unit we simply include among the m input lines one input whose value is always 1; the corresponding column of the weight matrix contains as its ith element the bias for unit i. In general, our naming convention dictates that we regard the weight w_{ij} as having x_j as its "presynaptic" signal and y_i as its "postsynaptic" signal. Figure 1 shows a fully connected network having 3 units, 2 input lines, and a 3 × 5 weight matrix.

For the semilinear units used here it is convenient to also introduce for each k the intermediate variable $s_k(t)$, which represents the net input to the kth unit at time t. Its value at time $t + 1$ is computed in terms of both the state of and input to the network at time t by

$$s_k(t + 1) = \sum_{l \in U} w_{kl} y_l(t) + \sum_{l \in I} w_{kl} x_l^{\text{net}}(t) = \sum_{l \in U \cup I} w_{kl} x_l(t). \quad (2)$$

We have written this here in two equivalent forms; the longer one clarifies how the unit outputs and the external inputs are both used in the computation, while the more compact expression illustrates why we introduced $\mathbf{x}$ and the corresponding indexing convention. Hereafter, we use only the latter form, thereby avoiding any explicit reference to $\mathbf{x}^{\text{net}}$ or its individual coordinates.

The output of such a unit at time $t + 1$ is then expressed in terms of the net input by

$$y_k(t + 1) = f_k(s_k(t + 1)), \tag{3}$$

where f_k is the unit's squashing function. Throughout much of this chapter we make no particular assumption abut the nature of the squashing functions used by the various units in the network, except that we require them to be differentiable. In those cases where a specific assumption about these squashing functions is required, it will be assumed that all units use the logistic function.

Thus the system of Equations 2 and 3, where k ranges over U, constitute the entire discrete-time dynamics of the network, where the x_k values are defined by Equation 1. Note that the external input at time t does not influence the output of any unit until time $t + 1$. We are thus treating every connection as having a one-time-step delay. It is not difficult to extend the analyses presented here situations where different connections have different delays. Later we make some observations concerning the specific case when some of the connections have no delay.

While the derivations we give throughout this chapter conform to the particular discrete-time dynamics given by Equations 2 and 3, it is worthwhile here to call attention to the use of alternative formulations obtained specifically from application of Euler discretization to continuous-time networks. For example, if we begin with the dynamical equations[3]

$$\tau_k \dot{y}_k(t) = -y_k(t) + f_k(s_k(t)), \tag{4}$$

where $s_k(t)$ is defined by Equation 2 as before, then discretizing with a sampling interval of Δt is easily shown to give rise to the discrete update equations

$$y_k(t + \Delta t) = \left(1 - \frac{\Delta t}{\tau_k}\right) y_k(t) + \frac{\Delta t}{\tau_k} f_k(s_k(t)). \tag{5}$$

Defining $\beta_k = \Delta t / \tau_k$ and altering the time scale so that $\Delta t = 1$, we then obtain the equations

$$y_k(t + 1) = (1 - \beta_k)y_k(t) + \beta_k f_k(s_k(t)), \tag{6}$$

and it is then clear that Equation 3 represents the special case when $\beta_k = 1$. It is straightforward to derive algorithms like those given throughout this chapter for these more general alternative forms of discrete-time dynamics if desired. The potential advantage of using such dynamics where $\beta_k \ll 1$ is that certain classes of task may be more readily learned by such systems, as has been observed by Tsung (1990).[4] The particular advantage possessed by such systems is that the

---

[3]Note that these particular equations are of essentially the same form as those considered by Pineda (Chapter 4, this volume), except that we assume that external input to the unit must pass through the squashing function.

[4]In fact, there is a strong similarity between Equation 6 and the form of recurrence Mozer (chapter 5, this volume) has used; some of his observations concerning the potential advantages of his focused architecture could be considered to apply more generally to any use of recurrence more like that found in continous-time systems.

gradient computation used in the learning algorithms to be described here falls off more gradually over time, which means that "credit assignment" is more readily spread over longer time spans than when $\beta = 1$.

Network Performance Measure

Assume that the task to be performed by the network is a *sequential supervised learning* task, meaning that certain of the units' output values are to match specified target values (which we also call *teacher signals*) at specified times. Once again, this is not the most general problem formulation to which these approaches apply, but it is general enough for our purposes here.

Let $T(t)$ denote the set of indices $k \in U$ for which there exists a specified target value $d_k(t)$ that the output of the kth unit should match at time t. Then define a time-varying n-tuple $\mathbf{e}$ by

$$e_k(t) = \begin{cases} d_k(t) - y_k(t) & \text{if } k \in T(t) \\ 0 & \text{otherwise.} \end{cases} \tag{7}$$

Note that this formulation allows for the possibility that target values are specified for different units at different times. The set of units considered to be "visible" can thus be time varying. Now let

$$J(t) = -\frac{1}{2} \sum_{k \in U} [e_k(t)]^2 \tag{8}$$

denote the negative of the overall network error at time t. A natural objective of learning might be to maximize[5] the negative of the total error

$$J^{\text{total}}(t',t) = \sum_{\tau=t'+1}^{t} J(\tau) \tag{9}$$

over some appropriate time period $(t', t]$. The gradient of this quantity in weight space is, of course,

$$\nabla_{\mathbf{w}} J^{\text{total}}(t',t) = \sum_{\tau=t'+1}^{t} \nabla_{\mathbf{w}} J(\tau). \tag{10}$$

In general, we let t_0 denote some starting time at which the network has its state initialized. For a continually running network there are no other times at which the state is ever reinitialized in this way, but with epochwise training there will be other such times $t_1, t_2, t_3, \ldots$ marking epoch boundaries. Alternatively,

---

[5]The problem of minimizing error is treated here as a maximization problem because it eliminates the need for annoying minus signs in many of the subsequent formulas.

one might consider time to begin anew at t_0 whenever the state is reinitialized in a epochwise approach. Throughout this chapter, whether considering the case of a network operating epochwise or continually, we let t_0 denote the last time at which a state reset occurred. In the epochwise case we also use t_1 to indicate the end of the current epoch.

We now introduce some specific definitions designed to pin down the relationship between the various notions concerning continual and epochwise operation on the one hand and the use of gradient computation on the other. For purposes of this chapter, we make the following definitions. An *exact gradient computation algorithm* is one having the property that at every time step τ during which the network runs there is an interval $(t', t]$ containing τ such that the algorithm computes $\nabla_{\mathbf{w}} J^{\text{total}}(t', t)$ at time t, under the assumption that the network weights are fixed. Any such exact gradient algorithm is called *epochwise* if it is applied to a network operating in epochwise fashion and it computes $\nabla_{\mathbf{w}} J^{\text{total}}(t_0, t_1)$ at t_1, the end of the epoch. It is called *real time* if it computes $\nabla_{\mathbf{w}} J(t)$ at each time t. If, instead, an algorithm computes what is considered only an approximation to $\nabla_{\mathbf{w}} J^{\text{total}}(t', t)$ at time t (under the assumption that the weights are fixed) it will be regarded as an *approximate gradient computation algorithm*.

It must be emphasized that an "exact" gradient algorithm in this sense is only exact if the weights are truly fixed. Such an algorithm may not compute the exact gradient for the current setting of the weights if the weights are allowed to vary. When such an exact gradient algorithm is used to adjust the weights in a continually operating network, what it computes will thus generally be only an approximation to the desired true gradient. Later we discuss this issue further.

A *gradient-based learning algorithm* is a learning algorithm which bases its weight changes on the result of an exact or approximate gradient computation algorithm. The complete specification of such a learning algorithm must include not only how it computes such gradient information, but also how it determines the weight changes from the gradient and when these weight changes are made. Since the main focus of this chapter is on the gradient computation itself, we will generally remain noncommittal about both of these details for the learning algorithms we discuss, occasionally even blurring the distinction between the learning algorithm itself and the gradient computation portion of the algorithm.

One natural way to make the weight changes is along a constant positive multiple of the performance measure gradient, so that

$$\Delta w_{ij} = \eta \frac{\partial J^{\text{total}}(t', t)}{\partial w_{ij}}, \tag{11}$$

for each i and j, where η is a positive learning rate parameter. In those cases where we describe the empirical behavior of particular gradient-based learning algorithms this is the precise weight-change strategy used.

With regard to the timing of the weight changes, it is natural with a continually operating network to adjust the weights at the point when the appropriate gradient has been computed, but, as already noted, for the epochwise case it may be appropriate to make weight adjustments only after multiple epochs. For purposes of this chapter, we consider an *epochwise learning algorithm* to be any learning algorithm appropriate for networks which operate epochwise and which has the property that weight updates are performed only at epoch boundaries, while a *real-time learning algorithm* is one in which weight updates can be performed at all time steps.

It is trivial to observe that any algorithm capable of computing the instantaneous performance gradient $\nabla_{\mathbf{w}}J(t)$ could be used in an epochwise manner by simply accumulating these values until time t_1 but we will discover below that this is not an efficient strategy.

Notation and Assumptions Used for Complexity Analyses

Here we summarize notation to be used in analyses of the computational complexity of the various algorithms to be discussed in this chapter. For completeness, we include some introduced earlier.

n = number of units

m = number of input lines

w_U = number of nonzero weights between units

w_A = number of adjustable weights

Δ_T = number of time steps between target presentations

n_T = average number of units given a target per time step and

L = total number of time steps

We also use the standard notation for describing the order of magnitude of the computational complexity of algorithms, where $O(\varphi(n))$ is the set of positive-integer-valued functions of n which are less than or equal to some constant positive multiple of $\varphi(n)$, $\Omega(\varphi(n))$ is the set of positive-integer-valued functions of n which are greater than or equal to some constant positive multiple of $\varphi(n)$, and $\Theta(\varphi(n)) = O(\varphi(n)) \cap \Omega(\varphi(n))$. Thus O is used to describe an upper bound on the order of magnitude of a quantity of interest, Ω is used to describe a lower bound on this order of magnitude, and Θ is used to describe the exact order of magnitude.

In all cases, we analyze the space complexity in terms of the number of real numbers stored and the time complexity in terms of the number of arithmetic operations required. For all the algorithms to be analyzed, the dominant computation is a form of inner product, so the operations counted are additions and multiplications, in roughly equal numbers. For the analyses presented here we ignore the computational effort required to run the dynamics of the network (which, of course, must be borne regardless of the learning algorithm used), and we also ignore any additional computational effort required to actually update the weights according to the learning algorithm. Our measurement of the complexity is based solely on the computational requirements of the particular exact or approximate gradient computation method used by any such learning algorithm.

For any fixed n, the worst case for all the algorithms discussed here occurs when the network is fully connected and all weights are adaptable. In this case, $w_A = n(n + m)$ and $w_U = n^2$. In all cases below where we perform an analysis of the worst case behavior we restrict attention to classes of networks for which $m \in O(n)$ just to make the resulting formulas a little simpler. This assumption applies, for example, to the situation where a variety of networks are to be taught to perform a particular fixed task, in which case $m \in O(1)$, and it also applies whenever we might imagine increasing the number of units in a network in proportion to the size of the input pattern representation chosen. For our worst-case analyses, then, we will use the fact that w_A and w_U are both in $\Theta(n^2)$.

Note that expressing the complexity in terms of the quantities w_A and w_U assumes that the details of the particular algorithm are designed to take advantage of the limited connectivity through the use of such techniques as sparse matrix storage and manipulation. Alternatively, one could regard multiplication by zero and addition of zero as no-cost operations. A similar remark applies to the use of Δ_T and n_T. All the complexity results derived throughout this chapter are summarized in Tables 1 and 2, which appear near the end of this chapter.

BACK PROPAGATION THROUGH TIME

Here we describe an approach to computing exact error gradient information in recurrent networks based on an extension of the standard back-propagation algorithm for feedforward nets. Various forms of this algorithm have been derived by Werbos (1974), Rumelhart, Hinton, and Williams (1986), and Robinson and Fallside (1987), and continuous-time versions have been derived by Pearlmutter (1989) and Sato (1990a; 1990b). This approach is called *back propagation through time* (BPTT) for reasons that should become clear.

Unrolling a Network

Let $\mathcal{N}$ denote the network which is to be trained to perform a desired sequential behavior. Recall that we assume that $\mathcal{N}$ has n units and that it is to run from time t_0 up through some time t (where we take $t = t_1$ if we are considering an epochwise approach). As described by Rumelhart et al. (1986), we may "unroll" this network in time to obtain a feedforward network $\mathcal{N}^*$ which has a layer for each time step in the interval $[t_0, t]$ and n units in each layer. Each unit in $\mathcal{N}$ has a

Time   Input   Unit Activities

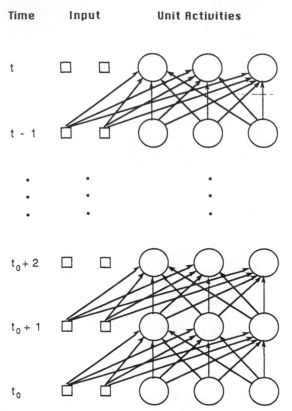

Figure 2.   The unrolled version of the network shown in Figure 1 as it operates from time t_0 through time t. Each connection in the network is assumed to have a delay of one time step.

copy in each layer of $\mathcal{N}^*$, and each connection from unit j to unit i in $\mathcal{N}$ has a copy connecting unit j in layer τ to unit i in layer $\tau + 1$, for each $\tau \in [t_0, t)$. An example of this unrolling mapping is given in Figure 2. The key value of this conceptualization is that it allows one to regard the problem of training a recurrent network as a corresponding problem of training a feedforward network with certain constraints imposed on its weights. The central result driving the BPTT approach is that to compute $\partial J^{\text{total}}(t', t)/\partial w_{ij}$ in $\mathcal{N}$ one simply computes the partial derivatives of $J^{\text{total}}(t', t)$ with respect to each of the $t - t_0$ weights in $\mathcal{N}^*$ corresponding to w_{ij} and adds them up. Thus, the problem of computing the necessary negative error gradient information in the recurrent net $\mathcal{N}$ reduces to the problem of computing the corresponding negative error gradient in the feedforward network $\mathcal{N}^*$, for which one may use standard back propagation.

Straightforward application of this idea leads to two different algorithms, depending on whether an epochwise or continual operation approach is sought.

Detailed mathematical arguments justifying all the results described may be found in the Appendix.

Real-Time Back Propagation through Time

To compute the gradient of $J(t)$ at time t, we proceed as follows. First, we consider t fixed for the moment. This allows us the notational convenience of suppressing any reference to t in the following. We compute values $\epsilon_k(\tau)$ and $\delta_k(\tau)$ for $k \in U$ and $\tau \in (t_0, t]$ by means of the equations

$$\epsilon_k(t) = e_k(t), \tag{12}$$

$$\delta_k(\tau) = f_k'(s_k(\tau))\epsilon_k(\tau), \tag{13}$$

and

$$\epsilon_k(\tau - 1) = \sum_{l \in U} w_{lk}\delta_l(\tau). \tag{14}$$

These equations represent the familiar backpropagation computation. The process begins by using Equations 12 to determine the $\epsilon_k(t)$ values. We call this step *injecting error*, or, if we wish to be more precise, *injecting* $e(t)$, at time t. Then the δ and ϵ values are obtained for successively earlier time steps (i.e., successively earlier layers in $\mathcal{N}^*$), through the repeated use of Equations 13 and 14. Figure 3 gives a schematic representation of this process.

When each unit in the network uses the logistic squashing function, the relation

$$f_k'(s_k(\tau)) = y_k(\tau)[1 - y_k(\tau)] \tag{15}$$

may be substituted in Equation 13. A corresponding observation applies to all the algorithms to be discussed throughout this chapter.

As described in the Appendix, $\epsilon_k(\tau)$ is just a mathematical shorthand for $\partial j(t)/\partial y_k(\tau)$ and $\delta_k(\tau)$ is just a mathematical shorthand for $\partial J(t)/\partial s_k(\tau)$. Thus $\epsilon_k(\tau)$ represents the sensitivity of the instantaneous performance measure $J(t)$ to small perturbations in the output of the kth unit at time τ, while $\delta_k(\tau)$ represents the corresponding sensitivity to small perturbations to that unit's net input at that time.[6]

Once the back-propagation computation has been performed down to time $t_0 + 1$, the desired gradient of instantaneous performance is computed by

---

[6]Note that all explicit references to ϵ could be eliminated by reexpressing the δ update equations entirely in terms of other δ values, resulting in a description of back propagation with which the reader may be more familiar. We have chosen to express the computation in this form for two reasons. One is that we will need to make explicit reference to these ϵ quantities later in this chapter; another is that it is useful to recognize that to back-propagate through a semilinear unit is to apply the chain rule through two stages of computation: application of the squashing function and weighted summation.

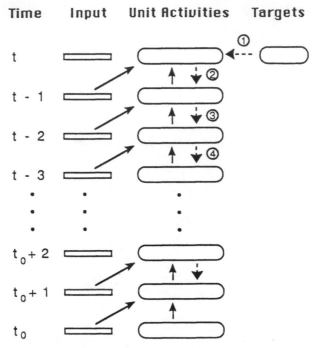

Figure 3. A schematic representation of the storage and processing required for real-time BPTT at each time step t. The history buffer, which grows by one layer at each time step, contains at time t all input and unit output values for every time step from t_0 through t. The solid arrows indicate how each set of unit output values is determined from the input and unit outputs on the previous time step. A backward pass, indicated by the dashed arrows, is performed to determine separate δ values for each unit and for each time step back to $t_0 + 1$. The first step is the injection of external error based on the target values for time step t, and all remaining steps determine virtual error for earlier time steps. Once the backward pass is complete the partial derivative of the negative error with respect to each weight can then be computed.

$$\frac{\partial J(t)}{\partial w_{ij}} = \sum_{\tau=t_0+1}^{t} \delta_i(\tau) x_j(\tau - 1). \tag{16}$$

To summarize, this algorithm, which we call *real-time back propagation through time* performs the following steps at each time t: (1) the current state of the network and the current input pattern is added to a history buffer which stores the entire history of network input and activity since time t_0; (2) error for the current time is injected and back propagation used to compute all the $\epsilon_k(\tau)$ and $\delta_k(\tau)$ values for $t_0 < \tau \leq t$; (3) all the $\partial J(t)/\partial w_{ij}$ values are computed; and (4) weights are changed accordingly. Because this algorithm makes use of potentially unbounded history storage, we will also sometimes denote it BPTT(∞). This algorithm is of more theoretical than practical interest, but later we discuss more practical approximations to it.

Epochwise Back Propagation through Time

An epochwise algorithm based on back propagation through time can be organized as follows. The objective is compute the gradient of $J^{total}(t_0, t_1)$, which can be obtained after the network has been run through the interval $[t_0, t_1]$. Essentially as before, we compute values $\epsilon_k(\tau)$ and $\delta_k(\tau)$ for $k \in U$ and $\tau \in (t_0, t_1]$, this time by means of the equations

$$\epsilon_k(t_1) = e_k(t_1), \tag{17}$$

$$\delta_k(\tau) = f_k'(s_k(\tau))\epsilon_k(\tau), \tag{18}$$

and

$$\epsilon_k(\tau - 1) = e_k(\tau - 1) + \sum_{l \in U} w_{lk}\delta_l(\tau). \tag{19}$$

These equations represent the familiar back-propagation computation applied to a feedforward network in which target values are specified for units in other layers than the last. The process begins at the last time step, using Equations 17 to determine the $\epsilon_k(t)$ values, and proceeds to earlier time steps through the repeated use of Equations 18 and 19. For this algorithm we speak of *injecting error* at time τ to mean the computational step of adding $e_k(\tau)$ to the appropriate sum when computing $\epsilon_k(\tau)$. The back-propagation computation for this case is essentially the same as that for computing the δ values for the real-time version, except that as one gets to layer τ one must inject error for that time step. Thus, not only are the δ values determined by a backward pass through the unrolled network, but the errors committed by the network are also taken into account in reverse order. Figure 4 gives a schematic representation of this process.

It is useful to regard the sum on the right-hand side of Equation 19 as a *virtual error* for unit k at time $\tau - 1$. We might also say that this unit has been given a *virtual target* value for this time step. Thus, in epochwise BPTT, virtual error is added to external error, if any, for each unit at each time step in the backward pass. Note that in real-time BPTT the only contribution to each ϵ is either external error, at the most recent time step, or virtual error, at all earlier time steps.

As with real-time BPTT, $\epsilon_k(\tau)$ is just a mathematical shorthand, this time for $\partial J^{total}(t_0, t_1)/\partial y_k(\tau)$; similarly, $\delta_k(\tau)$ is just a mathematical shorthand for $\partial J^{total}(t_0, t_1)/\partial s_k(\tau)$. Thus $\epsilon_k(\tau)$ represents the sensitivity of the overall performance $J^{total}(t_0, t_1)$ to small perturbations in the output of the kth unit at time τ, while $\delta_k(\tau)$ represents the corresponding sensitivity to small perturbations to that unit's net input at that time.

Time   Input   Unit Activities   Targets

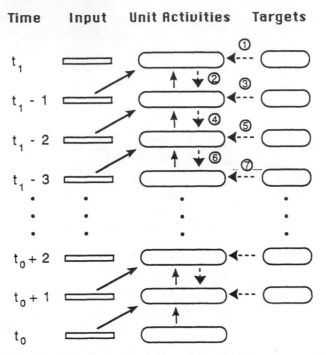

Figure 4.   A schematic representation of the storage and processing required for epochwise BPTT. All input, unit output, and target values for every time step from t_0 and t_1 are stored in the history buffer. The solid arrows indicate how each set of unit output values is determined from the input and unit outputs on the previous time step. After the entire epoch is complete, the backward pass is performed as indicated by the dashed arrows. Each even-numbered step determines the virtual error from later time steps, while each odd-numbered step corresponds to the injection of external error. Once the backward pass has been performed to determine separate δ values for each unit and for each time step back to $t_0 + 1$, the partial derivative of the negative error with respect to each weight can then be computed.

Once the back-propagation computation has been performed down to time $t_0 + 1$, the desired gradient of overall performance is computed by

$$\frac{\partial J^{\text{total}}(t_0, t_1)}{\partial w_{ij}} = \sum_{\tau = t_0 + 1}^{t_1} \delta_i(\tau) x_j(\tau - 1). \tag{20}$$

Epochwise BPTT thus must accumulate the history of activity in (and input to) the network over the entire epoch, along with the history of target values (or, equivalently, the history of errors) over this epoch, after which the following steps are performed: (1) the back-propagation computation is carried out to obtain all the $\epsilon_k(\tau)$ and $\delta_k(\tau)$ values for $t_0 < \tau \le t_1$; (2) all the $\partial J^{\text{total}}(t_0, t_1)/\partial w_{ij}$ values are computed; and (3) weights are changed accordingly. Then the network is reinitialized and this process repeated.

Epochwise BPTT Applied to Settling Networks

Although our main interest here is in the general problem of training networks to perform time-varying behaviors, the BPTT formulation leads to a simple algorithm for training settling networks with constant input, whenever certain assumptions hold. This algorithm, which is a discrete-time version of the algorithm described by Almeida (1987) and Pineda (1987; chapter 4, this volume) is obtained as follows.

First, suppose that a network is to be driven with constant input and that we have initialized it to a state which represents a fixed point for its dynamics. Suppose further that we intend to observe this state at the end of the epoch $[t_0, t_1]$ to compare it with some desired state. If we were to use epochwise BPTT for this situation, the appropriate equations would be

$$\epsilon_k(t_1) = e_k(t_1), \tag{21}$$

$$\delta_k(\tau) = f'_k(s_k(t_1))\epsilon_k(\tau), \tag{22}$$

and

$$\epsilon_k(\tau - 1) = \sum_{l \in U} w_{lk}\delta_l(\tau), \tag{23}$$

with weight changes determined by

$$\frac{\partial J^{\text{total}}(t_0, t_1)}{\partial w_{ij}} - \sum_{\tau=t_0+1}^{t} \delta_i(\tau)x_j(\tau - 1) = \sum_{\tau=t_0+1}^{t} \delta_i(\tau)x_j(t_1)$$

$$= x_j(t_1) \sum_{\tau=t_0+1}^{t} \delta_i(\tau). \tag{24}$$

Note that this last result takes into account the fact that all states and all input during the epoch are equal to their values at the end of the epoch. Thus there is no need to save the history of input and network activity in this case.

Now define

$$\epsilon_k^*(t) = \sum_{\tau=t+1}^{t_1} \epsilon_k(\tau) \tag{25}$$

and

$$\delta_k^*(t) = \sum_{\tau=t+1}^{t_1} \delta_k(\tau). \tag{26}$$

Then Equation 24 becomes

$$\frac{\partial J^{\text{total}}(t_0, t_1)}{\partial w_{ij}} = \delta_i^*(t_0) x_j(t_1). \tag{27}$$

Furthermore, it is easy to check by induction that

$$\epsilon_k^*(t_1) = e_k(t_1), \tag{28}$$

$$\delta_k^*(\tau) = f_k'(s_k(t_1)) \epsilon_k^*(\tau), \tag{29}$$

and

$$\epsilon_k^*(\tau - 1) = e_k(t_1) + \sum_{l \in U} w_{lk} \delta_l^*(\tau). \tag{30}$$

Thus the δ^* and ϵ^* values may be interpreted as representing the δ and ϵ values obtained from performing epochwise BPTT from t_1 back to t_0 while injecting the constant error $e(t_1)$ at each time step, while Equation 27 has the form of the usual feedforward backpropagation computation for determining the partial derivative of error with respect to any weight.

Now consider what happens in the limit as the epoch is made very long. In this case, the computation of the $\delta_i^*(t_0)$ values by means of Equations 28–30 can be viewed as a settling computation, assuming it converges. As it turns out, it can be shown that the BPTT computation given by Equations 21–23 will "die away" (meaning that the backpropagated quantities $\delta_k(\tau)$ and $\epsilon_k(\tau)$ will decrease to zero) exponentially fast as long as the network has reached a *stable* equilibrium state, which implies that the settling computation for the $\delta_i^*(t_0)$ values does indeed converge in this case.

The *recurrent back-propagation* (RBP) algorithm (Almeida, 1987; Pineda, 1987) for training settling networks having constant input consists of applying the following steps: (1) the network is allowed to settle (with the time at which settling has completed regarded as t_1); (2) the BPTT computation given by equations 28–30 is performed for as long as needed until the δ_i^* values converge; (3) all the $\partial J^{\text{total}}(t_0, t_1)/\partial w_{ij}$ values are computed using Equation 27; and (4) weights are changed accordingly. The appealing features of this algorithm are that it does not require the storage of any past history to implement and is entirely local. The reason it requires no history storage is that it implicitly assumes that all relevant past states and input are equal to their current values. This algorithm is thus applicable only to situations where both the desired and actual behaviors of the network are limited to stable settling.

The argument presented so far shows that RBP would compute the same thing as the BPTT computation given by Equations 21–23 over a very long epoch in which the network state is held constant at a stable equilibrium. Now, continue to assume that the input to the network is constant throughout the entire epoch, but assume instead that the network has settled to an equilibrium state from possibly some other starting state by the end of the epoch, at time t_1. Assume further that it has reached this equilibrium state long before t_1. Because the BPTT computation resulting from injecting error only at time t_1 dies away, as described earlier, even in this case RBP and this BPTT computation yield essentially the same result. That is, if error is injected only long after the network has arrived at its steady-state behavior, the full BPTT computation will also give the same result as RBP, because the BPTT computation dies away before reaching the transient portion of the network's behavior. This shows clearly that not only is RBP limited to training settling networks, but it is really only designed to directly influence their fixed points and cannot control their transient behaviors. In general, RBP is only capable of perturbing the equilibrium states already present in the network's dynamics.[7] On the other hand, as long as errors are injected within (or soon after) the transient behavior of a network, BPTT can directly influence such transient behavior.

These observations concerning the inability of even full BPTT to reach back into the transient behavior if error is injected too long after steady-state behavior is reached have some other interesting consequences for the problem of training continually operating networks, which we describe below when we discuss the teacher forcing strategy.

Computational Requirements of BPTT Algorithms

It is clear that to store the history of m-dimensional input to and n-dimensional activity of a network over h time steps requires $(m + n)h$ numbers. In addition, the number of target values over these h time steps is no greater than nh. Thus the gradient computation performed for epochwise BPTT has space complexity in $\Theta((m + n)h)$, where h represents the epoch length. However, for BPTT(∞) this history must continue to grow indefinitely. With L representing the total time over which the network is actually run, the space complexity of BPTT(∞) is thus in $\Theta((m + n)L)$.

To determine the number of arithmetic operations required for these algorithms, note that Equation 13 requires an evaluation of $f'_k(s_k(\tau))$ plus one multiplication for each k in U. For the logistic squashing function this amounts to two multiplications per unit for determining the δ values from the corresponding ϵ values. In general, the number of operations required for this part of the back-propagation computation is in $\theta(n)$. Application of Equation 14 for all $k \in U$ at each fixed τ clearly requires w_U multiplications and $w_U - 1$ additions, while

---

[7]However, as we discuss later, Pineda (1988; chapter 4, this volume) has shown that new equilibrium points can be created by combining RBP with the *teacher forcing* technique.

application of Equation 19 for all $k \in U$ at each fixed τ requires the same number of multiplications and up to n more additions and subtractions, depending on how many units have target values for that time step. As long as we assume $w_U \in \Omega(n)$, it follows that each stage of the back-propagation computation has time complexity in $\Theta(w_U)$, regardless of whether error is injected at all time steps during the backward pass, as in epochwise BPTT, or just at the last time step, as in real-time BPTT.

Now let $h = t - t_0$, where t represents the time at which BPTT is performed for either real-time or epochwise BPTT. (In the latter case, $t = t_1$.) It is clear that Equation 16, which must be evaluated once for each adaptable weight, requires h multiplications and $h - 1$ additions, leading to a total of $\Theta(w_A h)$ operations. Thus the total number of operations required to compute the gradient for one epoch in epochwise BPTT is in $\Theta(w_U H + w_A h)$.[8] Amortized across the h time steps of the epoch, the gradient computation for epochwise BPTT requires an average of $\Theta(w_U + w_A)$ operations per time step. For real-time BPTT, a back-propagation computation all the way back to t_0 must be performed any time a target is specified. Thus the total number of operations required over the entire training interval of length L is in $\Theta((w_U + w_A)T^2/\Delta_T)$, which is an average of $\Theta((w_U T + w_A)T/\Delta_T)$ operations per time step. These complexity results are summarized in Table 1.

The worst case for either of these algorithms for any fixed n is when the network is fully connected, all weights are adaptable, and target values are supplied at every time step, so that $\Delta_T = 1$. In this case, epochwise BPTT has space complexity in $\Theta(nh)$ and average time complexity per time step in $\Theta(n^2)$, while real-time BPTT has space complexity in $\Theta(nL)$ and average time complexity per time step in $\Theta(n^2 L)$, as shown in Table 2.

Note that when weights are changed throughout the course of operating the network, a variant of real-time BPTT is possible in which the history of weight values are saved as well and used for the backpropagation computation, by replacing w_{lk} by $w_{lk}(\tau)$ in Equation 14. For this algorithm, the storage requirements are in $\Theta((m + n + w_A)T)$ in the general case and in $\Theta(n^2 T)$ in the worst case.

While real-time BPTT could be used to train a network which is operated in epochwise fashion, it is clearly inefficient to do so because it must duplicate some computation which need only be performed once in epochwise BPTT. Epochwise BPTT computes $\nabla_{\mathbf{w}} J^{\text{total}}(t_0, t_1)$ without ever computing any of the gradients $\nabla_{\mathbf{w}} J(t)$ for individual time steps t.

---

[8]This assumes that there is some error to inject at the last time step. In general, it is also assumed throughout this analysis that the number of units given targets and the connectivity of the network are such that backpropagation "reaches" every unit. If this is not true, then the time complexity could be lower for an algorithm designed to take advantage of this.

THE REAL-TIME RECURRENT LEARNING ALGORITHM

While BPTT uses the backward propagation of error information to compute the error gradient, an alternative approach is to propagate activity gradient information forward. This leads to a learning algorithm which we have called *real-time recurrent learning* (RTRL). This algorithm has been independently derived in various forms by Robinson and Fallside (1987), Kuhn (1987), Bachrach (1988; Chapter 11, this volume), Mozer (1989; chapter 5, this volume), and Williams and Zipser (1989a), and continuous-time versions have been proposed by Gherrity (1989), Doya and Yoshizawa (1989), and Sato (1990a; 1990b).

The Algorithm

For each $k \in U$, $i \in U$, $j \in U \cup I$, and $t_0 \le t \le t_1$, we define

$$p_{ij}^k(t) = \frac{\partial y_k(t)}{\partial w_{ij}}. \tag{31}$$

This quantity measures the sensitivity of the value of the output of the kth unit at time t to a small increase in the value of w_{ij}, taking into account the effect of such a change in the weight over the entire trajectory from t_0 to t but assuming that the initial state of the network, the input over $[t_0, t)$, and the remaining weights are not altered.

From Equations 7 and 8 and use of the chain rule, we find that

$$\frac{\partial J(t)}{\partial w_{ij}} = \sum_{k \in U} e_k(t) p_{ij}^k(t) \tag{32}$$

for each $i \in U$ and $j \in U \cup I$. Also, differentiating Equations 2 and 3 for the network dynamics yields

$$p_{ij}^k(t+1) = f_k'(s_k(t+1)) \left[\sum_{l \in U} w_{kl} p_{ij}^l(t) + \delta_{ik} x_j(t) \right], \tag{33}$$

where δ_{ik} denotes the Kronecker delta. Furthermore,

$$p_{ij}^k(t_0) = \frac{\partial y_k(t_0)}{\partial w_{ij}} = 0 \tag{34}$$

since we assume that the initial state of the network has no functional dependence on the weights. These equations hold for all $k \in U$, $i \in U$, $j \in U \cup I$, and $t \ge t_0$.

Thus we may use Equations 33 and 34 to compute the quantities $\{p_{ij}^k(t)\}$ at each time step in terms of their prior values and other information depending on activity in the network at that time. Combining these values with the error vector $\mathbf{e}(t)$ for that time step via Equations 32 then yields the negative error gradient

453

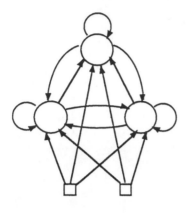

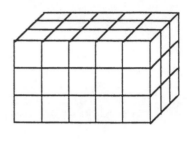

p Array

Network

Figure 5.   The data structures that must be updated on each time step to run the RTRL algorithm with the network of Figure 1. In addition to updating the three unit activities within the network itself on each time step (along with the 15 weights, if appropriate), the $3 \times 5 \times 3$ array of p_{ij}^k values must also be updated. It is assumed here that all 15 weights in the network are adjustable. In general, a p_{ij}^k value for each combination of adjustable weight and unit in the network must be stored and updated on each time step for RTRL.

$\nabla_{\mathbf{w}} J(t)$. Because the $p_{ij}^k(t)$ values are available at time t, the computation of this gradient occurs in real time. Figure 5 depicts the data structures that must be updated on each time step to run the RTRL algorithm with the network of Figure 1.

Computational Requirements

The computational requirements of the RTRL algorithm arise from the need to store and update all the p_{ij}^k values. To analyze these requirements, it is useful to view the triply indexed set of quantities p_{ij}^k as forming a matrix, each of whose rows corresponds to a weight in the network and each of whose columns corresponds to a unit in the network. Looking at the update equations it is not hard to see that, in general, we must keep track of the values p_{ij}^k even for those k corresponding to units that never receive a teacher signal. Thus, we must always have n columns in this matrix. However, if the weight w_{ij} is not to be trained (as would happen, for example, if we constrain the network topology so that there is no connection from unit j to unit i), then it is not necessary to compute the value p_{ij}^k for any $k \in U$. This means that this matrix need only have a row for each adaptable weight in the network, while having a column for each unit. Thus the minimal number of p_{ij}^k values needed to store and update for a general network having n units and w_A adjustable weights is nw_A. Furthermore, from Equation 33 it is clear that the number of multiplications and the number of additions required to update all the p_{ij}^k values are each essentially equal to $w_U w_A$. Note that this computation is performed on every time step, regardless of whether target values are specified for that time step.

In addition, Equation 32 requires one multiplication (and approximately one addition) at each time step for each unit given a target on that time step and each adjustable weight. This amounts to an average of $\Theta(n_T w_A)$ operations per time step. Thus the space complexity of the gradient computation for RTRL is in $\Theta(nw_A)$, and its average time complexity per time step is in $\Theta(w_U w_A)$, as indicated in Table 1. When the network is fully connected and all weights are adaptable, this algorithm has space complexity in $\Theta(n^3)$ and average time complexity per time step in $\Theta(n^4)$, as shown in Table 2.

While this time complexity is quite severe for serial implementation, part of the appeal of this algorithm is that it can run in $O(n)$ time per time step using $\Theta(n^3)$ processors. However, this raises the question of its communication requirements, especially in relation to the network being trained. Interestingly, update of the p_{ij}^k values can be carried out using a completely local communication scheme in the network being trained if one allows n-tuples to be communicated along network connections rather than single real numbers. The idea is to let each unit k store within it the set of numbers p_{ij}^k with (i, j) ranging over all weights in the network. If we regard this set of numbers as a vector $\mathbf{p}^k$, then the set of Equations 33 corresponding to each fixed value of k can be organized into a single vector update equation. In this way, one can imagine a network of units which pass not only their activations around, but also thee $\mathbf{p}^k$ vectors. However, the actual computation of $\nabla_{\mathbf{w}} J(t)$ by means of Equation 32 ultimately requires global access to the $\mathbf{p}^k$ vectors.

Without giving details, we note that the entire RTRL algorithm could be carried out in a more conventional scalar-value-passing network having, in addition to the n units of the network to be trained, an additional unit for each p_{ij}^k value and an additional unit for each connection in the network to be trained. Each unit in this last set would simultaneously gate numerous connections among the remaining units.

A HYBRID ALGORITHM

It is possible to formulate a hybrid algorithm incorporating aspects of both BPTT and the forward gradient propagation computation used in RTRL. This algorithm, first proposed in Williams 1989, and later described by Schmidhuber (1992), is interesting both because it helps shed light on the relationship between BPTT and RTRL and because it can yield exact error gradient information for a continually running network more efficiently than any other method we know. The mathematical derivation of this algorithm is provided in the Appendix. Here we describe the steps of the algorithm and analyze its computational complexity.

The Algorithm

This algorithm involves a segmentation of time into disjoint intervals each of length $h = t - t'$, with weight changes performed only at the end of each such interval. By our definition, then, this is not a real-time algorithm when $h > 1$. Nor is it an epochwise algorithm, since it does not depend on the artificial imposition of credit-assignment boundaries and/or state resets. The segmentation into intervals is purely arbitrary and need have no relation to the task being performed. Over each such interval $[t', t]$ the history of activity of (and input to) the network is saved; at the end of this time period, a computation to be described is performed. Then the process is begun anew, beginning with collecting the history of the network activity starting at time t (which becomes the new value of t').

This algorithm depends on having all the values $p_{ij}^k(t')$, as used in RTRL, for the start of each time period. For the moment, we assume that these are available; later we describe how they are updated by this algorithm. Then the equations

$$\epsilon_k(\tau) = \begin{cases} e_k(t) & \text{if } \tau = t \\ e_k(\tau) + \sum_{l \in U} w_{lk}\delta_l(\tau + 1) & \text{if } \tau < t \end{cases} \tag{35}$$

and

$$\delta_k(\tau) = f_k'(s_k(\tau))\epsilon_k(\tau) \tag{36}$$

are used to compute all the values $\epsilon_k(\tau)$ for $t' \leq \tau \leq t$ and $\delta_k(\tau)$ for $t' < \tau \leq t$. This computation is essentially identical to an epochwise BPTT computation over the interval $[t', t]$. In particular, note that each error vector $\mathbf{e}(\tau)$, for $t' < \tau \leq t$, is injected along the backward pass. Once all these ϵ and δ values are obtained, the gradient of $J^{\text{total}}(t', t)$, the cumulative negative error over the time interval $(t', t]$, is computed by means of the equations

$$\frac{\partial J^{\text{total}}(t', t)}{\partial w_{ij}} = \sum_{l \in U} \epsilon_l(t')p_{ij}^l(t') + \sum_{\tau = t'}^{t-1} \delta_i(\tau + 1)x_j(\tau), \tag{37}$$

for each i and j.

Note that the second sum on the right-hand side is what would be computed for this partial derivative if one were to truncate the BPTT computation at time t', while the first sum represents a correction in terms of the p values used in RTRL. There are two special cases of this algorithm worth noting. When $t' = t$, the second sum in Equation 37 vanishes and we recover the RTRL Equation 32 expressing the desired partial derivatives in terms of the current p values. When

$t' = t_0$, the first sum in Equation 37 vanishes and we recover Equation 16 for the BPTT(∞) algorithm.

Thus far we have described how the desired error gradient is obtained, assuming that the p values are available at time t'. In order to repeat the same process over the next time interval, beginning at time t, the algorithm must also compute all the values $p_{ij}^r(t)$. For the moment, consider a fixed r in U. Suppose that we were to inject error $\mathbf{e}^r(t)$ at time t, where $e_k^r(t) = \delta_{kr}$ (the Kronecker delta), and use BPTT to compute $\partial J(t)/\partial w_{ij}$. It is clear from Equation 32 that the result would be equal to $p_{ij}^r(t)$. Thus this gives an alternative view of what these quantities are. For each r, the set of numbers $p_{ij}^r(t)$ represents the negative error gradient that would be computed by BPTT if unit r were given a target 1 greater than its actual value. Furthermore, we may use the same approach just used to compute the partial derivatives of an arbitrary error function to compute the partial derivatives of this particular imagined error function. Thus, to compute $p_{ij}^r(t)$ for all i and j, the algorithm first performs a BPTT computation using the equations[9]

$$\epsilon_k(\tau) = \begin{cases} \delta_{kr} & \text{if } \tau = t, \\ \sum_{l \in U} w_{lk}\delta_l(\tau + 1) & \text{if } \tau < t, \end{cases} \tag{38}$$

together with Equations 36, to obtain a set of values[10] $\epsilon_k(\tau)$ for $t' \leq \tau \leq t$ and $\delta_k(\tau)$ for $t' < \tau \leq t$. These values are then used to compute $p_{ij}^r(t)$ for each i and j by means of the equations

$$p_{ij}^r(t) = \sum_{l \in U} \epsilon_l(t')p_{ij}^l(t') + \sum_{\tau=t'}^{t-1} \delta_i(\tau + 1)x_j(\tau). \tag{39}$$

In other words, to compute $p_{ij}^r(t)$, a 1 is injected at unit r at time t and BPTT performed back to time t', and the results substituted into Equation 39.

This process is repeated for each r in U in order to obtain all the p values for time t. Thus this algorithm involves a total of $n + 1$ different BPTT computations, one to compute the error gradient and n to update the p values. Because this algorithm involves both a forward propagation of gradient information (from time t' to time t) and backward propagation through time, we will denote this

---

[9]The reader is warned to avoid confusing the singly subscripted (and time-dependent) quantities denoted δ_l, which are obtained via back propagation, with the doubly subscripted Kronecker delta, such as δ_{kr}. Both uses of the symbol δ appear throughout the equations presented in this and the next section.

[10]The reader should understand that, although we are denoting the result of several different BPTT computations in the same way, the various sets of δ and ϵ values obtained from each BPTT computation are unrelated to each other. We have resisted introducing additional notation here which might make this clearer, on the grounds that it might clutter the presentation. A more precise formulation may be found in the Appendix.

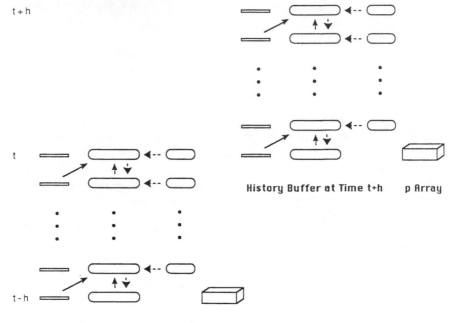

History Buffer at Time t   **p Array**

Figure 6.   A schematic representation of the storage and processing required for the FP/BPTT(h) algorithm for two consecutive executions of the error gradient computation, one at time step t and the next at time step $t + h$. From time step $t - h$ through time step t the network input, activity, and target values are accumulated in the history buffer. At time t the cumulative error gradient is computed on the basis of one BPTT pass through this buffer, also using the p values stored for time step $t - h$. In addition, n separate BPTT passes, one for each unit in the network, are performed to compute the p values for time t. Each such BPTT pass begins with the injection of 1 as "error" at a single unit at the top level. Once the weights have been adjusted on the basis of the cumulative error gradient over the interval $(t - h, t]$ and the p values have been updated at time t, accumulation of the history begins anew over the interval $[t, t + h]$.

algorithm FP/BPTT(h), where $h = t - t'$ is the number of past states which are saved in the history buffer. Figure 6 gives a schematic representation of the storage and processing required for this algorithm.

Computational Requirements

This hybrid algorithm requires $\Theta(nw_A)$ storage for the p_{ij} values, like RTRL, and $\Theta((m + n)h)$ storage for the history of network input, activity, and teacher signals over the interval $[t', t]$, like epochwise BPTT. In addition, each BPTT computation requires $\Theta(nh)$ storage for all the δ and ϵ values, but this space may be reused for each of the $n + 1$ applications of BPTT. Thus its overall storage requirements are in $\Theta(nw_A + (m + n)h)$.

To determine the number of arithmetic operations performed, note that each BPTT computation requires $\Theta((w_U + w_A)h)$ operations, and, for each such BPTT computation, equation 37, requiring $\Theta(n + h)$ operations, must be used for each adjustable weight, or w_A times. Thus the number of operations required for each of the $n + 1$ applications of BPTT requires $\Theta(w_U h + 2w_A h + nw_A) = \Theta(w_U h + w_A h + nw_A)$, giving rise to a total number of operations in $\Theta(nw_U h + nw_A h + n^2 w_A)$. Since this computation is performed every h time steps, the average number of operations per time step is in $\Theta(nw_U + nw_A + n^2 w_A/h)$. When the network is fully connected and all weights are adaptable, FP/BPTT(h) has space complexity in $\Theta(n^3 + nh)$ and average time complexity per time step in $\Theta(n^3 + n^4/h)$. Thus, by making h proportional to n, the resulting algorithm has worst-case space complexity in $\Theta(n^3)$ and time complexity per time step in $\Theta(n^3)$. Thee complexity results are summarized in Tables 1 and 2.

This means that of all exact gradient computation algorithms for continually operating networks, FP/BPTT(cn), where c is any constant, has superior asymptotic complexity properties. Its asymptotic space complexity is no worse than that of RTRL, and its asymptotic time complexity is significantly better. The reduction in time complexity in comparison to RTRL is achieved by only performing the update of the p_{ij}^k values after every cn time steps. The improvement in both time and space complexity over real-time BPTT over long training times is achieved because there is no need to apply BPTT further back than to the point where these p_{ij}^k values are available.

SOME ARCHITECTURE-SPECIFIC APPROACHES

Up to now, we have restricted attention to the case where every connection in the network is assumed to have a delay of one time step. It is sometimes useful to relax this assumption. In particular, a number of researchers have proposed specific mixed feedforward/feedback architectures for processing temporal data. In almost all of these architectures the feedforward connections are assumed to have no delay while the feedback connections are assumed to incorporate a delay of one time step. After briefly considering the case of arbitrary (but fixed) delays, we then focus in this section on exact gradient algorithms for certain classes of network architectures where all delays are 0 or 1.

Connection-Dependent Delays

To handle the general case in which various connections in the network have different delays, Equation 2 for the network dynamics must be replaced by

$$s_k(t) = \sum_{l \in U \cup I} w_{kl} x_l(t - \Delta_{kl}), \tag{40}$$

where Δ_{kl} represents the delay on the connection from unit (or input line) l to unit k. In general, we may allow each delay to be any nonnegative integer, as long as the subgraph consisting of all links having delay 0 is acyclic. This condition is necessary and sufficient to guarantee that there is a fixed ordering of the indices in U such that, for any t and k, $s_k(t)$ depends only on quantities $x_l(t')$ having the property that $t' < t$ or l comes before k in this ordering.

As an alternative to allowing multiple delays, one could instead transform any such setup into a form where all delays are 1 by adding "delay units" along paths having a delay larger than 1 and repeating computations along paths having delay 0, but this is generally undesirable in simulations. Because holding a value fixed in memory is a no-cost operation on a digital computer, it is always more efficient to simulate such a system by only updating variables when necessary. For example, in a strictly layered network having h layers of weights, although they both lead to the same result, it is clearly more efficient to update activity one layer at a time than to run one grand network update a total of h times. A similar observation applies to the backward pass needed for back propagation. Figure 7 illustrates a case where all links have delay 0 or 1 and shows a useful way to conceptualize the unrolling of this network.

Watrous and Shastri (1986) have derived a generalization of BPTT to this more general case, and it is straightforward to extend the RTRL approach as well. With a little more effort, the hybrid algorithm described here can also be generalized to this case. Rather than give details of these generalizations, we confine attention in the remainder of this section to some particular cases where all delays are 0 or 1 and describe some exact gradient computation algorithms for these involving both backward error propagation and forward gradient propagation. These cases represent modest generalizations of some specific mixed feedforward/feedback architectures which have been considered by various researchers.

Some Special Two-Stage Architectures

The architectures to be investigated here involve limited recurrent connections added to what would otherwise be a feedforward net. We regard these architectures as consisting of two stages, which we call a *hidden stage* and an *output stage*. The output stage must contain all units given targets, but it need not be confined to these. The hidden stage contains all units not in the output stage. As a minimum, each architecture has feedforward connections from the hidden stage to the output stage, and there may be additional feedforward connections within each stage as well. Thus, in particular, each stage may be a multilayer network. Let U_O denote the set of indices of units in the output stage, and let U_H denote the set of indices of units in the hidden stage.

Here we restrict attention to three classes of recurrent net which consist of this

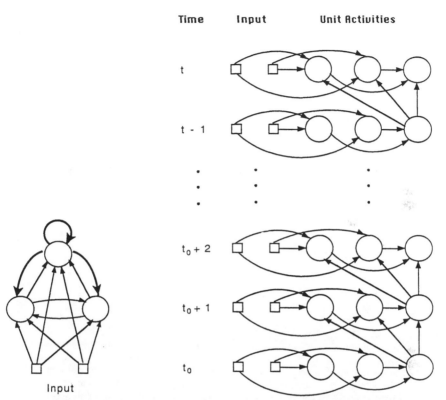

Time   Input   Unit Activities

t

t - 1

$t_0 + 2$

$t_0 + 1$

t_0

Input

Figure 7.   A network having connections with delays of 0 and 1 and its unrolling from time t_0 to t. The feedforward connections, indicated by the thinner arrows in the network itself, all have a delay of 0. These correspond to the within-level connections in the unrolled version. The feedback connections, indicated by the thicker arrows in the network, all have a delay of 1. These correspond to the connections from each level to the next level above it in the unrolled version. Other delays beside 0 and 1 are possible and would be represented by connections that skip levels. In the unrolled network, updating of activity is assumed to occur from left to right within each level and then upward to the next level. Thus a sequence of operations is performed within each single time step when computing the activity in the network. When errors are back-propagated, processing goes in the reverse direction, from higher levels to lower levels and from right to left within each level.

minimum feedforward connectivity plus some additional recurrent connections. In all cases, we assume that the feedforward connections have delay 0 and the added feedback connections have delay 1. For any given network which falls into one of these categories there may be many ways to decompose it into the two stages, and particular recurrent networks may be viewed as belonging to more

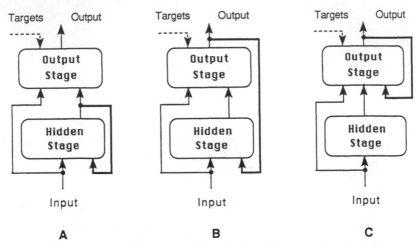

Figure 8.   Three special architectures where all connections have delays of 0 or 1 time step. In each case the hidden stage and the output stage have only 0-delay feedforward connections within them. They may each consist of multilayer networks, for example. It is also assumed that there is no delay on the input connections or the feedforward connections from units in the hidden stage to units in the output stage. The output stage must contain all units which receive target values. Input may optionally feed directly to the output stage, as indicated. The feedback connections, indicated by the heavier arrows, all have a delay of 1 time step. The three possible feedback configurations are where (a) all feedback is confined to the hidden stage; (b) all feedback goes from the output stage to the hidden stage; and (c) all feedback is confined to the output stage. A specialized mixture of back propagation and RTRL is applicable to each of these architectures.

than one category, depending on which units are assigned to which stage. We consider feedback connections confined to one of three possibilities: internal feedback within the hidden stage, feedback from the output stage to the hidden stage, and internal feedback within the output stage. Figure 8 depicts these three architectures. In this section we omit discussion of the computational complexity of the algorithms described.

Hidden-to-Hidden Feedback Only

Figure 8a illustrates a general architecture in which all feedback connections are confined to the hidden stage. One example of this architecture is provided by the work of Elman (1988), who has considered a version in which the hidden stage and the output stage are each one-layer networks, with feedback connections provided between all units in the hidden stage. Cleeremans, Servan-Screiber, and McClelland (1989; Chapter 9, this volume) have also studied this architecture extensively. One approach to creating an real-time, exact gradient algorithm for this architecture is to use a hybrid strategy involving both RTRL and back propagation. In this approach, the p_{ij}^k values need only be stored and updated for the hidden units, with back propagation used to determine other necessary quantities. Mathematical justification for the validity of this approach is based on essentially the same arguments used to derive the hybrid algorithm FP/BPTT(h).

The error gradient is computed by means of

$$\frac{\partial J(t)}{\partial w_{ij}} = \begin{cases} \delta_i(t)x_j(t) & \text{if } i \in U_O, \\ \displaystyle\sum_{l \in U_H} \epsilon_l(t)p_{ij}^l(t), & \text{if } i \in U_H, \end{cases} \qquad (41)$$

where $\delta_i(t)$ is obtained by back propagation entirely within the hidden stage.

The p_{ij}^k values, for $k \in U_H$, are updated by means of the equations

$$p_{ij}^k(t) = f_k'(s_k(t)) \left[\sum_{l \in U_H} w_{kl} p_{ij}^l(t-1) + \delta_{ik} x_j(t-1) \right], \qquad (42)$$

which are just the RTRL Equations 33 specialized to take into account the fact that w_{kl} is 0 if $l \in U_O$.

One noteworthy special case of this type of architecture has been investigated by Mozer (1989; chapter 5, this volume). For this architecture, the only connections allowed between units in the hidden stage are self-recurrent connections. In this case, p_{ij}^k is 0 except when $k = i$. This algorithm can then be implemented in an entirely local fashion by regarding each p_{ij}^i value as being stored with w_{ij}, because the only information needed to update p_{ij}^i is locally available at unit i. The algorithm described here essentially coincides with Mozer's algorithm except that his net uses a slightly different form of computation within the self-recurrent units.

Output-to-Hidden Feedback Only

Figure 8b illustrates a general architecture in which all feedback connections go from the output stage to the hidden stage. One example of this architecture is provided by the work of Jordan (1986), who has considered a version in which the hidden stage and the output stage are each one-layer networks, with feedback connections going from all units in the output stage to all units in the hidden stage. As in the preceding case, we consider a hybrid approach for this architecture involving both RTRL and back propagation. In this case, the p_{ij}^k values are only stored and updated for the output units. Mathematical justification for the validity of this approach is based on essentially the same arguments used to derive the hybrid algorithm FP/BPTT(h).

The error gradient is computed by means of the equation

$$\frac{\partial J(t)}{\partial w_{ij}} = \sum_{k \in U_O} e_k(t) p_{ij}^k(t), \tag{43}$$

which is just the RTRL Equation 32 specialized to take into account the fact that e_k is always 0 for $k \in U_H$.

The updating of the p values for units in the output stage is based on performing a separate backpropagation computation for each $k \in U_O$, in a manner very much like that used in the hybrid algorithm FP/BPTT(h). To compute $p_{ij}^k(t)$, for $k \in U_O$, inject a 1 as "error" at the kth unit and back-propagate all the way from the output stage, through the hidden stage, and through the feedback connections, right back to the output stage at the previous time step. Then compute

$$p_{ij}^k(t) = \sum_{l \in U_O} \epsilon_l(t - 1) p_{ij}^l(t - 1) + \delta_i(t) x_j(t - \Delta_{ij}), \tag{44}$$

where Δ_{ij} is 1 if $j \in U_O$ and 0 otherwise. The relevant $\delta_i(t)$ and $\epsilon_i(t - 1)$ values are obtained from the back-propagation computation, with a new set obtained for each k.

Output-to-Output Feedback Only

Figure 8c illustrates a general architecture in which all feedback connections are confined to the output stage. Just as in the previous cases, we consider a hybrid approach in which the p_{ij}^k values need only be stored and updated for the output units, with back propagation used to determine other necessary quantities. As before, the error gradient is computed by means of Equation 43.

Updating of the p_{ij}^k values is performed using a slightly different mix of back propagation and forward gradient propagation than in the previous case. To derive this, we write the equation computing net input for a unit in the output stage as

$$s_k(t) = \sum_{l \in U_H \cup I} w_{kl} x_l(t) + \sum_{l \in U_O} w_{kl} x_l(t - \Delta_{kl}), \tag{45}$$

where Δ_{kl} is 0 if the connection from unit l to unit k is a feedforward connection within the output stage and 1 if it is a feedback connection. Singling out the first sum on the right-hand side of this equation, we define

$$s_k^*(t) = \sum_{l \in U_H \cup I} w_{kl} x_l(t). \tag{46}$$

It then follows that

$$p_{ij}^k(t) = f_k'(s_k(t)) \frac{\partial s_k^*(t)}{\partial w_{ij}} + f_k'(s_k(t)) \left[\sum_{l \in U_O} w_{kl} p_{ij}^l(t) + \delta_{ik} x_j(t - \Delta_{ij}) \right]. \tag{47}$$

If $i \in U_O$, the first term on the right-hand side of this equation is zero and the updating of p_{ij}^k thus proceeds using a pure RTRL approach. That is, for k and i in U_O, p_{ij}^k is updated by means of the equation

$$p_{ij}^k(t) = f_k'(s_k(t)) \left[\sum_{l \in U} w_{kl} p_{ij}^l(t) + \delta_{ik} x_j(t - \Delta_{ij}) \right]. \qquad (48)$$

If $i \in U_H$, however, the first term on the right-hand side of Equation 47 is not necessarily zero, but it can be computed by injecting a 1 as "error" at the output of the kth unit and back-propagating directly into the hidden stage to the point where δ_i is computed. This backpropagation computation begins at the output of the kth unit and proceeds directly into the hidden stage, ignoring all connections to the kth unit from units in the output stage. Specifically, then, for each fixed $k \in U_O$, one such back-propagation pass is performed to obtain a set of $\delta_i(t)$ values for all $i \in U_H$. Then the p_{ij}^k values for this particular k are updated using

$$p_{ij}^k(t) = \delta_i(t) x_j(t) + f_k'(s_k(t)) \left[\sum_{l \in U_o} w_{kl} p_{ij}^l(t) + \delta_{ik} x_j(t - \Delta_{ij}) \right]. \qquad (49)$$

One special case of this architecture is a network having a single self-recurrent unit as its only output unit, with a feedforward network serving as a preprocessing stage. In this case, there is a single value of p_{ij}^k to associate with each weight w_{ij}, and we may imagine that it is stored with its corresponding weight. Then only local communication is required to update these p values, and a single global broadcast of the error $e_k(t)$ (where k is the index of the output unit) is sufficient to allow error gradient computation. This may be viewed as a generalization of the single self-recurrent unit architecture studied by Bachrach (1988). One of the algorithms he investigated coincides with that described here.

APPROXIMATION STRATEGIES

Up to this point we have confined our attention to exact gradient computation algorithms. However, it is often useful to consider algorithms which omit part of the computation required to fully compute the exact gradient. There are actually several reasons why this can be advantageous, some of which we discuss later. The primary reason is to simplify the computational requirements.

Truncated Back Propagation through Time

A natural approximation to the full real-time BPTT computation is obtained by truncating the backward propagation of information to a fixed number of prior time steps. This is, in general, only a heuristic technique because it ignores dependencies in the network spanning durations longer than this fixed number of time steps. Nevertheless, in those situations where the actual back-propagation computation leads to exponential decay in strength through (backward) time, which occurs in networks whose dynamics consist of settling to fixed points, this can give a reasonable approximation to the true error gradient. Even when this is not the case, its use may still be justified when weights are adjusted as the network runs simply because the computation of the "exact" gradient over a long period of time may be misleading since it is based on the assumption that the weights are constant. We call this algorithm *truncated back propagation through time*. With h representing the number of prior time steps saved, this algorithm will be denoted BPTT(h). Note that the discrepancy between the BPTT(h) result and the BPTT(∞) result is equal to the first sum on the right-hand side of Equation 37 for the FP/BPTT(h) algorithm. The processing performed by the BPTT(h) algorithm is depicted in Figure 9.

The computational complexity of this algorithm is quite reasonable as long as h is small. Its space complexity is in $\Theta((m + n)h)$ and the average number of arithmetic operations required per time step is in $\Theta((w_U + w_A)h/\Delta_T)$. The worst case for this algorithm for any fixed n is when the network is fully connected, all

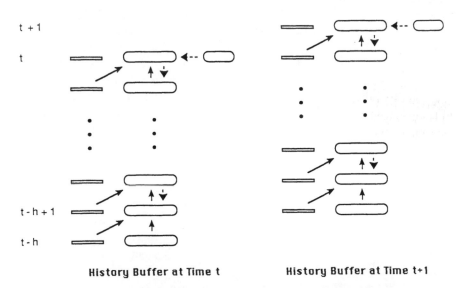

History Buffer at Time t   **History Buffer at Time t+1**

Figure 9.   A schematic representation of the storage and processing required for the BPTT(h) algorithm for two consecutive executions of the error gradient computation, one at time step t and the next at time step $t + 1$. The history buffer always contains the current network input, activity, and target values, along with the values of network input and activity for the h prior time steps. The BPTT computation requires injection of error only for the current time step and is performed anew at each subsequent time step.

weights are adaptable, and target values are supplied at every time step, so that $\Delta_T = 1$. In this case the algorithm requires $\Theta(nh)$ space and $\Theta(n^2h)$ time. These complexity results are summarized in Tables 1 and 2.

A number of researchers (Watrous & Shastri, 1986; Elman, 1988; Cleeremans, Servan-Schreiber, & McClelland, 1989, chapter 9, this volume) have performed experimental studies of learning algorithms based on this approximate gradient computation algorithm. The architecture studied by Elman and by Cleeremans et al. is an example of the two-stage type described earlier with hidden-to-hidden feedback only, but the learning algorithm used in the recurrent hidden stage is BPTT(1).

A More Efficient Version of Truncated Back Propagation through Time

Interestingly, it is possible to devise a more efficient approximate gradient computation algorithm for continually operating networks by combining aspects of epochwise BPTT with the truncated BPTT approach, as has been noted in Williams, (1989). Note that in the truncated BPTT algorithm, BPTT through the most recent h time steps is performed anew each time the network is run through an additional time step. More generally, one may consider letting the network run through h' additional time steps before performing the next BPTT computation. In this case, if t represents a time at which BPTT is to be performed, the algorithm computes an approximation to $\nabla_W J^{\text{total}}(t - h', t)$ by taking into account only that part of the history over the interval $[t - h, t]$. Let us denote this algorithm BPTT($h; h'$). Thus BPTT(h) is the same as BPTT($h; 1$), and BPTT($h; h$) is the epochwise BPTT algorithm, which, of course, is not an exact gradient algorithm unless there are state resets at the appropriate times. Figure 10 depicts the processing performed by the BPTT($h; h'$) algorithm.

In general, whenever it can be assumed that backpropagating through the most recent $h - h' + 1$ time steps gives a reasonably close approximation to the result that would be obtained from back-propagating all the way back to t_0, then this algorithm should be sufficient. The storage requirements of this algorithm are essentially the same as those of BPTT(h), but, because it computes the cumulative error gradient by means of BPTT only once every h' time steps, its average time complexity per time step is reduced by a factor of h'. Thus, its average time complexity per time step is in $\Theta((w_U + w_A)h/h')$ in general and in $\Theta(n^2h/h')$ in the worst case, as indicated in Tables 1 and 2. In particular, when h' is some fixed fraction of h, the worst-case time complexity per time step for this algorithm is in $\Theta(n^2)$. Furthermore, it is clear that making h/h' small makes the algorithm more efficient. Thus, a practical approximate gradient computation algorithm for continually operating networks may be obtained by choosing h and h' so that $h - h'$ is large enough that a reasonable approximation to the true gradient is obtained and so that h/h' is reasonably close to 1.

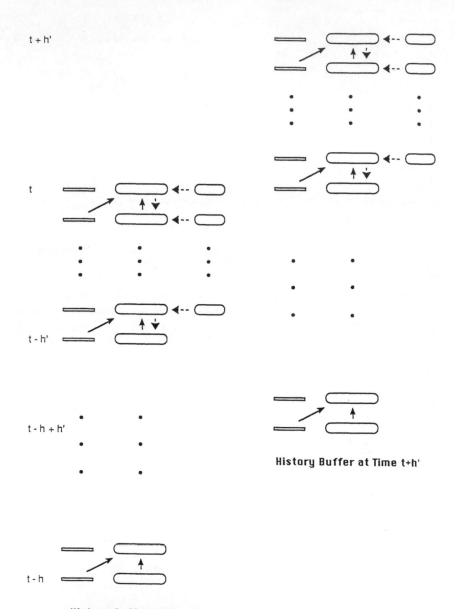

History Buffer at Time t+h'

History Buffer at Time t

Figure 10. A schematic representation of the storage and processing required for the BPTT(h; h') algorithm for two consecutive executions of the error gradient computation, one at time step t and the next at time step $t + h'$. The history buffer always contains the values of the network input and activity for the current time step as well as for the h prior time steps. It also contains target values for the most recent h' time steps, including the current time step. The BPTT computation thus requires the injection of error only at the h' uppermost levels in the buffer. This figure illustrates a case where $h' < h/2$, but it is also possible to have $h' \geq h/2$.

Subgrouping in Real-Time Recurrent Learning

The RTRL approach suggests another approximation strategy which is designed to reduce the complexity of the computation and which also has some intuitive justification. While truncated BPTT achieves a simplification by ignoring long-term *temporal* dependencies in the network's operation, this modification to RTRL, proposed in Zipser (1989), achieves its simplification by ignoring certain *structural* dependencies in the network's operation.

This simplification is obtained by viewing a recurrent network for the purpose of learning as consisting of a set of smaller recurrent networks all connected together. Connections within each subnet are regarded as the recurrent connections for learning, while activity flowing between subnets is treated as external input by the subnet which receives it. The overall physical connectivity of the network remains the same, but now forward gradient propagation is only performed within the subnets. Note that this means that each subnet must have at least one unit which is given target values.

More precisely, in this approach the original network is regarded as divided into g equal-sized subnetworks, each containing n/g units (assuming that n is a multiple of g, as we will throughout this discussion). Each of these subnetworks needs to have at least one target, but the way the targets are distributed among the subnetworks is not germane at this point. Then Equations 33 and 32 of the RTRL algorithm are used to update the p_{ij}^k values and determine the appropriate error gradient, except that the value of p_{ij}^k is regarded as being fixed at zero whenever units i and k belong to different subnetworks. If we regard each weight w_{ij} as belonging to the subnetwork to which unit i belongs, this amounts to ignoring $\partial y_k / \partial w_{ij}$ whenever the kth unit and weight w_{ij} belong to different subnets. The computational effect is that RTRL is applied to g decoupled subnetworks, each containing n/g units. We denote this algorithm RTRL(g). Clearly, RTRL(1) is the same as RTRL. Figure 11 illustrates how RTRL is simplified by using the subgrouping strategy.

The number of nonzero p_{ij}^k values to be stored and updated for this algorithm is $n w_A / g$. To analyze its time requirements, we assume for simplicity that every subnetwork has the same number of adjustable weights and that every unit receives input from the same number of units, which implies that each subnetwork then contains w_A / g adjustable weights and w_U / g^2 within-group weights. But then Equation 33 for updating the p_{ij}^k values requires $\Theta((w_U / g^2)(w_A / g))$ operations within each subnetwork on each time step, or a total of $\Theta(w_U w_A / g^2)$ operations on each time step. In addition, the average number of operations required for Equation 32 per time step is $n_T w_A / g$. Altogether, then, the time complexity of this algorithm per time step is in $\Theta(w_U w_A / g^2 + n_T w_A / g)$.

To examine the worst-case complexity, assume that the network is fully connected, all weights are adaptable, and n_T is in $\Theta(n)$. In this case RTRL(g) has space complexity in $\Theta(n^3 / g)$ and average time complexity per time step in $\Theta(n^4 / g^2 + n^3 / g) = \Theta(n^4 / g^2)$ (since $g \leq n$). In particular, note that if g is

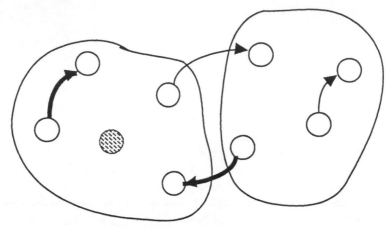

Figure 11.   A network divided into two subnetworks for subgrouped RTRL. The full RTRL algorithm requires keeping track of the sensitivity of each unit in the network with respect to each weight in the network. When subgrouping is used, each unit only pays attention to its sensitivity to weights on connections terminating in the group to which it belongs. Thus, among the four connections shown, only those two indicated with the heavy lines are considered when computing the sensitivity of the unit indicated by the shading to variations in the weights.

increased in proportion to n, which keeps the size of the subnets constant, the resulting algorithm has, in the worst case, space and time complexity per time step both in $\Theta(n^2)$. These complexity results are summarized in Tables 1 and 2.

One strategy which avoids the need for assigning specific target values to units from each subgroup is to add a separate layer of output units with 0-delay connections from the entire recurrent network to these output units, which are the only units given targets. This is then an example of a two-stage architecture having only hidden-to-hidden recurrence, and the training method described earlier for such networks, involving both back propagation and RTRL, can be modified so that the full RTRL is replaced by subgrouped RTRL. This approach amounts to giving the recurrent network virtual targets by means of back propagation from the output units.

Note also that this subgrouping strategy could be used to advantage in the hybrid algorithm FP/BPTT(h). Such an approximation algorithm would provide an interesting blend of aspects of both truncated BPTT and subgrouped RTRL.

TEACHER FORCING

An interesting strategy that has appeared implicitly or explicitly in the work of a number of investigators studying supervised learning tasks for recurrent nets

(Doya & Yoshizawa, 1989; Jordan, 1986; Narendra & Parthasarathy, 1990; Pineda, 1988; Rohwer & Renals, 1989; Williams & Zipser, 1989a; 1989b) is to replace, during training, the actual output $y_k(t)$ of a unit by the teacher signal $d_k(t)$ in subsequent computation of the behavior of the network, whenever such a target value exists. We call this intuitively sensible technique *teacher forcing*.

Formally, the dynamics of a teacher-forced-network during training are given by Equations 2 and 3, as before, but where $\mathbf{x}(t)$ is now defined by

$$x_k(t) = \begin{cases} x_k^{\text{net}}(t) & \text{if } k \in I, \\ d_k(t) & \text{if } k \in T(t), \\ y_k(t) & \text{if } k \in U \backslash T(t) \end{cases} \tag{50}$$

rather than by Equation 1. Because $\partial d_k(t)/\partial w_{ij} = 0$ for all $k \in T(t)$ and for all t, this leads to very slight differences in the resulting gradient computations, giving rise to slightly altered algorithms. It is an easy exercise to rework the computations given earlier for BPTT and RTRL using these modified dynamics. We omit the details and content ourselves here with a description of the results.

The one simple change necessary to incorporate teacher forcing into any version of BPTT is that the back-propagation computation from later times must be "blocked" at any unit in the unrolled network whose output has been set to a target value. Equivalently, any unit given an external target value at a particular time step should be given no virtual error for that time step. More precisely, for real-time BPTT or any of its variants, Equation 14 must be replaced by

$$\epsilon_k(\tau - 1) = 0 \tag{51}$$

whenever $k \in T(\tau - 1)$ for any $\tau \le t$. Similarly, for epochwise BPTT, Equation 19 must be replaced by

$$\epsilon_k(\tau - 1) = e_k(\tau - 1) \tag{52}$$

whenever $k \in T(\tau - 1)$ for any $\tau \le t_1$.

In the case of RTRL, the one simple change required to accommodate teacher forcing is to treat the value of $p_{ij}^l(t)$ as zero for any $l \in T(t)$ when computing $p_{ij}^k(t + 1)$ via Equation 33. Equivalently, Equation 33 is replaced by

$$p_{ij}^k(t + 1) = f_k'(s_k(t)) \left[\sum_{l \in U \backslash T(t)} w_{kl} p_{ij}^l(t) + \delta_{ik} x_j(t) \right]. \tag{53}$$

There seem to be several ways that teacher forcing can be useful. For one thing, one might expect that teacher forcing could lead to faster learning because it enables learning to proceed on what amounts to the assumption that the network is performing all earlier parts of its task correctly. In this way, all learning effort is focused on the problem of performing correctly at a particular time step given that the performance is correct on all earlier time steps. When teacher forcing provides this benefit, one would expect that its absence would simply slow down learning but not prevent it altogether. It may also play a useful, or even critical, role in situations where there is some approximation involved. For example, when using subgrouping in RTRL, it has sometimes been found to make the difference between success and failure.

Beyond these potential benefits of teacher forcing is what we now recognize as its sometimes essential role in the training of continually operating networks. One such situation we have studied involves training networks to oscillate auton-omously using RTRL. If the network starts with small enough weights, its dynamical behavior will consist of settling to a single point attractor from any starting state. Furthermore, assuming that the learning rate is reasonably small, it will eventually converge to its point attractor regardless of where it was started. Once it has stayed at this attractor sufficiently long the task can never be learned by moving along the negative error gradient in weight space because this error gradient information only indicates what direction to move to alter the fixed point, not what direction would change the overall dynamical properties. This is the same phenomenon described earlier in our discussion of the relationship between BPTT and the recurrent back-propagation algorithm for training settling networks. The gradient of error occurring long after the transient portion has passed contains no information about the overall dynamics of the network. Applying BPTT or RTRL to such a network is then equivalent to applying RBP; the only effect is that the point attractor is moved around. A network being trained to oscillate will thus simply adjust its weights to find the minimum error between its constant output and the desired oscillatory trajectory without ever becoming an oscillator itself.

We believe that this is a particular case of a much more general problem in which the weights need to be adjusted across a bifurcation boundary but the gradient itself cannot yield the necessary information because it is zero (or moving arbitrarily close to zero over time). The information lost when the net-work has fallen into its attractor includes information which might tell the weights where to move to perform the desired task. As long as the network is moving along a transient, there is some gradient information which can indicate the desired direction in which to change the weights; once the network reaches its steady-state behavior, this information disappears.

Another example of this justification for the use of teacher forcing is provided by the work of Pineda (1988; chapter 4, this volume), who has combined it with RBP as a means of attempting to add new stable points to an associative memory network. Without teacher forcing, RBP would just move existing stable point around without ever creating new ones.

Still another class of examples where teacher forcing is obviously important is where the weights are correct to perform the desired task but the network is currently operating in the wrong region of its state space. For example, consider a network having several point attractors which happens to be currently sitting on the wrong attractor. Attempting to get it onto the right attractor by adjusting the weights alone is clearly the wrong strategy. A similar case is an oscillator network faced with a teacher signal essentially identical to its output except for being 180° out of phase. Simulation of such problems using RTRL without teacher forcing leads to the result that the network stops oscillating and produces constant output equal to the mean value of the teacher signal. In contrast, teacher forcing provides a momentary phase reset which avoids this problem.

The usefulness of teacher forcing in these situations is obviously related to the idea that both the network weights and initial conditions determine the behavior of the network at any given time. Error gradient information in these learning algorithms allows control over the network weights, but one must also gain control over the initial conditions, in some sense. By using desired values to partially reset the state of the net at the current time one is helping to control the initial conditions for the subsequent dynamics.

There are situations for which teacher forcing is clearly not applicable or may be otherwise inappropriate. It is certainly not applicable when the units to be trained do not feed their output back to the network, as in one of the special two-stage architectures discussed earlier. Furthermore, a gradient algorithm using teacher forcing is actually optimizing a different error measure than its unforced counterpart, although any setting of weights giving zero error for one also gives zero error for the other. This means that, unless zero error is obtained, the two versions of a gradient algorithm need not give rise to the same solutions. In fact, it is easy to devise examples where the network is incapable of matching the desired trajectory and the result obtained using teacher forcing is far different from a minimum-error solution for the unforced network.

A simple solution is the problem of attempting to train a single unit to perform a sequence consisting of n zeros alternating with n ones. It is not hard to see that when $n \geq 2$ the best least-squares fit to this training data is achieved when the unit produces the constant output 0.5 at all times. This is the behavior to which a gradient algorithm will essentially converge for this problem if teacher forcing is not used. Such a solution is achieved by setting the unit's bias and recurrent weight to zero. Note that this actually makes 0.5 a global attractor for this dynamical system; if the output were somehow perturbed to some other value momentarily, it would converge back to 0.5 (in one time step, in this case).

However, when teacher forcing is used, the behavior tends toward creating point attractors for the output of the unit at $1/n$ and $1 - 1/n$. When $n = 2$ this is identical to the solution obtained without teacher forcing, but for $n \geq 3$ it is quite different. When $n \geq 3$, the weights obtained using teacher forcing lead to bistable behavior, with an output of 0.5 representing an unstable critical point separating the two basins of attraction for the system.

Teacher forcing leads to such a result because it emphasizes *transitions* in the training data. According to the training data, a correct output of either 0 or 1 is followed by that same value $1 - 1/n$ of the time and by the opposite value $1/n$ of the time; the result obtained using teacher forcing simply represents the minimum mean-square error for such transition data. In this particular problem only the transitions between successive output values are relevant because there are no other state variables potentially available to record the effect of earlier output values. More generally, teacher forcing attempts to fit transitions from the collections of all prior correct output values to the next correct output value, subject to the ability of the net to capture the relevant distinctions in its state of activity.

Pineda (1980; chapter 4, this volume) has pointed out some other potential problems with teacher forcing. One of these is that it may create trajectories which are not attractors but repellers. One potential way around this and other difficulties with teacher forcing is to consider a slight generalization in which $x_k(t)$ is set equal to $y_k(t) + \beta e_k(t)$ for $k \in U$, where $\beta \in [0, 1]$ is a constant. Teacher forcing uses $\beta = 1$ while $\beta = 0$ represents its absence. But other values of β represent a mix of the two strategies. For this generalization, the correct gradient computation involves attenuating the virtual error back-propagated from later times by the factor $1 - \beta$ in BPTT or multiplying $p_{ij}^l(t)$ by $1 - \beta$ before propagating the activity gradient forward in RTRL. A related strategy is to use teacher forcing intermittently rather than on every time step when target values are available. This has been tested by Tsung (1990) and found useful for dealing with the somewhat different but related problem of training network trajectories that vary extremely slowly.

Finally, we note that Rohwer (1990) has expanded on this idea of teacher forcing to develop an interesting new epochwise learning algorithm based on computation of the gradient of performance with respect to unit activities rather than network weights.

EXPERIMENTAL STUDIES

The important question to be addressed in studies of recurrent network learning algorithms, whatever the constraints to which they must conform, is how much total computational effort must be expended to achieve the desired performance. For many of the algorithms described here an analysis of the amount of computation required per time step has been presented, but this must be combined with knowledge of the number of time steps required and success rate obtained when training particular networks to perform particular tasks. Any speed gain from performing a simplified computation on each time step is of little interest unless it allows successful training without inordinately prolonging the training time.

To examine the relative performance of some of the more computationally attractive approximation algorithms for continually operating networks described here, both subgrouped RTRL and truncated BPTT were tested for their ability to train fully recurrent networks to emulate the finite state machine part of a Turing machine for balancing parentheses, a task that had previously been shown to be learnable by RTRL (Williams & Zipser, 1989b). For this task the network receives as input the same tape mark that the Turing machine "sees," and is trained to produce the same outputs as the Turing machine for each cell of the tape that it visits. There are four output lines in the version of the problem used here. They code for the direction of movement, the character to be written on the tape, and whether a balanced or unbalanced final state has been reached. It had previously been found that a fully recurrent network with 12 units was the smallest that learned the Turing machine task. Although this could be formulated as an epoch-wise task by resetting the network every time the Turing machine halts and begins anew, the network was allowed to run continually, with transitions from a halt state to the start state being considered part of the state transition structure which the network had to infer.

To test the subgrouping strategy on this task, a 12-unit fully connected network was divided for learning into four subnets of 3 units each, with one unit in each subnet designated as an output unit. The full RTRL algorithm allowed the network to learn the task with or without teacher forcing about 50% of the time after seeing fewer than 100,000 cells of the Turing machine tape. The RTRL(4) algorithm also allowed the network to learn the task about 50% of the time in fewer than 100,000 Turing machine cycles, but only in the teacher forcing mode. The subdivided network never learned the task without teacher forcing.

To test the truncation strategy on this task, BPTT(h) was tried, with various values of h.[11] No teacher forcing was used. It was found that with $h \leq 4$, BPTT(h) was successful in training the network only about 9% of the time, while BPTT(9) succeeded more than 80% of the time. The fact that BPTT(9) succeeded more often than the various RTRL algorithms, including the version with no subgrouping, may indicate that the error committed in computing an exact gradient as if the weights had been constant throughout the past may outweigh the error committed by discarding all effects of activity and input in the distant past. On the other hand, it might also represent a beneficial effect of failing to follow the exact gradient and thereby avoiding becoming trapped at a local optimum.

The relative actual running times of the these algorithms on a single-processor machine were also compared. It was found that BPTT(9) ran 28 times faster on this task than RTRL, while RTRL(4) ran 9.8 times faster than RTRL.

In another set of studies (Williams & Peng, 1990), BPTT(16;8) was found to succeed as often as BPTT(9) on this task, while running twice as fast.[12] Note that BPTT(16;8) is thus well over 50 times faster than RTRL on this task.

---

[11]For these studies the variant in which past weight values are stored in the history buffer was used.

[12]Careful analysis of the computational requirements of BPTT(9) and BPTT(16;8), taking into account the fixed overhead of running the network in the forward direction that must be borne by any algorithm, would suggest that one should expect about a factor of 4 speedup when using BPTT(16;8). Because this particular task has targets only on every other time step, the use of BPTT(9) here really amounts to using BPTT(9;2), which therefore reduces the speed gain by essentially one factor of 2.

TABLE 1
Order of Magnitude of Space and Time Requirements
for the Various General-Purpose Algorithms Discussed Here

Algorithm	Space	Average Time Per Time Step
Epochwise BPTT	$\Theta((m + n)h)$	$\Theta(w_U + w_A)$
BPTT (∞)	$\Theta((m + n)L)$	$\Theta((w_U + w_A)L/\Delta_T)$
RTRL	$\Theta(nw_A)$	$\Theta(w_U w_A)$
FP/BPTT(h)	$\Theta(nw_A + (m + n)h)$	$\Theta(nw_U + nw_A + n^2 w_A/h)$
FP/BPTT(cn)	$\Theta(nw_A + cn(m + n))$	$\Theta(nw_U + nw_A + nw_A/c)$
BPTT(h)	$\Theta((m + n)h)$	$\Theta((w_U + w_A)h/\Delta_T)$
BPTT($h;h'$)	$\Theta((m + n)h)$	$\Theta((w_U + w_A)h/h')$
BPTT($h;ch$)	$\Theta((m + n)h)$	$\Theta(w_U + w_A)$
RTRL(g)	$\Theta(nw_A/g)$	$\Theta(w_U w_A/g^2 + n_T w_A/g)$
RTRL(cn)	$\Theta(w_A)$	$\Theta(w_U w_A/cn^2 + n_T w_A/n)$

Here c denotes a constant and the meaning of all the other symbols used is summarized in the third section. For the variant of BPTT(h) in which past weight values are saved, the space requirements are in $\Theta(w_A h)$.

TABLE 2
Worst-Case Complexity for the Various
General-Purpose Algorithms Discussed Here
Expressed in Terms of the Number of Units n

Algorithm	Space	Average Time Per Time Step
Epochwise BPTT	$\Theta(nh)$	$\Theta(n^2)$
BPTT(∞)	$\Theta(nL)$	$\Theta(n^2 L)$
RTRL	$\Theta(n^3)$	$\Theta(n^4)$
FP/BPTT(h)	$\Theta(n^3 + nh)$	$\Theta(n^3 + n^4/h)$
FP/BPTT(cn)	$\Theta(n^3)$	$\Theta(n^3)$
BPTT(h)	$\Theta(nh)$	$\Theta(n^2 h)$
BPTT($h;h'$)	$\Theta(nh)$	$\Theta(n^2 h/h')$
BPTT($h;ch$)	$\Theta(nh)$	$\Theta(n^2)$
RTRL(g)	$\Theta(n^3/g)$	$\Theta(n^4/g^2)$
RTRL(cn)	$\Theta(n^2)$	$\Theta(n^2)$

These results are based on the assumption that m, the number of input lines, is in $O(n)$. Here c denotes a constant. For the variant of BPTT(h) in which past weight values are saved, the worst-case space requirements are in $\Theta(n^2 h)$.

DISCUSSION

In this chapter we have described a number of gradient-based learning algorithms for recurrent networks, all based on two different approaches to computing the gradient of network error in weight space. The existence of these various techniques, some of them quite reasonable in terms of their computational requirements, should make possible much more widespread investigation of the capabilities of recurrent networks.

In the introduction we noted that investigators studying learning algorithms for such networks might have various objectives, each of which might imply different constraints on which algorithms might be considered to meet these objectives. Among the possible constraints one might wish to impose on a learning algorithm are biological plausibility and locality of communication. Feedforward back propagation is generally regarded as biologically implausible, but its requirement for reverse communication along only the connections already in place allows it to be considered a locally implementable algorithm, in the sense that it does not require a great deal of additional machinery beyond the network itself to allow implementation of the algorithm. Except in very restricted cases involving severely limited architectures or extreme approximations, the algorithms described here cannot be considered biologically plausible as learning algorithms for real neural networks, nor do they enjoy the locality of feeforward back propagation.

However, many of the algorithms discussed here can be implemented quite reasonably and efficiently in either vector parallel hardware or special-purpose parallel hardware designed around the storage and communication requirements of the particular algorithm. Several of these algorithms are quite well suited for efficient serial implementation as well. Thus one might expect to see these algorithms used especially for off-line development of networks having desired temporal behaviors in order to study the properties of these networks. Some of these techniques have already been used successfully to fit models of biological neural subsystems to data on the temporal patterns they generate (Arnold & Robinson, 1989; Lockery, Fang, & Sejnowski, 1990; Tsung, Cottrell, & Selverston, 1990; Anastasio, 1991) and a number of studies have been undertaken to apply these methods to develop networks which carry out various language processing or motor control tasks as a means of understanding the information processing strategies involved (Elman, 1988; Jordan, 1986; Mozer, 1989, chapter 5, this volume; Cleeremans, Servan-Screiber, and McClelland, 1989, chapter 9, this volume; Smith & Zipser, 1990). One might also expect to see specific engineering applications of recurrent networks developed by these methods as well.

Thus there is much that can be done with the currently available algorithms for training recurrent networks, but there remains a great deal of room for further development of such algorithms. It is already clear that more locally implementable or biologically plausible algorithms remain to be found, and algorithms with improved overall learning times are always desirable. It seems reasonable to conjecture that such algorithms will have to be more architecture specific or task specific than the general-purpose algorithms studied here.

Of particular importance are learning algorithms for continually operating networks. Here we have described both "exact" and approximate gradient algorithms for training such networks. However, by our definition, the exact algorithms compute the true gradient at the current value of the weights only under the assumption that the weights are held fixed, which cannot be true in a continually operating learning network. This problem need not occur in a network which operates epochwise; when weight changes are only performed between epochs, an exact gradient algorithm can compute the true gradient of some appropriate quantity.

Thus all the algorithms described here for continually operating networks are only capable of computing approximate gradient information to help guide the weight updates. The degree of approximation involved with the "exact" algorithms depends on the degree to which past history of network operation influences the gradient computation and the degree to which the weights have changed in the recent past. Truncated BPTT alleviates this particular problem because it ignores all past contributions to the gradient beyond a certain distance into the past. Such information is also present in RTRL, albeit implicitly, and Gherrity (1989) has specifically addressed this issue by incorporating into his continuous-time version of RTRL an exponential decay on the contributions from past times. For the discrete-time RTRL algorithm described here, this is easily implemented by multiplying all the p_{ij}^k values by an attenuation factor less than 1 before computing their updated values. Unlike truncated BPTT, however, this does not reduce the computational complexity of the algorithm.

Another way to attempt to alleviate this problem is to use a very low learning rate. The effect of this is make the constant-weight approximation more accurate, although it may slow learning. One way to view this issue is in terms of time scales, as noted by Pineda (chapter 4, this volume). The accuracy of the gradient computation provided by an exact algorithm in our sense depends on the extent to which the time scale of the learning process is decoupled from the time scale of the network's operation by being much slower. In general, with the learning rate set to provide sufficiently fast learning, these time scales may overlap. This can result in overall dynamical behavior which is determined by a combination of the dynamics of the network activation and the dynamics of the weight changes brought about by the learning algorithm. At this point one leaves the realm of gradient-based learning algorithms and enters a realm in which a more general control-theoretic formulation is more appropriate. A particular issue here of some importance is the overall stability of such a system, as emphasized in the theory of *adaptive control* (Narendra & Annaswamy, 1989). It is to be expected that satisfactory application of the techniques described here to situations requiring on-line adaptation of continually operating recurrent networks will depend on gaining further understanding of these questions.

It is useful to recognize the close relationship between some of the techniques discussed here and certain approaches which are well known in the engineering literature. In particular, the specific backward error propagation and forward gradient propagation techniques which we have used here as the basis for all the algorithms investigated turn out to have their roots in standard optimal-control-theoretic formulations dating back to the 1960s. For example, leCun (1988) has pointed to the work of Bryson and Ho (1969) in optimal control theory as containing a description of what can now be recognized as error back propagation when applied to multilayer networks. Furthermore, it is also clear that work in that tradition also contains the essential elements of the back-propagation-through-time approach. The idea of back-propagating through time, at least for a linear system, amounts to running forward in time what is called in that literature the *adjoint system*. The two-point boundary-value problems discussed in the optimal control literature arise from such considerations. Furthermore, the idea of propagating gradient information forward in time, used as the basis for RTRL, was proposed by McBride and Narendra (1965), who also noted that use of the adjoint system may be preferable when on-line computation is not required because of its lower computational requirements. The teacher forcing technique has its counterpart in engineering circles as well. For example, it appears in the adaptive signal processing literature as an "equation error" technique for synthesizing linear filters having an infinite impulse response (Widrow & Stearns, 1985).

In work very similar in spirit to that we have presented here, Piche (1994) has shown how various forms of back propagation through time and forward gradient computation may be derived in a unified manner from a standard Euler-Lagrange optimal-control-theoretic formulation. Furthermore, he also discusses the computational complexity of the various algorithms described. Included among the algorithms covered by his analysis are some of those we have described in Section 7 for special architectures.

Finally, we remark that the techniques we have discussed here are far from being the only ones available for creating networks having certain desired properties. We have focused here specifically on those techniques which are based on computation of the error gradient in weight space, with particular emphasis on methods appropriate for continually operating networks. As described earlier in the discussion of the teacher forcing technique, Rohwer (1990) has proposed an epochwise approach based on computation of the error gradient with respect to unit activities rather than network weights. Also, another body of techniques has been developed by Baird (1989) for synthesizing networks having prescribed dynamical properties. Unlike the algorithms discussed here, which are designed to gradually perturb the behavior of the network toward the target behavior as it runs, these algorithms are intended to be used to "program in" the desired dynamics at the outset. Another difference is that these techniques are currently limited to creating networks for which external input must be in the form of momentary state perturbations rather than more general time-varying forcing functions.

ACKNOWLEDGMENT

R. J. Williams was supported by Grant IRI-8703566 from the National Science Foundation. D. Zipser was supported by Grant I-R01-M445271-01 from the National Institute of Mental Health and grants from the System Development Foundation.

REFERENCES

Almeida, L. B. (1987). A learning rule for asynchronous perceptrons with feedback in a combinatorial environment. *Proceedings of the IEEE First International Conference on Neural Networks. II* (pp. 609–618).

Anastasio, T. J. (1991). Neural network models of velocity storage in the horizontal vestibuloocular reflex. *Biological Cybernetics, 64,* 187–196.

Arnold, D. & Robinson, D. A. (1989). A learning neural-network model of the oculomotor integrator. *Society of Neuroscience Abstracts, 15,* part 2, 1049.

Bachrach, J. (1988). *Learning to represent state.* Unpublished master's thesis. University of Massachusetts, Amherst, Department of Computer and Information Science.

Baird, B. (1989). A bifurcation theory approach to vector field programming for periodic attractors. *Proceedings of the International Joint Conference on Neural Networks. I* (pp. 381–388).

Bryson, A. E., Jr. & Ho, Y-C. (1969). *Applied optimal control.* New York: Blaisdell.

Cleeremans, A., Servan-Schreiber, D., & McClelland, J. L. (1989). Finite-state automata and simple recurrent networks. *Neural Computation, 1,* 372–381.

Doya, K. & Yoshizawa, S. (1989). Adaptive neural oscillator using continuous-time back-propagation learning. *Neural Networks, 2,* 375–385.

Elman, J. L. (1988). *Finding structure in time* (CRL Technical Report 8801). La Jolla: University of California, San Diego, Center for Research in Language.

Gherrity, M. (1989). A learning algorithm for analog, fully recurrent neural networks. *Proceedings of the International Joint Conference on Neural Networks. I* (pp. 643–644).

Jordan, M. I. (1986). Attractor dynamics and parallelism in a connectionist sequential machine. *Proceedings of the Eighth Annual Conference of the Cognitive Science Society* (pp. 531–546).

Kuhn, G. (1987). *A first look at phonetic discrimination using a connectionist network with recurrent links* (SCIMP Working Paper No. 4/87). Princeton, NJ: Communications Research Division, Institute for Defense Analyses.

leCun, Y. (1988). *A theoretical framework for back-propagation* (Technical Report CRG-TR-88-6). Toronto: University of Toronto, Department of Computer Science.

Lockery, S., Fang, Y., & Sejnowski, T. (1990). Neural network analysis of distributed representations of dynamical sensory-motor transformations in the leech. In *Advances in neural information processing systems, 2.* San Mateo, CA: Morgan Kaufmann.

McBride, L. E., Jr., & Narendra, K. S. (1965). Optimization of time-varying systems. *IEEE Transactions on Automatic Control, 10,* 289–294.

Mozer, M. C. (1989). A focused back-propagation algorithm for temporal pattern recognition. *Complex Systems, 3,* 349–381.

Narendra, K. S., & Annaswamy, A. M. (1989). *Stable adaptive systems.* Englewood Cliffs, NJ: Prentice-Hall.

Narendra, K. S., & Parthasarathy, K. (1990). Identification and control of dynamic systems using neural networks. *IEEE Transactions on Neural Networks, 1,*4–27.

Pearlmutter, B. A. (1989). Learning state space trajectories in recurrent neural networks. *Neural Computation, 1,* 263–269.

Piche, S. W. (1994). Steepest descent algorithms for neural network controllers and filters. *IEEE Transactions on Neural Networks, 5.*

Pineda, F. J. (1987). Generalization of backpropagation to recurrent neural networks. *Physical Review Letters, 18,* 2229–2232.

Pineda, F. J. (1988). Dynamics and architecture for neural computation. *Journal of Complexity, 4,* 216–245.

Pineda, F. J. (1989). Recurrent backpropagation and the dynamical approach to adaptive neural computation. *Neural Computation, 1,* 161–172.

Robinson, A. J., & Fallside, F. (1987). *The utility driven dynamic error propagation network* (Technical Report CUED/F-INFENG/TR.1). Cambridge, England: Cambridge University Engineering Department.

Rohwer, R. (1990). The "moving targets" training algorithm. In L. B. Almeida & C. J. Wellekens (Eds.), *Proceedings of the EURASIP Workshop on Neural Networks,* Sesimbra, Portugal. *Lecture Notes in Computer Science* (vol. 412, p. 100). New York: Springer-Verlag.

Rohwer, R., & Renals, S. (1989). Training recurrent networks. In L. Personnaz & G. Dreyfus (Eds.), *Neural networks from models to applications.* Paris: I.D.E.S.T.

Rumelhart, D. E., Hinton, G. E., & Williams, R. J. (1986). Learning internal representations by error propagation. In D. E. Rumelhart, J. L. McClelland, & the PDP Research Group, *Parallel Distributed Processing: Explorations in the Microstructure of Cognition. Vol. 1: Foundations.* Cambridge: MIT Press/Bradford Books.

Sato, M. (1990a). A real time learning algorithm for recurrent analog neural networks. *Biological Cybernetics, 62,* 237–241.

Sato, M. (1990b). A learning algorithm to teach spatiotemporal patterns to recurrent neural networks. *Biological Cybenertics, 62,* 259–263.

Schmidhuber, J. (1992). A fixed size storage $O(n^3)$ time complexity learning algorithm for fully recurrent continually running networks. *Neural Computation 4,* 243–248.

Smith, A. W., & Zipser, D. (1990). Learning sequential structure with the real-time recurrent learning algorithm. *International Journal of Neural Systems, 1,* 125–131.

Tsung, F. S. (1990). Learning in recurrent finite difference networks. In D. S. Tourtetzky, J. L. Elman, T. J. Sejnowski, & G. E. Hinton (Eds.), *Proceedings of the 1990 Connectionist Models Summer School.* San Mateo, CA: Morgan Kaufmann.

Tsung, F. S., Cottrell, G. W., & Selverston, A. (1990). Some experiments on learning stable network oscillations. *Proceedings of the International Joint Conference on Neural Networks,* San Diego, CA.

Waibel, A., Hanazawa, T., Hinton, G., Shikano, K., & Lang, K. (1987). *Phoneme recognition using time-delay neural networks* (Technical Report TR-I-0006). Japan: Advanced Telecommunications Research Institute.

Watrous, R. L., & Shastri, L. (1986). *Learning phonetic features using connectionist networks: An experiment in speech recognition* (Technical Report MS-CIS-86-78). Philadelphia: University of Pennsylvania.

Werbos, P. J. (1974). *Beyond regression: new tools for prediction and analysis in the behavioral sciences.* Unpublished doctoral dissertation. Harvard University.

Werbos, P. J. (1988). Generalization of backpropagation with application to a recurrent gas market model. *Neural Networks, 1,* 339–356.

Widrow, B., & Stearns, S. D. (1985). *Adaptive signal processing.* Englewood Cliffs, NJ: Prentice-Hall.

Williams, R. J. (1990). Adaptive state representation and estimation using recurrent connectionist networks. In: W. T. Miller, R. S. Sutton, & P. J. Werbos (Eds.) *Neural Networks for Control.* Cambridge: MIT Press/Bradford Books.

Williams, R. J. (1989). *Complexity of exact gradient computation algorithms for recurrent neural networks* (Technical Report NU-CCS-89-27). Boston: Northeastern University, College of Computer Science.

Willaims, R. J., & Peng, J. (1990). An efficient gradient-based algorithm for on-line training of recurrent network trajectories. *Neural Computation, 2,* 490–501.

Williams, R. J., & Zipser, D. (1989a). A learning algorithm for continually running fully recurrent neural networks. *Neural Computation, 1,* 270–280.

Williams, R. J., & Zipser, D. (1989b). Experimental analysis of the real-time recurrent learning algorithm. *Connection Science, 1,* 87–111.

Zipser, D. (1989). A subgrouping strategy that reduces complexity and speeds up learning in recurrent networks. *Neural Computation, 1,* 552–558.

A. APPENDIX

A.1. Preliminaries

For completeness, we first summarize some of the definitions and assumptions from the main text. Given a network with n units and m input lines, we define an $(m + n)$-tuple $\mathbf{x}(t)$ and index sets U and I such that $x_k(t)$, the kth component of $\mathbf{x}(t)$, represents either the output of a unit in the network at time t, if $k \in U$, or an external input to the network at time t, if $k \in I$. When $k \in U$, we also use the notation $y_k(t)$ for $x_k(t)$. For each $i \in U$ and $j \in U \cup I$ we have a unique weight w_{ij} on the connection from unit or input line j to unit i.

Letting $T(l)$ denote the set of indices $k \in U$ for which there exists a specified target value $d_k(t)$ that the output of the kth unit should match at time t, we also define a time-varying n-tuple $\mathbf{e}(t)$ whose kth component is

$$
e_k(t) = \begin{cases} d_k(t) - y_k(t) & \text{if } k \in T(t), \\ 0 & \text{otherwise.} \end{cases} \tag{A.1}
$$

We then define the two functions

$$
J(t) = \frac{1}{2} \sum_{k \in U} [e_k(t)]^2 \tag{A.2}
$$

and

$$
J^{\text{total}}(t', \text{itt}) = \sum_{\tau = t' + 1}^{t} J(\tau), \tag{A.3}
$$

where $t_0 \leq t' < t$, with t_0 denoting some fixed starting time.

For purposes of analyzing the backpropagation-through-time approach, we replace the dynamical Equations 2 and 3 by the equations

$$s_k(t + 1) = \sum_{l \in U \cup I} w_{kl}(t)x_l(t), \qquad (A.4)$$

$$y_k(t + 1) = f_k(s_k(t + 1)), \qquad (A.5)$$

and

$$w_{ij}(t) = w_{ij}, \qquad (A.6)$$

for all $k \in U$, $i \in U$, $j \in U \cup I$, which give rise to equivalent dynamics for the s_k and y_k values. These equations can be viewed as representing the multilayer computation performed in the unrolled version $\mathcal{N}^*$ of the original arbitrary net $\mathcal{N}$, where t represents a layer index in $\mathcal{N}^*$ rather than a time index in $\mathcal{N}$.

Now suppose we are given a differentiable function F expressed in terms of $\{y_k(\tau) | k \in U, t' < \tau \leq t\}$, the outputs of the network over the time interval $(t', t]$. Note that while F may have an *explicit* dependence on some $y_k(\tau)$, it may also have an *implicit* dependence on this same value through later output values. To avoid the resulting ambiguity in interpreting partial derivatives like $\partial F / \partial y_k(\tau)$, we introduce variables $y_k^*(\tau)$ such that $y_k^*(\tau) = y_k(\tau)$ for all $k \in U$ and $\tau \in (t_0, t]$ and treat F as if it were expressed in terms of the variables $\{y_k^*(\tau)\}$ rather than the variables $\{y_k(\tau)\}$.[13]

Then, for all $k \in U$, define

$$\epsilon_k(\tau; F) = \frac{\partial F}{\partial y_k(\tau)} \qquad (A.7)$$

for all $\tau \in [t_0, t]$ and define

$$\delta_k(\tau; F) = \frac{\partial F}{\partial s_k(\tau)} \qquad (A.8)$$

for all $\tau \in (t_0, t]$. Also, define

$$e_k(\tau; F) = \frac{\partial F}{\partial y_k^*(\tau)} \qquad (A.9)$$

for all $\tau \in (t_0, t]$. Note that $e_k(\tau; F) = 0$ whenever $\tau \leq t'$ because we assume that F has no explicit dependence on the output of the network for times outside the interval $(t', t]$. Finally, for $i \in U$, $j \in U \cup I$, $k \in U$, and $\tau \in [t_0, t]$, define

---

[13]To see why this is necessary, consider, for example, the two possible interpretations of $\partial F / \partial x$ given that $F(x, y) = x + y$ and $y = x$. The confusion occurs because the variable named "x" represents two different function arguments according to a strict use of the mathematical chain rule, a problem easily remedied by introducing additional variable names to eliminate such duplication. Werbos (1974, 1988), in addressing this same problem, uses the standard partial derivative notation to refer to explicit dependencies only, introducing the term *ordered derivative*, denoted in a different fashion, for a partial derivative which takes into account all influences. Our use of partial derivatives here corresponds to this latter notion.

$$p_{ij}^k(\tau) = \frac{\partial y_k(\tau)}{\partial w_{ij}}, \qquad (A.10)$$

with

$$p_{ij}^k(t_0) = 0 \qquad (A.11)$$

for all such i, j, and k since we assume that the initial state of the network has no functional dependence on the weights.

A.2 Derivation of the Back-Propagation-through-Time Formulation

Since F depends on $y_k(\tau)$ only through $y_k^*(\tau)$ and the variables $s_l(\tau + 1)$, as l ranges over U, we have

$$\frac{\partial F}{\partial y_k(\tau)} = \frac{\partial y_k^*(\tau)}{\partial y_k(\tau)} \frac{\partial F}{\partial y_k^*(\tau)} + \sum_{l \in U} \frac{\partial s(\tau + 1)}{\partial y_k(\tau)} \frac{\partial F}{\partial s(\tau + 1)}, \qquad (A.12)$$

from which it follows that

$$\epsilon_k(\tau;F) = \begin{cases} e_k(t;F) & \text{if } \tau = t, \\ e_k(\tau;F) + \sum_{l \in U} w_{lk}\delta_l(\tau + 1;F) & \text{if } \tau < t. \end{cases} \qquad (A.13)$$

Also, for all $\tau \leq t$,

$$\frac{\partial F}{\partial s_k(\tau)} = \frac{dy_k(\tau)}{ds_k(\tau)} \frac{\partial F}{\partial y_k(\tau)}, \qquad (A.14)$$

so that

$$\delta_k(\tau; F) = f_k'(s_k(\tau))\epsilon_k(\tau; F). \qquad (A.15)$$

In addition, for any appropriate i and j,

$$\frac{\partial F}{\partial w_{ij}} = \sum_{\tau=t_0}^{t-1} \frac{\partial F}{\partial w_{ij}(\tau)} \frac{\partial w_{ij}(\tau)}{\partial w_{ij}} = \sum_{\tau=t_0}^{t-1} \frac{\partial F}{\partial w_{ij}(\tau)}, \qquad (A.16)$$

and, for any τ,

$$\frac{\partial F}{\partial w_{ij}(\tau)} = \frac{\partial F}{\partial s_i(\tau + 1)} \frac{\partial s_i(\tau + 1)}{\partial w_{ij}(\tau)} = \delta_i(\tau + 1;F)x_j(\tau). \qquad (A.17)$$

Combining these last two results yields

$$\frac{\partial F}{\partial w_{ij}} = \sum_{\tau=t_0}^{t-1} \delta_i(\tau + 1;F)ix_j(\tau). \qquad (A.18)$$

Equations A.13, A.15, and A.18 represent the back-propagation-through-time computation of $\partial F / \partial w_{ij}$ for any differentiable function F expressed in terms of the outputs of individual units in a network of semilinear units. With $F = J(t)$, these specialize to the real-time BPTT Equations 12–16 because $e_k(t; J(t)) = e_k(t)$ and $e_k(\tau; J(t)) = 0$ for $\tau < t$. Similarly, Equations 17–20 for epochwise BPTT are obtained by setting $t = t_1$ and $F = J^{\text{total}}(t_0, t_1)$ and observing that $e_k(\tau; J^{\text{total}}(t_0, t_1)) = e_k(\tau)$ for all $\tau \leq t_1$.

A.3. Derivation of the Hybrid Formulation

Continuing on from Equation A.16, we may write

$$\frac{\partial F}{\partial w_{ij}} = \sum_{\tau=t_0}^{t'-1} \frac{\partial F}{\partial w_{ij}(\tau)} + \sum_{\tau=t'}^{t-1} \frac{\partial F}{\partial w_{ij}(\tau)} . \tag{A.19}$$

But the first sum on the right-hand side of this equation may be rewritten as

$$\sum_{\tau=t_0}^{t'-1} \frac{\partial F}{\partial w_{ij}(\tau)} = \sum_{\tau=t_0}^{t'-1} \sum_{l \in U} \frac{\partial F}{\partial y_l(t')} \frac{\partial y_l(t')}{\partial w_{ij}(\tau)} = \sum_{l \in U} \frac{\partial F}{\partial y_l(t')} \sum_{\tau=t_0}^{t'-1} \frac{\partial y_l(t')}{\partial w_{ij}(\tau)}$$

$$= \sum_{l \in U} \frac{\partial F}{\partial y_l(t')} \frac{\partial y_l(t')}{\partial w_{ij}} = \sum_{l \in U} \epsilon_l(t'; F) p_{ij}^l(t').$$

Incorporating this result and equation A.17 into Equation A.19 yields

$$\frac{\partial F}{\partial w_{ij}} = \sum_{l \in U} \epsilon_l(t'; F) p_{ij}^l(t') + \sum_{\tau=t_0}^{t'-1} \delta_i(\tau + 1; F) x_j(\tau). \tag{A.20}$$

This last result, together with equations (66) and (68), represents the basis for the hybrid FP/BPTT algorithm described in the text. For that algorithm we apply Equation A.20 a total of $n + 1$ times, first to $F = J^{\text{total}}(t', t)$, and then to $F = y_k(t)$ for reach $k \in U$. That is, back propagation through time, terminating at time step t', is performed $n + 1$ different times. When $F = J^{\text{total}}(t', t)$, this computation yields the desired gradient of $J^{\text{total}}(t', t)$, assuming that the values $p_{ij}^l(t')$, for all appropriate i, j, and k, are available. Performing the back propagation with $F = y_k(t)$ yields the values p_{ij}^k for all appropriate i and j, so this must be performed anew for each k to yield the entire set of p_{ij}^k values for use in the next time interval.

Not surprisingly, this hybrid formulation can be s hown to subsume both the BPTT and RTRL formulations. In particular, the pure BPTT Equation A.18 is the special case where $t' = t_0$. Likewise, if we let $F = J(t)$ and $t' = t$, we see that the second sum vanishes and the result is

$$\frac{\partial F}{\partial w_{ij}} = \sum_{l \in U} e_l(t) p^l_{ij}(t),$$

(A.21)

while letting $F = y_k(t)$ and $t' = t - 1$ yields

$$p^k_{ij}(t) = \sum_{l \in U} w_{kl} f'_k(s_k(t)) p^l_{ij}(t - 1) + \delta_{ik} f'_i(s_i(t)) x_j(t - 1)$$

$$= f'_k(s_k(t)) \left[\sum_{l \in U} w_{kl} p^l_{ij}(t - 1) + \delta_{ik} x_j(t - 1) \right].$$

(A.22)

14 When Neural Networks Play Sherlock Holmes

Pierre Baldi
Jet Propulsion Laboratory and Division of Biology, California Institute of Technology, Pasadena, California

Yves Chauvin
Net-ID, Inc., San Francisco, California

ABSTRACT

After collecting a data base of fingerprint images, we first design a neural network algorithm for fingerprint recognition. When presented with a pair of fingerprint images, the algorithm outputs an estimate of the probability that the two images originate from the same finger. In one experiment, the neural network is trained using a few hundred pairs of images from the data base and its performance is subsequently tested using several thousand pairs. The error rate currently achieved is less than 0.5%. We then describe preliminary classification experiments. Additional results, extensions and possible applications are also briefly discussed.

INTRODUCTION

The fast, reliable, and computerized classification and matching of fingerprint images is a remarkable problem in pattern recognition which has not yet received a complete solution. Automated fingerprint recognition systems could have an extremely wide range of applications, well beyond the traditional domains of criminal justice. Such systems could in principle be used in any situation where identification, verification, and/or access control are paramount. A few examples include all identification cards systems, such as driver licenses, computer security systems, entitlement systems (such as welfare), access control systems (for instance, in airports or hospitals), and credit card (as well as several other types of financial transactions) validation systems. Automated fingerprint recognition systems could also render the use of locks and keys obsolete and be installed in cars, homes, and hotels. Although it is beyond our scope to discuss either the existence of real markets for such applications or their complex juridical implications, it seems intuitively clear that fingerprint recognition is a well-defined problem in pattern recognition within the reach of our current technology and which should be amenable to neural network techniques. Our purpose here is to give a brief account of our current results on the application of neural network ideas to the problem of fingerprint matching. In particular, we describe the architecture, training, and testing of a neural network algorithm which, when presented with two fingerprint images, outputs a probability p that the two images originate from the same finger.

There are several reasons to suspect that neural network approaches may be remarkably well suited for fingerprint problems. First, fingerprints form a very specific class of patterns with very peculiar flavor and statistical characteristics. Thus the corresponding pattern recognition problems seem well confined and constrained, perhaps even more so than other pattern recognition problems, such as the recognition of handwritten characters, where neural networks have already been applied with reasonable success (see, for instance, Gorman and Sejnowski (1988), Tesauro (1989), Le Cun et al., 1990, and references therein).

Second, neural networks could avoid some of the pitfalls inherent to other more conventional approaches. It has been known for over a century (see Moenssens, 1971 for an interesting summary) that pairs of fingerprint images can be matched by human operators on the basis of minutia and/or ridge orientations. Minutia are particular types of discontinuities in the ridge patterns, such as bifurcations, islands, and endings. There is typically around 50 to 150 minutia (Figure 2a) on a complete fingerprint image. Ten matching minutia or so are usually estimated as sufficient to reliably establish identity. Indeed, it is this strategy based on minutia detection and matching which has been adopted in most of the previous attempts to find automated solutions. The minutia-based approach has two obvious weaknesses: it is sensitive to noise (especially with inked fingerprints, small perturbations can create artificial minutia or disguise existing ones) and computationally expensive since it is essentially a graph-matching problem.

Third, neural networks can be robust, adaptive, and trainable from examples. This is particularly important since fingerprint images can include several different sources of deformation and noise ranging from the fingers and their positioning on the collection device (translation, roll, rotation, pressure, skin condition, etc.) to the collection device itself (ink/optical, etc.). Furthermore, it is important to observe that the requirements in terms of speed, computing power, probability of false acceptance and false rejection, memory, and data base size can vary considerably, depending on the application considered. To access a private residence or private car, one needs a small economic system with a small modifiable data base of a few people and a response time of at most a few seconds. On the other hand, forensic applications can require rapid searches through very large data bases of millions of records using large computers and a response time which can be longer. Neural networks can be tailored and trained differently to fit the particular requirement of specific applications.

In any case, it is difficult to assess what are the possibilities of a neural network approach in the area of fingerprint analysis short of trying it. From a technical standpoint, there are two different problems in the area of fingerprint analysis: classification and matching. The classification of fingerprints into sub-classes can be useful, for instance, to speed up the search through large data bases. It is of interest to ask whether neural networks can be used to implement some of the conventional classification schemes, such as the partition of finger-prints patterns into whorls, arches, and loops ("pattern level classification"), or to create new classifications boundaries. Here, we concentrate on the matching problem. At the core of any automated fingerprint system, whether for identifica-tion or verification purposes and whether for large or small data base environ-ments, there should be a structure which, when presented with two fingerprint images, decides whether or not they originate from the same finger. Accordingly, our goal is the design and testing of such a neural algorithm.

Because neural networks are essentially adaptive and need to be trained from examples, we describe our data base of training and testing examples, and how it was constructed. We then consider the matching algorithm, which consists of two stages: a preprocessing stage and a decision stage. The preprocessing stage basically aligns the two images and extracts, from each one of them, a central region. The two central regions are fed to the decision stage which is the proper neural network part of the algorithm and subject to training from examples. Whereas the preprocessing stage is fairly standard, the decision stage is novel and based on a neural network which implements a probabilistic Bayesian ap-proach to the estimate of p. In the main experiment, the network is trained by gradient descent using a training set of 300 pairs of images and its generalization tested with an additional set of 4650 pairs. After training, the network achieves an overall error rate of 0.5%. Additional results and possible extensions are discussed at the end.

DATA BASE

Although there exist worldwide many fingerprint data bases, these are generally not available for public use. In addition, and this is a crucial issue for connection-ist approaches, most data bases contain only one image or template per finger, whereas training a neural network to recognize fingerprint images usually re-quires that several noisy versions of the same record be available for learning. Therefore, to train and test a neural network, one must first construct a data base of digitized fingerprint images.

Such images can be obtained in a variety of ways, such as by digital scanner with inked fingerprints or by more sophisticated holographic techniques (Igaki et

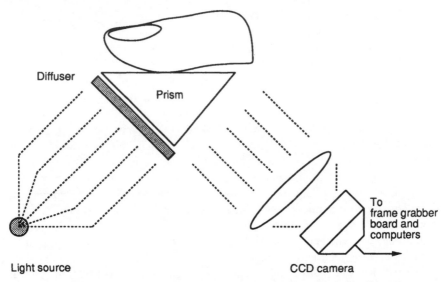

Figure 1. Collection device. Diffuse light entering the prism is not reflected where the ridges are in contact with the prism. The corresponding pattern of light and dark ridges is focused on a CCD camera, digitized on a personal computer and sent to a workstation for further processing.

al., 1990). We decided to build our own collection device, using a simple principle. The device basically consists of a prism placed in front of a charged-coupled device (CCD) camera connected to a framegrabber board installed on a personal computer (Figure 1). When a finger is positioned on the diagonal face of the prism, incoming rays of light from one of the square sides of the prism are refracted differently, depending on whether they encounter a point of contact of the finger with the prism (corresponding to a ridge) or a point of noncontact. This creates a pattern of bright and dark ridges in the refracted beam which can be easily focused, with a lense, on the CCD camera and then digitized and stored in the computer. Our resulting images are 512 × 464 pixels in size, with 8 bits gray scale per pixel. On the corresponding scale, the thickness of a ridge corresponds to 6 pixels or so. This is, of course, not a very economical format for the storage of fingerprint images which contain a much smaller amount of useful information. Yet, this format is necessary, at least in the developing phase, to fine-tune the preprocessing.

We have currently assembled a database of over 200 fingerprint images using various fingers from 30 persons. To address the matching problem, it is imperative that the data base contain several different images of the same finger taken at different times. Thus, for what follows, the most important part of the data base consists of a subset of 100 images. These are exclusively index finger images from 20 persons, five images being taken for each index finger at different times. At each collection time, we did not give any particular instruction to the person regarding the positioning of the finger on the prism other than to do so "in a natural way." In general, we made a deliberate attempt not to try to reduce the noise and variability which would be present in a realistic environment. For instance, we did *not* clean the surface of the prism after each collection. Indeed, we do observe significant differences among images originating from the same finger. This variability results from multiple sources, mostly at the level of the finger (positioning, pressure, skin condition, etc.) and the collection device (brightness, focus, condition of prism surface, etc.).

We have conducted several learning experiments using this data base, training the networks with image pairs originated from up to seven persons and testing the algorithm on the remaining pairs. Here, we report the typical results of one of our largest experiments, where, out of the $\binom{100}{2} = 4950$ image pairs in this data base, $\binom{25}{2} = 300$ image pairs originating from five persons are used to train the network by gradient descent. The remaining 4650 pairs of images are used to test the generalization abilities of the algorithm.

Given two fingerprint images A and B, the proposition that they match (resp. do not match) will be denoted by $M(A, B)$ (resp. $\bar{M}(A, B)$). The purpose then is to design a neural network algorithm which, when presented with a pair (A, B) of fingerprint images, outputs a number $p = p(M) = p(M(A, B))$ between 0 and 1 corresponding to a degree of confidence (Cox, 1946) or probability that the two fingerprints match. Here, as in the rest of the chapter, we tend to omit in our notation the explicit dependence on the pair (A, B) except the first time a new symbol is introduced.

PREPROCESSING STAGE

Any algorithm for fingerprint recognition may start with a few stages of standard preprocessing where the raw images may be rotated, translated, scaled, contrast-enhanced, segmented, compressed, or convolved with some suitable filter. In our application, the purpose of the preprocessing stage is to extract from each one of the two input images a central patch called the central region and to align the two central regions. Only the two aligned central regions are in turn fed to the decision stage. The preprocessing itself consists of several steps, first to filter out high-frequency noise, then to compensate for translation effects present in the images and to segment them and finally to align and compress the central regions. For ease of description, one of the input images will be called the reference image and the other one the test image, although there is no intrinsic difference between the two.

(a) Low-pass filtering.   To get rid of the numerous high-frequency spikes which seem to be present in the original images, we replace every pixel which

Figure 2a. A typical fingerprint image. The surrounding box is determined using an edge detection algorithm. Notice the numerous minutia and the noise present in the image, for instance in the form of ridge traces left on the prism by previous image collections.

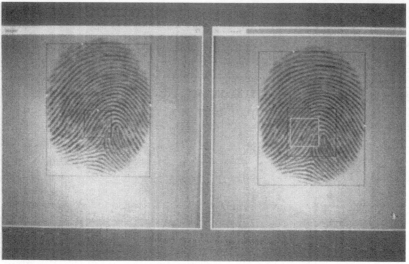

Figure 2b. Preprocessing of two images of the same finger. The left image is the reference image, the right image is the test image (same as 2a). The 65 × 65 central region of the reference image is shown in black right under the geometrical center (white dot). The 105 × 105 window of the test image is shown in black. The white square is the central region of the test image and corresponds to the 65 × 65 patch, within the window, which has a maximal correlation with the central region of the reference image.

significantly deviates from the values of its four neighbors by the corresponding average.

(b) Segmentation.   For each image, we first draw a tight rectangular box around each fingerprint using an edge detection algorithm and determine the geometrical center of the box. The central region of the reference image is then defined to be the 65 × 65 central square patch which occupies the region immediately below the previously described center. For the test image instead, we select a similar but larger patch of size 105 × 105 (extending the previous patch by 20 pixels in each direction). This larger patch is termed the window.

(c) Alignment.   We slide, pixel by pixel, the central region of the reference image across the window of the test image (by 20 pixels up, down, left, and right) and compute at each step the corresponding correlation, until we find the position where the correlation is maximal. This, aside from the training period, is the most computationally expensive part of the entire algorithm. The central region of the test image is then determined by selecting the central 65 × 65 patch corresponding to the position of maximal correlation (Figure 2b).

(d) Compression and normalization.   Finally, each one of the two 65 × 65 central regions is reduced to a 32 × 32 array by discrete convolution with a truncated Gaussian of size 5 × 5. This 32 × 32 compressed central region contains a low-resolution image which corresponds roughly to 10 ridges in the original image. The resulting pixel values are conveniently normalized between 0 and 1.

In our implementation, all the parameters and in particular the size of the various rectangular boxes are adjustable. The values given here are the ones used in the following simulations and empirically seem to yield good results. To avoid border effects, a 2-pixel-wide frame is usually added around the various rectangular boxes which explains some of the odd sizes. It is also natural to wonder at this stage, whether a decision regarding the matching of the two inputs could not already be taken based solely on the value of the maximal correlation found during the alignment step (c) by thresholding it. It is a key empirical observation that this maximal correlation, due in part to noise effects, is *not* sufficient. In particular, the correlation of both matching and nonmatching fingerprint images is often very high (above 0.9) and we commonly observe cases where the correlation of nonmatching pairs is higher than the correlation of matching pairs. It is therefore essential to have a nonlinear decision stage following the preprocessing. Finally, it should be noticed that, during training as well as during testing, the preprocessing needs only to be applied once to each pair of images. In particular, only the central regions need to be cycled through the neural network during the training phase. Although the preprocessing is not subject to training, it can be implemented, for the most part, in a parallel fashion compatible with a global neural architecture for the entire algorithm.

NEURAL NETWORK DECISION STAGE

The decision stage is the proper neural network part of the algorithm. As in other related applications (see, for instance, Le Cun et al., 1990), the network has a pyramidal architecture, with the two aligned and compressed central regions as inputs and with a single output p. The bottom level of the pyramid corresponds to a convolution of the central regions with several filters or feature detectors. The subsequent layers are novel. The final decision they implement results from a probabilistic Bayesian model for the estimation of p, based on the output of the convolution filters. Both the filtering and decision part of the network are adaptable and trained simultaneously.

Convolution

The two central regions are first convolved with a set of adjustable filters. In this implementation only two different filter types are used, but the extension to a larger number of them is straightforward. Here, each filter has a 7×7 receptive field, and the receptive fields of two neighboring filters of the same type have an overlap of 2 pixels to approximate a continuous convolution operation. The outputs of all the filters of a given type form a 6×6 array. Thus, each 32×32 core is transformed into several 6×6 arrays, one for each filter type. The output of filter type j at position (x, y) in one of this arrays is given (for instance for A) by

$$z^j_{x,y}(A) = f\left(\sum_{r,s} w^j_{x,y,r,s} I_{r,s}(A) + t^j \right), \tag{1}$$

where $I_{r,s}(A)$ is the pixel intensity in the compressed central region of image A at the (r, s) location, f is one of the usual sigmoids ($f(x) = (1 + e^{-x})^{-1}$), $w_{x,y,r,s}$ is the weight of the connection from the (r, s) location in the compressed central region to the (x, y) location in the array of filter outputs, and t^j is a bias. The sum in Equation 1 is taken over the 7×7 patch corresponding to the receptive field of the filter at the (x, y) location. The threshold and the 7×7 pattern of weights are characteristic of the filter type ("weight sharing"). They are shared within an image but also across the images A and B. Thus, $w^j_{x,y,r,s} = w^j(x - r, y - s)$, and, in this implementation, each filter type is characterized by $7 \times 7 + 1 = 50$ learnable parameters. In what follows, we simplify the notation for the location of the outputs of the filters by letting $(x, y) = i$. For each filter type j, we can now form an array $\Delta z^j(A, B)$ consisting of all the squared differences

$$\Delta^j_i(A, B) = (z^j_i(A) - z^j_i(B))^2, \tag{2}$$

and let $\Delta z = \Delta z(A, B)$ denote the array of all $\Delta z^j_i(A, B)$ for all positions i and filter types j (Figure 3).

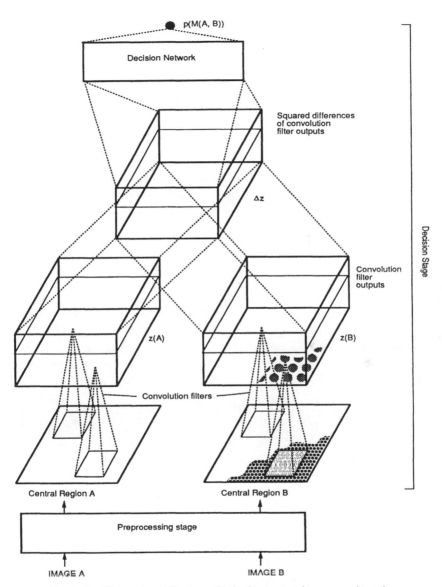

Figure 3. Network architecture. At the bottom, reference and test images *A* and *B* are presented to the network as two 32×32 arrays. The network extracts features from the images by convolution with several different 7×7 filter types.

495

Decision

The purpose of the decision part of the network is to estimate the probability $p = p(M(A, B)/\Delta z(A, B)) = p(M/\Delta z)$ of a match between A and B, given the evidence Δz provided by the convolution filters. The decision part can be viewed as a binary Bayesian classifier. There are four key ingredients to the decision network we are proposing.

(i) Because the output of the network is to be interpreted as a probability, the usual least-mean-square error used in most back-propagation networks does not seem to be an appropriate measure of network performance. For probability distributions, the cross entropy between the estimated probability output p and the true probability P, summed over all patterns, is a well-known information-theoretic measure of discrepancy (see, for instance, Blahut, 1987):

$$H(P,p) = \sum_{(A,B)} P \log \frac{P}{p} + Q \log \frac{Q}{q},\tag{3}$$

where, for each image pair, $Q = 1 - P$ and $q = 1 - p$. The function H is also known as the discrimination function and can be viewed as the expected value of the log-likelihood ratio of the two distributions. The discrimination is nonnegative, convex in each of its arguments, and equal to zero if and only if its arguments are equal.

(ii) Using Bayes' inversion formula and omitting, for simplicity, the dependence on the pair (A, B) give

$$p(M/\Delta z) = \frac{p(\Delta z/M)p(M)}{p(\Delta z/M)p(M) + p(\Delta z/\bar{M})p(\bar{M})}.\tag{4}$$

The effect of the priors $p(M)$ and $p(\bar{M})$ should be irrelevant in a large set of examples. Our data base is large enough for the decision to be driven only by the data, as confirmed by the simulations (see also Figure 4). In simulations, the values chosen are typically $p(M) = 0.1$ and $p(\bar{M}) = 0.9$ (the observed value of $p(M)$ is roughly 16% in the training set and 4% in the entire data base).

(iii) We make the simplifying independence assumption that

$$p(\Delta z/M) = \prod_{i,j} p(\Delta z_i^j/M),\tag{5}$$

$$p(\Delta z/\bar{M}) = \prod_{i,j} p(\Delta z_i^j/\bar{M}).\tag{6}$$

Strictly speaking, this is not true, especially for neighboring locations. However, in the center of a fingerprint, where there is more variability than in the periphery, it is a reasonable approximation which leads to simple network architectures and, with hindsight, yields excellent results.

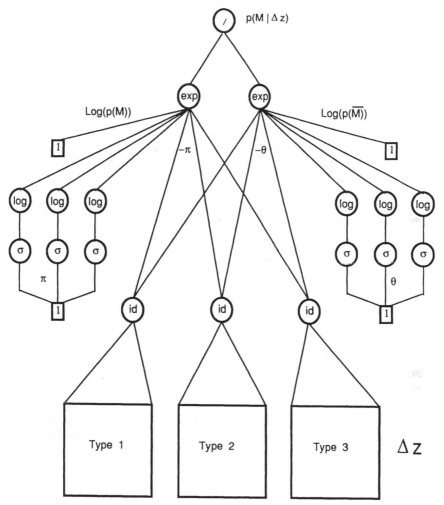

Figure 4. Neural decision network. This is just a neural network implementation of Equations 4–8. Except for the output unit, each unit computes its output by applying its transfer function to the weighted sum of its inputs. In this network, different units have different transfer functions, including $id(x) = x$, $\sigma(x) = (1 + e^{-x})^{-1}$, $\log x$, and $\exp(x) = e^x$. The output unit is a normalization unit which calculates $p(M/\Delta z)$ in the form of a quotient $x/x + y$. The coefficients p_j and q_j of Equations 7 and 8 are implemented in the form $p_j = \sigma(\pi_j)$ and $1 - q_j = \sigma(\theta_j)$. π_j and θ_j are the only adjustable weights of this part of the network, and they are shared with the connections originating from the convolution filter outputs. All other connection weights are fixed to 1 except for the connections running from $\log p_j$ to the exponential unit which have a weight equal to 36, the size of the receptive field of the convolution filters. The exponential unit on the left, for instance, computes $p(\Delta z/M)p(M) = p(M) \, \Pi_{i,j} \, p_j[(1 - p_j)/p_j]^{\Delta z^j_i}$ using the fact that $(1 - p_j)/p_j = -\Pi_j$. Notice that the priors play the role of a bias for the exponential units which, after training, ends up having little influence on the output.

497

(iv) To completely define our network, we still need to choose a model for the conditional distributions $p(\Delta z_i^j/M)$ and $p(\Delta z_i^j/\bar{M})$. In the case of a match, the probability $p(\Delta z_i^j/M)$ should be a decreasing function of Δz_i^j. It is therefore natural to propose an exponential model of the form $p(\Delta z_i^j/M) = C_{ij} s_{ij}^{\Delta z_i^d}$, where $0 < s_{ij} < 1$ and, for proper normalization, the constant C_{ij} must take the value $C_{ij} = \log s_{ij}/s_{ij} - 1$. In what follows, however, we use a less general but slightly simpler binomial model of the form

$$p(\Delta z_i^j/M) = p_j^{1-\Delta z_i^j} = p_j \left(\frac{1 - p_j}{p_j} \right)^{\Delta z_i^j}, \tag{7}$$

$$p(\Delta z_i^j/\bar{M}) = q_j^{\Delta z_i^j}(1 - q_j)^{1-\Delta z_i^j} = (1 - q_j) \left(\frac{q_j}{1 - q_j} \right)^{\Delta z_i^j}, \tag{8}$$

with $0.5 \le p_j, q_j \le 1$. This is again only an approximation used for its simplicity and because the feature differences Δz_i^j are usually close to 0 or 1. In this implementation and for economy of parameters, the adjustable parameters p_j and q_j depend only on the filter type, another example of weight sharing. In a more general setting, they could also depend on location.

In summary, the adjustable parameters of the neural network are $w_{x,y,r,s}^j$, t^j, p_j, and q_j. In this implementation, their total number is $(7 \times 7 + 1) \times 2 + 2 \times 2 = 104$. At first sight, this may seem too large since the network is trained using only 300 pairs of images. In reality, each one of the 50 shared parameters corresponding to the weights and bias of each of the convolution filters is trained on a much larger set of examples, since, for each pair of images, the same filter is exposed to 72 different subregions. The parameters are initialized randomly (for instance, the $w_{x,y,r,s}^j$ are all drawn independently from a Gaussian distribution with zero mean and standard deviation 0.5). They are then iteratively adjusted, after each example pair presentation, by gradient descent on the cross entropy error measure H. The specific formula for adjusting each of them can readily be derived from Equations 3–8 and will not be given here.

The network defined by Equations 3–8 is not a neural network in the most restrictive sense of a layered system of sigmoid units. It is rather a nonlinear model with adjustable parameters which can be drawn (Figure 4) in several different ways in a neural network fashion. The number of units and their types, however, depends on how one decides to decompose the algebraic steps involved in the computation of the final output p.

RESULTS

We have trained the network described in the previous sections using 300 pairs of images from our data base and only two different filter types (Figure 5). The network performance is then tested on 4650 new pairs. The network usually learns the training data base perfectly. This is not the case, however, when only one filter type is used. The separation obtained in the output unit between matching and nonmatching pairs over the entire population is good since 99% of the matching (resp. nonmatching) pairs yield an output above 0.8 (resp. below 0.2). The error rate on the generalization set is typically 0.5% with roughly half the errors due to false rejections and half to false acceptances. In many applications, these two types of error do not play symmetric roles. It is often the case, for instance, that a false acceptance is more catastrophic than a false rejection If, by changing our decision threshold on p, we enforce a 0% rate of false acceptances, the rate of false rejections increases to 4%. This error rate needs, of course, to be reduced, but even so it could be almost acceptable for certain applications. Consider, for instance, the case of a lock type of application. If, as we think, this error rate is mostly due to problems in the positioning of the finger and therefore to a failure in the preprocessing and not in the matching of particular ridge patterns, then this would roughly mean that on 4 occasions out of 100 one needs to reposition one's finger twice on the collection device before being able to open the lock. Of course, the probability of error could also be lowered by using, for each person, several fingers.

As in other related applications, the interpretation of the filter types discovered by the network during learning is not always straightforward (Figures 5 and 6). We have conducted various experiments with up to four filter types but on smaller data bases. Usually, at least one of the filter types always appears to be an edge or a ridge orientation detector. Some of the other filter types found in the course of various experiments may be interpretable in terms of minutia detectors, although this is probably more debatable.

Another observation is that upon the completion of the training phase, the outputs of the filters in the decision stage are close to being binary 0 or 1. Since the final decision of the network is entirely based on these outputs, these provide a very compressed representation of all the relevant matching information originally contained in the $512 \times 464 \times 8$ bits images. Thus, in this implementation, each image is roughly reduced to $36 \times 2 = 72$ bits which is within a factor of 2 from a rough estimate of the theoretical lower bound (the number of human beings, past and present, is approximately $2^{33} = 8.5 \times 10^9$).

It must also be pointed out that in a practical application, the algorithm would not be used in the same way as it has been during the training phase. In particular, only the central regions of the reference images need to be stored in the data base. Since the forward propagation through the decision stage of the algorithm is very fast, one can envision a variation on the algorithm where the alignment step in the preprocessing is modified and where the reference image is stored in the data base only in the most compressed form given by the corresponding outputs of the filters in the decision stage. In this variation, all the possible 65×65 square patches contained in the 105×105 window of the test image would be sent, after the usual compression and normalization preprocessing steps, through the convolution filter arrays and then matched through the neural network with the corresponding outputs for the reference image. The final decision would then

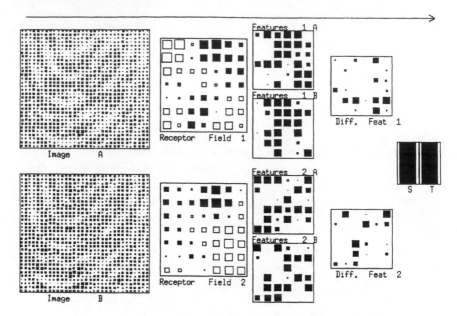

Figure 5.   Unit activation throughout the network when two matching fingerprint images are presented as inputs. Flow of activation is left to right. Images *A* and *B* are presented to the network as 32×32 arrays. The network has two filters 1 and 2, each represented by the corresponding 7×7 pattern of weights. Each filter is convolved with each array and generates the set of feature arrays 1*A*, 1*B*, 2*A*, and 2*B*. The next layer computes the squared feature differences for each filter. Finally, the similarity $S = p(M/\Delta z)$ is computed. In this example the similarity is close to 1 (represented by a black vertical bar), close to the target value $T = 1$. Notice the essentially binary values assumed by the features and the compact representation of the input images with 72 bits each.

be based on an examination of the resulting surface of p values. Whether this algorithm leads also to better decisions needs further investigation.

To reduce the error rate, several things can be tried. One possibility is to use more general exponential models in Equations 7 and 8 rather than binomial distributions. Alternatively, the number of filter types or the number of free parameters could be increased (for instance, by letting p_j and q_j depend also on location) and/or increase the data base. Another possibility is to use in the comparison larger windows or, for instance, two small windows rather than one, the second window being automatically aligned by the alignment of the first one. A significant fraction of the residual false rejections we have seems to be due to rotation effects, that is, to the fact that fingers are sometimes positioned at different angles on the collection device. The network we have described seems to be able to deal with rotations up to a $10°$ angle. Larger rotations could easily be dealt with in the preprocessing stage. It is also possible to include a guiding device to the collection system so as to entirely avoid rotation problems. There are many other directions in which this approach can be extended or improved, depending also on the type of application envisioned. Here are only a few examples. Exceptional fingerprints, for instance with large scars, probably need to be addressed separately. For certain applications, images originated from different collection devices could be included in the data base. False rejection and false acceptance errors could be weighted differently in the learning algo-

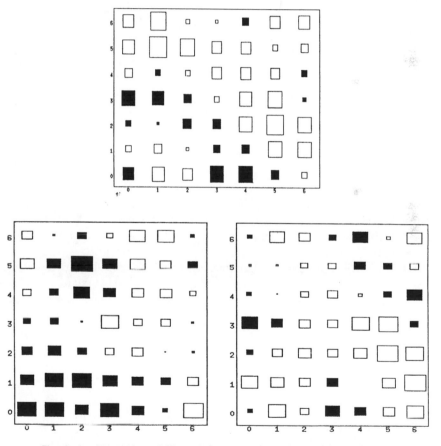

Figure 6. Examples of filters learned in different experiments: one filter is represented by the corresponding 7 × 7 patterns of weights. The size of each square represents the value of the corresponding weight. Black (resp. white) squares correspond to positive (resp. negative) weights. Whereas the first filter seems to be an edge or ridge orientation detector, the other two are more difficult to interpret. It may be tempting to describe them in terms of minutia detectors, such as an ending and a bifurcation detector, but this may not necessarily be the case.

rithm. The training and testing set could also be increased or varied, depending on the application.

In this study, we have attempted to find a general-purpose neural network matcher which could be able, in principle, to solve the matching problem over the entire population. In this regard, it is remarkable that the network, having been trained with image pairs associated with only 5 persons, generalizes well to a larger data base associated with 20 persons. Obviously, a general-purpose network needs also to be tested on a larger sample of the population. Specific applications, especially those involving a small data base, have particular characteristics which may be advantageously exploited both in the architecture and the training of networks and raise also some particular issues. For a car lock application, for instance, positive matches occur only with pair of fingerprints associated with a small data base of only a few persons. Positive matches corresponding to fingerprints associated with persons outside the data base are irrelevant. They may not be needed for training. In addition, in a normal functioning situation, the system may be exposed much more often to matching pairs than to non-matching ones. Furthermore, the system should be designed in a way that facilitates the addition or deletion of persons.

The approach we described and especially the Bayesian decision stage with its probabilistic interpretation is not particular to the problem of fingerprint recognition. It is rather a general framework which could be applied to other pattern matching problems where identity or homology needs to be established. This is the case, for instance, in the identification of humans based on the patterns of blood vessels revealed by retinal scans or in the analysis of homologies in nucleic or amino acid sequences.

Finally, the neural network algorithm can easily be embodied in hardware, especially once the learning has been done off-line. As pointed out earlier, most of the steps in the preprocessing and decision stages are convolutions and are amenable to parallel implementation. On a workstation it currently takes a few seconds to completely process a pair of fingerprint images. This time could be reduced by a few orders of magnitude with specially dedicated hardware.

CLASSIFICATION

We now briefly describe a few classification experiments. Classification of fingerprints into subclasses (such as whorls, arches, or loops) can be useful to speed up search through large data bases. For classification, we used the NIST data base, that contains 2,000 classified pairs of images, divided into 5 balanced classes of 400 each (these images are of variable quality, sometimes very poor, representative of a typical sample from the FBI data base). Our overall classification architecture consists of the following stages:

Preprocessing. A central 77 × 77 region is extracted from the original image and fed to the neural network. This central region is first convolved with a set of relatively small adjustable filters. Each filter has a 7×7 receptive field and the receptive fields of two neighboring filters of the same type have an overlap of two pixels in order to approximate a continuous convolution operation. The output of all the filters of a given type form a 15×15 array. For a given image A, the output of filter type j at position (x, y) in one of the arrays is given by

$$z^j_{x,y}(A) = f\left(\sum_{r,s} w^j_{x,y,r,s} I_{r,s}(A) + t^j \right),$$

where $I_{r,s}(A)$ is the pixel intensity in the central region of the input image A at the (r, s) location, f is one of the usual sigmoids $(f(x) = (1 + e^{-x})^{-1})$, $w_{x,y,r,s}$ is the weight of the connection from the (r, s) location in the central region to the (x, y) location in the array of filter outputs, and t^j is a bias. The sum in is taken over the 7×7 patch corresponding to the receptive field of the filter at the (x, y) location. The threshold and the 7×7 pattern of weights are characteristic of the filter type ("weight sharing technique"), so they can also be viewed as the parameters of a translation-invariant convolution kernel. Thus, $w^j_{x,y,r,s} = w^j_{x-r,y-s}$, and, in this implementation each filter type is characterized by $7 \times 7 + 1$ learnable parameters. During training, the network should find what are the most appropriate feature detectors or convolution kernels for the classification task.

An averaging layer is inserted between the feature extraction layer and the high level feature extraction layer. The same technique of weight sharing is used for the connections to this layer but in this case, the averaging units have a linear transfer function, instead of the previous sigmoid function, and the weights are equal and fixed at initialization. The role of this averaging layer is to "smooth out" the features extracted in the first layer. It acts as a filter and decreases the chances of extracting fingerprint idiosyncracies that may be contained in the training data base. The size of this averaging layer is 2×2 with an overlap of 1, reducing the original 15×15 feature map into a 14×14 array.

High-level feature extraction.   From a formal standpoint, this stage is similar to the previous one in the sense that we convolve the corresponding input with several different translation invariant kernels or feature detectors. The output unit at this stage, however, have access to information from a much larger patch of the original image. Again, it is up to the network and the training procedure to discover what are the proper features to use for proper classification. From our intuition, we can expect that some of the filters will become essentially "ridge curvature detectors", others may become "delta detectors" or "core detectors". The kernel size is 8×8 with an overlap of 7. The smoothed feature map in the 14×14 averaging layer is then transformed into a 7×7 layer. The activities of the units in this layer constitute a representation of the presence likelyhoods of location specific high-level features.

Probabilistic output classification.   Different variations in the basic architecture can be envisioned in order to calculate the quantities p_i from the outputs of the high-level feature extractors. In the most simple case, p_i is derived from the output of a sigmoidal unit that receives a weighted combination of the outputs of the high-level feature extractors. Alternatively, slightly more sophisticated Bayesian probabilistic models can be introduced to estimate the p_i's from the outputs of the previous layer. To train these architectures, we used gradient descent on the cross-entropy or Kullbach distance defined as

$$H(P,p) = \sum_i P_i \ln(P_i/p_i).$$

Clearly, depending on the final objectives and error rates to be achieved, different decision functions can be implemented based on the outputs p_i of the architecture. In particular, the decision boundaries for referencing and nonclassifiability can be tailored to the needs of a particular application.

From the NIST data base, we extracted images and corresponding classes and constructed network pattern files containing about 200 examples per file. As with other neural network applications, results can be described in terms of performance and in terms of the types of internal representations obtained after training. These internal representations usually indicate the relevance of the features extracted by the network and may constitute good indicators of the future performance of the network for large data bases.

The network performance can be analyzed for each class in terms of the probability distributions for the in-class and out-of-class samples after training (see architectures). Over several runs and for all classes, the observed training performance is usually perfect. Classification performance can be obtained by setting a probability threshold in which input images are classified in the target class and input images are classified in the nontarget classes. For the whorls, with a threshold set at .5, we obtain about 50% false negative and 10% false positive with an overall performance rate of about 70%. The proportion of false positive and false negative will change as a function of threshold setting. For right loops, left loops and arches, the performance is similar. Worse performance is obtained for the tented arches, again because all the referenced patterns were taken out from the original data bases, leaving few positive examples for the network to learn from.

One of the most interesting results observed in the simulations relates to the shape of the low-level receptor fields learned by the network. The profiles of these receptor fields clearly resemble ridge-orientation detectors. Furthermore, if several receptor fields are used, each of them becomes an orientation detector with a specific ridge-orientation preference. The first layers of the network, therefore, constitute nonlinear versions of ridge orientation matrices. The second layer of the network was designed to extract the overall shape of each basic class from the ridge-orientation matrices learned in the first layers. The architecture of the network and the associated learning algorithm were designed to make this extraction translation independent. As pointed out earlier, the number of free parameters in the network should then be adapted to the size of the training data base. Because the low-level receptor fields are learned with the technique of weight sharing, the number of patterns currently used in the simulations is probably sufficient to generate interesting receptor profiles. However, the next layer of the current network architecture is designed to capture the characteristics of each basic fingerprint class. There are 128 such parameters, 64 for each feature map, for each of these class detectors. The number of in-class samples in a training pattern file, therefore, is currently not sufficient for good validation performance. For example, we observed that when an unusual proportion of double loops are included in the whorl training data base, the network does not generalize to other types of whorl subclasses.

Considering the number of parameters, the size of the training patterns and of the input images, the results show that the network extracted information necessary for basic class discrimination. Although validation performance should be improved with refined network architectures and larger training data bases, the preliminary results we obtain are encouraging and show the potential of neural networks as fingerprint classifiers.

ACKNOWLEDGMENTS

Substantial portions of this chapter are reprinted from *Neural Networks for Fingerprint Recognition,* P. Baldi, and Y. Chauvin, in Neural Computation, 5, pp. 402–418 (1993) with permission from M.I.T. Press.

APPENDIX

In this appendix we briefly show that the architectures used in this chapter can also be viewed in the general framework outlined in the first chapter of this volume. The matching architecture, for instance, with its single decision output unit falls in the binomial case category. We have seen that the right cost function to be used in this case is the cross-entropy and that the proper transfer function, in the output layer, is the logistic function. Clearly, the matching architecture has been trained using a cross-entropy function. To study the output function of our decision network, recall that we have

$$p(M/\Delta z) = \frac{p(\Delta z/M)p(M)}{p(\Delta z/M)p(M) + p(\Delta z/\bar{M})p(\bar{M})}. \tag{A1}$$

By dividing the numerator and the denominator by $p(\Delta z/M)p(M)$ we immediately get:

$$p(M/\Delta z) = \cfrac{1}{1 + \cfrac{p(\Delta z/\bar{M})p(\bar{M})}{p(\Delta z/M)p(M)}}$$

$$= \frac{1}{1 + e^{-[\log p(\Delta z/M) + \log p(M) - \log p(\Delta z/\bar{M}) - \log p(\bar{M})]}}. \tag{A2}$$

Now, it is clear that in order for $p(M/\Delta z)$ to be a sigmoidal function of a linear weighted input, we need exactly to have a product decomposition of the form

$$p(\Delta z/M) = \prod_{i,j} p(\Delta_i^j/M) \tag{A3}$$

$$p(\Delta z/\bar{M}) = \prod_{i,j} p(\Delta_i^j/\bar{M}) \tag{A4}$$

with

$$p(\Delta z_i^j/M) = p_j^{1-\Delta z_i^j}(1 - p_j)^{\Delta z_i^j} \tag{A5}$$

$$p(\Delta z_i^j/\bar{M}) = q_j^{\Delta z_i^j}(1 - q_j)^{1-\delta z_i^j} \tag{A6}$$

with $0 \leq p_j$, $q_j \leq 1$, as used in the matching architecture described above. In this sense, our matching architecture is somewhat canonical and can be applied to other matching problems. It falls within the general framework of chapter 1 and shows, for a particular family of problems, how the general framework can be used practically not only for the design of the output layer but also for the design of some of the hidden layers.

Likewise, our classification architecture, falls within the general multinomial framework of chapter 1. As we have seen in both cases, the global cost function is again a cross-entropy function and the transfer functions in the output layer are normalized exponentials, with one output unit for each class. The hidden layers of the architecture are also somewhat canonical and generalize the design principles used by Keeler et al. (1991). When stripped of unnecessary algebraic details, their architecture for handwritten character segmentation and recognition is based on two essential computational layers. First, the computation of p_{ij}, the probability that character i is present at position j, by a sigmoidal unit for each i and j. Second, the computation of p_i, the probability that character i is present or not in the input window, independently of its position, and for each i. In general, p_i is apolynomial function of the p_{ij}'s. Which particular polynomial function and its order depend on the assumption one makes about the input: for instance, whether a given character can occur at most once in the input, at most twice or any number of times. The complexity of this polynomial function and the type of units used for its implementation dictate the number of units and layers required for its computation. The classification architecture described generalizes this approach by calculating first, a hierarchical series of location dependent probabilistic events, over larger and larger spatial scales, and in a feed-forward mode. Consider, for instance, three levels of successive calculations p_{ij}^1, p_{ij}^2 and p_{ij}^3 as representing, respectively, the probability of a certain orientation i at position j, the probability of a certain curvature i at position j and the probability of a "character" i, such as a core or a delta, at position j. A unit computing a term of the form p_{ij}^{k+1} has a receptive field in the layer associated with the computation of the p_{ij}^k's. From the location dependent "character" probabilities p_{ij}^3, we can calculate position independent probabilities p_i^4 (in a way similar to the Keeler et al. architecture), if we deem it useful for the final decision. Finally, the probability that the input belongs to any of the possible classes is computed using normalized exponentials, as in the general framework of chapter 1. It is clear how these ideas can be further generalized in several directions.

REFERENCES

Blahut, R. E. (1987). *Principles and practice of information theory.* Reading, MA: Addison Wesley.

Cox, R. T. (1946). Probability, frequency and reasonable expectation. *American Journal of Physics, 14*(1), 1–13.

Gorman, R. P., & Sejnowski, T. J. (1988). Analysis of hidden units in a layered network trained to classify sonar targets. *Neural Networks, 1,* 75–89.

Igaki, S., Eguchi, S., & Shinzaki, T. (1990). Holographic fingerprint sensor. *Fujitsu Technical Journal, 25*(4), 287–296.

Keeler, J. D., Rumelhart, D. E., & Leow, W. K. (1991). Integrated segmentation and recognition of hand-printed numerals. In *Neural information processing systems 3,* (pp. 557–563). San Mateo, CA: Morgan Kaufmann.

Le Cun, Y., Boser, B., Denker, J. S., Henderson, D., Howard, R. E., Hubbard, W., & Jackel, L. D. (1990). Handwritten digit recognition with a back-propagation network. In *neural information processing systems 2,* (pp. 296–404). San Mateo, CA: Morgan Kaufmann.

Mjolsness, E. (1986). Neural networks, pattern recognition and fingerprint hallucination. Unpublished doctoral thesis, California Institute of Technology.

Moenssens, A. A. (1971). *Fingerprint techniques.* Chilton Book Company.

Rumelhart, D. E., Hinton, G. E., & Williams, R. J. (1986). Learning representations by back-propagating errors. *Nature, 323,* 533–536.

Tesauro, G. (1989). Neurogammon wins computer olympiad. *Neural Computation, 1*(3), 321–323.

15

Gradient Descent Learning Algorithms: A Unified Perspective

Pierre Baldi
Jet Propulsion Laboratory and Division of Biology,
California Institute of Technology, Pasadena, California

ABSTRACT

We give a unified treatment of gradient descent learning algorithms for neural networks using a general framework of dynamical systems. This general approach organizes and simplifies all the known algorithms and results which have been originally derived for different problems (fixed point/trajectory learning), for different models (discrete/continuous), for different architectures (forward/recurrent) and using different techniques (back-propagation, variational calculus, adjoint methods, . . .). The general approach can also be applied to derive new algorithms. We then briefly examine some of the complexity issues and limitations intrinsic to gradient descent learning. Throughout this chapter we focus on the problem of trajectory learning.

INTRODUCTION

Learning in biological systems is widely believed to result from progressive modifications occurring at the level of synapses connecting neurons. While the detailed biophysical mechanisms by which a given connection may become stronger or weaker are being intensively investigated, it is clear that ultimately such modifications can depend only on the local electrochemical environment of a given synapse. This is not to say that there are no global signals; these indeed exist, for instance in the form of neuromodulators. But the central point is that a given synapse is not aware of their global nature. A single synapse does not know anything about the global tasks the organism is trying to learn. Synaptic modifications and global tasks belong to two very distant levels of the brain hierarchy. Therefore, the fundamental question of learning is: what are the principles according to which local synaptic changes are organized in order to yield global learning of complex behaviors for the organism? This puzzling question remains largely unanswered. There are, however, two basic and somewhat complementary ideas in the theoretical literature which have shed some light on this question.

The main contribution to the origin of the first idea is usually attributed to Hebb (1949). Loosely speaking, this is the idea that if the activities of two connected neurons are correlated over time, then the strength of the corresponding synapse should tend to increase. If the activities are not correlated, then the strength should tend to decrease. This formulation is obviously very vague, and various ways exist by which Hebbian learning rules can be implemented in neural networks. It is well known that, although these rules are very simple and local, they can lead to powerful self-organization effects in networks of simple model neurons (see, for instance, Linsker, 1988). Yet, it is also clear that a Hebb rule by itself cannot account for the learning of complex behaviors and that more global organizing principles are also required.

Gradient descent is the second main idea in the theory of learning, one which precisely attempts to offer a simple guiding principle for the overall organisation of synaptic changes across networks. Whether something vaguely similar to gradient descent occurs in biological organisms is still unclear. But the study of gradient descent learning remains worthwhile for at least two reasons: the numerous insights it sheds on the problems attached to learning and for its applications, in artificial neural systems, to the solution of many practical problems. This chapter is devoted to the study of gradient descent learning from an algorithmic point of view. In particular, we try to sort out all the different possible ways of actually implementing the basic gradient descent idea, and also examine some of its limitations.

Because gradient descent learning algorithms have been studied in the context of particular neural network models (discrete time, continuous time, additive model, higher-order models, etc.), particular problems (fixed-point learning, trajectory learning, etc.), and different techniques (variational calculus, adjoint methods, numerical integration, etc.), the general underlying principles have been somewhat obscured. Thus, numerous and apparently different algorithms have been published in the literature. Some examples include the back propagation and back propagation through time of Rumelhart et al. (1986), the recurrent back propagation of Pineda (1987), and the algorithms of Williams and Zipser (1989), Pearlmutter (1989), and Toomarian and Barhen (1991). This list is not intended to be exhaustive: the same algorithm, including the simple back propagation, has often been discovered independently by several authors at different times, and gradient descent ideas are quite ancient (see also Werbos, 1974, and Bryson & Denham, 1962 along these lines). One of our goals here is to give a general and unified treatment of all these approaches in terms of general dynamical systems. It is our hope that such a treatment should illuminate the simple underlying structure of all the known algorithms, which become special cases of the general approach. Another advantage of the general approach is that it can be readily applied to new models or to new situations, for instance the learning of parameters other than synaptic weights, such as gains, time constants, or delays.

For the purpose of generality, we want to consider the learning problem for an N-dimensional dynamical system of the form

$$\frac{d\mathbf{u}}{dt} = \mathbf{F}(\mathbf{u}, W, \mathbf{I}, \mathbf{u}^*), \tag{1}$$

with initial condition $\mathbf{u}(t_0)$. In this relation, the N-dimensional vector $\mathbf{u}$ represents the state variables of the system, W is an array of adjustable parameters, and $\mathbf{I}$ is a vector of external inputs. When present, the vector $\mathbf{u}^*$ is used to represent particular target values for some of the $\mathbf{u}$ variables. In neural network terminology, the $\mathbf{u}$'s describe the activity or internal membrane potential of the N neurons comprising the network. The parameters W consist mainly of connection weights between the units but may also include their time constants, their gains, and the time delays possibly existing between them. In some situations, one may require that the initial conditions themselves be adjustable. All the results to be derived can also be presented using the slightly different but equivalent framework of discrete dynamical systems. For completeness, these are discussed in the Appendix, where it is shown how to translate learning algorithms from one formalism to the other.

In this framework, the learning problem consists in adjusting the parameters W so that the trajectories of Equation 1 have certain specified properties. Gradient descent learning requires that, at any time, the performance of the dynamical system be assessable through a certain error function E which measures the discrepancy between the trajectories of the dynamical system and the desired behavior. The essence of gradient descent learning consists of iteratively adjusting the dynamical parameters in the direction opposite to the gradient of E so as to reduce this discrepancy according to

$$\frac{dw}{dt} = -\eta \frac{\partial E}{\partial w} \tag{2}$$

or some approximation to it. The parameter η is the usual learning rate or the relaxation time constant of the parameter dynamics. It is also possible to have different learning rates for different parameters or even learning rates which are themselves adaptable (see, for instance, Fang & Sejnowski, 1990). The results to be derived extend immediately to these cases.

In the case of the most commonly used form of supervised gradient descent learning, the target trajectories of the system are supposed to be known and available for training. In particular, the target trajectories $\mathbf{u}^*$ can be incorporated in the error function, for instance by using the usual least-mean-squares error function. In the case of supervised fixed-point learning, the dynamical system should converge to a prescribed fixed point **u***. In the more general case of supervised trajectory learning, the dynamical system should follow a prescribed trajectory $\mathbf{u}^*(t)$ over a certain time interval $[t_0, t_1]$. The target fixed point **u*** or the target trajectory $\mathbf{u}^*(t)$ is usually not defined for all the N units and at all times but only on a subset of the units, the visible units, and possibly only at certain times. The error function is computed only at the visible units and at the times where error information is available. In the most general gradient descent setting however, the target trajectories need not be known in advance or be explicitly present in the error function E.[1] In practice, it is usually desirable to learn several trajectory patterns at the same time so that $E = \Sigma_p E_p$, where E_p is the error for the pth pattern. Since $\partial E/\partial w = \Sigma_p \partial E_p/\partial w$, it is sufficient to study the computation of the gradient for only one pattern. Accordingly, in what follows we shall assume that the system is learning only one trajectory pattern.[2]

Most of the neural network models discussed in the literature are simple special cases of this general framework. It is helpful, for concreteness, to keep in mind some of the particular models to which the theory can be applied. In general, these can be viewed as simple one-compartment models for the neuron charging equations.

Examples of Neural Dynamical Systems

The usual additive model (see, for instance, Amari, 1972; Sejnowski, 1976; Grossberg & Cohen, 1983; Hopfield, 1984) is just a one-compartment model for each neuron and can be described by

$$\frac{du_i}{dt} = -\frac{u_i}{\tau_i} + \sum_j w_{ij} f_j(u_j) + I_i, \tag{3}$$

where τ_i is the time constant of the ith unit and f_i is its input-output transfer function, usually a sigmoid with gain g_i. The form of the transfer function is howerver irrelevant in most of what follows and the equations to be derived can be applied also to the case of nonsigmoidal transfer functions, such as exponential, Gaussian, or logarithmic units.

A different version of the additive model is

$$\frac{du_i}{dt} = -\frac{u_i}{\tau_i} + \alpha_i f_i\left(\sum_j w_{ij} u_j\right) + I_i. \tag{4}$$

---

[1]Contrastive learning (Baldi & Pineda, 1991), which is a generalization of Boltzmann machine learning, is also a special case of gradient descent learning on a particular type of error function. So far, it has mainly been applied only to the case of fixed-point learning and therefore will not be considered here in detail.

[2]The issue of batch learning versus on-line learning, that is, whether Equation 2 can be approximated by $dw/dt = -\eta \partial E_p/\partial w$ is completely outside the focus of this chapter.

It is easy to check that provided all the time constants are identical ($\tau_i = \tau$) and the matrix (w_{ij}) is invertible, the two systems Equations 3 and 4 are equivalent under a simple linear transformation. Indeed, if, for instance in Equation 4 we make the transformation $r_i = \Sigma_j \, w_{ij} u_j$, we immediately obtain a system for the vector r similar to Equation 3. The discretization of (1.4), with $\tau_i = \alpha_i = \Delta t = 1$, leads immediately to the usual connectionist models of Rumelhart et al. (1986).

In some cases (Williams & Zipser, 1989; Baldi & Pineda, 1991) it is useful to include a teacher signal (or error signal) in the charging equation of some of the units of the additive model, for instance in the form

$$\frac{du_i}{dt} = -\frac{u_i}{\tau_i} + \sum_j w_{ij} f_j(u_j) + I_i + \beta_i (u_i^* - u_i)^{\gamma_i}. \tag{5}$$

The additive model can also easily be modified to take into account higher-order interactions. In the case of certain models of shunting inhibition, for instance, one can have terms of the form $(1 - f_k(u_k)) w_{ij} f_j(u_j)$ where the kth unit can control the j to i connection. If the kth unit is active, $f_k(u_k)$ is close to 1, and the j-to-i connection is blocked. The more general additive system with, for instance, only first- and second-order interactions can be written in the form

$$\frac{du_i}{dt} = -\frac{u_i}{\tau_i} + \sum_{j,k} w_{ijk} f_j(u_j) f_k(u_k) + \sum_j w_{ij} f_j(u_j) + I_i. \tag{6}$$

An example of a different class of neural dynamical systems consists of networks of coupled oscillators (see, for instance, Baldi & Meir, 1990) or directional spins. These are modeled in the form

$$\frac{du_i}{dt} = \omega_i + \sum_j w_{ij} \sin(u_j - u_i), \tag{7}$$

where the variables u_i represent the phases of the corresponding oscillators. The general approach can also be applied to more complex models, such as Fitzugh (1961) and Hindmarsh and Rose (1984), where several coupled differential equations are used to model the behavior of a single neuron and its spiking activity.

Time delays seem to play an essential role in natural neural systems (for instance, Carr & Konishi, 1988) and can easily be taken into account in any of the previous models by introducing terms of the form $\mathbf{u}(t - \tau)$ in the corresponding differential equations. In the most general case, the introduction of time delays leads to somewhat more complicated notations because time delays may not be symmetric and because the current state of a synapse may depend on several events having occurred in the neighboring neurons at different times. For instance, in second-order interactions, one may have a charging equation of the form

$$\frac{du_i}{dt} = -\frac{u_i}{\tau_i} \sum_{j,k,P} w_{ijkP} f_j(u_j(t - \tau_{ijkP})) f_k(u_k(t - \tau_{ikjP}))$$

$$+ \sum_{j,Q} w_{ijQ} f_j(u_j(t - \tau_{ijQ})) + I_i, \tag{8}$$

where the first index of a delay refers to the postsynaptic neuron, the second index to the neuron with corresponding delayed activity in the interaction, the following indices to the other neurons participating in the synaptic interaction, and the last index to the corresponding event in the past. In most cases, only the most recent event in the past plays a role in the current charging equation. A more general formulation of delayed networks in terms of convolution kernels, which does not need discretized delays, is possible (see, for instance, de Vries & Principe, 1991). For a first-order additive model, for example, we can write

$$\frac{du_i}{dt} = -\frac{u_i}{\tau_i} + \int_j^t \sum_j w_{ij}(t - s) f_j(u_j(s)) \, ds + I_i. \tag{9}$$

This, however, requires the introduction of a time dependent matrix of synaptic interactions and results have been derived only in the most simple cases which often are essentially reducible to discrete delays.

In the second and third sections we derive the gradient descent learning algorithms for fixed points and trajectories in the framework of general dynamical systems. In both cases, the computation of the gradient depends crucially on the solution of a linear system with matrix L, where L is the Jacobian matrix of the function $\mathbf{F}$ which governs the dynamical system

$$L = (L_{ij}) = \left(\frac{\partial F_i}{\partial u_j} \right). \tag{10}$$

In fixed-point learning, it is a linear system of equations evaluated at equilibrium and basically L that needs to be inverted. In trajectory learning, it is a time-dependent linear system of differential equations which needs to be integrated over time. Different algorithms are possible, depending on how these linear systems are solved. In both cases, one of the algorithms is based on the solution of an auxiliary linear system (the adjoint system) governed by the transpose L^t of L. It is this transposition which is the signature of "back propagation." We briefly examine the connection of these algorithms to the "back propagation through time" concept of Rumelhart et al. (1986). We then extend the algorithms to the case of networks with time delays and where, in addition to the synaptic weights, the delays themselves and the other temporal parameters may also be adjustable and subject to learning. In the fourth section we examine the complexity of the algorithms and some of the limitations inherent to gradient descent procedures, especially for recurrent networks. Several technical results used in the sections are deferred to the Appendix.

Throughout this chapter, $\mathbf{v} = (v_i)$ or $M = (M_{ij})$ will denote a vector or a matrix (vector quantities are in boldface), $\|\mathbf{v}\|$ is the Euclidean norm of the vector $\mathbf{v}$. All vectors are column vectors, and $\mathbf{v}^t$ or M^t represent the transpose of the corresponding vector or matrix. The adjoint of a matrix M is the transpose of the matrix whose entries are the complex conjugate of the entries of M; that is, the adjoint of M is the matrix $\bar{M}^t = (\bar{m}_{ij})^t$. Because all the matrices considered here have real entries, adjoint and transpose matrices are identical. Unless otherwise specified, all functions (in particular $\mathbf{F}$ and f_i) are supposed to be continuously differentiable in all their variables over the range of interest. This ensures the existence and unicity of the solutions of the differential equations considered and allows certain manipulations such as interchanging the order of differentiation in mixed partial derivatives. Parameters such as synaptic weights or delays require multiple indices reflecting the interaction of several neurons. By convention, the first index always characterizes the unique equation in which this parameter appears. Thus a parameter such as $w_{i\ldots}$ appears only in the charging equation of the ith unit (i.e., in F_i). Finally, if an interval such as $[t_0, t_1]$ is discretized into intervals of length Δt, then for any function $g(t)$ we write $g(m) = g(t_0 + m\Delta t)$.

LEARNING FIXED POINTS

In this section, we assume that the system defined by Equation 1 with fixed initial condition $\mathbf{u}(t_0)$ is convergent and remains so in the course of learning. Accordingly, all the quantities to be considered will be evaluated at equilibrium. The system converges to a fixed point $\mathbf{u}^f$, which is a function of the parameters W for fixed initial conditions and fixed external input. The goal here is to modify the parameters so that $\mathbf{u}^f$ approaches a minimum of E. In the special case of supervised learning, $\mathbf{u}^f$ should approach a prescribed target value $\mathbf{u}^*$ defined for the visible units of the networks. The following derivation is unchanged whether the final state is to be considered a function of the external input or a function of the initial state. The error function is of the form

$$E = E(\mathbf{u}^f, \mathbf{u}^*). \tag{11}$$

For instance, in the usual LMS case

$$E = \tfrac{1}{2}(\mathbf{u}^f - \mathbf{u}^*)^2 \tag{12}$$

computed over the visible units. The fixed point $\mathbf{u}^f$ satisfies the relation

$$\mathbf{F}(\mathbf{u}^f, w, \mathbf{I}, \mathbf{u}^*) = 0. \tag{13}$$

To update the weights, we need to compute the gradient

$$\frac{\partial E}{\partial w} = \sum_i \frac{\partial E}{\partial u_i^f} \frac{\partial u_i^f}{\partial w} = \left(\frac{\partial E}{\partial \mathbf{u}^f}\right)^t \frac{\partial \mathbf{u}^f}{\partial w} = \left(\frac{\partial E}{\partial \mathbf{u}^f}\right)^t \mathbf{P}_{.w} \tag{14}$$

($\partial E/\partial u_i^f = 0$ for nonvisible units) where the coordinates

$$p_{iw} = \frac{\partial u_i^f}{\partial w} \tag{15}$$

of the vector $\mathbf{p}_{.w}$ represent how the coordinates u_i^f of the fixed point vary with a small change in w. In control theory, the numbers p_{iw} are often called sensitivities. To compute $\mathbf{p}_{.w}$, we differentiate the fixed-point equation, Equation 15, to get

$$\sum_j \frac{\partial F_i}{\partial u_j^f} p_{jw} + \frac{\partial F_i}{\partial w} = 0 \tag{16}$$

where the vector $\partial \mathbf{F}/\partial w = (\partial F_i/\partial w)$ results from the *explicit* dependence of F_i on w. In vector notation,

$$L\mathbf{p}_{.w} + \frac{\partial \mathbf{F}}{\partial w} = 0, \tag{17}$$

or, with the mild assumption that L be invertible,

$$\mathbf{p}_{.w} = -L^{-1} \frac{\partial \mathbf{F}}{\partial w}, \tag{18}$$

where $L = (\partial F_i/\partial u_j^f)$ is the Jacobian matrix at the equilibrium point. Then from Equations 14 and 18,

$$\frac{\partial E}{\partial w} = -\left(\frac{\partial E}{\partial \mathbf{u}^f}\right)^t L^{-1} \frac{\partial \mathbf{F}}{\partial w} = -\left(\frac{\partial \mathbf{F}}{\partial w}\right)^t (L^t)^{-1} \frac{\partial E}{\partial \mathbf{u}^f}. \tag{19}$$

Now, a few alternatives exist depending on how one chooses to deal with the inversion of the matrices in the right-hand side of Equation 19 and several observations can be made. First, what is really required is the calculation of the product $L^{-1}\partial \mathbf{F}/\partial w$ or $(L^t)^{-1}\partial E/\partial \mathbf{u}^f$. The second product $(L^t)^{-1}\partial E/\partial \mathbf{u}^f$ is preferable because *it does not depend directly on the parameter* w and therefore can be calculated once for all and used in the evolution equation of every parameter throughout the network. If so, we can write

$$\frac{\partial E}{\partial w} = \left(\frac{\partial \mathbf{F}}{\partial w}\right)^t \mathbf{v} \tag{20}$$

with $\mathbf{v} = -(L^t)^{-1}\partial E/\partial \mathbf{u}^f$, or using Equation 2,

$$\frac{dw}{dt} = -\eta \left(\frac{\partial \mathbf{F}}{\partial w}\right)^t \mathbf{v}. \tag{21}$$

Second, the vector $\partial \mathbf{F}/\partial w$ is very sparse for in fact it contains at most one' nonzero component because of our convention on the indices of the neural parameters. (The vector $\partial E/\partial \mathbf{u}^f$ can also be sparse if the proportion of visible units is small.) Therefore, if we write $w = w_{i...}$,

$$\frac{dw_{i...}}{dt} = -\eta \frac{\partial F_i}{\partial w_{i...}} v_i \qquad (22)$$

or

$$\frac{dw_{i...}}{dt} = \eta \frac{\partial F_i}{\partial w_{i...}} \sum_j (L^{-1})_{ji} \frac{\partial E}{\partial u_j^f}. \qquad (23)$$

In this form, the right-hand side of the parameter update equation is the product of two terms: a usually presynaptic activity term $\partial F_i/\partial w_{i...}$ and an error-propagated term v_i. This learning rule could be considered Hebbian only in a very limited sense, since some special machinery must be required to propagate the errors. The definition of $\mathbf{v}$ is based on the transpose L^t of L. It is this transposition which is the signature of "back propagation" and reverts the orientation of the edges in the network. Indeed, $\mathbf{v}$ can be computed by a relaxation method as the equilibrium solution of the system

$$\frac{d\mathbf{v}}{dt} = L^t\mathbf{v} + \frac{\partial E}{\partial \mathbf{u}^f}. \qquad (24)$$

(Notice that since the dynamical system is convergent, all the eigenvalues of L at $\mathbf{u}^f$ have negative real parts. Since L and L^t have the same eigenvalues, Equation 24 is also convergent.) This transposition appears also in the next section on trajectory learning and adjoint methods. In the case of feedforward networks, the matrices L and L^t are triangular and the calculations are somewhat simpler. In the appendix, we give a derivation from Equation 20 of the usual back-propagation equations for connectionist feedforward networks. One can then see that $\mathbf{v}$ is the usual back-propagated error. When Equations 22 and 24 are applied to the version of the additive model defined by Equation 14, one obtains exactly the recurrent back-propagation algorithm discussed in Pineda (1987) (see also Farotimi et al., 1991 for another general derivation based on optimal control theory).

LEARNING TRAJECTORIES

In the more general case of trajectory learning, the goal is to modify the parameters so that the output trajectory minimizes some measure of poor performance. In the supervised case as usual, $\mathbf{u}$ should follow a prescribed target trajectory $\mathbf{u}^*$ for the visible units over a time interval $[t_0, t_1]$. This is a well-defined task, although it is a simplification of what may happen in real situations where one may want to learn several trajectories or even a flow. Furthermore, the problems of stability and phase along the trajectory and whether the trajectory is an attractor are left out for the moment and will be partly addressed in the fourth section. The error function is of the form

$$\mathbf{E} = \int_{t_0}^{t_1} E(\mathbf{u},\mathbf{u}^*,t)\ dt. \tag{25}$$

Although $\mathbf{E}$ is a scalar, a boldface character is used to distinguish it from the instantaneous error $E(\mathbf{u},\ \mathbf{u}^*,\ t)$. For instance, in the usual LMS case

$$\mathbf{E} = \frac{1}{2}\int_{t_0}^{t_1} (\mathbf{u}^*(t) - \mathbf{u}(t))^2 dt \tag{26}$$

computed over the visible units and possibly over the subtime intervals at which $\mathbf{u}^*(t)$ is defined. To update the weights, we need to compute the gradient

$$\frac{\partial \mathbf{E}}{\partial w} = \int_{t_0}^{t_1} \sum_i \frac{\partial E}{\partial u_i}\frac{\partial u_i}{\partial w}\ dt = \int_{t_0}^{t_1}\left(\frac{\partial E}{\partial \mathbf{u}}\right)^t \frac{\partial \mathbf{u}}{\partial w}\ dt = \int_{t_0}^{t_1}\left(\frac{\partial E}{\partial \mathbf{u}}\right)^t \mathbf{p}_{.w}\ dt \tag{27}$$

$(\partial E/\partial u_i = 0$ for nonvisible units) where the coordinates

$$p_{iw}(t) = \frac{\partial u_i(t)}{\partial w} \tag{28}$$

of the sensitivity vector $\mathbf{p}_{.w}(t)$ represent how the coordinates u_i at time t vary with a small change in w. To compute $\mathbf{p}_{.w}$, we have

$$p_{iw}(t) = \frac{\partial}{\partial w}\int_{t_0}^{t}\frac{du_i}{ds}\ ds = \int_{t_0}^{t}\frac{\partial F_i}{\partial w}\ ds, \tag{29}$$

or, by differentiating,

$$\frac{dp_{iw}(t)}{dt} = \frac{\partial F_i(\mathbf{u},\mathbf{W},\mathbf{I},\mathbf{u}^*)}{\partial w} = \sum_j \frac{\partial F_i}{\partial u_j}\frac{\partial u_j}{\partial w} + \frac{\partial F_i}{\partial w}, \tag{30}$$

where $\partial F_i/\partial w$ denotes again the explicit derivative. In vector notation,

$$\frac{d\mathbf{p}_{.w}}{dt} = L\mathbf{p}_{.w} + \frac{\partial \mathbf{F}}{\partial w}, \tag{31}$$

where L is the time-dependent Jacobian matrix $L = L(t) = (\partial F_i(t)/\partial u_j)$. The similarity of this derivation to the one obtained in the case of fixed-point learning should be stressed. In particular, in the case of fixed-point learning, $dp_{iw}(t)/dt = 0$ at equilibrium and Equation 31 yields immediately Equation 17. If the choice of the initial condition $\mathbf{u}(t_0)$ is independent of any of the parameters w, as it is most often the case, then the initial condition for Equation 31 is $p_{iw}(t_0) = 0$. Now, to evaluate Equation 27 different algorithms are possible, depending on how one deals with the linear system of differential equations in Equation 31.

Numerical Integration of the System

The first possible algorithm is derived by simply integrating Equation 31 forward in time and using Equation 27. If the interval $[t_0, t_1]$ is discretized into M small steps of length Δt, then $\mathbf{p}_{.w}(m)$ can be evaluated recursively through the relation

$$\mathbf{p}_{.w}(m + 1) = \Delta t \left[L(k)\mathbf{p}_{.w}(m) + \frac{\partial \mathbf{F}}{\partial w}(m) \right] + \mathbf{p}_{.w}(m), \tag{32}$$

and the parameters can be updated by using Equation 27 in the form

$$\frac{\partial \mathbf{E}}{\partial w} \approx \sum_{m=1}^{M} \left(\frac{\partial E}{\partial \mathbf{u}}(m) \right)^t \mathbf{p}_{.w}(m)\Delta t. \tag{33}$$

When Equations 32 and 33 are applied with $\Delta t = 1$ to the discretized version of Equation 4, one immediately obtains the algorithm discussed by Williams and Zipser (1989) (see also the Appendix). This algorithm amounts to a direct computation of each partial derivative using the definition $\partial E/\partial w = \lim(E(w + h) - E(w))/h$ as $h \to 0$, that is, by slightly perturbing each weight, one at a time, leaving all the others fixed. This method can also be applied to conventional feedforward networks. Its main disadvantage lies in the fact that a lot of computations are required since each weight is dealt with separately. One advantage is that both unit and parameter dynamics can be evolved forward simultaneously. If the learning rate is small enough, it is also possible to approximate the gradient descent process by updating the parameters after each time step, instead of every M steps, resulting in an on-line learning procedure.

Explicit Solution of the System

Because Equation 31 is linear, its solution can be written explicitly (see the Appendix). Indeed, if we take for instance $\mathbf{p}_{.w}(t_0) = 0$, then

$$\mathbf{p}_{.w}(t) = \int_{t_0}^{t} K(t,s) \frac{\partial \mathbf{F}}{\partial w}(s) \, ds, \tag{34}$$

where $K(t, s) = H(t)H^{-1}(s)$ and $H(t)$ is a $N \times N$ invertible matrix whose columns form a set of N independent solutions of the homogeneous system associated with Equation 31. Thus, from Equation 27,

$$\frac{\partial \mathbf{E}}{\partial w} = \int_{t_0}^{t_1} \int_{t_0}^{t} \left(\frac{\partial E}{\partial \mathbf{u}}(t) \right)^t H(t)H^{-1}(s) \frac{\partial \mathbf{F}}{\partial w}(s) \, ds \, dt, \tag{35}$$

or, by transposing as in Equation 19,

$$\frac{\partial \mathbf{E}}{\partial w} = \int_{t_0}^{t_1} \int_{t_0}^{t} \left(\frac{\partial F}{\partial \mathbf{u}}(s) \right)^t (H^t(s))^{-1} H^t(t) \frac{\partial E}{\partial \mathbf{u}}(t) \, ds \, dt. \qquad (36)$$

By first interchanging the order of integration in Equation 35 (or Equation 36) and then exchanging the variables s and t, we successively get

$$\frac{\partial \mathbf{E}}{\partial w} = \int_{t_0}^{t_1} \int_{s}^{t_1} \left(\frac{\partial E}{\partial \mathbf{u}}(t) \right)^t K(t,s) \frac{\partial F}{\partial w}(s) \, dt \, ds = \int_{t_0}^{t_1} (\mathbf{x}(t))^t \frac{\partial F}{\partial w}(t) \, dt, \qquad (37)$$

which is the time-dependent version of Equation 20 and where

$$\mathbf{x}(t) = \int_{t}^{t_1} K(s,t)^t \frac{\partial E}{\partial \mathbf{u}}(s) \, ds. \qquad (38)$$

As discussed in the Appendix, $K(s, t)^t$ is the transition matrix of a new system, called the adjoint system. Thus, Equation 38 suggests that we look at the application of adjoint methods to our problem.

Adjoint Methods

Adjoint methods rest on a very simple trick (see Appendix). To solve the system in Equation 38, we construct an auxiliary N-dimensional system, the adjoint system, by introducing a new vector variable $\mathbf{v}$. The matrix of the auxiliary linear system of differential equations is the opposite of the adjoint of L, which in our case is just the transpose of L. The adjoint system is then defined by

$$\frac{d\mathbf{v}}{dt} = -L^t \mathbf{v} - \frac{\partial E}{\partial \mathbf{u}}. \qquad (39)$$

The reason for the choice of the nonhomogeneous term will soon become apparent. Notice that Equation 39 is essentially the same as Equation 24. Now we multiply, on the left, both hand sides of Equation 31 by $\mathbf{v}^t$ and of Equation 39 by $\mathbf{p}^t_{,w}$ and add the two resulting equations. After simple cancellations, this yields

$$\frac{d(\mathbf{v}^t \mathbf{p}_{,w})}{dt} = \mathbf{v}^t \frac{\partial \mathbf{F}}{\partial w} - \mathbf{p}^t_{,w} \frac{\partial E}{\partial \mathbf{u}}. \qquad (40)$$

From Equation 27 and integrating both sides of Equation 40, we get

$$\frac{\partial \mathbf{E}}{\partial w} = \int_{t_0}^{t_1} \mathbf{p}^t_{,w} \frac{\partial E}{\partial \mathbf{u}} \, dt = -(\mathbf{v}^t \mathbf{p}_{,w})_{t=t_1} + (\mathbf{v}^t \mathbf{p}_{,w})_{t=t_0} + \int_{t_0}^{t_1} \mathbf{v}^t \frac{\partial \mathbf{F}}{\partial w} \, dt. \qquad (41)$$

Except for the boundary terms, we see that in the adjoint methods the computation of the integral $\int_{t_0}^{t_1} \mathbf{p}^t_{,w}(\partial E/\partial \mathbf{u}) \, dt$ is replaced by $\int_{t_0}^{t_1} \mathbf{v}^t(\partial \mathbf{F}/\partial w) \, dt$. The advantage of this approach is that, whereas in the direct methods a linear system for $\mathbf{p}_{.w}$ must be solved *for each w,* in the adjoint approach only *one* linear system for the variable $\mathbf{v}$ needs to be solved and used in the update of any of the parameters.

To deal with the boundary terms, it must be noticed that the boundary conditions for $\mathbf{v}$ in Equation 39 can be chosen arbitrarily. Since usually, as we have seen, we can choose $\mathbf{p}_{.w}(t_0) = 0$, one possible approach is to fix $\mathbf{v}(t_1) = 0$. In this case

$$\frac{\partial \mathbf{E}}{\partial w} = \int_{t_0}^{t_1} \mathbf{v}^t \frac{\partial \mathbf{F}}{\partial w}\, dt \tag{42}$$

or, similar to Equation 22,

$$\frac{dw_{i...}}{dt} = -\eta \int_{t_0}^{t_1} v_i \frac{\partial F_i}{\partial w_{i...}}\, dt. \tag{43}$$

The application of Equations 39 and 43 to the version of the additive model defined by Equation 4 yields immediately the algorithm discussed by Pearlmutter (1989). This approach requires that Equation 39 be solved backwards in time with final condition $\mathbf{v}(t_1) = 0$. In the Appendix, it is shown that $K(s, t)^t$ is the transition matrix of the adjoint system. Therefore, by solving Equation 39 backwards in time with final condition $\mathbf{v}(t_1) = 0$, one gets $\mathbf{v}(t) = -\int_{t_1}^{t} K(s, t)^t \partial E / \partial \mathbf{u}(s)\, ds$. Comparing to Equation 38, we see that $\mathbf{x}(t) = \mathbf{v}(t)$ and therefore the algorithm derived by explicitly solving the sensitivity system is identical to the algorithm we just derived using adjoint methods. As we shall see, the discretized version of this algorithm is also identical to the back propagation through time of Rumelhart et al. (1986), and the variable $\mathbf{x}(t) = \mathbf{v}(t)$ can be interpreted as a vector of back-propagated error signals. Because the integration is backwards, this algorithm, which computationally is the fastest, has been considered as being "acausal" and thus probably not ideally suited for a collective implementation in a physical system. However, provided one is willing to pay the price of a matrix inversion, the solution of Equation 39 with final boundary condition can still be obtained through a forward calculation in time. This is because the solution of a linear system depends linearly on the initial condition and therefore the effect of the initial condition can be factored out. To be more precise, by using the theorem on the solution of linear systems we have

$$\mathbf{v}(t) = G(t,t_0)\mathbf{v}(t_0) + \int_{t_0}^{t} G(t,s)\frac{\partial \mathbf{E}}{\partial \mathbf{u}}\, ds, \tag{44}$$

where G is the usual forward state transition matrix (as already pointed out, $G(t, s) = K(s, t)^t$). Thus, from Equation 42, we can write

$$\frac{\partial \mathbf{E}}{\partial w} = \mathbf{v}^t(t_0) \int_{t_0}^{t_1} G^t(t,t_0) \frac{\partial \mathbf{E}}{\partial w} \, dt$$

$$+ \int_{t_0}^{t_1} \int_{t_0}^{t} \left(\frac{\partial E}{\partial \mathbf{u}}(s) \right)^t G^t(t,s) \frac{\partial \mathbf{F}}{\partial w}(t) \, ds \, dt. \tag{45}$$

Because $\mathbf{v}(t_0)$ factors out in Equation 44, the integral terms in Equation 42 can be computed in forward mode. At the end of the process, we can use Equation 44 and the final condition $\mathbf{v}(t_1) = 0$ to solve for $\mathbf{v}(t_0)$:

$$\mathbf{v}(t_0) = -G^{-1}(t_1,t_0) \int_{t_0}^{t_1} G(t,s) \frac{\partial E}{\partial \mathbf{u}} \, ds. \tag{46}$$

For completeness, we can derive the discretized version of this algorithm. From Equation 42,

$$\frac{\partial \mathbf{E}}{\partial w} \approx \sum_{m=1}^{M} \Delta t \mathbf{v}^t(m) \frac{\partial \mathbf{F}}{\partial w}(m). \tag{47}$$

Using Equation 39 the vector $\mathbf{v}(m)$ satisfies the recurrence relation

$$\mathbf{v}(m + 1) = A(m)\mathbf{v}(m) + \mathbf{b}(m), \tag{48}$$

where $A(m)$ is the $N \times N$ matrix

$$A(m) = (I - \Delta t L^t(m)) \tag{49}$$

and $\mathbf{b}(m)$ is the N-dimensional vector

$$\mathbf{b}(m) = -\Delta t \frac{\partial E}{\partial \mathbf{u}}(m). \tag{50}$$

Then, by induction,

$$\mathbf{v}(m) = C(m)\mathbf{v}(0) + \mathbf{d}(m), \tag{51}$$

where the matrix $C(m)$ is

$$C(m) = \prod_{j=m-1}^{0} A(j), \tag{52}$$

and the vector $\mathbf{d}(m)$ is

$$\mathbf{d}(m) = \mathbf{b}(m - 1) + \sum_{e=0}^{m-2} \prod_{j=m-1}^{l+1} A(j)\mathbf{b}(l) \tag{53}$$

(the order of the terms in the products appearing in Equations 52 and 53 is important since, in general, the matrices $A(j)$ do not commute). Therefore,

$$\frac{\partial \mathbf{E}}{\partial w} \approx \mathbf{v}^t(0) \sum_{m=1}^{M} \Delta t C^t(m) \frac{\partial \mathbf{F}}{\partial w}(m) + \sum_{m=1}^{M} \Delta t \mathbf{d}^t(m) \frac{\partial \mathbf{F}}{\partial w}(m). \qquad (54)$$

Again, the sums in Equation 54 can be computed entirely in feedforward mode and, at the end, we can find $\mathbf{v}(0)$ by inverting the matrix $C(M)$:

$$\mathbf{v}(0) = C^{-1}(M)(\mathbf{v}(M) - \mathbf{d}(M)) = -C^{-1}(M)\mathbf{d}(M). \qquad (55)$$

Provided the parameter dynamics is slow with respect to the network dynamics, this algorithm can be implemented on-ine in a way similar, but more economical, to the implementation of the algorithm derived from the numerical integration of the system.

Back Propagation through Time

In their original article on back propagation, Rumelhart et al. (1986) considered the problem of learning in discrete-time recurrent networks in terms of back propagation through time. Their analysis was based on the observation that the time evolution of a recurrent network can be represented by a stack of snapshots of the same network taken at successive time intervals with the proper feedforward connections. (Notice that with the proper time discretization, time delays in this representation result in feedforward connections between distant elements of the stack.) Error signals can then be injected in the stack at different levels, both in space and time, and their effect on the update of each weight assessed through the usual back propagation through space in the stack (i.e., layer by layer). Conversely, the usual back-propagation algorithm for feedforward networks can be seen as a back propagation through time as soon as the time taken by each unit in the network to compute its value is taken into consideration. In other words, there is no real distinction between back propagation through space and through time. What is then the relation of the different algorithms described to back propagation through time? All the different algorithms result from different ways of organizing the gradient calculation—that is, the propagation of errors throughout the previous stack. If the propagation is started at the top of the stack as in the usual back propagation, then back propagation through time is identical, as shown in the Appendix, to the discretized version of the algorithms derived in the previous sections by explicitly solving the sensitivity system or by using adjoint methods. This is also the algorithm that can be derived by variational methods (see Bryson & Denham, 1962 and Appendix) or which has been suggested by Pearlmutter (1989). If, on the other hand, each weight is perturbed in isolation and the effect of each perturbation is propagated forward in the stack starting from the bottom, then one obtains the algorithm of Williams and Zipser (1989), which corresponds to a forward numerical integration of the sensitivity equations. Thus, there seems to be only two basic ways of calculating the gradient in the literature we have reviewed. Several variations, however, seem possible and an example has been given at the end of the section on adjoint methods. Clearly, there are trade-offs between the amount of computation, the amount of memory required and the time direction (forward or backward in time) followed by the different learning algorithms. Whether these trade-offs and the theoretical limits of any algorithm can be formalized with precision and whether other algorithms exist which can perform better or achieve these theoretical limits remains to be seen.

Gradient Learning of Time Constants, Gains, and Delays

To extend gradient descent learning for fixed points or trajectories to include time constants or gains in any of the models listed in the introduction is entirely straightforward. Time constants and gains can be treated as any other parameter such as synaptic weights and all the learning algorithms derived can be applied without any modification. The treatment of delays requires a slightly more careful analysis.

The presence of delays in a network can affect learning algorithms in two different ways. First, they affect the learning of other parameters such as synaptic weights. Second, delays may themselves be part of the adaptable parameters. Although there is no conclusive evidence for continuously adjustable delays in biology, there exist numerous examples of fine-tuned delays and delay lines (Carr & Konishi, 1988; in this context, see also Lisberger & Sejnowski, 1992). Moreover, many delays are subject to variations, for instance during the growth of an organism. Certainly, several biophysical mechanisms can be envisioned to achieve adaptable delays. Whether in natural or artificial systems, delays could then be regarded as beneficial rather than detrimental, for they could enlarge the family of means through which neural networks can tailor their own dynamics.

First, in the case of fixed-point learning, it is easy to see that delays have no effect on the gradient descent learning equations. This is because all the relevant expressions such as $\partial E/\partial u^f$ or $\partial u^f/\partial w$ are computed at equilibrium, when the vector du/dt is constantly 0. Thus, the delays do not appear in the learning equations at all. Of course they affect the activation dynamics and can change the fixed point associated with a given initial state, thus still influencing the learning dynamics in an nondirect way.

For the case of trajectories, the learning equations need to be modified. To simplify the notation, we assume that neuron j can influence the charging equation of neuron i only through one term with corresponding delay τ_{ij}. This would, for instance, be the case of the simple additive model with delays given by

$$\frac{du_i}{dt} = -\frac{u_i}{\tau_i} + \sum_j w_{ij} f_j(u_j(t - \tau_{ij})). \tag{56}$$

The derivation for the case of more general delays is similar. There are two ways in which delays can affect the previous learning algorithms. First, the equations for the sensitivities of the usual parameters need to be slightly modified to take the delays into account, and then, in the case where the delays themselves are learnable, new sensitivity equations need to be added for the adjustment of the delays. More precisely, when delays are present, Equations 25 through 29 remain unchanged. However, in the case of Equation 56, Equation 30 need to be modified in the form

$$\frac{dp_{iw}(t)}{dt} = -\frac{1}{\tau_i} p_{iw}(t) + \sum_j w_{ij} f_j'(u_j(t - \tau_{ij})) p_{jw}(t - \tau_{ij}) + \frac{\partial F_i}{\partial w}, \tag{57}$$

where $\partial F_i / \partial w$ is the explicit derivative of F_i with respect to w; that is, $\partial F_i / \partial w_{jk} = \delta_{ij} f_k(u_k(t - \tau_{ik}))$. In vector notation

$$\frac{d\mathbf{p}_{.w}(t)}{dt} = L(t)\mathbf{p}_{.w}(t) + L(t - \tau)\mathbf{p}_{.w}(t - \tau) + \frac{\partial \mathbf{F}}{\partial w}, \tag{58}$$

where $L_{ij}(t) = \partial F_i / \partial u_j(t) = -\delta_{ij}/\tau_i$, $L_{ij}(t - \tau) = \partial F_i / \partial u_j(t - \tau_{ij})$, and $\mathbf{p}_{.w}(t - \tau)$ is the vector of components $p_{jw}(t - \tau_{.j})$. The adjoint methods or back propagation through time algorithms can easily be extended to this case. To see this, it suffice to remark that in the discretized and unfolded through time network, delays only introduce additional feedforward connections which may skip certain layers. Thus the overall connectivity matrix of the unfolded network remains triangular and therefore the usual back-propagation equations can be applied (see the appendix).

When in addition delays are learnable, we must add for each delay τ a new sensitivity equation

$$\frac{dp_{i\tau}(t)}{dt} = -\frac{1}{\tau_i} p_{i\tau}(t) + \sum_j w_{ij} f_j'(u_j(t - \tau_{ij})) p_{j\tau}(t - \tau_{ij}) + \frac{\partial F_i}{\partial \tau}, \tag{59}$$

where, as usual, $\partial F_i / \partial \tau$ denotes the explicit derivative, namely

$$\partial F_i / \partial \tau_{jk} = -\delta_{ij} w_{ik} f'(u_k(t - \tau_{ik})) \frac{du_k(t - \tau_{ik})}{dt}$$

$$= -\delta_{ij} w_{ik} f'(u_k(t - \tau_{ik})) F_k(t - \tau_{ik}).$$

In vector notation

$$\frac{d\mathbf{p}_{.\tau}(t)}{dt} = L(t)\mathbf{p}_{.\tau}(t) + L(t - \tau)\mathbf{p}_{.\tau}(t - \tau) + \frac{\partial \mathbf{F}}{\partial \tau}, \tag{60}$$

where $\mathbf{p}_{.\tau}(t - \tau)$ is the vector of components $p_{j\tau}(t - \tau_{.j})$. To evolve the dynamics forward over the interval $[t_0, t_1]$, the initial conditions on any $u_i(t)$ must be defined over the interval $[t_0 - \rho_i, t_0]$ where $\rho_i = \max_j \tau_{ji}$. If, as it is often the case, these conditions are chosen independently of the relevant parameters and kept constant, then we can set $p_{iw}(t) = 0$ for $t_0 - \rho_i \leq t \leq t_0$. In any case, once these initial conditions are determined, the sensitivity Equations 57 and possibly 59 can be evolved forward in time, as in Equation 32, although this is computationally expensive.

As in the case of systems without delays, similar alternatives approaches can be used to adjust the delays, including back propagation through time or adjoint methods for delayed differential equations (see also Hale, 1977). Intuitively, this is very clear using the same remark already made. If we represent a general delayed system as in Equation 9, then in the discretized and unfolded through time version of the network, forward connections with weight $w_{ij}(t - s)$, for all possible t and s, must be introduced between all pairs of layers. The weights $w_{ij}(t - s)$ can then be adjusted using the usual form of back propagation. Formally, in this case, it is easy to see that the derivation Equations 24–31, the adjoint system, Equation 39, and the update Equation 42 remain valid provided $\mathbf{p}_{.w}(t)$ is replaced by $\mathbf{p}_{.w(t-s)}(t)$.

Especially if implemented on a computer, the algorithm described here is not meant to be used for undiscriminate learning of delays throughout large, amorphous and densely interconnected networks with random initial conditions. Rather, it should be considered only for the fine tuning of a small set of parameters in architectures already endowed of a certain degree of structure. In this respect, it is remarkable that in the best studied examples of useful delays, both in natural (Carr & Konishi, 1988) and artificial (Unnikrishnan et al., 1991) neural systems, the delays are arranged in orderly arrays of delay lines. These delay lines are essentially part of a feedforward network for which the learning task is much simpler. In these examples, different delays are used in order to bring together the effects of temporally separated events onto a coincidence detector type of neuron. For instance, in Unnikrishnan et al., the successive parts of a spoken word are delayed differentially in order to arrive simultaneously onto a unit assigned to the recognition of that particular word. For a given input $I(t)$, the output of the ith delay line is given by the convolution

$$o_i(t) = \int_0^{+\infty} K(i,,t')I(t - t')dt', \qquad (61)$$

where here $K(i, t')$ is the Gaussian kernel

$$K(i,t') = \frac{1}{\sqrt{2\pi}\sigma} e^{-(t'-iT)^2/2\sigma^2} \qquad (62)$$

and T is a parameter used to discretize the possible delays. It is clear that in this approach based on fixed delays, delays could easily be made adjustable by allowing both the width σ and the center $t_i = iT$ of the delay kernel to vary. Both types of parameters could be adjusted by gradient descent since it is easy to derive $\partial o_i / \partial \sigma$ or $\partial o_i / \partial t_i$ from Equations 61 and 62.

COMPLEXITY AND LIMITATIONS

Complexity

For completeness, the purpose here is to give rough known estimates of the computational and storage requirement of the previous algorithms. We want also to keep into consideration whether the algorithm is causal or not, that is whether it requires any integration backward in time, for noncausal algorithms cannot be directly implemented in hardware. The complexity estimates one can derive depend on the type of machine on which the algorithms are implemented. We consider the case of a conventional computer implementation, but different estimates could result from a parallel implementation. This complexity analysis has several additional limitations. First of all, it assumes a fixed number of bits of precision for all the quantities involved and no distinctions are made between the costs of different operations such as additions, multiplications or input/output transfer functions f. Similarly, the costs of storing or reading from memory are considered negligible. These assumptions are easily violated in a physical implementation where different costs and durations may be attached to different operations and where precision on the connection weights may often be limited to just a few bits. They are also, strictly speaking, insufficient from a theoretical standpoint since it is well known (see, for instance, Minsky & Papert, 1969) that for certain problems the precision required on the parameters of a solution may scale with the dimension of the problem. However, the scaling of the precision with N may just behave, to a first approximation, as an amplification factor. Finally, these assumptions should be valid in the range of many simulations carried on current digital computers where high precision on all variables is easily achieved and where the number of neurons in the simulated networks is still often relatively small. It is also good to keep in mind that the complexity estimates to be derived correspond to rough asymptotic behavior. We shall assume that the number of adjustable parameters is n. In the usual case of densely interconnected networks, with first-order interactions only, $n = O(N^2)$. Complexity estimates based on the number of parameters rather than the number of neurons are more general since they extend to other models, such as higher-order networks.

Fixed-Point Learning by Direct Integration

Fixed point learning by direct integration corresponds to a direct calculation of the sensitivities and weight changes using Equations 18 and 19. For each pattern presentation and each modification cycle it requires

1. Integration of the N Equation 1 for the forward evolution of the system. Typically in the first-order additive model or in the usual connectionist networks, the main calculation during each integration step is the multiplication of the weight matrix by the vector of activations. This gives a number of operations which is of the order of $O(n)$ and if there are M time steps in the forward integration, this yields of the order of $O(nM)$ operations. The factor M should not matter very much in normal conditions since the convergence to fixed points is usually fast (for instance, in the case of Hopfield associative memories, corresponding essentially to symmetrically interconnected additive models, and under the proper assumptions, the convergence to fixed points occurs in less than $O(\log \log N)$ steps (Komlós & Paturi, 1988)).

2. Inversion of the $N \times N$ matrix L in Equation 18. The theoretical minimal cost of such an inversion on a serial machine is known to be of the form $O(N^{2+\alpha})$ where $0 < \alpha < 0.496$ (Pan, 1984). The precise value of α is not known, but explicit algorithms are available which can compute the inverse in less than $O(N^3)$ computations.

3. Evaluation of the sensitivities $\mathbf{p}_{,w}$ for each w according to Equation 18. The matrix vector multiplication $L^{-1} \partial F/\partial w$ requires in general $O(N^2)$ operations, and there are n parameters, so that the overall complexity scales like $O(nN^2)$. In general, however, (unless there is weight sharing), the vector of explicit derivatives $\partial F/\partial w$ is very sparse and has only one nonzero component for each w. So the overall complexity of this step scales more like $O(nN)$.

4. Evaluation of the weights adjustments, according to Equation 19. For each parameter w, the scalar product $(\partial E/\partial \mathbf{u}^f)^t \mathbf{p}_{,w}$ requires $O(N)$ operations, so that the complexity of this step is $O(nN)$.

Thus, in typical cases, fixed-point learning by gradient descent using direct integration takes $O(nN)$ operations. As far as memory requirement, if one needs to store all the sensitivities together then it is easy to see that this is the most demanding requirement and requires a storage capacity of $O(nN)$. If the implementation is such that the sensitivity to only one parameter at a time needs to be stored in memory, then one still needs to store the matrix L and the weights (in addition to evolving the dynamics forward) and it is easy to see that the storage requirement is about $\max(O(n), O(N^2))$.

Fixed-Point Learning by Back Propagation

Fixed point learning by back propagation corresponds to the calculation of the back-propagated errors $\mathbf{v}$ from the relaxation of Equation 24 and the parameters updates from Equation 21. This requires

1. Same as 1 for the direct algorithm for fixed-point learning.

2. Integration of the N Equations 24 for the forward evolution of the back-propagated errors **v**. This in general should require $O(N^2)$ operations at each time step for the vector/matrix multiplication. However, in typical cases, the matrix L contains roughly the same number of nonzero entries as W. So that the total cost for the calculation of the equilibrium value of **v** should scale like $O(nM')$, where M' is the number of time steps, which should not be too relevant in typical situations (the exact duration depends on the negative real parts of the eigenvalues of the matrix L which are the time constants of the time-decaying exponentials governing the relaxation of the linear system).

3. Evaluation of the weight adjustments according to Equation 21. For each parameter w, the scalar product $(\partial \mathbf{F}/\partial w)^t \mathbf{v}$ normally requires $O(N)$ operations. Again, because of the sparsity in general of $\partial \mathbf{F}/\partial w$, the total cost of this step for all parameters is $O(n)$.

In the usual case of connectionist feedforward architectures with a small number of hidden layers, the convergence can be considered instantaneous and the factors M or M' entirely neglected (otherwise one can introduce a factor of $\max(O(M), O(M'))$, so that the total number of operations is roughly equal to three times the number of weights (one time for each step). It therefore scales like $O(n)$, with a saving of a factor of N over the direct integration. It is easy to see that in usual conditions the main memory requirement in the back-propagation algorithm comes from the storage of the weights and thus scales also like $O(n)$.

Trajectory Learning by Direct Integration

Trajectory learning by direct integration corresponds to a direct forward integration of the sensitivity Equations 31 and using the result to estimate the parameter adjustments according to Equation 24. For each pattern presentation and each modification cycle it requires

1. Integration of the N Equations 1 for the forward evolution of the system. As in the previous similar cases, with M time steps, the total complexity typically scales like $O(nM)$. Here, however, the system does not necessarily converge to a fixed point and M can be an important large factor.

2. Evolving the sensitivity system of Equation 31 forward in time using Equation 32. In general the matrix vector multiplication in 32 should take $O(N^2)$ operations, which should yield with M time steps and n parameters a total complexity of $O(nMN^2)$. With the same remark on the matrix L already made, this complexity can be lowered to $O(n^2M)$. Of course, in the case of dense networks where $n = O(N^2)$ there is no difference between the two estimates.

3. Evaluation of the weight adjustments according to Equation 33. For each parameter w, the scalar product $(\partial E/\partial \mathbf{u})^t \mathbf{p}_{,w}$ requires $O(N)$ operations. With M steps and n parameters, the total complexity scales like $O(nMN)$.

Thus in the direct algorithm all integrations are forward in time. The total cost of an update for one patterns is likely to scale like $O(n^2 M)$, which is $O(MN^4)$ in dense networks. As far as memory requirement, for each adjustable parameter one must store the corresponding sensitivity vector so that the minimal memory requirement is roughly $O(nN)$. Unlike the fixed-point case, it is not possible to work with only one $\mathbf{p}_{,w}$ at a time since all the sensitivities need to be available to compute their evolution from one time step to the next.

Trajectory Learning by Back Propagation

Trajectory learning by back propagation corresponds to back propagation through time or adjoint methods and relies on the back propagation of the errors or, equivalently, the solution of the adjoint system in Equation 39 backward in time. This requires

1. Same as 1 for the direct algorithm for trajectory learning.
2. Integration of the N equations of the adjoint system, Equation 39, backward in time. Again, the vector matrix multiplication scales in general like $O(N^2)$ but this estimate can be reduced to $O(n)$ by using the fact that the number of nonzero entries in L is of the same order as the number of parameters in the most commonly used models. The complexity of solving the adjoint system backward in time thus scales like $O(nM)$ (rather than $O(MN^2)$).
3. Evaluation of the weight adjustments according to Equation 42. For each parameter w, the scalar product $(\partial \mathbf{F}/\partial w)^t \mathbf{v}$ normally requires $O(N)$ operations. Again, because of the sparsity in general of $\partial \mathbf{F}/\partial w$, the total cost of this step for all parameters is $O(nM)$ (rather than $O(nMN)$).

Thus learning trajectories by back propagation typically requires $O(nM)$ operations. This can also be seen immediately from the back propagation through time approach since the unfolded network has nM forward connections, and the number of operations for the usual back propagation is roughtly equal to three times the number of weights (one for the forward pass, one for the backward pass, and one for the updates). Back propagation leads to a reduction in computational costs by a factor of n over direct integration but requires that the error or adjoint system be evolved backward in time. As far as memory requirements, one must evolve the network dynamics forward and store the corresponding NM activities into memory before Equation 39 can be evolved backwards in time. Since $O(n)$ parameters are in memory anyway, the memory requirement can be seen to be $\max(O(NM), O(n))$. If one still wants to integrate Equation 39 forward in time as described in Equations 46 to 55, the price to pay is that of inverting an $N \times N$ matrix. As we have seen, this has a cot of the form $O(N^{2+\alpha})$ where $0 < \alpha < 0.496$. Thus if M is larger than $O(N^{\alpha})$, the matrix inversion is not relevant, at least asymptotically.

Limitations

In spite of its success, there are several problems with gradient descent learning. The problems are slightly different depending on the perspective adopted: hardware design, biological realism, numerical algorithm for digital computers, or as a general approach to learning. First of all, most of the time it has been used as a supervised mode of learning where the correct target patterns need to be known. It requires a fairly precise calculation of the gradient which, in many cases, is expensive. In biological systems, evidence for neural circuitry dedicated to the computation of gradients for learning is lacking and the existence of pathways for the precise back propagation of error signals is very debatable to say the least. More fundamentally perhaps, it seems intuitively clear that gradient descent applied to large amorphous networks cannot be successful on complex problems (see also Geman et al., 1992). For instance, nobody has tried to take a fully interconnected random network and train it to play chess by gradient descent, although we can reasonably expect that there exists a relatively small circuit, with at most a few thousand threshold gates, which outperforms any existing program or player. Even in the case of simpler games, such as backgammon (Tesauro, 1989), which have been successfully tackled by gradient descent learning, considerable additional structure must often be introduced in the learning system before the start of the learning procedure.

The exact reason for the limitations inherent to gradient descent learning applied to random starting networks is far from clear. Gradient descent can fail in several ways: by reaching a poor local minima, by reaching a global minima which is unsatisfactory, by encountering numerical precision problems and/or getting stuck in long plateaux, by becoming prohibitively slow for the given hardware or by failing to generalize properly. These reasons are not independent nor well understood. For instance, are local minima a characteristic of complex problems? Intuitively, it seems that for a given problem, as the number of units in a network is increased, the number of local minima in the LMS error should tend to decrease. Thus, either complex problems are characterized by error landscapes plagued with local minima irrespective of network size or, more likely, local minima tend to vanish but for infinite or prohibitively large networks. In fact, there is some circumstantial evidence (Baldi, 1991) that if we allow for a continuum of hidden units the problem of local minima disappears, at least in the case of normalized inputs. As fundamental, if not more, is the problem of the evolution of the generalization—that is, of the performance of the network on points which are not part of the training set. Of course, these questions are intimately related to other difficult problems in complexity theory, such as the $P \neq NP$ problem. Is it the case that, for reasonable problems, gradient descent cannot find, in polynomial time, polynomial size networks which execute the task sufficiently well?

There is an additional set of difficulties with gradient descent learning of fixed points or trajectories, which is particular to *recurrent* networks, and which has to do with the bifurcations of the system being considered. In the case of a recurrent[3] network, as the parameters of (1) are varied, the system may or may not undergo a series of bifurcations—that is, of abrupt changes in the structure of its trajectories and, in particular, of its attractors (fixed points, limit cycles, etc.). This in turn may translate into abrupt discontinuities, oscillations or non-convergence in the corresponding learning curve. At each bifurcation, the error function is usually discontinuous and therefore the gradient is not properly defined. Learning can be disrupted in two ways: when unwanted abrupt changes occur in the trajectory space of the dynamical system or when desirable bifurcations are prevented from occurring. A classical example of the second type is the case of a neural network with very small initial weights being trained to oscillate, in a symmetric and stable fashion, around the origin. With small initial weights, the network in general converges to its unique fixed point at the origin, with a large error. If we slightly perturb the weights, remaining away from any bifurcation, the network continues to converge to its unique fixed point which may be slightly displaced from the origin and yield an even greater error so that learning by gradient descent becomes impossible (the starting configuration of weights is a local minimum of the error function).

A few directions attempting to overcome the limitations of gradient descent are discussed in Baldi (1992). Learning is a form of model fitting, or inference. As such, two complementary levels of optimisation need to be considered: (1) the selection of the proper model, for instance in terms of network architecture; (2) the optimisation of the model parameters, for instance in terms of gradient descent. A number of other algorithms are available for the second task, including, for example, simulated annealing and other random perturbation methods, and conjugate gradient methods. Optimization techniques mathematically more sophisticated than gradient descent, such as conjugate gradient, can be useful, especially when the function to be optimised is given rather than the result of a deliberate construction. However, it seems unlikely to us that any such sophisticated scheme may be implemented in wetware or hardware. Rather, for the second task, one would expect simpler algorithms than gradient descent to be better suited for physical computations (for instance Cauwenberghs (1993)). It seems equally unlikely that sophisticated parameter optimisation algorithms may

---

[3]In a feedforward network where the transfer functions of the units are continuous, the output is a continuous function of the parameters and therefore there are no bifurcations.

be able to systematically overcome the limitations inherent to gradient descent. Overcoming these limitations is more likely to result from progress on the first task, the selection of the proper model, which remains the domain of an art.

CONCLUSION

Gradient descent learning is a simple but powerful principle for the global coordination of local synaptic changes in neural networks. In spite of its conceptual simplicity, it has led to the introduction of many different algorithms for different models and different problems. The general framework of dynamical systems enables one to give a unified treatment of all the known procedures, to reveal and stress the common underlying computational structures and provides a general flexible tool which can rapidly be adapted to new situations. It clarifies the relations between different approaches, the similarities between the static and time-dependent case and easily yields new algorithms for new models, for instance in the case of networks with adjustable delays. The analysis shows that to this date essentially two distinct algorithms have been used to evaluate gradients: one is based on a direct solution of the sensitivity equations and the other on the solution of the adjoint system equivalent to back propagation. The second algorithm is computationally superior but requires, in the time-dependent case, integrating a time-dependent linear system backward in time. In spite of several important limitations, gradient descent learning remains an important tool in the study of learning and the design of artificial intelligent machines. Understanding and overcoming these limitations while uncovering the secrets of learning in biological systems remains one of the main challenges in the field.

APPENDIX

Discrete Dynamical Systems and Back Propagation

Gradient descent learning has been studied in a framework of continuous-time dynamical systems. Equivalently, one could use discrete-time dynamical systems of the form

$$\mathbf{u}(m + 1) = \mathbf{G}(\mathbf{u}(m), W, \mathbf{I}(m), \mathbf{u}^*(m)). \tag{A.1}$$

There is a one-to-one correspondence between systems satisfying Equations 1 and A.1. Namely, if we discretize Equation 1 according to $d\mathbf{u}/dt \approx [\mathbf{u}(t + \Delta t) - \mathbf{u}(t)]/\Delta t = [\mathbf{u}(m + 1) - \mathbf{u}(m)]/\Delta t$ and use $\Delta t = 1$, we get $\mathbf{u}(m + 1) = \mathbf{u}(m) + \mathbf{F}(\mathbf{u}, W, \mathbf{I}, \mathbf{u}^*)$. So that the correspondence between Equations 1 and A.1 is established by having

$$\mathbf{G} = \mathbf{u} - \mathbf{F}. \tag{A.2}$$

It is important to notice that the correspondence between a continuous system and its discretized version is formal: the two can behave very differently unless the unit of time for which $\Delta t = 1$ is small enough so that discrete differences yield a good approximation to derivatives. Gradient descent learning in discrete systems can be expressed as

$$w(m + 1) = w(m) + \eta \frac{\partial E}{\partial w} (m). \tag{A.3}$$

It is straightforward to check that all the steps carried in the derivation of $\partial E / \partial w$ for continuous systems remain valid in the case of a discrete system. (In the case of trajectory learning, one must replace $\mathbf{u}(t)$ by $\mathbf{u}(m)$ and the integrals by the corresponding sums). Thus the learning rule for a discrete system such as Equation A.2 can be derived by calculating $\partial E / \partial w$ in the corresponding continuous system defined by Equations 1 and A.2 and substituting in Equation A.3, or, equivalently, by directly discretizing the learning rule of the associated continuous system, with $\Delta t = 1$. Again, for the evolution of the parameters to parallel each other in the discrete and continuous systems two conditions are necessary: both the activation and the parameter units of time corresponding to $\Delta t = 1$ must be sufficiently small to ensure first that both systems have similar activation dynamics and then similar parameter dynamics.

As an example we can easily derive the usual (Rumelhart et al., 1986) backpropagation equations for feedforward discrete time neural networks trained on fixed points. To begin with, let us give a description of back propagation which is as general as possible. Thus, we assume that we have a discrete dynamical system which has a layered feedforward structure and which is defined by

$$u_i^l(m + 1) = f_i^l(u^{l-1}(m), \ldots , u^1(m), u^0), \tag{A.4}$$

$l = 1, \ldots , p$, where u_i^l can be viewed as the activity of the ith unit in the lth layer which depends on the activities of the units in previous layers. More generally and throughout this section, upper indices will always refer to layers. The input and output layers correspond to layers 0 and p respectively. $\mathbf{u}^0$ can be viewed as the input which is held fixed so that the system converges in at most p steps to a vector $\mathbf{u}$ of stable activities. Only these stable activities are of importance and therefore the temporal indices in Equation A.4 can be neglected. The transfer functions f_i^l may depend on adjustable parameters w. In order to cover the case of "weight sharing," we assume that a given parameter w may appear in several different transfer functions. Thus let $\mathcal{F}(w)$ be the set of indices (i, l) such that w appears in the expression of f_i^l. If the performance of the system is measured by an error function E, then

$$\frac{\partial E}{\partial w} = \sum_{(i,l) \in \mathcal{F}(w)} \frac{\partial E}{\partial u_i^l} \frac{\partial u_i^l}{\partial w}. \tag{A.5}$$

Starting from the output layer p, the quantities $\partial E / \partial u_i^l$ can be calculatedly using the chain rule backward through the network. Thus back propagation is given by the recurrence relations

$$\frac{\partial E}{\partial u_i^l} = \sum_{(j,k),k>l} \frac{\partial E}{\partial u_j^k} \frac{\partial u_j^k}{\partial u_i^l} = \sum_{(j,k),k>l} \frac{\partial E}{\partial u_j^k} \frac{\partial f_j^k}{\partial u_i^l}. \qquad (A.6)$$

The quantities $\partial E / \partial u_i^p$ are of course given.

Connectionist neural networks are special cases of this framework and can be viewed as discretized versions of the additive model Equation 4 defined by

$$u_i^l(m + 1) = f_i^l \left(\sum_{k<l} \sum_j w_{ij}^{lk} u_j^k(m) \right) \qquad (A.7)$$

for $l = 1, \ldots, p$. The weight matrix W is a lower triangular block matrix. The $l - k$ block ($l > k$) represents the forward connections from layer k to layer l. A constant bias or threshold can easily be incorporated inside the sum appearing in the right hand side in the usual way by introducing a special unit with constant activity 1 connected to all the other units by a bias weight w_{i0}^{l0}. The usual LMS error function is given, for one pattern, by $E = \Sigma_i (u_i^p - U_i^*)^2/2$. From what we have seen, we can use Equation 20,

$$\Delta w = \eta \left(\frac{\partial \mathbf{F}}{\partial w} \right)^t (L^t)^{-1} \frac{\partial E}{\partial \mathbf{u}^t}, \qquad (A.8)$$

to update the weights. Here, L is the Jacobian matrix of $I - G$. Thus L is a lower triangular block matrix with

$$L = (l_{ij}^{lk}) = \begin{cases} -1 & \text{if } l = k \text{ and } i = j, \\ (f_i^l)' w_{ij}^{lk} & \text{if } l > k, \\ 0 & \text{otherwise.} \end{cases} \qquad (A.9)$$

The matrix L^t is an upper triangular block matrix with

$$L^t = (m_{ij}^{lk}) = (l_{ji}^{kl}) = \begin{cases} -1 & \text{if } l = k \text{ and } i = j, \\ (f_j^k)' w_{ji}^{kl} & \text{if } l < k, \\ 0 & \text{otherwise.} \end{cases} \qquad (A.10)$$

Thus for $l > k$ we finally have

$$\Delta w_{ij}^{lk} = \eta \left(\frac{\partial F_i^l}{\partial w_{ij}^{lk}} \right) v_i^l = \eta (f_i^l)' u_j^k v_i^l, \qquad (A.11)$$

where the solution $\mathbf{v}$ of $L^t \mathbf{v} = \partial E / \partial \mathbf{u}$ can be computed recursively, layer by layer, starting from the output layer. Indeed, one has immediately $v_i^p = u_i^p - u_i^*$ for the output layer and than, using the fact that L^t is upper triangular with a -1 diagonal

$$v_i^l = \sum_{k>l} \sum_j (f_j^k)' w_{ji}^{kl} v_j^k, \tag{A.12}$$

which is the usual formula for the back propagation of errors.

As a second example, we can derive the algorithm described in Williams and Zipser (1989). This time, we consider a recurrent network of units satisfying

$$u_i(m + 1) = f_i\left(\sum_j w_{ij} u_j(m)\right). \tag{A.13}$$

The usual LMS error function is written as

$$\mathbf{E} = \frac{1}{2} \sum_m \sum_i (u_i^*(m) - u_i(m))^2 = \sum_m \sum_i e_i(m), \tag{A.14}$$

with $e_i(m) = 0$ for the units i and the times m at which a target value is not defined. The corresponding continuous model is given by Equation 4. It is easy to check that all the steps carried in the derivation of the learning algorithm for continuous systems remain valid in the case of discrete systems. Thus, by using Equations 32 and 35 with $\Delta t = 1$ and $L_{ij}(m) = \partial F_i(m)/\partial u_j = -\delta_{ij} + f_i'(\Sigma_l w_{il} u_l(m)) w_{ij}$, we get

$$\frac{\partial \mathbf{E}}{\partial w} = -\sum_{m=1}^{M} \sum_i e_i(m) p_{iw}(m), \tag{A.15}$$

where the sensitivities $p_{iw}(m)$ satisfy the recurrence relation

$$p_{kw_{ij}}(m) = f'\left(\sum_l w_{kl} u_l(m)\right)\left[\sum_l w_{kl} p_{lw_{ij}}(m) + \delta_{ik} u_j(m)\right], \tag{A.16}$$

and, usually, the initial conditions $p_{iw}(0) = 0$ for any i and w. This is exactly the algorithm in Williams and Zipser (1989).

As a third and last example, we can derive the explicit solution or adjoint algorithm of the third section from the discrete back propagation through time. Indeed, if we discretize a continuous system satisfying Equation 1, we get

$$u_i(t + \Delta t) = u_i(t) + \Delta t F_i(u, W, I, u^*). \tag{A.17}$$

In back propagation through time, the recurrent network and its time evolution are replaced by a layered feedforward network, with one layer for each interval Δt. Therefore, using the same notation as in Equation A.4 we can write at equilibrium

$$u_i^{m+1} = u_i^m + \Delta t F_i(u, W, I, u^*) = f_i^{m+1}(u, W, I, u^*). \tag{A.18}$$

Here, each layer contains all the units of the original network and there are as many layers as time steps. For simplicity we can assume that there are no delays and therefore all connections in the unfolded network run from one layer to the next. The total error $\mathbf{E}$ is the sum of all the instantaneous errors $\mathbf{E} = \sum_{l}^{M} E(l)\Delta t = \sum E^l \Delta t$. Each instantaneous error $E^l \Delta t$ occurs at the lth level of the unfolded network and therefore gives rise to a correction signal of the form $\Delta t \partial E^l / \partial u^m$ which can be back-propagated in all the previous layers with index $m < 1$ as in Equations A.5 and A.6. Thus we have

$$\frac{\partial \mathbf{E}}{\partial w} = \sum_{m=1}^{M} \sum_{i=1}^{N} \sum_{l \geq m} \frac{\partial E^l}{\partial u_i^m} \frac{\partial u_i^m}{\partial w} \Delta t = \sum_{m=1}^{M} \sum_{i=1}^{N} z_i(m) \frac{\partial u_i^m}{\partial w}, \quad (A.19)$$

where

$$z_i(m) = \sum_{l \geq m}^{M} \frac{\partial E^l}{\partial u_i^m} \Delta t \quad (A.20)$$

is the sum of all the error signals arriving on layer m from all the other upper layers and from layer m itself. Using Equation A.6,

$$z_i(m) = \frac{\partial E^m}{\partial u_i^m} \Delta t + \Delta t \sum_{l=m+1}^{M} \sum_{j=1}^{N} \frac{\partial E^l}{\partial u_j^{m+1}} \frac{\partial f_j^{m+1}}{\partial u_i^m}. \quad (A.21)$$

Using the definition of f_i^{m+1} given in Equation A.18 we get

$$\frac{z_i(m+1) - z_i(m)}{\Delta t} = -\Delta t \sum_{l=m+1}^{M} \sum_{j=1}^{N} \frac{\partial E^l}{\partial u_j^{m+1}} \frac{\partial F}{\partial u_i^m} - \frac{\partial E^m}{\partial u_i^m}, \quad (A.22)$$

or, in continuous form,

$$\frac{d\mathbf{z}}{dt} = -L^t \mathbf{z} - \frac{\partial \mathbf{E}}{\partial \mathbf{u}}, \quad (A.23)$$

which, for instance, is exactly the same as Equation 39. Accordingly, updating the parameters using the continuous version of Equation A.19 yields immediately Equation 42. From Equation A.20, the boundary condition on $\mathbf{z}$ is $\mathbf{z}(t_1) = \mathbf{z}(M) = 0$, identical to the condition on $\mathbf{v}$ in the adjoint methods algorithm.

Solution of Linear Systems of Differential Equations and Adjoint Systems

The following is a classical theorem which gives in explicit form the solution of a general linear system of differential equations (see, for instance, Apostol, 1967).

Theorem: *Given an $n \times n$ matrix $A(t)$ and an n-dimensional vector function $\mathbf{b}(t)$, both continuous on an open interval containing t_0, the solution of the initial value problem*

$$\frac{dy}{dt} = A(t)\mathbf{y} + \mathbf{b}(t), \qquad \mathbf{y}(t_0) = \mathbf{c}, \tag{A.24}$$

exists and is unique and given by

$$\mathbf{y}(t) = H(t)H^{-1}(t_0)\mathbf{c} + H(t) \int_{t_0}^{t} H^{-1}(s)\mathbf{b}(s)\, ds, \tag{A.25}$$

where H(t) *is an* $n \times n$ *invertible matrix whose columns form n independent solutions of the homogeneous systems* dy/dt = A(t)y *associated with Equation A.24. Alternatively,*

$$\mathbf{y}(t) = K(t,t_0)\mathbf{c} + \int_{t_0}^{t} K(t,s)\mathbf{b}(s)\, ds, \tag{A.26}$$

where K(t, s) = H(t)H^{-1}(s) *is the transiton matrix of the system. Obviously, for any t,* K(t, t) = I *and K satisfies also the differential equaiton*

$$\frac{d}{dt} K(t,s) = A(t)K(t,s). \tag{A.27}$$

For instance, in the one-dimensional case,

$$H(t) = e^{\int_{t_0}^{t} A(s)\, ds}, \qquad K(t,s) = e^{\int_{s}^{t} A(r)\, dr}, \tag{A.28}$$

and in the *n*-dimensional case, *with constant A(t) = A,*

$$H(t) = e^{tA}, \qquad K(t,\, s) = e^{(t-s)A}. \tag{A.29}$$

Notice that it is easy from Equation A.25 to express the value of $\mathbf{y}(t_0)$ as a function of $\mathbf{y}(t)$. In other words, if Equation A.24 is to be solved backward in time from a final condition $\mathbf{y}(t_1)$, then

$$\mathbf{y}(t) = K(t,t_1)\mathbf{y}(t_1) + \int_{t_1}^{t} K(t,s)\mathbf{b}(s)\, ds. \tag{A.30}$$

Thus, the same equation, Equation A.25, describes the evolution of the system forward or backward in time and $K(t,\, s)^{-1} = K(s,\, t)$. By definition, the adjoint system associated with an homogeneous system governed by a matrix A is the homogeneous system governed by the opposite of the adjoint of A. Thus, in the case of real variables, the adjoint of $dy/dt = A(t)\mathbf{y}$ is $dv/dt = -A^t(t)\mathbf{v}$. Clearly, $d(\mathbf{y}^t\mathbf{v})/dt = \mathbf{y}^t d\mathbf{v}/dt + \mathbf{v}^t d\mathbf{y}/dt = 0$. Thus, for given initial conditions, the solutions $\mathbf{y}(t)$ and $\mathbf{v}(t)$ of the two systems maintain a constant angle. Let $L(t,\, s) = J(t)J^{-1}(s)$ be the transition matrix of the adjoint system. Then $\mathbf{y}(t) = H(t)H^{-1}(s)\mathbf{y}(t_0)$ and $\mathbf{v}(t) = J(t)J^{-1}(s)\mathbf{v}(t_0)$. By using the constancy of the angle, we see that the transition matrix of the adjoint system is given by $L(t,\, s) = K(s,\, t)^t$ (i.e., $J^{-1} = H^t$).

Variational Methods

Alternatively, to derive the learning algorithms one can use a variational approach (see Troutman, 1983 for more mathematical background). To minimize the error, Equation 25, under the constraint that $\mathbf{u}$ be a trajectory of Equation 1, we can extremize the functional

$$\mathcal{L} = \int_{t_0}^{t_1} \left[E(\mathbf{u},\mathbf{u}^*,t) + \sum_i v_i \left(F_i(\mathbf{u},W,\mathbf{I},\mathbf{u}^*) - \frac{du_i}{dt} \right) \right] dt$$

$$= \int_{t_0}^{t_1} \mathcal{E} \, dt, \tag{A.31}$$

which incorporates the constraints imposed by Equation 1 using the Lagrange multipliers $\mathbf{v}$. Taking a variation of Equation A.31, that is, by looking at how $\mathcal{L}$ varies, to a first order, with a small change in $\mathbf{u}$ or W, one first obtains the Euler equation

$$\frac{\partial \mathcal{E}}{\partial \mathbf{u}} - \frac{d}{dt} \frac{\partial \mathcal{E}}{\partial d\mathbf{u}/dt} = 0. \tag{A.32}$$

This immediately gives

$$\frac{dv_i}{dt} = - \sum_j \frac{\partial F_j}{\partial u_i} v_j - \frac{\partial E}{\partial u_i}, \tag{A.33}$$

which is exactly Equation 39, with the Lagrange multipliers being the back-propagated error. The boundary condition resulting from the final time t_1 being fixed is given by $\partial \mathcal{E}/\partial(d\mathbf{u}/dt)(t_1) = 0$, which yields $\mathbf{v}(t_1) = 0$. Finally, the variation $\delta\mathcal{L}$ is related to the variation δW by $\delta\mathcal{L} = [\int_{t_0}^{t_1} \mathbf{v}^t(\partial \mathbf{F}/\partial w) \, dt]\delta W$, which gives Equation 42.

ACKNOWLEDGMENTS

This work is supported by grants from the AFOSR, the ONR and the McDonnell-Pew Foundation. I would like to thank Geoffrey Hinton, Barak Pearlmutter, and Fernando Pineda for their useful comments.

This chapter is based on the article "Gradient Descent Learning Algorithms: A General Dynamical System Perspective," by P. Baldi, *IEEE Transactions on Neural Networks* (in press) © IEEE.

REFERENCES

Amari, S. (1972). Characteristics of random nets of analog neuron-like elements. *IEEE Transactions on Systems, Man and Cybernetics, SMC-2*, 643–657.

Apostol, T. (1967). *Calculus.* (2nd ed.). New York: Wiley.

Baldi, P., & Meir, R. (1990). Computing with arrays of coupled oscillators: an application to preattentive texture discrimination. *Neural Computation, 2,* 458–471.

Baldi, P., & Pineda, F. (1991). Contrastive learning and neural oscillations. *Neural Computation, 3,* 526–545.

Baldi, P. (1991). Computing with arrays of bell-shaped and sigmoid functions. In *Neural information processin gsystems,* (vol. 3). San Mateo: CA: Morgan Kaufmann.

Baldi, P. (1992). *Learning in dynamical systems. Gradient descent, random descent and modular approaches* (JPL Technical Report). California Institute of Technology.

Bryson, A. E., & Denham, W. (1962). A steepest-ascent method for solving optimum programming problems. *Journal of Applied Mechanics, 29,* 247–257.

Carr, C. E., & Konishi, M. (1988). Axonal delay lines for time measurement in the owl's brainstem. *Proceedings of the National Academy of Science, USA, 85,* 8311–8315.

Cauwenberghs, G. (1993). A Fast Stochastic Error-Descent Algorithm for Supervised Learning and Optimisation. In: *Advances in Neural Informaton Processing Systems 5,* S. J. Hanson, J. D. Cowan & C. Lee Giles (Eds.) p. 244–251. San Mateo, CA: Morgan Kaufmann.

de Vries, B., & Principe, J. C. (1991). A theory for neural networks with time delays. In: *Advances in neural information processing systems 3,* R. P. Lippmann, J. E. Moody & D. S. Touretzky (Eds.), 162–168, San Mateo, CA: Morgan Kaufmann.

Fang, Y., & Sejnowski, T. (1990). Faster Learning for Dynamic Recurrent Backpropagation. *Neural Compution, 2,* 270–273.

Farotimi, O., Dembo, A., & Kailath, T. (1991). A general weight matrix formulation using optimal control. *IEEE Transactions on Neural Networks, 2,* 378–394.

Fitzhugh, R. (1961). Impulses and physiological states in theoretical models of nerve membrane. *Biophysics Journal, 1,* 445–466.

Geman, S., Bienenstock, E., & Doursat, R. (1992). Neural networks and the bias variance dilemma. *Neural Computation, 4,* 1–58.

Grossberg, S., & Cohen, M. (1983). Absolute stability of global pattern formation and parallel memory storage by competitive neural networks. *IEEE Transactions on Systems, Man and Cybernetcs, SMC-13,* 815–826.

Hale, J. (1977). Theory of functional differential equations. New York: Springer Verlag.

Hebb, D. O. (1949). The organisation of behavior. New York: Wiley.

Hindmarsh, J. L., & Rose, R. M. (1984). A model of neuronal bursting using three coupled first order differential equations. *Proceedings of the Royal Society London, B, 221,* 87–102.

Hopfield, J. J. (1984). Neurons with graded response have collective computational properties like those of two-state neurons. *Proceedings of the National Academy of Science, USA, 81,* 3088–3092.

Komlós, J., & Paturi, R. (1988). Convergence results in an associative memory model. *Neural Networks, 1,* 239–250.

Linsker, R. (1988). Self-organisation in a perceptual network. *Computer, 21,* 105–117.

Lisberger, S. G., & Sejnowski, T. J. (1992). Computational analysis predicts sites of motor learning in the vestibulo-ocular reflex. (Tech. Rep. No. Technical Report 9201). UCSD Institute for Neural Computation.

Minsky, M., & Papert, S. (1969). *Perceptrons.* Cambridge, MA: MIT Press.

Pan, V. (1984). How can we speed up matrix multiplication? *SIAM Review, 26,* 393–415.

Pearlmutter, B. (1989). Learning state space trajectories in recurrent neural networks. *Neural Computation, 1,* 263–269.

Pineda, F. J. (1987). Generalization of back-propagation to recurrent neural networks. *Physical Review Letters, 59,* 2229–2232.

Rumelhart, D. E., Hinton, G. E., & Williams, R. J. (1986). Learning internal representations by error propagation. In D. E. Rumelhart, & J. L. McClelland, (Eds.), Parallel distributed processing, Cambridge, MA: MIT Press.

Sejnowski, T. J. (1976). On the stochastic dynamics of neuronal interaction. *Biological Cybernetics, 22,* 203–211.

Tesauro, G. (1989). Neurogammon wins computer olympiad. *Neural Computation, 1,* 321–323.

Toomarian, N., & Barhen, J. (1991). Adjoint-functions and temporal learning Algorithms in neural networks. In *Advances in neural information processing systems 3.* R. P. Lippman, J. E. Moody and D. S. Touretzky (Eds.), San Mateo, CA: Morgan Kaufmann.

Troutman, J. L. (1983). Variational calculus with elementary convexity. New York: Springer Verlag.

Unnikrishnan, K. P., Hopfield, J. J., & Tank, D. W. (1991). Connected-digit speaker dependent speech recognition using a neural network with time-delayed connections. *IEEE Transactions on Signal Processing, 39,* 698–713.

Werbos, P. (1974). Beyond regression: New tools for prediction and analysis in the behavioral sciences. Unpublished doctoral dissertation, Harvard University.

Williams, R. J., & Zipser, D. (1989). A learning algorithm for continually running fully recurrent neural networks. *Neural Computation, 1,* 270–280.

Author Index

Subject Index

Printed and bound by CPI Group (UK) Ltd, Croydon, CR0 4YY

17/10/2024

01775684-0014